Canada
Labour Relations Board
Policies and Procedures

Canada
Labour Relations Board
Policies and Procedures

by

Claude H. Foisy, Q.C.
Daniel E. Lavery, B.C.L.
and
Luc Martineau, B.C.L., LL.M.

Members of the Quebec Bar

Butterworths
Toronto and Vancouver

Canada Labour Relations Board Policies and Procedures
English language edition © 1986 Butterworths, A division of Reed Inc.

Printed and bound in Canada by John Deyell Company

The Butterworth Group of Companies

Canada:
Butterworths, Toronto and Vancouver
United Kingdom:
Butterworth & Co. (Publishers) Ltd., London and Edinburgh
Australia:
Butterworths Pty Ltd., Sydney, Melbourne, Brisbane, Adelaide and Perth
New Zealand:
Butterworths (New Zealand) Ltd., Wellington and Auckland
Singapore:
Butterworth & Co. (Asia) Pte. Ltd., Singapore
South Africa:
Butterworth Publishers (SA) (Pty) Ltd., Durban and Pretoria
United States:
Butterworth Legal Publishers, Boston, Seattle, Austin and St. Paul
D & S Publishers, Clearwater

Canadian Cataloguing in Publication Data

Foisy, Claude H.
    Canada Labour Relations Board policies and procedures

Includes index.
ISBN 0-409-81975-1

1. Canada Labour Relations Board.   2. Labour laws and legislation – Canada
– Interpretation and construction.   I. Lavery, Daniel E.'   II. Martineau,
Luc.   III. Title.

KE3153.F64 1986   344.71'01'0269   C86-093346-6

Sponsoring Editor – Derek Lundy
Managing Editor – Linda Kee
Supervisory Editor – Marie Graham
Editor – John Eerkes
Cover Design – Linda Kee
Production – Jim Shepherd
Typesetting and Assembly – Computer Composition of Canada, Inc.

To Louise, Isabelle and Jean-Hubert (*C.H.F.*)

To my father, Judge Pierre Lavery, and my mother, Mireille, and to Josée, Sylvain and Sophie (*D.E.L.*)

To Louisette, Valérie and Véronique (*L.M.*)

Preface

This book analyses the Labour Relations (Part V) and Health and Safety (Part IV) provisions of the *Canada Labour Code* and the interpretation given to them by the Canada Labour Relations Board. In the process, we have considered all the decisions of the "new" Board since it commenced operating in 1973, up to and including decision no. 500, dated March 6, 1985. It also outlines the subject-matters coming within the constitutional jurisdiction of Parliament and the enforcement and judicial review of the Board's decisions. This book is intended to be a snapshot of the legislation as it existed on March 6, 1985 and of the Board's interpretation. It has been organized in paragraphs to facilitate the reader's research and the updating of the book. To that effect, Butterworths, when publishing CLRB's decisions in its monthly publication, *Canadian Labour Relations Boards Reports*, will from now on refer to the appropriate paragraph numbers of this book.

We particularly wish to express our thanks to Phyllis MacRae, for her assistance in proofreading our initial draft; Louise Denoncourt, who was responsible for cross-referencing Appendix 8; Ruth Smith of the Canada Labour Relations Board for her cooperation in providing statistical information; Monique Pinet, our secretary; and the partners of Heenan, Blaikie and Associates of Montreal, who have graciously given us access to word processing and photocopying equipment.

Finally, we wish to express our thanks to the Law Reform Commission of Canada, the federal Department of Justice, and Labour Canada for their assistance in making this book a reality.

Claude H. Foisy
Daniel E. Lavery
Luc Martineau

CONTENTS

Contents

Contents

Contents

Contents

TABLE OF COURT AND BOARD CASES

All references are to paragraph numbers.

TABLE OF CANADA LABOUR RELATIONS BOARD DECISIONS

Note: Decisions having similar styles of cause (for example, banks and their branches) are listed in chronological order, by date of decision. All references are to paragraph numbers.

CHAPTER 1

FEDERAL LABOUR RELATIONS

1:1000   **THE SCOPE OF APPLICATION OF PART V OF THE CODE**

Part V of the *Canada Labour Code*,[1] according to s. 108, applies "in respect of employees who are employed upon or in connection with the operation of any federal work, undertaking or business and in respect of the employers of all such employees in their relations with such employees and in respect of trade unions and employers' organizations composed of such employees or employers". Although the Code does not apply in respect of employment by Her Majesty in right of Canada, it does apply to the federal crown corporations and their employees, except where the Government of Canada has excluded the agencies from the operation of the Code by adding their names to Parts I or II of Schedule I to the *Public Service Staff Relations Act*, which regulates employment by Her Majesty in right of Canada.[2]

---

[1]   R.S.C. 1970, c. L-1 [am. 1972, c. 18; 1977-78, c. 27; 1980-81-82-83, cc. 47, 121; 1984, cc. 39, 40].

[2]   See the *Canada Labour Code*, ss. 108, 109. Employment in the public sector is regulated not only by the *Public Service Staff Relations Act*, R.S.C. 1970, c. P-35, dealing with collective bargaining, but by other statutes as well. See the *Public Service Employment Act*, R.S.C. 1970, c. P-32; *Financial Administration Act*, R.S.C. 1970, c. F-10; and *Public Service Superannuation Act*, R.S.C. 1970, c. P-36. Not all crown agencies have identical status under the law. Under the *Financial Administration Act*, distinctions exist between departmental corporations, agency corporations, and proprietary corporations. Some crown corporations, such as the Canadian Broadcasting Corporation, created under the *Broadcasting Act*, R.S.C. 1970, c. B-11, have a status and exercise powers derived from an Act of Parliament. Others may have been incorporated under the *Canada Corporations Act*, S.C. 1974-75, c. 33, but all the companies' shares are owned by or held in trust for Her Majesty in right of Canada and hence come within the definition of "company" in the *Government Companies Operations Act*, R.S.C. 1970, c. G-7. This Act provides that the governor in council may issue a proclamation directing that the Act be applicable to the companies, which makes them "for all its purposes" agents of Her Majesty. See also *Canadian Forces Exchange System* (1977), 24 di 183, [1978] 1 Can LRBR 219, where the Board decided that a group of employees at a Canadian Forces base were employees of Her Majesty in right of Canada and by virtue of s. 109(4) were not within the jurisdiction of the Code.

1

1:2000   CONSTITUTIONAL JURISDICTION OVER LABOUR RELATIONS

Since 1925 it has been settled law that federal competence over labour relations cannot be asserted under either the "Peace, order and good government" clause or under s. 91(2) concerning "the Regulation of Trade and Commerce" of the *Constitution Act, 1867*. Constitutional jurisdiction over labour relations starts from the premise that labour relations are provincially regulated, but federal regulation will apply where the labour relations have a necessary relation to a federal object.[3] However, exclusive provincial competence over the field of labour relations is the rule. In exceptional circumstances, exclusive federal jurisdiction may be asserted if it is shown that such jurisdiction is an integral part of Parliament's primary competence over a head of power enumerated in ss. 91 and 92(10) of the *Constitution Act, 1867*.[4] This is precisely what Parliament has done by means of the non-exhaustive enumeration found in s. 2 of the Code. That section states that a federal work, undertaking, or business includes:

(a)   a work, undertaking or business operated or carried on for or in connection with navigation and shipping, whether inland or maritime, including the operation of ships and transportation by ship anywhere in Canada;

(b)   a railway, canal, telegraph or other work or undertaking connecting any province with any other or others of the provinces, or extending beyond the limits of a province;

(c)   a line of steam or other ships connecting a province with any other or others of the provinces, or extending beyond the limits of a province;

(d)   a ferry between any province and any other province or between any province and any other country other than Canada;

(e)   aerodromes, aircraft or a line of air transportation;

(f)   a radio broadcasting station;

(g)   a bank;

(h)   a work or undertaking that, although wholly situated within a province, is before or after its execution declared by the Parliament of Canada to be for the general advantage of Canada to or for the advantage of two or more of the provinces; and

(i)   a work, undertaking or business outside the exclusive legislative authority of provincial legislatures.

The above expressions are "characteristic appellations" in the terms of the constitutionalists, who can easily point to those federal heads of powers mentioned in ss. 91 and 92(10) of the *Constitution Act, 1867* under which most of the works, undertakings, or businesses enumerated by s. 2 fall. These heads are: s. 91(10), "navigation and shipping"; s. 91(13),

---

3   *Toronto Electric Commissioners v. Snider*, [1925] A.C. 396, [1925] 1 W.W.R. 785, [1925] 2 D.L.R. 5 (P.C.).

4   *Reference re Validity of Industrial Relations and Disputes Investigation Act (Can.); Re Eastern Canada Stevedoring Co.*, [1955] S.C.R. 529, 55 CLLC #15,223, [1955] 3 D.L.R. 721.

"ferries between a province and any British or foreign country or between two provinces"; s. 91(15), "banking, incorporation of Banks, and the issue of paper money"; s. 91(29), "such classes of subjects as are expressly excepted in the enumeration of the classes of subjects by this Act assigned exclusively to the legislature of the provinces"; s. 92(10)(a), "lines of steam or other ships, railways, canals, telegraphs, and other works and undertakings connecting the province with any other or others of the provinces, or extending beyond the limits of the province"; s. 92(10)(b), "lines of steamships between the provinces and any British or foreign country"; s. 92(10)(c), "such works as, although wholly situate within the province, are before or after their execution declared by the Parliament of Canada to be for the general advantage of Canada or for the advantage of two or more of the provinces".

The remaining paragraphs of the enumeration found in s. 2 are not taken from the actual wording of s. 91(2) or 92(10) of the *Constitution Act, 1867*. They are para. (e), referring to "aerodromes, aircraft or a line of air transportation", and para. (f), "a radio broadcasting station". These two paragraphs incorporate part of the heritage left by the Privy Council in its decisions of the 1930s.[5]

The question of whether an undertaking, service, or business is federal depends on the nature of its operation. In order to determine the nature of the operation, one must look at the normal or habitual activities of the business as those of "a going concern", without regard for exceptional or casual factors.[6] To rebut the presumption of provincial jurisdiction, it must be shown that the operation is "vital", "essential", or "integral" to the operation of a federal undertaking.[7] As a preliminary step, the Canada Labour Relations Board is called upon to determine whether there is a "federal undertaking" or not. This may prove to be a difficult task when more than one head of power is involved.

For example, para. (a) of the Code's definition of "federal work, undertaking or business" suggests that all forms of navigation and ship-

---

5   *Re Regulation and Control of Radio Communication*, [1932] A.C. 304 (P.C.); *Re Regulation and Control of Aeronautics*, [1932] A.C. 54 (P.C.).

6   Justice Dickson in *Northern Telecom Ltd. v. Communications Workers of Canada (No. 1)*, [1980] 1 S.C.R. 115, at 132, 28 N.R. 107, 79 CLLC #14,211, 98 D.L.R. (3d) 1, summarizing the two last principles enunciated by Mr. Justice Beetz in *Construction Montcalm Inc. v. Minimum Wage Commission*, [1979] 1 S.C.R. 754, 25 N.R. 1, 79 CLLC #14,190, 93 D.L.R. (3d) 641. See also *Letter Carriers' Union of Canada v. Canadian Union of Postal Workers*, [1975] 1 S.C.R. 178, [1974] 1 W.W.R. 452, 73 CLLC #14,190, 40 D.L.R. (3d) 105, where the court found that a trucking company which did 90 percent of its business for the post office was a federal undertaking.

7   *Reference re Validity of Industrial Relations and Disputes Investigation Act (Can.); Re Eastern Canada Stevedoring, supra*, note 4. "Navigation and shipping" is a head of federal competence contained in s. 91(10) of the *Constitution Act, 1867*. It is under this head that Parliament has been able to assert jurisdiction over the longshoring industry, since in the above decision the regulation of the employment of stevedores was characterized by the Supreme Court as an essential part of navigation and shipping, and was essentially connected to transportation by ship.

ping are covered by the Code. But this provision must be properly read with the provisions of ss. 91(29) and 92(10)(a) and (b) of the *Constitution Act, 1867.* The latter have been interpreted by the courts as excluding from the jurisdiction of Parliament maritime shipping undertakings whose operations are carried on entirely within the boundaries of a single province.[8]

Accordingly, notwithstanding the wording of s. 2 of the Code and the provisions of s. 91(10) of the *Constitution Act, 1867*, the Board has decided that a tug boat operation engaged in a log-towing on an inland lake within British Columbia was not a federal work, undertaking, or business.[9] In another case, the Federal Court of Appeal held that the Board should have asserted its jurisdiction over seamen working on vessels that plied between St. John's or Botwood in Newfoundland and the drilling rigs and ships, engaged in exploring for oil and gas on the Atlantic continental shelf, since this undertaking could be characterized as a "shipping" undertaking, the operation of which was not confined to the province of Newfoundland.[10]

However, there can be no dispute concerning the federal character of a bank, a television or radio station, a cable broadcasting company,[11] an airline company,[12] an enterprise involving employment in the Yukon and Northwest Territories,[13] or a declared work such as a grain elevator

---

8   *Agence Maritime Inc. v. Canada Labour Relations Board,* [1969] S.C.R. 851, 12 D.L.R. (3d) 722; *Three Rivers Boatman Ltd. v. Canada Labour Relations Board,* [1969] S.C.R. 607, 12 D.L.R. (3d) 710. It seems that it is no longer possible to rely on the view expressed by *Montreal v. Montreal Harbour Commissioners,* [1926] A.C. 299, [1926] 1 W.W.R. 398, [1926] 1 D.L.R. 840, at 840 (P.C.), to the effect that the power conferred by s. 91(10) should be construed widely enough to justify federal intervention into intraprovincial shipping and navigation.

9   *Finlay Navigation Ltd.* (1978), 25 di 411, [1978] 1 Can LRBR 516, 78 CLLC #16,143; compare with *Agences Maritime et Arrimages Madeleine Ltée* (1978), 32 di 264, [1979] 3 Can LRBR 322.

10   *Seafarers' International Union of Canada v. Crosbie Offshore Services Ltd.,* [1982] 2 F.C. 855, 82 CLLC #14,180, 135 D.L.R. (3d) 485 (C.A.). However, a somewhat different reasoning in another case led a majority of the Federal Court of Canada to state that the Board had jurisdiction over the employees of a dredging company, not because the enterprise was using floating material or was conducting business in several provinces, but rather because its activities were closely related to "navigation and shipping". See *Verrault Navigation Inc. v. Seafarers' International Union of Canada,* [1983] 2 F.C. 203, 50 N.R. 242 (C.A.). In *TAP Catering and Management Ltd.* (1983), 52 di 128, 3 CLRBR (NS) 168, 83 CLLC #16,057, the Board found that the operation of an oil rig outside the limit of the territorial sea is a "federal work, undertaking or business".

11   *Cable TV Ltée* (1979), 35 di 28, [1980] 2 Can LRBR 381, 80 CLLC #16,019.

12   Since federal jurisdiction over aeronautics is justified under the residual power clause of the constitution (see *Re Regulation and Control of Aeronautics, supra,* note 5; *Johannesson v. West St. Paul,* [1952] 1 S.C.R. 292, 69 C.R.T.C. 105, [1951] 4 D.L.R. 609); a company conducting intraprovincial flights would also come under the control of Parliament: *Butler Aviation of Canada Ltd. v. International Association of Machinists and Aerospace Workers,* [1975] F.C. 590, at 593, 12 N.R. 271, 76 CLLC #14,008 (C.A.).

13   *Yellowknife v. Canada Labour Relations Board,* [1977] 2 S.C.R. 729, 14 N.R. 72, 77 CLLC #14,073, 76 D.L.R. (3d) 85; *Yellowknife District Hospital Society* (1977), 20 di 281, 77 CLLC #16,083; *General Enterprises Ltd.* (1977), 23 di 26, [1977] 1 Can LRBR 432, 77

or a mill.[14] There are still uncertain areas where the Board must determine whether it is dealing with an interprovincial business or a connecting work between two or more provinces. The test in such cases is to determine whether the interprovincial portion of the business is regular and continuous. If it is, it falls within federal jurisdiction. Therefore the solution lies more in a proper interpretation of the factual situation than in the general principles of law involved.[15]

1:3000 THE FINDING OF "EMPLOYMENT IN CONNECTION WITH A FEDERAL WORK, UNDERTAKING OR BUSINESS"

Much difficulty arises where the employer and the employees in question are involved in an operation or activity that is related to another employer's work, undertaking, or business. In such cases, to establish whether the employment is in connection with a federal work, undertaking, or business, the Board has developed and applied a three-fold test:

1. Is there a federal work, undertaking, or business involved in the case?

CLLC #16,084; *Government of the Northwest Territories and Housing Corporation of the Northwest Territories* (1978), 31 di 165, 78 CLLC #16,171, [1979] 2 Can LRBR 521; *Geddes Contracting Co. Ltd. v. Teamsters Local Union No. 213 of the International Brotherhood of Teamsters, Chauffeurs, Warehousemen and Helpers of America*, unreported, June 10, 1981, file no. A-914-80 (Fed. C.A.).

[14] See the *Canada Grain Act*, S.C. 1970-71-72, c. 7, s. 43; *Canadian Wheat Board Act*, R.S.C. 1970, c. C-12, s. 45; *C.S.P. Foods Ltd. v. Canada Labour Relations Board*, [1979] 2 F.C. 23, 25 N.R. 91 (C.A.).

[15] *MacCosham Van Lines Ltd.* (1979), 34 di 716, [1979] 1 Can LRBR 498; *G. Courchesne Transport Inc.* (1979), 16 di 63; *Loughead Express Ltd.* (1980), 41 di 267, [1981] 1 Can LRBR 75; *Les Aviseurs en Déménagements Inc.* (1981), 45 di 111; *Hurdman Bros. Ltd.* (1982), 51 di 104, 83 CLLC #16,003; *G.M. Patry Ltée, Distripak Ltée* (1982), 50 di 71; *Ottawa Taxi Owners and Brokers Association*, decision no. 464, not yet reported, May 14, 1985 (C.L.R.B.); *Bernshine Mobile Maintenance Ltd.* (1984), 7 CLRBR (NS) 21, 84 CLLC #16,036; *Main d'Oeuvre Maska Inc.*, decision no. 487, not yet reported, November 26, 1984 (C.L.R.B.). Among the decisions of the Board dealing with interprovincial undertakings that have been the subject of judicial scrutiny, the following cases may usefully be examined: *Re Cannet Freight Cartage Ltd.*, [1976] 1 F.C. 174, 11 N.R. 606, 60 D.L.R. (3d) 473 (C.A.); *Transportaide Inc. v. Canada Labour Relations Board*, [1978] 2 F.C. 660, 86 D.L.R. (3d) 24 (C.A.); *Holmes Transportation (Quebec) Ltd. v. Transport Drivers, Warehousemen and General Workers, Local 106*, [1978] 2 F.C. 520, 20 N.R. 351 (C.A.); *Loomis Armored Car Service Ltd. v. Canada Labour Relations Board*, unreported, March 11, 1981, file no. A-586-80 (Fed. C.A.); *Ottawa-Carleton Regional Transit Commission v. Amalgamated Transit Union, Local 219* (1983), 83 CLLC #14,034, 144 D.L.R. (3d) 581; affd. 44 O.R. (2d) 560, 84 CLLC #14,006, 1 O.A.C. 77, 4 D.L.R. (4th) 452 (C.A.). In the latter case, the court found that the applicant undertaking was a fully integrated, public passenger-transport service operated by one corporate body connecting Ontario and Quebec, and that it therefore fell within s. 92(10)(a) of the *Constitution Act, 1867*. The court added that, even though the applicant was regulated by the *Regional Municipality of Carleton Act*, which in certain aspects could be regarded as legislation in relation to municipal institutions in the province, it could not have the effect of ousting the legislative jurisdiction of Parliament in relation to this federal undertaking.

2.   If so, is the work in question done upon or in connection with the operation of the federal work, undertaking, or business (that is, is it "vital", "essential", "necessarily incidental", "intimate", or "integral" to the federal work, undertaking, or business)?

3.   If so, can the employees in question be characterized as doing that work — is this work a major or insignificant part of their total time?[16]

This three-fold test represents a rationalization of the "functional" method, which courts have constantly applied since the 1950s to determine whether or not the subsidiary enterprise is in connection with a federal work, undertaking, or business.[17] Before the *Northern Telecom* case a similar test was used by some labour boards.[18] But even though the

---

[16]   *Marathon Realty Company Ltd.* (1977), 25 di 387, [1978] 1 Can LRBR 493, 78 CLLC #16,138. The Board has referred to or applied this test in a number of subsequent decisions: *Wardair Canada (1975) Ltd.* (1978), 32 di 248, [1979] 1 Can LRBR 49; affd. (*sub nom. Canadian Air Line Employees' Association v. Wardair Canada (1975) Ltd.*) [1979] 2 F.C. 91, 25 N.R. 613, 97 D.L.R. (3d) 38 (T.D.); *Agences Maritime et Arrimages Madeleine Ltée* (1978), 32 di 264, [1979] 1 Can LRBR 322; *MacCosham Van Lines Ltd.* (1979), 34 di 716, [1979] 1 Can LRBR 498; *Johnston Terminals and Storage Ltd.*(1980), 36 di 45, 80 CLLC #16,039, [1980] 2 Can LRBR 390; affd. [1982] 2 F.C. 549, 35 N.R. 325, 81 CLLC #14,094, 122 D.L.R. (3d) 391; *Northern Telecom Canada Ltd.* (1980), 41 di 44, [1980] 2 Can LRBR 122; affd. [1982] 1 F.C. 191, 37 N.R. 145, 123 D.L.R. (3d) 483; affd. (*sub nom. Northern Telecom Canada Ltd. v. Communications Workers of Canada (No. 2)*) 48 N.R. 161, 83 CLLC #14,148 (S.C.C.); *North Canada Air Ltd. and Norcanair Electronics Ltd.* (1979), 38 di 168, [1980] 1 Can LRBR 535; affd. (*sub nom. North Canada Air Ltd. v. Canada Labour Relations Board*) [1981] 2 F.C. 399 and 407, 34 N.R. 556 and 560, 81 CLLC #14,072, 117 D.L.R. (3d) 206 and 216 (Fed. Ct.); *Loughead Express Ltd.* (1980), 41 di 267, [1981] 1 Can LRBR 75; *G.M. Patry Ltée, Distripak Ltée* (1982), 50 di 71; *TAP Catering and Management Ltd.* (1983), 52 di 128, 3 CLRBR (NS) 168, 83 CLLC #16,057; *Main d'Oeuvre Maska Inc.*, decision no. 487, not yet reported, November 26, 1984 (C.L.R.B.).

[17]   Before the recent rationalization made by the Supreme Court of Canada in *Construction Montcalm Inc. v. Minimum Wage Commission, supra*, note 6, and *Northern Telecom Ltd. v. Communications Workers of Canada (No. 1), supra*, note 6, most courts referred to the "necessity" test enunciated in *Reference re Eastern Canada Stevedoring, supra*, note 4. For examples of different applications of this test by the Federal Court in relation to Board decisions, see *Butler Aviation of Canada Ltd. v. International Association of Machinists and Aerospace Workers, supra*, note 12; *Re Cannet Freight Cartage Ltd., supra*, note 15; *Holmes Transportation (Quebec) Ltd. v. Transport Drivers, Warehousemen and General Workers, Local 106, supra*, note 15; *Canadian Air Line Employees' Association v. Wardair Canada (1975) Ltd., supra*, note 16.

[18]   In *Northern Telecom Ltd. v. Communications Workers of Canada (No. 1), supra*, note 6, Mr. Justice Dickson referred to the method described in the decision of the British Columbia Labour Relations Board in *Arrow Transfer Co.*, [1974] 1 Can LRBR 29, to determine constitutional jurisdiction in a labour matter as "a useful statement of the method adopted by the courts". He then explained at p. 132 (S.C.R.) what this method consists of: "First, one must begin with the operation which is at the core of the federal undertaking. Then the courts look at the particular subsidiary operation engaged in by the employees in question. The court must then arrive at a judgment as to the relationship of that operation to the core federal undertaking, the necessary relationship being variously characterized as 'vital', 'essential' or 'integral'." The Board, in *Marathon Realty Co. Ltd.* (1977), 25 di 387, [1978] 1 Can LRBR 493, 78 CLLC #16,138, adopted fundamentally the same method as the one used by the British Columbia

Board and the tribunals agree on the method to follow in such cases, they may differ about the proper characterization of a particular operation, especially where such an operation can be segregated from the rest of the employer's enterprise.[19] The following examples illustrate this problem.

Although an employer's main activity was the manufacturing and selling of telephone equipment, it has been held both by the Supreme Court of Canada and the Federal Court of Appeal that a group of his employees who were almost exclusively engaged in the installation of this equipment for a federally regulated telecommunication enterprise fell under federal jurisdiction.[20] In this case, it was argued in support of the provincial jurisdiction that the installation of this material constituted the final phase of the performance of the company's sales contracts and accordingly that this operation should be regarded as necessary to the employer's provincial enterprise. The opposite argument was to the effect that the installation work was the first phase of the operation of the client company's federal telecommunication system and was therefore within federal competence.[21] Before the issue was finally decided by the Supreme Court, various panels of both the Board and the courts had entertained differing opinions in this case.

In a somewhat similar case,[22] the Board and the Federal Court both reached the conclusion that an application for certification filed with the Board for a group of employees employed by a company engaged in the business of providing administrative, personnel, and technical support services to its approximately thirty-five subsidiary companies had been filed before the proper body. The employees sought by the certification demand worked at the premises of a subsidiary company, which carried out stevedoring or terminal operator functions. These operations were considered to be an undertaking federal in nature. The employer's contention that the employees should be considered in the light of the parent company's main provincial activity (the supply of administrative, personnel, and technical services to its subsidiaries), was rejected. The Board and the court both held that the work in question was necessary to the successful operation of steamship lines engaged in the transportation of freight, the loading and unloading of this freight from ships, and its dispatch and delivery to customers.[23]

Labour Relations Board in *Arrow Transfer Co.*

[19] *Canadian Pacific Railway Co. v. Attorney General for British Columbia*, [1950] A.C. 122 (P.C.).

[20] *Northern Telecom Canada Ltd. v. Communications Workers of Canada (No. 2), supra*, note 16.

[21] Compare the comments of Justice Thurlow, who rendered the judgment of the Federal Court of Appeal at [1982] 1 F.C. 191, in particular at p. 201, with the dissenting opinion of Mr. Justice Beetz in the Supreme Court of Canada judgment at 147 D.L.R. (3d) 161.

[22] *Johnston Terminals and Storage Ltd. v. Vancouver Harbour Employees Association, Local 517, supra*, note 16.

[23] Compare this reasoning with *Main d'Oeuvre Maska Inc.*, decision no. 487, not yet reported, November 26, 1984 (C.L.R.B.), concerning an application for certification

However, in a previous decision, rendered before the 1978 amendment to s. 122, the privative clause, a writ of prohibition, was issued by the Trial Division of the Federal Court to prevent the Board from processing an application for the certification of a group of truck drivers, apparently employed by a company whose business appeared to have been the supply of drivers to trucking companies.[24] It was held that the supplying of drivers to a trucking company or companies that might or might not carry on business extending beyond the limits of the province was not in itself a work or undertaking over which the Board had jurisdiction.

In another case, the Federal Court of Appeal also quashed a decision of the Board that had included in a unit of longshoremen six employees of a grain company whose distribution centre was located in the port.[25] The work of these employees consisted of operating and maintaining the ultra-modern equipment that received the grain from self-unloading ships and distributed it to customers who came to pick it up with trucks. The Board felt that federal jurisdiction stopped where the grain was put on the customers' trucks. However, assuming that there was a navigation undertaking in this case, the court held that once the grain had been self-unloaded from the ships, this was the end of the process, since the grain was then taken over by its owner, the grain company.

The Board has determined that it has the power of, and the responsibility for, interpreting the Code in the first instance, and in a case[26] it has accordingly rejected the argument made that the only body competent to deal with the question of determining whether the House of Commons was a "federal work, undertaking or business" was the House of Commons itself. However, the finding by the Board of employment in connection with a federal work, undertaking, or business relates to the constitutional applicability of the Code, and accordingly it is a jurisdictional issue that may be reviewed by the Federal Court of Appeal and the superior courts of the provinces upon proper application.[27]

---

that had been presented with respect to drivers and garage employees employed by a company engaged in lending truck drivers and mechanics to transportation undertakings (in this case, provincial ones).

24   *Transportaide Inc. v. Canada Labour Relations Board, supra,* note 15.
25   *Cargill Grain Co. v. International Longshoremen's Association, Local 1739* (1983), 51 N.R. 182 (Fed. C.A.), which granted a s. 28 *Federal Court Act* application against the Board's decision in *Maritime Employers' Association* (1981), 45 di 314.
26   *House of Commons* (1984), 6 CLRBR (NS) 354, 84 CLLC #16,024.
27   See Chapter 19.

CHAPTER 2

THE CANADA LABOUR RELATIONS BOARD

2:0000 THE CANADA LABOUR RELATIONS BOARD

The Canada Labour Relations Board is a quasi-judicial and administrative body.[1] It also exercises regulatory powers. It is responsible for the administration of Part V and certain sections of Part IV (health and safety) of the *Canada Labour Code*.

The Board, under Part V of the Code, has jurisdiction in regard to the following matters:

    (i) certification of trade unions and councils of trade unions (ss. 124 to 136);

    (ii) statutory freeze of working conditions following the filing of a certification application (s. 124(4));

    (iii) revocation of bargaining rights conferred to certified and voluntary recognized bargaining agents (ss. 137 to 142);

    (iv) successorship provisions (ss. 143 to 145);

    (v) technological changes (ss. 149 to 153);

    (vi) referral of certain questions that arise in the course of arbitration proceedings (s. 158);

    (vii) modification of the expiry date of a collective agreement (s. 160(1) and (3));

    (viii) the exemption from compulsory union dues deductions because of religious beliefs (s. 162(2) and (3));

    (ix) the imposition of a first collective agreement (s. 171.1);

    (x) illegal strikes and lockouts (ss. 179 to 183.1);

    (xi) unfair labour practices (ss. 124(4), 136.1, 148, 161.1, 184 to 189);

    (xii) authorization to initiate penal prosecution (s. 194);

    (xiii) reference of certain questions by the Minister of Labour (s. 197);

    (xiv) access to employer's premises (s. 199);

---

[1] The quasi-judicial and administrative role and the jurisdiction of labour boards in general have been discussed by the Supreme Court of Canada in *Re Tomko and Nova Scotia Labour Relations Board*, [1977] 1 S.C.R. 112, 7 N.R. 317, 10 N.R. 35, 14 N.S.R. (2d) 191, 76 CLLC #14,005.

(xv) access to financial statements (s. 199.1).

In addition the Board has jurisdiction under Part IV of the Code (health and safety) to deal with the following matters:

(i) the review of decisions by security officers in cases of refusal to work for reason of imminent danger (s. 82.1);

(ii) the review of directives given by safety officers in case of imminent danger (s. 95);

(iii) complaints by employees who have been the object of sanctions for having exercised their right to refuse to work for reason of imminent danger (ss. 96.1 to 96.4).

Administratively the Board is independent of the Department of Labour and reports directly to Parliament through the Minister of Labour. The chief executive officer of the Board is its chairman.[2]

2:1000   COMPOSITION OF THE BOARD

The Board is composed of a chairman, a maximum of five vice-chairmen, eight full-time members, and such other part-time members as is necessary to assist the Board in carrying out its functions under Part IV of the Code. They are appointed by order-in-council.[3] Their terms of office are for a maximum of ten years for the chairman and the vice-chairmen, five years for the full-time Board members, and three years for part-time members.[4] The latter are appointed exclusively to assist the Board in carrying out its functions under Part IV and cannot sit in procedures initiated under Part V. Board members are non-representative in the sense that, even though they may have originally been identified with management or labour, once appointed they do not sit as either employer or union nominees. Eligibility for Board appointments is open to Canadian citizens who do not hold any other remunerative employment or office and who have not yet attained the age of seventy years. The same prerequisites apply to part-time members, with the exception that they may hold other remunerative employment at the same time.[5] A member may be reappointed in the same or in another capacity.[6] During his appointment he may be removed from office only by the Governor in Council for cause.[7] In order to hold office it is not necessary to be a member of the legal profession.[8]

---

[2]   *Canada Labour Code*, s. 116.
[3]   Section 111(2).
[4]   Section 111(3).
[5]   Section 111(5) and (5.1).
[6]   Section 111(6).
[7]   Section 111(4).
[8]   At the time of publication, the chairman, two vice-chairmen, and two full-time Board members were legally trained. Two vice-chairmen and five full-time Board members were not legally trained.

When a person ceases to be a member of the Board for any reasons other than his removal by the Governor in Council, he may continue to act in respect of matters that were before the Board and concerning which there were proceedings in which he participated when he was a member.[9]

2:2000 SITTINGS AND OPERATIONS OF THE BOARD

As an administrative tribunal, the Board renders decisions concerning Parts V and IV (health and safety) of the *Canada Labour Code*. Excepting those cases in which the Board must consider an uncontested application or question,[10] the quorum for decisions under Part V is at least three members, one of whom shall be either the chairman or a vice-chairman.[11] A decision of the majority of members present is a decision of the Board.[12] When dealing with health and safety applications under Part IV, one member may sit as the sole adjudicator.[13]

The Board's head office is located in Ottawa,[14] and it operates as well through regional offices located in Halifax, Montreal, Toronto, Winnipeg, and Vancouver.[15]

One facet of the Board's methods of operation is that it assigns investigating officers (I.O.s), either from the head office or from one of the regional offices, to assist the parties in preparing their submissions to the Board and in helping them settle their differences, where possible.[16]

Once the file is complete, it is referred to a panel of the Board for consideration and decision.[17]

2:3000 GENERAL POWERS OF THE BOARD— SECTIONS 117 TO 121

Some of the Board's general and specific powers in relation to proceedings before it will be succinctly dealt with below. They are the powers set out in ss. 117 to 121. Reference is made to these sections, along

---

9   Section 112.
10 Section 115(1.1). Before June 27, 1984, a single member could not render a decision in proceedings initiated under Part V.
11 Section 115(1).
12 Section 115(2).
13 Section 106.1.
14 Section 114(1).
15 The addresses and telephone and telex numbers of the Board's head office and regional offices are listed in Appendix 1.
16 Regarding the role of the investigating officer, see *Cablevision Nationale Ltée* (1978), 25 di 422, [1979] 3 Can LRBR 267. See also paragraphs 4:2500 and 15:4100, where the I.O.'s involvement is referred to.
17 See paragraphs 4:2500, 4:2600, and 15:4210, where the decisional processes of the Board in contested matters is reviewed.

with a more detailed discussion of their provisions in the appropriate chapters of this book.

2:3100   QUASI-JUDICIAL POWERS

Section 118 enumerates the extent of the Board's powers. These powers are exercised in relation to proceedings before it and constitute the tools with which the Board can efficiently exercise its jurisdiction.[18] Section 118(a) to (o) reads as follows:

118. The Board has, in relation to any proceeding before it, power

(a) to summon and enforce the attendance of witnesses and compel them to give oral or written evidence on oath and to produce such documents and things as the Board deems requisite to the full investigation and consideration of any matter within its jurisdiction that is before the Board in the proceeding;

(b) to administer oaths and affirmations;

(c) to receive and accept such evidence and information on oath, affidavit or otherwise as in its discretion the Board sees fit, whether admissible in a court of law or not;

(d) to examine, in accordance with any regulations of the Board, such evidence as is submitted to it respecting the membership of any employees in a trade union seeking certification;

(e) to examine documents forming or relating to the constitution or articles of association of

(i) a trade union or council of trade unions that is seeking certification, or

(ii) any trade union forming part of a council of trade unions that is seeking certification;

(f) to make such examination of records and such inquiries as it deems necessary;

(g) to require an employer to post and keep posted in appropriate places any notice that the Board considers necessary to bring to the attention of any employees any matter relating to the proceeding;

(h) subject to such limitations as the Governor in Council in the interests of defence or security may by regulation prescribe, to enter any premises of an employer where work is being or has been done by employees and to inspect and view any work, material, machinery, appliances or articles therein and interrogate any person respecting any matter that is before the Board in the proceeding;

(i) to order, at any time before the proceeding has been finally disposed of by the Board, that

(i) a representation vote or an additional representation vote be taken among employees affected by the proceeding in any case where the Board considers that the taking of such a representation vote or additional representation vote would assist the Board to decide any question that has arisen or is likely to arise in the proceeding, whether or not such a representation vote is provided for elsewhere in this Part, and

---

[18]   The subject-matters over which the Board has jurisdiction are enumerated in paragraph 1:2000.

(ii) the ballots cast in any representation vote ordered by the Board pursuant to subparagraph (i) or any other provision of this Part be sealed in ballot boxes and not counted except as directed by the Board;

(j) to enter upon an employer's premises for the purpose of conducting representation votes during working hours;

(k) to authorize any person to do anything that the Board may do under paragraphs (b) to (h) or paragraph (j) and to report to the Board thereon;

(l) to adjourn or postpone the proceeding from time to time;

(m) to abridge or enlarge the time for instituting the proceeding or for doing any act, filing any document or presenting any evidence in connection with the proceeding;

(n) to amend or permit the amendment of any document filed in connection with the proceeding;

(o) to add a party to the proceeding at any stage of the proceeding. . . .

The Board has made reference to its powers in most of its decisions, but has only rarely discussed the parameters of each of these powers. In *K.J.R. Associates Ltd.*[19] the Board stated that the power stipulated in s. 118(a) to summon and compel the attendance of witnesses, coupled with its power under s. 118(o) to add a party to the proceeding at any stage, confers on it not only the mandate to assume an inquisitory role, but also an obligation to do so in areas as fundamental to industrial relations as the status of an employer/employee or of a trade union.

In *Air West Airlines Ltd.*[20] the Board referred to s. 118(c), which gives it the power "to protect and accept . . . evidence whether admissible in a court of law or not", and s. 118(k), which enables the Board to authorize any person to do anything that the Board itself can do under paras. (b) to (h) or para. (g). It elected to proceed on the basis of a report consisting of testimony received during a hearing by only two Board members. The decision then made was based on the report of these two members to the three-member panel.[21]

Section 118(m), which gives the Board the power to abridge or enlarge the time for instituting proceedings, was interpreted by the Supreme Court of Canada[22] as not empowering the Board to alter a substantive provision of the statute prescribing a time limit for filing a complaint. It follows that the Board only has power to enlarge the time limits of a procedure already before it.

---

19   (1979), 36 di 36, [1979] 2 Can LRBR 445.
20   (1980), 39 di 56, [1980] 2 Can LRBR 197.
21   *Ibid.* In this case the Board, while dealing with urgent matters, had heard one week of evidence when it became necessary to adjourn to a date one month later. In the interim one of the original panel members suffered a stroke. In order to cope effectively with the resulting problem, the hearing continued with two Board members alone and the proceedings were recorded. The panel then filed the recording as a report, and the decision was ultimately rendered by the three original members who had sat during the first week of the hearing.
22   *Upper Lakes Shipping Ltd. v. Sheehan*, [1979] 1 S.C.R. 902, at 915, 25 N.R. 149, 79 CLLC #14,192.

The Board has used s. 118(m) to abridge the time delays of s. 31 of the Board's regulations.[23] The Board has also used s. 118(m) to abridge the time limits for filing certain procedures as prescribed in the regulations in order to deal at the same time with a number of applications and complaints arising out of the same facts, but which had been filed at different times.[24]

The most important powers of the Board are those enumerated at s. 118(p):

(p) to decide for all purposes of this Part any question that may arise in the proceeding, including, without restricting the generality of the foregoing, any question as to whether

(i) a person is an employer or employee,

(ii) a person performs management functions or is employed in a confidential capacity in matters relating to industrial relations,

(iii) a person is a member of a trade union,

(iv) an organization or association is an employers' organization, a trade union or a council of trade unions,

(v) a group of employees is a unit appropriate for collective bargaining,

(vi) a collective agreement has been entered into,

(vii) any person or organization is a party to or bound by a collective agreement, and

(viii) a collective agreement is in operation.

Because of the words "any question that may arise in the proceeding", the Federal Court of Appeal has decided that s. 118(p) did not give the Board an independent jurisdiction to issue declaratory judgments on the subject-matters enumerated within, unless it was already seized with a proceeding over which it had jurisdiction under Part V of the Code.[25]

Section 118.1 grants the Board, where it is required to determine the wishes of the majority of the employees, the power to determine those wishes as of the filing of the application or at any other date the Board considers appropriate.

The Board may also "review, rescind, amend, alter or vary any order or decision made by it, and may rehear any application before making an order in respect of the application".[26]

Where, in order to dispose finally of an application the Board must determine two or more issues, it may make a decision resolving only one

---

[23]   Section 31 of the *Canada Labour Relations Board Regulations*, S.O.R./78-499, states that an application for certification cannot be filed within six months from the date on which a first application for the same group was dismissed by the Board unless the Board enlarges the time limits pursuant to s. 118(m). See in this regard *Bell Canada* (1979), 30 di 104, [1979] 2 Can LRBR 429; and *Crosbie Offshore Services Ltd.* (1983), 54 di 81.

[24]   *Northern Sales Co. Ltd.* (1980), 40 di 128, [1980] 3 Can LRBR 15, 80 CLLC #16,033.

[25]   *Canadian Broadcasting Corp. v. Canada Labour Relations Board*, not yet reported, January 22, 1985, file no. A-720-84 (Fed. C.A.).

[26]   *Canada Labour Code*, s. 119. This section is analysed in Chapter 6.

or some of the issues and reserve its jurisdiction to later dispose of the remaining issues.[27]

The Board, where it is authorized to issue any order or decision under the Act, may do so, either generally or in any particular case or class of cases.[28] Section 121 directs the Board to exercise its powers in a manner consistent with the attainment of the objects of Part V.[29]

2:3200   REGULATORY POWERS (SECTION 117)

Section 117 specifically authorizes the Board to make regulations. The Board has effectively passed regulations in accordance with such powers.[30] These regulations are specifically referred to elsewhere in this book when discussing particular matters within the Board's jurisdiction.

2:4000   APPLICATIONS TO THE BOARD

The Board's regulations[31] define the manner in which an application, a complaint, a reply, or an intervention is filed with the Board and what information such applications, complaints, replies, or intervention must set out. Those regulations set out requirements of both general and specific application. The regulations requiring specific informations in the cases of applications for certification, revocation, unlawful strikes and lockouts, and unfair labour practices complaints will be dealt with in this book in the chapters relating to such matters. The following paragraphs deal exclusively with the regulations of general application. It must be emphasized that in any case, whether general or specific, no special form is necessary. An application will not be rendered invalid because of a defect in form or a technical irregularity.[32]

---

27   Section 120.1.
28   Section 120.
29   The Federal Court of Canada, in *Le Syndicat des employés de production du Québec et de l'Acadie v. Canada Labour Relations Board*, [1982] 1 F.C. 471, at 476 and 477, stated that s. 121 does not by itself authorize the Board to remedy violations of the Code. Section 121 must be read in conjunction with specific powers granted to the board in the Code to remedy violations. This decision of the appeal court has since been confirmed by the Supreme Court of Canada in [1984] S.C.R. 412. The Supreme Court said that even if s. 121 encompassed independent powers (as opposed to incidental or accessory powers) they could not constitute independent powers to remedy situations addressed elsewhere in the Code and for which specific remedial powers are granted.
30   S.O.R./78-499.
31   *Ibid.*
32   Section 6 of the regulations, S.O.R./78-499, and s. 203 of the Code. See *Saskatchewan Wheat Pool* (1977), 21 di 388, at 398, [1977] 1 Can LRBR 510, 77 CLLC #16,104. Note that the Board may permit the amendment of any document, according to s. 118(n) of the Code.

2:4100   FILING THE APPLICATION

The application must be in writing.[33] The date of its filing is the date it is posted, if sent by registered mail. If sent by any other means, the date is the date it is received by the Board.[34] Although s. 11 of the regulations provides that the application must be sent to the Board in Ottawa or elsewhere as directed or permitted by the Board, the Board encourages the parties to send their application to its regional offices.[35]

2:4200   WHO CAN SIGN THE APPLICATION, THE REPLY, OR THE INTERVENTION

If the application is made by a trade union it must be signed by its president, or secretary, or two officers, or a person authorized in writing to sign on its behalf.[36] Officers who are not selected according to the union's constitution cannot sign the application, which may be found to be a nullity on that ground.[37] The person authorized to represent the union must file his authorization with the Board,[38] but failure to do so will not invalidate the application, provided the default is subsequently remedied.[39]

If it is filed on behalf of the employer,[40] it must be signed by the employer, or by the general manager, or by the principal executive officer, or by a person authorized in writing to sign on his behalf.

Where the application is filed on behalf of an employee, it shall be signed by the employee himself or by a person authorized by him in writing to sign on his behalf.[41]

In all cases where a person has been authorized to sign an application, reply, or intervention on behalf of another person, a copy of the authorization must be filed with the Board.[42]

---

[33]   Section 4 of the regulations. However, in the case of illegal strike, the proceeding may be initiated by a telephone call, followed by a written application. See paragraph 9:2200.

[34]   Section 8(1)(a) and (b) of the regulations.

[35]   See Appendix 1, which lists the addresses of the head office and regional offices of the Board.

[36]   Section 9(1)(a) of the regulations.

[37]   *Canadian Pacific Ltd.* (1976), 13 di 13, [1976] 1 Can LRBR 361, 76 CLLC #16,018.

[38]   Section 9(1) of the regulations.

[39]   *Canadian Imperial Bank of Commerce (Branches at Creston, B.C. and St. Catharines, Ont.)* (1979), 35 di 105, [1980] 1 Can LRBR 307, 80 CLLC #16,002; *La Banque Nationale du Canada* (1981), 42 di 352, at 359, [1982] 3 Can LRBR 1; *A & M Transport Ltd.* (1983), 52 di 69; and *Ronald Wheadon* (1983), 54 di 134, 5 CLRBR (NS) 192, 84 CLLC #16,004.

[40]   S.O.R./78-499, s. 9(1)(b).

[41]   Section 9(1)(c) of the regulations.

[42]   Section 9(2) of the regulations.

2:4300   CONTENT OF THE APPLICATION

The application must set out the following information:[43]

(i) the full name and address of the applicant,

(ii) the full name and address of the employer of the employee affected by the application and of any trade union affected by the application,

(iii) a reference to the section of the Code under which the application is made,

(iv) a concise statement of the purpose of the application,

(v) the particulars of the facts and circumstances in support of the application, and

(vi) the date and nature of any order or decision of the Board that is affected by the application.

The application must be accompanied by a copy of any relevant documents.[44]

2:4400   NOTIFICATION OF THE APPLICATION

On receipt of an application or reply, the Board, through its registrar, gives notice of it in writing to any person who in its opinion may be affected by said application or reply.[45] In certain circumstances the Board may require the employer in writing to post notices of an application and require him to keep the notices posted for a period of seven days.[46] This is the case where applications may affect a number of employees, such as an application for certification or revocation. In other cases the registrar notifies persons the Board feels may be affected by the proceedings and exchanges with them the documents filed, unless these documents are considered to be evidence of a confidential nature,[47] such as evidence relating to the membership of any employee in a trade union, or objections by employees to the certification or to an employee's wish for union representation.

2:4500   REPLIES AND INTERVENTION TO THE APPLICATION

Persons affected by the application may respond to it by way of a reply or an intervention. However, the Board is under no statutory obligation to hold a hearing in many matters coming before it and may

---

43   Section 12 of the regulations.
44   Section 12(b) of the regulations.
45   Section 13(2) of the regulations.
46   *Ibid.*
47   Section 28. Failure by the Board to notify persons affected by the application may amount to a breach of the rules of natural justice. See paragraph 19:4110.

decide the application on the basis of the written representations.[48] In that context, it is important for the parties to make their case fully in writing and to file all pertinent documents with the Board.

The difference between a reply and an intervention appears to be one of form. A comparison of the requisites of s. 15 of the regulations for a reply with those of s. 16 for an intervention reveals that the latter appears to be less formal.

The reply,[49] if filed by a union, must be authorized in the manner previously described.[50] If it is filed on behalf of the employer,[51] it must be signed by the employer, or the general manager, or the principal executive officer, or a person authorized in writing to sign on his behalf. Where a person has been authorized to act on behalf of another person, a copy of the authorization must be filed with the Board.[52] The Board will not invalidate the reply or the application if the consent has not been filed, but it must be satisfied that the person is in fact authorized to represent the organization whose representative he claims to be. It follows that an authorization can be filed at a latter stage and any default remedied.[53]

A person wishing to reply must do so in writing within ten days of the date on which he received notice of the application.[54] In the case of a person employed by the employer who wishes to respond to the posted notice, the ten days' delay commences on the first day the application is posted by the employer.[55] If the person wishing to reply or intervene fails to do so within ten days of the posted notice, he will not be permitted to do so unless he obtains the prior consent of the Board.[56]

The written reply must contain the following information:

(i) the full name and address of the person filing the reply;

(ii) a clear identification of the application to which the reply relates;

(iii) the admission or denial of each of the statements made in the application;

(iv) a concise statement of the facts relied on; and

---

[48]   Section 19(2) of the regulations. *Bank of Nova Scotia (Main Branch, Regina)* (1978), 28 di 885, [1978] 2 Can LRBR 65; *Les Arsenaux Canadiens Ltée* (1978), 28 di 931. For a full discussion of this subject, see paragraph 19:4120.

[49]   Section 15 of the regulations.

[50]   See paragraph 2:4200.

[51]   Section 9(1)(b) of the regulations.

[52]   Section 9(2) of the regulations.

[53]   *La Banque Nationale du Canada* (1981), 42 di 352, at 359, [1982] 3 Can LRBR 1. See also *Canadian Imperial Bank of Commerce, (Branches at Creston, B.C. and St. Catharines, Ont.)* (1979), 35 di 105, [1980] 1 Can LRBR 307, 80 CLLC #16,002; *A & M Transport Ltd.* (1983), 52 di 69; and *Ronald Wheadon* (1983), 54 di 134, 84 CLLC #16,004, 5 CLRBR (NS) 192.

[54]   Section 18(1) of the regulations.

[55]   Section 14 of the regulations.

[56]   Section 18(2) of the regulations.

(v) a statement as to whether or not a hearing before the Board is requested for the purpose of making oral representations or presenting evidence in respect to the issues raised in the reply.[57]

A person who wishes to intervene in an application must do so in writing, setting out:

(i) his full name and address;
(ii) his ground for intervening; and
(iii) the facts relied on.[58]

2:4600 PROCESSING AND DECIDING THE APPLICATION BY THE BOARD

The reader is referred to paragraph 4:2500, where the procedure is explained in detail in the context of an application for certification. The same general process, with the necessary adjustments, applies to any application filed with the Board.

---

[57] Section 15 of the regulations.
[58] Section 16 of the regulations.

CHAPTER 3

INTERESTED PARTIES OR INTERVENANTS: THE CONCEPTS OF EMPLOYEE, EMPLOYER, AND TRADE UNION

3:0000   **INTERESTED PARTIES OR INTERVENANTS: THE CONCEPTS OF EMPLOYEE, EMPLOYER, AND TRADE UNION**

3:1000   **EMPLOYEE**

The Board has jurisdiction over employees who work for an employer operating a federal work, undertaking, or business.[1]

Employee status is fundamental for a person wishing to bargain collectively. The basic freedom to join a union[2] and subsequently to bargain collectively is restricted to employees as they are defined in s. 107(1) of the Code:[3]

> "employee" means any person employed by an employer and includes a dependent contractor and a private constable, but does not include a person who performs management functions or is employed in a confidential capacity in matters relating to industrial relations.

Section 118(p)(i) grants the Board power to decide for all purposes of Part V who is an employee. The Board views the definition as containing two aspects:[4]

> (1) *a positive one:* "'employee' means any person employed by an employer and includes a dependent contractor and a private constable";
>
> (2) *and a restrictive one:* "but does not include a person who performs management functions or is employed in a confidential capacity in matters relating to industrial relations".

---

[1]   See, generally, para. 1:3000.

[2]   *Canada Labour Code*, s. 110(a).

[3]   The Board has retraced the historical background of the definition in *Cominco Ltd.* (1980), 40 di 75, [1980] 3 Can LRBR 105, 80 CLLC #16,045; see also *British Columbia Telephone Co.* (1976), 20 di 239, [1976] 1 Can LRBR 273, 76 CLLC #16,015.

[4]   *Société Radio-Canada* (1982), 44 di 19, 1 CLRBR (NS) 129; affd. not yet reported, January 25, 1985, file no. A-467-82 (Fed. C.A.).

The definition is interpreted in light of the objectives of the Act,[5] using what is known as the "statutory purpose" test. The Board has explained that the definition must not be interpreted according to common-law objectives developed in the context of deciding whether damages should be awarded to an injured party for the faulty execution of work by a workman, but rather in the context of the Code's legislative intent favouring collective bargaining. For the purpose of labour relations, the Board has stated that a person is an employee if he is economically dependent on his employer for the establishment of his terms and conditions of employment. In practice, the Board will consider as employees all persons covered by the application unless there is evidence that these persons are entrepreneurs.[6]

The determination of "entrepreneur" status is a question of fact that must be decided on a case-by-case basis. In making that determination, the Board will try to identify "whose business it is", to use Lord Wright's expression in *Montreal v. Montreal Locomotive Works*.[7] The Board will use common-law criteria only to the extent that they are compatible with the objectives of the Code and with labour relations criteria.[8] The Board has indicated[9] that it will refer to, among others, the following criteria, which are not necessarily those determined by common law:

(i) whether the person is integrated into the employer's operation;

(ii) whether the person has any other business market than the one of the employer;

(iii) whether the person has invested capital in the enterprise;

(iv) whether the person is working under the administrative control of the employer;

(v) whether the performance of the work may result in profits or losses for the person;

(vi) whether the person's risk is limited to the time invested;

(vii) whether the person's income is guaranteed;

(viii) whether the person performs work similar to that of employees of the same employer under similar conditions;

(ix) whether the exclusion of the person who performs work similar to that performed by employees would undermine the union's authority in collective bargaining.

None of these criteria is determinative by itself, and all of these criteria will be weighed against the particular facts of each case.

---

5   *Ibid.; Bank of Montreal (Cloverdale Branch)* (1977), 23 di 92, [1978] 1 Can LRBR 148; and *Cominco Ltd.* (1980), 40 di 75, [1980] 3 Can LRBR 105, 80 CLLC #16,045.

6   *Société Radio-Canada, supra,* note 4.

7   [1946] 3 W.W.R. 748, [1947] 1 D.L.R. 161 (P.C.).

8   *Société Radio-Canada, supra,* note 4, at p. 106(di).

9   *Ibid.,* at p. 110(di).

On numerous occasions the Board has said that the Code is a public-interest statute that promotes collective bargaining as a means of achieving industrial peace. It follows that very serious reasons are required to deny a person employee status. Accordingly, an opposing party must bring such evidence that the person is an entrepreneur.[10] The Board alone has the responsibility to determine who is an employee, and it is not bound by an agreement of the parties to exclude a given individual from the bargaining unit.[11] On the other hand where, in the process of determining the appropriateness of a bargaining unit, the Board exercises its discretion under s. 125(2) to exclude individuals, it will not consider itself bound to determine their employee status.[12]

3:1100   STATUTORY INCLUSIONS

3:1110   Dependent Contractor

The notion of dependent contractor was introduced into federal legislation for the first time with the enactment of Part V of the Code in 1973. Section 107 includes a definition of "dependent contractor":

"dependent contractor" means
(a) the owner, purchaser or lessee of a vehicle used for hauling livestock, liquids, goods, merchandise, or other materials, other than on rails or tracks, who is not employed by an employer but who is a party to a contract, oral or in writing, under the terms of which he is
(i) required to provide the vehicle by means of which he performs the contract,
(ii) entitled to retain for his own use from time to time any sum of money that remains after the cost of his performance of the contract is deducted from the amount he is paid, in accordance with the contract, for that performance, and
(iii) required to operate the vehicle in accordance with the contract, and
(b) a fisherman who, pursuant to an arrangement to which he is a party, is entitled to a percentage or other part of the proceeds of a joint fishing venture in which he participates with other persons, and

---

10   *Société Radio-Canada, supra*, note 4; *CJRP Radio Provinciale Ltée* (1975), 11 di 33, 77 CLLC #16,074; *Vancouver Wharves Ltd.* (1974), 5 di 30, [1975] 1 Can LRBR 162, 74 CLLC #16,118; *Bank of Montreal (Cloverdale Branch)* (1977), 23 di 92, [1978] 1 Can LRBR 148; affd. (*sub nom. Bank of Montreal v. Canada Labour Relations Board*) [1979] 1 F.C. 87, 21 N.R. 214 (C.A.); *Transair Ltd.* (1974), 4 di 54, [1974] 1 Can LRBR 281, 74 CLLC #16,111; *Victoria Flying Services Ltd.* (1977), 23 di 13, 77 CLLC #16,072; *Canadian Imperial Bank of Commerce (Victory Square Branch)* (1977), 25 di 355, [1978] 1 Can LRBR 132, 78 CLLC #16,120; *Canadian Imperial Bank of Commerce (Alness Branch, Downsview)* (1978), 28 di 921, [1978] 2 Can LRBR 361, 78 CLLC #16,145; *British Columbia Maritime Employers' Association* (1981), 45 di 357; *Cominco Ltd.* (1980), 40 di 75, [1980] 3 Can LRBR 105, 80 CLLC #16,045.
11   *CJRP Radio Provinciale Ltée, supra*, note 10; *Bank of Nova Scotia (Port Dover Branch)* (1977), 21 di 439, [1977] 2 Can LRBR 126, 77 CLLC #16,090.
12   *Atomic Energy of Canada Ltd.* (1978), 33 di 415, [1979] 1 Can LRBR 252.

(c) any other person who, whether or not employed under a contract of employment, performs work or services for another person on such terms and conditions that he is, in relation to that other person, in a position of economic dependence on, and under an obligation to perform duties for, that other person. . . .

Because the definition of dependent contractor was, until the addition of para. (c) on June 27, 1984,[13] narrowly restricted to owner-operators in the trucking industry and to fishermen, the Board has had very few occasions to apply the provisions of the definition as it stood before the amendment. Indeed, in *Midland Superior Express Ltd.*[14] the Board questioned the propriety of the legislative characterization of owner-operators as dependent contractors, since a survey of its predecessor's decisions that dealt with the definition of "employee" in the *Industrial Relations and Disputes Investigations Act*,[15] which did not include any notion of "dependent contractor", revealed that such owner-operators had been considered as "employees" and, accordingly, had access to collective bargaining. Thus, the Board went on to find that, on the facts of that case, the individuals concerned were employees.

In *Byers Transport Ltd.*[16] as well, owner-operators were found to be dependent contractors. In this case, the Board raised the question, without answering it, whether a distinction should be made between the owner-operator who actually drives his vehicle and one who employs someone else to drive it. Finally, in *K.J.R. Associates Ltd.*[17] the Board said that it would look at the total business character of the dependent contractor, including his economic dependency, in order to decide whether he was a dependent contractor or an employer. Here, the Board held that K.J.R. was a dependent contractor.

In *Société Radio-Canada*[18] the Board was not directly concerned with the definition of dependent contractor as it was deciding whether freelancers in the television industry were independent contractors, but it did deal with the question at length in an effort to clarify the definition of employee. The Board retraced the history of the notion of dependent contractor and the reasons for its inclusion in the Code. It concluded that the notion of dependent contractor as found in s. 107 did not limit the generality of the first part, which reads: "employee means any person employed by an employer". Rather, the inclusion of the notion of dependent contractor was a legislative technique used by Parliament to ensure that persons who might not be considered at common law would

---

13   S.C. 1983-84, c. 39.
14   (1974), 4 di 30, [1974] 1 Can LRBR 267, 74 CLLC #16,104.
15   S.C. 1948, c. 54, s. 2(1)(i).
16   (1974), 5 di 22, [1974] 1 Can LRBR 434, 74 CLLC #16,113.
17   (1979), 36 di 36, [1979] 2 Can LRBR 445. See also *Mercury Tanklines Ltd.* (1984), 55 di 99.
18   (1982), 44 di 19, 1 CLRBR (NS) 129; affd. not yet reported, January 25, 1985, file A-467-82 (Fed. C.A.).

not be denied such a status under the Code. The Board went on to say that the inclusion of the notion in the Code did not add anything substantive to the general definition of employee.

On June 27, 1984, in addition to the enactment of para. (c) to the definition of dependent contractor, the following paragraph was added to the definition of employer:

> Employer means: . . .
>
> (b) in respect of a dependent contractor such person as, in the opinion of the Board, has a relationship with the dependent contractor to such extent that the arrangement that governs the performance of services by the dependent contractor for that person can be the subject of collective bargaining. . . .

These amendments suggest that the definition of dependent contractor has been enlarged to cover, in addition to owner-operator and fisherman, any person who is in a relation of economic dependance with and is under the obligation to perform duties for another person, where the arrangements that govern the performance of services by the dependent contractor are amenable to collective bargaining. It has also obviated the deficient 1972 definition of employer with respect to fishermen as determined by the Supreme Court of Canada.[19]

3:1120   Private Constable

Section 107 defines private constable as a person appointed a constable under the *Railway Act*[20] or the *Canada Ports Corporation Act*.[21]

In *Denison Mines*[22] the Board made it clear that the definition applied only to those constables appointed under the *Railway Act* or the *National Harbours Board Act* (now the *Canada Ports Corporation Act*) and found that security guards, even though sworn as special constables under the *Police Act* of Ontario,[23] were not private constables under the Code. Persons who do not fall within the ambit of the definition may nevertheless be considered as employees under the Code. The purpose of the definition is to ensure that private constables as defined by the Act are included in units of their own and represented by a distinct bargaining agent.[24]

3:1200   STATUTORY EXCLUSIONS

The Board has jurisdiction to determine whether a person performs management functions or is employed in a confidential capacity in mat-

---

[19]   *British Columbia Provincial Council v. British Columbia Packers Ltd.*, [1978] 2 S.C.R. 97, 19 N.R. 320, [1978] 1 W.W.R. 621, 82 D.L.R. (3d) 182.
[20]   R.S.C. 1970, c. R-2, as amended.
[21]   R.S.C. 1970, c. N-8, as amended (formerly the *National Harbours Act*).
[22]   *Denison Mines Ltd.* (1975), 8 di 13, [1975] 1 Can LRBR 313, 75 CLLC #16,150.
[23]   R.S.O. 1970, c. 351 (now R.S.O. 1980, c. 381).
[24]   *Canada Labour Code*, ss. 125(5) and 135.

ters relating to industrial relations.[25] The Federal Court of Appeal[26] said that the words "management" or "matters related to industrial relations" do not have a precise meaning and that the concept of "management functions" or "matters related to industrial relations" must be interpreted and applied according to the circumstances of each case. The precise ambit of these words is a question of fact or opinion for the Board rather than a question of law. The Federal Court of Appeal[27] has also expressly confirmed the Board's view that exclusions must be carefully interpreted and applied to ensure that the least number of persons are excluded from the freedoms granted by the Code.

The purpose of exclusion, whether for reasons of management function or confidential capacity in matters relating to industrial relations, lies in the need to avoid putting that person in a situation of conflict of interests and loyalties with respect to the employer and the union,[28] in a context where management and union relations are viewed as adversarial.[29] The conflict of interests sought to be avoided is the one that exists between the work responsibility owed to the employer and the one owed to the union as the instrument of collective bargaining, within a system that provides legal protection for the individual in his relationship to the union, both as bargaining agent and as organization.[30]

Before dealing with the specifics of the statutory exclusions, it is important to keep in mind the distinction between the exclusion of a person for reasons of lack of employee status and the exclusion of an employee for reasons related to the appropriateness of the unit.[31] The following paragraphs deal exclusively with the employee-status aspect and the resulting inclusion or exclusion of a person from a bargaining unit based on that reason.

3:1210   Managers and Supervisors

The exclusion of a person for management functions is based on the existence of a conflict of interest. The determination of the line where such conflict arises is not an easy one, and it will vary from case to case. It is particularly difficult under the *Canada Labour Code* where, since 1973,

25   *Canada Labour Code*, s. 118(p)(ii); and *Bank of Nova Scotia (Main Branch, Regina)* (1978), 28 di 885, [1978] 2 Can LRBR 65.

26   *Bank of Montreal v. Canada Labour Relations Board*, [1979] 1 F.C. 87, at 88-89, 21 N.R. 214 (C.A.); *Empire Stevedoring Co. Ltd. v. International Longshoremen's and Warehousemen's Union, Local 514*, [1974] 2 F.C. 742, 6 N.R. 485, 75 CLLC #14,262 (C.A.).

27   *Bank of Montreal v. Canada Labour Relations Board, supra*, note 26.

28   *Bank of Nova Scotia (Port Dover Branch)* (1977), 21 di 439, [1977] 2 Can LRBR 126, 77 CLLC #16,090; *Feed-Rite Ltd.* (1978), 29 di 33, [1979] 1 Can LRBR 296.

29   *British Columbia Maritime Employers Association* (1981), 45 di 357. In this case, employees working for an employer whose sole operation was the dispatching of longshoremen were found not to be "employees", on the basis of the existence of such a conflict of interest.

30   *Cominco Ltd.* (1980), 40 di 75, [1980] 3 Can LRBR 105, 80 CLLC #16,045.

31   *Feed-Rite Ltd.* (1978), 29 di 33, [1979] 1 Can LRBR 296.

persons exercising supervisory functions have been granted employee status. The intent of the legislator to that effect was made clear by the removal of the statutory exception contained in the previous definition of the term employee[32] and by the enactment of s. 125(4). The effect of these changes is that the existence of supervisory functions is no longer in itself a cause for exclusion.[33] Furthermore, the Board has held that the supervisory duties referred to in s. 125(4) should not be given a restrictive meaning so as to exclude employees from collective bargaining.[34] Because of this, the dividing line between management and employees is established at a higher level than that determined by other jurisdictions, where supervision is considered to be a management function.

In order to determine what constitutes management functions, the Board has elaborated a series of criteria, each of which must be weighed against the particular facts of the case[35] and viewed, not in isolation, but in relation to all the other factors.[36] The Board believes that managerial authority in today's business is spread over an ever-increasing range of persons. This dispersal of control varies in degree, according to the policy and personnel of each enterprise,[37] and it has the effect of diffusing managerial authority. The Board will also take into account the importance of any management functions allegedly performed, as well as the intensity and frequency with which they are performed.[38]

In trying to identify who manages the business as opposed to who merely supervises employees, the Board poses the following questions: Does the employee in question have the power to make binding policy decisions involving the exercise of independent judgment?[39] Does the individual act independently or as part of a team in setting the general

---

[32] "'[E]mployee' means a person employed to do skilled or unskilled manual, clerical or technical work, but does not include (i) a manager or superintendent, or any person who, in the opinion of the Board, exercises management functions or is employed in a confidential capacity in matters relating to labour relations, or (ii) a member of the medical, dental, architectural, engineering or legal profession qualified to practise under the laws of a province and employed in that capacity." (*Industrial Relations and Disputes Investigations Act*, S.C. 1948, c. 54, s. 2(1)(i)).

[33] *Niagara Falls Bridge Commission* (1974), 3 di 7, [1974] 1 Can LRBR 149, 74 CLLC #16,098; *Wardair (Can.) Ltd.* (1974), 4 di 62, 74 CLLC #16,103; *Vancouver Wharves Ltd.* (1974), 5 di 30, [1975] 1 Can LRBR 162, 74 CLLC #16,118; *British Columbia Telephone Co.* (1976), 20 di 239, [1976] 1 Can LRBR 273, 76 CLLC #16,015; and *Atomic Energy of Canada Ltd.* (1978), 33 di 415, [1979] 1 Can LRBR 252.

[34] *Niagara Falls Bridge Commission*, *supra*, note 33; *Transair Ltd.* (1974), 4 di 54, [1974] 1 Can LRBR 281, 74 CLLC #16,111.

[35] *Greyhound Lines of Canada* (1974), 4 di 22, 74 CLLC #16,112; *Vancouver Wharves Ltd.*, *supra*, note 33.

[36] *Greyhound Lines of Canada*, *supra*, note 35.

[37] *Vancouver Wharves Ltd.*, *supra*, note 33.

[38] *British Columbia Telephone Co.* (1976), 20 di 239, at 261, [1976] 1 Can LRBR 273, 76 CLLC #16,015.

[39] *Greyhound Lines of Canada*, *supra*, note 35; *Vancouver Wharves Ltd.*, *supra*, note 33; *British Columbia Telephone Co.*, *supra*, note 38; *Crown Assets Disposal Corp.* (1981), 43 di 203; *Radio Saguenay Ltée* (1981), 43 di 228.

policies of the enterprise[40] or in formulating the corporate policies that will be acted upon?[41] Is the decision-making centralized?[42] In this regard the Board inquires as to who decides, as opposed to who "effectively recommends", the latter factor not being grounds for denying status.[43] It is not because recommendations are followed that the person making them is a manager. It is expected that a report made to management will be thorough enough to be acted upon.[44] For the same reason, the power to make suggestions is not a case for denying employee status.[45] Likewise, a person acting merely as a conduit between employees and management is an employee.[46] The mere incidental function of reporting facts on which one's superior will act[47] is not a factor in denying employee status. Ultimately the board tries to determine whether the individual in question possesses independent authority to bind the business. The greater his decision-making discretion, the more likely he is to be qualified as management. The more he follows predetermined guidelines or acts in consultation with others, the more often he will be categorized as an employee.[48]

In general the Board has recognized that hiring, dismissal, promotion and demotion, discipline, planning of work and appointing people to do it, budgeting, and representing management in collective bargaining and contract administration are all management functions.[49] As we have seen above,[50] the Board qualifies these broad statements by the overriding guidelines that each factor must be weighed against the other aspects of the individual case and that the mere fact that a person occasionally performs some management functions is not itself cause for denial of employee status.[51]

In the specific area of hiring, the Board has found that only the final decision—accepting or rejecting a recommendation—is managerial.[52]

---

40   *Vancouver Wharves Ltd., supra,* note 33.

41   *British Columbia Telephone Co.* (1977), 33 di 361, [1977] 2 Can LRBR 385, 77 CLLC #16,107.

42   *British Columbia Telephone Co., supra,* note 38.

43   *Vancouver Wharves Ltd., supra,* note 33; *British Columbia Telephone Co., supra,* note 38; *CHLT Télé-7 Ltée* (1976), 13 di 49, [1976] 2 Can LRBR 76, 76 CLLC #16,025; *Cominco Ltd.* (1980), 40 di 75, [1980] 3 Can LRBR 105, 80 CLLC #16,045; *Québecair* (1978), 33 di 480, [1979] 3 Can LRBR 550.

44   *British Columbia Telephone Co., supra,* note 38.

45   *CHLT Télé-7 Ltée, supra,* note 43.

46   *Greyhound Lines of Canada, supra,* note 35; *Wardair (Can.) Ltd., supra,* note 33; *Vancouver Wharves Ltd., supra,* note 33.

47   *Greyhound Lines of Canada, supra,* note 35; *Canadian Broadcasting Corp.,* decision no. 461, not yet reported, April 30, 1984 (C.L.R.B.).

48   *Greyhound Lines of Canada, supra,* note 35; *Wardair (Can.) Ltd., supra,* note 33; *Canadian Broadcasting Corp., supra,* note 47.

49   *Vancouver Wharves Ltd., supra,* note 33; *British Columbia Telephone Co., supra,* note 41.

50   *Greyhound Lines of Canada, supra,* note 35; *Vancouver Wharves Ltd., supra,* note 33.

51   *Niagara Falls Bridge Commission, supra,* note 33; *British Columbia Telephone Co., supra,* note 38.

52   *Vancouver Wharves Ltd., supra,* note 33; *British Columbia Telephone Co., supra,* note 38.

Mere responsibility for the hiring of students and their training, supervision, discipline, and evaluation will not constitute a bar to the employee status of a supervisor.[53] The same applies in regard to probationary employees when the decision to deny them permanent status is made within strictly defined parameters.[54] The supervisor, working in direct contact with the employees he supervises, is generally qualified to know the requirements of the job because of his high degree of expertise. He is in the best position to make recommendations on hiring.[55] A producer who hires additional staff to complete his production, where it is normal for him to have control over the staff, will not lose his employee status.[56] Where the decision to hire is made in consultation with others, such as industrial relations personnel,[57] or is circumscribed by policies,[58] it will not be considered as a reason for denial of status.

Likewise, in matters relating to promotion and discipline, where the decision is taken in consultation with others or according to management guidelines or negotiated provisions of a collective agreement, the Board has stated that this will not disqualify a person from employee status.[59] A supervisor acting at the first step in the grievance procedure, whether dealing with a verbal complaint or a written grievance, will not be denied employee status if his decision is referred to higher-level management or if he decides in consultation with his superiors.[60] On the other hand, the determination of the organization's structure and staffing levels is a management function.[61] The appraisal of an employee, which may have serious repercussions on his career, is also a management function,[62] although the act of rating other employees[63] and the mere completion of performance evaluations with no follow-up[64] are not bars to employee status.

---

[53] *Greyhound Lines of Canada, supra,* note 35; *Canadian Broadcasting Corp., supra,* note 47.
[54] *British Columbia Telephone Co., supra,* note 41; *Canadian Broadcasting Corp., supra,* note 47.
[55] *Greyhound Lines of Canada* (1974), 4 di 22, 74 CLLC #16,112; *Atomic Energy of Canada Ltd.* (1978), 33 di 415, [1979] 1 Can LRBR 252.
[56] *CHLT Télé-7 Ltée* (1976), 13 di 49, [1976] 2 Can LRBR 76, 76 CLLC #16,025.
[57] *British Columbia Telephone Co.* (1976), 20 di 239, [1976] 1 Can LRBR 273, 76 CLLC #16,015.
[58] *British Columbia Telephone Co.* (1977), 33 di 361, [1977] 2 Can LRBR 385, 77 CLLC #16,107; *Canadian Broadcasting Corp., supra,* note 47.
[59] *Vancouver Wharves Ltd.* (1974), 5 di 30, [1975] 1 Can LRBR 162, 74 CLLC #16,118; *British Columbia Telephone Co., supra,* note 58.
[60] *Greyhound Lines of Canada, supra,* note 55; *Northern Electric Co. Ltd.* (1976), 16 di 237; *Atomic Energy of Canada Ltd., supra,* note 55; *Canadian Broadcasting Corp., supra,* note 47.
[61] *British Columbia Telephone Co., supra,* note 58.
[62] *British Columbia Telephone Co., supra,* note 57.
[63] *Niagara Falls Bridge Commission* (1974), 3 di 7, [1974] 1 Can LRBR 149, 74 CLLC #16,098.
[64] *Greyhound Lines of Canada, supra,* note 55.

The establishment of budgets and their administration is a management function.[65] But this is not the case if the budget is constructed by following higher management guidelines,[66] or where it is prepared with the aid of a large number of support staff and where standard targets have been established and must be followed.[67] The power to commit the employer financially within predetermined budgetary guidelines or via expenditures through a purchasing department for ongoing operations will not be considered a reason to deny employee status.[68] It is expected that authority to make decisions on the economic life of the business will be delegated to lower levels of management, but this does not make the recipient of such delegation a part of the management team.[69]

Job titles are of little help in assisting the Board in determining whether an individual is part of management.[70] The image that a person holds of himself or that the community or his employer holds of him is not a factor to be considered.[71] Employee status is not denied to professionals by ss. 107 and 125(3). Where they provide highly technical or professional advice without the power to make decisions on the basis of the advice, they do not exercise management functions.[72] The technical knowledge of dock supervisors in the loading or unloading of ships,[73] or the design of market plans from which a telephone company can make profits where the designer is part of a group of knowledgeable workers,[74] the supervising of a finance department where the supervisor's major role is to get the work done in a timely manner,[75] and the recommendation of technical data by a managing stewardess[76] have all been held to be employee functions. Likewise in the context of a nuclear plant operation, it has been held that a person does not lose his employee status because the function he performs is essential during a shut-down period.[77] Profes-

---

[65]   *Vancouver Wharves Ltd., supra,* note 59.

[66]   *British Columbia Telephone Co., supra,* note 57; *Canadian Broadcasting Corp., supra,* note 47.

[67]   *Northern Electric Co., supra,* note 60; *British Columbia Telephone Co., supra,* note 58; *Canadian Broadcasting Corp., supra,* note 47.

[68]   *Greyhound Lines of Canada, supra,* note 55; *Cominco Ltd.* (1980), 40 di 75, [1980] 3 Can LRBR 105, 80 CLLC #16,045; *Québecair* (1978), 33 di 480, [1979] 3 Can LRBR 550; *Canadian Broadcasting Corp., supra,* note 47.

[69]   *Cominco Ltd., supra,* note 68.

[70]   *Greyhound Lines of Canada, supra,* note 55; *Wardair (Can.) Ltd.* (1974), 4 di 62, 74 CLLC #16,103; *British Columbia Telephone Co.* (1976), 20 di 239, [1976] 1 Can LRBR 273, 76 CLLC #16,015.

[71]   *British Columbia Telephone Co.* (1979), 38 di 145.

[72]   *Greyhound Lines of Canada, supra,* note 55; *Oceanic Tankers Agency Ltd.* (1974), 4 di 41, 74 CLLC #16,110; *Vancouver Wharves Ltd.* (1974), 5 di 30, [1975] 1 Can LRBR 162, 74 CLLC #16,118; *British Columbia Telephone Co., supra,* note 57; *Northern Electric Co. Ltd.,* (1976), 16 di 237; *National Harbours Board* (1980), 41 di 126, [1980] 3 Can LRBR 265.

[73]   *Oceanic Tankers Agency Ltd., supra,* note 72; *Vancouver Wharves Ltd., supra,* note 72.

[74]   *British Columbia Telephone Co., supra,* note 57.

[75]   *National Harbours Board, supra,* note 72.

[76]   *Wardair (Can.) Ltd., supra,* note 70.

[77]   *Atomic Energy of Canada Ltd.* (1978), 33 di 415, [1979] 1 Can LRBR 252.

sional and highly technically qualified persons, especially in large enter-prises, may wield a measure of authority over other employees without necessarily performing management functions.[78]

A supervisor working in an isolated area in the country who was the only management representative present was held not to be an em-ployee.[79] Concerning the question of sole employer representative, the Board subsequently held that to argue that, because a person is the sole supervisor present at a given place or time, a conflict of interest is created because he represents management is to think of conflicting loyalties in an outdated framework.[80] The Board may also take into consideration the number of employees supervised.[81]

Since the performance of supervisory functions is not in itself equiv-alent to management functions, it follows that the percentage of time worked on bargaining-unit work by a supervisor will not be determinant, but rather will serve to reinforce the assertion that the supervisor is not part of management.[82] The fact that a supervisor earns less on a yearly basis than those he supervises is one indication that he is an employee.[83] He will not lose his employee status if he has access to personal employee files unless he plays a confidential role in matters relating to industrial relations.[84] His participation in a safety committee as the management representative is also not a reason to be denied employee status.[85]

If an employee is refused time off by his supervisor but has the possibility of appealing the decision to another level of supervision,[86] or if the supervisor is limited by management policies or directives or by the provisions of a collective agreement for the calling in of personnel for overtime,[87] chances are that the supervisor will not be denied employee status.

In conclusion, because of the clear legislative intent to give super-visory personnel access to collective bargaining, the Board has drawn a dividing line between management and employees that is much higher than the one traced in jurisdiction where this legislative intent is absent. The main characteristic of the Board's approach to supervisory person-

---

[78]   *British Columbia Telephone Co.* (1977), 33 di 361, [1977] 2 Can LRBR 385, 77 CLLC #16,107; *Canadian Broadcasting Corp.*, decision no. 461, not yet reported, April 30, 1984 (C.L.R.B.).

[79]   *British Columbia Telephone Co., supra,* note 78; *Canadian Broadcasting Corp., supra,* note 78.

[80]   *Cominco Ltd.* (1980), 40 di 75, [1980] 3 Can LRBR 105, 80 CLLC #16,045.

[81]   *British Columbia Telephone Co.* (1976), 20 di 239, [1976] 1 Can LRBR 273, 76 CLLC #16,015.

[82]   *Wardair (Can.) Ltd., supra,* note 70; *British Columbia Telephone Co., supra,* note 78.

[83]   *Greyhound Lines of Canada* (1974), 4 di 22, 74 CLLC #16,112.

[84]   *Greyhound Lines of Canada, supra,* note 83. This is discussed in paragraph 3:1220.

[85]   *British Columbia Telephone Company, supra,* note 71; *Cominco Ltd., supra,* note 80.

[86]   *Greyhound Lines of Canada, supra,* note 83.

[87]   *Atomic Energy of Canada Ltd., supra,* note 77.

nel exclusions lies in the identification of who "makes the decision" as opposed to who "effectively recommends".

3:1220   Persons Employed in a Confidential Capacity

The rationale for the confidentiality exclusion is based on the need to avoid conflicts of interest where the inclusion in the bargaining unit of a person exercising such functions might give the union access to matters that the employer wishes to hold close in its dealing with the union.[88] In order to ensure that employees will enjoy maximum rights and freedoms,[89] this exclusion has been narrowly interpreted to meet the circumstance where the employer has designated a disproportionate number of persons exercising confidential functions. This interpretation has been approved by the Federal Court of Appeal.[90] On the other hand, the Board has recognized that the employer must be in a position to operate efficiently and must have a sufficient number of persons exercising management functions.[91]

The Board has developed a three-tier test to decide whether a person is to be excluded for reasons of confidential capacity in matters relating to industrial relations.[92]

First, the confidential matters must be in relation to industrial relations[93] such as those relating to contract negotiations, the strategies used by the employer in processing grievances (not merely the communication of the final decision), and the strategies used by the employer in proceedings concerning a union in courts or before labour boards. Such confidential matters do not include industrial secrets such as product formulae[94] or information related to the competitive position of the employer[95] because the employee, while exercising his rights under the Code, is expected to continue to be loyal to his employer.[96] Such confidential matters do not include matters of which the unions or employees are aware, such as (1) salaries, (2) performance assessments discussed by the employer representative with an employee or that the employer representative may sign or initial, (3) or personal history or family infor-

---

88   *Bank of Nova Scotia (Port Dover Branch)* (1977), 21 di 439, [1977] 2 Can LRBR 126, 77 CLLC #16,090.

89   *Bank of Nova Scotia (Port Dover Branch), supra,* note 88.

90   *Per* Jackett J.A., in *Bank of Montreal v. Canada Labour Relations Board,* [1979] 1 F.C. 87, at 88-89, 21 N.R. 214 (C.A.).

91   *Transair Ltd.* (1974), 4 di 54, [1974] 1 Can LRBR 281, 74 CLLC #16,111.

92   *Greyhound Lines of Canada, supra,* note 83.

93   *Greyhound Lines of Canada, supra,* note 83; *Transair Ltd., supra,* note 91; *CJRP Radio Provinciale Ltée* (1975), 11 di 33, 77 CLLC #16,074; *Bank of Nova Scotia (Port Dover Branch), supra,* note 88; *Crown Assets Disposal Corp.* (1981), 43 di 203; *Canadian Broadcasting Corp., supra,* note 78.

94   *Bank of Nova Scotia (Port Dover Branch) supra,* note 88.

95   *Transair Ltd., supra,* note 91.

96   *Ibid.*

mation that may be available from other sources.[97] Security guards in an airport who had the responsibility to investigate the employees and had access to confidential information were found to be employees and not employed in matters related to industrial relations.[98]

Second, the disclosure of the confidential information must be likely to affect the employer adversely in his labour relations.

Third, the person must be involved with this information as a regular part of his duties. Merely having access to information on such matters as contract negotiations is not a reason for exclusion.[99] For this reason, persons who attend a regular management meeting or who take part in the consultative process initiated by the industrial relations department to gather information to prepare the employer's position in negotiations or to respond to union demands, and who do not themselves participate in the establishment of the bargaining tactics, are not deprived of their employee status.

3:1300 PRESERVATION OF THE EMPLOYEE STATUS

To conclude on the concept of employee, it should be noted that according to s. 107(2), no employee will lose status by reason of ceasing to work as the result of a lockout or strike or because of his dismissal contrary to Part V of the Code. The Board has stated[100] that in the context of a strike, s. 107(2) find its rationale in balancing the employer's right to operate and the strikers' right to return to work. Furthermore, the fact that a striker accepts temporary or permanent employment elsewhere during a strike does not deny him the protection of s. 107(2). By protecting an employee's status, s. 107(2) maintains the Board's jurisdiction under s. 108.[101] Similarly, when an employee is dismissed, the union, because of s. 107(2), is bound by its duty of fair representation under s. 136.1.[102] A resignation by an employee is not a bar to the application of s. 107(2) where the Board equates the resignation with a dismissal.[103]

3:2000 EMPLOYER

Section 107 defines "employer" as follows:

(a) any person who employs one or more employees, and

---

97 *Bank of Nova Scotia (Port Dover Branch), supra,* note 88.
98 *Eastern Provincial Airways (1963) Ltd.* (1978), 29 di 44, [1979] 1 Can LRBR 456.
99 *Transair Ltd., supra,* note 91.
100 *Arthur T. Ecclestone* (1978), 26 di 615, [1978] 2 Can LRBR 306, 78 CLLC #16,142.
101 *George Lochner* (1979), 37 di 114, 79 CLLC #16,209, [1980] 1 Can LRBR 149.
102 *John J. Huggins* (1979), 38 di 195, [1980] 1 Can LRBR 364.
103 *Purolator Courier Ltd.* (1982), 48 di 32.

(b) in respect of a dependent contractor such person as, in the opinion of the Board, has a relationship with the dependent contractor to such extent that the arrangement that governs the performance of services by the dependent contractor for that person can be the subject of collective bargaining.

This definition is self-evident and has not given rise to many decisions by the courts.[104]

In practice, the difficulty lies in the identification of the real employer. In identifying the employer,[105] the Board is not bound by the situation as it stands at the date of the application. It may, depending on the circumstances of each case, take into account subsequent events that are brought to its attention at the hearing.[106]

In *Northern Television Systems Ltd.*[107] the Board laid down the general principle that has been followed ever since.[108] It reiterated the position taken by its predecessor[109] that in determining who the employer is, the Board will examine the realities, as opposed to the appearances, of the employment relationship. In doing so, it will identify which person, corporation, or entity effectively exercises control over the essential elements that constitute the employment relationship. It identifies: (1) who hires the employees, (2) who controls their work, (3) who effectively establishes their wages and working conditions, and (4) who controls any negotiations with respect to wages and terms of employment.[110] In this regard, the Board is not concerned with the person, corporation, or entity who carries out the hiring formalities, but rather with the one who controls the actual selection.[111] In that case, the Board found Northern Television Systems to be the real employer because it had retained control of the employees, even though it had contracted out their work to another entity that used the same employees.[112] The employees did not need specific instructions for routine work assignments but they had to refer to Northern's station manager to solve technical problems. The latter retained control over the work that had to be done and over the

---

104 *British Columbia Packers Ltd. v. British Columbia Provincial Council United Fishermen and Allied Workers,* [1978] 2 S.C.R. 97, [1978] 1 W.W.R. 621, 19 N.R. 320, 82 D.L.R. (3d) 182.

105 *Canada Labour Code,* s. 118(p)(i).

106 *Northern Television Systems Ltd.* (1976), 14 di 136, 76 CLLC #16,031.

107 *Ibid.*

108 *Dome Petroleum Ltd.* (1977), 27 di 653, [1978] 1 Can LRBR 393, 78 CLLC #16,129; *MacCosham Van Lines Ltd.* (1979), 34 di 716, [1979] 1 Can LRBR 498; *K.J.R. Associates Ltd.* (1979), 36 di 36, [1979] 2 Can LRBR 445; *Newfoundland Steamships Ltd.* (1981), 45 di 156, 2 CLRBR (NS) 40.

109 *Kent Lines Ltd.* (1972), 72 CLLC #16,062; affd. (*sub nom. Seafarers' International Union of Canada v. Kent Lines Ltd.*) [1972] F.C. 573, at 578, 72 CLLC #14,145, 27 D.L.R. (3d) 105 (C.A.), where the court said that "the Board was not bound to have regard only for the appearances and to reject the realities".

110 *Northern Television Systems Ltd. supra,* note 106.

111 *MacCosham Van Lines Ltd., supra,* note 108; *Newfoundland Steamships Ltd., supra,* note 108.

112 *Northern Television Systems Ltd., supra,* note 106.

way it was to be carried out.[113] The Board also found that it was determinant that the real employer had control over the funds that could be committed at the bargaining table.

However, in another case, the Board found that the ultimate control over the remuneration paid to employees was not determinant where that control did not prevent the real employer from engaging in meaningful negotiations.[114]

The Board has stated[115] that, although the employer is free to initiate changes in the enterprise's structure to suit his legitimate business purposes, if he is found to be an employer in accordance with the criteria of *Northern Television Systems Ltd.*[116] he cannot use the corporate veil to avoid his obligations as an employer under Part V of the Code. The Board has also made it clear that corporate documents, declarations, statements, and arrangements made for purposes unrelated to the formation and maintenance of an employment relationship will not be given the same weight as that given to the evidence related to the actual control over the employees.[117]

3:3000   TRADE UNION, COUNCIL OF TRADE UNIONS, AND BARGAINING AGENT

The status of trade union is essential to the application of the *Canada Labour Code.* The determination that an organization is a trade union within the meaning of the Code has wide and important implications throughout the statute. It will determine, among other things, whether this organization may be certified or voluntarily recognized and, accordingly, whether it may acquire the status of bargaining agent. The status of bargaining agent is, in turn, essential to the validity of a collective agreement. Indeed, a collective agreement can only be concluded between an employer and a bargaining agent. The acquisition of the status of bargaining agent by a trade union also imposes upon it a duty of fair representation[118] and of establishing referral rules and applying them fairly and without discrimination if it is engaged in referral to employment.[119] However, whether the trade union has acquired the status of bargaining agent or not, various unfair labour practice prohibitions apply to it.

---

[113]   See also *Dome Petroleum Ltd., supra,* note 108, where it was found that Mercator, who hired, disciplined, and discharged employees, handled their grievances, and assumed the employer's responsibility before the Board, was perceived by the employees as their employer and was in fact the real employer.

[114]   *Dome Petroleum, supra,* note 108.

[115]   *Newfoundland Steamships Ltd., supra,* note 108.

[116]   *Northern Television Systems Ltd., supra,* note 106.

[117]   *MacCosham Van Lines Ltd., supra,* note 108, at p. 721(di).

[118]   *Canada Labour Code,* s. 136.1.

[119]   Section 161.1.

3:3100   DEFINITION OF TRADE UNION

Section 118(p)(iv) of the Code empowers the Board to determine whether an organization or an association is a trade union. As a matter of procedure, the Board will carefully examine the trade union's status when dealing with an employee organization for the first time.[120] This generally occurs in the context of an application for certification,[121] although the issue can be raised in other circumstances.[122]

The Code defines a trade union as "any organization of employees, or any branch or local thereof, the purposes of which include the regulation of relations between employers and employees".[123] The Board has decided[124] that the definition requires three essential elements: (1) an organization must exist, (2) it must be composed of employees, and (3) one of the objects or purposes or the organization must be the regulation of relations between employers and employees.

3:3110   "Any Organization"

In determining whether a trade union exists as an "organization", the Board has followed the practice of other Canadian labour boards[125] in requiring that the union be viable and that as a minimum, it be structured by a constitution and by-laws that will enable it to act with authority on behalf of the membership.[126]

The rationale behind this requirement is that the constitution sets the rules under which the organization operates. It binds the members in their relations to each other and establishes their rights and duties and those of the organization's officers.[127]

The Board has recognized at least two means of setting up a union:[128] a formal process, for example by incorporation under the *British Columbia*

---

[120] *Radio Côte-Nord Inc.* (1977), 23 di 39.

[121] The mere fact that a voluntarily recognized bargaining agent's name has been put on a ballot along with that of a trade union that has filed a certification application seeking to displace it is not an implicit recognition by the Board of the incumbent bargaining agent's status as a trade union. See *Société Radio-Canada* (1978), 27 di 765, at 783, [1979] 2 Can LRBR 41.

[122] *Claude Latrémouille* (1983), 50 di 197. In this case, the question was raised in the context of an unfair labour practice complaint.

[123] *Canada Labour Code*, s. 107(1).

[124] *Air West Airlines Ltd.* (1980), 39 di 56, [1980] 2 Can LRBR 197.

[125] See Jeffrey Sack and C. Michael Mitchell, *Ontario Labour Relations Board Law and Practice* (Toronto: Butterworths, 1985); J.E. Dorsey, *Employee / Employer Rights in British Columbia* (Vancouver: International Self-Counsel Press Ltd., 1979).

[126] *Air West Airlines Ltd., supra,* note 124; *Capital Coach Lines Ltd. (Travelways)* (1980), 40 di 5, [1980] 2 Can LRBR 407, 80 CLLC #16,011; *Air Canada* (1976), 18 di 66 (see pp. 81 and 82), 77 CLLC #16,062.

[127] In this regard see *Orchard v. Tunney*, [1957] S.C.R. 436, 8 D.L.R. (2d) 273, at 281-82; *Astgen v. Smith*, [1970] 1 O.R. 129, 7 D.L.R. (3d) 657, at 661 (C.A.).

[128] *Air West Airlines Ltd., supra,* note 124.

Societies Act[129] or the *Quebec Professional Syndicates Act,*[130] and an informal process, which requires the following steps:

(a) A group of employees meets to form a union. Following the adoption of a motion properly seconded and voted upon, they choose a committee to draft a constitution.

(b) The constitution and by-laws are prepared and amended or accepted as drafted by motion and vote.

(c) Interim officers (president, secretary-treasurer, and other officers) are elected.

(d) Members of the group join the union by making an application and paying minimum dues, generally in the form of initiation fees. The members are then accepted by the interim officers. Unions should be aware that under the federal jurisdiction a minimum of $5 must have been paid by the members during the six months preceding the filing of an application for certification, in order that these membership cards be considered by the Board as evidence of their membership in the trade union.[131] This does not mean that a constitution providing for the payment of a lesser amount would bar a trade union from being granted status under the *Canada Labour Code*. It simply means that the union must prove the payment of $5 by each member in order to show majority support by way of membership cards.

(e) The interim officers then resign, and new officers are elected according to the procedure set out in the constitution and by-laws.

(f) The union can subsequently accept new members according to its constitution and by-laws and can file an application for certification in accordance with the provisions of the Code.

The Board has said[132] that, in light of the clear intention of the legislator to favour access to collective bargaining, it will not be formalistic and will, whenever possible, permit the union to correct defects in its constitution. The Board has ruled[133] that the word "any" that precedes the word "organization" in the definition of "trade union" is not to be interpreted as granting union status to any type of organization, whether regulated by a constitution or not. Rather it refers to different forms of organizations that may have been set up in a formal or informal way, as discussed above. However, the incorporation of a union under a statute, or its voluntary recognition by an employer, will not in itself

---

[129] *Societies Act*, R.S.B.C. 1979, c. 390.
[130] R.S.Q. 1977, c. S-40. See also *Conseil des Montagnais du Lac St-Jean* (1982), 50 di 190.
[131] *Canada Labour Relations Board Regulations*, S.O.R./78-499, s. 27(2).
[132] *Capital Coach Lines Ltd. (Travelways)*, *supra*, note 126.
[133] *Ibid.*

suffice to confer upon it the status of a trade union within the meaning of the Code.[134]

There are limits to the Board's willingness to find that an adequate constitution exists. The Board refused to recognize as a valid constitution the preamble of a collective agreement that set out the goals of the agreement and was subject to modification by negotiations with the employer at the bargaining table.[135] The election of employees for the purpose of negotiations and the processing of grievances from time to time by the union will not cure the defect of the lack of a valid constitution.[136]

Financial viability was found not to be a factor in the recognition of trade union status, particularly where the trade union in question was represented by a lawyer and was using the physical facilities of another union.[137] It is not determinant of the validity of a constitution that the union officers hold office for a determinant period of time.[138] What is necessary is that they hold their office according to the provisions of the constitution.[139] Apart from what may be prescribed in other statutes, the constitution need not require the union to be unequivocally democratic and free of any potential for autocracy, since the Code provides the means under ss. 124 and 137 for employees to change bargaining agents.[140] It must be stressed that unlike provincial statutes such as the *Labour Code of British Columbia,*[141] the *Canada Labour Code* does not require a trade union to be local or provincial in nature. There is nothing in the Code that requires a trade union to have a permanent office in a given province or representatives based in Canada. Therefore, the Board can and has certified international unions as bargaining agents.

The definition of trade union in the *Industrial Relations and Dispute Investigation Act* of 1948 did not contain any reference to a "branch or local thereof" as does the current legislation. These words, it has been argued, were introduced by Parliament in 1972 following the emancipation of Canadian locals from American international unions and their acquisition of a greater degree of autonomy in the running of their affairs. The introduction of these words, furthermore, had the effect of

---

[134]   *Verreault Navigation Inc.* (1978), 24 di 227.

[135]   *Capital Coach Lines Ltd. (Travelways), supra,* note 126.

[136]   *Ibid.*

[137]   *Bank of Nova Scotia (Port Dover Branch)* (1977), 21 di 439, [1977] 2 Can LRBR 126, 77 CLLC #16,090.

[138]   *Ibid.*

[139]   *Transair Ltd.* (1974), 4 di 54, [1974] 1 Can LRBR 281, 74 CLLC #16,111; *Canadian Pacific Ltd.* (1976), 13 di 13, [1976] 1 Can LRBR 361, 76 CLLC #16,018 (the Board stated at 13 di 13, at 25, that it was fatal to union status if its officers were not selected according to the constitution).

[140]   Section 124 of the *Canada Labour Code* deals with certification and s. 137 with revocation of bargaining rights.

[141]   S.B.C. 1973, c. 122, s. 1, as amended and interpreted in *Carcoat Engineering Ltd.,* [1974] 1 Can LRBR 530 (B.C.L.R.B.).

dissipating any doubt as to the status of locals or branches of international unions for the purpose of federal labour legislation by providing them with express recognition. Finally, the addition of these words complemented the new union successorship provisions of s. 143, also introduced in 1972. For instance, in one case, the Board certified an international union that subsequently delegated to one of its locals the jurisdiction and the responsibility of the certificate and the administration of the collective agreement.[142] The Board stated that the union successorship provisions of the Code applied and referred to the definition of a trade union, which includes a branch or a local. The Board concluded that s. 143 clearly contemplated successions between a certified international union and one of its locals. It goes without saying that such a local or branch must be governed by a constitution and by-laws. In practice, the local constitution generally refers to the constitution of the national or international union of which it is a part.

3:3120   An Organization of Employees

The *Canada Labour Code* does not expressly deny trade union status because the organization is employer dominated,[143] as is the case with some provincial labour codes.[144] An employer-dominated union cannot be certified by the Board.[145] Must the organization be solely composed of "employees" within the meaning of the Code to conclude that it is a trade union? This question, which appears simple, is more complex. A trade union may represent employees in both provincial and federal jurisdictions. The provincial definitions of "employee" are not the same as the one in the *Canada Labour Code*. As a result, some persons who would be considered non-employees by a provincial statute may, under the *Canada Labour Code*, have employee status.[146]

---

142   *Banque Nationale du Canada (Sillery, Québec)* (1982), 50 di 91, 2 CLRBR (NS) 202.
143   *Bank of Nova Scotia (Port Dover Branch)*, *supra*, note 137; and *CJRC Radio Capitale Ltée* (1977), 21 di 416, [1977] 2 Can LRBR 578, 78 CLLC #16,124.
144   British Columbia, *Labour Code of British Columbia*, R.S.B.C. 1979, c. 212, s. 1: "'trade union' means a local or Provincial organization or association of employees, or a local or Provincial branch of a national or international organization or association of employees in the Province, that has as one of its purposes the regulation in the Province of relations between employers and employees through collective bargaining, and includes an association or council of trade unions, but not an organization or association of employees that is dominated or influenced by an employer . . ."; New Brunswick, *Industrial Relations Act*, R.S.N.B. 1973, c. I-4, s. 1; Newfoundland, *Labour Relations Act*, S. Nfld. 1977, c. 64; and Saskatchewan, *Trade Union Act*, R.S.S. 1978, c. T-17, s. 2(L).
145   *Canada Labour Code*, s. 134(1).
146   For example, contrast the decision of the Supreme Court of Canada in *Yellow Cab Ltd. v. Alberta Board of Industrial Relations*, [1980] 2 S.C.R. 761, 33 N.R. 585, 14 Alta. L.R. (2d) 39, 24 A.R. 275, 80 CLLC #14,066, 114 D.L.R. (3d) 427, interpreting the Alberta statute, with the interpretation given by the Board in *Société Radio-Canada* (1982), 44 di 19, 1 CLRBR (NS) 129; affd. not yet reported, January 25, 1985, file no. A-467-82 (Fed. C.A.).

In the context of collective bargaining, where it is understood that management and employees through their unions will each promote their own interest in defining the conditions of work, management representatives should not be part of a union.

Although the Board has not rendered a decision on the subject, it is doubtful that it would take such a narrow and literal interpretation.[147] In a number of industries such as construction or longshoring, where employees are dispatched through a hiring hall, it is an accepted practice that a person continues to be a member of the union and pays dues even when he is promoted to supervisory positions excluded from the bargaining unit. This is so because the nature of the industry is volatile and it is quite common that a person who is a supervisor at a given site may well be an employee at the next. In other industries such as radio, television, and the performing arts, a number of persons can be "employees" for one event and a theatre director may be considered an "entrepreneur" in other events.

3:3200   "THE PURPOSES OF WHICH INCLUDE THE REGULATION OF RELATIONS BETWEEN EMPLOYER AND EMPLOYEES"

One purpose of the organization of employees, that is, regulating employer-employee relations, is broadly stated. The Board will infer this purpose from the facts of each case and, more particularly, from the stated objectives of the union's constitution. This purpose will also be inferred from the practices of the trade union in its dealings with employees and employers.[148] A trade union that is not able to convince the Board of its good faith in its dealings with the employer by failing, for example, to establish an arm's-length relationship, will not be recognized as a trade union.[149] The Board will also take into account the manner in which the trade union was formed and whether it had previously been recognized by the Board or by a provincial board,[150] although it is not bound by any provincial recognition.

The regulation of employer-employee relations may not be the only purpose of the trade union. This is made clear by the utilization of the word "include" in the definition. For this reason, the political and social activity of a trade union is not a reason to deny status, as long as it is found that one of its purposes is the regulation of relations between employer

---

147   It is submitted that the element of the definition requiring a union to be composed of employees should be interpreted broadly and with flexibility to take the Canadian bargaining reality into account.

148   *Bank of Nova Scotia (Port Dover Branch), supra,* note 137; *Canadian Imperial Bank of Commerce (Victory Square Branch)* (1977), 20 di 319, [1977] 2 Can **LRBR** 99, 77 CLLC #16,089.

149   *Verreault Navigation Inc.* (1978), 24 di 227.

150   *Canadian Imperial Bank of Commerce (Victory Square Branch), supra,* note 148.

and employees. This interpretation conforms with today's reality and can be contrasted with a decision rendered in 1950,[151] which denied status to a trade union because of its communist affiliation.

3:3300   "COUNCIL OF TRADE UNIONS"

The expression "council of trade unions" is used in s. 130 of the Code. However, it is not defined in the Code. This section enables two or more trade unions, as defined by the Code, to be grouped on a voluntary basis and to apply for certification as a bargaining agent. Section 130(4)(b) provides that, except as otherwise stipulated, Part V applies as if the council of trade unions were a trade union. The status of trade union is bestowed on the council only by certification under s. 130.[152]

3:3400   BARGAINING AGENT STATUS

In order to represent employees for the purpose of collective bargaining under Part V of the Code, a trade union must meet the definition of "bargaining agent" provided in s. 107:

"bargaining agent" means
(a) a trade union that has been certified by the Board as the bargaining agent for the employees in a bargaining unit and the certification of which has not been revoked, or
(b) any other trade union that has entered into a collective agreement on behalf of the employees in a bargaining unit
(i) the term of which has not expired, or
(ii) in respect of which the trade union has, by notice given pursuant to subsection 147(1), required the employer to commence collective bargaining. . . .

A trade union can obtain bargaining agent status either by Board certification or by voluntary recognition from the employer. There are two conditions for the existence of a voluntarily recognized bargaining agent: first, it must have concluded a collective agreement; and second, the term of the collective agreement must not have expired, or a notice to bargain for renewal must have been given in accordance with s. 147. Where a trade union had been certified under provincial jurisdiction, and where it was subsequently found by the courts that the business fell under federal jurisdiction, the trade union was given status as a recognized bargaining agent under the *Canada Labour Code* based on the recognition clause in the collective agreement.[153] The Code, however, clearly favours certification over recognition,[154] as will be seen below.

---

[151]   *Branch Lines Ltd. v. Canadian Seamen's Union* (1950), 52 CLLC #16,622 (C.L.R.B.).
[152]   *MacCosham Van Lines Ltd.* (1984), 84 CLLC #16,051, 7 CLRBR (NS) 216.
[153]   *Cable T.V. Ltée* (1979), 35 di 28, [1980] 2 Can LRBR 381, 80 CLLC #16,019.
[154]   *Joseph Szabo and Jaro Jarkowvsky* (1977), 25 di 345, [1978] 1 Can LRBR 161.

By virtue of its certification and by giving notice to bargain, the certified bargaining agent has the power to compel the employer to negotiate a collective agreement.[155] The voluntarily recognized bargaining agent cannot claim bargaining agent status until a collective agreement has been signed with the employer, nor can it strike to obtain recognition.[156] In order to renew a collective agreement, s. 147 provides that both certified and voluntarily recognized bargaining agents must send the employer a notice to bargain in order to compel him to commence bargaining. However, failure to do so by the recognized bargaining agent may result in its loss of status. Furthermore, an application for certification will freeze the terms and conditions of employment of the employees, and it will constitute an unfair labour practice for the employer to change the conditions or privileges of employment without the Board's consent. This favours the trade union in collective bargaining if it is subsequently certified.[157]

The signing of a recognition clause by the agreement of the parties, if not followed by the signing of a collective agreement, will not preclude a rival union from seeking certification for the same unit. Furthermore, when the collective agreement expires, the voluntary recognized bargaining agent can be raided at any time unless the employees of the unit are engaged in a strike or lockout.[158] In such a case, a six-month bar is imposed by s. 124(3). By contrast, a certified bargaining agent can only be raided after the expiration of twelve months after certification,[159] or after the first six months of a strike, unless the Board consents otherwise.[160]

If there is a collective agreement in force, the delays for filing an application for certification are the same whether the union is voluntarily recognized or certified. However, the voluntarily recognized bargaining agent must be careful to give notice to bargain according to s. 147 in order to maintain its status.[161] Otherwise the employer is free to sign a collective agreement with another union without engaging in unfair labour practices.[162]

While the bargaining agent is certified, an application for revocation of the certificate may be brought only during the time limits provided for certification in s. 124[163] and not during the first six months of a strike, unless authorized by the Board.[164] Where the bargaining agent is not

---

[155] See *Canada Labour Code*, ss. 136(1), 146, and 148.
[156] *Radiodiffusion Mutuelle Ltée* (1977), 18 di 56.
[157] *Canada Labour Code*, ss. 124(4) and 187(1).
[158] Section 124(2)(a).
[159] Section 124(2)(b).
[160] Section 124(3).
[161] See the definition of "bargaining agent" in s. 107(1).
[162] Sections 184(3)(g) and 185(a).
[163] Section 137(1) and (2).
[164] Section 137(5).

certified and where it has concluded a first collective agreement, its mandate to represent the employees can be revoked at any time during the first year of the collective agreement.[165] In other cases it can be revoked during the period for the filing of a certification application in accordance with s. 124.

A further major distinction exists in the application of s. 138(2). In the case of first-agreement negotiations, this section immunizes the certified bargaining agent from a revocation order if it is demonstrated to the Board that the bargaining agent has made a reasonable effort to enter into a collective agreement for the bargaining unit for which it has been certified.[166]

---

[165] Section 137(3) and (4)(a)(i).
[166] For a review of the jurisprudence on the application of s. 138(2), see *La Sarre Air Service Ltée (Propair Inc.)* (1982), 49 di 52.

CHAPTER 4

CERTIFICATION

4:0000   **CERTIFICATION**

There are three conditions to be met before the Board can certify a union to represent a group of employees:

1. The application must be filed by a trade union, within the time limits set out in s. 124.
2. The Board must determine the appropriateness of the bargaining unit (s. 126).
3. The Board must be satisfied that a majority of employees in the unit which it has determined to be appropriate wishes to be represented by the applicant trade union (s. 126).

In dealing with the three conditions set out above, the timeliness of an application, the procedures followed by the Board in processing the application, its policies in regards to the determination of bargaining units, the expression of employee wishes in regard to union representation, and other related issues are examined.

4:1000   **TIMELINESS OF THE APPLICATION**

Section 124(2) sets out the time limits in relation to two variables: the existence or non-existence of a collective agreement, and the presence or absence of an incumbent bargaining agent for the unit.

Before dealing with the specific provisions of s. 124(2), it is important to focus on an important question. Indeed, since both variables taken into consideration by s. 124(2) relate to "the unit", it is essential to know which unit is referred to. For example, in this regard one must consider what happens when the unit sought is different from the existing unit, but includes employees who are represented by a bargaining agent or covered by a collective agreement.

The Board has dealt with this question in a case in which it identified three situations where the problem may arise:[1]

---

[1]   *Société Radio-Canada* (1982), 44 di 19, at 125 to 132, 1 CLRBR (NS) 129. On this point the Board referred to *White Spot Ltd.*, [1976] 1 Can LRBR 241 (B.C.L.R.B.) and adopted its conclusion.

45

1. *Fragmentation.* This occurs when a union seeks certification with respect to small units contained within a larger unit already represented by another union, when a collective agreement is in force and binding on all employees in the larger unit.

2. *Submergence.* A union seeks certification with respect to a unit encompassing a smaller unit for which a union is already certified, where a collective agreement is in force and is binding on all employees of the smaller unit.

3. *Overlap.* This situation occurs when a union seeks certification for a unit that overlaps on another unit already represented by a union, where a collective agreement is in force and is binding on all the employees of the second unit.

After reviewing the advantages and disadvantages of the arguments advanced by the parties in light of the competing policies of the Code,[2] the Board has decided that in the case of fragmentation, as all employees were covered by the same collective agreement, the application could only be made in the periods set out in s. 124(2)(c) and (d). In the case of the other two situations, the application could be filed at any time, since no collective agreement applied in relation to the precise unit sought by the union. The Board went on to say that it would not permit a union in such situations to use this interpretation as a device to evade the time limitation set out in s. 124 by applying for a unit that has little or few differences with the existing one.

It follows that in the second and third situations (submergence and overlap), the board will determine whether the unit sought is substantially different from the unit already certified or for which a collective agreement is in force. It is important to keep the above principle in mind when reading s. 124(2)(b), (c), and (d), as the question may always arise as to whether a collective agreement or a bargaining agent is in place in relation to the unit sought.

---

[2]   Unions have argued that in these three situations s. 124 permits the filing of an application at any time, because no collective agreement is in force and binding on *all* employees of the specific unit sought by an applicant union, nor is there a certified bargaining agent representing *all* employees of the unit. The opposite position required the Board to find any application concerning any employees covered by a collective agreement or represented by a bargaining agent, as the case may be, to be untimely.

The Board discussed the advantages and disadvantages of both positions in relation to the need to fashion a proper bargaining unit. It considered the opportunity presented to refashion the unit and avoid the proliferation of small units on the one hand, and on the other hand, the need to promote stability in the work place by artificially enlarging the existing units to avoid raids, which could be launched at any time. The Board chose an intermediate interpretation that gave it enough flexibility to balance the need to fashion proper bargaining units with the promotion of industrial stability.

Section 124(2)(a) to (d) contemplates four basic situations, which are considered below.

First Situation: No Collective Agreement and No Certified Trade Union — Paragraph (a)

In this case an application may be filed at any time. Such a situation arises not only when a group of employees is seeking to be represented for purposes of collective bargaining for the first time, but also where a collective agreement has expired and the bargaining agent in place is not certified.[3] Occasionally, however, serious issues may arise as to whether a collective agreement exists,[4] and if so, whether it is still in force.[5] Section 124(2)(a) embodies the legislator's preference for certified bargaining agents as opposed to voluntarily recognized bargaining agents. It enables a trade union to apply for certification even if the employer has recognized another trade union but has not yet concluded a collective agreement.[6]

Where a collective agreement was concluded between an employer and a union after an application for certification was filed by a rival union, the Board held that the application was not untimely under s. 124(2)(a).[7] In respect of the construction industry in the Northwest Territories, the Board decided that an application timely under s. 124(2)(a) did not become invalid if, because of the seasonal nature of the business, at the time of certification no more employees were employed by the employer. The Board reasoned that the certificate was attached to job functions rather than to employees, and that the jobs would be filled when the employer resumed its operations in the spring.[8]

Second Situation: No Collective Agreement But Certified Trade Union — Paragraph (b)

Here an application can be filed after the expiry of twelve months from the date of certification, or earlier with the consent of the Board.

---

3 *Wholesale Delivery Service (1972) Ltd.* (1978), 32 di 239, [1979] 1 Can LRBR 90.

4 See paragraph 8:2000. See also *Canadian Offshore Marine Ltd.* (1973), 1 di 20, 74 CLLC #16,089.

5 See, for example, *Austin Airways Ltd./White River Air Services Ltd.* (1980), 41 di 151, [1980] 3 Can LRBR 393, where the Board discussed whether a collective agreement had been continued or renewed. See also on this point *William E. Blonski* (1984), 84 CLLC #16,054, 8 CLRBR (NS) 111. In *J. Phillips* (1978), 34 di 603, at 608, [1979] 1 Can LRBR 180, in relation to s. 138(2), the Board interpreted the words "where no collective agreement is in force" as being "words of art . . . to describe a state or type of bargaining relationship that can exist under the Code rather than the exact legal obligations of parties".

6 It should be noted, however, that such a raid would be barred during the first six months of a strike or lockout, except with the consent of the Board. *Canada Labour Code*, s. 124(3).

7 *Northern Construction Co.* (1976), 14 di 127, 77 CLLC #16,071.

8 *Kevton Holdings Ltd.* (1977), 23 di 43, [1977] 2 Can LRBR 323, 78 CLLC #16,116.

The Board will not easily grant such consent, but will try to protect the incumbent newly certified union to give it a chance to fulfil its mandate to enter into a collective agreement. The Board has stated that the only possible reason to authorize the filing of a new application resides in the employees' interests, as opposed to interests between divergent factions within the union.[9]

Section 124(2)(b) deals with a situation where a trade union is newly certified and is trying to enter into a first collective agreement. Because of the sensitivity of the relation between the parties at this early stage of their "marriage of reason", unless there are very special circumstances the Board will exercise its discretion under s. 124(3) to protect the certified bargaining agent and bar applications until six months after the beginning of a strike or lockout, giving it a protection of up to eighteen months against raids.[10]

Third Situation: Where There Is a Collective Agreement With a Term of a Maximum of Three Years — Paragraph (c)

In this situation, an application can be made after the commencement of the last three months of the term of the agreement. In fact, this means that the application can be made at any time from that date until the collective agreement is renewed[11] and is not confined to the last three months,[12] save for the provisions of s. 124(3) in the case of a strike or lockout. Where the collective agreement provides that at expiry it shall remain in full force and effect from year to year, it was decided that the collective agreement had expired for the purpose of s. 124 when it came to its term,[13] and the application was timely if filed before the renewal of the agreement and was not restricted to the last three months.

Fourth Situation: Where There is a Collective Agreement With a Term of More Than Three Years — Paragraph (d)

An application can be made between the thirty-fourth and thirty-seventh month of the agreement.[14] An application can be made during the last three months preceding the end of each year that the collective agreement continues to operate after the third year of its operation.[15] An

---

9 *Terminal Maritime Pointe-au-Pic*, decision no. 477, not yet reported, August 17, 1984 (C.L.R.B.).
10 *CJMS Radio Montréal (Québec) Ltée* (1978), 28 di 946, at 951, [1979] 1 Can LRBR 426.
11 *Byers Transport Ltd.* (1974), 5 di 22, [1974] 1 Can LRBR 434, 74 CLLC #16,113; *Bell Canada* (1979), 30 di 104, [1979] 2 Can LRBR 429.
12 *Wholesale Delivery Service (1972) Ltd., supra*, note 3.
13 *Ibid.* See also *William E. Blonski, supra*, note 5.
14 *Canada Labour Code*, s. 124(2)(d)(i).
15 Section 124(2)(d)(ii).

application for certification can also be made after the commencement of the last three months of the agreement.[16]

4:1100   BARS TO THE APPLICATION

There are two situations in which the Code and Regulations bar certification:

(1)   a first application has been dismissed; and

(2)   an application is filed during the first six months of a strike or lockout.

Dismissal of the Original Application

This time bar is set out in s. 31 of the regulations, which was adopted in accordance with ss. 124(1) and 117(e) of the Code.[17] The six-month bar is justified by the need to assure some stability in the work place and to avoid perpetuating the periods of insecurity that characterize a union organization drive.[18] In exercising its discretion to abridge the time bar, the Board will take a close look at the circumstances surrounding the application, the uncertainty as to the number of employees sought by the applicant, the effect on the stability of the working relations of the parties and the employees, and the fact that the applicant union must have clean hands.[19]

In *Bell Canada*, where the number of employees affected was 7,658, the Board rejected the initial application because the raiding union did not show a minimum of 50 percent of the membership within the unit that it wanted to represent. The union subsequently made a new application, and the Board shortened the six-month bar on the basis that there had existed uncertainty as to the number of employees when the first application was made (there was a difference of six hundred employees between the applicant's estimate and the final count, which was determined only after a lengthy investigation). The employees were located in seventy cities in two provinces. The Board reasoned that the new application would not result in greater industrial instability than that which already existed, as the incumbent union, which was still in the process of renegotiating its expired collective agreement, needed majority support for that purpose. In that context, it was judged proper to clear the air. The Board went on to find that the raiding union in that case had clean hands and authorized it to file a new application within the six-month time-bar period.

---

16   Section 124(2)(d)(iii).
17   *Canada Labour Relations Board Regulations*, S.O.R./78-499, s. 31.
18   *Bell Canada, supra*, note 11.
19   *Ibid.*; and *Terminal Maritime Pointe-au-Pic supra*, note 9.

From time to time the Board is confronted with applications that are defective for reasons of untimeliness, insufficient representation, or other reasons. Where the Board has reason to believe that the applicant union has made a *bona fide* application, it will entertain an application to withdraw which, if granted, will permit the union to reapply regardless of s. 31 of the regulation. This is so because the decision of the Board does not dismiss the application, but rather grants a withdrawal. Such applications to withdraw are more likely to succeed if they are filed at an early stage of the investigation process rather than at the end, where it becomes apparent that the union could not be certified — as, for example, after a vote — and where it is clear that the union is manoeuvring to avoid the application of s. 31 of the regulations.

First Six Months of a Strike or Lockout — Section 124(3)

The Board has held that where a union has instituted a strike that was later followed by a lockout, the six-month period started to run from the commencement of the strike or the lockout, whichever came first, as both were viewed as part of the same economic warfare.[20] In that case, the Board reaffirmed that the bar was not absolute.

4:1200   TIMELINESS OF AN APPLICATION FILED BY A VOLUNTARILY RECOGNIZED BARGAINING AGENT

The Canada Labour Code does not give preferential status to a voluntarily recognized bargaining agent applying for certification. Indeed, the voluntarily recognized bargaining agent can only file an application for certification within the time limits prescribed by s. 124(2)(c) and (d). It follows that if the application is filed prematurely in regard to the prescriptions of s. 124(2)(c) and (d), it will be found to be untimely.[21] On the other hand, an application filed within the prescribed time period is not invalidated if a collective agreement is renewed before the Board certifies the applicant.[22]

4:2000   PRACTICE AND PROCEDURES

The procedure and the Board's practice and jurisprudence in relation to the filing of an application for certification, the filing of replies and interventions, the processing of the application up to and including the hearing where it is ordered by the Board, are set out below. As a rule,

---

20   *Air Canada* (1976), 18 di 66, 77 CLLC #16,062.
21   *Arctic Transportation Ltd.* (1978), 30 di 94, [1978] 2 Can LRBR 561.
22   *Ibid.; Byers Transport Ltd.* (1974), 5 di 22, [1974] 1 Can LRBR 434, 74 CLLC #16,113.

the documents received by the Board are exchanged between the parties to the proceedings.[23]

4:2100   FILING THE APPLICATION

The application must be in writing.[24] No special form is necessary, but the Board will supply one if requested.[25] Although s. 11 of the regulations provides that the application must be sent to the Board in Ottawa or elsewhere as directed or permitted by the Board, the Board encourages the parties to send the application to its regional offices.[26]

4:2200   CONTENT OF THE APPLICATION

The application must set out the following information:[27]

1. "The full name and address of the applicant." An application may be brought by the international or the local union.[28] A trade union is not restricted by its constitution as to what type of employees it can seek to represent in an application.[29] The application must be signed by its president or secretary or by two officers or by a person authorized in writing to sign on behalf of the union.[30] Officers who are not selected in accordance with the union's constitution cannot sign the application for certification, and their application may be found to be a nullity on that ground.[31] Nor, as a consequence, could such an illegally appointed officer authorize anyone else to act on behalf of the union. The person authorized to represent the union must file his authorization with the Board,[32] but the failure to do so will not invalidate the application, provided the default is subsequently remedied.[33]

---

[23] *Canada Labour Relations Board Regulations*, ss. 8, 9, and 10.
[24] See paragraph 2:4100.
[25] The form is reproduced in Appendix 2.
[26] See Appendix 1, which lists the addresses of the regional offices of the Board.
[27] Regulations, s. 30.
[28] *Air Canada, supra*, note 20; *Banque Nationale du Canada (Sillery, Québec)* (1982), 50 di 91, 2 CLRBR (NS) 202.
[29] *Air Canada, supra*, note 20.
[30] Regulations, s. 9(1)(a).
[31] *Canadian Pacific Ltd.* (1976), 13 di 13, [1976] 1 Can LRBR 361, 76 CLLC #16,018.
[32] Regulations, s. 9(2).
[33] *La Banque Nationale du Canada* (1981), 42 di 352, at 359, [1982] 3 Can LRBR 1; *Canadian Imperial Bank of Commerce (Branches at Creston, B.C. and St. Catharines, Ont.)* (1979), 35 di 105, [1980] 1 Can LRBR 307, 80 CLLC #16,002; *A & M Transport Ltd.* (1983), 52 di 69; *Ronald Wheadon* (1983), 54 di 134, 84 CLLC #16,004, 5 CLRBR (NS) 192.

2. "The full name and address of the employer affected by the application." This simple requisite may sometimes cause problems for an applicant. As seen earlier, it is occasionally difficult to identify correctly the real employer, and even more so, to determine its correct legal appellation.[34] The Board decided, on the basis of s. 203, that a misidentification of the employer is not fatal to the application where the employer is responsible for the situation that created confusion as to its corporate name.[35] The Board will identify the real employer and permit the applicant to amend the application or will add on its own motion the employer as a party pursuant to s. 118(o).[36]

3. "The general nature of the business carried on by the employer."

4. "A description and the location of the unit that the applicant considers is appropriate for collective bargaining and for which certification is sought."

5. "The full name and address of any trade union that is the bargaining agent for any employee affected by the application."

6. "Information respecting the commencement and termination dates of any existing or recently expired collective agreement covering any of the employees affected by the application and a description of the unit of employees covered by each such agreement."

7. "Particulars of any certification order covering any employees affected by the application."

8. "The approximate number of employees in the proposed bargaining unit."

9. "A statement of the number of employees in the proposed unit that the applicant claims as members." Although this statement must accompany the application, it should be sent in a separate document, as this information is treated confidentially by the Board and is not communicated to the employer.[37]

Occasionally, the Board has treated an application filed under s. 119 to amend an existing certificate to include a group of employees in the same manner as if it were an application for certification, where the application for review satisfied the essential elements of an application for certification.[38]

---

34   See paragraph 3:2000.
35   *Northern Construction Co.* (1976), 14 di 127, 77 CLLC #16,071.
36   *Reimer Express Lines Ltd.* (1973), 1 di 12, 74 CLLC #16,093.
37   Regulations, s. 28, and s. 117(m) of the Code. See also *Canadian National Railway Co.* (1983), 52 di 166; and *Crosbie Offshore Services Ltd.* (1983), 54 di 81.
38   *Eastern Provincial Airways (1963) Ltd.* (1978), 29 di 44, [1979] 1 Can LRBR 456; *Capital Coach Lines Ltd. (Travelways)* (1980), 40 di 5, [1980] 2 Can LRBR 407, 80 CLLC

4:2300   NOTIFICATION OF THE APPLICATION

When the Board receives the application, the date and hour of its reception are marked on it. It is then examined for timeliness or other apparent defect. The Board then must give notice in writing to any person who in its opinion may be affected by the application.[39] A letter is then prepared and sent to the employer, informing him of the application and requesting him, among other things,[40] to post a notice of the application for the attention of the employees covered by the application.[41] The employer is required to keep the notice posted for seven days in places where it is most likely to come to the attention of the employees.[42] The employer is also required to attest to the posting and to so inform the Board.[43] Although posting is the usual method of notifying employees and other parties concerned by the application, it is not the only one,[44] and the fact that an employer cannot[45] or will not[46] post is not a reason to dismiss the application, as this would result in denying the employees access to collective bargaining.

4:2400   REPLY AND INTERVENTION TO THE APPLICATION

Persons affected by the application may respond to it by way of a reply or by intervention. In practice, the Board will treat as a reply any representation of an employer or an incumbent union to an application for certification, and as an intervention representations of employees or other unions that have a lesser degree of interest in the proceedings. The characterization of an intervenor as opposed to a respondent will depend on the Board's evaluation of the interests of the party who is intervening or replying.

A person wishing to reply to an application for certification must do so in writing within ten days of the date on which he received notice of the application.[47] In the case of a person employed by the employer who wishes to respond to the posted notice, the ten days' delay commences on

---

#16,011. See also paragraph 6:2000.

[39]   Regulations, s. 13.1.

[40]   The investigating officer writes to the employer notifying him of the application and of the documents which the Board requests the employer to prepare. See paragraph 4:2500.

[41]   A form of this notice is reproduced in Appendix 3.

[42]   Section 117(k) of the Code and s. 13.2 of the regulations.

[43]   Regulations, s. 13(4).

[44]   *Kevton Holdings Ltd.* (1977), 23 di 43, [1977] 2 Can LRBR 323, 78 CLLC #16,116. In this case the Board found that notification by the union to the employees was deemed to be sufficient in the absence of posting by the employer.

[45]   *Northern Construction Co., supra,* note 35.

[46]   *North American Construction Ltd.* (1977), 24 di 220, [1978] 1 Can LRBR 462, 78 CLLC #16,147.

[47]   Regulations, s. 18(1).

the first day the application is posted by the employer.[48] If the person wishing to reply or intervene fails to do so within ten days of the posted notice, he will not be permitted to do so unless he obtains the prior consent of the Board.[49]

The admissibility of the intervention is subject to the Board's discretion.[50] The intervention is the means ordinarily used by employees to respond to an application for certification. It is exceptional for an employee to reply fully to an application. In most cases the intervention will refer to the employees' opposition to the application or alleged impropriety in recruiting.[51] Whenever an employee's intervention relates to his membership in the union, the Board acknowledges its reception to the employee but it is kept confidential.[52] Unless a formal request is made, the intervenor does not receive the correspondence exchanged between the parties. If a hearing is held, the Board will notify the intervenors. If they wish to participate in the hearing, then they will have to establish their interests.

Occasionally, interventions are also filed by third parties who have a certain interest in the proceeding but do not wish to participate actively. For example, interventions may be filed by other incumbent trade unions who want a copy of the proceedings to ascertain whether or not the applicant union is infringing on their own bargaining units.

4:2500   PROCESSING THE APPLICATION

Once the application for certification has been vetted, it is assigned to an investigating officer whose function is to assist the parties in preparing the documents and gathering evidence requested by the Board. When the investigation is complete, the investigating officer prepares a report for the Board. The file is then dealt with by a panel composed of three Board members, unless the matter is uncontested. When the matter is contested, the panel must necessarily be chaired by the chairman or a vice-chairman.[53] The role of the investigating officer and that of the Board in dealing with an application for certification is outlined below.[54]

---

48   Section 14.
49   Section 18(2).
50   Section 17 and *Les Moulins Maple Leaf Ltée* (1978), 23 di 114. In this case the Board refused the intervention filed shortly before a scheduled hearing because it would have resulted in delaying the hearing, and the Board was not satisfied by the explanation given for the tardiness of the intervention.
51   This issue is often raised in the context of raids and in relation to employer dominated allegations which is dealt with at paragraph 4:8100, where the application of s. 134 of the Code is discussed.
52   Regulations, s. 28. The question of the confidentiality of employee wishes is discussed at paragraph 4:6000. See also paragraph 4:6210, where reference is made to employee intervention and the weight to be given to such interventions. See also *Bank of Montreal (Tweed and Northbrook)* (1978), 26 di 591, [1978] 2 Can LRBR 123; and *Quebecair* (1978), 33 di 480, [1979] 3 Can LRBR 550.
53   *Canada Labour Code*, s. 115(a)(1.1), (2).
54   See *Québecair* (1978), 33 di 480, at 497-98, [1979] 3 Can LRBR 550, where the general

The investigating officer represents a particular and vital facet of the Board's operations.[55] The investigating officer's authority to investigate is found in s. 118(k) of the Code. Upon his assignment to a certification file, the investigating officer writes to the employer notifying him of the application and requesting, among other things, that the employer prepare a list of all his employees with names, functions, addresses, and telephone numbers. The employer is also required to prepare a list of employees without the addresses and telephone numbers. The second list will later be transmitted to the applicant union and other parties to the application. Except in very special circumstances, such as an application for a small unit of employees working for a very large employer, the employer is required to give a list of all employees and not only those covered by the application. The employer is also requested to prepare an organizational chart showing the totality of his operations, indicating line and staff relationships within the whole organization and not merely that part which is sought in the application. This document will guide the Board in understanding the employer's operations and in determining whether the unit is appropriate. The investigating officer meets with the employer and, where necessary, helps him to prepare these documents.

The investigating officer will also meet the applicant's representatives and will collect from them the signed membership cards in the possession of the union, together with the financial statements and receipts indicating that money was paid.[56] He will also require the applicant's representative to sign a form[57] attesting, among other things, that the members have paid the initiation fees on their own behalf and that the signatures appearing on the cards are those of the members who have paid the required amount on the date indicated. Unless there are complaints of irregularity by the employees concerned, the investigating officer does not, as a rule, check the signatures or make interviews at random to verify the veracity of the cards. The Board's practice rests on an honour system. Should the Board find out during the course of its inquiry that the representations made by an applicant union as to membership are not as they were represented to be, the application will be dismissed outright.[58]

The investigating officer is also assigned to investigate and mediate any related unfair labour practices complaints and will meet the parties to try to settle such complaints.[59] In certification proceedings, the inves-

---

procedure is outlined.

[55] *Cablevision Nationale Ltée* (1978), 25 di 422, [1979] 3 Can LRBR 267, where the Board had the occasion to discuss the role of the investigating officer.

[56] *Canada Labour Relations Board Regulations*, s. 27(1)(b).

[57] The text of this form is reproduced in Appendix 5.

[58] *Air West Airlines Ltd.* (1980), 39 di 56, [1980] 2 Can LRBR 197; and *Reimer Express Lines Ltd.* (1979), 38 di 213, [1981] 1 Can LRBR 336. This question is dealt with in a more detailed manner in the section concerning employee wishes at paragraph 4:6210.

[59] The role of the investigating officer in this regard is in compliance with the Code s.

tigating officer's main task is to identify the exact scope of the bargaining unit sought by the applicant and to direct the parties to justify their respective positions on inclusions and exclusions.[60]

Once the parties have exchanged their representations in accordance with Board regulations, the investigating officer prepares for the Board a report that sums up the positions of the parties and gives an outline of the nature of the employer's business. This report is exchanged with the parties so that they can comment on its content. A second report dealing solely with the union's representativeness, to which is attached a marked list of employees indicating who is a member of the applicant union, is sent to the Board and is kept confidential.[61]

When the investigating officer's report has been filed, the chairman and vice-chairmen are advised that the file is ready for disposition. It is then assigned to a single member in case of uncontested applications or to a three-member panel in other cases and put on an agenda to be dealt with *in camera* at the date and time set by the chairman of the panel. The members of the panel then study the file and decide whether it can be disposed of without a hearing.[62] The Board is under no obligation to hold a hearing;[63] it is therefore important for the parties to make their case fully in writing, as it may be too late to add to the record once the decision is rendered by the Board.[64]

In *Bank of Nova Scotia (Main Branch Regina)*,[65] the Board discussed the circumstances in which it will hold a hearing. These include: where certification applications are related to unfair labour practices complaints; where the application comes from a new industry; where job positions held by employees require closer examination to determine their content or where new provisions of the Code are involved and require interpretation; where there are several parties involved and a hearing would expedite the application more than would an exchange of written submissions; where the Board determines that a hearing is necessary to give the parties an opportunity to clear the air between themselves, or where the Board foresees a matter of policy that it wishes to have fully explored by the parties; and finally, where constitutional issues

---

188(1)(a).

60   *Majestic Wiley Contractors Ltd.* (1975), 11 di 43, 75 CLLC #16,179.

61   Section 117(m) of the Code and s. 28 of the regulations.

62   Where possible, the Board favours the non-hearing approach, because it permits the Board to decide the matter more rapidly.

63   Regulations, s. 19(2). See also *Bank of Nova Scotia (Main Branch, Regina)* (1978), 28 di 885, [1978] 2 Can LRBR 65; and *Les Arsenaux Canadiens Ltée* (1978), 28 di 931. See also paragraph 19:4120.

64   See in this regard *Canadian National Railways* (1975), 9 di 20, [1975] 1 Can LRBR 327, 75 CLLC #16,158, where the Board laid down the ground rules for reviewing its decisions. The Board will refuse to review its decision unless the party applying for review can demonstrate that it was impossible for it to make its representations before the decision was rendered.

65   *Bank of Nova Scotia (Main Branch, Regina)* (1978), 28 di 885, at 886, [1978] 2 Can LRBR 65; *British Columbia Telephone Co.* (1979), 38 di 145.

are raised. The Board will also take into consideration its own calendar and the possibility of disposing with the application more quickly. In practice, in certification applications the Board orders a hearing in less than 10 percent of the cases.[65a]

4:2600   HEARING BY THE BOARD

If, in the Board's opinion, a hearing is necessary, the panel will decide on a date, and notice of at least ten days will be given to the parties.[66] As a general rule, the Board will hold a hearing in the region where the file originated. The Board may cancel the scheduled hearing or restrict the scope of the hearing to specific issues,[67] or it may combine two or more applications as one.[68]

The Board views the determination of bargaining units and certification as its ultimate responsibility, and it is not bound by any agreement of the parties.[69] In certification matters, the Board acts as a fact-finder in order to collect the information it requires to make a sound decision. Because of its role as a fact-finder and because of its discretion to dispense with a hearing and its power to hear any relevant evidence under s. 118(c), the hearing procedure used by the Board differs from that used by common-law courts, which places the burden of proof and the duty to lead evidence on the applicant.[70]

The hearing is preceded by an informal pre-hearing meeting between the Board members and the parties' representatives. During this meeting, the Board discusses the procedure it intends to follow and any other pertinent matters. Although the applicant union has the onus to convince the Board that the unit sought is appropriate, the Board as a matter of convenience will require the employer to lead evidence to explain its administrative and corporate structures. In order to facilitate this, a full or partial hearing may be called. Once this background information is entered, the applicant union must convince the panel that the unit sought is appropriate. The other parties in turn will then present their evidence, to which the applicant may reply. The Board is an active participant in the hearing and intervenes as frequently as it deems necessary to enhance its understanding of the case.

65a   6.4% in fiscal 1982-83 and 9.7% in fiscal 1983-84. See the Board's annual reports.

66   Regulations, s. 20.

67   *CJRC Radio Capitale Ltée* (1977), 21 di 416, [1977] 2 Can LRBR 578, 78 CLLC #16,124; *CFTO-TV Ltd.* (1981), 45 di 306.

68   Regulations, s. 24. See also *CJRP Radio Provinciale Ltée* (1975), 11 di 33, 77 CLLC #16,074.

69   *CJRC Radio Capitale Ltée, supra,* note 67; *B.D.C. Ltée* (1981), 43 di 140; *Cablevision Nationale Ltée* (1979), 35 di 168; *Société Radio-Canada* (1982), 44 di 19, 1 CLRBR (NS) 129.

70   *Canadian Pacific Ltd.* (1976), 13 di 13, [1976] 1 Can LRBR 361, 76 CLLC #16,018. See also *Nordair Ltd.*, decision No. 458, unreported, April 30, 1984 (C.L.R.B.).

In order to fulfil its mandate to determine the appropriate unit, the Board is not formalistic in adducing evidence, except where the credibility of witnesses is of the essence. This attitude is warranted by the Board's view that since it can decide on the basis of written representations that contain hearsay evidence (and does so in 90 percent of the cases),[71] it would not be appropriate in a fact-finding hearing to require a formalistic standard of proof such as that used by the courts. The Board, as a general rule in certification proceedings, will admit pertinent evidence adduced subsequently to the application and up to the date of the hearing.[72]

A party requiring a subpoena must contact the Board to have them issued. A call to one of its regional offices is sufficient. The payment of witness fees is the responsibility of the party who subpoenas them, according to regional practices. The party requiring a particular witness is well advised to make the necessary arrangement for his presence at the hearing through subpoena or otherwise, rather than assuming that the witness will be present because of his anticipated interest in the case.[73] The Board has refused to suspend a hearing because one party requested the testimony of a person who it was anticipated would have been present, but who did not show up.[74]

If the employer is not required to lead evidence on specific issues, more particularly in regard to its administrative and organizational structure, the Board has decided that the obligation to lead evidence rests on the parties challenging an existing unit[75] or the employee status.[76]

Since 1978, the Board as a matter of policy has not permitted the recording of procedures during the hearings and has explained its reasons for this practice in *Canadian Pacific Ltd.*[77] The party wishing a recording must convince the Board that this will be a useful tool to decide the case. The Board has granted such requests where lengthy hearings were expected[78] or where constitutional jurisdiction was at issue.[79]

In an exceptional case,[80] acting on powers given to it by s. 118(k), the

---

71 Source: *Annual Reports* of the Board, 1982-83 and 1983-84.
72 *Northern Television Systems Ltd.* (1976), 14 di 136, at 145, 76 CLLC #16,031.
73 *Canada Labour Code*, s. 207.
74 *Wholesale Delivery Service (1972) Ltd.* (1978), 32 di 239, [1979] 1 Can LRBR 90.
75 *Transair Ltd.* (1974), 4 di 54, [1974] 1 Can LRBR 281, 74 CLLC #16,111.
76 *Ibid.*
77 (1980), 39 di 138, [1980] 3 Can LRBR 87, 80 CLLC #16,059.
78 *Société Radio-Canada, supra,* note 69; *Canadian Broadcasting Corp.*, decision no. 461, not yet reported, April 30, 1984 (C.L.R.B.).
79 *Northern Telecom Canada Ltd.* (1980), 41 di 44, at 93, [1980] 2 Can LRBR 122.
80 *Air West Airlines Ltd.* (1980), 39 di 56, [1980] 2 Can LRBR 197. In this case the Board was hearing a matter where employer interference was alleged in the context of a raid following a long and bitter strike, and it was requested to render a decision quickly. The Board, sitting as a three member panel, had heard a week's evidence in Vancouver and had peremptorily scheduled another week for a month later. Shortly before the resumption of the hearing a panel member became incapacitated, which resulted in his inability to sit as scheduled.

Board collected evidence by delegating two members to hear evidence and report to the three-member panel. The decision was then taken by the three-member panel on the basis of the report, which consisted of the filing of the recording of the evidence taken at the sub-hearing.

The Board is under no statutory obligation to give reasons for its decision,[81] although it will usually do so unless it is dealing with a routine matter. The reasons are normally given in writing by means of a formal numbered decision or a letter decision,[82] or they are included in the body of the certification order.

4:2700   APPLICATION TO WITHDRAW

An applicant wishing to withdraw its application may do so by applying in writing to the Board. The Board will not automatically grant the withdrawal and will inquire into the circumstances surrounding the application before deciding the matter. If the Board does not grant withdrawal, it will dispose of the matter on its merit and may dismiss it. The dismissal will constitute a bar to the filing of a new application within six months.[83]

4:3000   DETERMINATION OF THE APPROPRIATE BARGAINING UNIT

The Board's jurisdiction and powers to determine appropriate bargaining units, the criteria developed by the Board for this purpose, together with those imposed by the statute and those related to the inclusion and exclusion of persons in and from the unit, are examined below. Special multi-employer and multi-union bargaining units are also dealt with, as well as patterns of bargaining units found in certain industries.

The Code defines "bargaining unit" as:

a unit
(a) determined by the Board to be appropriate for collective bargaining, or
(b) to which a collective agreement applies. . . .[84]

"Unit" is defined as:

a group of two or more employees.[85]

---

81   *Cablevision Nationale Ltée* (1978), 25 di 422, at 427, [1979] 3 Can LRBR 267. This decision was affirmed by *Canadian Arsenals Ltd. v. Canada Labour Relations Board*, [1979] 2 F.C. 393 (C.A.).
82   *Les Arsenaux Canadiens Ltée* (1978), 28 di 931; *Cablevision Nationale Ltée, supra*, note 81.
83   *Terminal Maritime Pointe-au-Pic*, decision no. 477, not yet reported, August 17, 1984 (C.L.R.B.). See also the discussion in paragraph 4:1100 in relation to the application of s. 31 of the regulations.
84   *Canada Labour Code*, s. 107(1).
85   *Ibid.*

The jurisdiction and powers of the Board in determining bargaining units are found in ss. 118(p)(v), 125(1), (2), (3), (4), (5), 126(b), 130(2), and 132(1) of the Code.

The Supreme Court of Canada has recognized that it was within the Board's jurisdiction to determine the appropriate bargaining unit and that its decision on the subject was not reviewable.[86] Basing its decision on the above-cited sections of the Code, the Board has found that it has exclusive authority to determine the appropriateness of bargaining units.[87] It has concluded that the impact of the determination of the appropriate unit is too great to allow a union to have the final word;[88] nor can that decision be left strictly to the choice of any particular group of employees.[89] In fact, the determination of the appropriate bargaining unit goes beyond the mere agreement of the parties, and the Board has stated on numerous occasions that it is not bound by such agreements.[90] If the agreement makes sense in terms of industrial relations and conforms to its own criteria, the Board may ratify it.[91] In this regard, the Board's practice is quite different from that of other labour boards in Canada, which approve more readily the parties' agreement concerning the inclusion and exclusion of employees.[92] The Board has further stated that it is not bound by the existence of voluntarily recognized bargaining units when determining the appropriateness of a unit.[93]

The Board has the power to fashion a unit that is larger than the one sought by the applicant union.[94] In *B.D.C. Ltée* the Board explained that its role is different from that of common-law courts or of arbitration

---

86 *Canada Labour Relations Board v. Transair Ltd.*, [1977] 1 S.C.R. 722, 9 N.R. 181, 76 CLLC #14,024; *Noranda Mines Ltd. v. The Queen; Saskatchewan Labour Relations Board v. The Queen*, [1969] S.C.R. 898, 69 W.W.R. 321, 69 CLLC #14,205, 7 D.L.R. (3d) 1.

87 *Majestic Wiley Contractors Ltd.* (1975), 11 di 43, 75 CLLC #16,179; *Saskatchewan Wheat Pool* (1977), 21 di 388, [1977] 1 Can LRBR 510, 77 CLLC #16,104; *Atomic Energy of Canada Ltd.* (1977), 25 di 377, [1978] 1 Can LRBR 92, 78 CLLC #16,128; *Téléglobe Canada* (1979), 32 di 270, [1979] 3 Can LRBR 86, 80 CLLC #16,025; *B.D.C. Ltée* (1981), 43 di 140; *Société Radio-Canada* (1982), 44 di 19, 1 CLRBR (NS) 129.

88 *Canadian Imperial Bank of Commerce (Victory Square Branch)* (1977), 20 di 319, [1977] 2 Can LRBR 99, 77 CLLC #16,089.

89 *Canadian Pacific Ltd.* (1976), 13 di 13, [1976] 1 Can LRBR 361, 76 CLLC #16,018; *Téléglobe Canada*, *supra*, note 87.

90 *CJRP Radio Provinciale Ltée* (1975), 11 di 33, 77 CLLC #16,074; *Canadian Pacific Ltd.*, *supra*, note 89; *Enterprises Télé-Capitale Ltée* (1976), 16 di 230, 77 CLLC #16,075; *Canadian Imperial Bank of Commerce (Victory Square Branch)*, *supra*, note 88; *Cablevision Nationale Ltée*, *supra*, note 81; *Téléglobe Canada*, *supra*, note 89; *Wardair Canada (1975) Ltd.* (1983), 53 di 26, 2 CLRBR (NS) 129; *Québecair* (1978), 33 di 480, [1979] 3 Can LRBR 550; *Bell Canada* (1981), 46 di 90, [1982] 1 Can LRBR 274.

91 *CJRP Radio Provinciale Ltée*, *supra*, note 90; *Canadian Pacific Ltd.*, *supra*, note 89; *Téléglobe Canada*, *supra*, note 87; *Wardair Canada (1975) Ltd.*, *supra*, note 90.

92 As stated by the Board in *Québecair*, *supra*, note 90, at p. 497 (di). See *Bell Canada*, *supra*, note 90, in which the Board traced the evolution of the notion of "parties' agreement" in bargaining unit determination up to the 1970s, when the provisions of Part V of the *Canada Labour Code* were enacted.

93 *Murray Bay Marine Terminal Inc.* (1981), 46 di 55.

94 *B.D.C. Ltée*, *supra*, note 87.

tribunals seized by a request for a determination of a private dispute.[95] The notion of *ultra petita*[96] applies to conflicts of a private nature where monetary compensation is sought as a remedy, but this is not the case where the Board must fashion bargaining units with a view to promoting industrial peace and where its decision has sociopolitical consequences. For these reasons the Board may increase or decrease the scope of the unit originally sought by the applicant trade union.[97]

The scope of the bargaining unit determined as appropriate by the Board is not carved in stone. The Board has always recognized that the structure of an employer's organization is not static and that changes may become necessary.[98] Referring to ss. 118(p), 119, 121, and 158 of the Code, the Board stated that after the issuance of the original certificate the parties may not compel the negotiation of the boundaries of the bargaining unit determined therein to restrict its scope.[99] The Board considers it to be its duty and obligation to continue to redefine the unit as changes in the employer's structure make it necessary,[100] although it has made it clear that it will not make changes to a bargaining unit simply to give the advantage to one party at the bargaining table.[101]

In short, the Board, in view of its exclusive power and jurisdiction to fashion bargaining units, actively participates in the fact-finding process leading to its final determination, either by a written exchange of information between the parties and the Board, or at a hearing, should one be held.

The Board will entertain applications to modify existing bargaining units, but before agreeing to any changes it must be satisfied that such changes are in accordance with its policies and criteria.

4:3100   GENERAL CRITERIA DEVELOPED BY THE BOARD

The Board has adopted criteria to determine the configuration of bargaining units by drawing on its own experience over the years and that of all the other Canadian labour boards and the Quebec Labour Court,

---

95   *Ibid.* See also Code s. 125(2), which gives power to the Board to include employees in and exclude employees from the unit proposed by the trade union.
96   Wherein the judge cannot adjudicate on what is not sought in the plaintiff's conclusions.
97   *B.D.C. Ltée, supra,* note 87, at p. 150 (di).
98   *Téléglobe Canada, supra,* note 87.
99   *Ibid.; Société Radio-Canada, supra,* note 87.
100 *Bell Canada, supra,* note 90.
101 *British Columbia Telephone Co., Canadian Telephones and Supplies Ltd.* (1977), 24 di 164, [1978] 1 Can LRBR 236, 78 CLLC #16,122; *Inter-City Truck Lines (Canada) Inc., and Trans Canada Truck Lines Inc.* (1981), 45 di 119, 81 CLLC #16,120; *Bank of Montreal (Windsor, Ontario)* (1981), 45 di 266, [1982] 2 Can LRBR 380.

which it has adapted to suit the particularities of federal undertakings and its enabling statute, the *Canada Labour Code*.[102]

To better understand the Board's approach in developing or shaping bargaining units, it is important to bear in mind that the Board views its role in administering the provisions of the Code as one that must favour the attainment of the objectives of Part V, the most important of which are favouring access to collective bargaining and promoting labour peace.[103]

In an early case, the Board enunciated the criteria it would consider in determining appropriate bargaining units.[104] It referred to the following:

1.   The existence of an agreement between the parties that respects the provisions of the law and Board policy.

2.   The viability concept: Is the bargaining unit strong enough to effectively permit the bargaining agent to strike a deal with the employer?

3.   The existence of a community of interest. In subsequent cases,[105] the Board enumerated the factors to be considered in determining a community of interest:

      — similarity of work and duties among the employees;

      — similarity of salary and method of payment;

      — similarity of working conditions;

      — similarity of trade and qualifications;

      — interdependence and interchangeability of duties;

      — transferability and promotion of workers from one category to another.

4.   Administrative and organizational status of the employer, so that members will stand a reasonable chance of effectively engaging in collective bargaining.[106]

5.   The history of collective bargaining between the employer and the union representing its employees.

6.   The wishes of the employees.[107]

---

102   *B.A.C.M. Construction Co. Ltd.* (1978), 33 di 386, [1979] 1 Can LRBR 104, 79 CLLC #16,173. In *Téléglobe Canada, supra,* note 87, the Board stated the rationale for its approach in determining and reshaping bargaining units.

103   *Canada Labour Code,* s. 121 and Preamble.

104   *Soo-Security Motorways Ltd.* (1974), 4 di 51, 74 CLLC #16,109.

105   *Cablevision Nationale Ltée* (1978), 25 di 422, [1979] 3 Can LRBR 267; *Société Radio-Canada* (1978), 27 di 765, [1979] 2 Can LRBR 41.

106   *Bell Canada* (1976), 19 di 117, [1976] 1 Can LRBR 345, 76 CLLC #16,016; *Northern Electric Co. Ltd.* (1976), 16 di 237.

107   *Soo-Security Motorways Ltd., supra,* note 104; *Canadian Broadcasting Corp.* (1977), 19 di 166, [1977] 2 Can LRBR 481, 77 CLLC #16,102; *General Aviation Services Ltd.* (1979), 34 di 791, [1979] 2 Can LRBR 98; *Cyprus Anvil Mining Corp.* (1979), 37 di 92.

7. The territorial or geographical distribution of the employer's operations.[108]
8. The interchangeability of personnel.
9. Industrial peace.
10. The professional status of the employees.
11. The regular, occasional, or part-time nature of the jobs performed by employees.[109]

No single criterion is determinant, and different weight will be given to each depending on the particulars of each case.[110]

In subsequent cases[111] the Board reformulated these criteria to distinguish between small units on the one hand, and large, all-employee units, encompassing either all the employees of an employer or all the employees of a given department or craft on the other hand. Some of the factors favouring the creation of large units are:

(i) administrative efficiency and convenience in bargaining;
(ii) the potential for achieving a common framework of employment conditions and the attainment of industrial stability.

Those factors that favour the creation of smaller units are:

(i) lack of a community of interest;
(ii) geographical factors;[112]
(iii) the likelihood that a large unit will not be viable;
(iv) a concern to enable employees to gain representation;[113]
(v) specific statutory provisions.[114]

When the Board considers the submissions of the parties on the appropriateness of the unit, it is well aware that each party is defending very specific interests: the union is applying for a unit shaped so as to

---

108   *Feed-Rite Ltd.* (1979), 29 di 33, [1979] 1 Can LRBR 296.
109   *Charterways Co. Ltd.* (1974), 2 di 18, [1974] 1 Can LRBR 161, 74 CLLC #16,097.
110   *Soo-Security Motorways Ltd., supra,* note 104; *Canadian Pacific Ltd.* (1976), 13 di 13, [1976] 1 Can LRBR 361, 76 CLLC #16,018; *Canadian Imperial Bank of Commerce (Victory Square Branch)* (1977), 20 di 319, [1977] 2 Can LRBR 99, 77 CLLC #16,089; *Canadian Broadcasting Corp., supra,* note 107; *British Columbia Telephone Co.* (1977), 33 di 361, [1977] 2 Can LRBR 385, 77 CLLC #16,107; *British Columbia Telephone Co.* (1977), 22 di 507, [1977] 2 Can LRBR 404, 77 CLLC #16,108; *Feed-Rite Ltd., supra,* note 108; *Empire Stevedoring Co. Ltd.* (1981), 45 di 36; *Société Radio-Canada* (1982), 44 di 19, 1 CLRBR (NS) 129.
111   *Canadian Pacific Ltd., supra,* note 110; *Saskatchewan Wheat Pool* (1977), 21 di 388, [1977] 1 Can LRBR 510, 77 CLLC #16,104; *Canadian Imperial Bank of Commerce (Victory Square Branch), supra,* note 110.
112   *Feed-Rite Ltd., supra,* note 108.
113   *Canadian Imperial Bank of Commerce (Victory Square Branch), supra,* note 110; *Banque Canadienne Nationale (Centre de traitement des données)* (1979), 34 di 822, [1980] 1 Can LRBR 297; *Okanagan Helicopters Ltd.* (1980), 42 di 172, [1981] 1 Can LRBR 327. In *Canadian Pacific Ltd., supra,* note 110, at p. 27 (di), the Board stated that the application of the criteria it generally refers to must not be used to hamper the organizing of employees.
114   *Canada Labour Code,* s. 125(5).

facilitate to the maximum its representative character, and the employer is submitting arguments that are more likely to negate this representivity.[115] The Board sees its role as one that must take into account the long-term interest of the parties' relationship and the interest of the employees concerned.[116] This explains in part why, as stated earlier, the Board does not feel bound by the agreement of the parties.

The enumeration of the criteria is more easily done than is a determination with certainty of which one will be determinant. That is so because unit determination has always been approached on a case-by-case basis. How then will the practitioner who is preparing an application for certification or a reply to an application be best able to "guesstimate" what criteria or preference for large or small units the Board is most likely to consider determinant in his case?

One must be aware that the Board does not operate in a vacuum. The decision will be made in a specific context. Following are some background factors that will help determine which set of criteria will be applied.

First, the organizational factor and the nature of the employer's business is most important in determining unit appropriateness. What is the nature of the employer's business? Is it a large national employer with employees in locations across the country (such as the C.B.C., Canada Post, Air Canada, C.N.R., C.P.R.), or is it a small employer with ten to fifteen employees operating in a single location, as for example, a small radio station? What is the administrative and operational set-up of the employer? Are its operations centralized or decentralized? What is the certification pattern of the employer and of the industry in which it operates? As was mentioned earlier, the Board's practice in each file where the question of unit appropriateness arises is to require from the employer complete charts showing the line and staff relationship of all its employees, whether or not they are covered by the pending application. A party, whether applicant or respondent, should always be prepared to defend its position in the light of the employer's organizational chart. It is not always easy for an applicant union to have advance knowledge of this, because information of this sort is not made easily accessible by employers. Nevertheless, once the Board has obtained a copy of the employer's organizational chart, it will communicate it to the interested parties. Since the Board will necessarily take that factor into account, applicants are well advised to reassess their position and, if necessary, to amend their initial application when this information is made available to them. In short, the Board initially looks at what might be the ideal (the most appropriate) bargaining unit, that is, a large unit that will include all the employees of a given employer, because it will be less destructive to the

---

115 *CFTO-TV Ltd.* (1981), 45 di 306.
116 *Téléglobe Canada* (1979), 32 di 270, [1979] 3 Can LRBR 86, 80 CLLC #16,025.

operations of the business.[117] But, as is well known, the Board is not obliged to establish the most appropriate bargaining unit.[118]

Second, the Board will try to determine the likelihood of the applicant employees gaining real access to collective bargaining if the most appropriate bargaining unit is retained. The Board will look at the employer's business and the industry in which he operates, and at their record in terms of permitting employees to bargain collectively. In fact, the Board will weigh the competing interests of establishing the most appropriate bargaining unit on the one hand and, on the other hand, of making it possible for employees to realistically assert their rights to collective bargaining as enshrined in the preamble of the Code in general and in s. 110 in particular.[119] In a case dealing with an application for a unit of employees whose configuration purported to correspond to an administrative division of the employer, the Board put the issue this way:

> The question to finally be answered is not whether Purolator Courier's zone 516 is autonomous or may be operated in an autonomous fashion, but whether the certification of the employees envisioned by the application would create an industrial relations anomaly, disrupt the orderly flow of the employer's business, be counter productive in respect of the interest of the employees and ride rough shod over long recognized almost hallowed considerations of community of interest.[120]

In fact, although the Code imposes no burden of proof on either party, the task of convincing the Board that the proposed bargaining unit is appropriate has over the years shifted from the applicant alone to a situation in which it is equally shared by the trade union and the employer. This is so because more emphasis is now being placed on the employees' right to bargain collectively[121] and because the Board does not perceive its role as the arbitrator of a dispute of a purely private nature, but rather one that is sociopolitical, with the long-range goal of promoting industrial relations peace. An example of this more modern approach can be seen in the manner in which the Board processes the application. In the course of the proceedings, the union's position is not equated with that of a plaintiff at common law, who has the onus to lead evidence. Because of the importance of the information relating to his organizational structure, the employer is required to lead evidence in that respect. More often than not, it is the Board that takes the initiative

---

117 *Canadian Pacific Ltd., supra,* note 110; *Saskatchewan Wheat Pool, supra,* note 111; *Canadian Imperial Bank of Commerce (Victory Square Branch), supra,* note 110.

118 *British Columbia Telephone Co.* (1977), 33 di 361, [1977] 2 Can LRBR 385, 77 CLLC #16,107; *British Columbia Telephone Co.* (1977), 22 di 507, [1977] 2 Can LRBR 404, 77 CLLC #16,108; *Empire Stevedoring Co. Ltd., supra,* note 110.

119 *Canadian Pacific Limited, supra,* note 110; *Saskatchewan Wheat Pool, supra,* note 111; *Canadian Imperial Bank of Commerce (Victory Square Branch), supra,* note 110; *Banque Canadienne Nationale (Centre de traitement des données), supra,* note 113; *Purolator Courier Ltd.* (1983), 53 di 166, 83 CLLC #16,069.

120 *Purolator Courier Ltd., supra,* note 119, at p. 176 (di).

121 See s. 2(d) of the *Canadian Charter of Rights and Freedoms, Canada Act 1982,* c. 11 (U.K.).

of requiring more information to gain a better understanding of the consequences of establishing a given unit. This approach is more in line with the Board's thinking that unit-determination is within its exclusive jurisdiction and duty and that it is not bound by the agreement of the parties. Once the application is made, its disposition rests entirely on the hands of the Board.

Where the Board has initially created small units to give employees access to collective bargaining, it may modify the existing pattern and certify larger units to enhance the union's bargaining power. In *Banque Nationale* the Board applied the American National Labor Relations Board "cluster" concept and certified in a single unit the employees of four bank branches.[121a] Until that decision the Board had, as a rule, certified on a branch basis.

Third, the Board will consider the context and circumstances in which the application for certification is filed. What is the nature of the application calling for the determination of a bargaining unit? Is it an application for certification to represent employees who are not already covered by a collective agreement? Does it purport to raid an existing unit? On this issue, it is useful to know that the Board's stated policy in raiding situations is not to modify existing units, but rather to emphasize the employees' wishes to change bargaining agents.[122] Are there other employees of the employer included in other bargaining units? Does the certification application seek to include some of these employees? Is the application one that seeks to amend an existing certificate? Does it request the fragmentation of an existing bargaining unit? The Board has stated that when considering applications to fraction existing units and those seeking the creation of new units, the weight to be given to the criteria will not be the same.[123] On numerous occasions, the Board has stated its reluctance to fraction existing units[124] or to create an unduly large number of small units,[125] and it has placed the onus on the party proposing fragmentation.[126] Does the application arise out of s. 144(3), which requires the Board to determine the appropriateness of bargaining units following the sale of a business, or out of s. 132, requiring a compulsory multi-employer unit?

[121a] *Banque Nationale du Canada*, decision no. 542, not yet reported, December 18, 1985 (C.L.R.B.).

[122] *Bell Canada* (1981), 43 di 86, [1982] 3 Can LRBR 113; *CJMS Radio Montréal (Québec) Ltée* (1978), 33 di 393, [1980] 1 Can LRBR 270.

[123] *Feed-Rite Ltd.*, *supra*, note 108.

[124] *Canadian Pacific Ltd.*, *supra*, 110; *Entreprises Télé-Capitale Ltée* (1976), 16 di 230, 77 CLLC #16,075; *Canadian Broadcasting Corp.* (1977), 19 di 166, [1977] 2 Can LRBR 481, 77 CLLC #16,102.

[125] *Bell Canada* (1976), 19 di 117, [1976] 1 Can LRBR 345, 76 CLLC #16,016; *Seaspan International Ltd.* (1979), 37 di 38, [1979] 2 Can LRBR 213.

[126] *British Columbia Telephone Co.* (1977), 33 di 161, [1977] 2 Can LRBR 385, 77 CLLC #16,107; *Atomic Energy of Canada Ltd.* (1977), 25 di 377, [1978] 1 Can LRBR 92, 78 CLLC #16,128.

Parties appearing before the Board to seek bargaining-unit determination through certification, review of an existing certificate, or the declaration of a sale of a business must be conscious: (i) of the Board's general approach to the criteria, (ii) that each case will be treated on the basis of its facts, (iii) that the Board is not obliged to determine the most appropriate bargaining unit, and (iv) that it is not bound by its own precedents.[127] If they do so, the parties will be better able to appreciate the following comments made by the Board:

1.   "Carving out" will not be condoned by the Board.[128]

2.   The Board will not easily fragment existing national units.[129] It will fraction such units if they correspond to the employer's reorganized structure, however.[130]

3.   It is desirable to avoid the creation of unduly large numbers of small units.[131]

4.   In widely organized industries the emphasis is placed on large units. When the employees in these units were first being organized, they were included in smaller units in order to facilitate their access to collective bargaining.[132]

---

[127] *Canadian Broadcasting Corp., supra,* note 124.

[128] *Pacific Coast Terminals Co. Ltd.* (1974), 6 di 59. In this case the applicant union was seeking to represent a group of supervisors. The Board found that the appropriate unit included all the supervisors of the employer, not only those originally sought by the applicant. As a result, the applicant did not have majority status as of the date of application, and a vote was ordered under s. 127(2) of the Code.

[129] *Canadian Pacific Ltd.* (1976), 13 di 13, [1976] 1 Can LRBR 361, 76 CLLC #16,018. In this case the application sought to fraction an existing national unit, where the incumbent union since 1946 (the date of its certification) and traditionally before that date had negotiated for all engineers in C.P.R.'s four regions: Western, Prairies, Eastern, and Atlantic. The applicant was seeking certification for the Pacific region. The Board dismissed the application.

In *Entreprises Télé-Capitale Ltée* (1976), 16 di 230, 77 CLLC #16,075, the applicant union was seeking to fragment an existing all-employee unit of a privately owned broadcasting station in order to represent the journalists and filmmakers only. The Board dismissed the application because the unit sought was not viable.

In *Canadian Broadcasting Corp.* (1977), 19 di 166, [1977] 2 Can LRBR 481, 77 CLLC #16,102, the Board dealt with an application to cover office and professional employees of the C.B.C. working in Quebec and already included in a national bargaining unit. The Board denied the application on the basis that the union was seeking to represent a group of employees that did not correspond to the organizational structure of the C.B.C.

[130] *Canadian Broadcasting Corp. supra,* note 129. Here the Board considered an application seeking to cover production employees of the C.B.C. working in its French service division who were already part of a national unit. The Board fractioned the existing unit on the basis that it corresponded to the reorganized operational structure of the C.B.C., which provided for an autonomous French-service division.

[131] *Bell Canada* (1976), 19 di 117, [1976] 1 Can LRBR 345, 76 CLLC #16,016. The applicant sought to cover all professional engineers and architects at the employer's locations in Ontario and Quebec. The Board dismissed the application, as it found that the employees sought performed functions and duties that were identical or very similar to those performed by non-professionals employed by the employer.

[132] *Saskatchewan Wheat Pool* (1977), 21 di 388, [1977] 1 Can LRBR 510, 77 CLLC #16,104.

5.   The Board must fashion units in order to give employees realistic access to collective bargaining.[133]

6.   A conflicting interest between two unions is secondary in importance to the acceptance of the employer's position that a system-wide unit is preferable and appropriate.[134]

7.   Through the years, Board policy has shifted away from forming craft units.[135]

8.   The Board favours large units and wishes to avoid fractioning existing units, and favours the amalgamation of a plurality of employee groups with the same community of interest.[136]

The Board received two applications for certification: one from a trade union that represented employees of five employers in the port of Vancouver and had a history of bargaining with an employer's association of which the five employers were members; the other by a trade union seeking to represent employees working for one of the five employers. The Board dismissed the second application and established a multi-employer unit under s. 131 of the Code.

[133] *Canadian Imperial Bank of Commerce (Victory Square Branch)* (1977), 20 di 319, [1977] 2 Can LRBR 99, 77 CLLC #16,089. The Board dealt with an application to represent employees working in a single branch of the employer. The employer, who had 34,000 employees in all regions of Canada, had argued that the appropriate bargaining unit was one that should include all its employees, working in 1,693 branches across Canada. The Board granted the union's application, taking into consideration the nature of the industry and the employees' realistic chances of having access to collective bargaining.

In *Banque Canadienne Nationale (Centre de traitement des données)* (1979), 34 di 822, [1980] 1 Can LRBR 297, the union sought certification for two units: the Data Centre and the Chargex Department. The employer argued that these departments represented only two of forty-one departments and comprised a small minority of the employees among its 1,900 head-office employees. The Board granted both applications in order to favour access to collective bargaining.

In *Purolator Courier Ltd., supra*, note 119, the Board heard an application to cover employees working within an administrative district of the employer. The employer argued that the administrative division did not correspond to the operational reality of its business. The Board granted the application. The question of whether the unit sought corresponded to the administrative or operational reality was found not to be determinant.

[134] *Pacific Western Airlines Ltd.* (1980), 40 di 205, [1980] 3 Can LRBR 180. The Board considered an application for review by the employer following the merger of two airlines and an application for certification by a union to cover all maintenance, ramp employees, and traffic agents of the employer, according to the industry pattern. The Board found that where employees had longstanding bargaining rights, the industry pattern was not determinant; but it found to be appropriate two company-wide units, one for maintenance employees and one for ramp and traffic employees.

[135] *Air Canada* (1980), 42 di 114, [1981] 1 Can LRBR 153. The Board dealt with an application seeking to fraction a national bargaining unit of maintenance employees in favour of a small group based in Winnipeg who had a higher degree of technical knowledge in maintenance work. This small group represented 243 employees out of the 7,345 who were already members of the national maintenance employee unit. The Board dismissed the application.

[136] *Conseil des Ports Nationaux* (1983), 52 di 34. The Board heard an application from a union seeking to regroup four units of blue- and white-collar workers for which it was already certified. The Board granted the application, stating that it would grant applications to regroup units that have a community of interest. It went on to dismiss the union's second application to add to the amalgamated groups another unit of office

9. The Board will not easily set aside a collective bargaining relationship that has existed for more than twenty years.[137]

10. The goal of the Board in fashioning appropriate units must be to ensure an equilibrium of forces at the bargaining table between employer and union.[138]

To summarize, when confronted with an application to determine the appropriateness of a bargaining unit, the Board is more likely to fashion it in terms of larger units if it is dealing with an employer who is not opposed to his employees having access to collective bargaining. Indeed, the more difficulties the Board perceives in the employees gaining any access to collective bargaining due to employer opposition or other factors, the more likely the employer is to be saddled with smaller bargaining units that will give his employees more effective access to collective bargaining, which in the Board's view is a means to promote industrial peace in the work place.[139]

In addition to the general approach taken by the Board that is outlined above, certain tendencies emerge in the Board's decisions, although in some cases they may be overridden by other considerations.

The Board will generally recognize the blue collar–white collar division among employees of the same employer[140] and will not include part-time and full-time employees in the same unit if the former is in the majority.[141] In one occasion, where a union represented two groups of employees — production and office personnel — and sought to merge them, the Board found that both options were acceptable and ordered a vote allowing the employees to decide which option they preferred.[142] On another occasion, the same bargaining agent acted for a group of production employees and a group of office employees and negotiated collective agreements at the same table for both groups. In this case, the Board consolidated both units.[143]

The Board is not bound by the provisions of a union's constitution or by the extent of the union's organizational campaign in selecting the

---

employees which the union represented as the bargaining agent because it found no community of interest with the employees of the larger group.

137 *Conseil des Ports Nationaux, supra,* note 136.
138 *Téléglobe Canada* (1979), 32 di 270, [1979] 3 Can LRBR 86, 80 CLLC #16,025. Here the Board dealt with an application for review under Code s. 119 where the union sought to add a group of employees to its certified bargaining unit. The Board reviewed its policy concerning its approach to bargaining unit determination and found the inclusions sought to be appropriate.
139 *Canada Labour Code,* s. 110 and Preamble.
140 *Conseil des Ports Nationaux, supra,* note 136; *Transport Route Canada Inc., CNX/CN Trucking* (1984), 84 CLLC #16,056.
141 *Charterways Co. Ltd.* (1974), 2 di 18, [1974] 1 Can LRBR 161, 74 CLLC #16,097; *Feed-Rite Ltd.* (1978), 29 di 33, [1979] 1 Can LRBR 296.
142 *Cablevision Nationale Ltée* (1979), 35 di 168.
143 *CFTO-TV Ltd.* (1981), 45 di 306.

appropriate bargaining unit.[144] Except where it is in the presence of an employer-dominated union, the Board has no power to determine whether a particular trade union is the appropriate bargaining agent for a group of employees.[145] The Board has also stated that the raiding of a union by another, in breach of a jurisdictional agreement entered into by the two unions, is not an issue for determination by the Board and is not a reason to dismiss an application for certification.[146]

The Board does not accept the concept of "tag-end" units and will avoid leaving out a small number of employees unless there is a good reason for it.[147] It will not consider excluding employees to preserve the union's majority character,[148] and it will tend to include these employees in existing units.[149] The Board has recognized, however, that the dividing line between two or more units of employees of the same employer is not always clear and is often the product of forces other than current theories of bargaining-unit definition. It may be the result of agreements and negotiations between the parties, as a result of which the unit boundaries often cannot be rationally described.[150] In *British Columbia Telephone Co.*,[151] for example, the union (TEMPO) applied to represent a group of supervisory, professional, and managerial employees. The Board certified a unit of professional, supervisory, and technical employees, and commented that the group it found to be appropriate could perhaps have been more appropriately included in the two existing groups.

Except in the construction industry, craft units are held not to be appropriate, as such groupings result in a multiplicity of bargaining units and encourage industrial unrest.[152] In *Uranerz Exploration and Mining Ltd.*[153] the Board indicated that it had serious reservations about the adoption of the "build-up" principle into the guidelines of the Code for determining unit appropriateness. According to the "build-up" principle an application for certification may be held premature because, at the time of application, a substantial and representative segment of the work force in the bargaining unit has not yet been hired. The reasoning is that an existing small group of employees should not be able to determine the issue of union representation or choice of trade union on behalf of a

---

144   *Majestic Wiley Contractors Ltd.* (1975), 11 di 43, 75 CLLC #16,179.
145   *General Aviation Services Ltd.* (1979), 34 di 791, [1979] 2 Can LRBR 98.
146   *Saskatchewan Wheat Pool* (1977), 21 di 388, [1977] 1 Can LRBR 510, 77 CLLC #16,104.
147   A "tag-end" unit is a remnant group of employees excluded from a bargaining unit for various reasons, the main one being the lack of a community of interest with a larger bargaining group; another is that the group was simply forgotten. See *Québecair* (1978), 33 di 480, [1979] 3 Can LRBR 550.
148   *Maclean-Hunter Cable TV Ltd.* (1979), 34 di 752, [1979] 2 Can LRBR 1.
149   *Majestic Wiley Contractors Ltd., supra,* note 144.
150   *British Columbia Telephone Co.* (1979), 38 di 145.
151   *Ibid.*
152   *Cape Breton Development Corp.* (1979), 35 di 140, [1979] 3 Can LRBR 485; and *Atomic Energy of Canada Ltd.* (1977), 25 di 377, [1978] 1 Can LRBR 92, 78 CLLC #16,128.
153   (1978), 27 di 728, [1978] 2 Can LRBR 193, 78 CLLC #16,135.

larger group to be hired later on.[154] The Board went on to find that in light of ss. 124 and 137 of the Code, which permit employees to change or revoke their bargaining agent, this principle should not be the factor in determining the appropriateness of the unit. It recognized, however, that the "build-up" principle could be a factor in deciding to call a vote under s. 127(1) of the Code.

In conclusion, although the parties will want to rest their case on precedents, this is almost impossible in certification matters because each case is decided on its own merit. One must always bear in mind the Board's general approach as outlined above and focus the preparation on a good understanding of the context in which the application is made, acquiring the best possible knowledge of the employer's organization and of the certification pattern of the industry in which the employer operates.

4:3200 STATUTORY INSPIRED UNITS: SUPERVISORS, PROFESSIONALS, PRIVATE CONSTABLES, SECURITY AGENTS, MULTI-EMPLOYER, MULTI-UNION, AND MAJOR PROJECTS UNITS

4:3210 Supervisors

The definition of employee does not exclude persons who exercise supervising functions over other employees without being categorized as management.[155] Section 125(4) of the Code reads as follows:

> Where a trade union applies for certification as the bargaining agent for a unit comprised of or including employees whose duties include the supervision of other employees, the Board may, subject to subsection (2), determine that the unit proposed in the application is appropriate for collective bargaining.

The general criteria and approach to unit determination outlined earlier apply. The larger the employer, the more likely it is that supervisory personnel will be grouped together. A sizable number of supervisory employees makes a unit viable in a situation where it is usually recognized that supervisors have a different community of interest from those they supervise. Whether the supervisors are grouped in one homogeneous supervisory unit or in a plurality of supervisory units will depend on the facts of each case.[156]

---

154 *Noranda Mines Ltd. v. The Queen; Saskatchewan Labour Relations Board v. The Queen*, [1969] S.C.R. 898, 69 W.W.R. 321, 69 CLLC #14,205, 7 D.L.R. (3d) 1.

155 *Atomic Energy of Canada Ltd.* (1978), 33 di 415, [1979] 1 Can LRBR 252.

156 *British Columbia Telephone Co.* (1977), 33 di 361, [1977] 2 Can **LRBR 385, 77 CLLC** #16,107. In this case, the Board found appropriate a unit including all the first-line

The Board has interpreted s. 125(4) as permitting the formation of units that include only supervisory personnel, or units that group supervisory personnel with those they supervise.[157] However, the Board has indicated its preference for the former kind of units, where possible, which excludes the supervised employees.[158]

Indeed, on numerous occasions the Board has found units composed exclusively of supervisory personnel to be appropriate.[159] On another occasion it has been found proper to include them in an all-employee unit.[160] In *Bank of Nova Scotia (Port Dover Branch)*,[161] the Board enumerated the factors that it will consider in determining whether to include supervisory employees in a unit of employees whom they supervise. They are:

 (i) whether exclusion will effectively deny bargaining rights to supervisory employees;
 (ii) the effect of creating a separate supervisory unit;
 (iii) the degree of conflict created by a single unit;
 (iv) the limitation imposed on the employer's ability to operate efficiently.

The Board has also made it clear that the fact that a particular trade union is already the bargaining agent for a unit of employees who are under the direction of the supervisors is not a bar to that union's being certified as a bargaining agent for the supervisory group.[162]

4:3220   Professional Employees

Section 125(3) provides that the Board may group together professional employees, whether they exercise the same profession or not, or

---

supervisors of the employer. It was not satisfied that the distinction between plant, clerical, and traffic employees was sufficient at the supervisory level to warrant the creation of such a range of supervisory units.

[157] *British Columbia Telephone Co.* (1977), 22 di 507, [1977] 2 Can LRBR 404, 77 CLLC #16,108; *Québecair* (1978), 33 di 480, [1979] 3 Can LRBR 550; *General Aviation Services Ltd.* (1979), 34 di 791, [1979] 2 Can LRBR 98.

[158] *Cominco Ltd.* (1980), 40 di 75, [1980] 3 Can LRBR 105, 80 CLLC #16,045; *CFTO-TV Ltd.* (1981), 45 di 306; *Pacific Western Airlines Ltd.* (1983), 52 di 56; *Canadian Broadcasting Corp.*, decision no. 461, not yet reported, April 30, 1984 (C.L.R.B.).

[159] *Niagara Falls Bridge Commission* (1974), 3 di 7, [1974] 1 Can LRBR 149, 74 CLLC #16,098; *Northern Electric Co. Ltd.* (1976), 16 di 237; *Québecair, supra,* note 157; *British Columbia Telephone Co.* (1979), 38 di 145; *Cominco Ltd., supra,* note 158; *CFTO-TV Ltd., supra,* note 158; *Pacific Western Airlines Ltd., supra,* note 158; *Canadian Broadcasting Corporation, supra,* note 158.

[160] *Atomic Energy of Canada Ltd., supra,* note 152.

[161] (1977), 21 di 439, [1977] 2 Can LRBR 126, 77 CLLC #16,090.

[162] *Yellowknife District Hospital Society* (1977), 20 di 281, 77 CLLC #16,083; *Québecair, supra,* note 157.

include them in units with employees performing the same functions but lacking the qualifications of a professional. The section reads as follows:

> Where a trade union applies under section 124 for certification as the bargaining agent for a unit comprised of or including professional employees, the Board, subject to subsection (2),
>
> (a) shall determine that the unit appropriate for collective bargaining is a unit comprised of only professional employees, unless such a unit would not otherwise be appropriate for collective bargaining;
>
> (b) may determine that professional employees of more than one profession, be included in the unit; and
>
> (c) may determine that employees performing the functions, but lacking the qualifications of a professional employee, be included in the unit.

Section 107 defines "professional employee" as:

> an employee who
>
> (a) is, in the course of his employment, engaged in the application of specialized knowledge ordinarily acquired by a course of instruction and study resulting in graduation from a university or similar institution, and
>
> (b) is, or is eligible to be, a member of a professional organization that is authorized by statute to establish the qualifications for membership in the organization. . . .

For the purposes of the Code, "professional employees" were found to include not only persons having the necessary qualifications, but persons who perform work of such a nature that it requires the application of the special knowledge "acquired in the course of securing these qualifications".[163] Professionals such as engineers who work as managers but not as professionals will not be included in professional units.[164]

The Board has dealt with an application for a unit of professional employees in only two cases.[165] In *Bell Canada,* the Board was presented with an application seeking to cover all professional engineers and architects of the employer. The evidence had established, however, that the number of employees performing functions requiring similar knowledge to that of professional engineers and architects, but who lacked the qualifications, was more considerable than that of the professional employees applied for. The Board dismissed the application because the unit was found not to be appropriate, as it did not correspond to the employer's organizational structure.

---

[163] *Bell Canada* (1976), 19 di 117, at 124, [1976] 1 Can LRBR 345, 76 CLLC #16,016.

[164] *Ibid.*, at p. 125 (di): "are professional employees, in the course of their employment, engaged in the application of specialized knowledge, if it can be shown that they perform the same task and functions as other and more numerous employees who do not have professional qualifications?"

[165] *Bell Canada, supra,* note 163; *British Columbia Telephone Co., supra,* note 159, where the union sought a unit composed of all supervisory professionals and management employees of British Columbia Telephone Company. The Board refused to form a unit of professionals alone, since it was not appropriate in the circumstances.

In the course of its discussion, the Board indicated that it interpreted s. 125(3) as indicating a statutory preference for units composed exclusively of professionals. It hastened to add that, in fashioning such units, it would stick to the general criteria and approach developed in establishing standard bargaining units.

4:3230   Private Constables

Section 125(5) provides that "the Board shall not include a private constable in a unit with other employees". Section 135 expressly forbids the Board to certify a trade union that acts as bargaining agent for private constables and other employees of the same employer. The same section expressly denies a trade union the right to act as bargaining agent for both a unit of private constables and another unit of employees of the same employer. Section 107 defines "private constable" as:

> A person appointed as a constable under the *Railway Act* or the *Canada Ports Corporation Act.*

The Board in *Denison Mines Ltd.*[166] stated that security guards, even though sworn as special constables under the *Police Act* of Ontario,[167] were not private constables as they were not employed under the two statutes referred to in s. 107(1).

There is no provision in the Code that stipulates, as in the case of private constables, that security guards cannot be included in a unit comprising employees of the same employer over which they exercise surveillance or that a union cannot act as bargaining agent for both security guards and employees of the same employer, either in the same or different bargaining units. The Board, however, has developed the practice of including guards in a unit of their own[168] or of excluding them from an employee unit found to be appropriate even though they are employees under the Code.[169] The Board has also found that the same trade union can act as the bargaining agent for a unit of security guards and for a unit comprising employees over whom they exercise surveillance.[170]

4:3240   Council of Trade Unions Units

Section 130 provides that two or more trade unions may join together on a *voluntary* basis and apply to be the bargaining agent for a unit

---

[166]   (1975), 8 di 13, [1975] 1 Can LRBR 313, 75 CLLC #16,150.
[167]   R.S.O. 1980, c. 381.
[168]   *Eastern Provincial Airways (1963) Ltd.* (1978), 29 di 44, [1979] 1 Can LRBR 456; *British Columbia Telephone Co.* (1979), 38 di 145; and *CFTO-TV Ltd.* (1981), 45 di 306.
[169]   *British Columbia Telephone Co., supra,* note 168, at p. 163 (di).
[170]   *Eastern Provincial Airways (1963) Ltd., supra,* note 168.

in the same manner as a trade union. The certification of a council of trade unions entails various consequences. First, s. 130(4)(b) provides that where a council of trade unions is certified by the Board "as the bargaining agent" for a bargaining unit, Part V applies to it "as if the council of trade unions was a trade union".[171] It follows that upon certification, a council of trade unions acquires, simultaneously, the status of trade union as well as that of bargaining agent. This means that a council of trade unions does not draw the status of trade union solely from the various organizations that form part of it. This status is acquired through certification, which is granted only if, pursuant to s. 130(2), the Board is satisfied that the council meets the requirements prescribed by Part V for certification. Thus, although there is as yet no decision on this point, it is likely that before granting certification, the Board will, similarly to its practice in cases of certification demands filed by trade unions, ascertain whether each trade union that forms part of the applicant council satisfies the definition of trade union contained in the Code. Indeed, although a "council of trade unions" has not been defined by the legislator, it is clear that the trade unions referred to by s. 130(1), which have formed a council, must be "trade unions" within the meaning of s. 107(1). Furthermore, it is likely that the Board would require from a council of trade unions some guarantee that it possesses the necessary requirements to effectively act as, and assume the responsibilities and duties of, a bargaining agent under the Code. Such a guarantee would be found in the provisions of the document binding the unions together as a council. In other words, by analogy to the requirements imposed on voluntary multi-employer associations,[172] in all likelihood the Board will not certify a multi-union council if it is not reasonably satisfied that the council is sufficiently unified to be viable as a labour relations organization.[173]

Once recognized by the Board, the council must also satisfy the provisions of s. 124 on timeliness and s. 125 on the appropriate character of the unit, and it must establish its representative character. In that regard, s. 130(3) provides that membership in any of the trade unions forming the council is deemed to be membership in the council.

Once certified, the council of trade unions and each trade union that forms a part of it is bound by any collective agreement entered into by the council and an employer. It follows that if the council were to disband during the life of a collective agreement, each constituent trade union would continue to be bound by the collective agreement binding on the council and by any procedures initiated for the purpose of renegotiating it, such as a notice to bargain.

---

[171] *MacCosham Van Lines* (1984), 7 CLRBR (NS) 216, 84 CLLC #16,051.
[172] See para. 4:3251.
[173] *Saskatchewan Wheat Pool* (1977), 21 di 388, [1977] 1 Can LRBR 510, 77 CLLC #16,104.

Once certified, the council must represent fairly all the members of its bargaining unit,[174] and it is subject to all other obligations of a trade union under Part V. A council of trade unions certified as a bargaining agent for employees of a given employer cannot on that basis claim union status in regard to a bargaining unit comprising employees of another employer. Consequently, it will only acquire union status following certification under s. 124 of the Code and not through the application of s. 119.[175]

4:3250   Multi-Employer Units

4:3251   Voluntary Employer Organizations

The Board dealt with s. 131 for the first time in *Saskatchewan Wheat Pool*.[176] In this case, the application for certification was directed against an association of employers operating grain elevators in the Port of Vancouver in the context of a long history of bargaining through an employers' association. The Board initially indicated that it did not view ss. 124 and 131 as independent provisions, and that an application under s. 131 would first have to satisfy the requirements of s. 124 in regard to timeliness. The Board viewed s. 131 as requiring three prerequisites for its application:

1.   *There must be an application for certification of a unit* of employees of two or more employers.

2.   *The employers must have formed an employers' organization.* An "employers' organization" is defined in s. 107 of the Code as:

any organization of employers the purposes of which include the regulation of relations between employers and employees. . . .

In other words, it must be more than a business or a social club. The Board, either by a review of the history of collective bargaining involving the employers' organization or by the provisions in the organization's constitution, must be convinced that one of the organization's goals is the negotiation and administration of collective agreements. It is not necessary for the organization to be incorporated, but it must be bound by some enabling statute or document. The organization of employers does not have to exist as of the date of application, but it can be formed at any time prior to the Board's decision.

---

174   *Canada Labour Code*, s. 136.1.
175   *MacCosham Van Lines Ltd., supra*, note 171.
176   *Saskatchewan Wheat Pool, supra*, note 173.

3. *Each employer must grant appropriate authority to the employers'*
organization to enable it to discharge the duties and responsibilities
of an employer under Part V. This is important, as s. 131
provides that the employers' organization is voluntary and
that any member employer can withdraw its mandate at any
time.[177] In its assessment of what constitutes appropriate
authority, the Board will try to assess whether or not the
organization is in a position to bargain in good faith. In this
regard, it will try to ascertain whether the authority vested
in the organization includes the right to withdraw if a
member disagrees with the organization's proposed settlement or if the relations between the members and the union
become rough or whether the authority requires unanimity
of its members at the bargaining table. If so, it is likely that it
will not be in a position to bargain in good faith.

Once the Board is satisfied the three prerequisites have been met, it
will then decide whether the unit is appropriate and whether ultimately
the employees wish the union to represent them.

When an employer withdraws from the employers' organization, it
continues to be bound by the collective agreement applicable to its
employees that was entered into by the employers' organization. It may
also be required to commence collective bargaining in accordance with
s. 146 when no collective agreement binding on the employees is currently in force.[178]

4:3252   Compulsory Employer Organization: Longshoring and Other Industries

Section 132 provides for compulsory multi-employer certification if
the following prerequisites are met:

1. The application by a bargaining agent must seek to include in
the same bargaining unit the employees of two or more
employers.

---

[177] *Canadian National Railway Co.* (1981), 46 di 31, [1982] 1 Can LRBR 254, 82 CLLC
#16,147. This case involved the Railway Association of Canada, which grouped seven
railway employers, among whom were Canadian National and Canadian Pacific, and a
council of trade unions representing seven unions acting for shopcraft employees who
were part of a bargaining certificate granted by the Board. Canadian National with-
drew its mandate, and the Railway Association applied to have its certificate amended.
The union opposed this, arguing that it would fragment the existing unit. The Board
reaffirmed the voluntary nature of the provisions of Code s. 131 and the fact that it was
powerless to stop an employer from withdrawing from an employer's organization.
[178] *Canada Labour Code*, s. 131(3)(b).

2.   The employees must be employed in either:

(a) the longshoring industry; or

(b) any other industry "recommended" to Cabinet by the Board. In order to make such a recommendation, the Board, after an inquiry, must be satisfied that the employers operating in a particular geographic area draw their employees from a group whose members are employed from time to time by some or all of the employers. Furthermore, the Board's recommendation as to the designation of the industry and the area must be officially ratified by a regulation of the Governor in Council.[179]

3.   The Board must be satisfied that the employees of the employers in the geographic area constitute an appropriate bargaining unit.

4.   The application must satisfy the requisites of Part V of the Code.

The Board has dealt with applications relating only to the longshoring industry.[180] Most decisions[181] centred on the determination of what constitutes an appropriate bargaining unit and what interpretation should be given to the purpose and the scope of application of s. 132. Another decision dealt with the problem arising out of the fact that, by the time that certification had been granted and an order had been given to the employers to appoint an agent in accordance with s. 132(3), there remained only one employer in operation. The Board then had to decide whether it was proper to suspend the application of its original order to name an agent.

In *Maritime Employers' Association* the Board dealt with an application for review under s. 119 to redefine the existing certificate issued under s. 132. The latter bound the employees represented by one trade union to several employers individually named on the certificate who were operating in the longshoring industry in the Port of Quebec.[182] The applicant wished the revised certificate to read, "*all* employees of all employers operating in the longshoring industry in the Port of Quebec". The Board held that the certificate should read, "all employees of all employers", and that the appropriate unit should be one that maintained the *status quo* in regard to the employers operating at the time of the filing of the

---

179   At the time of publication, the Board had made no such recommendation.

180   *Maritime Employers' Association* (1981), 45 di 314; *Murray Bay Marine Terminal Inc.* (1981), 46 di 55; *St. John's Shipping Association* (1983), 53 di 114, 3 CLRBR (NS) 314, 83 CLLC #16,039; *Murray Bay Marine Terminal Inc.* (1983), 54 di 38; *W.S. Anderson Co. Ltd.* (1984), 84 CLLC #16,023; *Maritime Employers' Association*, decision no. 470, not yet reported, September 21, 1984 (C.L.R.B.); *Gilles Drapeau*, decision no. 483, not yet reported, September 29, 1984 (C.L.R.B.).

181   *Ibid.*, except for *Murray Bay Marine Terminal Inc.* (1983), 54 di 38.

182   *Maritime Employers' Association* (1981), 45 di 314.

application. As a result, it obliged all future employers operating in the longshoring industry to be bound by the certificate. In its decision, the Board reviewed the labour relations history of the St. Lawrence ports in general and of the Quebec port in particular, where security of employment was guaranteed in the collective agreement and financed by the employers' association. It concluded that there was a need to favour the development of situations that would minimize the risk of work stoppages and create a labour relations climate that would enhance productivity. In other words, s. 132 should, as much as possible, favour the regrouping of bargaining units and serve as a means to avoid creating new units.[183]

The Board also held that an employer who had started to operate a business in the Port of Quebec after the filing of the application and who had opposed the application was covered by the all-employer certificate, as he was operating in the longshoring industry. The Federal Court of Appeal overturned the Board's decision on that point, reasoning that the employer was operating a local undertaking and was not involved in longshoring operations.[184]

In *W.S. Anderson Co. Ltd.* the Board granted an application under s. 132 to group the employees of four employers.[185] Taking into consideration the particular conditions that prevailed in the port of Miramichi, New Brunswick, and the small scale of longshoring operations, the Board refused to grant an order certifying "all employees of all employers", as was done in *Maritime Employers' Association.*[186] It further decided that employers whose businesses were related to the forest industry were not engaged in work encompassed by the longshoring industry.

In *St. John's Shipping Association*[187] the Board dealt with an application under s. 119. The union sought to amend a bargaining certificate that bound it to an association grouping four employers, in order to include all employees working for any employer in the longshoring industry and other related operations in the Port of St. John's, Newfoundland. Granting the application would have resulted in sweeping-in the employees of eighteen employers not previously covered by the existing certificate and collective agreement. The Board refused to amend the existing certificate and interpreted s. 132 in a more restrictive manner than it did in *Maritime Employers' Association.*[188] In this case it said that s. 132 was to be applied in the same spirit as s. 131, that is, there must exist an initial

---

183   This view of the interpretation of s. 132 was reaffirmed in *Murray Bay Marine Terminal Inc., supra,* note 180; and in *W.S. Anderson Co. Ltd., supra,* note 180. In *St. John's Shipping Association, supra,* note 180; *Maritime Employers' Association, supra,* note 180; *Gilles Drapeau, supra,* note 180, the Board took a different view.
184   *Cargill Grain Co. v. International Longshoremen's Association, Local 1739* (1983), 51 N.R. 182 (Fed. C.A.).
185   *W.S. Anderson Co. Ltd., supra,* note 180.
186   *Supra,* note 180.
187   *Supra,* note 180.
188   *Supra,* note 182.

agreement between the employers indicating that they wanted to be part of an employers' association. It went on to say that certification under s. 132 only had the effect of negating the voluntary element of an application under s. 131. In other words, prior to certification under s. 132, the Board had to be convinced that the employers concerned had agreed to be part of an employers' association. Certification under s. 132 was considered to be the means to assure that employers could not withdraw from the association. The Board concluded that certification under s. 132 could only be granted for compelling reasons and could not be used to sweep into a unit employers who were unwilling. However, in *W.S. Anderson Co. Ltd.*[189] the Board did certify under s. 132, although the four employers mentioned in the order had opposed the application. In this latter case, the Board went on to state that the existence of a hiring-hall system was not a prerequisite for certification under s. 132.

Section 132(3) stipulates that once the Board has certified a trade union as the bargaining agent to deal with a unit of employers, the Board must direct the employers to appoint an agent to act on their behalf. The employers must grant to their agent the appropriate authority to discharge the duties and responsibilities of an employer under Part V.

In *Murray Bay Marine Terminal Inc.* the Board suspended its earlier order to the employers concerned to name an agent and to confer on the agent the necessary authority.[190] In that case it was shown that, following certification, one of the employers had been granted exclusive jurisdiction for longshoring operations by the port's administration. The Board refused to amend the certificate and indicated that, if in the future the situation were to change and other employers were to join the longshoring industry in the Port of Becancour, it would then reactivate its order under s. 132(3).

The Code is silent about the manner in which the Board can resolve difficulties arising out of a disagreement in appointing the agent. That problem was mentioned in *St. John's Shipping Association*, but no answer was suggested.[191]

4:3260   Common Employer Declaration

Section 133 is designed primarily to avoid the frustration of the free collective bargaining scheme provided under the Code by the simple creation of different legal entities or by the utilization of "corporate veils",[192] which would hide the true relationship between an employer

---

[189]   *Supra*, note 180.
[190]   *Murray Bay Marine Terminal Inc.* (1983), 54 di 38.
[191]   *St. John's Shipping Association, supra*, note 180.
[192]   *British Columbia Telephone Co. and Canadian Telephones and Supplies Ltd.* (1977), 24 di 164, [1978] 1 Can LRBR 236, 78 CLLC #16,122.

and his employees.[193] It is also a means to permit the rationalization of bargaining structures where there are good labour relations reasons to do so, and where certain conditions set out in s. 133 are met.[194]

Section 133 serves no purpose on its own; it must be applied in conjunction with other sections of the Code, whether to facilitate collective bargaining, as in the determination of an appropriate bargaining unit, or to avoid the fractioning of an existing bargaining unit through the creation of spin-off companies.[195]

The Board stated that five criteria must initially be met simultaneously before it can exercise its discretion to make a single employer declaration.[196] They are as follows:

1. The enterprise must constitute a federal work, undertaking, or business.[197]

2. There must be more than one such undertaking or business.

3. They must be associated or related.

4. They must be under common control or direction.

5. There must be two or more employers as defined by the Code.

Often the third and fourth conditions overlap. The interrelation between employers will be evidenced by the degree of common control or direction found.[198] In *Canadian Press,* in order to determine the degree of interrelation, the Board indicated that it would identify whether the undertakings in question provided similar services and production, or whether they are part of a vertically integrated process whereby one business carries out one function, for example the mining of ore, while another business in the organization processes it.[199] For the same reasons, in *Les Aviseurs en Déménagements Inc.*[200] and in *Music Mann Leasing Ltd., Bus Drivers (London) Inc.,*[201] where companies were set up to

---

193   *Canadian Press* (1976), 13 di 39, [1976] 1 Can LRBR 354, 76 CLLC #16,013.
194   *Canadian Press, supra,* note 193; *North Canada Air Ltd., and Norcanair Electronics Ltd.* (1979), 38 di 168, [1980] 1 Can LRBR 535, affd. *North Canada Air Ltd. v. Canada Labour Relations Board,* [1981] 2 F.C. 407, 34 N.R. 560, 81 CLLC #14,072, 117 D.L.R. (3d) 216 (C.A.). See also *British Columbia Telephone Co. and Canadian Telephones and Supplies Ltd.* (1979), 38 di 205; *Les Aviseurs en Déménagements Inc.* (1981), 45 di 111; *Music Mann Leasing Ltd., Bus Drivers (London) Inc.* (1982), 51 di 51, [1982] 1 Can LRBR 337.
195   *North Canada Air Ltd., and Norcanair Electronics Ltd., supra,* note 194; *Canadian Press, supra,* note 193.
196   *Canadian Press, supra,* note 193; *Victoria Flying Services Ltd.* (1979), 35 di 73, at 86, [1979] 3 Can LRBR 216.
197   See paragraph 1:2000. See also *North Canada Air Ltd. and Norcanair Electronics Ltd., supra,* note 194; *Paul L'Anglais Inc.* (1978) 28 di 934, [1979] 2 Can LRBR 332; quashed (*sub nom. Paul L'Anglais Inc. v. Le Conseil canadien des relations du travail*) [1981] C.A. 62, 81 CLLC #14,090, 122 D.L.R. (3d) 583; affd. [1983] 1 S.C.R. 147, 47 N.R. 351, 83 CLLC #14,033, 146 D.L.R. (3d) 202. See also *Intermountain Transport Ltd.* (1984), 8 CLRBR (NS) 141.
198   *Canadian Press, supra,* note 193, at p. 45 (di).
199   *Ibid.*
200   *Les Aviseurs en Déménagements Inc., supra,* note 194.
201   *Supra,* note 194.

provide manpower to other companies owned by the same interests, the Board found the companies to be interrelated and under common control and direction.

Whether undertakings are related or associated and whether they are under common control or direction is a question of fact. The Board found to be interrelated and commonly controlled or managed: (i) a group of press undertakings controlled by Canadian Press;[202] (ii) a telephone company providing communication services, and its wholly owned subsidiary, which carried out the retailing and installation of telephone equipment;[203] (iii) a television station and its wholly owned subsidiary television station operating in Lethbridge, Alberta;[204] (iv) two construction undertakings coming under the same corporate umbrella and operating in the Yukon;[205] (v) two airline companies commonly owned and operated;[206] (vi) one airline and a company providing avionic services to the airline in the proportion of 95 percent of its total business;[207] and (vii) a trucking company and its wholly owned subsidiary.[208]

Concerning the fifth condition, the Board found that the undertakings must be in operation and employ employees as of the date of its decision. The Board refused to join, in a declaration of a common employer, companies that were dormant and/or had no employees.[209] Section 133 is designed to deal with ongoing situations, not situations where one employer moves out and another moves in. Such circumstances are more appropriately considered under the sale of business provisions of s. 144.[210]

Although the five criteria have been met, a declaration of common employer will not automatically ensue. The Board must be convinced that the interest of the employees concerned and sound labour-management relations warrant such a declaration.[211] In the construction industry, however, because of the special nature of the industry, the onus is

---

202   *Canadian Press, supra,* note 193.

203   *British Columbia Telephone Co. and Canadian Telephones and Supplies Ltd., supra,* note 192; and *British Columbia Telephone Company and Canadian Telephones and Supplies Ltd., supra,* note 194.

204   *Calgary Television Ltd.* (1977), 25 di 399, [1978] 1 Can LRBR 532.

205   *General Enterprises Ltd. and Herschel Construction Ltd.* (1978), 27 di 790.

206   *Victoria Flying Services Ltd., supra,* note 196.

207   *North Canada Air Ltd. and Norcanair Electronics Ltd., supra,* note 194.

208   *Inter-City Truck Lines (Canada) Inc., and Trans Canada Truck Lines Inc.* (1981), 45 di 119, 81 CLLC #16,120. See also, in regard to transportation undertakings, *Les Aviseurs en Déménagements Inc., supra,* note 194; *Music Mann Leasing Ltd., Bus Drivers (London) Inc., supra,* note 194; *Transport Route Canada Inc., CNX/CN Trucking* (1984), 84 CLLC #16,056.

209   *Canadian Press, supra,* note 193; *Victoria Flying Services Ltd., supra,* note 196. This is also implied in *Freight Emergency Service Ltd.* (1984) 84 CLLC #16,031.

210   *Intermountain Transport Ltd., supra,* note 197.

211   *Canadian Press, supra,* note 193; *Inter-City Truck Lines (Canada) Inc., and Trans Canada Truck Lines Inc., supra,* note 208.

reversed on the respondent and a declaration will be made unless the Board is otherwise convinced.[212]

The Board will identify the applicant's motivation to determine whether it should exercise its discretion to make a declaration.[213] Where the applicant sought the creation of appropriate bargaining units[214] or where existing bargaining structures were already in place,[215] the Board made a declaration of a single employer to promote sound labour relations purposes. Where the applicant sought a declaration for two or more employers so as to enhance its position at the bargaining table, the Board found that a declaration was not appropriate.[216] In order to identify the purpose of the applicant, the timing of the application will be taken into consideration.[217] In short, once the five conditions are met, the Board will examine closely the motives of the applicant and will only make a declaration if it is satisfied that the declaration will benefit free collective bargaining as encouraged by the Code.

4:3270   Major Projects — Section 109.1

When a major project has been identified as such by the minister, s. 109.1 implies that the Board should determine the appropriate unit or units on a project-wide basis. This section is aimed at facilitating collective bargaining in projects, such as pipeline construction, that relate to numerous employers and cut across many union jurisdictions in the

---

212   *General Enterprises Ltd. and Herschel Construction Ltd.*, *supra*, note 205.
213   *Canadian Press* (1976), 13 di 39, [1976] 1 Can LRBR 354, 76 CLLC #16,013; *British Columbia Telephone Co. and Canadian Telephones and Supplies Ltd.* (1977), 24 di 164, [1978] 1 Can LRBR 236, 78 CLLC #16,122; *Calgary Television Ltd.* (1977), 25 di 399, [1978] 1 Can LRBR 532; *North Canada Air Ltd. and Norcanair Electronics Ltd.* (1979), 38 di 168, [1980] 1 Can LRBR 535; *British Columbia Telephone Company and Canadian Telephones and Supplies Ltd.* (1979), 38 di 205; *Les Aviseurs en Déménagements Inc.* (1981), 45 di 111; *Inter-City Truck Lines (Canada) Inc., and Trans Canada Truck Lines Inc.* (1981), 45 di 119, 81 CLLC #16,120; *Music Mann Leasing Ltd., Bus Drivers (London) Inc.* (1982), 51 di 51, [1982] 1 Can LRBR 337.
214   *Canadian Press*, *supra*, note 213; *North Canada Air Ltd. and Norcanair Electronics Ltd.*, *supra*, note 213; *Victoria Flying Services Ltd.* (1979), 35 di 73, [1979] 3 Can LRBR 216; *Les Aviseurs en Déménagements Inc.*, *supra*, note 213; *Music Mann Leasing Ltd., Bus Drivers (London) Inc.*, *supra*, note 213.
215   *General Enterprises Ltd. and Herschel Construction Ltd.*, *supra*, note 205; *British Columbia Telephone Co. and Canadian Telephones and Supplies Ltd.*, *supra*, note 213; *Transport Route Canada Inc., CNX/CN Trucking*, *supra*, note 208.
216   In *British Columbia Telephone Co. and Canadian Telephones and Supplies Ltd.* (1977), 24 di 164, [1978] 1 Can LRBR 236, 78 CLLC #16,122, the Board found that the union wanted to use s. 133 to impose a particular bargaining format. In *Calgary Television Ltd.*, *supra*, note 213, the Board found that the union wanted to join a mature bargaining unit that had been negotiating for fifteen years with a newly certified unit comprising employees who were on strike to improve their picketing position. In *Inter-City Truck Lines (Canada) Inc., and Trans Canada Truck Lines Inc.*, *supra*, note 213, the Board found that the union wanted to use s. 133 to renege on a deal it had made with the employer.
217   *Calgary Television Ltd.*, *supra*, note 213.

construction industry. To date, no decision has been rendered in this connection.

4:4000   CERTIFICATION PATTERN BY INDUSTRIES

An outline of the general pattern of bargaining units by industry determined by the Board to be appropriate is found below. It is based on an analysis of the certificates issued by the Board, sorted by industries since 1973.[218]

4:4100   AIR TRANSPORTATION[219]

The Board deals with a variety of airline organizations ranging from large national employers, such as Air Canada or CP Air, to very small

---

[218]   In the process of analysing all certificates by industry, we have noted that a reference to each certificate does not necessarily result in obtaining a comprehensive picture of the industry, because the inclusions and exclusions may vary in each case according to the job content of each position in each enterprise. In cases where there are enumerative certificates, the description in the certificates gives a clear indication of which positions are included or excluded. Unfortunately, most of these certificates predate 1973 and have been amended through the years, and in a significant number of cases the job classifications referred to no longer correspond to the modern terminology employed by the parties in current collective agreements. "All-employees" or inclusive certificates, descriptions in use since 1973, do not give a complete picture of the inclusions unless one is very well aware of the particularity of the employer's organization. As to the exclusions, the job content varies in each case, and classifications included in some are excluded in others. References to the Board's published decisions will not necessarily be reflective of the industry pattern, because each decision is tailor-made to the situation and is not directed at defining an industry-wide pattern. Occasionally, however, the Board will make allusion to the certification pattern of the industry.

The Board also deals with very large employers such as national airlines, the railroad industry, national broadcasters, and telecommunication undertakings which, over the years, have developed their own particular patterns and are of little help for an applicant seeking to represent employees of small employers, such as a ten- to fifteen-employee radio station. The purpose of the following exercise is to give the reader a broad, general understanding of bargaining unit patterns, while making the reader aware that each case is different and that, in the end, it is the particularity of a given employer's organization and structure, together with the Board's assessment of the employees' chances of gaining access to collective bargaining, that will determine the shape of the unit and the inclusion or exclusion of particular job functions. For those who wish to reconstruct a more detailed picture of each industry pattern, we have compiled in Appendix 8 a list of all the Board's certification orders since 1973, which have been reproduced in *di*, the Board's publication, where the reader may find the actual description of the unit contained in the order.

[219]   The Board has issued reasons for decision dealing with appropriateness in the following certification cases: *Transair Ltd.* (1974), 4 di 54, [1974] 1 Can LRBR 281, 74 CLLC #16,111; *Wardair (Can.) Ltd.* (1974), 4 di 62, 74 CLLC #16,103; *Victoria Flying Services Ltd.* (1977), 23 di 13, 77 CLLC #16,072; *Eastern Provincial Airways (1963) Ltd.* (1978), 29 di 44, [1979] 1 Can LRBR 456; *Québecair* (1978), 33 di 480, [1979] 3 Can LRBR 550; *General Aviation Services Ltd.* (1979), 34 di 791, [1979] 2 Can LRBR 98; *North Canada Air Ltd. and Norcanair Electronics Ltd.* (1979), 38 di 168, [1980] 1 Can LRBR 535; *Pacific Western Airlines Ltd.* (1980), 40 di 205, [1980] 3 Can LRBR 180; *Air Canada* (1980), 42 di 114, [1981] 2 Can LRBR 153; *Okanagan Helicopters Ltd.* (1980), 42 di 172, [1981] 1 Can LRBR 327; *Airwest Airlines Ltd.* (1980), 42 di 247, [1981] 1 Can LRBR 427;

regional organizations, such as one concerned with flying fishermen or supplies into isolated areas. The larger the employer organization, the more likely the units are to be specialized. Conversely, the smaller the organization, the more likely it is that the employees will be regrouped in a single unit. This was discussed in *Airwest Airlines Ltd.* where, following a merger of several small airline companies whose employees were included in single, all-employee units, the Board redefined the units according to the industry pattern.[220] Where the number of employees warrants it, the Board will group in separate bargaining units pilots, maintenance crew, flight attendants, ground services personnel (who may include baggage and cargo handling and customer services staff), and office and clerical employees. Depending on the circumstances, any combination of these groups is possible in addition to supervisory units.[221]

Where possible, the Board will create units that are company-wide as opposed to units that attach to a single location.[222] On certain occasions the Board will not follow a company-wide pattern so as to permit employees to have easier access to collective bargaining.[223]

4:4200   CONSTRUCTION INDUSTRIES IN THE NORTH[224]

The Board's jurisdiction over construction stems from its jurisdiction over employers operating in the Northwest Territories and the Yukon. In a full-Board decision, it stated that it would recognize standardized craft units on a territory-wide basis.[225] It indicated that, in the Yukon, the standardized units would correspond to those recognized in

---

Wardair Canada (1975) Ltd. (1983), 53 di 26, 2 CLRBR (NS) 129; *Pacific Western Airlines Ltd.* (1983), 52 di 56; *Pacific Western Airlines Ltd.* (1983), 52 di 178, 5 CLRBR (NS) 260; *North Canada Air Ltd.* (1978), 35 di 129, [1979] 3 Can LRBR 239, 79 CLLC #16,194; *Québecair* (1984), 55 di 88. See also Appendix 8. In *Wardair Canada (1975) Ltd.* (1978), 32 di 248, [1979] 1 Can LRBR 49, the Board ruled that Nordair's reservation clerk fell under provincial jurisdiction.

220   *Airwest Airlines Ltd.* (1980), 42 di 247, at 261-64, [1981] 1 Can LRBR 427.

221   *Pacific Western Airlines Ltd.* (1983), 52 di 56.

222   *Airwest Airlines Ltd., supra,* note 220; *Pacific Western Airlines Ltd.* (1980), 40 di 205, [1980] 3 Can LRBR 180.

223   *Okanagan Helicopters Ltd., supra,* note 219. In this case, the Board certified helicopter pilots of the Western and Logging Division of the undertaking without including the Eastern and International divisions.

224   The Board has issued reasons for decisions dealing with appropriateness in the following cases: *Majestic Wiley Contractors Ltd.* (1975), 11 di 43, 75 CLLC #16,179; *North American Construction Ltd.* (1977), 24 di 220, [1978] 1 Can LRBR 462, 78 CLLC #16,147; *Uranerz Exploration and Mining Ltd.* (1978), 27 di 728, [1978] 2 Can LRBR 193, 78 CLLC #16,135; *Interior Contracting Co. Ltd.* (1979), 29 di 51, [1979] 1 Can LRBR 248; *Cominco Ltd.* (1980), 40 di 75, [1980] 3 Can LRBR 105, 80 CLLC #16,045; *Mitchell Installations Ltd.* (1980), 42 di 266; *P.C.L. Construction Ltd.,* decision no. 481, not yet reported, September 21, 1984 (C.L.R.B.). See also Appendix 8.

225   *Interior Contracting Company Ltd., supra,* note 224. See also *B.A.C.M. Construction Co. Ltd.*

British Columbia, where the majority of the construction unions servicing the Yukon are based. It indicated that, for the Northwest Territories, it would most likely certify according to the standardized craft unit patterns of Alberta.

4:4300   BANKING INDUSTRY[226]

In the banking industry, the Board has determined that it will certify on a branch basis.[227] The Board has also included the employees of four branches in a single unit by applying the "cluster" concept developed in the United States.[227a] Bank managers and accountants who have direct supervisory responsibilities over branch employees, manager trainees,[228] and casual, part-time employees[229] are excluded from the units. In larger branches, assistant managers may be excluded. As a rule secretaries are included, although the Board has decided that in an isolated area, where it dealt with a large branch, the manager's secretary should be excluded.[230] Credit officers are included.[231] With respect to bank employees working in locations other than bank branches, the Board has

---

(1978), 33 di 386, [1979] 1 Can LRBR 104, 79 CLLC #16,173; *Mitchell Installations Ltd.*, *supra*, note 224; and *P.C.L. Construction Ltd.*, *supra*, note 224.

226   The Board has issued reasons for decisions dealing with appropriateness in the following cases: *Canadian Imperial Bank of Commerce (Victory Square Branch)* (1977), 20 di 319, [1977] 2 Can LRBR 99, 77 CLLC #16,089; *Bank of Nova Scotia (Port Dover Branch)* (1977), 21 di 439, [1977] 2 Can LRBR 126, 77 CLLC #16,090; *Canadian Imperial Bank of Commerce (Victory Square Branch)* (1977), 25 di 355, [1978] 1 Can LRBR 132, 78 CLLC #16,120; *Bank of Montreal (Cloverdale Branch)* (1977), 23 di 92, [1978] 1 Can LRBR 148; *Bank of Montreal (Clinton Branch)* (1977), 24 di 198, [1978] 1 Can LRBR 157; *The Royal Bank of Canada (Gibsons Branch)* (1977), 26 di 509, [1978] 1 Can LRBR 326; *Banque Canadienne Nationale (Centre de traitement des données)* (1979), 34 di 822, [1980] 1 Can LRBR 297; *Bank of British Columbia (Abbotsford)* (1980), 41 di 188, 81 CLLC #16,068, [1980] 1 Can LRBR 576. *Banque Provinciale du Canada (Roberval)* (1978), 34 di 633; *Toronto Dominion Bank (Maple Ridge Square Branch)* (1977), 22 di 536, [1978] 1 Can LRBR 156; *Bank of Montreal (Tweed and Northbrook)* (1978), 26 di 591, [1978] 2 Can LRBR 123; *Bank of Nova Scotia (Main Branch Regina)* (1978), 28 di 885, [1978] 2 Can LRBR 65; *Banque Canadienne Nationale (Rouyn)* (1978), 23 di 107; *Canadian Imperial Bank of Commerce (Simcoe, Ontario)* (1977), 21 di 462, [1977] 2 Can LRBR 137, 77 CLLC #16,091; *Canadian Imperial Bank of Commerce (Alness Branch, Downsview)* (1978), 28 di 921, [1978] 2 Can LRBR 361, 78 CLLC #16,145; *Banque Nationale du Canada*, decision no. 542, not yet reported, December 18, 1985 (C.L.R.B.). In this decision the board reviews the entire evolution of collective bargaining in the banking industry. See also Appendix 8.

227   *Canadian Imperial Bank of Commerce (Victory Square Branch)*, *supra*, note 226; *Bank of Nova Scotia (Port Dover Branch)*, *supra*, note 226; *Banque Provinciale du Canada (Roberval)*, *supra*, note 226.

227a   *La Banque Nationale du Canada*, decision no. 542, not yet reported, December 18, 1985 (C.L.R.B.).

228   *Bank of Montreal (Cloverdale Branch)*, *supra*, note 226.

229   *Canadian Imperial Bank of Commerce (Victory Square Branch)* (1977), 25 di 355, [1978] 1 Can LRBR 132, 78 CLLC #16,120.

230   *Banque Canadienne Nationale (Rouyn)*, *supra*, note 226.

231   *Bank of Montreal (Cloverdale Branch)*, *supra*, note 226.

applied its general criteria and has found to be appropriate units of employees of a data centre and a credit card centre.[232]

4:4400   COMMUNICATIONS[233]

4:4410   Broadcasting and Cable Distribution

The general rule to the effect that the larger the number of employees is, the more likely it is that units will be specialized, also applies in this industry. At one end of the spectrum stands the C.B.C. with twenty-nine bargaining units,[234] and at the other end are found small radio stations with ten to fifteen employees who are all included in single units. Where numbers warrant, a first division between units will be made between office and clerical employees on the one hand and technicians on the other.[235] When dealing with still larger organizations, the Board will likely group together production and program employees.[236] The broadcasting industry is one where, in general, collective bargaining is not easily accessible. This is especially true in the case of small or medium-size employers. Accordingly, the Board will often fashion units to give employees a realistic chance to accede to collective bargaining.[237] In *Cablevision Nationale Ltée*, the Board found appropriate a small group of employees in the programming department in a context where upon becoming aware of the certification application the employer had dismissed seven employees, among them all the union officers.[238] Where the employer has many locations in its organization, the Board will likely certify by location initially and then regroup the units if warranted.

---

[232] *Banque Canadienne Nationale (Centre de traitement des données), supra*, note 226.

[233] The Board has issued reasons for decisions dealing with appropriateness in the following certification cases: *Radio Station CHQM* (1975), 11 di 16, [1976] 1 Can LRBR 110, 75 CLLC #16,166; *Co-opérative de Télévision de l'outaouais* (1975), 10 di 27, [1975] 2 Can LRBR 278, 75 CLLC #16,178; *CJRP Radio Provinciale Ltée* (1975), 11 di 33, 77 CLLC #16,074; *Entreprises Télé-Capitale Ltée* (1976), 16 di 230, 77 CLLC #16,075; *Radio Côte-Nord Inc.* (1977), 23 di 39; *Canadian Broadcasting Corp.* (1977), 19 di 166, [1977] 2 Can LRBR 481, 77 CLLC #16,102; *Canadian Broadcasting Corp.* (1977), 19 di 162, [1977] 2 Can LRBR 515; *Cablevision Nationale Ltée* (1978), 25 di 422, [1979] 3 Can LRBR 267; *Société Radio-Canada* (1978), 27 di 765, [1979] 2 Can LRBR 41; *Maclean-Hunter TV Ltd.* (1979), 34 di 752, [1979] 2 Can LRBR 1; *CFTO-TV Ltd.* (1981), 45 di 306; *Skeena Broadcasters Ltd.* (1982), 49 di 27, 82 CLLC #16,165; *Société Radio-Canada* (1982), 44 di 19, 1 CLRBR (NS) 129; *Canadian Broadcasting Corp.*, decision no. 461, not yet reported, April 30, 1984 (C.L.R.B.); *CHLT Télé 7 Ltée* (1976), 13 di 49, [1976] 2 Can LRBR 76, 76 CLLC #16,025; *Northern Television Systems Ltd.* (1976), 14 di 136, 76 CLLC #16,031; *CJRC Radio-Capitale Ltée* (1977), 21 di 416, [1977] 2 Can LRBR 578, 78 CLLC #16,124. See also Appendix 8.

[234] See *Canadian Broadcasting Corp.*, decision no. 461, *supra*, note 233, where the CBC's bargaining groups are listed.

[235] *Maclean-Hunter Cable TV Ltd., supra*, note 233.

[236] *Cablevision Nationale Ltée, supra*, note 233.

[237] *Ibid.*

[238] See also, in this regard, *Maclean-Hunter Cable TV Ltd., supra*, note 233.

In this industry, freelance personnel hired on contracts are as a rule found to be employees, and the question of their inclusion or exclusion is often a source of contention between the parties. The Board, in *Société Radio Canada*, defined the criteria that it will use to determine whether freelancers are employees.[239] If they are, they will be included in the unit unless their number warrants a unit of their own. Salesmen will be excluded if evidence is adduced that their community of interest differs from that of other employees.[240]

4:4420   Telephone and Telecommunications[241]

The Board in this regard deals with large organizations such as Bell Canada, British Columbia Telephone, and Teleglobe Canada, and because of their size their certification patterns are not of great help in dealing with smaller employers in the same industry, if indeed they are to be found at all. The dividing lines between units are drawn to separate office and clerical employee technical staff units. These enterprises employ large groups of engineering personnel who may form appropriate bargaining units of their own.[242] Supervisors, because of their large number, are also likely to be included in units of their own.

4:4500   ROAD TRANSPORTATION[243]

4:4510   Trucking

The Board's jurisdiction over trucking arises out of the extra-provincial nature of the employers' activity. The main clientele in this

---

239   *Société Radio-Canada* (1982), 44 di 19, 1 CLRBR (NS) 129. See also paragraph 3:1000, "Definition of employee".

240   *Radio Côte-Nord Inc., supra*, note 233.

241   The Board has issued reasons for decisions dealing with appropriateness in the following certification cases: *Bell Canada* (1976), 19 di 117, [1976] 1 Can LRBR 345, 76 CLLC #16,016; *Northern Electric Co. Ltd.* (1976), 16 di 237; *British Columbia Telephone Co.* (1977), 33 di 361, [1977] 2 Can LRBR 385, 77 CLLC #16,107; *British Columbia Telephone Co.* (1977), 22 di 507, [1977] 2 Can LRBR 404, 77 CLLC #16,108; *British Columbia Telephone Co.* (1979), 38 di 145; *Téléglobe Canada* (1979), 32 di 270, [1979] 3 Can LRBR 86, 80 CLLC #16,025; *British Columbia Telephone Co.* (1976), 20 di 239, [1976] 1 Can LRBR 273, 76 CLLC #16,015; *British Columbia Telephone Co.* (1977), 33 di 361, [1977] 2 Can LRBR 385, 77 CLLC #16,107. See also Appendix 8.

242   *Bell Canada, supra*, note 241.

243   The Board has issued reasons for decisions dealing with appropriateness in the following certification cases: *Charterways Co. Ltd.* (1974), 2 di 18, [1974] 1 Can LRBR 161, 74 CLLC #16,097; *Greyhound Lines of Canada* (1974), 4 di 22, 74 CLLC #16,112; *Soo-Security Motorways Ltd.* (1974), 4 di 51, 74 CLLC #16,109; *Loughead Express Ltd.* (1980), 41 di 267, [1981] 1 Can LRBR 75; *Les Aviseurs en Déménagements Inc.* (1981), 45 di 111; *Purolator Courier Ltd.* (1983), 53 di 166, 83 CLLC #16,069; *Reimer Express Lines Ltd.* (1979), 38 di 213, [1981] 1 Can LRBR 336; *Mercury Tanklines Ltd.* (1984), 55 di 99; *Ottawa Taxi Owners and Brokers Association*, decision no. 464, not yet reported, May 14, 1984 (C.L.R.B.); *Transport Route Canada Inc., CNX/CN Trucking* (1984), 84 CLLC #16,056; *Holmes Transportation (Quebec) Ltd.* (1977), 20 di 306; *B.D.C. Ltée* (1981), 43 di 140. See also Appendix 8.

area includes general and specialized cargo and moving companies and courier services.

Most of the trucking units are the result of numerous amalgamations of small companies over a period of time. Consequently, the primary pattern is one related to terminal locations as opposed to company-wide units. On a terminal basis, in most cases the Board includes drivers and garage employees in the same unit, while excluding office and clerical employees who are generally few in number and are most likely part of the employer's family. In smaller terminals, dispatchers are often equated with foremen and are likely to be excluded. If the evidence reveals, however, that the dispatchers have no real authority, then they will be included.

In larger companies, where possible, the Board will favour the re-grouping of certificates so that the bargaining units will become regional or company-wide,[244] and if the number of concerned employees warrants it, drivers and garage employees will be certified in different units. The same pattern occurs with long-distance drivers and brokers (owner-operators), who do not often share the same community of interest.[245] Important elements in determining whether the unit will be company-wide are the employer's own organizational structure[246] and the past patterns of certification. As mentioned earlier, most of today's large trucking enterprises are the result of successive mergers of smaller firms. This explains why certification patterns are not necessarily rational, and on occasion large trucking companies will have to deal with different unions representing employees performing similar job functions. The Board also takes into consideration the union's geographical jurisdiction, as is the case with the International Brotherhood of Teamsters locals.

In dealing with trucking firms the Board often addresses the question of occasional and part-time employees, the former being excluded. As to part-timers and regular employees, the Board tries to balance the interests of both groups, showing a clear tendency to include part-timers in the unit if they are a minority.

In the trucking industry, companies often recruit drivers from an employee referral firm, and it is difficult to identify who is the real employer.[247]

---

244   *Purolator Courier Ltd.*, *supra*, note 243; *Transport Route Canada Inc.*, *CNX / CN Trucking* (1984), 84 CLLC #16,056.
245   *Byers Transport Ltd.* (1974), 5 di 22, [1974] 1 Can LRBR 434, 74 CLLC #16,113.
246   *Provost Cartage Inc.* (1983), 53 di 155, 4 CLRBR (NS) 248; *Transport Route Canada Inc.*, *CNX / CN Trucking*, *supra*, note 244.
247   See, in this regard, the definition of "employer" and "employee" as discussed in Chapter 3.

4:4520   **Passenger Transportation**

Employees of bus companies are generally divided into three units: drivers, garage employees, and office and clerical employees. Where possible, the Board will either group the dispatchers in single units if the numbers warrant it, or it will include them in units other than the one comprising employees whom they dispatch.

4:4600   MINING

The Board will determine bargaining units along operational lines, as opposed to craft lines.[248]

4:4700   MARITIME INDUSTRY

4:4710   **Shipping**[249]

The Board will certify units on a ship-by-ship basis, but will regroup the units if requested to do so. Different bargaining units are created for licensed and unlicensed personnel working on the same ship. Captains are excluded, but in certain circumstances the Board will certify captains in separate units.

Office employees of shipping companies who perform their duties in offices located on the docks will be grouped together in units separate from those of other office employees of the same employer who work downtown and who do not come in contact with the dock workers.[250]

Shipyard workers employed by dredging companies are included in units separate from those of employees working on dredges.[251] Employees working on dredges are included in units of licensed or unlicensed personnel, following the pattern in shipping.

---

[248]   *Cape Breton Development Corp.* (1979), 35 di 140, [1979] 3 Can LRBR 485; *Uranerz Exploration and Mining Ltd.* (1978), 27 di 728, [1978] 2 Can LRBR 193, 78 CLLC #16,135; *Cominco Ltd.* (1980), 40 di 75, [1980] 3 Can LRBR 105, 80 CLLC #16,045.

[249]   The Board has issued reasons for decisions dealing with appropriateness in the following certification cases: *Oceanic Tankers Agency Ltd.* (1974), 4 di 41, 74 CLLC #16,110; *North Arm Transportation Ltd.* (1975), 9 di 17, 75 CLLC #16,155; *Verreault Navigation Inc.* (1981), 45 di 72; *Northern Construction Co.* (1976), 14 di 127, 77 CLLC #16,071; *Arctic Transportation Ltd.* (1978), 30 di 94, [1978] 2 Can LRBR 561. See also Appendix 8.

[250]   *Empire Stevedoring Co. Ltd.* (1981), 45 di 36; and *Johnston Terminals and Storage Ltd.* (1980), 36 di 45, [1980] 2 Can LRBR 390, 80 CLLC #16,039.

[251]   *Verreault Navigation Inc., supra,* note 249.

4:4720   Longshoring[252]

Longshoremen are included in units of their own, which usually include foremen, although on some occasions foremen have been regrouped in their own bargaining units.[253] Longshoring operations usually include the loading and unloading of merchandise and its handling from the ship holds to railway cars or truck tail gates. They include, among others, terminal operations and the operation of equipment related to the movement of cargo such as cranes and forklifts and their maintenance. These functions are not necessarily performed by members of the longshoremens' unions, and the functions longshoremen actually do perform may vary from port to port; thus the units may vary accordingly.[254]

The Board has also indicated that, when possible, it will regroup bargaining units comprising employees working in connection with ocean-going vessels or coastal shipping.[255] In the St. Lawrence ports the Board has favoured wide geographical units covering all employees and all employers,[256] while it has refused to do so in the Port of St. John's, Newfoundland.[257] The type of units to be fashioned by the Board in any given case will vary according to the particular situation found in each

---

252   The Board has issued reasons for decisions dealing with appropriateness in the following certification case: *Vancouver Wharves Ltd.* (1974), 5 di 30, [1975] 1 Can LRBR 162, 74 CLLC #16,118; *Cassiar Asbestos Corp. Ltd.* (1974), 6 di 17, 74 CLLC #16,122; *Empire Stevedoring Co. Ltd.* (1974), 6 di 25, 74 CLLC #16,123; *Fraser-Surrey Docks Ltd.* (1974), 6 di 32, 74 CLLC #16,124; *Northland Shipping (1962) Co. Ltd.* (1974), 6 di 7, 74 CLLC #16,125; *Pacific Coast Terminals Co. Ltd.* (1974), 6 di 59; *Lynn Stevedoring Co. Ltd.* (1974), 6 di 39; *Associated Stevedoring Co. Ltd.* (1974), 6 di 44; *Western Stevedoring Co. Ltd.* (1974), 6 di 48; *Squamish Terminals Ltd.* (1974), 6 di 79; *British Yukon Navigation Co. Ltd.* (1974), 6 di 88; *Neptune Terminals Ltd.* (1974), 6 di 97; *Canadian Stevedoring Co. Ltd.* (1974), 6 di 107; *Casco Terminals Ltd.* (1974), 6 di 117; *Westcan Terminals Ltd.* (1974), 6 di 127; *Westshore Terminals Ltd.* (1974), 6 di 141 (foremen cases); *Empire Stevedoring Co. Ltd.* (1981), 45 di 36; *Maritime Employers' Association* (1981), 45 di 314; *Murray Bay Marine Terminal Inc.* (1981), 46 di 55; *St. John's Shipping Association* (1983), 53 di 114, 3 CLRBR (NS) 314, 83 CLLC #16,039; *Murray Bay Marine Terminal Inc.* (1983), 54 di 38; *W.S. Anderson Co. Ltd.* (1984), 84 CLLC #16,023; *Murray Bay Marine Terminal Inc.* (1983), 50 di 163; *Maritime Employers' Association*, decision no. 470, not yet reported, September 21, 1984 (C.L.R.B.); *Gilles Drapeau*, decision no. 483, not yet reported, October 29, 1984 (C.L.R.B.); *Maritime Employers' Association* (1981), 45 di 314.

253   *Vancouver Wharves Ltd.*, *supra*, note 252.

254   *Maritime Employers' Association* (1981), 45 di 314, at 342-46. See also the notes of Judge Huggessen in *Cargill Grain Co. v. International Longshoremen's Association, Local 1739* (1983), 51 N.R. 182 (Fed. C.A.), which inferred a distinction between longshoring and stevedoring. See also *St. John's Shipping Association* (1983), 53 di 114, 3 CLRBR (NS) 314, 83 CLLC #16,039; and *W.S. Anderson Co. Ltd.* (1984), 84 CLLC #16,023.

255   *Maritime Employers' Association*, *supra*, note 254; *Murray Bay Marine Terminal Inc.* (1981), 46 di 55.

256   *Ibid.*

257   *St. John's Shipping Association* (1983), 53 di 114, 3 CLRBR (NS) 314, 83 CLLC #16,039. See also *Maritime Employers' Association*, decision no. 470, not yet reported, September 21, 1984 (C.L.R.B.); *Gilles Drapeau*, *supra*, note 252.

port.[258] The Board will give special consideration to the local bargaining history and to the type of business handled in the port.

4:4730   Ports Employees[259]

Employees working for different harbour commissions are re-grouped along white collar and blue collar lines.[260] Harbour policemen are regrouped in units of their own.[261]

4:4800   GRAIN-HANDLING INDUSTRY[262]

Employees working in grain elevators in the ports have their own bargaining units in relation to a single employer and may be part of a multi-employer unit, as is the case in the Port of Vancouver.[263]

Employees who operate elevators across the western provinces at various locations are employed by large wheat pool employers such as the Manitoba, Saskatchewan, and Alberta wheat pools, and they are grouped in units comprising employees of all elevators operated by their employer.[264] Other employees of these employers are included in industrial units.

4:4900   RAILWAY INDUSTRY[265]

The railway industry, because of its size, is another field where employees have been regrouped in a number of specialized units. Large railway companies such as Canadian National Railways, Canadian Pacific

---

[258]   *W.S. Anderson Co. Ltd., supra,* note 254.

[259]   See Appendix 8, "Crown Corporations".

[260]   *Conseil des Ports Nationaux* (1983), 52 di 34.

[261]   See Code s. 107(1), definition of "private constable". See also ss. 125(5) and 135.

[262]   The Board has issued reasons for decisions dealing with appropriateness in the following certification cases: *Saskatchewan Wheat Pool* (1977), 21 di 388, [1977] 1 Can LRBR 510, 77 CLLC #16,104; *Feed-Rite Ltd.* (1978), 29 di 33, [1979] 1 Can LRBR 296. See also Appendix 8. For a more detailed picture of the bargaining structure in this industry, see Francis Bairstow, *Report of the Inquiry Commission on Wider-Based Collective Bargaining* (Ottawa: Labour Canada, 1978).

[263]   *Saskatchewan Wheat Pool, supra,* note 262.

[264]   *Atomic Energy of Canada Ltd.* (1978), 33 di 415, [1979] 1 Can LRBR 252; *Manitoba Pool Elevators* (1973), 2 di 9, [1974] 1 Can LRBR 168, 74 CLLC #16,091.

[265]   The Board has issued reasons for decisions dealing with appropriateness in the following certification cases: *Canadian Pacific Ltd.* (1976), 13 di 13, [1976] 1 Can LRBR 361, 76 CLLC #16,018; *Canadian National Railway Co.* (1981), 46 di 31, [1982] 1 Can LRBR 254, 82 CLLC #16,147; *Canadian National Railways* (1982), 44 di 170, [1982] 3 Can LRBR 384, 82 CLLC #16,197; *Canadian National Railway Co.*, decision no. 468, not yet reported, June 26, 1984 (C.L.R.B.). The collective bargaining relationship in this industry was also discussed in *Len Larmour* (1980), 41 di 110, [1980] 3 Can LRBR 407; and *Robert Hogan* (1981), 45 di 43, [1981] 3 Can LRBR 389, 81 CLLC #16,132. See also Appendix 8.

Railways, and Via Rail are, together with various trade unions, covered by a great number of certificates that have evolved since the early 1900s.

In the railway industry, the bargaining agents representing the different units have regrouped themselves for the purpose of collective bargaining. The main groups that negotiate nationally at separate tables are:

> (i) operating groups, including locomotive engineers;[266] and
>
> (ii) conductors, breakmen, yard foremen, and yardmen;[267]

Over the years these two groups have sometimes bargained together and at other times separately.

> (iii) non-operating groups, such as clerks, office employees, and labourers;[268]
>
> (iv) track maintenance workers;[269]
>
> (v) shop craft employees, whose four larger groups include carmen, machinists, electricians, and boiler makers;[270]
>
> (vi) police constables;[271]
>
> (vii) train dispatchers and operators;[272]
>
> (viii) signal men.[273]

4:5000 INCLUSIONS AND EXCLUSIONS

Once the scope of the unit has been determined, the Board must decide whether certain persons should be included or excluded even though they are employees or may occupy positions included in the general scope of the unit. This determination is often critical for the union applicant, as it may have repercussions in regard to its representative character at the certification stage and in regard to its negotiating strength later. In this section, we will only consider criteria for the exclusion or inclusion of persons already found to be employees as defined by the Code.

---

[266] Represented by the Brotherhood of Locomotive Engineers (B.L.E.).

[267] Represented by the United Transportation Union (U.T.U.).

[268] Represented mainly at C.N.R. by the Canadian Brotherhood of Railway, Transport and General Workers, a C.L.C. affiliate (C.B.R.T. and G.W.), and at C.P.R. by the Brotherhood of Railway, Airline and Steamship Clerks Freight Handlers and Express and Station employees (B.R.A.C.) (AFL-CIO, CLC).

[269] Represented by the Brotherhood of Maintenance of Way Employees (AFL-CIO, CLC) (B.M.W.E.).

[270] Shop craft unions have been regrouped under the Canadian Council of Shop Craft Unions.

[271] Represented by railway police associations.

[272] Represented by Rail Canada Traffic Controllers (R.C.T.C.).

[273] Represented by the Brotherhood of Railroad Signal Men (AFL-CIO, CLC).

The Board's power to include or exclude employees in the unit is found in s. 125(2).[274] The exclusivity of this power was confirmed by the Supreme Court of Canada,[275] which found that a decision of the Board in this regard is not reviewable. The Board, as stated earlier, is not bound by the agreement of the parties,[276] but it will consider it and may agree with it if it makes labour relations sense.[277] Apart from the consideration of the exclusion of employees on the basis of the appropriateness of the unit,[278] the inclusion or exclusion of employees is decided on a case-by-case basis. In so doing, the Board tries to balance the right of the excluded employees to negotiate collectively with factors that militate in favour of their exclusion, such as an absence of community of interest with the main group[279] and the existence of conflicts of loyalty in regard to the union-employer relationship.[280] In doing so, the Board will not only look at the job functions exercised by the employees but will also consider factors that are particular to the employee as an individual. It is impossible to set out guidelines applicable to all cases of exclusions, as the possible combinations are infinite. We will now examine how the Board has made its decisions in regard to the exclusion or inclusion of part-time employees, students, casual part-time staff, secretaries, salesmen, and dispatchers.

4:5100   PART-TIME EMPLOYEES

Part-time workers are considered to be employees regardless of the number of hours they work in a week. What characterizes them is the regularity with which they perform their functions.[281] The rule is that regular, part-time employees are included with regular employees per-

---

[274]   The general power of labour boards to include or exclude employees from the unit proposed by the trade union has been upheld in *La Commission des relations ouvrières de la province de Québec v. Burlington Mills Hosiery Co. of Canada Ltd.*, [1964] S.C.R. 342, 45 D.L.R. (2d) 730. See also *Canadian Broadcasting Corp.* (1977), 19 di 166, [1977] 1 Can LRBR 481, 77 CLLC #16,102.

[275]   *Canada Labour Relations Board v. Transair Ltd.*, [1977] 1 S.C.R. 722, 9 N.R. 181, 76 CLLC #14,024, 67 D.L.R. (3d) 421; *CKCV Québec Ltée v. Canada Labour Relations Board*, [1981] 1 S.C.R. 411, 38 N.R. 181, 81 CLLC #14,127, 125 D.L.R. (3d) 348.

[276]   *CJRP Radio Provinciale Ltée* (1975), 11 di 33, 77 CLLC #16,074; *Canadian Pacific Ltd.* (1976), 13 di 13, [1976] 1 Can LRBR 361, 76 CLLC #16,018; *Entreprises Télé-Capitals Ltée* (1976), 16 di 230, 77 CLLC #16,075; *Canadian Imperial Bank of Commerce (Victory Square Branch)* (1977), 20 di 319, [1977] 2 Can LRBR 99, 77 CLLC #16,089; *Cablevision Nationale Ltée* (1978), 25 di 422, [1979] 3 Can LRBR 267; *Téléglobe Canada* (1979), 32 di 270, [1979] 3 Can LRBR 86, 80 CLLC #16,025; *Wardair Canada (1975) Ltd.* (1983), 53 di 26, 2 CLRBR (NS) 129.

[277]   *CJRP Radio Provinciale Limitee, supra,* note 276.

[278]   See, generally, paragraph 4:3100.

[279]   Exclusion of casual employees and salesmen, for example.

[280]   *Canadian Imperial Bank of Commerce (Victory Square Branch)* (1977), 25 di 355, at 363, [1978] 1 Can LRBR 132, 78 CLLC #16,120.

[281]   *Radio Station CHQM* (1975), 11 di 16, [1976] 1 Can LRBR 110, 75 CLLC #16,166.

forming the same or similar functions.[282] They will be excluded if their inclusion offsets the power of the regular employees to negotiate their working conditions.[283] If the inclusion of part-time employees would render regular employees a minority within the unit, chances are that the Board will create two units to allow for the different communities of interest of the two groups.[284]

4:5200   CASUAL EMPLOYEES

These employees work for an employer on an irregular basis, where generally there are no obligations on the part of the employer to call in the employees and no obligation on the part of the employees to answer such calls.[285] In order to determine whether the employees sought to be excluded are regular part-time or casuals, the Board will require the employer to list all hours worked by the employees in the three months preceding the application.[286] In certain circumstances, the Board has required the employer to list the hours worked for a period of one year preceding the application.[287] Employees who do not work on a regular basis during that period are considered to be casuals. The rule is that casual employees are excluded because they do not share the same community of interest as regular or part-time employees,[288] and their inclusion would permit the employer to hire casuals only and thus flood the unit.[289] The Board has indicated it will consider the following factors

---

282   *Ibid; Co-opérative de Télévision de l'Outaouais* (1975), 10 di 27, [1975] 2 Can LRBR 278, 75 CLLC #16,178; *Victoria Flying Services Ltd.* (1977), 23 di 13, 77 CLLC #16,072; *Canadian Imperial Bank of Commerce (Victory Square Branch), supra,* note 280; *Cablevision Nationale Ltée, supra,* note 276; *Les Aviseurs en Déménagements Inc.* (1981), 45 di 111.

283   *Capital Coach Lines Ltd. (Travelways)* (1980), 40 di 5, [1980] 2 Can LRBR 407, 80 CLLC #16,011. In this case the Board refused to include, in a unit of 37 regular garage maintenance employees, 205 bus drivers' positions on the basis that they did not have the same community of interest.

284   *Cablevision Nationale Ltée, supra,* note 276; *Capital Coach Lines Ltd. (Travelways), supra,* note 283.

285   *Murray Bay Marine Terminal Inc.* (1983), 50 di 163, at 173-74.

286   *Cablevision Nationale Ltée, supra,* note 276; *Murray Bay Marine Terminal Inc., supra,* note 285; *Canadian Imperial Bank of Commerce (Victory Square Branch), supra,* note 280.

287   *Société Radio-Canada* (1982), 44 di 19, 1 CLRBR (NS) 129. The Board examined the contracts of freelancers who had worked for the CBC in the year preceding the filing of applications for certification and review. In *Murray Bay Marine Terminal Inc., supra,* note 285, the Board examined the hours worked by stevedores in the fourteen months preceding the filing of the application for certification.

288   *Charterways Co. Ltd.* (1974), 2 di 18, [1974] 1 Can LRBR 161, 74 CLLC #16,097; *City and County Radio Ltd.* (1975), 11 di 22, [1975] 2 Can LRBR 1, 75 CLLC #16,171; *Canadian Imperial Bank of Commerce (Simcoe, Ontario)* (1977), 21 di 462, [1977] 2 Can LRBR 137, 77 CLLC #16,091; *Canadian Imperial Bank of Commerce (Victory Square Branch)* (1977), 25 di 355, [1978] 1 Can LRBR 132, 78 CLLC #16,120; *Cablevision Nationale Ltée* (1978), 25 di 422, [1979] 3 Can LRBR 267; *Les Aviseurs en Déménagements Inc.* (1981), 45 di 111; *Murray Bay Marine Terminal Inc.* (1983), 50 di 163; *Pacific Western Airlines Ltd.* (1984), 7 CLRBR (NS) 346, 84 CLLC #16,040.

289   *Cablevision Nationale Ltée, supra,* note 288; *Pacific Western Airlines Ltd., supra,* note 288.

when assessing whether or not it will join casuals with regular employees:[290]

> (i) the danger that the unit of regular employees be dominated by casuals;
> (ii) whether the casuals perform essentially the same work as regular employees;
> (iii) although the casuals work irregular hours, they maintain a continuous relationship with their employer;
> (iv) whether casuals have a community of interest with regular employees;
> (v) the Board is dealing with an application for certification or review. The Board is looking at whether the inclusion of casuals will affect the right of regulars to bargain collectively;
> (vi) the wishes of the casuals.

4:5300   DISPATCHERS

Dispatchers' positions are found in the transportation industry. The question is often raised as to whether they should be included in the same unit as the employees they dispatch. In a number of enterprises, especially small trucking companies, the dispatcher is often equated to a supervisor and is excluded on that basis, although he may be an employee. Dispatchers are rarely found in numbers sufficient to warrant a unit of their own. As far as possible the Board will refuse to include dispatchers in the same unit as those they dispatch.[291] However, it is quite possible that, in the absence of other units in which they might be included and in the absence of strong reasons to deny the dispatchers their right to negotiate collectively, they will be included in the same unit as those whom they are called upon to dispatch.

4:5400   SALESMEN

Salesmen are usually excluded on the ground that they have a different community of interest from other employees.[292] This is so because salesmen usually enjoy different working conditions from other regular employees, such as being paid on a commission basis, working outside the office, having the use of company cars, or having to use their own cars. When possible, the Board will include them in a unit of their own. The exclusion of salesmen is not automatic. If they are not paid on a commission basis but on the same basis as other employees, and if they enjoy generally the same benefits, they will be included in the same unit as

---

290   *Pacific Western Airlines Ltd., supra,* note 288.
291   *Airwest Airlines Ltd.* (1980), 42 di 247, [1981] 1 Can LRBR 427.
292   *Radio Côte-Nord Inc.* (1977), 23 di 39.

other employees. The party wishing to exclude salesmen must convince the Board that there are good reasons to do so.

4:5500   SECRETARIES

Secretaries are employees and are generally included in clerical units. Only in exceptional cases will they be excluded. In order to have them excluded, it must be shown to the Board that their inclusion would put them in a position of a conflict of interest regarding their loyalty to the employer and their union.[293] The criteria for the exclusion of secretaries discussed in *Bank of Montreal (Cloverdale Branch)* centred on whether the information to which the secretary was privy was confidential in regard to industrial relations. Confidentiality in regard to other matters will not be a factor for exclusion, as the Board is of the opinion that an employee does not become disloyal to his employer merely because he has joined a union.[294] In *Banque Canadienne Nationale (Rouyn)*[295] the Board excluded the secretary on the basis of confidentiality in regard to labour relations, where the issue concerned a large bank branch in an isolated area.[296]

4:5600   STUDENTS AND TRAINEES

Students and trainees are considered employees and are not excluded unless they also fall into other categories, such as casuals, or are associated with management.[297] Trainees in bank branches who are not related to management have been included.[298]

4:5700   FAMILY MEMBERS

Where special family ties bind employees occupying positions included in the bargaining unit to senior management, such employees will be excluded on the basis of the existence of a conflict of loyalty counters the principle of collective bargaining under the Code.[299] The Board has

---

[293] *Canadian Imperial Bank of Commerce (Victory Square Branch)* (1977), 25 di 355, at 362-63, [1978] 1 Can LRBR 132, 78 CLLC #16,120; *Toronto-Dominion Bank (Maple Ridge Square Branch)* (1977), 22 di 536, [1978] 1 Can LRBR 156.

[294] *Bank of Montreal (Cloverdale Branch)* (1977), 23 di 92, at 99, [1978] 1 Can LRBR 148.

[295] (1978), 23 di 107.

[296] As to what constitutes information related to industrial relations, see paragraph 3:1220.

[297] *Canadian Imperial Bank of Commerce (Victory Square Branch)*, *supra*, note 293. Bank manager trainees were excluded on the basis of a lack of community of interest with other employees in the unit.

[298] *Canadian Imperial Bank of Commerce (Victory Square Branch)*, *supra*, note 293; *Bank of Montreal (Cloverdale Branch)*, *supra*, note 294. Bank tellers and credit officer trainees were included.

[299] *Feed-Rite Ltd.* (1978), 29 di 33, [1979] 1 Can LRBR 296. In this case two fourteen-year-old students, sons of vice-presidents of the employer, were excluded on the basis of an existing conflict of loyalty.

stated that the degree of the possibility of a conflict decreases with the remoteness of family relationship.

4:6000   DETERMINING EMPLOYEE WISHES

Section 126(c) provides that, before the Board can certify a trade union, it must be

> satisfied that, as of the date of the filing of the application, or of such other date as the Board considers appropriate, a majority of the employees in the unit wish to have the trade union represent them as their bargaining agent.
> . . .

This section raises three questions:[300]

1. As of what date must the Board determine the employee's wishes?
2. How is the Board to satisfy itself that the majority of employees in the unit wishes to be represented by the applicant union?
3. Who is entitled to express his wishes?

Before we deal with the specifics of these three elements of s. 126(c), it is important to note that the expression of wishes by the employees is confidential in nature[301] and will be revealed only in exceptional cases.[302] The confidential aspect not only covers the membership cards but also protects any objection raised by employees to the certification of a trade union or any employee intervention to the effect that they do not wish to be represented by a trade union. The names of employees signing petitions or resignation forms will not be revealed to the employer. The wishes of the employees may be revealed in the case of an unfair labour practice complaint, where it is necessary to identify, for example, who participated in the formation of a union,[303] or where improprieties arise in the signing of membership cards.[304] The percentage of union representation is also kept confidential. However, it may be revealed when the application is dismissed because it does not meet the minimum require-

---

[300]   *Bank of Montreal (Tweed and Northbrook)* (1978), 26 di 591, [1978] 2 Can LRBR 123. For an overview of the Board's practices in regards to these three questions, see *Murray Bay Marine Terminal Inc.* (1983), 50 di 163, at 168-172.

[301]   Section 117(m) of the Code and s. 28 of the regulations. See also *North Arm Transportation Ltd.* (1975), 9 di 17, 75 CLLC #16,155; and *Canada Labour Relations Board v. Transair Ltd.*, [1977] 1 S.C.R. 722, 9 N.R. 181, 76 CLLC #14,024, 67 D.L.R. (3d) 421. The principle of confidentiality is also highlighted by the Board's practice of not revealing the number or percentage of the union's representation when possible.

[302]   *Québecair* (1978), 33 di 480, [1979] 3 Can LRBR 550.

[303]   Such a situation occurred in *Air West Airlines Ltd.* (1980), 39 di 56, [1980] 2 Can LRBR 197, where the question raised was whether the employer had participated in the formation of the association.

[304]   Such a situation occurred in *Air West Airlines Ltd.*, *supra*, note 303; and in *Reimer Express Lines Ltd.* (1979), 38 di 213, [1981] 1 Can LRBR 336.

ments of representation.[305] Majority rule takes precedence, and the Board does not have to assure itself that all employees have been consulted by the applicant union.[306]

4:6100 THE DATE OF DETERMINATION OF THE WISHES

Sections 118.1 and 126(c) establish that the Board has the power to determine that the employees wish to be represented by a trade union at the date of application, or at such other date as it considers appropriate.

Once the parameter of the bargaining unit has been determined, the Board will compare the number of membership cards valid at the time of application with the total number of employees in the unit. Where the union has a majority, in the absence of unfair labour practices or improprieties, the percentage arrived at will determine the question of employee wishes. If it becomes necessary for whatever reason to hold a vote, then all employees in the unit will be notified of the upcoming vote and it will be up to each employee to express his wish.

The practice is that, as a rule, the Board will consider the wishes of employees as of the date of application.[307] In *Swan River — The Pas Transfer Ltd.*[308] the Board expressed its preference for referring to the application date, because to consider the request at a later date would invite the employer to organize counter-petitions and would encourage electioneering to defeat the union's application. The main exception to the rule arises when a vote is ordered. In such a case, the employees' wishes will necessarily be assessed at a later date. In *Arctic Transportation Ltd.*[309] the Board heard a certification application from the Yukon where, because of the seasonal nature of the employer's operations, no employees were employed at the time the application was filed. In this case the Board considered the wishes of the employees at the date when the operations were to resume, that is, in the spring.

In *Canadian Imperial Bank of Commerce (Sioux Lookout)*[310] the Board indicated that it could consider the wishes of the employees at a date

---

305   The application will normally be dismissed if the applicant cannot at the time of filing show support of 35 percent where no union represents the employees as bargaining agent or 50 percent if it is raiding an incumbent bargaining agent.

306   *Téléglobe Canada* (1979), 32 di 270, [1979] 3 Can LRBR 86, 80 CLLC #16,025; *North Canada Air Ltd. and Norcanair Electronics Ltd.* (1979), 38 di 168, [1980] 1 Can LRBR 535; *B.D.C. Ltée* (1981), 43 di 140; *Bell Canada* (1981), 46 di 90, [1982] 1 Can LRBR 274; *Société Radio-Canada* (1982), 44 di 19, 1 CLRBR (NS) 129.

307   *Swan River — The Pas Transfer Ltd.* (1974), 4 di 10, [1974] 1 Can LRBR 254, 74 CLLC #16,105; *Banque Provinciale du Canada (Roberval)* (1978), 34 di 633; *Bell Canada* (1979), 30 di 112, [1979] 2 Can LRBR 435; *Air West Airlines Ltd.* (1980), 39 di 56, [1980] 2 Can LRBR 197; *B.D.C. Ltée* (1981), 43 di 140; *Murray Bay Marine Terminal Inc., supra,* note 300.

308   *Supra,* note 307.

309   (1978), 30 di 94, [1978] 2 Can LRBR 561.

310   (1978), 33 di 432, [1979] 1 Can LRBR 18.

preceding the application if, for example, the union's majority or minimum of 35 percent representation[311] had been reduced as a consequence of the employer's interference. The Board also considers the employee wishes at a later date when a long period of time has elapsed between the time the application is filed and the time the decision is rendered.[312]

In the course of the proceedings, a party may contest the eligibility of an employee to cast a vote. This question is most often raised in regard to inclusions or exclusions.[313] When the question of inclusion or exclusion is decided by the Board, then the wishes of the employees included will be considered if they have signed a membership card valid at the terminal date. If the employees have not signed a membership card, the Board will apply the general majority rule without verifying whether the employees in the minority have been canvassed prior to the filing of the application. However, the Board will necessarily take into consideration the fact that the minority employees have been included in the unit, and this factor is an important one in establishing the majority support in the unit.

4:6200   MEANS TO DETERMINE WISHES

4:6210   Membership Cards

The primary means used by the Board to ascertain employee wishes is the reference to signed membership cards. Section 26(1) and (2) of the regulations establishes that membership in a trade union is evidence that an employee wishes to be represented by that trade union.[314] In order for the evidence to be accepted by the Board, it must be shown that the individual has signed an application for membership and has paid to the trade union a sum of at least $5 for, or within, the six-month period immediately preceding the date of the filing of the application for certification. The Board, in *City and Country Radio Ltd.*[315] and *American Airlines Inc.*,[316] explained why it, together with the majority of Canadian labour relations boards, relies on membership evidence rather than taking votes. Simply stated, it is the best method to prevent employer interference when the holding of a vote is not possible in the few days immediately following the filing of the application, and the best method to permit employees to have easier access to collective bargaining.

---

311   As stipulated by the *Canada Labour Code*, s. 127(2).
312   See *Empire Stevedoring Co. Ltd.* (1981), 45 di 36; and *Verreault Navigation Inc.* (1981), 45 di 72, where a period of two years elapsed before the decision. In both these cases the Board ordered a vote.
313   See, in this regard, paragraph 4:5000.
314   *Bank of Montral (Tweed and Northbrook)* (1978), 26 di 591, [1978] 2 Can LRBR 123; *Téléglobe Canada* (1979), 32 di 270, [1979] 3 Can LRBR 86, 80 CLLC #16,025; *Murray Bay Marine Terminal Inc.* (1983), 50 di 163.
315   (1975), 11 di 22, [1975] 2 Can LRBR 1, 75 CLLC #16,171.
316   (1981), 43 di 114, [1982] 3 Can LRBR 90.

The Board has interpreted s. 27(2) of the regulations as requiring that the signing of the membership cards and the $5 contributions be witnessed by the person receiving payment.[317] The Board requires the duly authorized representative of the applicant union to sign a certificate attesting, *inter alia,* that the membership cards and payments were signed and made at the time indicated on the cards and the receipt, and that they were duly witnessed.[318] The financial contribution is an essential element, as it adds weight to the card as evidence of membership.[319] Where there is evidence that the initiation fee was paid by a social club and not by the employees[320] or where the money was not paid by the employee in the presence of the person receiving the payment, as attested to by the union,[321] the application will be dismissed outright. In *Bank of Montreal (Tweed and Northbrook),*[322] the Board indicated that the membership card plan operates on an honour system and that the cards are not regularly verified by the Board, although there are occasional spot checks. The system's guarantee rests both on the fact that a union will deal regularly with the Board and it would serve no useful purpose for it to undermine its credibility, and also on the fact that the Board will dismiss the application outright if it discovers irregularities in regard to the cards.[323]

The fact that a trade union admits persons as members without regard to the eligibility requirements of its charter, constitution, or by-laws is no ground for invalidating the membership of the applicant employee or the application of the trade union, if the Board is satisfied that the union has an established practice of admitting persons without regard to such requirements.[324]

As to petitions, evidence contradicting membership, and evidence received by the Board after the date of application, the Board has indicated that it will give no weight to them unless improprieties are alleged.[325] Petitions and letters of objections do not by themselves deter-

---

[317] *Soo-Security Motorways Ltd.* (1974), 4 di 31, 74 CLLC #16,109.

[318] See Appendix 5.

[319] *Cape Breton Development Corp.* (1977), 20 di 301, [1977] 2 Can LRBR 148, 77 CLLC #16,087.

[320] *Oceanic Tankers Agency Ltd.* (1974), 4 di 41, 74 CLLC #16,110.

[321] *Reimer Express Lines Ltd.* (1979), 38 di 213, [1981] 1 Can LRBR 336; and *Air West Airlines Ltd.* (1980), 39 di 56, [1980] 2 Can LRBR 197.

[322] *Supra,* note 314.

[323] *Ibid.*

[324] *Canada Labour Code,* s. 127(3). See also *W.S. Henderson Co. Ltd.* (1984), 84 CLLC #16,023 (C.L.R.B.).

[325] *Canadian Imperial Bank of Commerce (Sioux Lookout)* (1978), 33 di 432, [1979] 1 Can LRBR 18; and *American Airlines Inc.* (1981), 43 di 114, at 130, [1982] 3 Can LRBR 90; and *Victoria Flying Services Ltd.* (1977), 23 di 13, 77 CLLC #16,072. In the latter case, the Board said that employer-initiated petitions would be given no weight in the context where, prior to the amendments of June 1978, the Board had to consider petitions filed during the ten-day period following posting of the application by the employer. The Supreme Court of Canada, in *Canadian Brotherhood of Railway, Transport and General Workers v. Victoria Flying Services Ltd.,* [1979] 1 S.C.R. 95, 78 CLLC #14,182, upheld the Board's decision, affirming that the Board's refusal to consider such petitions was not

mine the question of representation. They may, however, cause the Board to order a vote.[326]

4:6220   Votes

The Board's power to order a vote is found in ss. 118.1, 127(1), (2), 128, and 129 of the Code. The Board's order of a vote is an administrative decision which, when it is not mandatory, cannot be reviewed.[327] If it deems it necessary, the Board may cancel a vote already taken and order a new one.[328] This, however, is exceptional and it is up to the party or person requesting the annulment of a vote to convince the Board that serious irregularities warrant such an action.[329] The Board is not compelled to count the ballots once a vote has been ordered, and s. 129(1) provides no authority for such a proposition. It merely directs the manner in which the results of a vote, if counted, are to be determined.[330] It is important to bear in mind that membership cards are the primary method of ascertaining employee wishes and that votes are the exception.[331]

4:6221   Mandatory Votes

Section 127(2) of the Code requires the Board to order a vote when a union applies for certification for a unit for which no other trade union is the bargaining agent, and where the applicant union can show that it has between 35 and 50 percent of the members in the unit. In such circumstances, a vote is mandatory,[332] notwithstanding the existence of any employer's unfair labour practices.[333] As mentioned earlier, the Board is not obliged to verify the employee wishes as of the date of the application for certification. If it can be shown to the Board that the trade union had a

reviewable. With the amendments to Code s. 126 and the enactment of s. 118.1, the Board no longer has to take into consideration the expression of employee wishes subsequent to the date of the application, as it was obliged to do prior to June 1978.

[326] *Cape Breton Development Corp.* (1977), 20 di 301, [1977] 2 Can LRBR 148, 77 CLLC #16,087.

[327] *Voyageur Inc. v. Syndicat des chauffeurs de Voyageur Inc.*, [1975] F.C. 533 (C.A.); *Syndicat des employés de CJRC (CNTU) v. Canada Labour Relations Board* (1978), 24 N.R. 454, 78 CLLC #14,179 (Fed. C.A.).

[328] *Air Canada* (1976), 18 di 66, 77 CLLC #16,062; *CJMS Radio Montréal (Québec) Ltée* (1978), 33 di 393, [1980] 1 Can LRBR 270; *Air West Airlines Ltd.* (1980), 39 di 56, [1980] 2 Can LRBR 197.

[329] *CJRC Radio Capitale Ltée* (1977), 21 di 416, [1977] 2 Can LRBR 578, 78 CLLC #16,124.

[330] *Bank of Montreal (Tweed and Northbrook)* (1978), 26 di 591, [1978] 2 Can LRBR 123.

[331] *Ibid.; Murray Bay Marine Terminal Inc.* (1983), 50 di 163.

[332] *Pacific Coast Terminals Co. Ltd.* (1974), 6 di 59; *Bank of Montreal (Tweed and Northbrook)*, **supra**, note 330; *North Canada Air Ltd.* (1978), 15 di 129, [1979] 2 Can LRBR 239, 75 CLLC #16,194.

[333] *Maclean-Hunter Cable TV Ltd.* (1979), 34 di 752, [1979] 2 Can LRBR 1.

majority status at some point prior to the filing of the application, but that its majority had been eroded due to employer interference, the Board can then consider the date on which the union had a majority as the determinant date and thus decline to call a vote, even though the trade union had a representation of only 35 to 50 percent at the time of its application. Where the applicant does not show a minimum membership support of 35 percent at the time of its application, the application will be dismissed and will not be processed further, once the percentage of representation is established.[334]

The Board has decided that the requirements of s. 127(2) do not apply to a trade union raiding an incumbent bargaining agent.[335] In order to succeed, the raiding union must show majority support at the date of application; otherwise its application will be dismissed.[336] However, in exceptional circumstances such as unfair labour practices or employer interference favouring one union or another, the Board may order a vote under s. 127(1).[337]

4:6222 Discretionary Votes

Sections 118.1 and 127 empower the Board "in any case" to order a vote or an additional vote before the proceeding is finally disposed of, for the purpose of satisfying itself that the employees of a unit wish to be represented by a trade union as their bargaining agent. Even though most votes are ordered in the context of certification applications, they are also ordered in other proceedings such as revocation[338] and, on occasion, in cases of successorship.[339]

Keeping in mind that the taking of votes is an exceptional method of ascertaining employee wishes,[340] when then are such votes ordered? The decision will depend on the particulars of each case.

Raids

In the case of raids, the raiding union as a rule must, to qualify, show a majority support at the time of application.[341] If the trade union initially

---

334 *British Columbia Telephone Co.* (1977), 33 di 361, [1977] 2 Can LRBR 385, 77 CLLC #16,107; *Murray Bay Marine Terminal Inc., supra,* note 331, at pp. 172-73 (di).

335 *CJMS Radio Montréal (Québec) Ltée* (1978), 33 di 393, [1980] 1 Can LRBR 270; *Bell Canada* (1979), 30 di 112, [1979] 2 Can LRBR 435.

336 *Ibid.*

337 *Bell Canada, supra,* note 335.

338 See ss. 137-142.

339 See s. 144 and *La Sarre Air Service Ltée (Propair Inc.)* (1982), 49 di 52; *Pacific Western Airlines Ltd.* (1980), 40 di 205, [1980] 3 Can LRBR 180; *Airwest Airlines Ltd.* (1980), 42 di 147, [1981] 1 Can LRBR 427; s. 143 and *Canadian National Railway Co., Telecommunications Department* (1980), 40 di 136, [1980] 3 Can LRBR 140.

340 *Murray Bay Marine Terminal Inc.* (1983), 50 di 163.

341 *CJMS Radio Montreal (Quebec) Ltée* (1978), 33 di 393, [1980] 1 Can LRBR 270; *Bell Canada* (1979), 30 di 112, [1979] 2 Can LRBR 435. See also *Québecair* (1984), 55 di 88.

has majority support, the Board has stated that, as a matter of policy, it will then order a vote in order to clear the air by giving the employees a choice between the incumbent and the raiding union.[342] However, if the raiding union can show an overwhelming support and if it appears that the holding of a vote will be a waste of time, the Board will not order a vote. In *Les Moulins Maple Leaf Ltée*[343] the Board did not order a vote where all the employees in the unit had signed membership cards with the raiding union. In numerous unreported cases, the Board has certified a raiding union without a vote where the union had a majority support of approximately 75 percent or more, or where the incumbent union had not filed an opposition to the application.

Irregularities in the Membership Evidence

The Board will order a vote in cases where the applicant union has shown more than 50 percent initial support, but where the Board has doubts in regards to the voluntariness of the membership. It is a question of fact in each case that will determine whether the Board will order a vote in such circumstances. The Board has stated that petitions which are employer-initiated will not warrant ordering a vote.[344] Irregularities in the filing of membership cards may result in a vote.[345]

Build-Up and Lapse Evidence

The Board has also indicated that in cases of build-up, if a substantial number of employees have been hired after the filing of the application, it may order a vote, even though the union may have had majority support at the time of its application.[346] The Board has ordered a vote where a substantial period of time had elapsed between the filing of the application and the decision.[347]

---

[342] *Les Moulins Maple Leaf Ltée* (1978), 23 di 114; *CJMS Radio Montreal (Quebec) Ltée, supra,* note 341; *Bell Canada, supra,* note 341.

[343] *Supra,* note 342. The policy concerning the advisability of ordering a representation vote in raiding situations was also discussed in *Québecair, supra,* note 341.

[344] *Victoria Flying Services Ltd.* (1977), 23 di 13, 77 CLLC #16,072. This decision was made in a context where the Board, prior to June 1, 1978, had to consider petitions filed within ten days of the date of posting, and where the union majority had to be established at the date of the decision.

[345] *Cominco Ltd.* (1980), 40 di 75, [1980] 3 Can LRBR 105, 80 CLLC #16,045.

[346] *Swan River — The Pas Transfer Ltd.* (1974), 4 di 10, [1974] 1 Can LRBR 254, 74 CLLC #16,105; *Uranerz Exploration and Mining Ltd.* (1978), 27 di 728, [1978] 2 Can LRBR 193, 78 CLLC #16,135.

[347] *Empire Stevedoring Co. Ltd.* (1981), 45 di 36; *Verreault Navigation Inc.* (1981), 45 di 72. In both these cases, a two-year period had elapsed.

New Votes and Run-Off Votes

The Board has the power to order a vote and to reorder a new one. This is likely to happen if substantial irregularities occur in the first representation vote or if employer interference casts doubts as to the free expression of the employee wishes.[348] Employer interference may also result in the Board's refusing to order a new vote to determine the employee wishes if the Board comes to the conclusion that, because of the employer's actions, another vote would not guarantee the free expression of the employees' wishes.[349] In *CJMS Radio Montréal (Québec) Ltée* the Board stated that the boycott of a vote by a trade union is no ground for ordering a second vote.[350] Where the Board has ordered a representation vote and the employees were given a choice between two or more unions and no union, and employees participating in the ballot have voted in majority for union representation without giving a majority to any union, a runoff vote between the unions will be ordered.[351]

The Board has a statutory obligation to cancel a vote where, upon considering the results, it appears that less than 35 percent of the eligible voters in the unit have voted.[352] In such cases the Board has the discretion to order a new vote or to dismiss the application.

4:6223   Who Can Cast a Ballot

When a vote is ordered, the general practice is to include as eligible those employees in the employ of the employer at the time of the application who are still employed at the time of the vote.[353] This practice, however, has not been uniform and on many occasions the Board has set the date of eligibility as of the date it orders the vote.[354] On this question the Board will try to determine whether the addition of new employees by the employer after the application date was directed at flooding the

---

[348]   *Crosbie Offshore Services Limited* (1982), 51 di 120, where the Board cancelled the first representation vote for the reason that, after the application, an employee was promoted to personnel manager and voted while acting in his new capacity. A new vote was ordered.

[349]   *Bank of Montreal (Tweed and Northbrook)* (1978), 26 di 591, [1978] 2 Can LRBR 123, where the Board annulled the first vote and refused to order another one because of employer interference. The same occurred in *La Sarre Air Service Ltée (Propair Inc.)* (1982), 49 di 52, in the context of a sale of business where the Board rescinded its order to vote because of employer interference and resorted to another method of determining employee wishes.

[350]   (1978), 33 di 393, [1980] 1 Can LRBR 270.

[351]   *Canada Labour Code*, s. 128(3). See also *CJRC Radio Capitale Ltée* (1977), 21 di 416, [1977] 2 Can LRBR 578, 78 CLLC #16,124; *Uranerz Exploration and Mining Ltd.*, *supra*, note 346; *Crosbie Offshore Services Ltd.* (1983), 54 di 81.

[352]   *Canada Labour Code*, s. 129(2).

[353]   *Williamson Trucking and Leasing Ltd.* (1975), 8 di 15, [1975] 1 Can LRBR 325, 75 CLLC #16,159; *Bank of Montreal (Cloverdale Branch)* (1977), 23 di 92, [1978] 1 Can LRBR 148; and *Murray Bay Marine Terminal Inc.* (1983), 50 di 163.

[354]   *Murray Bay Marine Terminal Inc.*, *supra*, note 353, at pp. 171-72.

bargaining unit and causing the union to lose its representative character. In *Canadian Imperial Bank of Commerce (Sioux Lookout)*,[355] the Board refused to consider the votes of two employees added to the unit on the date of application, when it found that their addition was designed to "water-down" the union's majority.

Where a vote is ordered, the practice of the Board is to have the contested employees vote and then segregate their ballots pending a decision on their inclusion or exclusion.[356] Employees who hold job functions included in the unit will normally have their wishes taken into consideration.

There may be occasions, other than those related to usual inclusions or exclusions, where the Board is called upon to decide who is eligible to express his wish.

Striking Employees

A striking employee who takes other employment, whether temporary or permanent, continues to have a job interest with the struck employer and therefore may vote[357] unless he has resigned.[358] In *CJMS Radio Montréal (Québec) Ltée*,[359] the Board decided that employees hired by the employer to replace striking employees were not eligible to vote in a raid situation unless they were occupying positions held prior to the strike by employees who had subsequently resigned.

Dismissed Employees

Employees who have been dismissed, but who have filed unfair labour practice complaints and grievances contesting their dismissal are permitted to vote in accordance with s. 107(2).

Laid-Off Employees and Employees on Maternity Leave

In other cases employees on lay-off who were subject to recall rights according to the collective agreement[360] and employees on maternity leave[361] were declared eligible to vote. Replacements of employees on maternity leave were not.

---

355   (1978), 33 di 432, [1979] 1 Can LRBR 18.
356   *Bank of Montreal (Cloverdale Branch), supra,* note 353.
357   *Arthur T. Ecclestone* (1978), 26 di 615, [1978] 2 Can LRBR 306, 78 CLLC #16,142.
358   *CJMS Radio Montréal (Québec) Ltée* (1978), 33 di 393, [1980] 1 Can LRBR 270.
359   *Ibid.*
360   *Robin Hood Multifoods Ltd.* (1978), 25 di 449, [1978] 2 Can LRBR 369, 78 CLLC #16,165; *Québecair, supra,* note 341.
361   *Canadian Imperial Bank of Commerce (Alness Branch, Downsview)* (1978), 28 di 921, [1978] 2 Can LRBR 361, 78 CLLC #16,145.

Seasonal Employees

In *Verreault Navigation Inc.*[362] the Board, in a vote held in January 1982, declared to be eligible all employees who had worked during the shipping season of 1980 and who had been recalled to work in 1981, as well as all those hired in 1981. In *Murray Bay Marine Terminal Inc.*[363] the Board considered the wishes of employees who had worked during an entire shipping season and who had worked a minimum number of hours during that period.

4:6224   Procedure in the Holding of a Vote

How does the Board proceed in the holding of a representation vote? As a rule, when the Board orders a representation vote, it merely gives a general direction that a vote be taken indicating which trade union shall appear on the ballot.[364] In this regard, s. 128(2) of the Code stipulates that, where a trade union is applying for certification for a unit that no other trade union represents as bargaining agent, the employees must be given the choice of not being represented by any trade union named on the ballot. However, this requirement is not applicable in run-off votes where the name of two or more trade unions appeared on the first ballot and the result indicated that a majority of employees who had cast ballots favoured union representation.[365]

The Board may direct that the ballots be segregated and sealed.[366] This often occurs where the Board is not in a position to make a final determination of the issues before it, and where it becomes necessary to hold the vote before the issues can be decided. Following final determination it may not become necessary to consider the results of the vote, and the ballots may then be ordered destroyed.[367] The Board may also in exceptional cases direct that the vote be taken by mail.[368]

Where a vote has been ordered, the chief returning officer of the Board will appoint a returning officer or deputy returning officers, as needed, who are required to hold the vote. The returning officer will contact the parties and come to an agreement as to the list of eligible voters and other questions of procedure.[369]

---

[362] (1981), 45 di 72.
[363] *Murray Bay Marine Terminal Inc., supra,* note 353.
[364] *Société Radio-Canada* (1978), 27 di 765, [1979] 2 Can LRBR 41.
[365] *Canada Labour Code,* s. 128(3).
[366] Section 118(i).
[367] *CJMS Radio Montreal (Québec) Ltée, supra,* note 358; *Société Radio-Canada* (1982), 44 di 19, 1 CLRBR (NS) 129.
[368] Such a vote was taken in *Société Radio-Canada, supra,* note 367, because the employees to be canvassed were dispersed all over the country.
[369] *Crosbie Offshore Services Ltd.* (1983), 54 di 81.

The vote is held by secret ballot and is normally held on the employer's premises. The employer and each trade union appearing on the ballot have the right to one representative at each polling station. If a problem arises that cannot be resolved at the returning officer level, it is submitted to the Board for decision. Electioneering is permitted between the unions involved and the concerned employees, but it should not occur at the place of employment without the employer's permission.[370] Solicitation is permitted where the employees take their free-time periods, such as in a cafeteria, or where the Board, in special cases, may direct.[371] Employers should note that their involvement in such electioneering is not welcome because of the special nature of their relationship with the employees and their evident interest in convincing employees not to join a union or to favour one union over the other.[372] In the exceptional circumstances of *Crosbie Offshore Services Ltd.* the Board ordered a silent period during the electioneering campaign.[373] In this case the Board referred to the numerous votes held over the years and the acrimony that had resulted between the competing trade unions.

When the vote is completed, unless otherwise ordered the ballots are counted by the returning officer in the presence of the parties' representatives, and the results are attested to by them. The result is then sent to the Board for consideration.

Where a vote is held by mail, the parties will attest to the list of eligible employees and their addresses. Unless all ballots or some of them are ordered segregated, the Board will send a ballot to each employee addressed to his residence. In the envelope the employee will find the ballot and a pre-addressed unmarked envelope in which to return his marked ballot. Upon receipt of the ballots, they are placed in boxes and later opened in the presence of the parties' representatives, who will attest to the results.

4:6300   DETERMINING THE MAJORITY STATUS

Once the Board has determined the parameters of the unit, the date at which the employees' wishes are to be considered, and who is eligible to express his wish, it then becomes a simple question of arithmetic to determine whether the union has more than 50 percent of the wishes expressed in its favour.[374] If the union has less than 35 percent at the time of application or at any other date determined by the Board, absent unfair labour practices, the Board will dismiss the application.[375] If the

---

[370] *Canada Labour Code*, s. 185(d).
[371] Section 199.
[372] *American Airlines Inc.* (1981), 43 di 114, [1982] 3 Can LRBR 90.
[373] *Crosbie Offshore Services Ltd., supra,* note 369.
[374] *Murray Bay Marine Terminal Inc.* (1983), 50 di 163, at 172.
[375] *British Columbia Telephone Co.* (1977), 33 di 361, [1977] 2 Can LRBR 385, 77 CLLC #16,107; *Murray Bay Marine Terminal Inc., supra,* note 374.

union has a majority the Board will then certify it, or it may in certain circumstances order a vote.[376] If the union has between 35 and 50 percent membership, a vote will be ordered.[377] If there are no reasons to discard the vote, the Board will certify or dismiss the application.

It must be stressed that, because certification is based on majority rule, up to 49.99 percent of the employees may be swept into collective bargaining without ever having been solicited by the applicant union.

It is important to note that the majority referred to in s. 126(c) may be as low as 17.5 percent by virtue of applying s. 129(2) and (3). Where a vote is taken and at least 35 percent of the employees eligible to vote have voted, the wishes expressed by the majority of the 35 percent who have voted is evidence of the wishes of the majority of all the employees in the bargaining unit.

4:7000 CERTIFICATION ORDER

The last paragraph of s. 126 states that, if the provisions of subss. (a), (b), and (c) are satisfied, the Board "shall certify the trade union making the application subject to this part". The order is signed by the chairman or one of the vice-chairmen. The description of the unit in the order will, as a rule, be couched in terms that include all employees of the employer except those who occupy jobs or functions expressly excluded. This is known as a universal or "all employee" description.[378]

4:8000 BARS TO CERTIFICATION

Where a trade union is "so dominated or influenced by an employer that its fitness to represent the employees is impaired",[379] or where the trade union denies membership to any employees or class of employees in a bargaining unit by virtue of a policy or practice that the trade union applies relating to qualifications for union membership,[380] or where a trade union acts as a bargaining agent for both private constables and other employees of the same employer,[381] then the Board cannot grant it a certificate.

4:8100 DOMINATION OR INFLUENCE BY THE EMPLOYER

Pursuant to s. 134(1) of the Code, the Board must refuse to certify a trade union where these two conditions are met:

---

[376] *Canada Labour Code*, ss. 127(1) and 118(i).
[377] Section 127(2).
[378] *British Columbia Telephone Co.* (1977), 22 di 507, [1977] 2 Can LRBR 404, 77 CLLC #16,108; *British Columbia Telephone Co.* (1978), 28 di 909, [1978] 2 Can LRBR 387, 78 CLLC #16,146.
[379] *Canada Labour Code*, s. 134(1).
[380] Section 134(2).
[381] Section 135.

(i) the trade union must be dominated or influenced by the employer; and

(ii) the Board must be satisfied that the domination or influence is so important, that the trade union's fitness to represent employees of the employer for the purpose of collective bargaining is impaired.

What constitutes domination or influence is a question of fact to be decided in each case.[382] In *CJRC Radio Capitale Ltée*[383] the Board identified indicia which, when found to be present, could result in domination or influence. It referred to the following factors:

1. The applicant association is an independent union created in the wake of an organizing campaign by a recognized trade union.

2. The applicant association is created in great haste and recruits a majority of members very quickly.

3. The applicant association's meetings are held at the work place during working hours.

4. The applicant association recruits members during working hours, often with the knowledge and assistance of the employer.

5. The applicant association has few financial resources, but it can afford technical and professional help.

6. Management representatives attend the applicant union's meetings or encourage employees to attend.

The Board has not found it necessary to differentiate between domination and influence.[384]

The second condition of s. 134(1) particular to the federal jurisdiction requires that, once the Board has come to the conclusion that domination or influence is present it must go a step further and decide whether in its opinion the domination or influence is such that the trade union's ability to bargain collectively has been impaired.[385] The issue here is not the employer's conduct, but rather the ability of the trade union to effectively represent employees at the bargaining table. The domination or influence must be substantial and of such a nature as to

---

[382] *CJRC Radio Capitale Ltée* (1977), 21 di 416, [1977] 2 Can LRBR 578, 78 CLLC #16,124; *Reimer Express Lines Ltd.* (1979), 38 di 213, [1981] 1 Can LRBR 336; *Air West Airlines Ltd.* (1980), 39 di 56, [1980] 2 Can LRBR 197; and *Nordair Ltd.*, decision no. 458, unreported, April 30, 1984 (C.L.R.B.).

[383] *CJRC Radio Capitale Ltée, supra,* note 382.

[384] *Reimer Express Lines Ltd., supra,* note 382.

[385] *CJRC Radio Capitale Ltée, supra,* note 382; *Reimer Express Lines Ltd., supra,* note 382; *Air West Airlines Ltd., supra,* note 382; and *Nordair Ltd., supra,* note 382.

render the union incapable of representing the employees.[386] In *Airwest Airlines Ltd.*[387] the Board asked whether a sufficient arm's-length relationship existed, so that meaningful collective bargaining of the kind contemplated by the Code could be undertaken and sustained. The Board went on to say that such an appreciation was necessarily subjective and that the whole of the evidence had to be considered before coming to a conclusion.

The existence of the second prerequisite of s. 134(1) necessarily implies that a trade union can be dominated or influenced without that factor being determinant of its status as a trade union.[388]

The Board has dealt directly with s. 134(1) in few cases. In *CJRC Radio Capitale Ltée* the Board found that some influence existed, but that it was not of such a degree as to prevent the union from engaging in meaningful collective bargaining.[389] In *Reimer Express Lines Ltd.* the Board dealt with two applications for certification, one by a *bona fide* trade union and the other by an association.[390] It found that some drivers who had been terminated had been rehired on the condition that they became members of the association. It also found that the posting of notices by the association was done on the company's bulletin board, while the union had been denied access to these boards; that the association had access to management offices; and that it used management's internal mailing and distribution system to distribute its literature to the employees. The Board went on to find that the influence or domination was such that it could not certify the association. In *Airwest Airlines Ltd.* the Board heard an application by an association that was raiding the incumbent bargaining agent. The Board found that the employer had initiated the formation of the association, had suggested the name of a lawyer, had guaranteed payment of the lawyer's fees, and had permitted the association to hold a vote on its premises. It had strongly suggested that the employees join the association, and it had initiated proceedings to obtain authorization from the Board to change existing working conditions under s. 124(4) of the Code with the intention of favouring the association's credibility over that of the union. The Board found that s. 134(1) applied, and denied certification. In *Nordair Ltd.* the Board found that the raiding association was not employer-dominated. The employees had sided with the employer in a strike because they were disenchanted with their bargaining agent and their applying for certification through the association was a means of repudiating their bargaining agent.[391]

---

386 *CJRC Radio Capitale Ltée, supra,* note 382.
387 *Air West Airlines Ltd., supra,* note 382.
388 *CJRC Radio Capitale Ltée, supra,* note 382; *Reimer Express Lines Ltd., supra,* note 382; *Air West Airlines Ltd., supra,* note 382.
389 *CJRC Radio Capitale Ltée, supra,* note 382.
390 *Reimer Express Lines Ltd., supra,* note 382.
391 *Nordair Ltd., supra,* note 382.

If the Board concludes that the union is so influenced or dominated that it cannot represent the employees at the bargaining table, then s. 134(1)(a) and (b) provide that the Board cannot certify.[392] If the union had concluded a collective agreement, s. 134(1)(b) provides that any collective agreement concluded between the trade union and the employer in regard to employees of the bargaining unit shall be deemed not to be a collective agreement for the purpose of Part V of the Code. In *Verreault Navigation Inc.*[393] the Board found that the union was dominated to such an extent that s. 134(1) applied, and it held invalid a collective agreement that had been entered into between the association and the employer even though the agreement had been filed in accordance with s. 204 of the Code.[394] The Board said that the union could not circumvent the imperative requirements of s. 134(1)(b), which concern public order, by merely filing the agreement in accordance with s. 204.

4:8200   DENIAL OF UNION MEMBERSHIP

Pursuant to s. 134(2), where a trade union seeking certification denies membership to any employees or class of employees in a bargaining unit by virtue of a policy or practice that it applies relating to qualifications for membership in the union, the Board shall not certify the union. The Board has considered the application of this provision in *West Shore Terminals Ltd.*, where it was alleged that a union's constitution restricted membership to Canadian citizens and British subjects, thus discriminating against immigrants.[395] The Board found that s. 134(2) did not apply. The Board's practice is to avoid incisive analysis of the union's constitution, because the union could always demonstrate a broad interpretation or practice, or failing this it could undertake to amend its constitution at the first opportunity.[396] It went on to say that it would be contrary to the Code's objectives to apply s. 134(2) rigidly. In *Majestic Wiley Contractors Ltd.* the employer argued that certain exclusions from the bargaining unit were warranted because the employees did not fall within the "craft jurisdiction" of the union,[397] but the Board said that it should be wary to interpret the union's constitution in a manner so restrictive as to bring s. 134(2) into operation. In *W.S. Anderson Co. Ltd.* the Board found that a clause in the union's constitution that barred from membership "those whose philosophy, principles, teachings or purposes are subversive" did not trigger the application of s. 134(2), where it

---

392   This is what happened in *Reimer Express Lines Ltd.*, *supra*, note 382; and *Air West Airlines Ltd.*, *supra*, note 382.
393   (1978), 24 di 227.
394   Section 204 provides that a collective agreement has to be filed with the minister.
395   *Westshore Terminals Ltd.* (1974), 6 di 141.
396   *Ibid.*, at p. 155 (di).
397   *Majestic Wiley Contractors Ltd.* (1975), 11 di 43, 75 CLLC #16,179.

appeared on the facts that the union had never refused membership on those grounds.[398]

Because of this approach, it is not likely that s. 134(2) will be a bar to certification. Where a problem arises, the Board will likely offer the union the possibility of amending its constitution or procedures.

Where s. 134(2) applies, the Board cannot certify the applicant union, and the collective agreement between the union and the employer is deemed not to be a collective agreement for the purpose of Part V.

4:8300 TRADE UNION REPRESENTING PRIVATE CONSTABLES AND OTHER EMPLOYEES OF THE SAME EMPLOYER

Pursuant to s. 135 of the Code, the Board cannot certify a trade union acting as a bargaining agent for both private constables and other employees of the same employer. The Board has not yet had the opportunity to apply this provision, although it had occasion to refer to it in *Dennison Mines Ltd.*[399] In order for this section to apply, the applicant trade union would have to potentially be placed in the position of representing, as bargaining agent, both private constables and other employees of the same employer, whether these employees and the private constables are included in a common or different units. In practice, because of the restrictive definition of "private constables",[400] s. 135 is not likely to be the subject of many decisions by the Board.

4:9000 THE EFFECTS OF CERTIFICATION

4:9100 EXCLUSIVE AUTHORITY FOR THE PURPOSE OF COLLECTIVE BARGAINING

When certification is granted by the Board, there is no room left for private negotiation between the employer and his employees. The employer must now necessarily deal with the certified bargaining agent, which not only represents employees but is a party in his own right to the new relationship.[401] However, certification does not abolish management's residual rights, and the notice to bargain given under s. 146

---

[398] *W.S. Anderson Co. Ltd.* (1984), 84 CLLC #16,023.
[399] (1975), 8 di 13, [1975] 1 Can LRBR 313, 75 CLLC #16,150.
[400] *Canada Labour Code*, s. 107(1).
[401] *British Columbia Telephone Co.* (1977), 33 di 361, at 374, [1977] 2 Can LRBR 385, 77 CCLC #16,107; *Syndicat catholique des employés de magasins du Quebec Inc. v. Paquet Ltée*, [1959] S.C.R. 206, 18 D.L.R. (2d) 346. See also s. 154. *McGavin Toastmaster Ltd. v. Ainsclough*, [1976] 1 S.C.R. 718, 4 N.R. 618, [1975] 5 W.W.R. 444, 75 CLLC #14,277, 54 D.L.R. (3d) 1.

following certification obliges the employer to negotiate all matters that are negotiable.[402]

Section 136(1)(a) provides that the bargaining agent has exclusive authority to bargain collectively on behalf of the employees in the bargaining unit. Section 136(1)(b) provides that the certification of any trade union that formally included employees covered by the new certificate is deemed to be revoked in regard to those employees covered by the new certificate. This, in fact, grants the bargaining agent a monopoly of representation over employees in its bargaining unit. This monopoly is stated in s. 136(1)(a) and (b) and is specifically protected by ss. 148(a), (b),[403] 184(1)(a), (3)(g), and 185(a), (b).[404]

This monopoly of representation for the purpose of collective bargaining also means that employees can no longer individually negotiate their working conditions with the employer unless so authorized by the bargaining agent.

The exclusivity of representation imposes on a bargaining agent, whether certified or voluntarily recognized, a duty to represent fairly all employees in the bargaining unit.[405]

4:9200   SUBSTITUTION OF THE BARGAINING AGENT IN THE COLLECTIVE AGREEMENT

Section 136(1)(c) provides that the certified bargaining agent is deemed to be substituted as a party to any collective agreement that affects any employee included in its newly certified bargaining unit. In fact, the newly certified bargaining agent is called upon to replace the former bargaining agent in the collective agreement to which it was a party. In *Bell Canada (George W. Adams)* the Board discussed the authority of a newly certified bargaining agent, which displaced an incumbent bargaining agent.[406] It said that the newly certified trade union could continue grievances initiated by the former bargaining agent or could initiate new grievances as a party, even when the collective agreement signed between the former bargaining agent and the employer had

---

402 *Bank of Nova Scotia (Sherbrooke and Rock Forest, Quebec)* (1982), 42 di 398, 82 CLLC #16,158.

403 These sections provide that where a notice to bargain is given, the employer must bargain in good faith and the conditions of work of employees in the bargaining unit cannot be modified unless agreed to by the bargaining agent. These sections are discussed in detail at paragraphs 12:1200 and 12:2000.

404 These sections are discussed in detail in paragraphs 12:4210 and 12:4310. They specifically forbid an employer to bargain collectively in relation to a bargaining unit that is already represented by a bargaining agent. They also prohibit a trade union from forcing an employer to bargain collectively if it is not the bargaining agent of the bargaining unit for which it wishes to bargain.

405 *George Lochner* (1979), 37 di 114, [1980] 1 Can LRBR 149, 79 CLLC #16,209.

406 *Bell Canada* (1981), 43 di 238, [1981] 2 Can LRBR 284, 81 CLLC #16,099.

expired but where the right to strike and lockout had not yet been acquired.

The substitution of the certified bargaining agent as a party to a collective agreement may result in the bargaining agent becoming a party to more than one collective agreement that was applicable to employees comprised in its newly certified bargaining unit. When such a situation arises, s. 136(2) provides that the certified bargaining agent may require the employer to bargain collectively with respect to the bargaining unit to which it has been substituted as a party. The thrust of this section is to make uniform the working conditions of all employees in the same bargaining unit.

Where no collective agreement binding on the employees in the unit is in force, the certified bargaining agent may require the employer by notice to commence collective bargaining,[407] or it may be required by the employer to do so.[408] Such is not the case for the voluntarily recognized bargaining agent that is negotiating its first collective agreement.

4:9300 EFFECT OF CERTIFICATION IN RELATION TO SUBSEQUENT BARGAINING UNIT MODIFICATIONS

Since its reconstitution in 1973 the Board has abandoned the practice of describing bargaining units in terms of enumerated included and excluded functions. It now uses a universal type of description or, in other words, an all-employee description, followed by specific exclusions.[409] Because of this practice, once a certificate has been issued by the Board, the parties will often include a more detailed definition of the bargaining unit in their collective agreement.[410] This may be done either in the scope clause of the agreement or in the monetary clauses, where the work functions, occupational categories, or classifications to which the agreement applies are listed. However, as the Board stated in *Bell Canada*,[411] ideally there should be no discrepancy between the scope of the unit as described in the certification order and the description of the unit to which the collective agreement is made applicable.

---

[407]   *Canada Labour Code*, s. 146(a).
[408]   Section 146(b).
[409]   *Téléglobe Canada* (1979), 32 di 270, [1979] 3 Can LRBR 86, 80 CLLC #16,025; see also *British Columbia Telephone Co.* (1977), 22 di 507, [1977] 2 Can LRBR 404, 77 CLLC #16,108; and *British Columbia Telephone Co.* (1978), 28 di 909, [1978] 2 Can LRBR 387, 78 CLLC #16,146, for the consequences of this practice. When new classifications are created following the issuance of a certification order, the burden is on the employer to demonstrate that they do not fall within the intended scope of the unit.
[410]   *British Columbia Telephone Co.* (1978), 28 di 909, [1978] 2 Can LRBR 387, 78 CLLC #16,146.
[411]   *Bell Canada* (1981), 43 di 86, [1982] 3 Can LRBR 113; *Bell Canada* (1982), 50 di 105.

In practice, however general the language of the certification order, the parties may demonstrate by their behaviour, as reflected in the clauses mentioned above, that they understand the bargaining unit to be smaller than the one apparently originally determined. Where this situation occurs inadvertently the Board has held, in *British Columbia Telephone Co.*,[412] that little more can be done than to give effect to the new description of the bargaining unit as evidenced by the behaviour of the parties over a long period of time. However, the union may suffer the consequences of this shrinkage of the unit in periods of union raiding should it wish, subsequently, to acquire bargaining rights for the "forgotten employees".[413]

Alternatively, where this situation occurs deliberately and the parties enter into a collective agreement that is expressly made applicable to a unit smaller than the one described in the certification order by excluding certain employees, work functions, occupational categories, or classifications, more serious consequences may ensue. The union may lay itself open to charges under s. 136.1[414] and may suffer the consequences, again, in periods of union raiding.[415] The employer, on the other hand, would be remiss in his duty to bargain in good faith under s. 148(a) should he attempt to impose and negotiate to an impasse such exclusions at the bargaining table in return, for example, for a few concessions to the union.[416]

In bargaining collectively with a certified trade union an employer may, by contrast, recognize the trade union for a unit larger than the one to which the certification order originally applied. In such a case the execution of the collective agreement will amount to the voluntary recognition of the trade union as bargaining agent for the additional group of employees.[417] Therefore, once a bargaining relationship has been established the bargaining unit defined by the Board in the certification order may expand and may, by this process of incremental recognition, extend to cover a larger group of employees. The parties may, however, by the same token, foster the development of work assignment or jurisdictional disputes among unions and lay themselves open to unfair labour practice complaints under ss. 184(3)(g) and 185(a) and (b), where two or more unions have been certified by the Board and one of the bargaining agents extends its unit into the other's unit. The ability to extend bargaining units through negotiations is circumscribed by the

---

412 *British Columbia Telephone Co.* (1977), 22 di 507, [1977] 2 Can LRBR 404, 77 CLLC #16,108.
413 *Ibid.; Bell Canada* (1982), 50 di 105.
414 *British Columbia Telephone Co., supra,* note 412. The duty of fair representation also applies in the context of contract negotiations: *Len Larmour* (1980), 41 di 110, [1980] 3 Can LRBR 407. On this subject, see paragraph 13:1200.
415 *British Columbia Telephone Co., supra,* note 412; *Bell Canada, supra,* note 413.
416 *Ibid.; Wardair Canada (1975) Ltd.* (1983), 53 di 184, 84 CLLC #16,005.
417 *British Columbia Telephone Co., supra,* note 412.

existence of bargaining rights granted to other trade unions in the same enterprise.[418]

As is the case at the initial stage of certification, the Board is not bound by an agreement between the parties that either enlarges or shrinks the unit originally defined. The Board views its role as that of an ongoing supervisor and as an exclusive arbiter of unit boundaries or composition.[419] It may give *a posteriori* effect to party covenants or behaviour affecting the scope of the unit, but as a matter of policy the intervention of the Board is required to modify the people or work-function content of the unit.

---

[418] *Eastern Provincial Airways (1963) Ltd.* (1978), 30 di 82, [1978] 2 Can LRBR 572; affd. [1980] 2 F.C. 512, 108 D.L.R. (3d) 743.
[419] *Bell Canada* (1981), 46 di 90, [1982] 1 Can LRBR 274.

CHAPTER 5

REVOCATION — SECTIONS 137 AND 139

5:0000 REVOCATION

The *Canada Labour Code* provides avenues for employees to have the certification of their bargaining agent revoked in certain circumstances. Section 137(1) and (3) provides for revocation on the grounds that a majority of employees no longer wishes to be represented by a certified or a voluntarily recognized bargaining agent. Section 139 provides for revocation where a trade union has been certified by fraud. Section 141 deals with the revocation of the certification of a council of trade unions. This chapter does not deal with the automatic revocation that occurs when a new bargaining agent displaces an incumbent trade union following certification or successorship.[1]

5:1000 REVOCATION FOR LOSS OF REPRESENTATIVITY

The Code, at s. 137(1) and (3), provides that any employee who claims to represent a majority of employees within the bargaining unit may apply to the Board to revoke the right of the bargaining agent to represent them.[2]

5:1100 TIMELINESS

The timeliness of an application for revocation may vary, depending on whether the incumbent bargaining agent is certified or voluntarily recognized. In either case an application shall not be made during the first six months of a legal strike or lockout, except with the consent of the Board.[3] The Board has clearly indicated that the time limits indicated in s. 137 are to be strictly adhered to, and that employees and employers cannot circumvent the time limits by using s. 119 (review proceedings) to obtain the modification or annulment of the Board's certification order.[4]

---

[1] *Canada Labour Code*, ss. 136(1), 144(3)(a)(ii)
[2] *Jean-Claude Harrison* (1983), 53 di 85, 4 CLRBR (NS) 258.
[3] *Canada Labour Code*, s. 137(5).
[4] *North West Community Video Ltd.* (1976), 14 di 132, 77 CLLC #16,085; *Northern Construction Ltd.* (1976), 19 di 128, 76 CLLC #16,032; *Inland Broadcasters (1969) Ltd. and Twin Cities Radio Ltd.* (1979), 37 di 96, [1980] 1 Can LRBR 193.

5:1110   Certified Bargaining Agent

The time of filing an application depends on whether a collective agreement covering the bargaining unit is in force or not. The Board has interpreted the words "where no collective agreement is in force" in s. 138(2) as being "words of art . . . to describe a state or type of bargaining relationship that can exist under the Code rather than the exact legal obligations of the parties".[5] It concluded that the state of the employer-employee relationship is not fixed by the terms of the collective agreement, but rather by the provisions of the Code. When a collective agreement continues to be applicable by reason of a continuation clause, or by the effect of s. 148(b)[6] or s. 160(4) and (5) of the Code, applications for revocation are not barred as a result. A bargaining agent cannot claim that an otherwise timely application under s. 137(2) or (4) is untimely because the collective agreement that was to expire at a fixed date continues in force by virtue of a bridging clause.[6a]

First Situation: Collective Agreement in Force — Section 137(2)(a)

In this case an application may only be filed during the period of time in which an application could be made under s. 124, unless the Board agrees that it be made at some other time.

Section 124(2)(c) and (d) sets out the time in which an application can be made where a collective agreement is in force. It may be filed:

> (i) if the term of the collective agreement is for three years or less, after the commencement of the last three months of the collective agreement;
>
> (ii) if the term of the collective agreement is more than three years
>
> — after the commencement of the thirty-fourth month and before the commencement of the thirty-seventh month;
>
> — during the three-month period immediately preceding the end of each year that the collective agreement continues to operate after the third year of its operation;
>
> — after the commencement of the last three months of its operation.

Second Situation: No Collective Agreement in Force — Section 137(2)(b)

In this case an application may be filed at any time after a period of one year from the date of certification. Here the protection of the

---

5   *J. Phillips* (1978), 34 di 603, at 608, [1979] 1 Can LRBR 180.
6   For freeze provisions, see paragraph 12:1200.
6a   *William E. Blonski* (1984), 8 CLRBR (NS) 111, 84 CLLC #16,054.

incumbent certified bargaining agent is absolute during that year, as the Board does not have the discretion to abridge the time limits that it has under s. 137(2)(a) where a collective agreement is in force.

5:1120   Voluntarily Recognized Bargaining Agent

Under s. 134(3) an employee claiming to represent a majority of employees in the unit may seek an order declaring that the bargaining agent is not entitled to represent them. The time limit for such an application will vary, depending on whether the applicable collective agreement is the first collective agreement concluded between the employer and the bargaining agent or is a subsequent agreement.

First Situation: During the First Collective Agreement — Section 137(4)(a)

The application may be filed:

(i) at any time during the first year of the term of that collective agreement, and

(ii) thereafter, except with the consent of the Board, only during a period in which an application for certification of a trade union is authorized to be made pursuant to section 124. . . .[7]

Second Situation: Other Cases — Section 137(4)(b)

In any other case, unless the consent of the Board is obtained, a revocation application can only be brought during the period in which a union can apply for certification under s. 124.[8]

5:1130   Bars to Application

By virtue of s. 137(5) an application made during the first six months of a legal strike or lockout would be untimely unless the Board decides otherwise, regardless of the effects of s. 124(2)(c) and (d).

5:1200   PRACTICE AND PROCEDURE

5:1210   Content of the Application

An application for revocation must set out the following information:

(i) the full name and address of the applicant,

---

7 See paragraph 4:1000.
8 See paragraph 4:1000.

(ii) the full name and address of the trade union affected by the application,

(iii) the full name and address of the employer of the employees affected by the application,

(iv) the date of the order of the Board, if any, certifying the trade union as a bargaining agent for the bargaining unit,

(v) particulars concerning the collective agreement, if any, covering the employees in the bargaining unit, and

(vi) the approximate number of employees in the bargaining unit. . . .[9]

The application must be accompanied by a statement signed by each employee supporting the application and attesting that

(i) he does not wish the bargaining agent to represent him;

(ii) he authorizes the applicant to make the application on his behalf.[10]

5:1220   Processing the Application

Upon receipt of an application, the file is vetted as to timeliness and other possible defects and is assigned to an investigation officer (I.O.). An investigation is then conducted in the same manner as in cases of certification.[11] The I.O. will see to it that the proceedings are exchanged between the parties and that the applicant employee signs a form[12] attesting that he is an employee of the employer, that he represents a majority of employees in the bargaining unit, that the signatories in support of the application have expressed their wishes, and that he understands that any misrepresentation or irregularity could result in the rejection of the application. Once the investigation is complete, a report is made and distributed to the parties and the file is then placed before a panel of the Board for decision.

In a situation where the investigation had revealed that the actual number of employees was larger than that represented by the applicant in his application, with the result that the applicant did not represent a majority of the employees, the Board, convinced that it was a *bona fide* miscalculation on the part of the applicant, ordered a vote.[13] It felt that to do otherwise and dismiss the application because at the time of application it did not represent a majority would be to put form over substance, particularly where the applicant could, the day following the dismissal of the application, make a new timely application and where there was no employer interference or unfair labour practice.

---

9   *Canada Labour Relations Board Regulations 1978,* SOR/78-499, s. 32(b).

10   Regulations, s. 32(b).

11   See paragraph 4:2500.

12   *Donna English* (1980), 40 di 179, at 181-82, [1980] 3 Can LRBR 213. See Appendix 6, where the form is reproduced.

13   *Donna English, supra,* note 12.

An application made under s. 137 is a means to provide employees with the opportunity to revoke the certificate of their bargaining agent, and its determination rests on the evidence that a majority of the employees in the bargaining unit wishes the bargaining agent to be removed.[14] The wishes of the employees may be ascertained by a representation vote or by other means.[15] The Board has indicated that, as a rule, it will favour a determination of employee wishes by a representation vote,[16] but where the wishes of the employees are not in doubt, no vote will be ordered.[17] Where the wishes of the employees are rendered doubtful because of employer interference, a previous order calling for a representation vote may be cancelled and the question decided by other means,[18] or the application may simply be dismissed.[19]

The wishes of the employees are the determinant factor for granting a revocation application under s. 137(1).[20] If the Board is satisfied that the majority of employees in the bargaining unit do not wish to be represented by the bargaining agent, the Board must, by order, revoke the certification of the bargaining agent[21] or, in the case of a voluntarily recognized bargaining agent, declare that the bargaining agent is not entitled to represent the employees in the bargaining unit.[22]

5:1300   BAR TO REVOCATION

The one exception to the use of employee wishes as the determinant factor in a revocation application is found in s. 138(2). This section provides that where the bargaining agent is certified and no collective agreement applicable to the unit is in force, no order revoking the certification shall be made unless the Board is satisfied that the bargaining agent has failed to make a reasonable effort to enter into a collective agreement in relation to the bargaining unit. This section only applies in the case of a certified bargaining agent.[23]

---

14 *Arleen Allen* (1979), 34 di 811, [1979] 2 Can LRBR 72; *William E. Blonski, supra,* note 6a.
15 *Société Radio-Canada* (1978), 27 di 765, [1979] 2 Can LRBR 41.
16 *Ralph Gordon Chatwin* (1979), 34 di 707, [1979] 1 Can LRBR 481, 79 CLLC #16,176.
17 See *Allan Martin* (1979), 37 di 50, [1979] 3 Can LRBR 184, 80 CLLC #16,004, where the employees had voted for revocation before the application was made and all employees had signed the application. See also *Joseph Szabo and Jaro Jarkowvsky* (1977), 25 di 345, [1979] 1 Can LRBR 161, where there were only two employees remaining in the bargaining unit and both had signed the application for revocation. In *William E. Blonski, supra,* note 6a, the applicant was the only employee left in the unit; the Board granted the application.
18 *La Sarre Air Service Ltée (Propair Inc.)* (1982), 49 di 52.
19 *CJRP Radio Provinciale Ltée* (1977), 19 di 140, [1977] 2 Can LRBR 238, 77 CLLC #16,106; *Jean-Claude Harrison* (1983), 53 di 85, 4 CLRBR (NS) 258.
20 *Arleen Allen, supra,* note 14.
21 *Canada Labour Code,* s. 138(1)(a).
22 Section 138(1)(b).
23 *Joseph Szabo and Jaro Jarkowvsky, supra,* note 17; *Ralph Gordon Chatwin, supra,* note 16.

The Board has interpreted s. 138(2) as being applicable in only two circumstances:[24]

1. Where a bargaining agent is certified and has not concluded a first collective agreement. It does not apply where a collective agreement has previously been concluded and is in the process of being renewed, nor does it apply following a successorship application (under s. 143 or 144) where the employer or the union, as successor parties to a collective agreement, are dealing with one another for the first time.[25]

2. Where a lawful strike or lockout is permitted, whether the strike or lockout occurs in the course of negotiating a first collective agreement or during a renewal negotiation.

If the application is filed in these two circumstances, then the certified bargaining agent may avail itself of the provisions of s. 138(2), and the onus then falls on the applicant to satisfy the Board that the bargaining agent has failed to make a reasonable effort to enter into a collective agreement. If a hearing is called under s. 138(2), the bargaining agent will be required to lead evidence because its actions relating to its efforts to negotiate are within its knowledge, but it is the applicant who will assume the ultimate burden of proof.[26] In *Ralph Gordon Chatwin*[27] the Board commented on the employer's participation in the hearing. It said that the employer had an interest in regard to allegations that it had not negotiated in good faith under s. 148(a), but that it had no interest in regard to his employees' wishes nor in regard to the union's reasonable efforts to negotiate, as these were matters between the trade union and the employees only.

In deciding what will constitute reasonable efforts to enter into a collective agreement, the Board has said that the touchstone is to be found in the expression of the duty to bargain in good faith under s. 148(a), and that it is composed of two elements:[28]

(i) efforts to negotiate a collective agreement with the employer;

(ii) communications with bargaining unit employees.

Whether these two criteria are satisfied is a question of fact to be determined in each case.[29] In *Arthur T. Ecclestone*, where a legal strike was in progress over the renewal of the agreement and where complaints of

---

[24] *J. Phillips* (1978), 34 di 603, [1979] 1 Can LRBR 180; *Ralph Gordon Chatwin, supra,* note 16.

[25] *Ibid.*

[26] *Ralph Gordon Chatwin, supra,* note 16; *Jean-Claude Harrison, supra,* note 19.

[27] *Ralph Gordon Chatwin, supra,* note 16.

[28] *Joseph Szabo and Jaro Jarkowvsky, supra,* note 17; *Ralph Gordon Chatwin, supra,* note 16; *Allan Martin, supra,* note 17; *Donald Nosworthy* (1981), 45 di 153; *La Sarre Air Service Ltée (Propair Inc.)* (1982), 49 di 52.

[29] *Ralph Gordon Chatwin, supra,* note 16; *Jean-Claude Harrison, supra,* note 19.

alleged bad-faith bargaining by the employer had been heard and dismissed by the Board, the Board found that the failure of the union to meet with the employer during the three months prior to the revocation application was not abnormal and did not constitute a failure to make reasonable efforts to negotiate.[30]

In *Ralph Gordon Chatwin*[31] the union had been certified for a bargaining unit of six employees, and a further application for a larger group of fifty-six employees had been dismissed on constitutional grounds. The union sought and won certification for the larger group with the provincial board fifteen months later. During that period, the bargaining agent met with the employer for the purpose of obtaining voluntary recognition for the larger group and not for the purpose of negotiating a collective agreement for the smaller unit already certified by the Board. The bargaining agent gave its notice to bargain fourteen months after certification in regard to the unit of six employees. The Board therefore found that the union had not made reasonable efforts to negotiate a collective agreement for the unit it had certified, and the revocation application was allowed.

In *Arleen Allen*[32] the union gave notice to bargain and pressed the employer to commence bargaining, even though the latter had applied for judicial review of the certification decision. Regarding communication with the employees, the union had had meetings with its members, had held a vote on the propositions tabled with the employer, and had included an employee on the negotiating committee at all bargaining sessions. The Board found the union had satisfied its obligations and had made reasonable efforts to negotiate and to communicate. The Board also found that the union had no obligation to communicate with non-union members in the unit. Applying s. 138(2), the Board dismissed the application.

In *Allan Martin*[33] the union, following certification, gave notice to bargain. However, the employer applied for judicial review. His application was dismissed by the Federal Court of Appeal, but he was later granted permission to appeal by the Supreme Court of Canada. At the bargaining table the employer opposed the union with its legal proceedings. The union accepted this refusal to bargain, although judicial review proceedings in themselves do not stay the execution of Board orders. The employer had frozen salaries in accordance with s. 148(b), and although the union was aware of the hardship this was creating for the employees in its unit, it did nothing to try to remedy the situation. In fact, the only meeting the union held with the employees occurred when they were

---

30   *Arthur T. Ecclestone* (1978), 26 di 615, [1978] 2 Can LRBR 306, 78 CLLC #16,142.
31   *Ralph Gordon Chatwin, supra,* note 16.
32   *Supra,* note 14.
33   *Allan Martin, supra,* note 17.

originally contacted to obtain union representation. The Board found the union had not made sufficient efforts to negotiate nor to communicate with its members. The application was allowed.

In *Donald Nosworthy*[34] and *LaSarre Air Service Ltée (Propair Inc.)*,[35] where evidence was adduced showing that the union had made efforts to negotiate with the employer, the Board found the lack of communication not to be determinant, since there was nothing to communicate; nothing was happening in the negotiations, due to the employer's resistance. In both cases, the applications were dismissed.

5:2000   REVOCATION FOR FRAUD

Where a trade union has been certified as the bargaining agent for a unit of employees, s. 139 provides that any employees in the bargaining unit, the employer, or any trade union that appeared before the Board in the certification proceedings may apply for revocation if it alleges that the certification was obtained by fraud. In such cases, the application can be made at any time.

Upon receipt of such an application, the Board investigates the matter. Section 140 sets out the conditions that, if present, compel the Board to order the revocation of the certification. The Board must be satisfied that the evidence adduced in support of the allegations

(a) was not and could not, by the exercise of reasonable diligence, have been presented to it in the certification proceeding, and

(b) is such that the Board would have refused to certify the trade union as the bargaining agent for the bargaining unit if the evidence had been presented to it in the certification proceeding. . . .

The Board has yet to render a decision on an application under s. 140. In *Murray Bay Marine Terminal Inc.*[36] the Board, while investigating an application for review of an existing certificate, discovered facts that, if they had been known at the time of certification, would have significantly changed the Board's order. The Board notified the parties to give reasons why it should not rescind its certification order. Following representations by the parties it rescinded the order under s. 119.

---

34   *Donald Nosworthy, supra,* note 28.
35   *La Sarre Air Service Ltée (Propair Inc.), supra,* note 18. The decision of the Board here was partially quashed by the Federal Court of Appeal, not yet reported, file no. A-370-82, because the employees had not had the opportunity to make representations. The file was returned to the Board, which subsequently applied s. 138(2) and dismissed the application.
36   (1981), 46 di 55.

5:3000   REVOCATION OF A COUNCIL OF TRADE UNIONS' CERTIFICATE

Where a council of trade unions has been certified as a bargaining agent pursuant to s. 130, any employee in the bargaining unit, the employer of the employees, or a trade union that forms part of the council of trade unions may apply to the Board for revocation on the grounds that, in addition to those circumstances covered by ss. 137 and 139, the council of trade unions no longer meets the requirements for certification as a council of trade unions.

The Board has yet to receive an application under s. 141 and to define what it considers to be "the requirements for certification of a council of trade unions". No requirements are set out in s. 130 other than that the council must be formed of two or more trade unions. Section 141 could apply following amendments to the council's constitution, which would result in a situation where it could not be said that the council could effectively negotiate a collective agreement. If evidence is presented to the Board that the council of trade unions no longer meets the requirements for certification as a council, the Board has the discretion, but not the obligation, to revoke the certificate. It is likely that the Board would give the council of trade unions and its members the opportunity to make the necessary adjustments so as to avoid the application of s. 141.[37] An application made under s. 141 can be filed during the same period of time as that provided for in s. 137.

5:4000   EFFECTS OF THE REVOCATION

Section 142 provides that any collective agreement between the trade union or the council of trade unions and the employer that applies to the employees of the bargaining unit ceases to have effect from the time the order to revoke is made, or at such later time as provided for by the Board.

The employer is further enjoined not to bargain collectively for a period of one year with the trade union or the council of trade unions whose certificate has been revoked, unless during that period the Board certifies the trade union as the bargaining agent for the employees of the employer. In fact, in regard to the employees in the bargaining unit, the employer cannot even negotiate on a voluntary basis with a bargaining agent that has lost its certificate or has been declared not to be entitled to represent the employees.

---

[37] This is affirmed by analogy to the Board's approach in dealing with ss. 130, 131, and 132. See paragraph 4:3240.

CHAPTER 6

REVIEW

6:0000   **REVIEW**

6:1000   POWERS OF THE BOARD: GENERALLY

Although s. 122(1) provides that every order or decision of the Board is final, Parliament has given the Board the power in s. 119 to "review, rescind, amend, alter or vary any order or decision made by it". The second part of s. 119 provides that the Board may "rehear any application before making an order in respect of the application" and is concerned with the power, following the hearing of a demand, to re-open the hearing and rehear on application before making an order. The first part of s. 119 concerns the Board's power, once a decision has been made or an order issued, to review that decision or order. It confers upon the Board what has been called an "independent plenary power" entitling it to deal with cases not specifically provided for by Part V.[1]

It is established law that the kind of power conferred by s. 119 may also be invoked in the following circumstances:

---

[1]   *Genaire Ltd. v. International Association of Machinists* (1958), 58 CLLC #18,101; *Oliver Co-Operative Growers Exchange v. British Columbia Labour Relations Board*, [1963] S.C.R. 7, 40 W.W.R. 333, 35 D.L.R. (2d) 694, 62 CLLC #15,428; *Bakery and Confectionery Workers International Union of America, Local 468 v. White Lunch Ltd.*, [1966] S.C.R. 282, 55 W.W.R. 129, 66 CLLC #14,110, 56 D.L.R. (2d) 193; *Zeballos District Mine and Mill Workers Union, Local 851 v. British Columbia Labour Relations Board*, [1966] S.C.R. 465, 56 W.W.R. 530, 66 CLLC #14,128, 57 D.L.R. (2d) 295; *United Brotherhood of Carpenters and Joiners of America v. Alberta Board of Industrial Relations*, [1971] 2 W.W.R. 105, (*sub nom. R. v. Alberta Board of Industrial Relations*) 17 D.L.R. (3d) 302 (Alta. C.A.); *Canadian Union of Public Employees, Local 41 v. Alberta Board of Industrial Relations* (1978), 5 Alta. L.R. (2d) 219, 8 A.R. 174, 79 CLLC #14,206, 84 D.L.R. (3d) 710 (C.A.); *National Association of Broadcast Employees and Technicians v. Western Ontario Broadcasting Ltd.* (1979), 30 N.R. 75, 102 D.L.R. (3d) 547 (Fed. C.A.); *Northern Taxi Ltd. v. Manitoba Labour Board* (1958), 27 W.W.R. 12, 18 D.L.R. (2d) 122 (Man. Q.B.). See also *Télévision St-François Inc. (CKSH-TV) v. Canada Labour Relations Board*, [1977] 2 F.C. 294 (T.D.); *Société Radio-Canada v. Canada Labour Relations Board*, not yet reported, January 22, 1985, file no. A-467-82 (Fed. C.A.); *Re Canadian Pacific Express Ltd. and Ontario Highway Transport Board* (1979), 26 O.R. (2d) 193, 12 C.P.C. 273, 102 D.L.R. (3d) 228 (Div. Ct.); *R. v. Ontario Labour Relations Board; Ex parte Nick Masney Hotels Ltd.*, [1969] 2 O.R. 797, 70 CLLC #14,110, 7 D.L.R. (3d) 119; revd. [1970] 3 O.R. 461, 70 CLLC #14,020, 13 D.L.R. (3d) 289 (C.A.); *Re Davisville Investment Co. Ltd. and Toronto*, (1976), 12 O.R. (2d) 455, 76 D.L.R. (3d) 218; affd. 15 O.R. (2d) 553, 2 M.P.L.R. 81 (C.A.).

    (i) where minor, clerical mistakes were committed in the decision that need to be corrected;

    (ii) where there is new evidence that was not brought before in the earlier proceeding for good and sufficient reasons that might have changed the Board's original decision or order;

    (iii) when the decision or order is vitiated by an error on a question of law or on a question of fact or of jurisdiction;

    (iv) where the order or decision is vitiated by a breach of the rules of natural justice;

    (v) where the order or decision raises an important question of policy or construction of the law.

The Board has recognized that s. 119 may be invoked not only in all of the above circumstances,[2] but also in a host of other circumstances:

> We should say at the start that since 1973, all applications under this section have been treated under the general heading *"applications for review"*. In reality, there can be a host of other categories of applications pursuant to Section 119 . . . .
>
> It should be noted that the English text in Section 119 speaks of the power to *"revise"*, *"annul"*, *"amend"*, *"alter"* and *"vary"* while the French text stipulates that the Board may only *"revise"*, *"annul"*, or *"modify"*. We do believe this divergence has no significance.
>
> But a review of the definitions of these terms in both French and English dictionaries illustrates the extent of the jurisdiction created by this section and the many diverse situations it may encompass. In practice, in Board decisions dealing with Section 119, this inventory of situations has led to several nuances like *"applications to bring up-to-date"*, *"to clarify"*, *"to correct"*, *"to amend"*, *"to modify"*, *"to enlarge"*, *"to aggrandize"*, to quote a few.[3]

In practice, the Board has used Section 119 mainly to:

    (i) enlarge the intended scope of an existing bargaining unit;

    (ii) clarify the scope of a bargaining unit;

    (iii) consolidate and merge existing bargaining units;

    (iv) revoke bargaining certificates;

    (v) review the merits of a previous decision or order.

6:2000   REVIEW OF BARGAINING UNITS AND CERTIFICATES

    In cases involving the composition of bargaining units, the Board has held that as a result of the public-interest role it assumes in the initial unit

---

2   *Canadian National Railways* (1975), 9 di 20, [1975] 1 Can LRBR 327, 75 CLLC #16,158; *Calgary Television Ltd.* (1977), 25 di 399, [1978] 1 Can LRBR 532; *British Columbia Telephone Co.* (1979), 38 di 124, [1980] 1 Can LRBR 340, 80 CLLC #16,008; and *Ronald Guy*, decision no. 494, not yet reported, December 20, 1984 (C.L.R.B.).

3   *Téléglobe Canada* (1979), 32 di 270, at 305, [1979] 3 Can LRBR 86, 80 CLLC #16,025.

determination and subsequent redetermination, it may exercise the powers of s. 119 on its own initiative.[4] However, whether the proceedings are initiated by the Board or by the parties, there are three limitations on the use of the powers of s. 119.

First, the powers conferred by that section can only be used in reference to previous Board decisions or orders.[5] Second, in applying s. 119, the Board must act in conformity with the other provisions of the Code.[6] This limitation requires that in the appropriate cases the wishes of employees affected by modifications to an existing unit be canvassed and that the appropriateness of the revised unit be determined, as provided by s. 126. The problem encountered in practice is to determine whether modifications made pursuant to a review initiated by the Board or upon an application by the parties raise such questions of appropriateness or representation and, therefore, whether the Board must take them into account before modifying an existing unit. The Board has written extensively on this subject, and its policy will be discussed below. The third limitation on the Board's powers to review an existing unit flows from the requirements of natural justice. All the parties who may be affected by the projected modifications of the unit must be given proper notice and afforded an opportunity to make representations.[7]

The questions raised by certification cases do not cease with the initial unit determination and the establishment of the representative character of the union. In *Canadian National Railways*[8] the Board described two situations illustrating the point. First, where the Board has certified a bargaining agent, it can later be asked to review its original order so as to enlarge the unit. Second, whenever an order or decision of the Board has continuing effects — and this is typically the case with a certification order — various circumstances may change, which may require clarifications of the original decision. For example, new positions or classifications may have been created following the issuance of the certificate, or the duties and responsibilities of certain positions may have varied. As a result, it may be unclear whether they are covered by the original decision of the Board and included in the existing unit.

In either situation, s. 119 may be invoked. In either situation, whether the demand seeks an enlargement of the unit or simple clarifications of the latter, the decision of the Board on an application for review

---

4   *Ibid.*; see also *Société Radio-Canada* (1982), 44 di 19, 1 CLRBR (NS) 129; affd. not yet reported, January 22, 1985, file no. A-467-82 (Fed. C.A.). In both these cases, the proceedings were initiated, in part, by the Board.

5   A consequence of this limitation is that parties to a voluntarily recognized bargaining relationship not founded on any earlier Board order or decision are barred from invoking s. 119 to have the bargaining unit reviewed by the Board.

6   *Ibid.*; see also *British Columbia Telephone Co.* (1979), 38 di 14, [1979] 3 Can LRBR 350.

7   *Télévision St-François Inc. (CKSH-TV) v. Canada Labour Relations Board, supra,* note 1; *Société Radio-Canada v. Canada Labour Relations Board, supra,* note 1.

8   *Canadian National Railways* (1975), 9 di 20, [1975] 1 Can LRBR 327, 75 CLLC #16,158.

may result in the addition to an existing unit of employees or functions not previously unionized. This does not mean that the conditions applicable to certification applications specified by the Code in ss. 124(2) and 126 must be met in both kinds of applications. In the exercise of its discretion, the Board has decided that only demands seeking an enlargement of a unit are basically of the same nature as applications for certification and therefore require that the wishes of the employees added to the existing unit and the appropriateness of the revised unit be taken into consideration.[9] The question of timeliness, on the other hand, has been dealt with in the same manner in either type of review application and is not a factor taken into consideration. A review application may be filed at any time, irrespective of the delays set out in s. 124(2) for applications for certification.[10]

Since only demands seeking an enlargement of the existing unit require that the conditions set out by s. 126 for applications for certification be met (excluding the timeliness provisions of s. 124(2)), it becomes imperative for any applicant to know how the Board distinguishes between applications seeking an enlargement of the unit and those that seek simple clarification of the latter.

6:2100   DETERMINING WHETHER A DEMAND SEEKS AN ENLARGEMENT OR CLARIFICATIONS OF THE UNIT

In this endeavour, the Board applies what has been referred to as the "Téléglobe test". The latter was evolved in the *Canadian National Railways*[11] and the *Téléglobe Canada*[12] cases. In *Canadian National Railways* the Board stated that a decision on an application involving clarifications of the unit does not change the nature and effect of the original order. By contrast, if an application involving an enlargement of the unit is granted, the revised order may be substantially different from the original one. In *Téléglobe Canada* the Board expanded on the implications of this distinction and stated the following:

> When the revised ordinance is substantially different from the original one, it would be more exact to state that it is far less an enlargement of the bargaining unit for which the bargaining agent was certified than a modification or transformation which so changes the nature and very essence of the original unit by way of enlargement or shrinking or otherwise, and this independently from the number of employees involved, that it would no

---

9   *British Columbia Telephone Co.* (1977), 22 di 507, [1977] 2 Can LRBR 404, 77 CLLC #16,108; *Téléglobe Canada* (1979), 32 di 270, at 305, [1979] 3 Can LRBR 86, 80 CLLC #16,025; *British Columbia Telephone Co.* (1979), 38 di 14, [1979] 3 Can LRBR 350.
10   *Ibid.*
11   *Supra*, note 8.
12   *Supra*, note 3.

longer be the same unit as originally designed by the certified union and found appropriate by the Board.[13]

According to this test, it must therefore be determined whether the very nature and essence of the existing unit would be altered by the addition of the functions or classifications sought by the union. An affirmative answer means an enlargement of the unit. A negative answer means mere clarifications of the unit. In order to determine whether the very nature and essence of the unit would be altered by the additions sought by the union, the Board resorts to the two criteria outlined below, namely that of the intended scope of the original certification order and the accretion doctrine.

6:2110 The Intended Scope of the Original Certification Order

From Quebec case law,[14] the Board has imported the concept of the intended scope of a certification order. This concept originates in the principle that, beyond simple reliance on the normal meaning of the words, or despite the generality of the terms employed in the description of a bargaining unit, one must refer to its intended scope in order to ascertain its true meaning. To that end, and among other means, one must resort to the Board's original file in order to examine the procedures and representations of the parties and analyse what was the scope that both the union and the Board intended to give to the initial certification. Various factors must be examined. Among these are the list of employees obtained from the employer, along with their corresponding classifications; the reaction of the union to that list; and any geographical factors present. Following the issuance of the certificate, the behaviour of the parties concerning the unit originally defined must also be examined. This will be reflected in the history of their negotiations and collective agreements concluded thereafter.

Although bargaining certificates issued since 1973 use a universal description, the methods used by the Board in cases of application for certification have allowed it to adopt the concept of the intended scope of the certificate as a tool for determining whether the addition of employees or functions to an existing unit would alter the nature and essence of the original order. By referring to, among other factors, the detailed organizational charts of the enterprise required from the employer and to the joint letter of understanding describing the final position of the

---

13   *Supra,* note 9, at p. 310 (di).
14   *Hôtel-Dieu de Roberval,* [1970] T.T. 1; *Ecole Notre-Dame de Liesse,* [1973] C.E. 351; *Commission Scolaire Régionale Lalonde,* [1973] T.T. 241; *La Ganterie Auclair Inc.,* [1974] C.E. 430; *Inter Cité Construction Ltée,* [1974] C.E. 231; *E. & R. Woodworking Co. (Division of E-1 Ran Furniture Ltd),* [1977] T.T. 10; *Produits Béton R.B.R. Inc.,* [1977] T.T. 146; *Asbestos Corp. Ltd.,* [1973] T.T. 98; *Coronet Carpets Ltd.,* [1974] T.T. 257.

parties, the Board can determine the composition and the scope that it originally intended to give to the unit. It is thereby able to compare the nature of the functions originally included with that of the functions sought to be added.[15] Subsequently created functions of a nature similar to those originally included must be viewed as having been intended to be encompassed in the existing unit. Thus their addition will not alter the nature and essence of the original order.[16] Conversely, where the functions sought for inclusion are different from those originally included, they may be viewed as not having been intended to be encompassed in the existing unit. Accordingly, if the application for review is granted, the revised order will be substantially different from the original one.[17]

However, the intended scope of a bargaining certificate issued prior to 1973, in an era where the Board's current practices in certification demands were non-existent, may not always be clearly ascertainable. Little or no information may be disclosed in the Board's predecessor's files with regard to the employer's organizational structures at the time of certification, or with regard to the reasons that warranted the exclusion of certain classifications from the unit. In such instances the Board relies on various elements, such as the history of dealings and bargains struck between the union and the employer over the composition of the bargaining unit, the interest of the employees sought to be included in the unit, the purpose for which the application for review is made, and the labour relations history within which the parties operate.[18]

The extent to which the board is able to trace the origins of the disputed positions back to the original exclusions will also be a relevant factor, although not necessarily a determining one.[19] For instance, in one case, the Board found that the exclusions from the original certificate had been based solely on management functions and therefore excluded those newly created positions sought by the union that fell into this category. However, while certain supervisory positions had been included in the original certificate, the Board excluded the newly created supervisory positions on the ground that these employees had no community of interest with the other employees.[20]

Pursuant to the prevailing policy at the time of certification, the Board's predecessor might have merely endorsed a bargaining unit that had specifically been agreed upon by the parties. In such cases, where the appropriateness of the original unit has never really been determined,

---

15   See, for example, *Millar & Brown Ltd.* (1977), 26 di 572, [1979] 1 Can LRBR 245; and *Neptune Bulk Terminals Ltd.* (1979), 35 di 149, 79 CLLC #16,199.
16   *Supra*, notes 3 and 8.
17   *Ibid.*
18   *Ibid.*
19   *National Harbours Board* (1980), 41 di 126, [1980] 3 Can LRBR 265.
20   *Ibid.*; see also *Canadian Broadcasting Corp.*, decision no. 461, not yet reported, April 30, 1984 (C.L.R.B.).

the Board has declined, on review applications, to rely on the apparent intended scope of the unit as suggested by the certificate. For example, although a certificate dating as far back as 1949 contained an all-employee description, the Board, in *British Columbia Telephone Co.*,[21] determined that only those classifications agreed upon by the parties at the time of certification and covered by the collective agreement fell within the scope of the certificate. Thus, the true intended scope of the unit was held to be precisely that which had been originally agreed upon by the parties, and no more than that. As a result, the expansion of bargaining rights to subsequently created functions that seemed to fall within the intended scope of the certificate was held to constitute an enlargement of unit boundaries and was subject to the requirements of review applications of that kind.

Alternatively, whether the unit originally defined by the Board's predecessor had been agreed upon by the parties or not, subsequent modifications may have been negotiated between them following certification. By such agreements, the union may have abandoned part of its representational rights. Conversely, these may have been expanded by voluntary recognition of classifications not covered by the original certification order.

In cases where the original intended scope of the unit cannot be clearly ascertained, effect will be given in preference to subsequent clear agreements concluded by the parties concerning the scope of the unit. It was determined that it would be wholly unrealistic and impractical in labour relations terms to expect that the Board would turn back the pages of history and several collective agreements to interpret the language of a certification order ignored by the parties for decades.[22] Here again, the true, intended scope of the unit is precisely and no more than that which has been agreed upon by the parties in such post-certification agreements. Hence, expansion of bargaining rights to functions that had been abandoned by the union in a post-certification agreement constitutes an enlargement of unit boundaries.[23] Similarly, where a union seeks the expansion of its bargaining rights to functions similar to those included in the unit by voluntary recognition, its demand under s. 119 will also be held to involve an enlargement of unit boundaries.[24] The Board held that

21   *British Columbia Telephone Co.* (1977), 22 di 507, [1977] 2 Can LRBR 404, 77 CLLC #16,108; *British Columbia Telephone Co.* (1978), 28 di 909, [1978] 2 Can LRBR 387, 78 CLLC #16,146.

22   *British Columbia Telephone Co.* (1977), 22 di 507, [1977] 2 Can LRBR 404, 77 CLLC #16,108; *Téléglobe Canada* (1979), 32 di 270, [1979] 3 Can LRBR 86, 80 CLLC #16,025.

23   *British Columbia Telephone Co.* (1977), 22 di 507, [1977] 2 Can LRBR 404, 77 CLLC #16,108; *British Columbia Telephone Co.* (1978), 28 di 909, [1978] 2 Can LRBR 387, 78 CLLC #16,146; *National Harbours Board* (1980), 41 di 126, [1980] 3 Can LRBR 265; *Bell Canada* (1981), 46 di 90, [1982] 1 Can LRBR 274.

24   *British Columbia Telephone Co.* (1977), 22 di 507, [1977] 2 Can LRBR 404, 77 CLLC #16,108.

voluntary recognition of classifications not covered by the original certi-fication does not result in the acquisition of representational rights over the work jurisdiction content of these classifications.[25]

6:2120   The Accretion Doctrine

The second criterion used by the Board in determining whether the addition of newly created functions or classifications would alter the nature and essence of the existing unit is embodied in the accretion doctrine, imported from American case law. According to the case law, disputed employees constitute an accretion when a community of interest exists between them and persons already included in the unit. To that end, various factors are examined by the National Labor Relations Board, such as the history of the bargaining unit, the geographic prox-imity or isolation of the new employees, the functions, duties, and skills of the entire work force, and the administrative territories or subdivisions of the employer.[26] For its own purposes the Board has adopted the following definition of what constitutes an accretion:

> In the future, when the Board uses the term *"accretion"* it shall do so to designate an enlargement or widening of an existing bargaining unit by the addition of a number of employees, for whatever reason, when said em-ployees, as compared to the actual members of the bargaining unit in-volved, shall occupy classifications the incumbents of which will perform similar work. There will then be a sufficient community of interest so as not to betray the essential nature of the original unit. The intended scope of the certification shall thus be respected.[27]

6:2200   UNIT ENLARGEMENT

Some examples of review applications involving an enlargement of unit boundaries have been given above when discussing the concept of the intended scope of a bargaining unit. As a matter of principle, of course, had the nature and essence of the existing unit been altered by the additions sought, all those cases where the demand was held to involve no more than a clarification of the original order (as will be discussed below)[28] would constitute, *a contrario*, other examples of applications seeking an enlargement of unit boundaries. However, there are circum-stances where, even if the nature and essence of an existing unit is not altered by the additions sought, the applicant must nevertheless meet the requirements of applications seeking an enlargement of unit boundaries. Such is the case with an application filed by a bargaining agent who has

---

25   *Ibid.*

26   See *Téléglobe Canada* (1979), 32 di 270, at 326, [1979] 3 Can LRBR 86, 80 CLLC #16,025.

27   *Ibid.*, at p. 327 (di); see also *Millar & Brown Ltd.* (1977), 26 di 572, [1979] 2 Can LRBR 245, for a typical example.

28   See paragraph 6:2300.

abandoned part of its representational rights either by (i) express agreement with the employer or by (ii) implicit agreement, as evidenced by a failure to act diligently to secure the integrity of the unit.[29]

In one case where the original intended scope of the certificate seemed clear from the universal type of description used, the Board nevertheless refused to implement this original intention, as a study of the history of the negotiations between the parties revealed that the functions included in the unit had been specifically excluded in the scope clause of the collective agreements they had concluded over the years.[30] The union had thereby abandoned the advantage flowing from the original universal description and had to gain anew the representational rights over the functions it had abandoned.

In another case, by relying on the original intended scope of its certificate covering all sales representatives of the enterprise, a union sought to have included in its unit a group of account representatives whose functions were similar to those of the employees included in the unit.[31] The functions sought had been created some twenty years earlier and excluded by the employer after consultation with the union. The Board acknowledged that there was clearly a community of interest among the account and sales representatives and even found an overall majority of union members in the combined group. It declined, nonetheless, to accede to the union demand and refused to exercise its discretionary authority under s. 119 as it found no compelling labour relations reasons for intervening in the bargaining unit boundary lines established so long ago by the parties. The acceptance by the union of a situation created twenty years before, as evidenced by its lack of effort during that period to alter the employer's decision, was treated as a delay in seeking to secure the integrity of the unit.[32]

6:2210   Requirements

The requirements to be met on a review application seeking an enlargement of unit boundaries were established in *Téléglobe Canada*.[33]

With respect to the representative character of the applicant, the latter must be ready, either by showing membership cards or through a Board-ordered vote pursuant to s. 127(1), or by virtue of a union membership clause in the collective agreement, to prove that it has the support of a majority of the employees to be added to the unit, as well as an overall majority in the combined group. The applicant must also demonstrate to

---

29 See paragraph 6:2310.
30 *British Columbia Telephone Co., supra*, note 24.
31 *Bell Canada, supra*, note 23.
32 The Board further cautioned that it would not introduce structural changes purely to assist a party seeking to gain advantages at the bargaining table.
33 *Supra*, note 26.

the Board that the addition is wanted by its members, excluding those members among the group to be added.[34] Furthermore, since the addition to an existing unit of functions or classifications dissimilar to those originally included by the Board and which do not fall within the intended scope of the certificate affects the appropriateness of the unit as initially determined, the applicant must convince the Board of the appropriateness of the revised unit.[35] Of course, where the union seeks to include in its unit functions that it has inadvertently or deliberately abandoned, it is not required to demonstrate the appropriateness of the revised unit. In such situations, however, the wishes of the employees are relevant and are taken into consideration.

The appropriateness and representational requisites are maintained in review applications seeking an enlargement of the unit because their fundamental nature is the same as that of applications for certification. Nonetheless, such a review application may be filed with the Board at any time, irrespective of any time limit set by the Code for applications for certification. The policy reasons for this practice have been explained by the Board in *Téléglobe Canada*.[36]

6:2220   Effects of the Revised Order

If an application for review seeking an enlargement of the unit is granted, a new order or decision will issue to amend or replace the original one. It will substantially alter the original decision, but the change will have no retroactive effects. The order will sanction a new unit.[37]

The terms and conditions of employment of the new employees, whether they are already covered by a collective agreement at the time of the decision or not, are governed in the same way as are those of newly added employees on review applications seeking clarifications of the unit.[38]

6:2300   UNIT CLARIFICATION

By interpreting and clarifying its certification orders, disputes concerning (i) the erosion of the bargaining unit,[39] (ii) the identification of employees bound by a collective agreement or jurisdictional conflicts,[40]

---

[34]   *Ibid.*
[35]   *Ibid.*
[36]   *Ibid.*
[37]   *Ibid.*
[38]   See paragraph 6:2312.
[39]   See paragraph 6:2310.
[40]   See paragraph 6:2320.

and (iii) the territorial scope of a bargaining unit[41] can be solved by the Board.

6:2310   Securing the Integrity of the Bargaining Unit

When the original certificate contains an enumerative description, the classification titles referred to in the order may have been replaced by new ones with the passage of time. Some may have been abolished. Changes in the employer's structure and operational methods may result in the description inadequately reflecting the union's representational rights. When such a situation arises, the Board may, on a review application, update the wording of the certificate and substitute a universal description for the old one.

Unless the applicant union meets the requirements for an enlargement of the bargaining unit in fashioning the new universal description, the Board will not change the nature and scope of the unit originally defined.[42] In other words, it will amend the original order in such a manner as to reflect generally the scope of the existing bargaining unit. Nevertheless, as a result of such an amendment, a certain number of employees not previously unionized but who perform functions similar to those included in the unit, as revised by the Board, may be added in the process.[43]

For instance, in *Millar & Brown Ltd.* a bargaining certificate covering clerical employees working at all the specifically enumerated locations of the employer was amended to substitute a universal description including all locations, present or future.[44] Although the revised order had the effect of bringing into the unit clerical employees at locations that did not exist at the time of certification, the nature and scope of the unit originally defined was not altered by such an amendment. As the Board stated, the newly added employees performed functions and occupied positions similar to those already included in the original unit. Thus, it was obviously not a situation of new categories or classifications of employees being added to the revised unit.

In reviewing original bargaining certificates, the Board has determined that persons who did not qualify as "employees" under the legislation current at the time of certification will not automatically be swept into existing certified units as a result of the 1972 amendments to the definition of "employee" and of the expanded coverage of Part V to

---

41   See paragraph 6:2330.
42   See, for example, *British Columbia Telephone Co.* (1977), 22 di 507, [1977] 2 Can LRBR 404, 77 CLLC #16,108; and *British Columbia Telephone Co.* (1978), 28 di 909, [1978] 2 Can LRBR 387, 78 CLLC #16,146.
43   *Millar & Brown Ltd.* (1977), 26 di 572, [1979] 1 Can LRBR 245; *Neptune Bulk Terminals Ltd.* (1979), 35 di 149, 79 CLLC #16,199.
44   *Millar & Brown Ltd., supra*, note 43.

supervisors and professionals.[45] On the other hand, when an application for review seeks to include in an existing unit functions that were originally excluded under the old legislation, it is not enough for an employer to argue that they should continue to be excluded because the functions have not varied since their exclusion. Unless evidence is adduced that the incumbents perform management functions or are employed in a confidential capacity in matters relating to industrial relations according to today's standards as developed by the Board, they will be included in the unit whose nature and scope encompasses similar functions.[46]

The erosion of the bargaining unit may result from causes other than the simple passage of time and the normal evolution of the enterprise. As stated in *British Columbia Telephone Co.*, an employer may not, simply by creating new classifications and labelling the incumbents "managers", alter the bargaining unit as defined by the Board in a certification order.[47] If the nature of the duties and responsibilities of those persons are such that the positions are clearly included in the bargaining unit for which the Board has certified the union, only the Board can determine whether those persons perform functions that would disqualify them as "employees". Accordingly, unless the union fails to act diligently or by its behaviour acquiesces in the contention of the employer, an application for review seeking the addition of those persons to the existing unit will be treated as requiring only a clarification of the unit.

The same holds true whenever new classifications created by the employer are excluded from a unit whose scope comprises similar functions.[48] For example, in a case where all the employees of an enterprise had been included in various units, the Board determined that the new functions created subsequently to the issuance of the various certificates and whose nature did not differ fundamentally from the functions already in existence in the enterprise had necessarily to come within the ambit of one or another of the certificates. Thus the scope of the certificate within which the new functions were included was determined by reference to the other certificates in the same enterprise.[49] Such determination required no more than a clarification of unit boundaries.

By contrast, in a case where all the employees of a small enterprise had originally been included in a single unit although performing different functions, the Board held that it was appropriate to include within the existing unit newly created functions of a nature similar to those

---

45 *British Columbia Telephone Co.* (1978), 28 di 909, [1978] 2 Can LRBR 387, 78 CLLC #16,146.
46 *CKCV (Québec) Ltée* (1977), 23 di 104; *Algoma Central Railway* (1980), 36 di 73.
47 *British Columbia Telephone Co.* (1977), 22 di 507, [1977] 2 Can LRBR 404, 77 CLLC #16,108.
48 *Société Radio-Canada* (1982), 44 di 19, 1 CLRBR (NS) 129.
49 *Télé-Metropole Inc.* (1980), 41 di 286.

already included, since the existing unit covered the job functions of all the operations of the enterprise.[50]

6:2311   Requirements

The requirements to be met on a review application seeking simple clarifications of the unit, that is, where the additions sought do not radically change the original intended scope of the unit, were established in *Téléglobe Canada*.[51]

With respect to the representative character of the applicant union, it was determined that, save for exceptional cases, the Board would not take into account the wishes of the employees in the group to be added to an existing unit, whether the application is initiated by the union or the Board.[52] The applicant only has to show that it has an overall majority of support in the revised unit, since in reality it is composed of one homogeneous group. This can be done either by exhibiting valid membership cards, by a Board-ordered vote under s. 127(1), or by way of a union membership clause in the collective agreement.

The latter overall majority support requirement in the revised unit has not met with complete unanimity, however. The question of employee wishes has been characterized as representational, whereas the question of the propriety of the union's representing a certain group or the issue of whether the union's bargaining rights should extend to certain work functions have been considered as issues of unit appropriateness.[53] Whenever an employer refuses to include newly created functions in the unit whose nature and scope comprises similar functions, the question raised on an application for review is not a representational one but is related to the interpretation and determination of the appropriateness of the unit.[54] As a result, it was held in *Société Radio-Canada*[55] that if the Board were to question the overall majority status of an already certified bargaining agent whenever it considers that it is appropriate for collective bargaining purposes to join another group to the existing one, it would be abdicating its responsibility provided in s. 125 by subordinating the appropriateness of the unit to the wishes of employees. The loss, by a union, of its majority status during the life of a collective agreement does not result in the loss of its status as bargaining agent.

---

50   *Sunwapta Broadcasting Ltd.* (1981), 43 di 218.
51   (1979), 32 di 270, [1979] 3 Can LRBR 86, 80 CLLC #16,025.
52   *Crosbie Offshore Services Ltd.* (1982), 51 di 120; *Téléglobe Canada, supra*, note 51.
53   *British Columbia Telephone Co.* (1979), 38 di 14, [1979] 3 Can LRBR 350.
54   *Ibid.; B.D.C. Ltée* (1981), 43 di 140; *Sunwapta Broadcasting Ltd.* (1981), 43 di 218.
55   *Société Radio-Canada, supra*, note 48.

As a consequence, the proponents of this approach, which was followed in *Northwestell Inc.*[56] but not in a subsequent decision,[57] do not take into account the representative character of the union in the overall revised unit or the wishes of employees to be added to the existing unit.

With respect to the appropriateness of the revised unit, the applicant union is not required to demonstrate that the latter retains its appropriate character, since the nature and essence of the unit originally determined by the Board is not affected by the addition of functions similar to those already included therein. The composition of the original unit remains homogeneous.[58]

Finally, a review application seeking clarifications of the bargaining unit may be filed at any time, irrespective of any time limit set by the Code for applications for certification.[59]

6:2312   Effects of the Revised Order

From the moment of their creation, functions of a nature similar to those originally included in the unit fall within the intended scope of the certification order. As a result, a decision of the Board on a review application that adds such functions to the existing unit has a retroactive effect.[60]

Another effect of the revised order is that the new employees are automatically covered by the collective agreement in force in the unit in which they have been added. However, as the Board originally held, this is so only to the extent that the collective agreement is applicable to them or, in other words, only to the extent that they are not already covered by a collective agreement at the time of their inclusion.[61] Thus, where newly added employees are not already governed by a collective agreement at the time of their inclusion in an existing unit, the collective agreement in force in the unit in which they have been added is integrally applicable to them. Some adjustments can be made to suit their needs, and specific conditions not already included in the agreement can be negotiated in an addendum, just as it is possible to renegotiate certain provisions during the life of a collective agreement. If differences arise, however, they can be resolved only through voluntary arbitration, if the parties so agree.

---

56   *Northwestell Inc.*, letter decision of the Board, no. 530-827, September 22, 1982; affd. (*sub nom. Northwestell Inc. v. International Brotherhood of Electrical Workers*, unreported, May 5, 1983, file no. A-895-82 (Fed. C.A.).

57   *Canadian National Railways* (1982), 44 di 170, [1982] 3 Can LRBR 384, 82 CLLC #16,197.

58   *Téléglobe Canada, supra,* note 51.

59   *Ibid.*

60   *Canadian National Railways* (1975), 9 di 20, [1975] 1 Can LRBR 327, 75 CLLC #16,158.

61   *Téléglobe Canada, supra,* note 51; *Premier Cablesystems Ltd.* (1981), 45 di 221, [1982] 1 Can LRBR 163, 82 CLLC #16,140; *Société Radio-Canada* (1982), 44 di 19, 1 CLRBR (NS) 129.

The union cannot resort to the strike weapon or the employer to the lockout until the entire group has acquired that right. The Board's rationale in this regard is based on the fact that since a collective agreement is applicable in the unit in which the new employees have been added, that collective agreement negates the parties' right to serve notice requiring the commencement of collective bargaining under s. 146.[62] The right to serve notice now resides in s. 147 and is, of course, dependent upon the term of the collective agreement. Since the service of notice to commence bargaining under s. 146 or 147 is a prerequisite of s. 180(1)(a), it follows that the right to strike or lockout cannot be attained by the parties for that part of the unit composed of the new employees until a notice to commence bargaining under s. 147 for the whole unit can be served and the other preconditions to the acquisition of the right to strike or lockout have been met.

Where, in the course of redefining the bargaining units in an enterprise, the Board transferred various functions from one unit to another, it was held, in the first *Société Radio-Canada* case,[63] that the employees already governed by a collective agreement at the time of their inclusion in another bargaining unit continued to be governed by the terms and conditions provided in the collective agreement in force in the unit from which they originated. The administration of the contract of these employees was, however, entrusted to their new bargaining agent.

However, on an application filed under s. 119 to have the merits of that decision reconsidered, the Board reversed its earlier decision and held that the employees who were already covered by a collective agreement at the time of their inclusion in another unit did not continue to be governed by the terms and conditions provided by the agreement in force in the unit from which they originated. Rather, in view of s. 154(b), they were governed by the collective agreement in force in the unit in which they had been included. The Board concluded in the following manner:

> Accordingly, the decision of December 1, 1982 is rescinded, and the employees added to the bargaining units for which the above-mentioned three unions were certified are subject to the collective agreements entered into between those unions and the Canadian Broadcasting Corporation.[64]

On judicial review, the Federal Court of Appeal did not address the correctness of the Board's rationale in the first *Société Radio-Canada* decision but left intact that part of the Board's conclusion in the second decision that read: "Accordingly the decision of December 1, 1982 is rescinded . . .". However, the court went on to quash the second part of the Board's conclusions in the second decision, reading: ". . . the em-

---

[62]   *Premier Cablesystems Ltd., supra,* note 61.
[63]   (1982), 50 di 141.
[64]   *Canadian Broadcasting Corp.,* decision no. 457, not yet reported, May 11, 1984 (C.L.R.B.).

ployees added to the bargaining units for which the above-mentioned three unions were certified are subject to the collective agreements entered into between those unions and the Canadian Broadcasting Corporation".[65] In other words, while concluding that the second panel of the Board had exceeded its jurisdiction in holding that the new employees were governed by the collective agreement in force in the unit in which they had been added, the court also affirmed the second panel's conclusion that the first panel had been wrong in law in holding that these employees continued to be governed by the collective agreement in the unit from which they originated. As a result, the solution to the problem of the employment conditions of employees transferred from one bargaining unit to another where a collective agreement is in force in both units is still to be decided. If anything, the Court of Appeal's decision points to the lack of appropriate powers in the Board to resolve such issues.

The court's decision, however, does not affect the Board's rulings with respect to the right to strike of newly added employees who are not already governed by a collective agreement at the time of their inclusion and their coverage by the collective agreement in force in the unit in which they have been added.

6:2320   Work Assignment and Jurisdictional Disputes

Whenever the Board has certified more than one union as bargaining agent for an employer, jurisdictional and work assignment disputes may arise. In the federal jurisdiction, parties have secured determinations from the Board on a number of occasions either through a review application under s. 119 or pursuant to a referral under s. 158.[66] The conflicts in which the Board intervened had arisen as a result of either (i) a unilateral expansion of the bargaining rights of one or another of the unions to include a disputed function[67] or (ii) an assignment or subsequent reassignment of work to members of one or another union across allegedly traditional jurisdictional lines in the enterprise.[68]

---

[65]   See *Société Radio-Canada v. Canada Labour Relations Board*, not yet reported, January 22, 1985, file no. A-467-82 (Fed. C.A.); and *Union des artistes v. Canada Labour Relations Board*, not yet reported, January 22, 1985, file no. A-725-82 (Fed. C.A.).

[66]   *Eastern Provincial Airways (1963) Ltd.* (1978), 30 di 82, [1979] 2 Can. LRBR 572; affd. [1980] 2 F.C. 512, 108 D.L.R. (3d) 743; see, however the dissenting opinion of Mr. Justice LeDain and the Board's decision in *Northern-Loram–Joint Venture*, decision no. 498, not yet reported, January 21, 1985 (C.L.R.B.), which commented on Mr. LeDain's opinion. See also *New Brunswick International Paper Co.* (1977), 21 di 466; *Cape Breton Development Corp.* (1979), 35 di 140, [1979] 3 Can. LRBR 485; and *Bell Canada* (1982), 50 di 105. For a detailed discussion of the Board's jurisdiction under s. 158, see paragraph 8:4000.

[67]   *Eastern Provincial Airways (1963) Ltd., supra,* note 66.

[68]   *Cape Breton Development Corp., supra,* note 66; *Bell Canada, supra,* note 66; *Northern-Loram–Joint Venture, supra,* note 66.

For instance, in *Cape Breton Development Corp.*[69] a work-assignment dispute arose between two unions and the employer as a result of a newly purchased truck. One union claimed, on the basis of its alleged jurisdiction over all drivers of the company, that members of its unit should have been assigned the work of driving the new vehicle. The Board decided that the applicant's claim was without merit, because the pattern of the vision of bargaining rights in the enterprise followed operational and not craft lines.

In *Eastern Provincial Airways (1963) Ltd.*[70] the Board addressed the problem of overlapping collective agreements where one union had clearly been granted the authority, in its certificate, to bargain for a given function and the other union had, through negotiations with the employer, expanded the bargaining rights granted by its certificate to cover the same function. The dispute concerned the performance of a waybilling function that was covered by both unions' collective agreements. The practice had developed, however, that members of one union performed this function at major cargo facilities but members of the other union did so otherwise. This eventually led to grievances and conflicting arbitration awards.

A reference was made by one of the arbitrators under s. 158, and the Board took jurisdiction. It was determined that where the bargaining authority for the employees of an employer is divided between two or more unions, one of those unions and the employer cannot bilaterally extend that union's bargaining authority into another union's bargaining unit without the latter's consent. In this case the Board found that such a consent had occurred, implicit in agreements achieved by the parties over the years, but that such agreements or accommodations between the unions were not reflected in the respective collective agreements. The Board resolved the dispute by giving effect to the accommodations achieved by the parties, thus rendering invalid those parts of the respective collective agreements that did not conform to the accommodations.

In *Bell Canada*[71] a dispatcher function unlisted in either the bargaining certificates or the collective agreements, which had allegedly been traditionally accomplished by members of a technical unit, had been reassigned to members of a clerical unit. The scope of the respective collective agreement being coextensive with the certification orders, the Board stated that the solution to this kind of jurisdictional conflict lay in the interpretation of the respective bargaining certificates and the determination of the intended scope of the units. This process revealed which of the competing unions' bargaining rights encompassed the function at issue once the nature of the latter had been thoroughly examined. It also

---

[69]   *Cape Breton Development Corp., supra,* note 66.
[70]   *Eastern Provincial Airways (1963) Ltd., supra,* note 66.
[71]   *Bell Canada* (1982), 50 di 105.

identified, at the same time, the collective agreement that was applicable. The Board came to the conclusion that the duties performed were of a clerical nature and were accordingly governed by the collective agreement in force in the unit comprising such functions. As a result, the members of the clerical unit to which the dispatching work had been reassigned had the right to accomplish such work. The Board then used its powers under s. 119 to amend the appropriate certification orders.

In the type of situations described above, it has been suggested that Board intervention is justified where the arbitral process is not suited to settling tripartite disputes and where there is a possibility of contradictory arbitral awards.[72] The Board's policy to intervene in jurisdictional or work assignment disputes was not approved, however, by all members of the Board. In *Wardair Canada (1975) Ltd.*[73] some bargaining unit work had been reassigned outside the bargaining unit to non-unionized employees following the reorganization of a service of the employer — a situation that must be distinguished from one where bargaining unit work is reassigned to members of another bargaining unit. In response, the union filed an unfair labour practice complaint under s. 184(1)(a) and a demand under s. 119. It argued that a logical extension of the Board's supervisory role of bargaining certificates is that when a craft or classification unit is certified as in that case, the Board's duty is to supervise the work-function content of the unit and prevent its erosion. Thus, if an employer assigns bargaining unit work out of the unit, he is engaging in interference prohibited by s. 184(1)(a) because the work function in a craft or classification unit is at the heart of the union's representational rights. In dismissing both applications, the panel of the Board disagreed with the *Bell Canada*[74] decision and held that it would not assume the role of the exclusive arbitrator of work jurisdiction by supervising the bargaining unit pursuant to the powers of s. 119.

Given the facts of that case, the Board's decision on the unfair labour practice complaint is in accordance with the general principles established in this area. The Board was concerned with avoiding lending credence to a claim that the bargaining certificate conferred a propriatary right to the union and the employees in the work performed in the unit. Had the Board endorsed such a proposition, this would have prevented the introduction of changes and the implementation of better methods of operation at odds with the employer's management rights, defined in the collective agreement applicable in that case, and with the right to innovate, which is explicitly recognized in the technological change provisions of the Code.

---

[72]   *Eastern Provincial Airways (1963) Ltd., supra,* note 66.
[73]   (1983), 53 di 26, 2 CLRBR (NS) 129.
[74]   See discussion accompanying note 71.

On the issue of the Board's authority to dispose of work-assignment disputes, however, two important features must be kept in mind when reading the *Wardair Canada (1975) Ltd.* decision. First, the Board was not faced with a multi-party dispute, as it was in the *Cape Breton Development Corp., Eastern Provincial Airways (1963) Ltd.,* and *Bell Canada* decisions. Second, implicit in the Board's reasoning is a distinction between work assignment or jurisdictional disputes on the one hand, and representational disputes on the other. The apparent importance of that distinction lies in a theory that holds that the powers and procedures provided in the Code were designed to settle representational conflicts and that, accordingly, these are not to be used as tools to resolve work-assignment or jurisdictional disputes.

In this connection, the Board took the position in *Northern-Loram Joint Venture*[75] that it clearly has the power under s. 158(1) to deal with multi-party work-assignment disputes. In that case, the arbitrator to whom a grievance had been submitted by one of the competing unions relied on the same distinction between work-assignment and representational disputes that had been referred to by the Board in *Wardair Canada (1975) Ltd.* and refused to refer the matter to the Board under s. 158(1). On a reference made by the employer, the Board dealt with the usefulness of that distinction. It wrote that the line between work-assignment and representational disputes is "blurred" and that, in any event, it is not useful to determine which kind of dispute is involved, since a situation can be characterized as both jurisdictional and representational at the same time, depending on one's perspective. In support of this conclusion the Board referred to its decision in *British Columbia Telephone Co.,*[76] in which the validity of the distinction had been rejected in the certification context. There, the Board said:

> This view contains implicitly the belief that the Board's role with respect to certification orders was representational in character only and not related to its work function character. Time, however, has overtaken this view. . . .
>
> But collective bargaining has become more sophisticated today and the role of labour relations board has expanded. There is a need for boards to act as instruments for resolving jurisdictional disputes. . . .[77]

In the same decision, the Board had justified its practice of interpreting bargaining certificates pursuant to the powers of s. 119 with a view to solving multi-party work-assignment disputes in the following manner:

> These authorities [ss. 119 and 121], aided by section 158, allow the Board to play a role in assisting parties to solve differences that may be multi-party. . . . Work assignments are often sources of friction that flower into work disruptions and job action. If misunderstandings or differences over the scope and content of bargaining units is the cause, then the Board which

---

[75]   *Northern-Loram–Joint Venture, supra,* note 66.
[76]   (1979), 38 di 14, [1979] 3 Can **LRBR** 350.
[77]   *Ibid.,* at p. 76 (di).

defines or sanctions the unit description must act to clarify its unit description and resolve the cause of the conflict. The concept of bargaining units
which are appropriate was a partial response to recognition warfare. It must
not be allowed to be the cause of interunion or employer-union jurisdictional warfare.[78]

Thus, the Board stated that the issue under s. 158 is not whether the
problem is properly characterized as work jurisdiction, representational,
or both. The real issue is whether the question raised falls within the
scope of s. 158. In multi-party conflicts such as those in the *Eastern
Provincial Airways (1963) Ltd.* and *Bell Canada* cases, which were similar to
the one with which the Board was confronted in *Northern-Loram–Joint
Venture*, the source of the Board's jurisdiction under s. 158 is found in the
words "the identification of . . . employees bound by a collective agreement". Indeed, in those cases there was no issue about the existence of
the respective collective agreements of the competing unions, nor was
there any issue as to whether the respective unions or the employer were
bound by the collective agreements in question. However, in those cases
it would have been inaccurate to say that the members of the competing
unions were bound by their respective union's collective agreement and
that, accordingly, there was no genuine question concerning the identification of employees bound by a collective agreement. The Board gave
the following example to illustrate the point:

> Take an example involving only one union, the Teamsters. The employer
> hires a person to do some trucking work. The employer takes the position
> that the job is not covered by the Teamsters' collective agreement and does
> not apply it to the employee in question. The employer, in fact, applies no
> collective agreement at all. The Teamsters take the position that the job
> does fall within the Teamsters' agreement and the matter ends up in
> arbitration. There is an obvious issue of whether the person is an employee
> bound by the Teamsters' collective agreement. It can be no different just
> because the employee in question happens to be a member of another
> union, the C.B.R.T., in respect of whom the employer happened to be
> applying another collective agreement, the C.B.R.T. agreement. To say
> that the employee is question is not bound by the Teamsters' collective
> agreement because he is a member of the C.B.R.T. is to misconstrue the
> situation.[79]

The implications of determining that an employee is bound by a
collective agreement is reflected in the fact that although the wrong
individual is doing the disputed work, that individual remains an employee bound by the collective agreement applicable to the work. This
simply means that the person is bound to the extent of not having any
right under the agreement to be doing the work.

In identifying the employees bound by a collective agreement, the
Board stated that it will consider the scope clause of the collective agree-

---

[78]   *Ibid.*, at pp. 78-79 (di).
[79]   *Northern-Loram–Joint Venture, supra,* note 66, at p. 39.

ments and whether the unions are certified or voluntarily recognized. Where the scope clause of two collective agreements overlap, there will obviously have been some over-bargaining by one or more of the unions, that is, the inclusion of more employees in the collective agreement than were included in the certificate. In such a case, the Board's interpretation of its certificates will determine the permissible reach of the respective collective agreements. That will enable the Board to determine, under s. 158, which employees are validly bound by the collective agreement referred to the Board.

When the scope clause of a collective agreement is coextensive with the certification order, a determination on whether an employee is covered by a certification order is equivalent to a determination on whether an employee is bound by a collective agreement.

6:2330   Territorial Scope

On a reference under s. 158(1), the Board has used the powers of s. 119 to clarify the territorial scope of a union's representational rights. In one case, after a thorough study of all the procedures and representations of the parties to a certification application, the Board found that the representational rights of a union had no extra-territorial applications and therefore did not extend to employees of the unit who were assigned to work outside Canada in Saudi Arabia.[80] It was held that neither the union nor the Board had intended to include extra-territorial operations of the employer within the scope of the certificate.

6:2400   UNIT CONSOLIDATION AND MERGER

The powers conferred by s. 119 have also been used to consolidate existing units in the better interest of labour relations. When it merges units, the Board may take into account the wishes of the employees, among other factors, but it will not necessarily canvass their wishes.

In one case, the merger of two unions raised the question of the appropriateness of also merging the two bargaining units. The Board determined that the consolidation of the units was appropriate, but as the employees had not favoured such a merger in a previous general meeting called by the unions for that purpose, a vote of preference between one or two units was ordered.[81]

In another case,[82] what had really occurred was a merger of bargaining units and an intermingling of the employees as a result of a corporate reorganization. These employees were represented by different unions. The Board decided that a single bargaining unit was appropriate and

---

80   *Bell Canada* (1981), 43 di 86, [1982] 3 Can LRBR 113.
81   *Cablevision Nationale Ltée* (1979), 35 di 168.
82   *Canadian Pacific Ltd.* (1984), 8 CLRBR (NS) 378, 84 CLLC #16,060.

decided to add the employees of the smaller unit to the larger unit without considering their wishes in view of the sizes of the units that were merged. In response to a challenge from the union that was losing its bargaining rights that the wishes of the employees of the smaller unit should prevail, the Board found that its disposition of the applications did not infringe on the employees' "freedom of association" as entrenched in s. 110(1) of the Code and as guaranteed by the *Canadian Charter of Rights and Freedoms.*

The consolidation of separate units has also been granted on the employer's initiative. For example, in one case a successorship situation resulted from the merger of two airline companies whose employees were represented by different unions. However, no application under s. 144 had been filed by either union. As a result, the incumbents of functions comprised in similar customer services operated by both companies before the merger continued to be distinctly represented in two units. On an application for certification filed by one of the bargaining agents to represent the incumbents of part of the functions represented by the other union in the customer services, the employer filed a demand under s. 119 for a review of the entire bargaining structure within the service. The Board granted the application and determined that a system-wide unit of all the customer service employees was appropriate. It ordered a representation vote to determine which union would represent the consolidated unit.[83]

6:2500   REVOCATION OF BARGAINING CERTIFICATES

The powers conferred by s. 119 also enable the Board to rescind previous certification orders. Applications under that section seeking revocations of bargaining rights have, however, seldom been granted.

Such an application presented by an employer in the guise of a review application under s. 119 was dismissed in *Inland Broadcasters (1969) Ltd.*[84] The Board stated that the legislative policy underlying the revocation of bargaining rights which provides, among other things, that only employees may present applications under s. 137 was not to be subverted by the use of the Board's authority under s. 119. By contrast, on a review application filed by an employee to have the bargaining rights of a recently certified union revoked, the Board stated that the fact that a demand under s. 119 might have the same consequences as an application for revocation under ss. 137 and 138 does not mean that it is necessarily subject to the same legislative restrictions or conditions applicable in the

---

[83]   *Pacific Western Airlines Ltd.* (1980), 40 di 205, [1980] 3 Can LRBR 180.
[84]   *Inland Broadcasters (1969) Ltd. and Twin Cities Radio Ltd.* (1979), 37 di 96, [1980] 1 Can LRBR 193.

case of an application for revocation.[85] Thus, in this case, the application filed no more than one month after the issuance of the Board's certification order was held to be timely. The Board held, however, that only in exceptional circumstances would it use its discretion under s. 119 to revoke or rescind a certification order as a result of an application for review founded on the very circumstances expressly dealt with in ss. 137 and 138 or other sections of the Code.[86]

In another decision, the Board stated that unless proof is made of the existence of facts undisclosed in the course of its initial investigation that are serious enough to warrant reconsidering the application for certification, it would not use its powers under s. 119 to revoke a bargaining certificate.[87]

Exceptionally, on an application filed under s. 119 to amend a bargaining certificate and substitute the name of a new trade union that had allegedly succeeded to the incumbent bargaining agent within the meaning of s. 143, the Board found that the applicant had abandoned its representational rights as a result of fifteen years of inactivity. Accordingly, the Board revoked the original certification order.[88]

6:3000   REVIEW OF THE MERITS OF A PREVIOUS DECISION OR ORDER

6:3100   GROUNDS FOR REVIEW

The Board may, pursuant to s. 119, reconsider the merits of an earlier decision or order, even in the case of a purely administrative decision such as an order directing that a representation vote be held,[89] in three types of situations:

(i) where the Board erred in its interpretation of the Code or of its policy or where a decision raises an important issue of policy;[90]

---

85   *North West Community Video Ltd.* (1976), 14 di 132, 77 CLLC #16,085.
86   *Ibid.*
87   *Northern Construction Ltd.* (1976), 19 di 128, 76 CLLC #16,032.
88   *Whitehorse Hotels Ltd.* (1977), 21 di 410, [1977] 1 Can LRBR 477, 77 CLLC #16,080.
89   *B. Williamson Trucking and Leasing Ltd.* (1975), 8 di 15, [1975] 1 Can LRBR 325, 75 CLLC #16,159.
90   *Canadian National Railways* (1975), 9 di 20, [1975]1 Can LRBR 327, 75 CLLC #16,158; *Kevton Holdings Ltd.* (1977), 23 di 43, [1977] 2 Can LRBR 323, 78 CLLC #16,116; *Calgary Television Ltd.* (1977), 25 di 399, [1978] 1 Can LRBR 532; *British Columbia Telephone Co.* (1979), 38 di 124, 80 CLLC #16,008, [1980] 1 Can LRBR 340; *Mitchell Installations Ltd.* (1981), 43 di 302; *Wardair Canada (1975) Ltd.* (1983), 53 di 184, 84 CLLC #16,005.

(ii) where there is new evidence that was not brought before the Board in the earlier proceeding for good and sufficient reasons;[91]

(iii) where the Board has failed to respect a principle of natural justice.[92]

6:3110   Error in the Interpretation of the Code or Its Policy

Errors of law committed by the Board in good faith or resulting from a not patently unreasonable interpretation of a provision of the Code that it is required to apply within the limits of its jurisdiction are not reviewable by the courts.[93] Thus, the Board will agree to review its order or decision where it was wrong in law or deviated from its stated policy in other decisions.[94]

The first decision whose merits were reconsidered by the Board in the course of a full plenary session involved a finding that the craft unit traditionally represented by the appellant union in British Columbia was not an appropriate bargaining unit. The union alleged that that decision contradicted the policy of the Code.[95] In a subsequent case, the Board refused to reconsider a previous decision because the differing opinions of the members of the original panel had resulted from their individual assessments of the facts of the case.[96] In another case, an enlarged quorum of the Board considered the validity of a previous decision in light of a Federal Court of Appeal judgment reversing the Board's interpretation of s. 126. The Board decided that the cessation of work should not constitute a bar to certification in the construction industry and that the first panel ought not to have rejected the certification application.[97]

The Board has also been called, in plenary sessions, to resolve conflicting interpretations of certain provisions of the Code made by various panels. In *British Columbia Telephone Co.*[98] a full panel of the Board

---

91 *Canadian National Railways* (1975), 9 di 20, [1975] 1 Can LRBR 327, 75 CLLC #16,158; *Les Arsenaux Canadiens Ltée* (1978), 28 di 931; *CJMS Radio Montréal (Québec) Ltée* (1979), 34 di 803, [1980] 1 Can LRBR 170.

92 *Cablevision Nationale Ltée* (1978), 25 di 422, [1979] 3 Can LRBR 267; *Wholesale Delivery Service (1972) Ltd.* (1978), 32 di 239, [1979] 1 Can LRBR 90.

93 Section 122(1) of the Code, which refers to the grounds mentioned in s. 28(1)(a) of the *Federal Court Act* (excess or absence of jurisdiction and breach of a rule of natural justice). See the decision of the Supreme Court of Canada in *Syndicat des employés de production du Québec et de l'Acadie v. Canada Labour Relations Board*, [1984] 2 S.C.R. 412, at 420-21. See also paragraph 19:4220.

94 *Wardair Canada (1975) Ltd.* (1983), 53 di 184, 84 CLLC #16,005.

95 *Mitchell Installations Ltd.* (1981), 43 di 302.

96 *Wardair Canada (1975) Ltd., supra,* note 94.

97 *Kevton Holdings Ltd.* (1977), 23 di 43, [1977] 2 Can LRBR 323, 78 CLLC #16,116.

98 *British Columbia Telephone Co.* (1979), 38 di 124, 80 CLLC #16,008, [1980] 1 Can LRBR 340.

decided that s. 184(3)(c) protects the employee who refuses to perform the duties and responsibilities of another employee on a lawful strike only if he is employed by the same employer as the striking employee. In *Brenda Haley*[99] a full panel of the Board affirmed a previous decision rejecting a complaint filed by an employee against its union under s. 136.1. The Board determined that seriously negligent conduct on the part of a union is a breach of this provision, while simple negligence is not. In *Bank of Nova Scotia*[100] a full panel of the Board met to resolve the conflicting interpretations made by various panels of s. 148(b), which establishes a freeze in the employees' working conditions following the serving of a notice to bargain. In *British Columbia Telephone Co.* a full panel of the Board met to decide whether a decision by a panel was "wholly irreconcilable" with earlier policy decisions concerning the appropriateness of units and applications to review. It concluded that it was not.[101] However, the Board will not necessarily wait to have a review application to sit in plenary sessions. In *Terminus Maritime Inc.*[101a] the Board examined, in a plenary session, the interpretation given in previous cases to s. 144.

6:3120 New Evidence

The Board will entertain an application to review an order or decision where the applicant alleges facts that were not brought to its attention at the time the original order or decision was made, if these facts are such that, had they been known to the Board, they might have changed its original order or decision. However, some explanation must be given by the applicant for the failure to bring these facts before the Board at the original investigation. The applicant for review must come to the Board "with clean hands".[102]

6:3130 Failure to Respect a Principle of Natural Justice

Although a failure to respect a principle of natural justice is reviewable by the Federal Court of Appeal pursuant to s. 28(1)(a) of the *Federal Court Act*,[103] nevertheless the Board will, either upon a request of a party

---

99 *Brenda Haley* (1981), 41 di 311, [1981] 2 Can LRBR 121, 81 CLLC #16,096.

100 *Bank of Nova Scotia (Sherbrooke and Rock Forest, Quebec)* (1982), 42 di 398, 82 CLLC #16,158.

101 *British Columbia Telephone Co.* (1980), 40 di 97.

101a (1983), 50 di 178.

102 *Canadian National Railways* (1975), 9 di 20, at 26-27, [1975] 1 Can LRBR 327, 75 CLLC #16,158; *Les Arsenaux Canadiens Ltée* (1978), 28 di 931; *Bell Canada* (1979), 30 di 112, [1979] 2 Can LRBR 435.

103 See paragraph 19:4100.

or on its own motion, review a decision where it appears that a principle of natural justice was not observed.[104]

In a case where no public hearing had been held before a certification order was issued, the Board, upon finding that it had not given sufficient opportunity to the parties to make representation, eventually decided to rescind the certification order and advised the parties that it was prepared to continue the investigation as soon as possible at a public hearing.[105] By contrast, although the Board admitted, in another case, its failure to give notice of the certification procedures to an interested party and offered it the opportunity to address the merits of the certification order by entertaining a review application and scheduling a hearing, the Board rejected the argument that, as a first step, it should rescind the certification order and then have the proceedings commenced again with appropriate notice.[106] However, in another case, the Federal Court of Appeal held that an offer by the Board to the parties to make representations and to call evidence, once the decision had been communicated and was the subject of a court challenge, did not have the effect of validating the decision or estopping the applicant from pursuing its right to judicial review.[107]

6:3200   TIMELINESS

Neither the Code nor the Board's regulations establish any specific time limit within which an application for review pursuant to s. 119 must be made. However, the Board has established a general rule to the effect that the party who wishes to have the merits of a decision reconsidered must act within a reasonable period of time.[108] In an earlier case, the Board mentioned that it would place a heavy onus on the applicant to establish that it has not acted with undue delay where it has failed to file an application within two weeks of the receipt of the Board's decision.[109] The Board then expressed doubts about the practical impact of a two-week time limit.[110] Currently, the Board's rule of thumb is that an application filed within three weeks meets the goal of access to Board review and serves the interest of the finality of Board decisions, necessary

---

104   *Cablevision Nationale Ltée* (1978), 25 di 422, [1979] 3 Can LRBR 267; *Wholesale Delivery Service (1972) Ltd.* (1978), 32 di 239, [1979] 1 Can LRBR 90.

105   *Cablevision Nationale Ltée, supra*, note 104.

106   *Wholesale Delivery Service (1972) Ltd., supra*, note 104.

107   *Eastern Provincial Airways Ltd. v. Canada Labour Relations Board*, [1984] 1 F.C. 732, 50 N.R. 81, 2 D.L.R. (4th) 597 (C.A.). See particularly the comments of Mr. Justice Mahoney, at pp. 752-53 (F.C.). See also paragraph 19:4160.

108   *CJMS Radio Montréal (Québec) Ltée* (1979), 34 di 803, at 806, [1980] 1 Can LRBR 170, and cases cited therein. A two-month delay was held to be an unreasonable period of time in this case and in *Calgary Television Ltd.* (1977), 25 di 399, [1978] 1 Can LRBR 532. See also *Jean-Paul Roy*, decision no. 495, not yet reported, January 7, 1985 (C.L.R.B.).

109   *Calgary Television Ltd., supra*, note 108.

110   *Cablevision Nationale Ltée* (1978), 25 di 422, [1979] 3 Can LRBR 267.

in labour relations matters.[111] However, this rule is for guidance only and non-compliance with it may be overlooked by the Board when serious grounds are alleged in support of an application for review.[112] Furthermore, the applicant seeking review must come to the Board with clean hands.[113]

6:4000 PRACTICE AND PROCEDURE

6:4100 CONTENT OF THE APPLICATION

Section 32 of the regulations provides that an application under s. 119 of the Code requesting the Board to review, rescind, amend, alter, or vary any order or decision made by it shall be dated and shall contain the following information:

(a) the full name and address of the applicant;

(b) the full name and address of:

(i) the employer of the employees in the bargaining unit affected by the application, and

(ii) the trade union, if any, affected by the application;

(c) the date and the nature of the order or decision of the Board that is the subject of the application; and

(d) particulars of the facts and circumstances in support of the application.

The board has stated that in applications for review of the merits of a previous decision, subs. (d) is extremely important and that it expects the applicant to set out both the reasons for its request and a detailed argument in support of its positions.[114]

6:4200 PROCESSING THE APPLICATION

6:4210 Generally

Challenges to the merits of a previous decision will generally be decided on the basis of written submissions. Therefore, both parties must

---

[111]   *Wholesale Delivery Service (1972) Ltd.* (1978), 32 di 239, [1979] 1 Can LRBR 90; *Wardair Canada (1975) Ltd.* (1983), 53 di 184, 84 CLLC #16,005; *Jean-Paul Roy, supra,* note 108.

[112]   *Calgary Television Ltd., supra,* note 108. Further, in *Wholesale Delivery Service (1972) Ltd., supra,* note 111, the application was made one month after the Board's original decision. Nevertheless, the Board entertained the application because of the seriousness of the grounds alleged, which were that the Board had breached the rules of natural justice, that the union and employer had acted in concert to circumvent the provincial certification and accreditation orders, and that the employer's operations were not a federal work, undertaking, or business.

[113]   *Jean-Paul Roy, supra,* note 108.

[114]   *Calgary Television Ltd., supra,* note 108.

detail their full argument in their original submissions. If no convincing case is made by the applicant, the Board will usually dismiss the application without hearing the submissions of the other parties.[115] Cases that raise issues of an evidentiary nature will be referred back to the panel that made the original finding of fact.

Cases that allege breaches of the rules of natural justice may be reviewed by the original panel or by another panel, depending on the nature of the allegation. For example, a procedural irregularity, such as the failure to transmit the submissions to the other parties, will not bar the original panel from deciding the review application. Conversely, where more substantial breaches such as bias are alleged, the original panel will not be assigned to the file.

Some cases raise issues of law extraneous to labour relations, which require legal expertise to resolve. Such is the case of difficult questions of constitutional law or the interpretation of other statutes. These may be referred to a panel mainly or entirely composed of members with a legal background. Cases where fundamental issues of interpretation of the Code or of its policies are raised may be considered by the full Board sitting in plenary session.[116]

Therefore, unless serious allegations of impartiality are directed at the members of the Board who rendered the original decision, they will participate in the debate on the policy issues with their colleagues or in the reconsideration of their previous decision. The Federal Court of Appeal has upheld the Board's practice.[117]

6:4220   Special Procedure

Applications alleging errors in the interpretation of the Code or its policies that may be considered by the full Board sitting in a plenary session were, until recently, referred back to the panel that had rendered the original decision. The latter was charged with making the initial determination as to whether the alleged error in law or policy was real or whether the application should be referred to a plenary session of the Board.

---

[115]   *British Columbia Telephone Co.* (1979), 38 di 124, 80 CLLC #16,008, [1980] 1 Can LRBR 340; *Calgary Television Ltd.* (1977), 25 di 399, [1978] 1 Can LRBR 532; *Les Arsenaux Canadiens Ltée* (1978), 28 di 931; *Bell Canada* (1979), 30 di 112, [1979] 2 Can LRBR 435; *CJMS Radio Montréal (Québec) Ltée* (1979), 34 di 803, [1980] 1 Can LRBR 170; and *Wardair Canada (1975) Ltd.* (1983), 53 di 184, 84 CLLC #16,005.

[116]   *British Columbia Telephone Co., supra,* note 115.

[117]   *Air B.C. Ltd. v. International Association of Machinists and Aerospace Workers,* unreported, file no. A-725-81, June 9, 1981 (Fed. C.A.); *Canadian Brotherhood of Railway, Transport and General Workers v. Canada Labour Relations Board,* unreported, file no. T-3165-81, August 7, 1981 (Fed. T.D.). See also paragraph 19:4150, dealing with bias as a ground for judicial review of Board decisions.

In *Wardair Canada (1975) Ltd.*[118] the Board re-examined certain aspects of this practice. It stated that the screening process by the original panel was the source of some apprehension and decided to modify this procedure so as to eliminate what could be the cause for at least a perception of conflict or bias. Applications for reconsideration involving issues of misinterpretation of law or policy are now referred to a "summit review panel" at the chairman or vice-chairman level, excluding any vice-chairman who has participated in the original decision.[119] The guidelines for bringing such applications may be summarized as follows:

1. Applications are to be filed with the Board within three weeks of the issuance of the decision to be reviewed.

2. If the application is filed with one of the Board's regional offices, a copy should be forwarded forthwith to the office of the chairman.

3. Section 12 of the Regulations and its spirit must be fully complied with.

4. Cases of this nature will be disposed of on the basis of written submissions. The parties must therefore elaborate their full argument in their original submissions.

5. Submissions will be examined in order of priority by a "summit panel", and if there are no substantial or persuasive reasons to entertain the request, the application will be dismissed immediately without submissions from the other parties. The request may also be disposed of in the same manner after replies and further submissions have been received.

6. Decisions of a "summit panel" of the Board dismissing a review application will not normally be accompanied by published reasons.

7. The filing of such an application does not suspend or interrupt the operation of the decision sought to be reviewed unless the Board so directs.

8. If the circumstances warrant, an application of this nature may be referred for consideration by the full Board. In such a case, a decision by a majority of members of the Board will be treated as binding on all members of the Board unless the issue is again addressed by the full Board.[120]

---

118 *Supra,* note 115.
119 *Ibid.*
120 *Ibid.*

CHAPTER 7

SUCCESSORSHIP

7:0000   **SUCCESSORSHIP**

Central to the legislative framework established by the *Canada Labour Code* are its successorship provisions. Their general purpose is to assure that the fundamental right of the employees to be represented by a union is not adversely affected by the union, corporate, and sometimes governmental changes that may take place.

These provisions cover three types of successorship: union succession, employer succession, and government succession.

By reason of a merger or amalgamation of trade unions or a transfer of jurisdiction among trade unions, one union may succeed another as the bargaining agent of the employees. This case is regulated by s. 143. When an employer decides to lease, transfer, or otherwise dispose of all or part of his business, the applicability of s. 144 must be considered.

Finally, the government of Canada may find it appropriate to transform a government department into a Crown corporation, to which the Code will then apply. Section 145 deals with such a situation.

In the present chapter we will deal first with employer succession. Comments on union and then governmental successions will follow.

7:1000   **EMPLOYER SUCCESSION**

The most familiar type of successorship is probably that in which a new employer assumes the conduct of another employer's business or businesses. As under provincial legislation, the Code uses the expression "sale of business" to describe the variety of circumstances leading to the change of employers. Although s. 144 uses the word "sell", it is not exhaustive but "includes the lease, transfer and other disposition of the business".[1] As to the word "business", it is also comprehensive; it means "any federal work, undertaking or business and any part thereof".[2]

There is an implied constitutional restriction to the application of s. 144. The constitutional application of the Code set out in ss. 2 and 108 must be respected. In consequence, where a sale of business crosses

---

[1]   *Canada Labour Code*, s. 144(1), "sell".
[2]   Section 144(1), "business".

constitutional boundaries, no employer successorship occurs under the Code.[3]

7:1100   DETERMINATION OF SALE OF BUSINESS

7:1110   Jurisdiction of the Board

In view of the broad effects of the successorship provision, it becomes particularly important to identify the situations that come within the ambit of the definition of "sale of business" in s. 144(1) of the Code.

The determination of any question as to whether or not a business has been sold or as to the identity of the purchaser of a business is left explicitly to the Board by s. 144(5) of the Code.

Since the Board is specifically empowered to determine the existence of a sale of business, the interpretation it will make of the elements of the definitions constituting a "sale of business" is not a preliminary or a collateral question, but constitutes an exercise within the Board's authority. Accordingly any such ruling, even where wrong in law, would not be reviewable by the courts unless it is so unreasonable that it cannot be rationally supported by the Code.[4]

7:1120   "Sale of Business" Concept

Before analysing the several situations leading to a "sale of business" under the successorship provisions, it is necessary to insist first on the Board's understanding of the "sale of business" concept referred to in the Code. The Board has adhered to a concept of "sale of business" that is

---

[3]   See *Marathon Realty Co. Ltd.* (1977), 25 di 387, [1978] 1 Can LRBR 493, 78 CLLC #16,138. In this case, due to constitutional jurisdiction, the Board rejected an application for a declaration under s. 144 with respect to an alleged sale of business from Canadian Pacific to Marathon Realty. The latter company had taken charge, through a subcontractor, of the janitorial services previously performed by CP employees at the building known as the "CP station", but in which CP had become a minor tenant. In this decision the Board referred to the "three-fold test" examined in Chapter 1 concerning constitutional jurisdiction over labour relations.

[4]   Moreover, in *National Bank of Canada v. Retail Clerks' International Union,* [1984] 1 S.C.R. 269, 53 N.R. 203, 84 CLLC #14,037, 9 D.L.R. (4th) 10, the Supreme Court of Canada held that the Board did not exceed its jurisdiction by ruling that the integration of two branches of the bank constituted a sale of business, since under s. 144(5) it clearly had jurisdiction to determine this question. The court stated further that the Board's interpretation did not seem to be so unreasonable that it could not be rationally supported by the relevant legislation and that it required intervention by the court upon review. Prior to this judgment, the Federal Court had taken the same approach in other cases where the jurisdiction of the Board to make a declaration of sale had been challenged: see *Seafarers' International Union of Canada v. Canada Labour Relations Board,* unreported, October 25, 1979, file no. A-385-79 (Fed. C.A.); *Québec Sol Services Ltée v. Canada Labour Relations Board,* unreported, November 1, 1982, file no. A-612-81 (Fed. C.A.); *J.T. Aviation Services Ltd. v. Canada Labour Relations Board,* unreported, January 11, 1983, file no. A-351-82 (Fed. C.A.).

directly related to the enhancement of the objective contemplated by the preamble to the Code: the encouragement of free collective bargaining through the support of freedom of association.

The successorship provisions prevent an undermining of bargaining rights and provide for their permanence, not only where there is a deliberate attempt by an employer to avoid his legal and contractual obligations toward his employees and their agent, but also in the context of ordinary business transactions.

The words used by the Code to define the concept of "sale of business" have led the Board to state that when a business changes hands by means other than those readily recognizable as a sale in the normal commercial sense, its decision will not concentrate on the formalities of ownership or on the particular method whereby the business has changed hands.[5] A full and liberal interpretation of the concept of successorship is indicated by the definitions contained in s. 144. The terms "business" and "sell" have been defined in a loose fashion. "Business" extends to "any part of a federal work, undertaking, or business. The word "sell" is defined in this way:

> "sell", in relation to a business, includes the lease, transfer and other dispositions of the business.

Therefore, the broad words used by the legislator in s. 144(1) of the Code and the general intent of this provision have led the Board to insist that a liberal interpretation should be given to the expression "sale of business".[6]

In its strict sense, the term "sell" ordinarily means a commercial transaction whereby the vendor disposes of his proprietary interest in an object or an intangible good in consideration of a sum of money or its equivalent, paid or agreed to be paid by the purchaser. However, under the regime of the Code, the word "sell" is not understood in this strict sense, since it is deemed to include also "the lease, transfer and other disposition of the business".[7]

Although the term "lease" has a somewhat restricted meaning, the words "transfer" and "other disposition" are obviously very wide in scope and are capable of describing a multitude of transactions, whether by sale, exchange, gift, trust, or otherwise. Consistent with the remedy envisaged by the successorship provision, which seeks to protect and to ensure the permanence of bargaining rights, the Board has interpreted the expression "and other disposition of the business" as an omnibus

---

5   *Seaspan International Ltd.* (1979), 37 di 38, at 44, [1979] 2 Can LRBR 213.
6   *Reimer Express Lines Ltd.* (1973), 1 di 12, at 18, 74 CLLC #16,093; *Eastern Canada Towing Ltd.* (1977), 24 di 152, at 159-61; *Newfoundland Broadcasting Ltd.* (1978), 26 di 576, at 582-85, [1978] 1 Can LRBR 565; *Seaspan International Ltd.* (1979), 37 di 38, at 42-43, [1979] 2 Can LRBR 213.
7   *Newfoundland Broadcasting Ltd.* (1978), 26 di 576, at 586, [1978] 1 Can LRBR 565.

provision intended to include dispositions of the business by any mode or means not included within the meaning of "lease or transfer".[8]

Central to an understanding of the concept of "sale" is the scope of the "business". Pursuant to s. 144(1) of the Code, the term "business" extends to "any part" of a federal work, undertaking, or business. This is the only definition of the concept of "business" provided by the Code, and accordingly its interpretation must be found in the Board jurisprudence.[9]

In defining the word "business" for the purpose of the successorship provision, the Board has focused on the classifications or job content for which the union was originally certified. If the object of the successorship provision is to preserve bargaining rights, it would be incorrect to focus upon whether there has been an actual transfer of the vendor's employees to the purchaser, since this would invite new employers to avoid the successorship provisions by refusing to maintain the employment continuity of the original employees. A more relevant consideration must be the nature of the work performed subsequent to the transaction, whether it is carried out by the same or by different employees.[10]

However, the "business" mentioned in the successorship provision cannot only be defined in relation to the work functions covered by the certificate. In 1983, a full Board panel explicitly opted for a global and dynamic definition of "business".[11] In this decision, which is discussed at length at paragraph 7:1143, the Board rejected any definition that would take into account only the work classifications. The Board decided that what should be considered as a "business" must be the sum of certain material and human elements, having in mind a certain finality. The business of the employer is seen in the light of its different activities as an "ongoing concern".

Therefore in order to determine whether or not the "business" has been transferred, the Board will look to such indicia as transfer of assets, continuity of management, continuity of product, and actual transfer of goodwill. This should indicate that what the Board calls a "business" has in fact been acquired by the "purchaser".[12]

---

8   *Ibid.; Terminus Maritime Inc.* (1983), 50 di 178.

9   This definition has been commented on in many decisions. See, in particular, *Newfoundland Broadcasting Ltd., supra*, note 7, at 587 (di); *Newfoundland Steamships Ltd.* (1981), 45 di 156, 2 CLRBR (NS) 40; *Terminus Maritime Inc., supra*, note 8.

10   *Newfoundland Broadcasting Ltd., supra*, note 7, at 587 (di).

11   *Terminus Maritime Inc., supra*, note 8; *Freight Emergency Service Ltd.* (1984), 84 CLLC #16,031.

12   *Ibid.* See also *Newfoundland Steamships Ltd., supra*, note 9; *Newfoundland Broadcasting Ltd., supra*, note 7. In *K.J.R. Associates Ltd.* (1979), 37 di 12, [1979] 2 Can LRBR 245, it was determined that within the meaning contemplated by s. 144, a leaseholder could not transfer his operations to another leaseholder when it appeared that they were both bound to a third company under the terms of contracts stipulating that the latter company leased vehicles to the other two, which were then leased back to it with the services of drivers under a lease transfer plan. See especially p. 18 (di) of this decision,

7:1130   The Board's Inquiry

Besides examining all the contracts or documents between the vendor and the purchaser in order to determine whether or not the business of the employer has been continued by the purchaser, the Board will also want to have a complete picture of both the vendor's and the purchaser's enterprises before and after the date of the sale.[13] This may include a description of the totality of the operations conducted by both employers, such as can be illustrated by organizational charts dealing with the administrative, corporative, and operational aspects of the business or organization. The vendor will likely have to furnish a list of all its employees (unionized and not unionized) who were working before and after the date of the sale, as well as an inventory of all its assets before and after the date of the sale.

The reason for such a thorough examination of both employer's operations in addition to a consideration of the details of the sale transaction (which might include its financing) comes from the Board's decision to adopt an inductive approach. Each case is assessed according to a number of indicia that indicate whether or not an actual transfer of the vendor's enterprise has taken place.[14]

7:1140   Situations Constituting a Sale of Business

In this section we will furnish a brief outline of the situations wherein the Board has been called upon to exercise its power to determine whether a sale of business has occurred under the Code.

7:1141   Take-overs, Mergers, and Amalgamations

The Board has consistently ruled that a sale of business occurs within the meaning of the Code anytime where, after a take-over, or a merger, or an amalgamation of companies, one or several entities continued the business of the former employer.[15] Technical arguments to the effect that the successorship provisions should not be applied, because under

    where the Board concluded that in view of the indicia enunciated above (transfer of assets, continuity of management, continuity of product, actual transfer of goodwill), the leaseholders had "little or no business to sell".

13   See *Terminus Maritime Inc., supra,* note 8.

14   *Ibid.;* and see also *Newfoundland Broadcasting Ltd., supra,* note 7 at pp. 588-89 (di).

15   *Reimer Express Lines Ltd.* (1973), 1 di 12, 74 CLLC #16,093; *Newfoundland Broadcasting Ltd.* (1978), 26 di 576, [1978] 1 Can LRBR 565; *Victoria Flying Services Ltd.* (1979), 35 di 73, [1979] 3 Can LRBR 216; *Airwest Airlines Ltd.* (1980), 42 di 247, [1981] 1 Can LRBR 427; *Pacific Western Airlines Ltd.* (1980), 40 di 205, [1980] 3 Can LRBR 180; *Seaspan International Ltd.* (1979), 37 di 38, [1979] 2 Can LRBR 213; *Newfoundland Steamships Ltd.* (1981), 45 di 156, 2 CLRBR (NS) 40.

corporate law such arrangements do not amount to a disposition of the business, have not been successful.[16]

The fact that the purchasing company does not employ any of the employees of the former employer will not in the case of a take-over have a significant impact because the key in determining if a sale of business has occurred resides in the continuity of the business, not in the actual persons who perform it.[17]

7:1142   Sales, Leases, and Transfers of Assets

The sale, lease, or transfer of a single asset will not normally constitute a sale of business within the scope of s. 144 unless some indication of a continuation of the business by the purchaser can be found. For example, the Board found that the movement and bare-bottom charter of a large salvage tug was not a sale of a "business and any part thereof", but was merely the transfer of a single asset. Accordingly, the Board rejected the successorship application.[18]

However the Board found an exception in a case where the single asset sold or transferred was a licence upon which the whole existence and continuance of the business of the vendor depended. It declared that a sale of business had taken place where two companies under common control and direction had acquired an exclusive right to operate on another company's licences, for which they acquired equipment to run in the licenced area, and also where one of them had hired some of the drivers displaced by this contractual arrangement.[19]

7:1143   Contracting Out, Subcontracting, and Loss of Business to a Competitor

In 1983, the Board issued an important policy decision concerning the determination of the application of the successorship provisions in the event of a contracting-out of the business or a change of subcontrac-

---

16   See *Seaspan International Ltd., supra*, note 15, where the Board discarded the argument made by an opposing union against a successorship application to the effect that a corporate amalgamation under British Columbia law did not amount to a disposition of the businesses amalgamated, as the effect of this action was to continue the amalgamated companies under the name of one of them. The Federal Court of Appeal refused to find an excess of jurisdiction in the Board's declaration of sale of business: *Seafarers' International Union of Canada v. Canada Labour Relations Board, supra*, note 4.

17   *Newfoundland Broadcasting Ltd., supra*, note 15, at p. 587 (di); *Victoria Flying Services Ltd., supra*, note 15.

18   *Eastern Canada Towing Ltd.* (1978), 24 di 152, at 160.

19   *Music Mann Leasing Ltd., Bus Drivers (London) Inc.* (1982), 51 di 51, [1982] 2 Can LRBR 337. Similarly, the Board also found a sale of business in a case where a company subcontracted the execution of the fixed-term transportation contract it had with another company and which constituted its whole business, in an engagement whereby the subcontracting company leased from the contractor eight trucks during the remainder of the contract: *Transports Provost Inc.* (1983), 50 di 225, 2 CLRBR (NS) 196.

tors.[20] In *Terminus Maritime Inc.*, the Board had to determine whether or not the legal and contractual obligations assumed by one subcontractor under the Code had passed to a subsequent subcontractor. More particularly, a shipping company that was using the services of a stevedoring company to load and unload its ships had decided to use the services of another stevedoring company which was a competitor of the former company. The latter had continued to operate its business without the benefit of the contract lost to the other stevedoring company.

In this decision, the Board explicitly recognized that the application of the successorship provision was not limited to transfers involving a transaction between the alleged purchaser and vendor (sale, lease, or contracting-out), but that it could also apply to indirect transfers of businesses following a tender or submission.[21]

Nevertheless, in *Terminus Maritime Inc.*, the Board refused to find a "sale of business", since the basic aim or purpose of the stevedoring company that had lost the contract was not transferred to the other company, which remained one of its competitors. This conclusion is in line with the more demanding school of thought within the Board, which holds that there must be something more than mere continuity in the nature of the work done, but that there must also be continuity in the employing enterprise.[22] The Board thereby rejected the "organic" approach to the concept of "business" referred to in other earlier decisions, which had relied exclusively on the transfer of work classifications covered by the bargaining certificate.[23]

---

[20]   *Terminus Maritime Inc.* (1983), 50 di 178.

[21]   *Ibid*, at p. 184.

[22]   See *Newfoundland Broadcasting Ltd.* (1978), 26 di 576, at 587-88, [1978] 1 Can LRBR 565: "But continuity of the work done is not sufficient alone to satisfy section 144. There must be some nexus between two employers other than the fact that one employed persons to do certain work that the other does or will do, before one can be declared the successor of the other. Otherwise a loss of work to a competitor employer would result in a successorship. There must be some continuity in the employing enterprise for which a union holds bargaining rights as well as continuity in the nature of the work. The two go hand in hand."

[23]   For instance in *Quebec Sol Services Ltée* (1981), 45 di 233, [1982] 2 Can LRBR 369, a panel of the Board used this "organic concept" and determined that there had been a sale of business following a tender by an airline company for the performance of certain duties in loading and unloading its planes at a particular airport, when these duties previously carried out by a subcontractor became the responsibility of another subcontractor. An application to quash this decision for grounds of excess of jurisdiction was unsuccessfully brought before the Federal Court: see *Québec Sol Services Ltée v. Canada Labour Relations Board*, unreported, November 1, 1982, file no. A-612-81 (Fed. C.A.). Approval of this organic definition of business is also found in the following Board decisions: *Newfoundland Steamships Ltd.* (1981), 45 di 156, 2 CLRBR (NS) 40; *La Banque Nationale du Canada* (1981), 42 di 352, [1982] 3 Can LRBR 1; affd. on the question of sale of business by the Supreme Court of Canada, [1984] 1 S.C.R. 269, 53 N.R. 203, 84 CLLC #14,037, 9 D.L.R. (4th) 10; *General Aviation Services Ltd.* (1982), 50 di 82; affd. not yet reported (Fed. C.A.); see note 12, *supra*. However, since the Board's policy decision adopted in 1983 in *Terminus Maritime Inc.* (1983), 50 di 178, there is no doubt that the "organic concept" developed in the above decisions has no chances of

Two fundamental principles can be extracted from the policy decision issued in 1983. First, the method by which a business is transferred is
not a determining factor once the "business" of the alleged "vendor" has
been identified. Second, the concept of "business" must be understood in
a dynamic sense by taking account of the basic aim of the employer's
enterprise as an ongoing concern and representing the sum of certain
material and human elements.

Different panels of the Board have interpreted and applied the
principles enunciated above in cases of changes of competing subcontractors with different results. In later decisions, however, a panel of the
Board indicated that the loss of a contract resulting from tendering does
not result in a sale of business, and another panel suggested that successor
rights were never intended to apply to genuine circumstances of subcontracting, to a loss of business to a competitor, or where there is a
corporate dissolution.[24]

---

revival. See *Freight Emergency Service Ltd.* (1984), 84 CLLC #16,031; and *CAFAS Inc.*
(1984), 7 CLRBR (NS) 1, 84 CLLC #16,034. In *National Bank of Canada v. Retail Clerks'
International Union,* [1984] 1 S.C.R. 269, 53 N.R. 203, 84 CLLC #14,037, 9 D.L.R.
(4th) 10, the Supreme Court of Canada held that the Board did not exceed its
jurisdiction by ruling that the integration of the two branches of the bank constituted a
sale of business, since under s. 144(5) it clearly had jurisdiction to determine this
question, and its interpretation did not seem to be so unreasonable that it could not be
rationally supported by the relevant legislation. Prior to this judgment, the Federal
Court had taken the same approach in other cases where the jurisdiction of the Board
to make a declaration of sale had been challenged.

[24]   In *Patrick Larkin* (1983), 50 di 208, the Board found no sale of business in circumstances
where a transportation company, although it had lost two mail contracts, had nevertheless continued its operations as mail contractor on a reduced scale. Therefore, in
the Board's view, the purpose of its enterprise had not been transferred. However, in
Les Transports Provost Inc. (1983), 50 di 225, 2 CLRBR (NS) 196, the Board found a sale
of business because the subcontractor had voluntarily assigned to another subcontractor its only contract of road transportation, and had subsequently abandoned road
transportation activities. In *CAFAS Inc.* (1983), 50 di 231; affd. unreported, April 17,
1985, file no. A-662-83 (Fed. C.A.), a panel of the Board also ruled that there had been
a sale of business between two subcontractors who were competing to obtain the same
contract from the Ministry of Transport for the operation and maintenance of pas-
senger transport vehicles (P.T.V.) for transporting passengers from Mirabel Airport
to aircrafts, and *vice versa*. In this case, the Board found that there were sufficient
indicia to show a transfer of business. Among these elements, the following were
mentioned: The P.T.V. contract with the Ministry of Transport was the only contract
the predecessor subcontracting company had at Mirabel Airport; the successor continued this contract without interruption, with the same equipment, and with a large
number of former employees of the predecessor who also constituted experienced and
valuable personnel. However, following this decision CAFAS applied to the Board
under s. 119 for a review of its decision. This application for review was allowed by a
differently constituted panel of the Board which had to hear the facts of the case:
CAFAS Inc. (1984), 7 CLRBR (NS) 1, 84 CLLC #16,034; affd. unreported, April 17,
1985, file no. A-674-84. Following the rehearing on the facts, the Board found that the
loss of a contract resulting from tendering does not result in a sale of business within
the meaning of s. 144. The position expressed by that panel runs contrary to the
fundamental principle that the method of transfer is not a determining factor as stated
in the full Board policy decision of *Terminus Maritime.* In *Freight Emergency Service Ltd.*
(1984), 84 CLLC #16,031, the Board took the opportunity of reviewing the evolution
and the inconsistency in its developing jurisprudence relating to a sale of business

7:1144   Receivership and Bankruptcy

In *Ontario Worldair Ltd.*, the Board refused to declare that the appointment of a receiver-manager pursuant to debentures granted by the employer, an airline company, constituted a sale of business within the meaning of s. 144 of the Code. Although by the terms of these debentures the receiver-manager acted as the agent of the employer and exercised extensive care and control of the enterprise, the airline company remained the employer. The contracts between the company and third parties were not terminated upon the appointment of the receiver-manager, and the collective agreement remained enforceable against the employer.[25]

In this case, the Board drew a distinction between the court-appointed receiver-managers and those appointed by the instrument. In the case of a court appointed receiver-manager, all the contracts between the debtor and third parties are terminated. A court-appointed receiver-manager should be considered as a successor employer within the meaning of the Code because his appointment involves a "transfer" or "disposition" of the business.[26]

7:1145   Internal Reorganizations and Closures of Departments, Plants, or Branches

In one instance involving a bank, the Board decided that the closure of a branch, followed by a transfer of the client's accounts to another branch and transfer of branch employees to that and other branches in the same city, constituted a sale of business. This particular ruling was upheld by the Supreme Court of Canada.[27]

In the decision mentioned above, the Board found it inconceivable that an employer conducting the same type of activities in two establishments located near each other, one of which was covered by a bargaining certificate while the other was not, could claim that it was not required to

---

under the Code. This panel of the Board rejected the concept that bargaining rights bestow proprietary rights over the work function performed by employees in a bargaining unit and a guarantee of permanence to that right regardless of which employees perform the work or how their employer came by the work. The panel also concluded that successor rights contained in s. 144 were never intended to apply to subcontracting, a loss of business to a competitor, or where there is a corporate dissolution.

However, contracting out is something different from the loss of business resulting from a change in subcontractors. In *Bernshine Mobile Maintenance Ltd.* (1984), 7 CLRBR (NS) 21, 84 CLLC #16,036, it was decided that the contracting out by an employer of its wash and tire-repair facilities to another company had resulted in a sale of a "part" of the employer's business.

25 *Ontario Worldair Ltd.* (1981), 45 di 22, [1981] 2 Can LRBR 405, 81 CLLC #16,117.
26 *Ibid.* at pp. 26-27 (di).
27 *La Banque Nationale du Canada* (1981), 42 di 352, [1982] 3 Can LRBR 1; affd. [1984] 1 S.C.R. 269, 53 N.R. 203, 84 CLLC #14,037, 9 D.L.R. (4th) 10.

respect this certificate simply because it had decided to amalgamate the activities of the unionized establishment with those of the non-unionized establishment. The Board therefore concluded that the term "transfer" used in the successorship provision could in fact cover an internal reorganization, bearing in mind that bargaining rights attach to the work classifications and not to the person of the employer or the employees.[28]

However, this decision was rendered before the 1983 policy decision discussed above, which rejected the purely organic understanding of the concept of "business" used by the Board to justify the ruling in *Terminus Maritime*.[29]

7:1200   EFFECTS OF SALE

Whenever there is a sale of business within the meaning of s. 144, the collective bargaining relationship established under the Code will be wholly transferred to the purchaser of the business. Section 144(2) provides that "a trade union that is the bargaining agent for the employees employed in the business continues to be their bargaining agent", and also that "the person to whom the business is sold is bound by any collective agreement that is, on the date on which the business is sold, applicable to the employees employed in the business".[30]

Continuity in any proceedings taken by a union or by employees under Part V of the Code is assured by the successorship provision. Neither certification proceedings nor any other proceeding are disturbed by the sale of a business.

Section 144(2) also provides that "a trade union that made application for certification in respect of any employees employed in the business before the date on which the business is sold may, subject to this Part, be certified by the Board as their bargaining agent" and also that "the person to whom the business is sold becomes a party to any proceeding taken under this Part that is pending on the date on which the business was sold and that affects the employees employed in the business or their bargaining agent".[31]

---

28   *Ibid.*, at pp. 375-76 (di).
29   (1983), 50 di 178. See the cases mentioned in notes 31 and 32. Moreover, a declaration under s. 144 is not the only recourse open to employees affected by an internal reorganization or closure. If the latter are motivated by anti-union reasons, this would certainly constitute an unfair labour practice, and the Board could use its remedial powers under s. 189 to rectify the situation. See *Bernshine Mobile Maintenance Ltd.* (1984), 7 CLRBR (NS) 21, 84 CLLC #16,036. Notwithstanding the employer's animus, we also believe that the Board could use its powers of review under s. 119 of the Code to declare that the employer continues to be bound by the certification at the new location.
30   *Canada Labour Code*, s. 144(2)(a), (c).
31   Section 144(2)(b), (d).

There are far-reaching effects of making the person to whom the business is sold a party to proceedings pending at the date of the sale of business.

For example, in one instance it was decided that the purchasers had become bound by a previous order made by the Board against the vendor, who prior to the date of sale had been found guilty of illegally dismissing two of his employees. The fact that the purchaser did not employ any of the employees of the former employer was not considered a significant factor by the Board. The latter mentioned that if the successor employer was not aware of the illegality because the vendor had not disclosed the pending proceedings, then his proper recourse was against his vendor.[32]

Similarly, in another case, the Board cautioned that, under the successorship provision, unresolved grievances and pending arbitrations, if left unsettled by the predecessor employer and the union at the date of the sale, will still become liabilities of the successor, and therefore that the disclosure of such liabilities is a commercial consideration of which prudent parties should take account.[33]

Although the collective agreement may have expired at the date of the sale of the business, in the authors' opinion, where notice to bargain collectively had been given by the union according to the Code prior to the actual date of sale, the purchaser would be compelled to maintain the same rates of pay as well as all the other conditions of employment specified in the collective agreement. This is so because a notice to bargain constitutes a proceeding under the Code affecting the employees and their bargaining agent.[34] It follows that the purchaser employer would have to respect s. 148, imposing on employer and union the duty to bargain collectively, and as well the obligation not to change the terms and conditions of employment until the right to declare a lockout or strike has been acquired by the parties.

Since a strike may be considered to be a "proceeding under the Code", an impending strike could also, in the authors' opinion, be carried out against the employer to whom the business has been sold. However, as yet no Board decision has been rendered on the effect of s. 144 in a strike situation.

An interesting issue raised by the successorship provision concerns the operative seniority date of the employees of the vendor once the sale has occurred.

---

[32] *Victoria Flying Services Ltd.* (1979), 35 di 73, at 82, [1979] 3 Can LRBR 216.
[33] *Radio CJYQ-930 Ltd.* (1978), 34 di 617, at 628, [1979] 1 Can LRBR 233.
[34] *Quebec Sol Services Ltée* (1981), 45 di 233, [1982] 2 Can LRBR 369. In this case the Board held that the purchaser was bound by the collective agreement negotiated by the vendor and the trade union before the date of the sale of business, but only effective at a date posterior to the date of sale.

In a case where the Board as a side issue examined the status of a particular employee following the sale of a part of the employer's business, it suggested that, as far as the seniority provisions of the collective agreement were concerned, the application of the benefits payable to the employees of the vendor should refer to the date on which they were hired by the successor employer.[35] However, this opinion may have been influenced by the fact that when terminated by the vendor, these employees had accepted separation pay credits in lieu of any rights they might have had under the collective agreement.[36]

In this case, the Board was not specifically asked to determine the operative seniority dates of the employees hired by the purchaser. It had to decide whether it was the obligation of the vendor or the purchaser to assume the potential liability resulting from a grievance made by an employee who was terminated by the vendor following the sale of business. Since, prior to his termination, this employee had remained in the employ of the vendor for one day after the date of the sale of business, the Board concluded that he was not employed in the part of the business sold and consequently was not an employee bound by the collective agreement transferred to the purchaser employer.

The effects discussed above take place by reason of the operation of the Code alone, and accordingly the intervention of the Board is not required. Any decision by the Board that a sale of business has taken place is purely declaratory in nature and its effects will be retroactive to the date of sale.

Except where the employees of the vendor are intermingled with the employees of the purchaser within the meaning of s. 144(3), the Board is not expressly empowered to modify or to suspend the effects contained in s. 144(2) of the Code. However, the Board has not considered that this absence of an express statutory power constitutes an obstacle to its exercise of a discretionary power to bar certain effects of s. 144(2) where it appears that the collective agreement between the vendor and the trade union was negotiated only with the view of prejudicing a competitor employer. In such a case, the Board has recognized that it possesses an implicit authority to declare that the purchaser should not be bound by such an agreement.[37]

---

35   *Radio CJYQ-930 Ltd., supra,* note 33.
36   *Ibid.,* at pp. 629-30 (di).
37   See *Terminus Maritime Inc.* (1983), 50 di 178; and *General Aviation Services Ltd.* (1982), 50 di 82. This presumed authority has not been examined by a reviewing court. In our opinion, these statements of the Board on the scope of its own jurisdiction should be taken with caution until they have received some sort of judicial approval.

7:1300 DETERMINATION OF RIGHTS IN CASE OF INTERMINGLING OF EMPLOYEES

Under s. 144(3)(a) of the Code, where an employer sells his business, and his employees are intermingled with employees of the purchaser employer, the Board is specifically empowered, on an application made by any trade union affected, to determine whether the employees affected constitute one or more units appropriate for collective bargaining, to determine which trade union shall be the bargaining agent for the employees in each such unit, and to amend any certificate issued to a trade union or the description of a bargaining unit contained in any collective agreement.

Once the Board has determined which trade union shall be the bargaining agent of the employees in the appropriate unit, s. 144(3)(b) and (c) provides that any applicable collective agreement will continue to be binding on that trade union, unless the Board grants leave to either party to serve on the other a notice to bargain collectively.

Before the Board may exercise the powers mentioned above, it is essential that a situation of employee intermingling exist. However, the question of determining what constitutes an intermingling of employees is left to the judgment of the Board, which will look at the particularities of each case.

The Board has not placed any limitations on the extent or the nature of the mixing required to constitute an intermingling of employees under the Code.[38] It has already ruled that a complete intermingling was not required and that a liberal and broad interpretation should be given to the word "intermingling".[39] It has also accepted that the form and the degree of intermingling could vary from one particular industry to another.[40]

---

[38]   *Seaspan International Ltd.* (1979), 37 di 38, at 45, [1979] 2 Can LRBR 213.

[39]   *Airwest Airlines Ltd.* (1980), 42 di 247, at 259, [1981] 1 Can LRBR 427. See also *Québecair et Régionair (1981) Inc.* (1983), 54 di 161.

[40]   *Eastern Canada Towing Ltd.* (1977), 24 di 152, at 161: "We recognize that in the commonly accepted sense '*intermingling*' of employees contemplates a situation where stable workforces are combined. In this shipping industry, with its extensive reliance on the union hiring hall, intermingling results from the identity of the hiring hall from which employees are dispatched." See also *Seaspan International Ltd.* (1979), 37 di 38, at 45, [1979] 2 Can LRBR 213: "In our opinion the method of operation in the circumstances described above constitutes an intermingling of employees. There is a mixing of members of two unions in separate bargaining units performing the same function. While the employer desired degree of intermingling does not exist the nature of the tugboat industry on the west coast with its stable force and the identification of unlicensed employees with particular vessels creates an intermingling of a type different from that usually seen in an industrial plant or that known to its counterpart on the east coast." See also *Newfoundland Steamships Ltd.* (1981), 45 di 156, 2 CLRBR (NS) 40.

In intermingling situations the Board has the task of determining the appropriate bargaining unit or units. In an application made under s. 144(3) the Board, in addition to applying the normal criteria respecting the determination of appropriate bargaining units,[41] will also consider the degree of intermingling.[42] If the extent of intermingling is not sufficient to eliminate the significant distinguishing features of the individual bargaining units, the Board will maintain their separate identities so as to reduce the possibility that employees' rights and benefits will be adversely affected.[43]

In that context, it may be asked of a union making the application under s. 144(3) that an undertaking be given to the effect that the employees represented by the other union will retain their seniority and will not lose their benefits if the union wishes the Board to create one bargaining unit.[44]

Once the Board has determined the appropriate bargaining unit or units, it must decide which trade union is to be the bargaining agent for the employees in the unit or units. If several bargaining units are maintained, the question of determining which of the two or more unions involved will act as the bargaining agent of the several groups of employees will not pose any particular problem — each union continuing to represent its own employees — unless the Board is also seized of an application for certification made by another union.[45]

However, when it has determined that one bargaining unit is appropriate, the question of the representative character of each union must be resolved by the Board. The employees' wishes may be determined by an examination of the membership evidence or by a representation vote ordered under the discretionary power given to the Board by s. 118(i) of the Code. In most cases, however, the Board is able to decide the issue on the basis of the relative size of the two employee groups, and a representation vote will not be necessary.[46]

---

[41] For instance, on the ground that the employees of a division of an airline company did not share the same community of interest, three distinct units were created by the Board in *Airwest Airlines Ltd.* (1980), 42 di 247, at 263, [1981] 1 Can LRBR 427. Moreover, In *La Sarre Air Service Ltée (Propair Inc.)* (1982), 49 di 52, the Board decided to regroup the pilots and the maintenance employees with the other employees of a small seasonal airline company in view of the small number of employees affected.

[42] *Seaspan International Ltd.* (1979), 37 di 38, at 47, [1979] 2 Can LRBR 213.

[43] *Ibid.* See also *Newfoundland Steamships Ltd.* (1981), 45 di 156, 2 CLRBR (NS) 40.

[44] Such an undertaking was asked and given in *Seaspan International Ltd.*, *supra*, note 42, at p. 48 (di). In *Les Transports Provost Inc.* (1983), 50 di 225, 2 CLRBR (NS) 196, although the Board did not have to make a determination under s. 144(3) in view of the fact that the issue was resolved under s. 119, the Board nevertheless considered the guarantees of seniority provided by the collective agreement of the applicant and union before amending the bargaining certificate of the applicant union to include within a single bargaining unit a group of employees integrated into the enterprise.

[45] See *Airwest Airlines Ltd.* (1980), 42 di 247, at 264, [1981] 1 Can LRBR 427.

[46] *Eastern Canada Towing Ltd.* (1977), 24 di 152, at 162; *Seaspan International Ltd.*, *supra*, note 42, at p. 49 (di). In *La Sarre Air Service Ltée (Propair Inc.)*, *supra*, note 41, following

The Board is empowered under s. 144(3)(c) to grant leave to one of the parties to give notice to bargain collectively, provided that an application is made to it at any time after the sixtieth day from the date when the Board disposed of an application under s. 144(3)(a).

However, where an application to serve notice to bargain collectively is heard by the Board, pursuant to s. 144(4), the latter must take into account the extent to which and the fairness with which the provisions of the collective agreement, particularly those dealing with seniority, could be applied to all the employees to whom the collective agreement is applicable.[47]

7:2000   UNION SUCCESSION

Another case of legal successorship under the Code occurs where there is a merger or amalgamation of trade unions or a transfer of jurisdiction among trade unions. In such circumstances, s. 143(1) provides that "the successor union shall be deemed to have acquired the rights, privileges and duties of its predecessor, whether under a collective agreement or otherwise". The words "merger", "amalgamation", and "transfer of jurisdiction among trade unions" are not defined in the Code. Accordingly, clarification must be found in the Board's jurisprudence.[48]

In addition, the Board is specifically empowered to determine "what rights, privileges and duties have been acquired or retained" on application to it by any trade union affected,[49] and for this purpose "it may make

---

an application under s. 144(3), the Board had ordered a representation vote. However, the Board was later asked to rescind its order of a vote on the grounds that the employer had interfered with the representation of the employees by a trade union. This being found to be true in this case, the Board cancelled the vote. It was also satisfied that a representation vote would not reflect the true wishes of the employees. Therefore, the Board relied solely on the comparative size of the former units at a date before the amalgamation in order to determine which of the two trade unions would represent the employees. The bargaining agent of the largest unit was confirmed as bargaining agent for the new unit. An unsuccessful application to quash this ruling was made to the Federal Court of Appeal (see file no. A-371-82).

[47]   *Seaspan International Ltd., supra*, note 42, at pp. 47-48.

[48]   Very few decisions of the Board have dealt with s. 143 of the Code: See *Canadian National Railways* (1975), 9 di 20, [1975] 1 Can LRBR 327, 75 CLLC #16,158; *Whitehorse Hotels Ltd.* (1977), 21 di 410, [1977] 1 Can LRBR 477, 77 CLLC #16,080; *Canadian National Railway Co., Telecommunications Department* (1980), 40 di 136, [1980] 3 Can LRBR 140; *Banque Nationale du Canada (Sillery, Québec)* (1982), 50 di 91, 2 CLRBR (NS) 202. None of these has attempted to give a precise definition to the expressions mentioned above, although in *Banque Nationale du Canada (Sillery, Québec)* the Board referred to comments made about similar words or expressions by the Ontario Labour Relations Board in *Hydro-Electric Power Commission of Ontario* (1957), 57 CLLC #18,080 at p. 1,654. In *Banque Nationale du Canada (Sillery, Québec)* the Board ruled that a transfer of jurisdiction from the international union holding the bargaining certificate to one of its local unions was covered by s. 143 of the Code.

[49]   See *Canadian Telecommunications Union, Division No. 1 of United Telegraph Workers v. Canadian Brotherhood of Railway, Transport and General Workers*, [1982] 1 F.C. 603, 42 N.R. 243, 81 CLLC #14,126, 126 D.L.R. (3d) 228 (C.A.), where it was held that the

such enquiry or direct such representation votes be taken as it considers necessary".[50]

The Board has already ruled that the holding of a hearing under s. 143 is not mandatory.[51] It has also ruled that the delays concerning the filing of a certification application are not applicable to applications made pursuant to the union successorship provision, although the Board may verify that the majority of the concerned employees are in favour of the merger or the amalgamation.[52]

7:3000   CROWN SUCCESSION

Section 145 of the Code specifically provides for what happens when a portion of the public service of Canada is transferred to a part of a public corporation to which the Code applies.[53] To pass from the public-service domain regulated by the *Public Service Staff Relations Act* to the status of a corporation acting on behalf of the government is not as traumatic as moving from the public to the private sector.[54] Section 145 provides that the collective agreement that applies to the employees in that portion of the public service continues in force until its term expires.[55] However, the bargaining agent must reapply to the Board with a certification application within the delays provided in s. 124 if it wishes to consolidate its bargaining rights.[56] Where the employees of the Crown

---

applicant union had no standing to bring an application for review of a decision of the Board made pursuant to s. 143, in which the Board had refused to grant intervenor status to the applicant union. See *Canadian National Railway Co., Telecommunications Department* (1980), 40 di 136, [1980] 3 Can LRBR 140.

50   See s. 143(2) and (3). Once the Board has determined that a trade union is the successor of another union under s. 143, it will make any necessary amendments to the bargaining certificate in order to reflect the change of union by means of s. 119. See *Banque Nationale du Canada (Sillery, Québec), supra,* note 48.

51   See *Canadian National Railways* (1975), 9 di 20, at 27-28, [1975] 1 Can LRBR 327, 75 CLLC #16,158, where the Board rejected an application under s. 119 to review a previous decision in which it had decided without a hearing to reject an application claiming that a merger had taken place under s. 143.

52   *Banque Nationale du Canada (Sillery, Québec), supra,* note 48. In *Whitehorse Hotels Ltd., supra,* note 48, where it appeared that a certified bargaining agent had been inactive in the bargaining unit for a period of some fifteen years, the Board did not hesitate to reject an application made by the applicant union which did not attempt to prove that it enjoyed the support of a majority of the employees in the unit.

53   See s. 109. Concerning crown corporations and the scope of s. 109, see *Government of the Northwest Territories and Housing Corp. of the Northwest Territories* (1978), 31 di 165, [1979] 1 Can LRBR 521, 78 CLLC #16,171.

54   In *Northern Sales Co. Ltd.* (1980), 40 di 128, [1980] 3 Can LRBR 15, 80 CLLC #16,033, the Board decided that the successorship provisions in s. 145 of the Code did not preserve a collective agreement concluded under the provisions of the *Public Service Staff Relations Act* when the Government of Canada transfers its operations from the public to the private sector. Section 145 applies only to corporations referred to in s. 109 of the Code. See note 53, *supra.*

55   *Canada Labour Code,* s. 145(1)(a).

56   Section 145(2).

corporation are already covered by a collective agreement or represented by a trade union, the Board may make determinations similar to those made in the case of an intermingling of employees following a sale of business.[57]

By legislative enactment, some of the effects of s. 145 of the Code were discarded in the case of the employees of the post office department.[58]

---

[57] Section 145(3) and (7). See s. 144(3) and paragraph 7:1300.

[58] *Canada Post Corporation Act*, S.C. 1980-81-82-83, c. 54 (passed by the House of Commons April 14, 1981), s. 70; particularly under s. 70(1), each trade union that, immediately prior to the coming into force of this section, was certified under the *Public Staff Relations Act* as the bargaining agent for any employees of the post office department, was deemed to have been certified as the bargaining agent for those employees under Part V of the *Canada Labour Code* on the day when s. 70(1) came into force.

CHAPTER 8

COLLECTIVE BARGAINING UNDER THE CODE

8:0000 COLLECTIVE BARGAINING AND COLLECTIVE AGREEMENTS

This chapter describes the mechanisms that govern collective bargaining under the *Canada Labour Code* following certification by the Board or that take place for the renewal of a collective agreement.

The Board's role in regard to collective bargaining is minimal compared with that of the Department of Labour's mediation and conciliation branch. The Board's involvement in the process of collective bargaining, except where specifically provided for,[1] is merely incidental to the exercise of its jurisdiction under other sections of the Code. In this chapter, the process the parties must go through to conclude a collective agreement is discussed (paragraph 8:1000). Those sections of the Code that refer to the content and renewal of collective agreements are summarized (paragraph 8:2000). The Board's jurisdiction in regard to technological change to considered (paragraph 8:2300). The statutory jurisdiction and powers of the arbitration (paragraph 8:3000) and reference to the Board of certain matters raised in arbitration (paragraph 8:4000) are also studied. Finally, the imposition of a first collective agreement is considered (paragraph 8:5000).

8:1000 NEGOTIATION OF A COLLECTIVE AGREEMENT

8:1100 NOTICE TO BARGAIN

Following certification, where no collective agreement already binds the employees of the unit, a bargaining agent or the employer may, by notice, require the other party to commence collective bargaining for the

---

[1] *Canada Labour Code*, s. 148(a) — bad faith bargaining; ss. 149 to 153 — technological changes; s. 158 — matters referred to an arbitrator or an arbitration board; s. 161.1 — hiring hall provisions; s. 171.1 — imposition of a first collective agreement; s. 160(3) — application for altering the termination dates of a collective agreement; s. 162(2), (3) — Board's jurisdiction to decide compulsory check-off provisions of a collective agreement do not apply to an employee for reasons of his religious conviction or beliefs; s. 197 — Board's jurisdiction to deal with matters referred to it by the minister.

purpose of entering into a collective agreement.[2] In the case of the renewal of a collective agreement, either party within the period of three months preceding the termination date of the agreement or of any longer period of time provided in the agreement, or within the term of the collective agreement if it is provided that certain provisions may be revised, may by notice require the other party to commence collective bargaining for the purpose of renewing or revising the collective agreement.[3]

The notice shall:

(i) designate a convenient time within twenty days from the date of the giving of the notice and a convenient place for the collective bargaining to commence; and

(ii) be dated and signed by or on behalf of the party giving the notice, and shall require the other party to commence collective bargaining for the purpose of entering into a collective agreement (s. 146) or renewing a collective agreement (s. 147).[4]

Once the notice to bargain has been given, the bargaining agent and the employer must meet and bargain in good faith and make every reasonable effort to enter into a collective agreement.[5] During this period the employer cannot alter the working conditions of his employees without the consent of the bargaining agent.[6]

8:1200   CONCILIATION

If, within twenty days of the notice, collective bargaining has not commenced, or the parties have negotiated but have been unable to reach an agreement, either party may, by notice, inform the Minister of Labour of their failure to enter into a collective agreement.[7]

This notice shall:

(a) state the name and address of the party giving the notice;
(b) state the name and address of the other party to the dispute;
(c) state the date upon which notice to commence collective bargaining was given;
(d) state the steps that have been taken, the progress that has been made and the difficulties that have been encountered in collective bargaining following the giving of the notice. . . .

The notice must also:

---

2   *Canada Labour Code,* s. 146.
3   Section 147.
4   *Canada Industrial Relations Regulations,* C.R.C. 1978, c. 1012, s. 5.
5   *Canada Labour Code,* s. 148(a). This question is discussed in paragraph 12:2000.
6   Section 148(b). This question is discussed in paragraph 12:1200.
7   Section 163. The conciliation procedure under the Code is summarized in Appendix 9.

(e) be accompanied by a copy of the notice to commence collective bargaining;

(f) be accompanied by a copy of any existing collective agreement between the parties; and

(g) be signed by or on behalf of the party giving the notice.[8]

Where the minister has received a notice under s. 163, he is obliged, no later than fifteen days after the receipt of the notice, to appoint a conciliation officer, a conciliation commissioner, or a conciliation board, or to notify the parties, in writing, of his intention not to appoint any of the preceding.[9] Where the minister finds it to be advisable, he may at his discretion, even in the absence of a notice, appoint any of the aforementioned.[10]

When the parties have met with a conciliator but have been unable to reach an agreement, the conciliation officer shall report this to the minister[11] who then, within fifteen days of receiving the report, must either appoint a conciliation commissioner or board, or must give the parties written notice of his intention not to do so.[12]

The manner in which conciliation boards are set up is described in ss. 172, 173, and 174 of the Code. The powers and jurisdiction of conciliation commissioners and boards are further defined at ss. 175 to 178.

8:1210   Establishment of Conciliation Boards

Conciliation boards consist of three members who must not have a pecuniary interest that may be directly affected by any matter referred to the Board.[13] When the minister decides to appoint a conciliation board, he must send forthwith a written notice to the parties requiring each one of them to appoint, within seven days, a nominee to sit as member of the Board.[14] The minister must nominate to the Board the nominee chosen by the parties.[15] If the parties fail to appoint their nominee, the minister has the power to appoint one instead.[16] The nominees must each, within five days of the appointment of the second nominee, nominate a chairman who is willing and ready to act, and the minister must appoint that chairman.[17] If the nominees fail to nominate a chairman within five days, the minister appoints one.[18] When the conciliation board is appointed, the minister must forthwith give notice to the parties of the name of the

---

8   *Canada Industrial Relations Regulations*, s. 6.
9   *Canada Labour Code*, s. 164(1).
10   Section 164(2).
11   Section 165.
12   Section 166.
13   Section 172(1), (2).
14   Section 173(1a).
15   Section 173(1b).
16   Section 173(2).
17   Section 173(3).
18   Section 173(4).

members of the board.[19] The appointment of a conciliation board or of a commissioner or the decision not to appoint cannot be questioned in court.[20] If a person ceases to be a member of a conciliation board, a new member is appointed following the procedure outlined above.[21]

8:1220   Powers of a Conciliation Commissioner or Conciliation Board and Procedure to be Followed in the Execution of Their Mandate

The conciliation board and the conciliation commissioner determine their own procedure,[22] can summon and enforce the attendance of witnesses,[23] administer oaths and affidavits,[24] receive evidence as they see fit, whether admissible in a court of law or not,[25] examine records and make such inquiries as they see fit,[26] enter any premises of an employer, and inspect any work material, machinery, appliances, or articles therein except where limited by the governor in council in the interests of defence and security.[27] They may also delegate their authority to administer oaths and make inquiries.[28]

The chairman of the conciliation board has the power to fix the time and place of the sittings after consultation with the board members[29] and notify the parties of the time and place of sittings. The chairman and one member of the conciliation board constitute a quorum. The board, however, cannot proceed in the absence of a member unless that member has been given reasonable notice of the sitting.[30] No testimony or record of proceeding before the conciliation commissioner or a conciliation board or their report are receivable in evidence in a court of law.[31] A conciliator, a conciliation commissioner, or a member of a conciliation board cannot be required to give evidence in any civil action, suit, or other proceeding respecting information obtained in the discharge of their duties under Part V.[32] At the conclusion of the sittings, the chair-

---

[19]   Section 174.
[20]   Section 177.
[21]   Section 176(2).
[22]   Section 175(a).
[23]   *Canada Labour Code,* ss. 175(b) and 118(a). A person who refuses to answer any proper question put to him by either a conciliation commissioner or a conciliation board may be the subject of penal prosecution in accordance with s. 192(b), providing authorization has been granted by the Canada Labour Relations Board in accordance with s. 194.
[24]   *Canada Labour Code,* ss. 175(b) and 118(b).
[25]   Sections 175(b) and 118(c).
[26]   Sections 175(b) and 118(f).
[27]   Sections 175(b) and 118(h).
[28]   Sections 175(c) and 118(b), (f).
[29]   Section 176(1a).
[30]   Section 176(2).
[31]   Section 178.
[32]   Section 208.

man must report to the minister, in a certified statement, the details of each sitting and the names of the members of the conciliation board and witnesses present at each sitting.[33]

8:1230   Report

Upon their appointment the conciliation officer, the conciliation commissioner, or board must endeavour to assist the parties in reaching an agreement.[34] They then must file, within fourteen days of their nomination or later with the agreement of the parties or the authorization of the minister, a report with the minister advising the minister of their success or failure in assisting the parties to the dispute and of their findings or recommendations.[35] The failure of the conciliation commissioner or board to file their report within the predetermined period does not invalidate the proceeding, nor does it terminate their authority.[36] The report of the majority of the board's members or, if each writes a report, the chairman's report is the report of the conciliation board.[37] The minister may either accept the report or ask the conciliation commissioner or board to review or clarify it.[38] In such a case, the report of the conciliation board or the commissioner is deemed not to have been received by the minister until the revised report is received by him.[39] The final report must be given to the parties,[40] and the minister may also release it to the public.[41]

In cases where a conciliation commissioner or board has been appointed, the parties may agree in writing, at any time before the filing of the report, that it will be binding on them.[42]

8:1300   LEGAL STRIKE OR LOCKOUT

Ultimately, if the parties are unable to agree to the terms of a collective agreement, they may resort to strike or lockout action as a means to resolve their differences. This action is only legal when certain conditions spelled out in s. 180 have been met. These conditions are:

1.   A notice to bargain collectively has been given under s. 146 or 147.

---

33   Section 176(1)(c).
34   Section 167(b).
35   Section 168(1).
36   Section 202.
37   Section 168(2).
38   Section 169(a).
39   Section 169(b).
40   Section 170(a).
41   Section 170(b).
42   Section 171.

2.   The parties have failed to meet to bargain within twenty days of the notice, or have bargained in accordance with s. 148, but have been unable to enter into a collective agreement.

3.   The minister has received a notice in writing under s. 163 informing him of their failure to enter into or revise a collective agreement or, having failed to receive such a notice, has seen appropriate to appoint a conciliation officer, a conciliation commissioner, or a conciliation board.

4.   Seven days have elapsed from the date on which the minister

(a) notified the parties of his intention not to appoint a conciliation officer, a conciliation commissioner, or a conciliation board under s. 164(1); or

(b) notified the parties of his intention not to appoint a conciliation commissioner or board under s. 166; or

(c) released a copy of the report of the conciliation commissioner or board to the parties.

An employee member of a bargaining unit may not legally participate in a strike unless he is a member of a bargaining unit in respect of which a notice to bargain has been given and the conditions set out above have been met in respect of the bargaining unit of which he is a member.[43] In other words, employees of another bargaining unit in respect of which the right to strike is not acquired may not participate in a legal strike of another bargaining unit. If employees strike without having met these requirements, their action is illegal and they may be ordered back to work by the Board if proceedings are initiated under s. 182 of the Code.[44]

8:1400   SUSPENSION OF THE RIGHT TO STRIKE OR LOCK-OUT

When a strike or lockout that would be legal under s. 180 occurs in a period commencing on the date Parliament is dissolved and ending when Parliament is recalled, the governor in council, at any time during the period, may suspend the right to strike or lockout by ordering that the period of seven days referred to above elapse only after the return of Parliament, if he is of opinion that the exercise of such right would adversely affect the national interest.[45] When the governor in council has made such an order, he must on any of the first ten sitting days of the first session of the new Parliament lay before Parliament a report setting out the reasons for the making of the order.

---

43   Section 180(1), (2).
44   See Chapter 9.
45   *Canada Labour Code*, s. 180(1), (2).

8:2000 THE COLLECTIVE AGREEMENT

8:2100 DEFINITION

A collective agreement is defined at s. 107(1) as "an agreement in writing entered into between an employer and a bargaining agent containing provisions respecting terms and conditions of employment and related matters".

In the context of a proceeding brought before it, the Board, in accordance with s. 118(p)(vi), (vii), and (viii), has the power to determine whether a collective agreement has been entered into, who is bound by the collective agreement, and whether a collective agreement is in operation. This paragraph will only deal with the question of what constitutes a collective agreement under the above definition. The questions of whether a collective agreement has been renewed or continued,[46] whether it continues to apply following the certification of a new bargaining agent and to what extent,[47] whether it continues following a transfer of employer,[48] whether certain clauses are valid or invalid,[49] and to what extent the statutory provisions of the Code affect the existence or validity of a collective agreement,[50] are not dealt with here.

The above definition refers to three essential elements conditioning the existence of a collective agreement under Part V of the Code:

1. "an agreement in writing"
2. "entered into between an employer and a bargaining agent"
3. "containing provisions respecting terms and conditions of employment and related matters."

"An Agreement in Writing"

A verbal agreement made between the parties at the negotiating table and ratified by the union membership at a general meeting was found not to be a collective agreement, where there was no evidence showing that the agreement had been put in writing.[51]

On the other hand, the Board is not formalistic and does not require that a formal document entitled "Collective Agreement" be executed,

---

[46] *Austin Airways Ltd. / White River Air Services Ltd.* (1980), 41 di 151, [1980] 3 Can LRBR 393.

[47] *Bell Canada* (1981), 43 di 238, [1981] 2 Can LRBR 284, 81 CLLC #16,099.

[48] *Northern Sales Co. Ltd.* (1980), 40 di 128, [1980] 3 Can LRBR 15, 80 CLLC #16,033; *Newfoundland Steamships Ltd.* (1981), 45 di 156, 2 CLRBR (NS) 40; *Ontario Worldair Ltd.* (1981), 45 di 22, [1981] 2 Can LRBR 405, 81 CLLC #16,117; and *Cable T.V. Ltée* (1979), 35 di 28, [1980] 2 Can LRBR 381, 80 CLLC #16,019.

[49] *Canadian Broadcasting Corp.* (1981), 45 di 29, [1981] 2 Can LRBR 462, 81 CLLC #16,128.

[50] *Bell Canada, supra,* note 47.

[51] *Donald William Murray Movers Ltd.* (1974), 7 di 11, [1975] 2 Can LRBR 317, 75 CLLC #16,148.

where the evidence shows that a written memorandum of agreement has been entered into by the parties purporting to continue the existing collective agreement except as otherwise amended by the provisions contained in the memorandum, as long as the memorandum of agreement has been ratified by the union membership and confirmed by letters exchanged between the parties and the provisions of the memorandum have been implemented.[52]

"Entered into between an Employer and a Bargaining Agent"

This aspect will often be raised in certification proceedings brought in the context of raid where the employer has voluntarily recognized and entered into an agreement with an incumbent independent association of employees. The incumbent "union" must be a trade union as defined by the Code. If not, it then follows that it cannot be a bargaining agent and the agreement entered into with the employer is not a collective agreement. In *Verreault Navigation Inc.*[53] the Board found that the association was not a *bona fide* trade union and that there was therefore no collective agreement in force. The same situation was found in *Capital Coach Lines Ltd. (Travelways).*[54] In *Canadian Offshore Marine Ltd.*[55] the Board found that the agreement had not been entered into with the employer whose employees were applying to be certified, and consequently there was no collective agreement in force.

"Containing Provisions Respecting Terms and Conditions of Employment and Related Matters"

In *Canadian Offshore Marine Ltd.*[56] the Board found that the agreement contained no duration clause, no clause providing for final and binding arbitration for the settlement of disputes, and no clause prohibiting strikes and lockouts while the agreement was in force. Noting that these clauses were the very essence of a collective agreement under the Code, the Board concluded that the agreement did not constitute a collective agreement.

In deciding what constitutes "terms and conditions of employment and related matters", the Board draws on its experience in the field of labour relations[57] and takes into account the legislative intent as contained in the preamble to the Code. The Board also takes into account whether the agreement entered into between the parties is contrary to

---

52   *Giant Yellowknife Mines Ltd.* (1976), 13 di 54, [1976] 1 Can LRBR 314, 76 CLLC #16,002.
53   (1978), 24 di 227.
54   (1980), 40 di 5, [1980] 2 Can LRBR 407, 90 CLLC #16,011.
55   (1973), 1 di 20, 74 CLLC #16,089.
56   *Ibid.*
57   *Ibid.*

other legislation, and to what extent the illegality of certain clauses invalidates the whole collective agreement.[58] For example, in *Cyprus Anvil Mining Corp.*[59] the employer and the union had concluded a written collective agreement. The agreement violated the provisions of the federal *Anti-Inflation Act*[60] as to the agreed-upon compensation package and exceeded the Anti-Inflation Board approved guidelines. The Board referred to the usual practices of collective bargaining but stated that it was obliged to take into account the provisions of the *Anti-Inflation Act*. It went on to say that, although the invalidity of certain clauses does not as a consequence render invalid the whole agreement, in this case, since the compensation package covered a wide range of benefits that had been agreed to in exchange for other concessions not necessarily related to compensation, its illegality rendered the entire agreement invalid.

In *Verreault Navigation Inc.*[61] the Board held further that the filing of an agreement with the minister of labour under s. 204 does not validate a collective agreement if it does not otherwise contain the essential elements required by the definition.

In *CAFAS Inc.* the Board decided that a letter of understanding that incorporated by reference the terms of an expired collective agreement constituted a collective agreement.[62]

8:2200   COMPULSORY PROVISIONS

Sections 154 to 162 impose on the parties certain restraints on what provisions must or may be included in a collective agreement negotiated under the authority of Part V of the *Canada Labour Code*. The latter relates to arbitration procedures, including the appointment and powers of arbitrators and their obligations in regard to the filing of awards with the minister's office, their remuneration, judicial review of arbitral awards, the filing of the award in the Federal Court, the term of a collective agreement, the right of parties to negotiate clauses requiring membership in the union as a condition of employment or the granting of preference in employment to members of a union, and those related to check-off provisions.

It is not within the Board's jurisdiction to deal with the administration, interpretation, application, or alleged violation of a collective agreement.[63] Nevertheless, in exercising its specific jurisdiction under the

---

58   *Cyprus Anvil Mining Corp.* (1976), 15 di 194, [1976] 2 Can LRBR 360, 76 CLLC #16,045.
59   *Ibid.*
60   S.C. 1974-75-76, c. 75.
61   (1978), 24 di 227, at 296.
62   *CAFAS Inc.* (1983), 50 di 231; affd. unreported, April 17, 1985, file no. A-662-83 (Fed. C.A.).
63   *Bell Canada* (1981), 43 di 238, at 240 and 252, [1981] 2 Can LRBR 284, 81 CLLC #16,099.

Code, the Board has had to take into consideration these aspects of collective bargaining, and in so doing it has made certain comments on them. Where significant, reference will be made to them.

Provisions for the Final Settlement of Disputes

Section 155 imposes on the parties the obligation to include, in their collective agreement, provisions for the final settlement without a work stoppage of disputes in regard to the interpretation, application, administration, or alleged violation of the agreement. Provision must be made for dispute resolution by way of arbitration or "otherwise".[64] Sections 155 and 180 oblige the parties bound by a collective agreement to resolve their differences without resorting to strikes or lockouts.[65]

Where a collective agreement does not contain a provision for the final settlement of disputes, or where it provides that differences must be submitted to an arbitration board, and either party fails to name its nominee to the board, then regardless of any other provision in the agreement the dispute must be submitted either to an arbitrator named by the parties or to one appointed by the minister at the written request of one of the parties.[66]

Where the collective agreement provides for final dispute settlement, without stoppage of work, by an arbitrator or an arbitration board, and the parties or their nominees are unable to agree on the arbitrator or the chairman of the board, either party may request in writing that the minister appoint one.[67] A request to the minister to appoint an arbitrator or chairman of an arbitration board shall:[68]

(a) state the name and address of the party making the request, or his representative;

(b) state the name and address of the other party to the dispute, or his representative;

(c) where an arbitration board is to be established, it must state the names and addresses of the parties' nominees;

(d) state the nature and date of occurrence of the dispute;

(e) be accompanied by a copy of the grievance form, if any, required by the collective agreement;

(f) be accompanied by a copy of the applicable collective agreement between the parties. . . .

---

64   *Canada Labour Code*, s. 155(1). The Supreme Court of Canada has held that the expression "by arbitration or otherwise" used in s. 155(1) imposes on the parties a statutory tribunal: *Roberval Express Limited v. Transport Drivers, Warehousemen and General Workers Union, Local 106*, [1982] 2 S.C.R. 888, 47 N.R. 34, 83 CLLC #14,023, 144 D.L.R. (3d) 673. *Volvo Canada Ltd. v. United Automobile, Aerospace and Agricultural Implement Workers of America (U.A.W.), Local 720* (1979), 79 CLLC #14,210, 33 N.S.R. (2d) 22, 57 A.P.R. 22, 27 N.R. 502 (S.C.C.).

65   *Shell Canada Ltd. v. United Oil Workers of Canada*, [1980] 2 S.C.R. 181.

66   *Canada Labour Code*, s. 155(2).

67   Section 155(3).

68   *Canada Industrial Relations Regulations*, C.R.C. 1978, c. 1012, s. 10.

Term of the Collective Agreement — Section 160

If the collective agreement is for a term of less than a year, or if it contains no provision as to its term, it is deemed to be for the term of one year from the date on which it comes into force.[69]

When two or more collective agreements are binding on the same employer, the parties to one of the agreements may jointly apply to the Board to alter the termination date of their agreement so that a common termination date may be established for all agreements.[70]

Union Security Clauses — Section 162

The parties may agree on provisions in the collective agreement that require membership in a specified trade union as a condition of employment,[71] or that grant preferential employment to members of a specified trade union.[72]

Where the bargaining agent so requests, compulsory check-off provisions providing that the employer deduct regular union dues from the wages of each employee in the bargaining unit and that the dues must be remitted to the union must be inserted in the collective agreement.[73] Regular union dues in respect of a member of the trade union are those that are regularly paid in accordance with the union's constitution and by-laws. In respect to employees who are not union members, dues are those paid by union members less the amount related to pension, superannuation, sickness insurance, or any other benefit available only to members of the union.[74]

An employee who objects to joining a union or to paying regular union dues to the union for reasons of religious conviction or beliefs may apply to the Board to obtain permission to pay an amount equal to the amount of the regular union dues into a registered charity that has been agreed to by the union. If the objecting employee and the union cannot agree on the charity, the matter is decided by the Board.[75]

8:2300 TECHNOLOGICAL CHANGES

The purpose of the provisions of the Code related to technological changes (ss. 149 to 153) is not to prevent the introduction of such changes

---

[69]   *Canada Labour Code,* s. 160(1)(a), (b).
[70]   Section 160(3).
[71]   Section 161(a).
[72]   Section 161(b).
[73]   Section 162(1). Section 162 has not always provided for a compulsory check-off. This new provision establishing a minimum union security in a form known as the Rand Formula came into force on July 18, 1984. The effect of the amendment was immediate. See *Okanagan Helicopters Ltd.* (1984), 85 CLLC #16,009.
[74]   Section 162(4).
[75]   Section 162(3), (4).

but rather to minimize the adverse effects of their implementation on employees.[76]

So far, the Board has rendered very few decisions under the latter provisions of the Code.[77] In *Ottawa-Carleton Regional Transit Commission* it discussed the historical background and the purpose of these provisions and denied the orders sought by an applicant union who wished to be granted permission to serve notice to bargain on the employer. The Board postponed its final decision in order to allow the parties to discuss the proposed change between themselves. In *Prince Rupert Grain Terminal Ltd.* the Board decided that the transfer of grain operations from an old grain elevator to a new one constituted a technological change as defined by s. 149(a) and (b). It also found that the employer had given notice pursuant to s. 150(2).

Sections 149 to 153 of the Code are analysed in the following paragraphs.

8:2310   Definition and Employer's Obligations

For the purpose of ss. 149 to 153, "technological change" is defined as meaning, pursuant to s. 149(1)(a),

(a) the introduction by an employer into his work, undertaking or business of equipment or material of a different nature or kind than that previously utilized by him in the operation of the work, undertaking or business; and
(b) a change in the manner in which the employer carries on the work, undertaking or business that is directly related to the introduction of that equipment or material.

Although the Board did not state it outright in *Ottawa-Carleton Regional Transit Commission,* the introduction of an automated vehicle monitoring system (A.V.M.), combined with a time communications and information system (T.I.C.C.S.), was considered to be a technological change. The Board found that technological change may take place progressively over a period of time.[78]

In *Prince Rupert Grain Terminal Ltd.* the Board found that the transfer of operations from one terminal, where the operations were performed manually, to a new computerized terminal constituted a technological change. The Board in doing so stated that paras. (a) and (b) of s. 149 must be read conjunctively. In assessing whether a change constituted a technological change as defined by s. 149(a) and (b), the Board answered three questions:

---

[76] On this subject see *Len Larmour* (1980), 41 di 110, [1980] 3 Can LRBR 407, where the Board discusses the policy and history of this legislation.

[77] *Ottawa-Carleton Regional Transit Commission* (1981), 45 di 365, 82 CLLC #16,143, [1982] 2 Can LRBR 172; *Prince Rupert Grain Terminal Ltd.* (1984), 9 CLRBR (NS) 1.

[78] *Ottawa-Carleton Regional Transit Commission, supra,* note 77, at pp. 397-98 (di).

1. What is the work, undertaking, or business of the employer?
2. Did the employer introduce some equipment or material of a nature or kind different from that previously utilized in the operation of the work?
3. Is there a change in the manner in which the employer carries out his business that is related to the introduction of that equipment or material?[79]

The Non-Application of Sections 150, 152, and 153

Section 150 provides that the employer bound by a collective agreement must give to the bargaining agent a 120-day notice of a proposed technological change. Section 152 authorizes a bargaining agent to apply to the Board when notice is given or deemed to be given for authorization to serve notice to bargain on the employer in regard to the proposed technological change and seniority-related issues. Section 153 bars the employer from effecting the proposed technological change until the Board has rendered a decision under s. 152 or, where the Board has authorized the bargaining agent to serve a notice to bargain, until the parties have concluded an agreement or have acquired the right to strike. These sections do not apply to an employer and a bargaining agent who are bound by a collective agreement[80] in any of the following cases:

1. a notice has been given that is substantially in accordance with s. 150(2)
    (i) prior to the day on which the parties entered into collective bargaining, if the notice to bargain was given under s. 146, *e.g.*, when no collective agreement is binding on the employees, or
    (ii) at least three months immediately preceding the date of expiration of the term of the collective agreement, or of any longer period provided for in the collective agreement, when the notice to bargain has been given under s. 147;[81]

    or
2. the collective agreement specifies procedures by which matters that relate to terms and conditions or security of employment likely to be affected by a technological change may be negotiated and settled during the term of the collective agreement;[82]

    or

---

79   *Prince Rupert Grain Terminal Ltd.*, *supra*, note 77.
80   *Canada Labour Code*, s. 149(2).
81   Section 149(2)(a).
82   Section 149(2)(b).

3. the collective agreement contains provisions that are intended to assist employees affected by a technological change to adjust to the effect of the change and that specify that ss. 150, 152, and 153 do not apply during the term of the collective agreement.[83]

Employers to Whom a Requirement to Give Notice of Technological Change Applies

Where ss. 150, 152, and 153 are applicable, the employer is bound to give a notice of at least 120 days prior to implementing the technological change when the following circumstances are present:

1. The employer is *bound* by a collective agreement and
2. he proposes to effect a *technological change*
3. *as defined* by s. 149(1)
4. which is *likely* to affect
5. the terms and conditions *or* security of employment
6. of a *significant* number[84]
7. of *his* employees
8. *to whom* the collective agreement applies.[85]

The notice must be in writing and must state, in accordance with s. 150(2):

(a) the nature of the technological change;

(b) the date upon which the employer proposes to effect the technological change;

(c) the approximate number and type of employees likely to be affected by the technological change;

(d) the effect that the technological change is likely to have on the terms and conditions or security of employment of the employees affected; and

(e) such other information as it is required by the regulations made pursuant to subsection (3).[86]

There are currently no regulations made by the governor in council under s. 150(3).

---

[83] Section 149(2)(c).

[84] See the reference in s. 152(2)(b) to "significant number" and "affect substantially and adversely", both discussed at paragraph 8:2322.

[85] Section 150(1).

[86] Section 150(3): "The Governor in Council, on the recommendation of the Board, may make regulations (a) specifying the number of employees or the method of determining the number of employees that shall, in respect of any federal work, undertaking or business or any type of federal work, undertaking or business, be deemed to be 'significant' for the purposes of subsection (1) and subsection 152(2); and (b) requiring any information in addition to the information required by subsection (2) to be included in a notice of technological change."

The notice must be stylized, in writing, and contain the information required by s. 150(2). It is not sufficient for the employer to have sent letters to all employees and the union informing them of the new operation and to have held discussions with the union.[87]

Furthermore, an employer that has given the required notice must on request provide to the bargaining agent a written statement, setting out in accordance with s. 150(2.1):

(a) a detailed description of the nature of the proposed technological change;

(b) the names of the employees who will initially be likely to be affected by the proposed technological change; and

(c) the rationale for the change.

8:2320   Role and Jurisdiction of the Board

The Board may be involved in technological change proceedings where a bargaining agent requests it to determine that the employer should have given the notice required by s. 150 and, when notice has been given or is deemed to have been given, to authorize the bargaining agent to serve notice to bargain on the employer.[88]

8:2321   Application to the Board under Section 151

A bargaining agent may apply to the Board within thirty days from the date it became aware or, in the opinion of the Board ought to have become aware, of the failure of the employer to give the notice of technological change provided for in s. 150.

The bargaining agent's application must allege that

(a)   sections 150, 152, and 153 apply to the employer, and that

(b)   the employer has failed to comply with s. 150.[89]

In *Ottawa-Carleton Regional Transit Commission*[90] the Board held that the reference to ss. 150, 152, and 153 contained in s. 151 was merely a matter of establishing the Board's jurisdiction and did not require that the criteria of ss. 152 and 153 be met before the Board could make an order under s. 151(2). The Board's jurisdiction is to be established by verifying whether or not the employer is excluded from the application of the technological changes provisions as stated in s. 149(2).

After affording the parties the opportunity to be heard, the Board may, by order pursuant to s. 151(2),

---

[87]   *Prince Rupert Grain Terminal Ltd., supra,* note 77.
[88]   Section 151(2), (4).
[89]   Section 151(1).
[90]   *Supra,* note 77, at p. 387 (di).

(a) determine that sections 150, 152 and 153 do not apply to the employer in respect of the alleged technological change; or

(b) determine that sections 150, 152 and 153 apply to the employer in respect of the alleged technological change and that the employer has failed to comply with section 150 in respect of the technological change.

When the Board makes such a determination, the employer is deemed to have given a notice under s. 150 and the Board must in a concurrent order grant leave to the bargaining agent to serve notice on the employer to commence collective bargaining for the purpose set out in s. 152(1).[91]

The Board may also, pursuant to s. 151(3), after consultation with the parties[92] and *before* deciding whether the employer was required to give the notice, or after having so decided pursuant to s. 151(2)(b),

(a) direct the employer not to proceed with the technological change or alleged technological change for such period, not in excess of ninety days, as the Board considers appropriate;

(b) require the reinstatement of any employees displaced by the employer as a result of the technological change; and

(c) where an employee is reinstated pursuant to paragraph (b), require the employer to reimburse the employee for any loss of pay suffered by the employee as a result of his displacement.

8:2322 Application to the Board under Section 152

When a bargaining agent has received notice of a technological change[93] it may, within thirty days of the reception of the notice, apply to the Board seeking leave to serve notice to bargain on the employer

1. to review the existing provisions of the collective agreement related to terms and conditions or security of employment, or

2. to include new provisions in the collective agreement to assist the employees affected by the technological change to adjust to the effect of these changes.[94]

The Board may grant leave to the bargaining agent to serve such a notice to bargain when the following conditions have been met:[95]

(i) it has received an *application* to that effect, and

(ii) the *technological change* contemplated by the notice

(iii) is *likely*

(iv) to *substantially* and *adversely*

(v) *affect*

---

[91] Section 151(4).
[92] The Code does not require the consent of the parties.
[93] In accordance with s. 150.
[94] Section 152(1).
[95] Section 152(2).

(vi) the terms and conditions *or* security of employment

(vii) of a *significant* number of employees to which the collective agreement applies.[96]

Even when all the conditions have been met, the Board has the discretion to make or deny the order, or to stay its execution. In practice, and as evidenced by the conclusion arrived at in *Ottawa-Carleton Regional Transit Commission*,[97] the Board's discretion will be exercised in a manner that in its opinion is compatible with the objectives of the Code.

When an application is made under s. 152(1), the employer cannot effect the proposed technological change until

1.   the Board has refused leave to give notice to bargain, or

2.   following leave to serve notice to bargain, the parties have:

   (a) reached an agreement, or

   (b) acquired the right to strike or lockout.

8:3000   STATUTORY JURISDICTION AND POWERS OF THE ARBITRATOR

8:3100   GENERALLY

The arbitrator appointed by the minister is deemed to have been appointed pursuant to the collective agreement.[98] The arbitrator or arbitration board must give the parties an opportunity to present evidence and make submissions.[99]

The arbitrator has the power:

---

[96]   In regard to the question of determining the extent to which employees are affected both qualitatively and quantitatively, the Board, in *Ottawa-Carleton Regional Transit Commission* (1981), 45 di 365, at 398, 82 CLLC #16,143, [1982] 2 Can LRBR 172, said: "In a similar vein the Board must not narrow its sights so that it concentrates only on those directly affected by the change. Although the change must be *'directly related to the introduction'* of equipment or material (section 149(1)(b)), the effect upon employees may be both direct, as in the case of the despatchers and inspectors, or indirect, as in the case of others. . . . The qualitative measure of the change as *'substantially and adversely'* affecting employees may not be directly related to whether the change is major or minor, in the words of the Woods Task Force (Canadian Industrial Relations . . . p. 194-6. See also *Re International Nickel Company of Canada Limited* (1972), 1 L.A.C. (2d) 85 (Weatherill)). It may be a measure of the extent of effect on some individuals. In this respect the vague compartmentalizing of the quantity of impact (*"significant number"*) and quality of impact (*"substantially and adversely"*) serve to emphasize the overriding discretionary authority of the Board to balance competing interests and legislative purposes when deciding to issue orders under either sections 151 or 152. . . . An important factual ingredient influencing that decision must be the extent to which the employer had adhered to the advance notice spirit of the Code which seeks to promote early exchange of information and discussion — 'at *least* ninety days prior' [120 days, since July 1984] (section 151)."

[97]   *Supra*, note 96, at p. 399 (di).

[98]   *Canada Labour Code*, s. 155(4).

[99]   Section 157(a).

1. to determine his own procedure;
2. to summon and enforce the attendance of witnesses and compel them to give oral or written evidence on oath and to produce such documents and things as he deems requisite to the full investigation and consideration of any matter within his jurisdiction that is before him;
3. to administer oaths and solemn affirmations;
4. to receive and accept such evidence and information on oath, affidavit, or otherwise, as he sees fit, whether or not it would be admissible in a court of law.[100]

The arbitrator has jurisdiction to determine any question as to whether a matter referred to him is arbitrable.[101] Where the arbitrator has determined that an employee has been discharged or disciplined for cause, and the collective agreement does not provide a specific penalty for the infraction, he has the power to substitute for the penalty imposed by the employer any other that he deems just and reasonable in the circumstances.[102]

The arbitrator's jurisdiction is statutorily maintained in regard to differences that arise after the collective agreement has expired but before the parties acquire the legal right to strike or lockout. This is provided for by s. 160(4) and (5).[103]

The Code confers on the arbitrator the jurisdiction to settle differences arising out of the interpretation, application, administration, or alleged violation of a collective agreement. Parties to the collective agreement cannot agree between themselves that certain differences may not be arbitrable, unless they have agreed to peaceful means other than arbitration for the resolution of their differences.[104]

However, when a question arises that relates to the existence of a collective agreement or to the identification of the parties or employees bound by a collective agreement, the arbitrator or board may refer the question to the Canada Labour Relations Board for hearing and determination. In such a case, the arbitrator or the Board may suspend the arbitration proceedings.[105]

---

[100] Section 157(b).
[101] Section 157(c).
[102] Section 157(d). *Port Arthur Shipbuilding Co. v. Arthurs*, [1969] S.C.R. 85, 70 D.L.R. (2d) 693; *Heustis v. New Brunswick Electric Power Commission*, [1979] 2 S.C.R. 768, 27 N.R. 103, 25 N.B.R. (2d) 613, 51 A.P.R. 613, 79 CLLC #15,000, 98 D.L.R. (3d) 622; *Blouin Drywall Contractors Ltd. v. United Brotherhood of Carpenters and Joiners of America* (1975), 8 O.R. (2d) 103, 75 CLLC #14,195, 57 D.L.R. (3d) 199 (C.A.).
[103] On this subject, see *Bell Canada* (1981), 43 di 238, at 246 and 250, [1981] 2 Can LRBR 284, 81 CLLC #16,099.
[104] *Larry Elliston* (1982), 47 di 103, [1982] 2 Can LRBR 241. In this case, the Board found that because of the provisions of s. 155, the discharge of a probationary employee is arbitrable even when the parties have provided otherwise. See also, in this connection, *Transair Ltd.* (1978), 27 di 739, [1978] 2 Can LRBR 354.
[105] Section 158(1), (2). See also paragraph 8:4000.

8:3200   DECISION OF THE ARBITRATOR

When the difference has been submitted to an arbitration board, decisions are taken on a majority basis, but if there is no majority, the decision of the chairman is binding.[106] The arbitrator's decision is final and is protected by a privative clause.[107] However, notwithstanding the existence of this privative clause and the wording of s. 155(1), the arbitrator or arbitration board is considered to be a statutory tribunal,[108] and the decision may therefore be the object of a judicial review.[109]

The arbitral award must be rendered within sixty days of the appointment of the chairman, unless the collective agreement provides otherwise or the parties consent to an extension.[110] However, the failure by the arbitrator to render his decision within the sixty days does not affect his jurisdiction, nor does it invalidate his decision.[111] The arbitrator must file his award with the minister within fifteen days of the date it is rendered.[112]

8:3300   FILING OF THE ARBITRAL AWARD IN COURT

Any person or organization affected by any arbitrator's decision or who wishes to enforce the terms of the decision may do so by filing a copy of the arbitration order, exclusive of reasons, in the Federal Court of Canada.[113] The order may be registered in the court after fourteen days from the date of the decision or the date of compliance set out in the award. Upon registration it will have the same force and effect as a judgment of the court.[114]

---

[106] Section 157.1.
[107] Section 156.
[108] *Roberval Express Ltd. v. Transport Drivers, Warehousemen and General Workers Union, Local 106*, [1982] 2 S.C.R. 888, 47 N.R. 34, 83 CLLC #14,023, 144 D.L.R. (3d) 673.
[109] *Bell Canada v. Office and Professional Employees' International Union, Local 131*, [1974] S.C.R. 335, 37 D.L.R. (3d) 561; *Metropolitan Toronto Police Association v. Metropolitan Toronto Board of Commissioners of Police*, [1975] 1 S.C.R. 630, 2 N.R. 95, 74 CLLC #14,223, 45 D.L.R. (3d) 548; *Association of Radio and Television Employees of Canada (CUPE — CLC) v. Canadian Broadcasting Corp.*, [1975] 1 S.C.R. 118; *Air-Care Ltd. v. United Steel Workers of America*, [1976] 1 S.C.R. 2, 3 N.R. 267, 49 D.L.R. (3d) 467; *Syndicat des professeurs du Collège d'Enseignement général et professionel du Vieux-Montréal v. College d'Enseignement général et professionnel du Vieux-Montréal*, [1977] 2 S.C.R. 568, 76 CLLC #14,030, 74 D.L.R. (3d) 685; *United Steelworkers of America, Local 4589 v. Bombardier — M.L.W. Ltée*, [1980] 1 S.C.R. 905; *R. v. Leeming*, [1981] 1 S.C.R. 129, 34 N.R. 480, 33 N.B.R. (2d) 490, 80 A.P.R. 490, 81 CLLC #14,087, 118 D.L.R. (3d) 202; *Miriam Home v. Canadian Union of Public Employees, Local 2115*, not yet reported, March 14, 1985 (S.C.C.).
[110] Canada Labour Code, ss. 257.3(1) and 157.3(2).
[111] Section 157.3(3).
[112] Section 156.1; and *Canada Industrial Relations Regulations*, C.R.C. 1978, c. 1012, s. 11.
[113] *Canada Labour Code*, s. 159(1).
[114] Section 159(2). See *Banque Nationale du Canada v. Granda*, not yet reported, April 19, 1984, file nos. A-1690-83 and A-137-84 (Fed. C.A.), where it was decided by the

8:3400   REMUNERATION OF THE ARBITRATOR

The parties to an arbitration proceeding must each bear half of the fees and expenses of the arbitrator or chairman of the arbitration board, unless this is otherwise provided for in the collective agreement. Each party is responsible for its own costs and for the fees and expenses of its nominee on the arbitration board.[115]

8:4000   REFERENCE TO THE BOARD OF MATTERS RAISED IN ARBITRATION

Section 158(1) permits the arbitration board, the Minister of Labour, or any alleged party to an arbitration proceeding to refer to the Canada Labour Relations Board two specific issues that are fundamental to the jurisdiction of an arbitrator or arbitration board. These issues are: "the existence of a collective agreement" and "the identification of the parties or employees bound by a collective agreement". It is uncertain whether or not questions related to these issues can form the subject-matter of an independent proceeding before the Board under s. 118(p)(vi), (vii), and (viii) in view of the wording of the opening part of s. 158(1), which speaks of "any question that may arise in the proceeding". Section 158(1) removes any doubt to this effect.

A reference can be made by either the arbitrator or arbitration board, the minister, and any alleged party. The meaning of the words "any alleged party" in s. 158(1) arose in a case where a jurisdictional or work-assignment dispute had been submitted at arbitration by one of the competing unions. The other union made a reference to the Board under s. 158(1), arguing that its interest might be affected by the arbitrator's decision and that, accordingly, it should have access to the Board under the provisions of that section. The Board held that the words "any alleged party" meant an "alleged party to the collective agreement" rather than "a potential party to an arbitration". Thus the applicant was not a party authorized to make a reference under s. 158(1). The Board stressed, however, that in any event the applicant was likely to have access to the Board through a reference made either by the arbitrator or the employer.[116] The latter as well as the minister are independently given the right to make a reference under s. 158(1). The fact that the arbitrator declines to do so cannot preclude the employer from so doing.

On the issue of jurisdiction over the questions encompassed by s. 158(1), the Board held in earlier decisions that it had exclusive jurisdic-

---

115   Federal Court of Appeal that the trial division had jurisdiction to stay the execution of an arbitrator's award filed pursuant to s. 61.5(12), which is a provision similar to s. 159(2).
115   Section 157.2.
116   *Northern-Loram — Joint Venture*, decision no. 498, not yet reported, January 21, 1985 (C.L.R.B.).

tion over these subject-matters.[117] This conclusion was reached on the basis of s. 118(p)(vi), (vii), and (viii). However, the Board pointed out in *Northern-Loram-Joint Venture*[118] that if that was the case, the arbitrator would be bound to make a reference whenever a question encompassed by s. 158(1) arose. Since that section permits a person other than the arbitrator to make a reference, it had to be inferred that the arbitrator is under no obligation to do so. As a result, the Board held in the latter case that it had a concurrent jurisdiction with arbitrators to determine the questions encompassed by s. 158(1), but that in the circumstances of each case, there are clear policy reasons dictating which forum is preferable. For instance, where the answer to the question covered by s. 158(1) depends on the interpretation of a provision of the Code, the Board has an obvious interest in the matter. The same applies to the interpretation of certification orders, given the Board's policy that certificates have a continuing effect and its position that it has a supervisory role in relation to them. In such circumstances, the Board normally expects an arbitrator to defer to it just as, in appropriate cases, the Board will defer to the arbitrator under s. 188(2) of the Code.

Once a reference is made, the Board's role under s. 158 is simply to answer the referred question. The Board does not dispose of the grievance. After its determination is made, the matter goes back to the arbitrator, who has jurisdiction to consider the grievance and to order any remedy that may be appropriate. However, the arbitrator is bound by any answer given by the Board to the referred question and must dispose of the grievance in light of the Board's determination.

In *Radio CJYQ-930 Ltd.*,[119] a case decided before *Northern-Loram Joint Venture*, the Board stated that s. 158(1) does not impose a deadline to make a reference. Furthermore, the Board expressed the opinion that, presumably, a reference might even be made after an arbitration board has rendered an award dealing with a question encompassed by s. 158(1). In support of this opinion, the Board referred to s. 158(2) and stated that the latter, by permitting the suspension of the arbitration proceeding, provides an element of supervision when the arbitrator has become involved in matters raising the determination of questions reserved to the Board. Although the Board has not discussed this issue in its *Northern-Loram-Joint Venture* policy decision, it is doubtful the Board would entertain the same opinion today. Indeed, the *Radio CJYQ-930 Ltd.* decision was rendered in an era when the Board had taken the position that it had exclusive jurisdiction over the matters mentioned in s. 158(1). More fundamentally, it would appear that once the arbitrator has made a decision, whether by final or interim award, on a matter mentioned in s.

---

117   *Radio CJYQ-930 Ltd.* (1978), 34 di 617, [1979] 2 Can LRBR 233; *Bell Canada* (1981), 43 di 86, [1982] 3 Can LRBR 113; *Bell Canada* (1982), 50 di 105.
118   *Supra*, note 116.
119   *Radio CJYQ-930 Ltd.*, *supra*, note 117.

158(1), the purpose of the machinery provided in that section is spent. To suggest that a reference to the Board might be made after the arbitrator has rendered such an award is equivalent to saying that s. 158(1) creates a statutory right of appeal, which it does not. As a result, one would be inclined to think that a reference to the Board under s. 158(1) made after the arbitrator has rendered his award dealing with a question mentioned in that section would not be entertained by the Board.

For the purpose of making its determination under s. 158(1), the Board is given a limited jurisdiction to interpret a collective agreement.[120] If there is an issue as to the existence of a collective agreement, the Board may examine and interpret the termination provisions. If there is an issue as to whether an employer or union is bound by the agreement, the Board may have to examine and interpret the provisions relating to the identifiction of the parties who are bound by the agreement, provisions relating to successorship, and other provisions. Similarly, if there is an issue as to the identification of employees bound by a collective agreement, it is not possible for the Board to avoid interpreting the scope clause of a collective agreement. The Board's jurisdiction to interpret a collective agreement does not extend, however, to the determination of how a collective agreement applies. For instance the Board may interpret the collective agreement to determine whether certain persons are bound by a collective agreement but it cannot determine how they are bound.[121] Where two or more collective agreements overlap, the Board has the power to determine whether those parts of the collective agreements, *i.e.*, the parts that overlap, are legally invalid insofar as they purport to apply to disputed employees.[122] The Board may also look at any and all collective agreements that are relevant in identifying the parties bound by a collective agreement, and it is not limited only to the particular agreement whose application gave rise to the grievance.[123]

Where the Board interprets a bargaining certificate to determine whether employees are covered by a collective agreement, the Board may also decide, either on its own initiative or pursuant to a party's request, that a review of the entire certificate is appropriate. In such cases, the basis of the Board's procedure for enlarging the inquiry originally undertaken under s. 158 lies in the power of review conferred by s. 119. The Board has justified the exercise of this discretionary power by the fact that the parties are faced with a problem more fundamental than a simple question of the application of the collective agreement. This kind of problem is one which necessitates a review of the bargaining rights

---

120   *Bell Canada, supra,* note 117; *Northern-Loram-Joint Venture, supra,* note 116.
121   *CJMS Radio Montréal (Québec) Ltée* (1979), 34 di 803, [1980] 1 Can LRBR 170.
122   *Eastern Provincial Airways (1963) Ltd.* (1978), 30 di 82, [1978] 2 Can LRBR 572; see *Société Radio-Canada v. Canada Labour Relations Board,* not yet reported, January 22, 1985, file no. A-467-82 (Fed. C.A.); and *Re Union des Artistes and Canadian Union of Public Employees,* not yet reported, January 22, 1985, file no. A-725-82 (Fed. C.A.).
123   *Eastern Provincial Airways (1963) Ltd., supra,* note 122.

granted to the union by the original certificates.[124] Such is the case where, in the course of its inquiry under s. 158, it becomes apparent to the Board that a reorganization of the employer's enterprise and the resulting creation of new positions might generate further disputes with respect to the application of the agreement.[125]

So far, referrals have been made to the Board where grievances raised questions of (i) the extraterritorial application of a collective agreement;[126] (ii) the coverage or application of a collective agreement to newly created functions;[127] (iii) the application of a collective agreement to certain employees in the context of the sale of part of a business;[128] and (iv) the application of one or another of the collective agreements to disputed functions in work-assignment or jurisdictional disputes.[129]

8:5000   IMPOSITION OF A FIRST COLLECTIVE AGREEMENT

Division V of Part V of the *Canada Labour Code*, which includes ss. 163 to 178, deals with conciliation and first agreements. This division empowers the conciliation and mediation branch of the Department of Labour, under certain conditions, to appoint conciliators, conciliation commissioners, and conciliation boards to assist parties who are unable to conclude a collective agreement by themselves. The Board is not involved in this process except when directed by the minister under s. 171.1 to inquire into the dispute and, if advisable, to settle the terms and conditions of the first collective agreement between the parties.

8:5100   MINISTER OF LABOUR'S INVOLVEMENT

An employee or a bargaining agent who is required to bargain collectively may apply to the minister in order that the Board be ordered to inquire into the dispute and impose a collective agreement. It is important to note that the minister may refer the matter to the Board even when the parties have not requested him to do so.[130] Section 171.1 provides the prerequisites that must be satisfied before the minister may refer the matter to the Board:

1.   The bargaining agent must be certified.

---

124   *Regional Harbours Board* (1980), 41 di 126, [1980] 3 Can LRBR 265.
125   *Télé-Métropole Inc.* (1980), 41 di 286.
126   *Bell Canada* (1981), 43 di 86, [1982] Can LRBR 113.
127   *British Columbia Telephone Co.* (1979), 38 di 14, [1979] 3 Can LRBR 350; *Télé-Métropole Inc., supra,* note 125.
128   *Radio CJYQ-930 Ltd.* (1978), 34 di 617, [1979] 2 Can LRBR 233; *Bell Canada* (1981), 43 di 238, [1981] 2 Can LRBR 284, 81 CLLC #16,099.
129   The Board's jurisdiction under s. 158(1) to deal with jurisdictional or work assignment disputes is discussed in paragraph 6:2320.
130   *Banque Royale du Canada (Kénogami, Québec)* (1980), 41 di 199, [1982] 1 Can LRBR 16.

2.   A notice to bargain under s. 146 must have been sent.
3.   The dispute between the parties must concern the settlement of the first collective agreement between them.
4.   The requirements of s. 180(1)(a) to (d) must have been met. Or, put another way, the parties must have acquired the right to strike or lockout.

When these requisites have been met, the minister has the discretion to refer the matter to the Board. There currently exist no guidelines or interpretation policies from the minister's office in regard to the exercise of this discretion. If the minister does not find it advisable to refer the matter to the Board, then the latter will not be involved. If, on the contrary, the minister feels that it is desirable to refer the dispute to the Board, the parties are so advised in writing and an order is directed to the Board enjoining it to inquire into the dispute and to settle the terms of the first collective agreement if the Board should determine that this is appropriate.

8:5200   THE JURISDICTION OF THE CANADA LABOUR RELATIONS BOARD

Upon receipt of an order from the minister pursuant to s. 171.1, the Board appoints an investigating officer to gather the pertinent information. The investigating officer contacts the parties and compiles the history of their relationship from the outset to the date of the inquiry. He gathers information on the ongoing negotiations, such as proposals and counter-proposals, and tries to isolate the issues still remaining in dispute. The investigating officer may also attempt to mediate the issues if he deems it advisable. He also gathers information concerning other collective agreements in the industry or the region to assist the Board in settling the terms of the collective agreement.

In the meantime, the parties are requested to exchange their respective positions in writing. When the information has been gathered, the file is then placed before the Board for decision. There is no obligation on the part of the Board to hold a hearing. In practice, however, the Board has, where reasons for decision were given, called a hearing on each occasion.[131]

The Board has stated[132] that it derives its jurisdiction from the Minister's order and therefore does not have to verify that the prerequisites to the minister's own jurisdiction have been met.

---

[131]   *CJMS Radio Montréal Ltée* (1978), 27 di 796, [1970] 1 Can LRBR 332; *Banque Royale du Canada (Kénogami, Québec), supra,* note 130; *Maclean-Hunter Cable TV Ltd.* (1980), 42 di 274, [1981] 1 Can LRBR 454; *Huron Broadcasting Ltd.* (1982), 49 di 68, [1982] 2 Can LRBR 227; *Fort Alexander Indian Band,* decision no. 462, not yet reported, August 23, 1984 (C.L.R.B.). The hearings lasted from one to three weeks.
[132]   *CJMS Radio Montréal Ltée, supra,* note 131, at p. 837 (di).

8:5210   Decision to Impose

The Board's decision on the imposition of a first collective agreement is entirely discretionary. The Board has stated that s. 171.1 must be viewed in the context of free collective bargaining that promotes responsibility, lucidity, and reason on the part of the parties, and that it will impose a collective agreement only in exceptional cases.[133] The Board has interpreted s. 171.1 in a restrictive manner.[134] The fact that a strike or lockout is ongoing is not a determinative factor *per se* in the Board's decision to impose an agreement.[135]

The Board views s. 171.1 as a remedy against bad faith and intransigence. It may take into account the fact that the parties have or have not bargained in good faith. This factor is not essential, and the Board may impose an agreement regardless of bad faith.[136] In *Banque Royale du Canada (Kénogami, Québec)*[137] the Board distinguished between bad-faith bargaining and hard bargaining. Bad-faith bargaining will be inferred from circumstantial evidence, and it will be decided on the facts of each case.[138] The Board has said that, in reaching its decision, it will look at the parties' relationship from the time certification is sought to the time of the hearing, including their relationship at the bargaining table.[139] It has also stated that s. 171.1 is not a means to equilibrate the relative force of the parties engaged in collective bargaining, and that there may be a winner and a loser in each contest.

In *CJMS Radio Montréal Ltée*[140] the Board found the situation to be exceptional and arrived at the conclusion that the relationship between the parties was such that it had to impose an agreement to break the impasse. The parties were not on speaking terms, and the Board characterized the situation as total warfare, where rational collective bargaining was impossible.

In *Huron Broadcasting Ltd.*[141] the Board found to be determinant the fact that the employer had initiated petitions to foil the union's application for certification and that, subsequent to the certification, it had tried to influence the employees in their choice of representatives on the bargaining committee. Furthermore, the employer had communicated directly with the employees in a manner aimed at undermining the

---

[133]   *Ibid.*, at 833, 838, 846. See paragraphs 12:2120 to 12:2500, where the duty to bargain in good faith and the obligation to make every reasonable effort to conclude a collective agreement is discussed.
[134]   *Ibid.*, at 836.
[135]   *Ibid.*
[136]   *Huron Broadcasting Ltd.*, *supra*, note 131; *CJMS Radio Montréal Ltée*, *supra*, note 131.
[137]   *Supra*, note 130.
[138]   See also *Huron Broadcasting Ltd.*, *supra*, note 131.
[139]   *Supra*, note 130, at p. 212 *et seq.*
[140]   *Supra*, note 131.
[141]   *Ibid.*

union's authority. The Board came to the conclusion that the employer's concessions at the bargaining table were minimal and were directed merely at gaining time, as the employer never really wished to enter into a collective agreement.

In *Fort Alexander Indian Band*,[142] where the Band council, following certification, did not accept the jurisdiction of the Board or of the Code and thus did not negotiate with the certified bargaining agent, the Board did impose a first collective agreement.

In *Banque Royale du Canada (Kénogami, Québec)*[143] the Board did not impose an agreement because it came to the conclusion that the differences between the parties were negotiable and that the union's attitude, as manifested by an illegal strike and bargaining through the media, was mainly responsible for the impasse. The Board found also that the employer's direct communication with his employees through letters was not a factor in the context, where the union was in a legal strike position and where no negotiation sessions were scheduled. The Board came to the conclusion that the union, which had neither requested the minister to impose an agreement nor filed an unfair labour practice complaint regarding bad-faith bargaining, merely wanted to use the proceeding to get what it could not obtain through negotiation.

In *Maclean-Hunter Cable TV Ltd.*[144] the Board refused to impose an agreement because it believed that the union was trying to use s. 171.1 as a bargaining tool. In that case, the union had gone on strike when only seven of the eighteen bargaining unit members had approved the strike, and it had applied to the minister for referral to the Board when, on the first day of picketing, eleven members of the unit had crossed the picket line. The Board noted that, although the employer had been found guilty of unfair labour practices at the certification stage, it had complied with the Board's remedial orders and no subsequent unfair labour practice complaints in regard to bad-faith bargaining had been brought by the union. The Board further said that the employer was ready to sign a collective agreement, albeit on his own terms, but that it was difficult to ask the employer to make concessions when he was aware the union was negotiating from a minority position.

8:5220   Decision Fixing Terms and Conditions

In settling the terms of a first collective agreement, the Board may take into account the extent to which the parties have or have not bargained in good faith,[145] the terms and conditions of employment

---

142   *Ibid.*
143   *Supra*, note 130.
144   *Supra*, note 131.
145   *Canada Labour Code*, s. 171.1(3)(a).

negotiated by employees performing the same or similar functions in the same or similar circumstances,[146] and other such matters as may be fair and reasonable in the circumstances.[147] Section 171.1(4) provides that the terms of the collective agreement imposed by the Board shall not exceed one year from the date on which the Board imposes the agreement. Although the Board has not yet made a decision on this point, s. 171.1(4) implies that the Board's decision would not have a retroactive effect. The Board has stated that it will not be innovative and will stay as close as possible to the positions expressed by the parties. The Board has not published the terms and conditions of any of the collective agreements that it has so far imposed, but on two occasions it incorporated into the agreement back-to-work provisions.[148] Section 171.1(2) provides that the parties are bound by the collective agreement imposed by the Board, but that they may amend it by agreement in writing. In the *Canada Labour Code*, there are no express provisions granting power to the Board to impose a return-to-work "agreement". When the Board did so, it made the "agreement" an integral part of the collective agreement.[149]

---

[146] Section 171.1.3(b).

[147] Section 171.1.2(c).

[148] *CJMS Radio Montréal Ltée, supra*, note 131. In *Huron Broadcasting Ltd., supra*, note 131, the back-to-work "agreement" is reproduced at the end of the decision.

[149] It is not settled law whether a return-to-work agreement separate or part of the imposed first collective agreement is a work condition. Assuming it is not, it is doubtful that s. 121 alone can support the Board's jurisdiction to impose such a return-to-work agreement. On this matter, see *Syndicat des employés de production du Québec et de l'Acadie v. Canada Labour Relations Board*, [1984] 2 S.C.R. 412.

CHAPTER 9

ILLEGAL STRIKES AND LOCKOUTS

9:0000 ILLEGAL STRIKES AND LOCKOUTS

The *Canada Labour Code* provides that the parties may legally resort to the ultimate economic weapons of strike and lockout to resolve their collective bargaining differences. However, the use of such economic weapons is strictly regulated.[1] The Code authorizes the parties to resort to a strike or lockout only after they have had the opportunity of obtaining the assistance of officers of the conciliation and mediation branch of the Department of Labour. If differences between the parties arise when a collective agreement is, or is deemed to be, in force,[2] they must be settled by arbitration or by means other than a stoppage of work.[3] If no collective agreement is in force and the conditions set out in s. 180(1)(a) to (d) have been met, then, and only then, may the parties legally resort to strike or lockout action.

Sections 182, 183, and 183.1 give jurisdiction to the Board to intervene in case of an illegal strike or lockout, that is, when the conditions set out at s. 180(1)(a) to (d) have not been met. In such cases, the Board may declare that the strike or lockout is illegal and may issue cease and desist orders enjoining the parties to refrain from their illegal actions.

This chapter deals with the jurisdiction of the Board, the procedure it has established to process applications concerning illegal strikes and lockouts, and its powers to remedy such illegal actions as provided in ss. 182, 183, and 183.1. The definition of a strike and lockout under the Code is examined, as is the jurisdiction of the Board under the Code. The discussion then deals with the procedure followed by the Board in dealing with applications alleging illegal strikes or lockouts and with the Board's remedial powers.

9:1000 DEFINITIONS

9:1100 STRIKE

Section 107(1) defines the word "strike" as including

---

[1]   *Canada Labour Code*, s. 180(1)(a) to (d).
[2]   Section 160(5).
[3]   Section 155.

(a) a cessation of work or a refusal to work or to continue to work by employees, in combination or in concert or in accordance with a common understanding, and

(b) a slowdown of work or other concerted activity on the part of employees in relation to their work that is designed to restrict or limit output. . . .

From the outset the Board has considered this definition to be an objective one and has stated that the motivation or objective pursued by the parties is not an element of the definition.[4] This approach was confirmed by the Supreme Court of Canada.[5] On the issue of motivation, the Board found that a concerted ban on overtime, even though voluntary under the collective agreement, constituted a strike regardless of the motivation of the employees or the union.[6] This view, however, is not unanimous, and certain panels of the Board have interpreted the definition of a strike as containing subjective elements.

In *British Columbia Telephone Co.*[7] the Board reviewed the definitions of a strike in the various provincial statutes and concluded that the requirement of objective or subjective elements varied from province to province, depending on the particular wording of the statute. In that case, the parties were at the conciliation stage and the prerequisites of s. 180(1)(a) to (d) had not been met. The employer announced that it might have to proceed with layoffs. The union responded by instituting a ban on overtime, and the employer applied to the Board under s. 182. There was no doubt that the activities by the employees were concerted. One member of the panel found that the ban on overtime, which had not been alleged to be contrary to the collective agreement or to any purposes related to collective bargaining, was designed to restrict or limit output, but he felt that it should be considered as "an understandable response to a threatened loss of jobs".[8] Another member found the overtime ban not to constitute a strike because the collective agreement

---

4   *Cyprus Anvil Mining Corp.* (1976), 15 di 194, at 210, [1976] 2 Can LRBR 360, 76 CLLC #16,045; *Société Radio-Canada* (1980), 40 di 35, at 45, [1981] 2 Can LRBR 52; *Canada Post Corp.* (1983), 54 di 152, 5 CLRBR (NS) 280; *Canadian Pacific Ltd.* (1980), 39 di 138, [1980] 3 Can LRBR 87, 80 CLLC #16,059. In the latter case the Board dealt with an application for a declaration of an illegal lockout, and in the course of the discussion said that, unlike a strike, a lockout required a specific motivation. In *Radiodiffusion Mutuelle Ltée* (1977), 18 di 56, at 63, the Board said that s. 182 was not concerned with the nature of a strike in itself.

5   *International Longshoremen's Association, Local 273 v. Maritime Employers' Association,* [1979] 1 S.C.R. 120, at 137-39, 23 N.R. 386, 23 N.B.R. (2d) 458, 78 CLLC #14,171, 89 D.L.R. (3d) 289.

6   *Société Radio-Canada* (1980), 40 di 35, [1981] 2 Can LRBR 52. On the question of whether a ban on overtime constituted a strike, the Federal Court of Appeal in *Le Syndicat des employés de production du Québec et de l'Acadie v. Canada Labour Relations Board*, [1982] 1 F.C. 471, sitting in review of the decision of the Board, confirmed that the Board had jurisdiction to determine what action constituted a strike. The Federal Court decision was affirmed by the Supreme Court of Canada at [1984] 2 S.C.R. 412. See also *Air Canada* (1984), 8 CLRBR (NS) 397.

7   (1980), 40 di 163, [1980] 3 Can LRBR 31, 80 CLLC #16,062.

8   *Ibid.*, at p. 177 (di).

permitted voluntary overtime, and the fact that the activities were concerted did not take away the negotiated right. The third member found the ban to constitute a strike.

In *Canadian Pacific Ltd.*[9] the employees had changed working procedures, particularly in regard to lunch breaks, with the result that work which took from seven-and-a-half to eight hours to perform prior to the change of work procedures now required from eleven to twelve hours. The Board found that there was a strike, as the members and officers of the union had acted in concert, "with the express aim of compelling C.P. Rail to negotiate conditions of employment". The Board mentioned in its discussion that the real strike issue could not be disguised by the fact that an employee could not be punished under the collective agreement for taking meal breaks or for compliance with other regulations.[10]

In *Canadian Broadcasting Corp.*[11] the Board continued its shift away from the objective definition. In this case the union members had refused to cross the legal picket line of the members of another bargaining unit of the same employer. The Board held that the purpose of the refusal to work is an element to be considered.[12] In this case the Board said that the negotiated right to refuse to cross a picket line was legal, but that, in the absence of such a right or some reason related to the exercise of this right or of another lawful or negotiated right, a concerted refusal to cross a picket line constituted a strike.[13]

In *Canada Post Corp.*,[14] the Board dealt with an application under s. 182 where the union had given directives to its members not to tax letters that did not bear the regulatory amount of postage. The Board found that the verification of postage and the taxing of insufficient postage was part and parcel of the union members' jobs and that a concerted failure to do so constituted a strike. The Board reaffirmed that the definition of a strike in the *Canada Labour Code*, unlike certain definitions found in some provincial statutes, was an objective one, and that "no subjective or intentional element test will apply. It does not depend upon an intention to obtain concessions from an employer".[15]

---

9   (1980), 42 di 40, [1981] 1 Can LRBR 121.
10   This remark is to be contrasted with the Board's decision in *British Columbia Telephone Co.*, *supra*, note 7, where a member of the panel expressed the view that a ban on overtime was not a strike because it was voluntary under the collective agreement (*e.g.*, not contrary to the collective agreement).
11   (1981), 45 di 29, [1981] 2 Can LRBR 462, 81 CLLC #16,128.
12   *Ibid.*, at p. 33 (di), where the Board said that "the purposes of the refusal to work measured against the purposes of the Code is the central test for determining the scope of the definition of strike". In *Air Canada*, *supra*, note 6, the Board seems to have considerably narrowed the scope of that statement by inferring it would only apply to determine whether the absences of employees were related to working-conditions related issues as opposed to extraneous factors such as a group of employees being absent for reasons of hunting or fishing.
13   *Canadian Broadcasting Corp.*, *supra*, note 11, at p. 33 (di).
14   (1983), 54 di 152, 5 CLRBR (NS) 280.
15   *Ibid.*, at p. 154 (di).

In conclusion, the Board originally stated that the definition of a strike found in the Code contained only objective elements. Subsequently, other panels of the Board have held that the reasons for the refusal to work must be measured against the purposes of the Code. By "purposes of the Code", the Board was particularly referring to negotiated rights such as the right to refuse to cross picket lines and the right to voluntary overtime. In a subsequent decision of *Canada Post Corp.*,[16] the Board panel, which included the chairman and a vice-chairman, reaffirmed the earlier opinion that the definition is an objective one.[17]

In addition to the usual situation of a work stoppage, the Board has found that a strike exists when concerted action has been organized in a variety of other circumstances. Among them are a ban on overtime,[18] the refusal to cross a picket line in the absence of a negotiated right to that effect,[19] employees' booking-off sick or unavailable for work,[20] the refusal by C.B.C. technicians and members of two different bargaining units to work in mixed crews on the production and broadcast of a sporting event,[21] a hunger strike,[22] work slowdowns occurring when employees changed their usual work practices, taking longer lunch breaks and more time in inspecting equipment,[23] the refusal to handle goods being transported to and from the premises of another employer,[24]

---

[16]   *Canada Post Corp., supra,* note 14.

[17]   The view expressed by the Board in *Société Radio-Canada* (1980), 40 di 35, [1981] 2 Can LRBR 52, that an overtime ban, whether the overtime was compulsory or voluntary under the collective agreement, constituted a strike, and that the definition in s. 107 was objective and that motivation was irrelevant, was upheld by the Federal Court of Appeal in its decision reported at [1982] 1 F.C. 471 (*sub nom. Syndicat des employés de production du Québec et de l'Acadie v. Canada Labour Relations Board*). The court affirmed that it was within the Board's jurisdiction to determine what constituted a strike and that its interpretation was not unreasonable. This was reaffirmed by the Supreme Court of Canada at [1984] 2 S.C.R. 412. The Board, in *Air Canada* (1984), 8 CLRBR (NS) 397, expressed the opinion the definition was an objective one.

[18]   *Conseil des Ports Nationaux* (1979), 33 di 530, [1979] 3 Can LRBR 502, 79 CLLC #16,204; *Société Radio-Canada* (1980), 40 di 35, [1981] 2 Can LRBR 52; *British Columbia Telephone Co.* (1980), 40 di 163, [1980] 3 Can LRBR 31, 80 CLLC #16,062 (opinion of Board member L. Shaffer); *Air Canada* (1984), 8 CLRBR (NS) 397; *Canadian National Railways,* Board file no. 725-106, see Appendix 10.

[19]   *Canadian Broadcasting Corp.* (1981), 45 di 29, [1981] 2 Can LRBR 462, 81 CLLC #16,128; *Premier Cablesystems Ltd.* (1981), 45 di 221, [1982] 1 Can. LRBR 163, 82 CLLC #16,140; *Purolator Courier Ltd.* (1981), 45 di 300; *Northumberland Ferries Ltd.,* Board file no. 725-95, see Appendix 10.

[20]   *Canadian National Railway Co.* (1983), 52 di 166; *La Compagnie des chemins de fer nationaux du Canada,* decision no. 479, not yet reported, September 11, 1984 (C.L.R.B.).

[21]   *Canadian Broadcasting Corp.,* Board file no. 725-44 (concerning anticipated refusal to work), see Appendix 10.

[22]   *Société Radio-Canada* (1980), 40 di 35, [1981] 2 Can LRBR 52.

[23]   *Canadian Pacific Ltd.* (1980), 42 di 40, [1981] 1 Can LRBR 121.

[24]   *Newfoundland Steamships Ltd.,* Board file no. 725-107, see Appendix 10.

the refusal to tax insufficient postage on letters,[25] and the refusal to accept acting supervisory assignments.[26]

On another occasion the Board found that an overtime ban did not constitute a strike, because the overtime was voluntary under the collective agreement and the ban was aimed at avoiding layoffs rather than at bargaining strategy.[27]

9:1200   LOCKOUT

Section 107(1) specifies that a "lockout"

> includes the closing of a place of employment, a suspension of work by an employer or a refusal by an employer to continue to employ a number of his employees, done to compel his employees, or to aid another employer to compel his employees, to agree to terms or conditions of employment. . . .

This definition requires a subjective element —that is, the action of the employer must be directed at forcing his employees or the employees of another employer to agree to terms and conditions of employment.[28] This subjective element is important in differentiating between a layoff and a lockout. The Board has had the opportunity to deal with only a few cases involving lockouts. In *Cable T.V. Ltée*[29] the Board came to the conclusion that the layoffs constituted a lockout, as they were directed at compelling the employees to accept certain terms and conditions of employment. In *Canadian Pacific Ltd.*[30] the Board found on the facts that the layoffs were not directed at compelling the employees to agree to change their working conditions. It held that the union should have referred its differences with the employer to arbitration, in accordance with the provisions of a collective agreement.

---

25   *Canada Post Corp.* (1983), 54 di 152, 5 CLRBR (NS) 280.

26   *Air Canada* (1984), 8 CLRBR (NS) 397.

27   *British Columbia Telephone Co., supra,* note 18.

28   *Cable T.V. Ltée* (1979), 35 di 28, [1980] 2 Can LRBR 381, 80 CLLC #16,019; *Canadian Pacific Ltd.* (1980), 39 di 138, [1980] 3 Can LRBR 87, 80 CLLC #16,059; *International Longshoremen's Association, Local 273 v. Maritime Employers' Association,* [1979] 1 S.C.R. 120, 23 N.R. 386, 23 N.B.R. (2d) 458, 78 CLLC #14,171, 89 D.L.R. (3d) 289.

29   (1979), 35 di 28, [1980] 2 Can LRBR 381, 80 CLLC #16,019. This case is unusual in that the employer was certified under the *Quebec Labour Code,* R.S.Q. 1977, c. C-27, which recognizes only collective bargaining relationships established through certification. The employer, who had had a certified bargaining relationship for a number of years, ran into difficulties in negotiating contracting-out provisions. At one point, he applied to the Quebec Superior Court and obtained a declaration that his business and operations were within the federal jurisdiction, and that consequently his labour relations were governed by the *Canada Labour Code.* The employer then took the position that the collective agreement signed under the ambit of the *Quebec Labour Code* was invalid, and proceeded with layoffs and then contracted out the work as previously discussed in negotiations with the union. The union applied to the Board to obtain a restraining order. The Board ultimately found the collective agreement negotiated under the *Quebec Labour Code* to be valid under the *Canada Labour Code,* since the latter applied to voluntarily recognized bargaining units. The collective agreement signed between the employer and the union did contain a recognition clause.

30   (1980), 39 di 138, [1980] 3 Can LRBR 87, 80 CLLC #16,059.

9:2000   DECLARATIONS AND ORDERS

9:2100   JURISDICTION OF THE BOARD AND THE COURTS

The power of labour relations boards to issue cease and desist orders has been held to be constitutional by the Supreme Court of Canada.[31] The Canada Labour Relations Board was also granted similar powers in 1978. However, the latter is not exclusive, and superior courts of the provinces can continue to exercise the powers they possessed in that regard before the Board was given jurisdiction in 1978.[32] On the other hand, the Federal Court has held[33] that it has no concurrent jurisdiction with that of the Board to issue injunctions in cases of illegal strikes and lockouts.

Sections 182, 183, and 183.1 define the Board's jurisdiction to act in cases of strikes and lockouts. An application must be made to the Board, seeking declaratory or injunctive relief. When such an application is made, the Board acquires jurisdiction to inquire into the matter of whether there is a strike or lockout and whether the strike or lockout is illegal. The existence of a strike and its legality are integral parts of the Board's jurisdiction under s. 182 and are not to be considered as preliminary questions of jurisdiction.[34]

9:2200   PRACTICE AND PROCEDURE

Applications for declarations under ss. 182 and 183 are urgent matters, and the Board has developed an approach to meet this requirement.

An employer confronted with an illegal strike, or a union confronted with an illegal lockout, can initiate proceedings by telephoning the Board either in Ottawa or at one of its regional offices.[35] Upon being so advised, the Board will appoint an investigating officer who will meet the parties concerned and will try to determine the underlying cause of the work

---

[31]   *Re Tomko and Nova Scotia Labour Relations Board*, [1977] 1 S.C.R. 112, 7 N.R. 317, 10 N.R. 35, 14 N.S.R. (2d) 191, 76 CLLC #14,005.

[32]   S.C. 1977-78, c. 27, s. 64. In *National Association of Broadcast Employees and Technicians v. The Queen*, [1980] 1 F.C. 820, 31 N.R. 19, 79 CLLC #14,231, 107 D.L.R. (3d) 186, the Federal Court of Appeal ruled that the 1978 amendments that gave the Board its cease and desist powers did not specifically remove such powers from the superior courts, who had prior to the 1978 amendments.

[33]   *National Association of Broadcast Employees and Technicians v. The Queen, supra,* note 32; *McKinlay Transport Ltd. v. Goodman,* [1979] 1 F.C. 760, 7 C.P.C. 233, 78 CLLC #14,161, 90 D.L.R. (3d) 689 (T.D.).

[34]   *Canada Labour Relations Board v. Syndicat des employés de production du Québec et de l'Acadie,* [1984] 2 S.C.R. 412.

[35]   Addresses and telephone and telex numbers of the Board's regional offices and head office are listed in Appendix 1.

stoppage or lockout.[36] At the same time, the Board will make arrangements to have a panel hear the matter. In most instances, the Board is able to hear the application within two or three days, or sooner if necessary.

Although the Board's involvement may be initiated by a telephone call, the applicant is subsequently required to file a written application.[37] In the case of a strike this application must set out pursuant to s. 37(1) of the *Canada Labour Relations Board Regulations*:

(a) (i) the full name and address of the applicant,
   (ii) the full particulars of the facts and circumstances on which the employer relies in alleging that the strike was, is or would be unlawful,
   (iii) the full name and address of any trade union or employee against whom the allegation is made,
   (iv) a statement of the nature of any order sought under paragraphs 182(a) to (d) of the Code, and
   (v) if a hearing is requested forthwith, the reasons therefor; and
(b) be accompanied by a copy of any collective agreement relevant to the application.

In the case of a lockout, the application must set out pursuant to s. 38(1) of the regulations:

(a) (i) the full name and address of the applicant,
   (ii) the full name and address of the employer who is alleged to have declared or caused or is about to declare or cause the alleged lockout of employees,
   (iii) full particulars of the facts and circumstances on which the trade union relies in alleging that the lockout was, is or would be unlawful,
   (iv) a statement of the nature of any orders sought under paragraphs 182(a) to (d) [sic] of the Code, and
   (v) if a hearing is requested forthwith, the reasons therefor; and
(b) be accompanied by a copy of any collective agreement relevant to the application.

If the applicant wishes to have a hearing forthwith, he must deliver a copy of his written application to the opposing party and inform the Board of the time and manner of such delivery.[38] In cases of illegal strikes where a large number of employees must be notified, the applicant may notify the investigation officer of this problem so that a practical solution may be found. It may be decided to give notice by posting a notice, by way of a newspaper announcement, or by advising a certain percentage of the employees concerned. A trade union, the employee, or the employer who has received a copy of such an application is deemed to have received

---

[36]   *Conseil des Ports Nationaux* (1979), 33 di 530, [1979] 3 Can LRBR 502, 79 CLLC #16,204.
[37]   *Canada Labour Relations Board Regulations*, S.O.R. 78/499, s. 37(1)(a), (b).
[38]   Sections 37(2) and 38(2).

notice that a hearing may be held forthwith.[39] Once the arrangements for holding the hearing are made, the parties are notified by the Board of the date and place.[40] The party against whom the application is sought may file a reply,[41] which shall contain, pursuant to s. 39(2) of the regulations,

(a) the full name and address of the persons replying;

(b) a clear identification of the application to which the reply relates;

(c) an admission or a denial of each of the statements made in the application; and

(d) a statement of the grounds and facts relied on in reply to the application.

However, in practice, depending on how quickly the hearing takes place, a reply may or may not be filed. The lack of a reply will not preclude the Board from proceeding with the scheduled hearing.

The investigating officer (I.O.) assigned by the Board will try to identify the underlying causes of the disputes and find a settlement. In the process the I.O. will meet with both parties and the employees if necessary and will make whatever suggestions he deems proper in the circumstances. If he cannot settle the matter, it will be dealt with more formally by the Board. Depending on the circumstances, the Board, if it finds it advisable, may itself engage in a mediation process to settle the dispute. In cases involving strikes and lockouts, once the hearing has started, the Board will usually sit around the clock, until a final decision is rendered.

The applicant must prove:

1. The existence of a strike or lockout as defined in s. 107(1).

2. The strike or lockout is illegal.[42] The Board can only issue orders if the strike or lockout is illegal. Section 182 refers to "a strike in contravention with this Part". The Board will verify that the conditions set out by s. 180(1)(a) to (d) have been met. If they have not, as a rule, the Board will conclude that the action is illegal.[43] This conclusion, however, is not necessarily automatic, as the Board may determine that certain actions are not illegal since they do not contravene Part V of the Code. This will be the case when employees refuse to perform the work of other employees of the same employer who are staging a legal strike.[44] The question may also be raised in terms of

---

39 Sections 37(3) and 38(3).

40 Sections 37(4) and 38(4).

41 Section 39(1).

42 See paragraph 8:1300.

43 *Cyprus Anvil Mining Corp.* (1976), 15 di 194, at 210, [1976] 2 Can LRBR 360, 76 CLLC #16,045; *Radiodiffusion Mutuelle Ltée* (1977), 18 di 56, at 63; *Conseil des Ports Nationaux* (1979), 33 di 530, at 531, [1979] 3 Can LRBR 502, 79 CLLC #16,204; *Société Radio-Canada* (1980), 40 di 35, at 45, [1981] 2 Can LRBR 52.

44 On this, see also Code s. 184(3)(c) as interpreted in *British Columbia Telephone Co.* (1979), 37 di 20, [1979] 2 Can LRBR 297, 80 CLLC #16,007; and *British Columbia Telephone Co.*

whether such action constitutes a strike or not as, for example, in regard to overtime bans,[45] or the refusal to cross picket lines when that right is protected in the agreement. The question as to whether the parties can legally contract out of the requirements of s. 180 through a clause of the collective agreement allowing the employees to refuse to cross a picket line set up by another union has been raised by the Board.[46]

9:2300   RELIEF GRANTED BY THE BOARD

9:2310   Generally

The Board's power to grant relief by way of declaration or injunction is discretionary. From the outset, the Board has indicated that this discretion would be exercised in accordance with the purposes expressed in the preamble to the Code, and that it would approach the question in a manner different from that taken by common-law superior courts.[47]

(1979), 38 di 124, [1980] 1 Can LRBR 340, 80 CLLC #16,008.

45   *British Columbia Telephone Co.* (1980), 40 di 163, [1980] 3 Can LRBR 31, 80 CLLC #16,062. One Board member found the refusal to do overtime not to constitute a strike or to be illegal because it was a negotiated right.

46   *British Columbia Telephone Co., supra*, note 45. As a general principle, it is recognized law that parties to a collective agreement cannot contract out of provisions of a public statute: *Bradburn v. Wentworth Arms Hotel Ltd.*, [1979] 1 S.C.R. 846, particularly at 861-63, 24 N.R. 417, 79 CLLC #14,189, 94 D.L.R. (3d) 161; *Ontario Human Rights Commission v. Etobicoke*, [1982] 1 S.C.R. 202, particularly at 213-14, 40 N.R. 159, 82 CLLC #17,005, 3 C.H.R.R. D/781, 132 D.L.R. (3d) 14.

47   *Purolator Courier Ltd.* (1981), 45 di 300; *Canadian National Railway Co.* (1983), 52 di 166; *La Compagnie des chemins de fer nationaux du Canada*, decision no. 479, not yet reported, September 11, 1984 (C.L.R.B.). Concerning the role of the courts in labour disputes, see Assistant Chief Justice Thurlow's remarks in *McKinlay Transport Ltd. v. Goodman*, [1979] 1 F.C. 760, at 763-64, 7 C.P.C. 233, 78 CLLC #14,161, 90 D.L.R. (3d) 689: "There is a further consideration that appears to me to bear on whether or not discretion should be exercised to grant an interlocutory injunction, even if the court has jurisdiction to entertain the action and the application and the case for an injunction is otherwise made out. Parliament has recently enacted extensive amendments to the *Canada Labour Code* which, in my view, demonstrate that the purpose was to vest in the Canada Labour Relations Board extensive and far reaching powers to deal with labour relations in the works and undertakings to which the statute applies including the granting of injunctions enjoining employees from participating in strikes, and the making of orders requiring employees to perform the duties of their employment — a power not exercised by a Court of equity. Not only has the Board been vested with powers more extensive and particular than those of the courts in such situations but the area in which the Board's decisions are open to attack and review has been narrowed by the amendments. The power previously reserved to the Minister of authorizing prosecution for violation of the Act has also been vested in the Board. In the face of these provisions, even though the legislation does not specifically purport to withdraw from the Superior Court's jurisdiction to issue injunctions in respect of conduct arising out of labour disputes, it seems to me that the Court can and ought to take into account in exercising its discretion that Parliament has shown its disposition that such matters be dealt with by the Board on the principles which it applies in the search for achievement of the objects of the legislation rather than by the courts. It is perhaps unnecessary to add that court injunctions have not been notoriously successful as a device for achieving harmonious labour relations or for resolving labour disputes."

Consistent with this view, the Board has refused to make a declaration or issue an injunctive order when the strike or lockout had already ended by the time of the hearing,[48] even though s. 182 expressly empowers the Board to do so. The Board has stated that it will identify the source of the problem causing the illegal action in order to remedy it properly, and that the investigating officer will play a major role in identifying the underlying source of the dispute between the parties.[49] It then follows that the Board may not issue an order even when confronted with the fact that a work stoppage has occurred, is occurring, or may occur.[50]

The Board may exercise its discretion under ss. 182 and 183 even if, at the time it does so, the illegal work stoppage or lockout has not yet commenced but the Board is of the opinion that "the employees are likely to participate in a strike",[51] or the employer "is about to declare or cause a lockout of employees".[52]

The Board's remedial powers may only be exercised after it has afforded to the party against which allegations of illegal strike or lockout have been made the opportunity to be heard. The normal practice of the Board is to hold hearings before issuing orders, although it may, in certain circumstances, issue orders without a formal hearing.

Sections 182 and 183 provide for specific remedies. Section 182 provides that the Board may make a declaration that the strike is illegal and/or that the union has declared or authorized it, or that employees have participated, are participating, or are likely to participate in it.

The Board may also issue "cease and desist" orders as provided by s. 182:

(a) requiring the trade union to revoke the declaration or authorization to strike and to give notice of such revocation forthwith to the employees to whom it was directed;

(b) enjoining any employee from participating in the strike;

(c) requiring any employee who is participating in the strike to perform the duties of his employment; and

(d) requiring any trade union of which any employee with respect to whom an order is made under paragraph (b) or (c) is a member, and any

---

48   *Newfoundland Steamships Ltd.* (1974), 7 di 8, [1975] 2 Can **LRBR** 275, 75 CLLC #16,147; *Purolator Courier Ltd.* (1981), 45 di 300; *Canadian National Railway Co.* (1983), 52 di 166; and *La Compagnie des chemins de fer nationaux du Canada, supra,* note 47. The Board's opinion that it possesses the discretion to make a declaration or not, once it has made a finding that the work stoppage is illegal, has not been tested by the courts. In *Air Canada* (1984), 8 CLRBR (NS) 397, the Board issued a restraining order, although the illegal activities had ceased at the time of the hearing because of particularly tense relations between the parties.

49   *Conseil des Ports Nationaux* (1979), 33 di 530, at 531, [1979] 3 Can LRBR 502, 79 CLLC #16,204; *Société Radio-Canada* (1980), 40 di 35, at 46, [1981] 2 Can LRBR 52.

50   *Conseil des Ports Nationaux, supra,* note 49, at p. 537 (di); *Société Radio-Canada, supra,* note 49, at p. 46 (di).

51   *Canada Labour Code,* s. 182.

52   Section 183.

officer or representative of that union, forthwith to give notice of any order made under paragraph (b) or (c) to any employee to whom it applies.

Likewise, s. 183 authorizes the Board to make a declaration that the employer has declared or is about to declare or cause a lockout and that such action was, is, or would be unlawful. The Board may also issue against the employer a "cease and desist" order:

(a) enjoining the employer or any person acting on behalf of the employer from declaring or causing the lockout;

(b) requiring the employer or any person acting on behalf of the employer to discontinue the lockout and to permit any employee or the employer who was affected by the lockout to return to the duties of his employment; and

(c) requiring the employer forthwith to give notice of any order made against the employer under paragraph (a) or (b) to any employee who was affected or would likely have been affected by the lockout.

Orders issued under ss. 182 and 183 may also be fashioned in such terms and for such time as the Board considers necessary and sufficient to meet the circumstances of the case.[53] The Board may also, upon application from any interested parties or persons, continue the order with or without modification or revoke it.[54]

Before prescribing a remedy, the Board will look for the underlying cause of the labour problem with which it is confronted.[55] The Board approaches the problem globally, and its decision to apply a specific remedy provided by s. 182 as adjusted to meet the circumstances of the case in accordance with s. 183.1,[56] is dictated by its desire to find a labour relations solution conducive to labour harmony in the work place.[57] The Board's approach in fashioning remedies is not punitive.[58] Its remedial powers under ss. 182, 183, and 183.1, its powers to authorize criminal proceedings under s. 194, and the filing of Board orders in the Federal Court[59] are all different means to achieve these goals.[60]

---

[53]   Section 183.1(1).

[54]   Section 183.1(2).

[55]   *Conseil des Ports Nationaux, supra*, note 49, at p. 537 (di).

[56]   The Supreme Court of Canada, in *Canada Labour Relations Board v. Syndicat des employés de production du Québec et de l'Acadie*, [1984] 2 S.C.R. 412, said that the Board did not have power under ss. 183.1, 121, 118(p), and the preamble of the Code to fashion remedies to an illegal strike different from those specifically referred to in s. 182. It may only adjust those specific remedies to the circumstances of the case as provided for by s. 183.1.

[57]   *Conseil des Ports Nationaux, supra*, note 49, at p. 537 (di), where the Board said, "everything depends on the higher interest to be satisfied in given circumstances". The higher interests are those "creating or helping to create the factual situation most likely to promote healthy and orderly labour relations". This statement, however, must now be read in light of the comments of the Supreme Court of Canada; see note 56, *supra*.

[58]   *Donald William Murray Movers Ltd.* (1974), 7 di 11, [1975] 1 Can LRBR 317, 75 CLLC #16,148; *Canadian National Railway Co.* (1983), 52 di 166.

[59]   *Canada Labour Code*, s. 123.

[60]   This view is more specifically expressed in *British Columbia Telephone Co.* (1979), 37 di

One area of contention was the power of the Board to fashion remedies other than those specifically provided for in ss. 182, 183, 183.1(1)(b), and 183.1(2). As we have said, the Board tries to find an appropriate labour relations solution, and in order to do so, it fashions remedies to fit the circumstances. The Board for this reason had viewed the source of its power in the language of s. 183.1(a) and s. 121. The contention was put to rest by the Supreme Court of Canada,[61] which affirmed the decision of the Federal Court of Appeal, which had said that s. 183.1(a) does not permit the Board to render orders other than those encompassed specifically by ss. 182 and 183.[62]

9:2320   Specific Remedies Fashioned by the Board

The Board has issued specific remedies in the case of illegal strikes or lockouts. An outline of such remedies is given below, whether the latter were accompanied by reasons for decision or not. This will serve to illustrate how the Board reacts in practice to labour conflicts and tries to solve them. Samples of Board orders are reproduced in Appendix 10.[63] As mentioned earlier, the Board will not as a rule issue orders if the strike or the lockout has already been settled. It will not direct an order against the union if it is satisfied that the union is not favouring or encouraging the illegal work stoppage and that it has seriously taken steps to put an end to it.[64]

In *Conseil des Ports Nationaux*[65] the Board ordered the union to refrain from authorizing a strike and to distribute a copy of the order to all its members and keep it posted. It further ordered the employees to perform the duties of their employment. This is an example of the standard order issued by the Board when the union is found to have authorized or declared a strike and the employees are participating in it.

In *Société Radio-Canada*[66] the Board dealt with two specific problems. The first was a hunger strike by twelve procurement specialists. The Board ordered them back to work, proposing that their problem should be settled at the negotiating table, and it directed the parties to meet with a conciliation commissioner previously appointed. It also directed them, as a priority, to deal with the jurisdictional dispute between the procure-

---

20, [1979] 2 Can LRBR 297, 80 CLLC #16,007.

[61]   *Canada Labour Relations Board v. Syndicat des employés de production du Québec et de l'Acadie, supra,* note 56.

[62]   *Le Syndicat des employés de production du Québec et de l'Acadie v. Canada Labour Relations Board,* [1982] 1 F.C. 471.

[63]   See page 507.

[64]   *Canadian National Railway Co.* (1983), 52 di 166.

[65]   (1979), 33 di 530, [1979] 3 Can LRBR 502, 79 CLLC #16,204. See also Appendix 10, Board file no. 725-39.

[66]   *Société Radio-Canada* (1980), 40 di 35, [1981] 2 Can LRBR 52. See also Appendix 10, Board file no. 725-54. See paragraph 9:2320 and note 67, *infra.*

ment employees and the set designers, which the Board had identified as the source of the problem.

The second problem was a ban on overtime, organized by the union in Montreal, Quebec City, and Moncton. In regard to the Montreal location, the Board found that the ban had been in effect for three months and that the employer had not applied for injunctive relief during that time. It decided not to make an order in respect of the Montreal employees, because no serious inconvenience would result for the C.B.C. As to the Quebec City and Moncton employees, the Board ordered them to desist from their overtime ban and ordered the union to so inform its members. The Board further ordered the parties to submit to expedited arbitration the question as to whether overtime was voluntary or compulsory.[67]

In *Canada Post Corp.*[68] the Board found that the action of C.U.P.W.'s members in refusing to tax letters carrying insufficient postage constituted an illegal strike. It ordered the union to revoke its declaration or authorization, to give notice of the order by posting it on all union bulletin boards, and to give evidence to the Board, supported by affidavit, that it had complied with the letter and intent of the order.

In *Cable TV Ltée*[69] the Board found the employer to have participated in an illegal lockout and ordered it to terminate the lockout, to take back into its employ those employees locked out, not to cause or order a lockout for a future date, to reimburse the employees for all benefits guaranteed by the collective agreement that they had lost as a result of the lockout, and finally, to notify all employees of the order.

In *Clark Transport Canada Inc.*[70] the union went on strike when the employer introduced a punch-clock system. The Board found the strike to be illegal and ordered the employees back to work, but compelled the parties to submit to accelerated arbitration the question of the employer's right to institute a punch-clock system. The order stated that the parties had agreed to the arbitrator and would not raise an objection to the arbitrator's jurisdiction. The arbitrator was instructed to proceed to hear the merits of the case.

On certain occasions, as was the case in *Canadian National Railways*,[71] the Board has addressed its order expressly to employees. In this case it elected to write short reasons for its decision and to have them distributed by the employer together with the order.

---

[67] However, the Federal Court of Appeal quashed paragraph 4 of the Board order relating to expedited arbitration for reason of lack of jurisdiction. This judgment was affirmed by the Supreme Court of Canada. See note 56 and 62, *supra*.

[68] (1983), 54 di 152, 5 CLRBR (NS) 280. See also Appendix 10, Board file no. 725-138.

[69] (1979), 35 di 28, [1980] 2 Can LRBR 381, 80 CLLC #16,019. See also Appendix 10, Board file no. 725-37.

[70] See Appendix 10, Board file no. 725-56. This order must now be viewed in the context of note 67, *supra*.

[71] See Appendix 10, Board file no. 725-106.

In *Thibaudeau-Finch Express Ltd.*[72] the Board had evidence that the strike taking place at the time of the hearing was illegal, but refrained from so declaring in the order. Instead it ordered that, if the employees were not at work at the start of their next scheduled shift, their absence from work would constitute an illegal strike. This approach gave the union the opportunity to call a meeting on a Sunday morning, where it convinced its members to return to work.

9:2400   ENFORCEMENT OF BOARD ORDERS AND PENAL PROSECUTION

As a rule, orders are enforced voluntarily by those against whom they are directed. In the event of non-compliance, a party may require the Board to authorize the filing of the order in the Federal Court in accordance with s. 123.[73] Illegal strikes and lockouts constitute a penal offence.[74] However, no prosecutions may be initiated without the prior consent of the Board.[75] If such an application is made, the Board will try to ascertain the reasons for non-compliance, and it will only authorize a filing of penal proceedings if it is convinced that there is no other way to deal with the situation.[76]

---

[72]   See Appendix 10, Board file no. 725-66.
[73]   In this regard, see paragraph 19:5000.
[74]   *Canada Labour Code*, ss. 180, 190, and 191.
[75]   Section 194.
[76]   *Conseil des Ports Nationaux* (1979), 33 di 557, [1979] 3 Can LRBR 513, 79 CLLC #16,204. In this case the Board authorized penal proceedings but made their filing conditional on the employer acting in their regard before the renewal of the collective agreement.

CHAPTER 10

UNFAIR LABOUR PRACTICES

10:0000   UNFAIR LABOUR PRACTICES

An unfair labour practice may be defined as a form of conduct that, though not unlawful at common law, is prohibited by statute because it permits either of the parties to thwart the normal functioning of the collective bargaining process envisaged by statute or to render illusory the right of association, which is a fundamental postulate of the *Canada Labour Code*.[1] These statutory prohibitions are found in s. 124(4) (statutory freeze of terms and conditions of employment following the filing of an application for certification); s. 136.1 (duty of fair representation); s. 148 (statutory freeze following the serving of a notice to bargain; duty to bargain in good faith); s. 161.1 (duty of fair referral); s. 184 (general prohibitions directed against employees); s. 185 (general prohibitions directed against unions); and finally s. 186 (general prohibitions directed against the use of intimidation or coercion). Section 199.1, which deals with the right of access to financial statements of unions, must also be added to that list. These prohibitions and the remedial authority given to the Board to enforce them are essential to give meaning to the rights granted by the Code.

Section 187 provides for the filing of a complaint when a contravention to any of these provisions has been committed within certain delays. The last subsection of s. 187 imposes the obligation to obtain the minister's consent before a complaint alleging a breach of ss. 148, 184(3)(g), and 185(a) or (b) can be filed with the Board.

Section 188 is related to the role of the Board where a complaint is filed by virtue of s. 187 and deals as well with the burden of proof. Finally, s. 189 spells out the Board's remedial powers.

The unfair labour practices prohibited by the Code may be divided according to the rights or institutions they are concerned with and designed to protect, namely the freedom of association, the institution of collective bargaining, the relationship between the members of the union

---

[1]   See A.W.R. Carrothers, *Collective Bargaining Law in Canada* (Toronto: Butterworths, 1965), at 111. See also *Air Canada* (1975), 11 di 5, [1975] 2 Can LRBR 193, 75 CLLC #16,164. In *Cominco Ltd.* (1980), 40 di 75, [1980] 3 Can LRBR 105, 80 CLLC #16,045, the Board traced the fundamental right of association embodied in s. 110(1) of the Code back to July 11, 1918, when it first received expression in Order in Council P.C. 1743.

and the members of the unit or the right to participate in the union's activities, and the free access to the Board charged with the administration of the Code. They can be further re-divided according to the persons they are designed to protect: the union, the employer, and the employee. The discussion of the unfair labour practice provisions of the Code in the following chapters follows that plan.

10:1000   PARTIES TO AN UNFAIR LABOUR PRACTICE COMPLAINT

A complaint filed under s. 187(1) may be brought by any "organization" or "person", which includes an employer, a union, an employee, an employer's organization, a council of trade unions, or a group of employees.[2] The complaint may be brought against an employer or a union or a person acting on their behalf, an employer's organization, or a council of trade unions.[3] The Board may add a party to the proceedings at any stage pursuant to its powers under s. 118(o).

The procedural requirements of an unfair labour practice complaint, its form and content, and other related questions such as its timeliness will be discussed in a later chapter.[4]

10:2000   BENEFICIARIES OF THE LEGAL PROTECTION: "EMPLOYEE" VERSUS "PERSON"

Before considering the unfair labour practice provisions of the Code, it is necessary to identify the beneficiaries of the protection afforded by such provisions. In this respect, the definition of "trade union" refers to an "organization of employees", s. 110(1) grants the basic freedoms to "employees" as defined in s. 107(1),[5] and s. 107(2) preserves

---

[2]   See the definitions of "party" and "person" in s. 2 of the *Canada Labour Relations Board Regulations* and the definition of "parties" in s. 107(1) of the *Canada Labour Code*.

[3]   Sections 184, 185, and 186 of the *Canada Labour Code* are directed against employers and unions as defined by s. 107(1), but for the purposes of Division VI of Part V of the Code, which includes the unfair practices provisions, the words "employers" and "trade union" include an employer's organization and a council of trade unions (s. 179).

[4]   See Chapter 15.

[5]   The definition of "employee" in the longshoring industry, with its extensive use of hiring halls, must be interpreted in the light of the decision of the Supreme Court of Canada in *International Longshoremen's Association, Local 273 v. Maritime Employers' Association*, [1979] 1 S.C.R. 120, 23 N.R. 386, 23 N.B.R. (2d) 458, 78 CLLC #14,171, 89 D.L.R. (3d) 289, which was applied by the Board in *Terrance John Matus* (1980), 41 di 278, [1981] 1 Can LRBR 155 and *Roland Arsenault* (1982), 50 di 51, [1982] 3 Can LRBR 425, 82 CLLC #17,018.

an employee's status notwithstanding his dismissal contrary to Part V.[6] Nonetheless the terminology used to identify the beneficiaries of the provisions of ss. 184 to 186 refers to "employee" and "person". The wording of s. 184 carefully distinguishes between unfair labour practices that may be committed against a "person" and those that may be committed against an "employee". The importance of the distinction lies in the fact that an individual may be barred from seeking the protection of the Code if, by reason of the terminology used, Parliament has failed to extend the Code's coverage to such individuals.[7]

In other sections of the Code that deal with practices relating to the relationship between the bargaining agent and the employees of the unit, the terminology used may be "employee" (ss. 136.1, 185(e), (f), (g)), "person" (s. 161.1), or "member" (s. 199(1)).

10:2100   EMPLOYER VIOLATIONS

10:2110   Protection Afforded to "Employees"

The Board has determined that several subsections of s. 184 are expressly and logically restricted to the sole benefit of employees.[8] Subsections (b), (c), and (d) of s. 184(3) have purposes that naturally reserve protection to employees.

10:2120   Protection Afforded to "Persons"

In *General Aviation Services Ltd.*[9] the Board determined that subparas. (iii) to (v) of s. 184(3)(a) and subparas. (i) to (iii) of s. 184(3)(e), dealing with participation in Board proceedings, were necessarily intended to afford protection to employees as well as to non-employees. This protection is essential to the orderly administration of the Code by the Board, and the word "person" used in those subparagraphs is not to be restricted to "employee".

The same holds true of subpara. (i) of s. 184(3)(a), and also of the introductory phrases in s. 184(3)(e) of the Code. The word "person" used therein was meant by Parliament to have a broader meaning than the scope of the definition of "employee" in s. 107(1) of the Code.[10] The interpretation adopted by the Board means, in effect, that lower-level management personnel who participate in union organizing activities or

---

6   *Purolator Courier Ltd.* (1982), 48 di 32, where, for instance, the issue was whether the complainant who had resigned was still an "employee" at the time of her alleged discriminatory dismissal.

7   See, for instance, *Mike Sheehan* (1976), 17 di 14, [1976] 2 Can LRBR 187, 76 CLLC #16,030, and paragraph 13:3200.

8   *General Aviation Services Ltd.* (1978), 34 di 587, [1979] 1 Can LRBR 285.

9   *Ibid.*

10   See also *Arnold Bros. Transport Ltd.* (1976), 19 di 132, [1977] 2 Can LRBR 86.

seek union membership may not be disciplined by an employer for their union activities, as the protection afforded by s. 184(3)(a)(i) and (e) extends to such persons. However, the Board qualified this policy approach in an important way. It held[11] that Parliament was undoubtedly aware of the uncertainty that would be created by the new extension of collective bargaining right to professionals and supervisory employees. Parliament anticipated the uncertainty and did not intend that individuals be penalized should they mistakenly consider themselves to be employees and seek to exercise rights under the Code. It expressed this concern by the use of the word "person" in s. 184(3)(a)(i) and (e) and by restricting certification rights to "employees" in s. 110(1). However, Parliament cannot be taken, at the same time, to have intended to extend this policy approach to every person regardless of how clear it is that this person ought to have known that union support was in direct conflict with its job responsibilities. In the Board's opinion, to extend the protection to such persons would not be compatible with the goal of s. 184(3), which is to provide protection for persons who may reasonably be in doubt as to their status under Part V of the Code. Thus, in cases where it is clear the person ought to have known that his support or participation in union activity would conflict with the terms of his employment, such as the company's sole industrial relations officer who exercises most confidential responsibilities in labour relations, Parliament did not intend to prohibit the employer from disciplining or dismissing such a person because of the liability to which his actions exposed the employer.

The Board has also held that s. 184(3)(f), which provides protection to persons who have refused to perform an act prohibited by Part V, is also a clear case where the coverage naturally extends beyond "employees".[12] For example, a managerial non-employee who refuses to commit an unfair labour practice would be the logical candidate for the protection of this section.

10:2200   UNION VIOLATIONS

10:2210   Protection Afforded to "Employees"

In *George Lochner*[13] the Board noted that the use of the word "employee" in s. 136.1 may raise problems. Indeed, if an individual is dismissed contrary to the provisions of the collective agreement and the actions of the union complained of occur subsequently to the dismissal, could it be argued that the duty of fair representation is no longer owed

---

[11]   *General Aviation Services Ltd., supra*, note 8.
[12]   *Arnold Bros. Transport Ltd., supra*, note 10. See also *General Aviation Services Ltd., supra*, note 8, which expanded on this subject.
[13]   (1979), 37 di 114, [1980] 1 Can LRBR 149, 79 CLLC #16,209.

to the individual? The Board determined in subsequent cases[14] that the duty of fair representation extends to persons who are no longer employees in the bargaining unit when the cause of their grievance arose while they were still employees.

In *Gerald Abbott*[15] the Board considered the problems associated with the use of the word "employee" in s. 185(e), (f), and (g), which relate to questions of internal union discipline and the discriminatory application of membership rules and disciplinary standards. Although it did not provide a final resolution to this problem, the Board did point to certain questions with respect to the extent of Parliament's constitutional competence in the area of the regulation of internal trade union affairs as a possible explanation for the use of the word "employee" rather than "member" in those subsections. This question will be discussed more extensively below,[16] but it is appropriate to keep in mind throughout this study of the unfair labour practice provisions of the Code that the choice of words made by Parliament may have been dictated, in some cases, by constitutional considerations.

10:2220   Protection Afforded to "Persons"

Subsections 185(i)(i) to (iii), dealing with participation in Board proceedings, refer to the word "person", as do subss. 184(3)(a)(iii) to (v) and (e)(i) to (iii). Its protection extends, therefore, to employees as well as to non-employees. Section 185(h), which is the counterpart to s. 184(3)(f), also protects non-employees who refuse to perform acts prohibited by Part V.

---

[14]   *John J. Huggins* (1979), 38 di 195, [1980] 1 Can LRBR 364.
[15]   (1977), 26 di 543, [1978] 1 Can LRBR 305.
[16]   See paragraph 13:3100.

CHAPTER 11

PROTECTION OF THE FREEDOM OF ASSOCIATION

11:0000 PROTECTION OF THE FREEDOM OF ASSOCIATION

11:1000 INTERFERENCE WITH TRADE UNIONS AND EMPLOYERS' ORGANIZATIONS

Interference with trade union and employers' organizations is considered in the following paragraphs. Section 184(1) of the *Canada Labour Code* prohibits employer participation or interference in the formation and administration of a trade union or in its representation of employees, while s. 184(2) provides for exceptions where an employer will be deemed not to contravene s. 184(1). The counterpart with respect to an employer's organization is provided in s. 185(c), which prohibits trade unions from participating or interfering in the formation or administration of employers' organizations.

11:1100 EMPLOYER INTERFERENCE: SECTION 184(1), (2)

11:1110 Scope of the Prohibitions

The Board has determined that, although the Code does not, as is the case in some other jurisdictions, expressly prohibit employer acts that interfere with the exercise of "any other rights under this Act",[1] nevertheless the ambit of s. 184(1) is intended to be broad enough to encompass rights granted under s. 110(1) that are not specifically addressed in s. 184(3). In other words, s. 184(1) is an "umbrella provision" that encompasses matters specified in s. 184(3) as well as others not specified therein.[2] For this reason, as will be discussed later,[3] breaches of various

---

[1]   See, for example: *Labour Relations Act*, C.C.S.M., 1973, c. I-4, s. 5(3); *Trade Union Act*, S.S. 1972, c. 137, s. 11(1)(a); *Labour Act*, R.S.P.E.I. 1974, c. L-1, s. 9(1)(a).

[2]   *Canadian Imperial Bank of Commerce (North Hills Shopping Centre)* (1979), 34 di 651, [1979] 1 Can LRBR 266, 80 CLLC #16,001; *Canadian Pacific Air Lines Ltd.* (1981), 45 di 204, [1982] 1 Can LRBR 3, 82 CLLC #16,138.

[3]   See paragraph 11:1121.

unfair labour practice provisions of the Code have often been found to involve a contravention of s. 184(1)(a) as well.

More specifically, in s. 184(1)(a) Parliament has prohibited, first, by the use of the word "participate", the domination and attempted domination of the formation and administration of a trade union, and the domination and attempted domination of the representation of employees by a trade union. This reading of the meaning of the word "participate" in that section is borne out by s. 134(1) of the Code. The second prohibition is "interference" with the formation and administration of a trade union or "interference" with the representation of employees by a trade union. Both employer domination of trade unions and interference with their formation, administration, and representation of employees are prohibited by s. 184(1)(a).[4]

To breathe life into the words "formation", "administration", and "representation of employees" by a trade union, the Board started from the proposition that the protection afforded by s. 184(1)(a) was intended to have a continuous effect. The prohibitions of this section, designed to discourage employers from illegally involving themselves in matters that are the concern only of employees and their trade union, are applicable during the formation and establishment of a collective bargaining relationship with the employer. In these early stages, trade unions and their members are particularly vulnerable to employer interference. The prohibitions of this section remain in effect after the formation of the trade union and during the normal collective bargaining relationship with the employer. The Board has stated that there is, indeed, nothing in the Code that would indicate any relaxation of the restraints contained in s. 184(1)(a) even after the parties to collective bargaining have attained the right to strike or lockout.[5]

11:1111   The "Formation" of a Trade Union

The "formation" of a union includes the organizing activities of the employees. Although the formation also involves the adoption of a constitution, the election of officers, or the acquisition of a charter, it does not begin and end with such actions.[6] It continues, for the purposes of s. 184(1)(a), during the organization of employees who, as members of the union, are essential to its existence and to its bid to acquire the status of a bargaining agent.[7]

---

4   *Banque Royale du Canada (Jonquière et Kénogami)* (1980), 42 di 125.
5   *Air Canada* (1976), 18 di 66, 77 CLLC #16,062; *Television Saint-François Inc.* (1981), 43 di 175; *Eastern Provincial Airways Ltd.* (1983), 54 di 172, 5 CLRBR (NS) 368, 84 CLLC #16,012.
6   *ATV New Brunswick Ltd. (CKCW-TV)* (1978), 29 di 23, [1979] 3 Can LRBR 342; *Canadian Imperial Bank of Commerce (Toronto)* (1979), 34 di 677, [1979] 1 Can LRBR 391.
7   *Canadian Imperial Bank of Commerce, Toronto, supra,* note 6.

The "formation" of a union also includes the selection of a bargaining agent by the employees. The Board has held that it would be too narrow an interpretation of the Code to view the formation of the union as excluding the selection of the union by the employees to become their bargaining agent. In *Canadian Imperial Bank of Commerce (Toronto)*,[8] the Board gave the following example: a group of employees decides that they wish to bargain collectively with their employer and they meet to discuss the best approach; they discuss the alternatives of establishing their own union at the plant, or of asking an existing union to represent them; they decide that they want a bargaining agent in any event; the employer hears of the meeting and takes steps to prevent further meetings or discussions by the employees. In the Board's opinion, such interference would relate to the formation of a trade union regardless of an eventual decision by the employees to select the outside union. The activity of the employees involved in deciding that they want a bargaining agent to represent them is part of the formation of a union. What is essential, as the Board held here, is the objective of the employees involved, not the procedure followed. Thus, the interference with the formation of a union prohibited by s. 184(1)(a) is not confined solely to events relating to the creation of the union as an entity.[9]

11:1112 The "Administration" of the Union

The prohibition against employer participation or interference with the "administration" of a trade union is directed at the protection of the union as a legal entity. The "administration" of a trade union encompasses such matters as the initial and subsequent elections of officers, the collection of money, the expenditure of this money, and general meetings of the members. In a word, all the internal matters of a trade union considered as an enterprise are covered. This is to ensure that the employer will not be able to control the union with which it must negotiate, and thus ensure that the negotiations will be conducted at arm's length.[10]

11:1113 The "Representation" of Employees by a Trade Union

The word "representation" as used in s. 184(1)(a) is addressed mainly but not exclusively to collective bargaining.[11] There are, indeed, many occasions where unions represent, with their authorization, individual employees in a variety of applications or complaints under the Code

---

8   *Ibid.*
9   *Amok Ltd.* (1981), 43 di 289.
10   *ATV New Brunswick Ltd. (CKCW-TV)*, *supra*, note 6.
11   *Ibid.; Canadian Imperial Bank of Commerce (North Hills Shopping Centre)*, *supra*, note 2.

outside of collective bargaining situations. On these occasions the union is clearly the representative of the employee. Such representation may take place, as it often does in unfair dismissal cases, in the absence of any bargaining relationship between the union and the employer. The absence of such a relationship does not affect the representative nature of the union's role on behalf of the employee.[12]

Thus, the concept of "representation" embraces matters arising both before and after certification and includes employee participation in the union's "lawful activities". As seen above, the most common forms of prohibited conduct by employers, addressed in s. 184(3) and encompassed in s. 184(1)(a), relate to actions that occur before as well as after certification or voluntary recognition. It follows that the protection afforded by s. 184(1)(a), as it relates to the representation of employees, extends to union activities that occur even before certification and the acquisition of the exclusive rights derived from s. 136(1)(a).[13] It is not confined solely to post-certification representation,[14] and the protection begins as soon as the employees initiate discussions to join a union.[15]

To conclude, the "formation", "administration", and "representation of employees" by a trade union clearly must not be viewed as compartmentalized concepts.

11:1120   The Application of Section 184(1)

11:1121   Umbrella Provision

A breach of various unfair labour practice provisions of the Code may involve a breach of s. 184(1)(a) as well. A typical example of this situation is found in *Canadian Imperial Bank of Commerce (Toronto),*[16] where the Board held that the dismissal by an employer of one of his employees who had been actively engaged in recruiting membership support in the course of an organizing campaign was due solely to the union activities of that employee and so contravened s. 184(3)(a)(i) of the Code. The same act was also held to be an interference by the employer in the formation of a trade union and the representation of employees in contravention of s. 184(1)(a). In addition, the dismissal contravened s. 184(3)(e) since, by reason of its anti-union motivation, the firing had become a means by which the employer sought to compel the other employees to refrain from joining the union or to abandon their membership. Dismissal and

---

12   *Canadian Imperial Bank of Commerce (Toronto), supra,* note 6.
13   *Canadian Imperial Bank of Commerce (North Hills Shopping Centre), supra,* note 2.
14   *Amok Ltd., supra,* note 9.
15   *La Banque Nationale du Canada* (1981), 42 di 352, [1982] 3 Can LRBR 1.
16   *Canadian Imperial Bank of Commerce (Toronto), supra,* note 6.

other actions may also be found to be in contravention of s. 186 as well as the above sections.[17]

Where the complaint involves alleged breaches of the statutory freeze provisions with respect to terms and conditions of the employment, it has been determined that the employer's actions may constitute a violation of ss. 124(4) and 148(b) on the one hand and of s. 184 on the other. The Board ruled that, in some circumstances, a violation of s. 184 could be found and, concomitantly, a violation of either or both of the freeze mechanisms. Conversely, the correct application and respect of the freeze provisions will not automatically absolve employers from scrupulously avoiding, in the implementation and application of the freeze periods, any action that could be viewed as a prohibited act under s. 184.[18]

Where the complaint involves a refusal to bargain or bad-faith negotiations, the Board has held, in some instances, that an employer's actions may be both a refusal to bargain contrary to s. 148(a) and a prohibited act under s. 184.[19] A single act can contravene both s. 148(a) and s. 184 of the Code.

The Board has held indeed that it may find, on the facts, that there have been contraventions of other sections of the Code as well, notwithstanding that the formal complaint refers only to one particular section.[20] Although this approach, together with the Board's interpretation of s. 184(1) as encompassing both matters specified in s. 184(3) and others not specified therein, may appear to contain an element of double jeopardy, the Board feels that such is not the case. One action may violate several laws or provisions of a statute. Under the Code, the remedial focus is not punitive but is intended to be "equitable" and to "counteract consequences" adverse to the fulfilment of its objectives.[21]

11:1122   Prohibited Motive

An anti-union animus is not a necessary ingredient of a contravention of s. 184(1)(a) when the effect of the employer's action seriously affects the basic rights bestowed under s. 110(1) of the Code. The Board has adopted the American test to the effect that, if it can reasonably be concluded that the employer's discriminatory conduct was "inherently

---

17   *Oakville Cablevision Ltd.* (1980), 40 di 189; *American Airlines Inc.* (1981), 43 di 114, [1981] 3 Can LRBR 90; *Loomis Armored Car Service Ltd.* (1983), 51 di 185.

18   *Canadian Imperial Bank of Commerce, (Branches at Creston, B.C. and St. Catharines, Ont.)* (1979), 35 di 105, [1980] 1 Can LRBR 307, 80 CLLC #16,002.

19   *Royal Bank of Canada (Kamloops & Gibsons, B.C.)* (1978), 27 di 701, [1978] 2 Can LRBR 159, 78 CLLC #16,132; *Eastern Provincial Airways Ltd.* (1983), 51 di 209, 3 CLRBR (NS) 75; *Eastern Provincial Airways Ltd.* (1983), 54 di 172, 5 CLRBR (NS) 368, 84 CLLC #16,012.

20   *American Airlines Inc., supra,* note 17.

21   *Canadian Imperial Bank of Commerce (North Hills Shopping Centre), supra,* note 2.

destructive" of important employee rights, no proof of an anti-union motivation is needed.[22] All the Board must seek to determine is whether, in a specific case, the freedom of association protected by s. 110 has been safeguarded; whether the freedom of an employee to join the union of his choice has been respected; whether the freedom of a union or an employee to exercise the rights provided for in the Code has been preserved — in other words, whether there has been a departure from the objectives and intentions set forth in the Code stemming from the employer's course of action. It is the course of action and its consequences, far more than the motivation behind it, that is examined by the Board. Although it is not necessary to scrutinize the employer's motivation to find a violation of s. 184(1), the presence of an anti-union animus will, of course, make otherwise permissible actions a violation of s. 184(1).[23]

11:1123   Cases Where No Breaches Were Found

Section 184(1) does not require that the employer actively protect the interests of a bargaining agent with which it has a legal relationship against the organizational drives of competing trade unions during open periods, such as after the lapse of six months from the beginning of a strike. The obligation an employer has in this regard is to continue to recognize the incumbent trade union for such time as it continues to enjoy representation rights with respect to the employees in the bargaining unit and to give effect to these rights. Thus, although organizational meetings had been held by a rival union during working hours among employees who had returned to work during the strike, the Board dismissed a complaint under s. 184(1)(a) filed by the incumbent union. The Board found that the employer had not actively involved itself in the organizational campaign of the rival union.[24] Attempts by an employer to dissuade an employee from grieving or attending an arbitration hearing were held not to be interference with the administration of a trade union nor to necessarily constitute interference with the representation of employees by the union in the circumstances of that case.[25]

An employer's failure to credit service for the period of a legal strike to employees who had participated in the strike was held not to constitute prohibited interference contrary to s. 184(1)(a). The fact that the em-

---

22   *Banque Canadienne Nationale (Montréal)* (1979), 35 di 39, [1980] 1 Can LRBR 470.
23   *Royal Bank of Canada (Kamloops & Gibsons, B.C.), supra,* note 19; *Bank of Nova Scotia (Vancouver Heights Branch)* (1978), 28 di 901, [1978] 2 Can LRBR 191; *Canadian Imperial Bank of Commerce (North Hills Shopping Centre)* (1979), 34 di 651, [1979] 1 Can LRBR 266, 80 CLLC #16,001; *Banque Canadienne Nationale (Montreal), supra,* note 22; *Bell Canada* (1981), 42 di 298, [1981] 2 Can LRBR 148, 81 CLLC #16,083; *Canadian Pacific Air Lines Ltd.* (1981), 45 di 204, [1982] 1 Can LRBR 3, 82 CLLC #16,138; *La Banque Nationale du Canada* (1981), 42 di 352, [1982] 3 Can LRBR 1; *Wardair Canada (1975) Ltd.* (1983), 53 di 26, 2 CLRBR (NS) 129.
24   *Air Canada* (1976), 18 di 66, 77 CLLC #16,062.
25   *ATV New Brunswick Ltd. (CKCW-TV)* (1978), 29 di 23, [1979] 3 Can LRBR 342.

ployer had credited service to employees in the bargaining unit who had worked during the strike was found not to be discriminatory conduct prohibited by s. 184(3)(a)(i) and (vi). The denial of seniority to the strikers, for the period of the strike, was found not to be motivated by anti-union animus. The Board noted that it could have had the effect of restraining an employee from exercising his right to strike, but found no contravention of the Code.[26]

An employer was found not to have breached s. 184(1) by awarding a financial advantage to union members who had crossed a picket line set up by another union. The employer's actions were found to be ill-advised, imprudent, and probably illegal, but in the particular circumstances of the case, considering the questionable legality of the picket line, the Board did not find anti-union animus in the employer's motive and declined to find a violation of the Code.[27]

In another decision the Board determined that, where the employer had properly sought and obtained the Board's consent pursuant to s. 124(4) while several applications for certification by competing unions were pending, the implementation of wage increases prior to a representation vote was not, in the circumstances of the case, animated by anti-union animus and could not support an unfair labour practice charge by one of the unions under s. 184(1) of the Code.[28]

The Board also determined that the reassignment of work formerly performed by bargaining unit employees to a newly created supervisory classification outside the unit, pursuant to rights acquired by the employer at the bargaining table as part of a strike settlement, did not constitute an interference in the representation of employees by the trade union. The Board held that the employer's rights, newly acquired at the bargaining table, had not been exercised in order to evade or erode the union's representational rights to an extent that constituted conduct prohibited by s. 184(1).[29]

11:1124   Cases Where Breaches Were Found

The Board has found contraventions to s. 184(1) in a variety of situations. The most common form of interference by an employer in the formation or administration of a union or its representation of employees consists in the dismissal of employees who are either leaders of union-

---

26   *Bell Canada, supra,* note 23.
27   *Canadian Pacific Air Lines Ltd., supra,* note 23.
28   *Crosbie Offshore Services Ltd.* (1982), 51 di 120.
29   *Wardair Canada (1975) Ltd., supra,* note 23. See also *Wardair Canada (1975) Ltd.* (1983), 53 di 184, 84 CLLC #16,005 where, on a review application under s. 119 a new panel of the Board confirmed this decision. It was determined that the union's claim that the employer could not properly pursue to an impasse in negotiations the issue of the scope of the bargaining unit might have been well taken, if the Board had had a complaint under s. 148(a) before it at that time.

organizing drives promoting membership support, union representatives, or employees who are very active in their union. The dismissals usually occur contemporaneously with the employer's knowledge of the union activities. They may be part of an overall strategy to discourage employees from exercising their rights and so may have a chilling effect on other employees. The cases where the Board has found that such dismissals contravened s. 184(1) among others are legion.[30]

Where the Board orders the reinstatement of such employees who had been the instigators of an organizing drive, an employer cannot justify its refusal to comply with the order by resuscitating events or alleged improper conduct that had occurred prior to the application for certification. The failure to comply with the original reinstatement order has been held to constitute a further contravention of s. 184(1).[31]

In one case, the Board determined that an employer had breached s. 184(1) when, on being informed of a union organizing campaign in one of its branches, personnel changes were effected and employees from other locations were transferred to the branch to dilute the union's membership support.[32]

The wearing of a dress pin was held to be a protected lawful activity and the Board found that an employer had contravened s. 184(1) by issuing a directive prohibiting employees from wearing them on its premises during working hours.[33] An employer was found to have breached s. 184(1) by announcing a general increase in wages across the company and circulating to all his employees a circular to that effect bearing the express proviso that such increase would not apply to certified branches and to those that had applied for certification. In the board's view, that action was undoubtedly aimed at creating a chilling effect on potential organizing and also among the members of the union.[34]

Where an employer continues to communicate exclusively with the union after it has been displaced by a rival bargaining agent, the employer breaches s. 184(1) by refusing to recognize the newly certified union as the authorized bargaining agent.[35] Where an employer imple-

---

[30]   *City and Country Radio Ltd.* (1975), 11 di 22, [1975] 2 Can LRBR 1, 75 CLLC #16,171; *Canadian Imperial Bank of Commerce (Toronto)* (1979), 34 di 677, [1979] 1 Can LRBR 391; *Oakville Cablevision Ltd.* (1980), 40 di 189; *Transx Ltd.* (1980), 40 di 214; *Banque Royale du Canada (Jonquière et Kénogami)* (1980), 42 di 125; *American Airlines Inc.* (1981), 43 di 156; *T.E. Quinn Truck Lines Ltd.* (1981), 45 di 254; *Highland Helicopters Ltd.* (1981), 46 di 50; *Purolator Courier Ltd.* (1982), 48 di 32; *Loomis Armored Car Service Ltd.* (1983), 51 di 185.

[31]   *Crosbie Offshore Services Ltd.*, *supra*, note 28; *T.E. Quinn Truck Lines Ltd.* (1982), 47 di 87.

[32]   *Canadian Imperial Bank of Commerce (Sioux Lookout)* (1978), 33 di 432, [1979] 1 Can LRBR 18.

[33]   *Canadian Imperial Bank of Commerce (North Hills Shopping Centre)*, *supra*, note 23.

[34]   *Canadian Imperial Bank of Commerce, (Branches at Creston, B.C. and St. Catharines, Ont.)*, *supra*, note 18.

[35]   *Austin Airways Ltd. / White River Air Service Ltd.* (1980), 41 di 151, [1980] 3 Can LRBR 393.

ments a pension plan and wage increases without any prior consultation with or consent by the bargaining agent after notice to bargain has been given, the employer contravenes s. 148(b) as well as s. 184(1) by interfering in the representation of employees by the union.[36]

In another decision the Board held that an employer's unilateral action in reorganizing the structure of his enterprise, in an attempt to remove elevator managers from the bargaining unit and placing them in managerial functions by creating positions outside the scope of the unit, was motivated by an anti-union animus. The implementation of individual contracts with these employees amounted to an interference by the employer in the representation of employees by a bargaining agent. In the Board's opinion, the creation and filling of the so-called "out of scope" positions could not be compared to any normal progression of bargaining unit employees through the ranks to managerial posts.[37]

In another case, in the absence of any evidence of disruption in the employer's operations, its decision not to allow the distribution of union literature in employee mail boxes on the company premises was held to be an interference with the representation of the employees by the union contrary to s. 184(1)(a).[38]

Where an employer had fostered and encouraged the creation of an "in-house" bargaining committee among the unionized employees and had negotiated a collective agreement directly with members of the committee over the heads of the union representatives, the Board held that by its actions, the employer had interfered in the administration of the union as well as in the representation of employees by the trade union.[39]

The closure by a bank of one of its recently unionized branches was found to be animated by the desire to get rid of the union and therefore constituted unlawful interference with the representation of employees by a trade union.[40] In another decision, the Board held that by negotiating to an impasse a no-reprisal clause as part of a return-to-work agreement in order to prevent union discipline against employees who had worked during a strike, an employer had contravened s. 184(1) in the particular circumstances of that case and had interfered in the internal administration of the trade union.[41]

The Board held that although s. 162 of the *Canada Labour Code* did, at the time, refer only to voluntary check-off of union dues, an employer had engaged in predetermined tactics designed to undermine the union

---

[36]   *Ibid.*
[37]   *Manitoba Pool Elevators* (1980), 42 di 27, [1981] 1 Can LRBR 44.
[38]   *American Airlines Inc.* (1981), 43 di 114, [1982] 3 Can LRBR 90.
[39]   *Television Saint-François Inc.* (1981), 43 di 175.
[40]   *La Banque Nationale du Canada* (1981), 42 di 352, [1982] 3 Can LRBR 1.
[41]   *Eastern Provincial Airways Ltd.* (1983), 51 di 209, 3 CLRBR (NS) 75; *Eastern Provincial Airways Ltd.* (1983), 54 di 172, 5 CLRBR (NS) 368, 84 CLLC #16,012.

and divide the employees by bringing the issue of voluntary deduction of union dues to an impasse. By doing so, the employer had interfered in the union's exclusive representation of the employees in the bargaining unit contrary to s. 184(1).[42]

11:1125   Permissible Employer Communications

The exposé of the policy of the Board with respect to permissible employer communications with employees is hereunder divided into two phases. They are, first, employer communications in the context of union-organizing activities and representation votes, and second, employer communications that occur after certification or in the course of labour disputes. Much of what the Board has said, however, with respect to ante-certification employer communications also applies in the context of post-certification communications. The policy evolved in the former situation reflects the Board's attitude in the latter and, save for few variances, one should not be segregated from the other.

Communications in the Context of Union Organizing and Representation Votes

In *City and Country Radio Ltd.*[43] the Board studied the effect of the prohibitions of s. 184(1) of the Code on the exercise of the employer's freedom of expression in the context of union-organizing campaigns and representation votes. In order to sensibly construe and apply the prohibitions of that section to avoid abrogating, abridging, or infringing on the freedom of expression previously recognized by the *Canadian Bill of Rights,*[44] and now guaranteed to everyone by s. 2(b) of the *Canadian Charter of Rights and Freedoms,* the Board stated that it would, in each case, take into account the context within which the events alleged to be in contravention of the Code had occurred, the overall circumstances, the whole climate, and the interplay of the relationship between unions and employers, in order to determine whether the employer's communication to his employees constituted prohibited interference in the formation or administration of a trade union.

On this issue the Board declined to introduce into its jurisprudence the American theory of "free speech", which had evolved in the early 1950s. This theory, based on the belief that the employer had a legitimate interest in defeating a union, had resulted in an increasing latitude, in the name of such freedom, which allowed legal employer interference in the

---

42   *Austin Airways Ltd.* (1983), 54 di 49, 4 CLRBR (NS) 343. It must be noted, however, that s. 162 was amended by s. 31 of Bill C-34, passed by the House of Commons on June 27, 1984. Section 162 now provides for compulsory check-off of union dues ("Rand Formula").

43   (1975), 11 di 22, [1975] 2 Can LRBR 1, 75 CLLC #16,171.

44   Originally passed in 1960; now R.S.C. 1970, app. III.

selection or formation of a union by his employees. The Board distinguished the American jurisprudence on the basis of the practice of the National Labor Relations Board of ascertaining the majority character of unions by means of a vote in the case of union-organizing campaigns and certification petitions. This practice is more prevalent under the *National Labor Relations Act*[45] than it is in Canada, where the primary method of ascertaining employee wishes is by counting membership cards.[46] The Canadian approach is aimed at eliminating as much employer interference as possible by putting him in a situation where it would be pointless to mount an opposition.

Except for short periods such as in the early 1950s, however, the prevailing view in the United States was that the privilege of free speech, like other privileges, is not absolute. This view led the National Labor Relations Board to set a number of restrictions on the exercise of the freedom of expression by an employer, in order to ensure that he could not unduly influence his employees during the campaign. Among others, this view led to the creation of the "captive audience" concept by the American board and to its policy that the freedom of speech in labour relations is not an all-encompassing and overriding right to be used indiscriminately or evoked in disregard of statutory enactments that create other rights, obligations, or prohibitions.

The Board adopted the *"captive audience"* concept[47] and, similarly to its American counterpart, held that the issue of free speech for employers

---

[45]   1935 (Wagner Act), 29 U.S.C. 151-68; amended by the *Labor Management Relations Act,* 1947 (Taft-Hartley Act), 29 U.S.C. 141-97.

[46]   As the Board stated in *American Airlines Inc.* (1981), 43 di 114, [1982] 3 Can LRBR 90, in the United States a union can be certified only following an election that is equated to a political election. In that context, the employer, in the name of his freedom of expression as entrenched in the First Amendment to the United States Constitution, has the right to campaign prior to the election to try to convince his employees not to join a union. By contrast, in Canada, the approach consists of verifying the wishes of the employees and the union's support through membership cards. For this reason, the Board has developed a procedure designed to impress upon the employee signing a card, and on the union applying for certification, the importance of their actions. Concurrently with the important changes enacted by Parliament in 1978, which clearly indicated its preference for establishing the union's majority by documentary evidence, the Board raised from $2 to $5 the minimum fee required for an employee to join a union. In addition, the union must certify to the Board that the money was personally paid by the employee who signed the membership card, and if there is any impropriety in these procedures, the Board, as a policy, will dismiss the application for certification on that basis alone. These important safeguards and procedures constitute the *quid pro quo* for declining to hold a vote in all cases, as is done in the United States, and they serve and are designed to avoid the employer's participation in the process by which his employees decide to join a union or not.

[47]   The "captive audience" concept refers to an assembly of workers called together during working hours to hear their employer's views on unionization or union activities. For examples of what, in the Board's opinion, does not constitute the holding of a "captive meeting" and does not exceed the bounds of permissible communication between employer and employee, see *National Bank of Canada* (1982), 51 di 60. For examples where the Board found that such meetings contravened the Code, see *City*

in labour relations must be interpreted in the light of the peculiar relationship that exists between them and their employees. The employer must bear in mind the force and weight his expression of views may have upon the minds of his employees, which derives from the nature and extent of his authority over them as employer. In the Board's opinion, words from an employer have an impact that is far more personal and immediate than those from politicians or many others who affect an employee's life. A threat or promise, no matter how veiled, is quickly translated by an employee into tangible consequences that can have a serious and readily perceived cost to him or her.[48]

Because employer pressure on employees may be exercised with all the more weight on account of their economic dependence, and in view of the fact that a union has far less opportunity to communicate with employees than does the employer as a result of the prohibitions contained in s. 185(d), the Board has stated that it will be most vigilant and circumspect in assessing the employer's actions, words, and overt or tacit support of movements against union representation during the period when the union is soliciting support from employees. As a result, the scope of permissible employer communication in this context is necessarily limited. In order to promote an environment where employees can and do feel confident that their rights under s. 110 are real, the Board, in administering s. 184, places rigid limitations on employer communications. The Board stated that the safest attitude, and the one it would most favourably countenance, is that of an absolute neutrality by an employer on the subject of the union representation of his employees.[49]

This does not mean, however, that the Board's interpretation of s. 184(1) of the Code prohibits all manner of comment by an employer. He may express his views and give facts in an appropriate manner and circumstances on the issues involved in representation proceedings, insofar as these directly affect him. An employer may do so provided that his expression of views is not transmitted to the employees in such a manner or circumstances as to bring their dependence to the fore or to remind them of it.[50]

The employer may reply to inaccurate propaganda directed at him or his business. He may respond to unequivocal and identifiable, adversarial, or libellous statements.[51] An employer may also accurately publicize the existing terms and conditions of employment, but if he does so,

---

and *Country Radio Ltd.* (1975), 11 di 22, [1975] 2 Can LRBR 1, 75 CLLC #16,171; *Canadian Imperial Bank of Commerce (Sioux Lookout)* (1978), 33 di 432, [1979] 1 Can LRBR 18; *Banque Royale du Canada (Jonquière et Kénogami)* (1980), 42 di 125; *American Airlines Inc.* (1981), 43 di 156.

48   *Bank of Nova Scotia (Selkirk, Manitoba)* (1978), 27 di 690, [1978] 1 Can LRBR 544.
49   *Ibid.*
50   *City and Country Radio Ltd.* (1975), 11 di 22, [1975] 2 Can LRBR 1, 75 CLLC #16,171.
51   *Ibid.; American Airlines Inc.* (1981), 43 di 114, [1982] 3 Can LRBR 90; *Re Taggart Service Ltd.* (1964), 64 CLLC #16,015 (C.L.R.B.).

he must not make or imply any promises or forecast or imply changes either to the benefit or detriment of the employees. By doing so, he would be inviting obvious conclusions about his authority over the employees and about how he may exercise it in response to any choice they may make. He would thereby interfere with his employees' rights under Part V of the Code.[52] Communications related to the efficient operation of the business are, of course, permissible.[53] In all communications the employer must take care, however, that his expression of views does not constitute and may not reasonably be construed by his employees to be an attempt, by means of intimidation, threats, or other forms of coercion, to interfere with their freedom to join a trade union of their choice or to otherwise select a bargaining agent of their choice.[54]

The Board has stated that, in its opinion, the above construction and application of s. 184(1) does not abrogate, abridge, or infringe on the freedom of expression now entrenched in s. 2(b) of the *Canadian Charter of Rights and Freedoms.*[55] However, the courts of the country will certainly be called to decide whether or not such an interpretation infringes on this guaranteed right.[56]

To date, the Board has held that a bank employer had not breached s. 184(1) when two of its senior representatives toured all the branches of the bank in a province, including one where a union organizing campaign was underway, and held meetings during working hours with the purpose of publicizing the bank's employment benefits and employee-relations policies. The Board was satisfied that the employer had done no more than highlight the employees' current employment conditions and had not adversely commented on unions or collective bargaining, or made any promises or threats or used coercion, intimidation, or undue influence on the employees.[57]

---

[52]   *Bank of Nova Scotia (Selkirk, Manitoba), supra,* note 48.

[53]   *American Airlines Inc., supra,* note 46.

[54]   *City and Country Radio Ltd., supra,* note 50.

[55]   *Constitution Act, 1982* (enacted by *The Canada Act, 1982* (U.K.), c. 11, sched. B). See *Eastern Provincial Airways Ltd.* (1983), 51 di 209, 3 CLRBR (NS) 75; revd. *Eastern Provincial Airways Ltd. v. Canada Labour Relations Board and Canadian Airline Pilots,* [1984] 1 F.C. 732, 50 N.R. 81, 2 D.L.R. (4th) 597 (C.A.), where the Federal Court of Appeal summarily dismissed the employer's contention that the Board's interpretation of s. 184(1) offended the *Canadian Charter of Rights and Freedoms,* but it did not explain its rationale or discuss the question of whether a limit on the freedom of expression imposed by s. 184(1) would be demonstrably justified in a free and democratic society such as Canada, in light of the Charter.

[56]   *National Bank of Canada v. Retail Clerks' International Union,* [1984] 1 S.C.R. 269, 53 N.R. 203, 84 CLLC #14,037, 9 D.L.R. (4th) 10. In this case, Justice Beetz of the Supreme Court of Canada suggested that the Board could not force the president of the bank to declare publicly that he believed in the freedom of association principle, as a remedial measure to an unfair labour practice committed by the bank in this case, because such remedy was contrary to the fundamental freedom of thought and belief guaranteed by the Charter.

[57]   *Bank of Nova Scotia (Selkirk, Manitoba)* (1978), 27 di 690, [1978] 1 Can LRBR 544.

By contrast, the Board found contraventions of s. 184(1) in a case where the president and general manager of the company had actively communicated to the employees their views concerning unionization both in various memos and verbally, and had incited them to form a staff association, and where some members of the management team had made some very disparaging statements against unions to employees and had held captive audiences.[58]

In another decision it was held that an employer had breached s. 184(1) in seeking to discourage his employees from attending union meetings and by prophesying harsh consequences if they participated in union activities.[59] Generally, the Board has found interferences in the representation of employees where, in the course of union-organizing campaigns, memos and letters sent to them were clearly intended to convince them not to join the union or contained veiled threats that they would lose existing special advantages, if a union succeeded in organizing them.[60]

Post-Certification or Labour Disputes Communications

Once a trade union has been certified by the Board, it does not mean that an employer cannot speak to his employees anymore without the consent of the union. Indeed, certification and s. 136(1) of the Code, in particular, create an exclusive power of representation in favour of the union, but they do not by law cast the union into the role of the sole spokesman for an employee in all of his or her dealings with the employer. The latter has always the right, within the confines discussed above, to speak to his employees even in post-certification situations. As the Board stated, to forbid an employer from speaking to his employees would seriously undermine the work relation between them, and more particularly the loyalty and the climate of confidence that are essential to good productivity. Whether such communications constitute interference with the representation of employees by a union contrary to s. 184(1) is a question of fact.[61]

For instance, in a post-certification situation it was determined that, where employees were planning to participate in the picketing of a third enterprise, to which their employer was a subcontractor, in order to support a sister union, that employer might address his employees to convey to them the consequences that would follow if they were to put their plan into action. The Board held that statements made about what the employer believes will in fact be the outcome of the action proposed by his employees do not go over the line that separates valid communica-

---

58   *City and Country Radio Ltd.* (1975), 11 di 22, [1975] 2 Can LRBR 1, 75 CLLC #16,171.
59   *Oakville Cablevision Ltd.* (1980), 40 di 189.
60   *American Airlines Inc.* (1981), 43 di 114, [1982] 3 Can LRBR 90; *Amok Ltd.* (1981), 43 di 289.
61   *ATV New Brunswick Ltd. (CKCW-TV)* (1978), 29 di 23, [1979] 3 Can LRBR 342.

tion from activities that interfere with trade union administration contrary to the Code. This is especially the case where the employer has no control over the eventual outcome of the actions proposed by his employees. To advise others that you have good reasons to believe that they will suffer consequences flowing from a third party if they do something to that third party can hardly be considered as a threat, unless the person giving the advice is at less than arm's length from the third party.[62]

A letter sent to employees by their employer while the parties were in conciliation was found not to contravene s. 184(1). The letter had been written in response to a perceived misunderstanding of the employer's position by the bargaining agent, and it described in a manner factually accurate the state of negotiations and the employer's proposition to the union.[63] The Board came to the same conclusion with respect to a letter sent by an employer to his employees on the eve of the acquisition of the right to strike, informing them of their terms of employment once the statutory freeze imposed by s. 148(b) expired and offering no term that had not already been offered to the union in negotiations. The letter was held to be a legally permissible communication and not an effort to undermine the union by negotiating directly with the individual employees.[64]

When the right to use economic sanctions has been legally acquired, the parties are then free to use every legal means up to and including the strike and lockout to compel each other to agree to terms and conditions of employment. The employer is entitled to use compulsion to obtain his desired terms and conditions of employment. He can shut down his operation either in whole or in part, with a view to compelling employees to agree with his position in negotiations. As the Board stated in an early decision, such action is clearly exercised by an employer directly against his employees, and it is his legal right to attempt to persuade them, either collectively or individually, to agree to his terms.[65]

It must be remembered, however, that the Board has made it clear that the prohibitions contained in s. 184(1) also apply during a strike period.[66] Where, in the midst of a strike, an employer distributed to his employees a negotiations bulletin, the Board found no contravention of s. 184(1). The communication contained no gross misstatements of facts tending to unjustly malign the bargaining agent to the extent that its legitimate representation of the employees in the bargaining unit might have been jeopardized and interfered with.[67]

---

[62] *Eastern Aviation Contractors Ltd.* (1983), 52 di 145, 83 CLLC #16,067.
[63] *CKLW Radio Broadcasting Ltd.* (1977), 23 di 51, 77 CLLC #16,110.
[64] *Ibid.*
[65] *Air Canada* (1976), 18 di 66, 77 CLLC #16,062.
[66] *Ibid.; Television Saint-François Inc.* (1981), 43 di 175; *Eastern Provincial Airways Ltd., supra,* note 55; *Austin Airways Ltd.* (1983), 54 di 49, 4 CLRBR (NS) 343.
[67] *Air Canada, supra,* note 65.

By contrast, the employer was found to have overstepped the fine line dividing permissible from impermissible communications in *Eastern Provincial Airways Ltd.*[68] In that case, the Board held that, by communicating directly with his employees who were on strike and inciting them to return to work on the terms and conditions of employment outlined in the communications, the employer had contravened s. 184(1) of the Code by interfering with the union's exclusive representation of the employees. Such communications, in the Board's opinion, were intended to malign the union and to demean it in the eyes of its members, thereby dividing them from their trade union and undermining its right and ability to engage in collective bargaining on their behalf.[69]

Whether direct communication with employees in the course of a strike constitutes an attempt to negotiate with them exclusive of their bargaining agent, and hence constitutes an interference in the representation of employees, is a question of fact. The fate of the complaint will turn on the particular circumstances of each case and on the context within which the events alleged to be in contravention of the Code have occurred.

11:1130   The Relation Between Sections 134(1) (Employer Domination) and 184(1) (Employer Interference)

The issue in an inquiry under s. 134(1) is not the legality of the conduct of the employer or his representatives, but rather whether the union "is so dominated or influenced by an employer" that the fitness of the trade union to represent employees of the employer for the purpose of collective bargaining is impaired. The evidence that the employer has contravened or allegedly contravened, either recently or in the past, the provisions of s. 184 is consequently irrelevant to a determination under s. 134(1). Such evidence can, at the very most, warrant the Board's carrying-out of an investigation to determine whether there is reason to apply s. 134(1) of the Code.[70]

11:1140   Effect of Employer Domination or Influence

Under s. 184(1), employers are prohibited from negative interference in the formation of a trade union. In other words, they are prohibited from using their privileged position in relation to their em-

---

68   *Supra*, note 55; *Eastern Provincial Airways Ltd.* (1983), 54 di 172, 5 CLRBR (NS) 368, 84 CLLC #16,012; affd. (*sub nom. Eastern Provincial Airways Ltd. v. Canada Labour Relations Board*), 84 CLLC #14,042 (Fed. C.A.).
69   The Board came to the same conclusion with respect to direct employer communications with the employees after notice to bargain had been given in *Austin Airways Ltd. / White River Air Service Ltd.* (1980), 41 di 151, [1980] 3 Can LRBR 393.
70   *CJRC Radio Capitale Ltée* (1977), 21 di 416, [1977] 2 Can LRBR 578, 78 CLLC #16,124.

ployees in attempting to influence their right to be represented by a bargaining agent of their choice. On the other hand, support or approval, that is, positive interference, is prohibited only insofar as it interferes with the freely expressed wishes of the employees and their freedom of choice in selecting a bargaining agent. For example, in a situation where two or more trade unions are competing for the support of employees, an employer who openly favours one union over the other would, while having a positive effect on behalf of one union, clearly have a negative impact on the other. Such action would be regarded as unlawful interference.[71]

In situations where employees are not represented by a bargaining agent and there are no competing unions, the support or involvement in a union-organizing drive by an individual identified as a member of management must be viewed in the following light: Would it be likely to deprive the employees of their freedom of choice? Would it influence them unduly in this regard? To make such a decision, the Board stated that it must determine whether the actions of the individual concerned are in fact consistent with the recognized interests or wishes of the employer. In the Board's opinion, the actions of a member of the management team with respect to the interest and position of the employer are easily identified by the employees. Normally, when a member of management acts in opposition to an application for certification, the employees identify this action as being in conformity with the interests and wishes of the employer. When, however, a member of the management team speaks in favour of a union, where there is no other rival union in the picture and when this support is given in a manner that the employees can easily identify as being contrary to the wishes of the company, it cannot really be said that this individual is representing the employer by his actions. The employees are not likely to be unduly influenced by this support of the union's position.

In other words, where the situation is such that the employees are not likely to consider the activities of a member of management as that of the employer, or where such activities are easily identified as being contrary to the wishes of the employer, then the employees cannot be said to have been or likely to be unduly influenced by these activities.[72] Thus, where the employer's sole industrial relations officer employed in a confidential capacity in matters relating to industrial relations had been actively soliciting membership support among the supervisory personnel of the company, the ensuing application for certification was not dismissed by the Board as bearing the taint of employer support, because it found no evidence that the employee's exercise of their freedom to select

---

71   *General Aviation Services Ltd.* (1979), 34 di 791, [1979] 2 Can LRBR 98.
72   *Radio Station CHQM* (1975), 11 di 16, [1976] 1 Can LRBR 110, 75 CLLC #16,166.

a union and the free expression of their wishes had been negatively interfered with by such management involvement.[73]

11:1150   Presumption of Non-Domination or Influence: Section 184(2)

In the cases mentioned in s. 184(2), an employer, by way of exception, is deemed not to contravene s. 184(1). The Board has determined that the matters referred to in s. 184(2) are obviously not the only forms of employer-union co-operation that are outside the ambit of s. 184(1). A narrow construction of subss. (1) and (2) would preclude all relationships of a business nature between the union and employer. Employers would not be able to lease property from unions, retain professional or technical services from a union, support union educational programs, or even purchase union literature, because it would be a "financial or other support to a trade union". Such a severe demarcation between union and management relations would promote a non-communicative entrenchment of labour and management and would be totally counter to "co-operative efforts" and "the development of good industrial relations" referred to in the preamble of the Code.

As the Board has stated,[74] the test is not intended to be the form of the relationship between the union and employer, but whether the employer's relationship with the union affects the union's ability to act as a bargaining agent independent of the employer. This test is implicit in Parliament's enactment of s. 134(1) of the Code, by which collective agreements are deemed not to exist and certification must be denied if the Board is satisfied a union "is so dominated or influenced by an employer that the fitness of the trade union to represent employees of the employer for the purpose of collective bargaining is impaired".

Thus, where an employer contributes financially to the dispatch services provided by a union through a hiring hall, this type of contribution does not affect the union's effective performance as an independent representative of employee interests. This type of contribution most resembles a fee for services in the nature of a business transaction and does not violate s. 184(1).

11:1200   UNION INTERFERENCE: SECTION 185(c)

Section 110(2) provides that every employer is free to join the employer's organization of his choice and to participate in its lawful activities. Section 107(1) defines an employer's organization as "any

---

[73]   *General Aviation Services Ltd., supra,* note 71.
[74]   *Pacific Maritime Agencies Ltd.* (1977), 24 di 148, [1977] 2 Can LRBR 168, 77 CLLC #16,078.

organization of employers the purpose of which include the regulation of relations between employers and employees". An employer thus enjoys the same basic freedom as is conferred on employees by s. 110(1). As a corollary, s. 185(c) provides that no trade union, and no person acting on behalf of a trade union, shall participate in or interfere with the formation or administration of an employer's organization.

Very seldom is this section raised in the Board's administration of the Code, and it has not yet had the opportunity to evolve a policy on this subject. In the only case in which it was raised, fifteen employees occupying dispatcher functions in an employer's organization that bargained for and represented sixty-five employers sought to be represented by a local union affiliated with the only union the employer's organization was mandated to deal with. In response, the employer's organization complained that the union's application was, in itself, a contravention of s. 185(c) of the Code. As the Board found that the dispatchers sought by the union were not employees within the meaning of the Code, the application for certification was dismissed. The Board, therefore, did not deal with the complaint under s. 185(c).[75] However, the facts of this case afford an interesting glance at the type of situation that might be envisioned by s. 185(c).

11:2000   UNFAIR PRACTICES RELATING TO UNION MEMBERSHIP OR ACTIVITIES

The following paragraphs deal with unfair labour practices related to union membership and to the exercise of rights protected by Part V. Prohibitions against positive actions by the employer directed at a person because of his membership or office in a union are provided in s. 184(3)(a)(i) and (e). Prohibitions against employer actions directed against a person or an employee because of the exercise of any right or the participation in activities protected by Part V are provided in s. 184(3)(a)(vi), (b), (d)(ii), and (f).

With respect to the practices of unions, prohibitions related to membership solicitation and canvassing are provided in s. 185(d), with an exception in s. 199. Finally, both unions and employers are prohibited by s. 186 from intimidating or coercing a person to become or to cease to be a member of a trade union.

11:2100   EMPLOYER-PROHIBITED CONDUCT

11:2110   Acts Motivated by Union Activities: Section 184(3)(a)(i), (e)

There are at least three categories of positive acts referred to in s. 184(3)(a). The first category concerns the refusal to employ. The

---

[75]   *British Columbia Maritime Employers Association* (1981), 45 di 357.

second category includes all forms of discipline, including (i) the refusal to continue to employ, or dismissal, (ii) suspension, (iii) transfer, (iv) lay-off, or (v) other discrimination against a person in regards to employment, pay, or any other term or condition of employment. The third category concerns intimidation or threats against a person. The prohibited reasons for these acts are listed in s. 183(a)(i) to (vi). Among the latter, subpara. (i) provides that the positive acts mentioned above cannot be taken against a person for the reason that "the person is or proposes to become, or seeks to induce any other person to become, a member, officer or representative of a trade union or participates in the promotion, formation or administration of a trade union".

The first part of s. 184(3)(e) enumerates specific acts such as intimidation, threats of dismissal, any other kind of threats, and the imposition of a pecuniary or other penalty, which are essentially to the same effect as those prohibited by the second and third category of s. 184(3)(a). These acts are prohibited when they are taken by an employer "to compel a person to refrain from becoming or to cease to be a member, officer or representative of a trade union". Section 184(3)(e) also refers to other unspecified "means".

These specific acts are studied in paragraphs 11:2111 to 11:2117.

11:2111   Refusal to Employ

There have been very few cases in which the Board has dealt with an alleged refusal to employ or to hire under s. 184(3)(a)(i).[76] In one such case,[77] a complaint brought under this section alleging that the employer had failed to hire nine union members who were employees of the predecessor firm for reasons of anti-union animus was dismissed by the Board. The union had been certified to represent all employees of a company that had a contract with an airline company to provide security services at Newfoundland airports. The respondent firm subsequently tendered for and displaced the previous company in the contract with the airline enterprise. Although the issue of the union's successor rights was not raised by either party, the new employer rehired some, but not all, of the former employees who were union members, in spite of the past practice of incumbent security firms of hiring the employees of their predecessors. The Board accepted the reasons given by the employer for the hiring of its security staff and dismissed the allegation of anti-union animus.

---

[76]   In *Mike Sheehan* (1976), 17 di 14, [1976] 2 Can LRBR 187, 76 CLLC #16,030, the Board considered an alleged refusal to employ for a reason prohibited by s. 184(3)(a)(ii). This decision is considered at paragraph 13:4110. Another case before the Board involved an alleged refusal to employ for a consideration prohibited by s. 184(3)(a)(iii): see *Northern Telecom Canada Ltd.* (1982), 48 di 78. This decision is considered at paragraph 14:0000.

[77]   *Ancon Corp. Security and Investigation Ltd.* (1981), 43 di 47, [1981] 2 Can LRBR 137.

In another decision,[78] a complaint filed by a retired employee under s. 184(3)(a)(i) alleging that his former employer had denied him an employment opportunity because of his past union activities was dismissed. The Board determined that the complainant was not a person falling within the category of retired employees eligible for employment opportunities in accordance with the criteria established by the employer and found that the denial of employment was not related to any reason prohibited by the Code. In another decision on this issue,[79] the Board found that an employer's refusal to employ the complainant was motivated by the latter's involvement in union activities and a fear that he would organize other employees into a union.

11:2112   Dismissal and Layoff

The cases in which the Board has dealt with alleged discriminatory dismissals because of membership or office in a union are legion.[80]

The manner in which a dismissal or termination is carried out may vary from one case to another. It may take the shape of a constructive or

---

[78]   *Northern Telecom Canada Ltd., supra*, note 76.

[79]   *Scotian Shelf Traders Ltd.* (1983), 52 di 151, 4 CLRBR (NS) 278, 83 CLLC #16,070.

[80]   For cases where complaints alleging discriminatory dismissals were upheld, see *CHUM Western Ltd., Radio CKVN* (1974), 3 di 18; *Radio Ste-Agathe (CJSA) Inc.* (1974), 4 di 66, 74 CLLC #16,108; *Aero-Club de Montréal Inc.* (1974), 4 di 44, 74 CLLC #16,106; *Les Ailes du Nord Ltée, Northern Wings Ltd.* (1974), 5 di 17, 74 CLLC #16,136; *Donald William Murray Movers Ltd.* (1975), 8 di 9, 75 CLLC #16,157; *Central Broadcasting Co. Ltd.* (1975), 10 di 8, [1975] 2 Can LRBR 65, 75 CLLC #16,169; *Arnold Bros. Transport Ltd.* (1976), 19 di 132, [1977] 2 Can LRBR 86; *CJRP Radio Provinciale Ltée* (1977), 19 di 136; *Victoria Flying Services Ltd.* (1977), 23 di 13, 77 CLLC #16,072; *Soo-Security Motorways Ltd.* (1977), 19 di 155, 77 CLLC #16,096; *Brazeau Transport Inc.* (1978), 33 di 520; *Brazeau Transport Inc.* (1978), 34 di 572; *Canadian Imperial Bank of Commerce (Toronto)* (1979), 34 di 677, [1979] 1 Can LRBR 391; *Victoria Flying Services Ltd.* (1979), 35 di 73, [1979] 3 Can LRBR 216; *British Columbia Telephone Co.* (1979), 38 di 14, [1979] 1 Can LRBR 350; *Banque Provinciale du Canada (Jonquière)* (1979), 36 di 58; *ADGA Systems International* (1979), 38 di 190; *G. Courchesne Transport Inc.* (1979), 36 di 63; *CJVA Radio-Acadia Ltée* (1980), 40 di 145; *Oakville Cablevision Ltd.* (1980), 40 di 189; *Transx Ltd.* (1980), 40 di 214; *Banque Royale du Canada (Jonquière et Kénogami)* (1980), 42 di 125; *Transvision Magog Inc.* (1981), 43 di 56; *American Airlines Inc.* (1981), 43 di 156; *T.E. Quinn Truck Lines Ltd.* (1981), 45 di 254; *Highland Helicopters Ltd.* (1981), 46 di 50; *Sorel-O-Vision Inc.* (1981), 46 di 73; *Purolator Courier Ltd.* (1982), 48 di 32; *A & M Transport Ltd.* (1983), 52 di 69; *International Sea-Land Shipping Services Ltd.* (1983), 54 di 63; *Worldways Canada Ltd.* (1984), 55 di 151.

For cases where complaints alleging discriminatory dismissals were dismissed, see: *Radio Ste-Agathe (CJSA) Inc.* (1975), 8 di 8, 75 CLLC #16,154; *Radio Côte-Nord Inc.* (1977), 20 di 270; *Radio Côte-Nord Inc.* (1977), 20 di 275; *Canadian Imperial Bank of Commerce (Gibsons, B.C.)* (1978), 27 di 748; *Brazeau Transport Inc.* (1978), 31 di 208; *Brazeau Transport Inc.* (1978), 34 di 572; *Bank of Montreal (Guelph)* (1979), 37 di 64; *Banque Provinciale du Canada (Jonquière)* (1979), 36 di 58; *Banque Nationale du Canada (Fermont, Québec)* (1979), 36 di 69; *Bank of Montreal (Carrall and Hastings Street)* (1980), 39 di 122; *Cabano Transport Ltée* (1981), 42 di 318; *Transvision Magog Inc.* (1981), 43 di 56; *Services Managers Roy Ltée* (1981), 43 di 212; *Amok Ltd.* (1981), 43 di 282; *Canadian Pacific Ltd.* (1981), 43 di 305; *Ed Finn* (1982), 47 di 49, 82 CLLC #16,155, [1982] 1 Can LRBR 399; *Air Mistassini Inc.* (1982), 48 di 73; *Hill Security Ltd.* (1982), 49 di 90; *Paul Godin and Robert Letang*, decision no. 451, not yet reported, January 13, 1984 (C.L.R.B.).

disguised dismissal, where an employee overburdened with work or responsibilities is forced to resign.[81] It may result from the employer's termination of the contracts held by dependent contractors.[82] It may result in the abolition of an employee's position.[82a] Such dismissals may also result from an employer's subcontracting out a number of services, thus rendering various work functions redundant.[83]

The persons whose dismissal is covered by s. 184(3)(a)(i) include foremen[84] and probationary employees.[85]

The failure to recall an employee who is laid-off because of a lack of work becomes a dismissal as soon as a recall is possible and another person is hired instead to perform the same functions. The Board has held that, when an employer fails to recall some employees at the resumption of seasonal operations because of their union membership and replaces them with newly hired employees, he is in violation of s. 184(3)(a)(ii).[86] Similarly the lay-off of an employee according to seniority constitutes a dismissal when the employer's intention is not to recall him. A lay-off on the basis of seniority must be followed by a recall on the same basis. Otherwise, the lay-off is in reality a dismissal.[87] Where an employer introduces new methods of operations that render some functions redundant, the resulting lay-offs may be found to contravene s. 184(3)(a)(i) if the new methods are used as tools of convenience to dilute the union's support in the bargaining unit.[88]

Board Inquiry Into the Causes of Dismissal

The Prohibited Reason

Unlike the *Quebec Labour Code*, which provides that the employer must prove that the employee has been disciplined or dismissed "for another good and sufficient reason", or the *Saskatchewan Trade Union Act*, which requires the employer to prove that the employee was discharged

---

81   *Purolator Courier Ltd.* (1982), 48 di 32.
82   *Arnold Bros. Transport Ltd.* (1976), 19 di 132, [1977] 2 Can LRBR 86.
82a *Task Terminal Ltée* (1980), 40 di 52.
83   *British Columbia Telephone Co.* (1979), 38 di 14, [1979] 1 Can LRBR 350.
84   *Highland Helicopters Ltd.* (1981), 46 di 50.
85   *Radio Côte-Nord Inc.* (1977), 20 di 270; *Verreault Navigation Inc.* (1978), 24 di 227; *Brazeau Transport Inc.* (1978), 33 di 520; *American Airlines Inc.* (1981), 43 di 156; *Amok Ltd.* (1981), 43 di 282.
86   *Verreault Navigation Inc., supra,* note 85.
87   *McAllister Towing & Salvage Ltd.* (1978), 27 di 784.
88   *International Sea-Land Shipping Services Ltd.* (1983), 54 di 63. For cases where complaints alleging discriminatory lay-offs were upheld, see *Verreault Navigation Inc., supra,* note 85; *McAllister Towing & Salvage Ltd., supra,* note 87; *Road Runner Courrier Services* (1979), 34 di 783, [1979] 2 Can LRBR 20; *Transvision Magog Inc.* (1981), 43 di 56; *International Sea-Land Shipping Services Ltd., supra.* For cases where complaints alleging discriminatory lay-offs were dismissed; see *Canadian Imperial Bank of Commerce (Gibsons, B.C.)* (1978), 27 di 748; and *Transvision Magog Inc., supra.*

"for good and sufficient reason", the *Canada Labour Code* does not prescribe what the employer must do or prove in order to rebut the presumption created by s. 188(3).

The Code does not provide that an employer may only discipline an employee for just cause, but rather it stipulates that he may not discipline an employee for certain prohibited reasons such as those found in s. 184(3)(a)(i). As a result, an employer may discipline an employee for a good reason, a poor reason, or no reason at all, so long as the provisions of the *Canada Labour Code* are not violated.

Obviously, the question of whether or not the dismissal was for a "just cause" or a "good and sufficient reason" will be an important consideration. However, the provisions of the *Canada Labour Code* do not confer on the Board a broad jurisdiction to determine whether an employee has been dismissed for just cause as they would confer on an arbitrator.[89] The Board hears this evidence, not to rule on it or to make a value judgment, but to make sure that the cause alleged by the employer is not associated with anti-union motive. The cause of dismissal put forward by the employer serves the sole purpose of establishing an absence of anti-union motive.

In *Oshawa Flying Club*,[90] the Board considered the applicability of s. 61.5 of Part III of the Code. The notion of just cause for persons qualifying under that section is the normal standard for dismissal. The benefit of this statutory employment condition is maintained by s. 124(4) of Part V following the filing of a certification application, and then by s. 148(b) until the conclusion of a collective agreement.[91] Thus, when the complainant qualifies under s. 61.5 of Part III, the Board has stated that it will evaluate the alleged cause more closely.

An examination of the sufficiency of the alleged reasons for dismissal alone rarely provides, however, a means to determine the motivation of the employer. Thus all events surrounding a dismissal are considered by the Board in order to arrive at a sound judgment. Evidence of events occurring prior to and immediately after the dismissal provides a reliable means of assessing the motivation behind the employer's action.[92]

The Board must satisfy itself that the action taken was not due to the employee's membership or participation in a union.[93] On this issue, what really matters is not whether the employee is a union member, but whether the employer believed he was and terminated him for this reason. Thus, to defend himself against a complaint of illegal dismissal, it is not enough for an employer to demonstrate that the person aggrieved

---

[89]   *CKOY Ltd.* (1976), 17 di 24, [1976] 2 Can LRBR 329; *Radio Côte-Nord Inc.* (1977), 20 di 270; *Oshawa Flying Club* (1981), 42 di 306, [1981] 2 Can LRBR 95; *Canpar* (1981), 43 di 169; *Pierre Fiset*, decision no. 473, not yet reported, April 23, 1985 (C.L.R.B.).

[90]   *Supra*, note 89.

[91]   See also *Highland Helicopters Ltd., supra,* note 84.

[92]   *Victoria Flying Services Ltd.* (1977), 23 di 13, 77 CLLC #16,072.

[93]   *Road Runner Courrier Services, supra,* note 88.

never in fact became a union member, particularly if that person did participate in union activities in such a manner as would reasonably suggest to the employer that he was a union member.[94] Whether the reason for the dismissal was the union activities of the complainant in particular or those of the employees in general, a breach of s. 184(3)(a)(i) will be found.[95] If, on the other hand, the employer can satisfy the Board that the disciplinary action had no relation to the employee's union membership or activities, the Board will not find a violation of the Code even though the employer's actions might very well have been arbitrary, discriminatory, or unjust.[96]

In order to determine whether such a relationship existed between the dismissal and the employee's union membership or activities, the Board will take various elements into consideration. These include, first, the contemporaneity of the dismissal with an organizing campaign and a certification demand, or with the employer's knowledge of the union activity.[97] An element of contemporaneity between the exercise of rights granted by the Code and the termination of employees creates a strong inference that their dismissals were motivated by such union activities.[98] The Board may not however, always conclude that anti-union animus must be inferred for the sole reason that some dismissals were contemporaneous to the exercise of union activities. For instance, the Board found in one case[99] that the occurrence of performance reviews of complainants and their subsequent dismissals were not related to pending certification proceedings. The Board held the events to be merely coincidental and found that there was no anti-union animus on the employer's part.

A second element taken into consideration is the employer's knowledge of the union's activities in general, or those of the complainant in particular. This element alone, however, cannot serve as a defence. For instance, in one case[100] the firing of a complainant was found to be contrary to s. 184(3)(a)(i) when it resulted from his supervisor's misrepresentation of the facts to the employer in retaliation for the complainant's seeking union representation. The employer's ignorance of the real reason for the dismissal recommendation did not vitiate his responsibility.

A third element is the timing of the dismissal.[101] For example, in one case[102] it was determined that dismissals which resulted from the sub-

---

94   *Central Broadcasting Co. Ltd.* (1975), 10 di 8, [1975] 2 Can LRBR 65, 75 CLLC #16,169.
95   *Purolator Courier Ltd.* (1982), 48 di 32.
96   *Road Runner Courrier Services, supra,* note 88.
97   *A.J. (Archie) Goodale Ltd.* (1977), 21 di 473, [1977] 2 Can LRBR 309; *T.E. Quinn Truck Lines Ltd.* (1981), 45 di 254.
98   *Transx Ltd.* (1980), 40 di 214; *Hill Security Ltd.* (1982), 49 di 90.
99   *Bank of Montreal (Guelph)* (1979), 37 di 64.
100   *ADGA Systems International* (1979), 38 di 190.
101   *A.J. (Archie) Goodale Ltd., supra,* note 97.
102   *British Columbia Telephone Co.* (1979), 38 di 14, [1979] 1 Can LRBR 350.

contracting of a number of services of the employer violated s. 184(3)(a)(i). Although the concept of transferring a number of services to a subcontractor had not originally been planned by the employer for the purpose of defeating the union, the timing and the inexplicable urgency to implement the contracting-out, once the employer had learned of the organizing campaign, led the Board to conclude that an anti-union animus existed.

A fourth element considered by the Board is the role of the complainant in the events preceding the discipline or dismissals. For example, in the context of an application for certification, the Board will consider whether the complainant was actively engaged in recruiting membership support in the course of the organizing drive.[103]

Finally, the Board will consider the demeanour of the witnesses at the hearing.[104]

Incompetence of the Complainant

A cause often advanced by employers to defend themselves against illegal dismissal charges is that of the incompetence of the complainant. On this subject, the Board has cautioned on a number of occasions[105] that, although the Code imposes a burden of proof on the employer to show that s. 184(3)(a)(i) was not violated, it is axiomatic that union membership should not be used to shelter the employee's incompetence.

However, where it is demonstrated that the employer had legitimate concerns over the complainant's lack of performance that might have led to dismissal in any event, if the termination was premature and was precipitated by the employer's knowledge of the complainant's union activities, a contravention of the Code will be found. Similarly, if the employer's knowledge of the complainant's union activities is used as a culminating incident that precipitates the dismissal, there will also be a violation of the Code. In other words, if a combination of anti-union motive and legitimate concerns with respect to an employee's lack of performance is found, there is, due to the presence of anti-union animus, a violation of the Code.[106]

---

103   *A.J. (Archie) Goodale Ltd., supra,* note 97; *Canadian Imperial Bank of Commerce (Toronto)* (1979), 34 di 677, [1979] 1 Can **LRBR** 391.
104   *A.J. (Archie) Goodale Ltd., supra,* note 97.
105   See *Brazeau Transport Inc.* (1979), 35 di 158; *Lawrence Schumph* (1980), 40 di 123; *Amok Ltd.* (1981), 43 di 282; *Pierre Fiset, supra,* note 89; and in particular see *National Bank of Canada* (1982), 51 di 60, where the incompetence of the complainant was accepted as the sole reason for the dismissal, and the complaints were therefore dismissed; and *Les Ailes du Nord Ltée, Northern Wings Ltd.* (1974), 5 di 17, 74 CLLC #16,136, where the same reason given by the employer was rejected.
106   *Canadian Imperial Bank of Commerce (Toronto), supra,* note 103.

Economic Difficulties

Another reason commonly advanced against unfair dismissal charges is that of economic difficulties. Where terminations are motivated solely by administrative and financial reasons, complaints under s. 184(3)(a)(i) of actions that are in no way attributable to the union membership of the employees will be dismissed. The Board holds the view that it is not its responsibility to determine whether the employer's decision to reduce expenditures that resulted in the terminations was truly inevitable in the light of the enterprise's financial situation. Rather, the Board seeks to determine whether these financial constraints were merely used as a pretext by the employer to dismiss employees who were union members.[107]

Moreover, the Board will not rule on the method the employer chooses to assess the capabilities of his employees in order to determine who should be laid-off. Whenever it becomes necessary to make reductions in staff for economic reasons, it is not unusual to take into account the quality of the work performed by the employees in question and their respective contributions to the success of the enterprise. This is a matter that, in the absence of a collective agreement, is within the exclusive managerial discretion of the employer. However, the Board will receive evidence as to the method of selection in order to determine the presence or absence of a prohibited motive for the rejection of one or another of the employees. In the Board's opinion, an illogical or inconsistent application of an established employer policy in assessing employee performance, while not establishing a violation of the Code, might be some evidence of the state of mind of the employer which, coupled with the fact of union activity on the part of the rejected employee, could permit a conclusion of the existence of anti-union animus.[108]

Other Causes and Illegal Union Activities

According to s. 110(1), employees have the right to freely join a union of their choice and to participate in the lawful activities of that union. The exercise of these rights, protected and enforced by s. 184(3)(a) among others, is not absolute, however, and they must be exercised in a manner consistent with the purpose for which they exist. Thus, although the Code imposes a burden upon the employer to prove that a dismissal was not motivated by membership or office in a union, or by the union activities of the complainant, union activities must not serve as a pretext

---

[107]   *Radio Côte-Nord Inc.* (1977), 20 di 275; *Radio CKML Inc.* (1982), 51 di 115.

[108]   *Canadian Imperial Bank of Commerce (Gibsons, B.C.)* (1978), 27 di 748. See also *Hasan Ergen* (1979), 34 di 776, [1979] 1 Can LRBR 571; and *Transvision Magog Inc.* (1981), 43 di 56 (for three of the complainants), where a defence of economic difficulties was accepted by the Board; *Transvision Magog Inc.*, *supra* (for one of the complainants); *Bessette Transport Inc.* (1981), 43 di 64, and *T.E. Quinn Truck Lines Ltd.* (1981), 45 di 254, where such a defence was rejected.

for misconduct or abusive language of the sort that could lead to a disruption of business operations or could provoke management representatives.[109] No employee, whether unionized or not, may disregard his normal obligations in the performance of his work, or fail to respect disciplinary rules in force in the enterprise.[110]

On this issue, the Board stated[111] that the issuing of a previous reinstatement order does not confer permanent immunity on the employee concerned or exempt him from the obligation to effectively carry out his duties as required by the employer. The Board found that the complainant, who had been previously reinstated by Board order, had not carried out his obligations conscientiously in accordance with his work contract. Accordingly, the employer had a valid reason for dismissal.

With respect to the participation in an illegal work stoppage, the Board stated in an early decision that it had no jurisdiction to decide that because a group of employees violated one of the provisions of Part V, it was automatically deprived of the protection of the unfair labour practice provisions of the Code.[112] In that case, which was decided before the judgment of the Supreme Court of Canada in *Lafrance v. Commercial Photo Service Inc.*,[113] the Board found that the dismissal of employees who had participated in an illegal picketing was in contravention of s. 184(3)(a)(i), as the fact that the employer believed the participants were union members constituted a proximate cause of their termination. By contrast, in a subsequent decision,[114] union officers who had been the leaders of an illegal strike were selected for special attention and disciplined by the employer after the Board had issued an order directing the employees to cease and desist from their illegal activities. It was determined that the employer had disciplined those whom it thought to be the leaders of the concerted action because they were the leaders, and not because of their union office or membership. In dismissing the complaint, the Board stated that, by leading an illegal strike, the officers were not engaged in activities related to their office or membership and, moreover, that union membership or office is not an armour to protect against any discipline imposed in the course of normal employment responsibilities.[115]

---

109   *Radio Ste-Agathe (CJSA) Inc.* (1974), 4 di 66, 74 CLLC #16,108.
110   *Jacques Lecavalier* (1983), 54 di 100.
111   *Radio Ste-Agathe (CJSA) Inc.* (1975), 8 di 8, 75 CLLC #16,154.
112   *Central Broadcasting Co. Ltd.* (1975), 10 di 8, [1975] 2 Can LRBR 65, 75 CLLC #16,169.
113   [1980] 1 S.C.R. 536, 32 N.R. 46, 80 CLLC #14,028.
114   *Canadian Pacific Ltd.* (1981), 43 di 305.
115   See also *Transvision Magog Inc.*, *supra*, note 108; *Services Managers Roy Ltée* (1981), 43 di 212; and *Jacques Lecavalier* (1983), 54 di 100, involving union officers. See also paragraph 11:2120.

Quantum of Compensation and Duty to Mitigate the Damages

When a dismissal is found to contravene s. 184(3)(a)(i), the Board has the power, under s. 189(b)(i) and (ii), to order the reinstatement of the complainant with compensation. As to the determination of the quantum of the compensation, the Board usually leaves this matter to be settled by the parties with or without the assistance of an investigating officer. The Board can and always does reserve jurisdiction on this question, however, of whether or not the parties consent to it.[116]

When reinstating and awarding compensation to employees who have been illegally dismissed, the Board does not impose on the complainants a duty to mitigate their damages by demonstrating that they have tried to find employment elsewhere during the period of their dismissal. The Board stated, in one case,[117] that although the duty to mitigate, derived from the law of contracts, is applied by arbitration boards to dismissals without cause under collective agreements, it is not always appropriate to impose this duty in the context of unfair labour practice dismissals. Thus, even where an employee illegally dismissed had refused a job offered to him by another company after his dismissal, the Board did not reduce the amount of compensation owed him by the employer.[118] Where another employee returned to school after his illegal dismissal rather than seek alternate employment, the Board dismissed the employer's claim that this demonstrated the complainant's greater interest in studying than in returning to work. Had the employer offered to reinstate the complainant, the Board would have been able to ascertain whether or not he really wanted to go back and, thus, determine compensation accordingly.[119]

The Board does, however, deduct from the amount of compensation awarded to employees illegally dismissed any sums they may have earned in the period between their dismissal and the date of reinstatement.[120]

11:2113   Suspension

In *Bell Canada*,[121] the Board held that the main reason for a complainant's two-day suspension was his union activities. The complainant

---

116   *Soo-Security Motorways Ltd.* (1977), 19 di 155, 77 CLLC #16,096. The acceptance of the practice of reserving jurisdiction on the quantum of compensation with or without the parties' consent is implicit in the decision of the Federal Court of Appeal in *Arnold Bros. Transport Ltd. v. Canada Labour Relations Board*, unreported, March 28, 1977, file no. A-548-76 (Fed. C.A.).

117   *Victoria Flying Services Ltd.* (1979), 35 di 73, [1979] 3 Can LRBR 216; see also, on this issue, *British Columbia Telephone Co.* (1979), 38 di 14, [1979] 1 Can LRBR 350.

118   *Victoria Flying Services Ltd., supra*, note 117.

119   *Ibid.*

120   *Ibid.*

121   (1977), 20 di 312.

had conducted various meetings and had been elected chairman of a movement supporting the displacement of the incumbent union.

11:2114   Transfer

In *La Banque Nationale du Canada*[122] the Board held that a transfer of recently certified employees to non-union branches of the enterprise was motivated by a desire to intimidate those employees as well as the employees of the other branches, with the aim of compelling them to resign from union membership or refrain from becoming members of the union.

11:2115   Discrimination in Terms and Conditions of Employment

As an illustration of this sort of discrimination, the Board found employer violations of the Code in a trucking enterprise where, while a certification application was pending, the employer had significantly altered the working conditions of the drivers who were responsible for the organizing campaign. He had severely reduced the number of local and long-run trips and had assigned the drivers to old vehicles.[123] In another decision, the Board held that when, in combining the seniority lists of employees working out of different terminals, an employer singles out one employee for special favourable treatment and applies to him criteria other than those applied to the integration of the seniority of all other employees, he violates the Code with respect to the employees whose positions on the list were displaced as a consequence.[124]

Where an employer issued a letter of warning to the complainant informing him that the use of a company truck outside working hours would be limited in future, contrary to past practice, the Board held that the complainant had been discriminated against for a prohibited reason.[125] By contrast, the Board dismissed a complaint filed by a union alleging an employer violation of the Code by refusing to pay his members one day's pay when they had refused to cross the picket line of another union and to handle goods that were brought from behind the line.[126]

---

[122]   (1981), 42 di 352, [1982] 3 Can LRBR 1.
[123]   *Bessette Transport Inc.* (1981), 43 di 64.
[124]   *Cabano Transport Ltée* (1981), 42 di 318.
[125]   *Sorel-O-Vision Inc.* (1981), 46 di 73.
[126]   *Purolator Courier Ltd.* (1981), 45 di 300; see also *Canadian Imperial Bank of Commerce (Branches at Creston, B.C. and St. Catharines, Ont.)* (1979), 35 di 105, [1980] 1 Can LRBR 307, 80 CLLC #16,002; *Bell Canada* (1981), 42 di 298, [1981] 2 Can LRBR 148, 81 CLLC #16,083.

11:2116   Intimidation and Threats

In most cases where an employer's actions were held to amount to intimidation or threats prohibited by s. 184(3)(a)(i), a contravention of other sections of the Code was also found.[127] For instance, the dismissal of an employee actively engaged in an organizing drive and recruiting union support was held to contravene s. 184(3)(a)(i) as well as ss. 184(1)(a) and 186. By his actions the employer had tried to intimidate his employees to prevent them from participating in union activities and obtaining certification.[128] A typical example of a breach of ss. 184(3)(a)(i) (threaten and intimidate because of union activities) and 186 (seek by intimidation or coercion to compel a person to cease to be a member of a trade union) is found in a decision where a bank branch manager had pressed his anti-union views upon an employee who was a senior official of the union as well as upon other employees of the branch.[129] Similarly, where wage increases were announced throughout a bank with the proviso that they did not apply to unionized branches, the employer was found to have breached the freeze provisions of ss. 124(4) and 148(b) as well as s. 184(3)(a)(i) by discriminating against and intimidating those who had opted for collective bargaining.[130]

11:2117   Other Means

The first part of s. 184(3)(e) enumerates specific acts such as intimidation, threats of dismissal, any other kind of threats, and the imposition of a pecuniary or other penalty. These words, similarly to those of s. 184(3)(a)(i), contemplate direct action by an employer against a person for the purpose of compelling him to refrain from becoming or to cease to be a member, officer, or representative of a trade union.

Section 184(3)(e) also refers to other unspecified "means". The Board has determined that an unlawful dismissal constitutes such a "means" of a nature similar to the acts specifically enumerated.[131] Other "means" that have been found unlawful and that illustrate that a breach of other sections of the Code such as ss. 184(1)(a), (3)(a)(i), 124(4), and 148(b), often involve a breach of s. 184(3)(e) as well, include a ban by the employer on the distribution of union literature in employee mail boxes

---

[127]   These other sections may be ss. 124(4), 148(b), 184(1)(a), (3)(e), and 186. See, for instance, *Canadian Imperial Bank of Commerce (Toronto)* (1979), 34 di 677, [1979] 1 Can LRBR 391; *Canadian Imperial Bank of Commerce (Branches at Creston, B.C. and St. Catharines, Ont.), supra,* note 126; *Oakville Cablevision Ltd.* (1980), 40 di 189; *American Airlines Inc.* (1981), 43 di 114, [1982] 3 Can LRBR 90; *Highland Helicopters Ltd.* (1981), 46 di 50.

[128]   *Highland Helicopters Ltd., supra,* note 127.

[129]   *Bank of Montreal (Devonshire Mall Branch, Windsor)* (1982), 51 di 160, 83 CLLC #16,015.

[130]   *Canadian Imperial Bank of Commerce (Branches at Creston, B.C. and St. Catharines, Ont.), supra,* note 126.

[131]   *Canadian Imperial Bank of Commerce (Toronto), supra,* note 127; *Oakville Cablevision Ltd., supra,* note 127; *Highland Helicopters Ltd., supra,* note 127.

on company premises during non-working hours;[132] the issuing of a directive prohibiting employees from wearing union insignia or dress pins on company premises during working hours;[133] the sending, in the course of an organizing campaign, of letters or memos to employees intended to convince them not to join a union;[134] the announcement of a general increase applying to all branches of a bank except the unionized ones;[135] or the implementation of payments pursuant to a profit-sharing plan to employees outside the bargaining unit only.[136] All these actions, which were in themselves unlawful, had become "means" by which the employer sought to compel the employees to refrain from becoming or to cease to be members of the trade union.

The above examples also illustrate that the protection afforded by s. 184(3)(e) extends to the person directly affected, as well as to those indirectly affected by the use of such "means". For instance, the unlawful dismissal of an employee for the sole reason that he is actively engaged in recruiting membership support has a chilling effect upon the union drive and may compel the other employees to refrain from becoming members of the union. The direct effect on the employee dismissed as well as the indirect effect on the other employees then becomes a remedial issue to be handled by the Board.[137]

11:2120   Acts Motivated by the Exercise of Any Rights under Part V: Section 184(3)(a)(vi)

One of the prohibited reasons listed by subpara. (vi) for the acts enumerated in s. 184(3)(a) is the exercise by a person of "any right" under Part V. This is an umbrella provision that encompasses any activity related to the freedom granted in s. 110(1) to join a trade union and to participate in its lawful activities. It includes the right not to be discriminated against because of the participation in a legal strike,[138] although an employee is not shielded against any offences that he may commit while participating in such a strike for the sole reason that it is legal.[139]

Moreover, s. 184(3)(a)(vi) cannot serve as an umbrella for all union activities regardless of their merit. For instance, a union president who speaks on behalf of his organization's members is clearly taking an action that can always be associated with the performance of union activities.

---

132   *American Airlines Inc., supra,* note 127. See also paragraph 11:2210.
133   *Canadian Imperial Bank of Commerce (North Hills Shopping Centre)* (1979), 34 di 651, [1979] 1 Can LRBR 266, 80 CLLC #16,001. See also paragraph 11:2210.
134   *American Airlines Inc., supra,* note 127; *Amok Ltd.* (1981), 43 di 289.
135   *Canadian Imperial Bank of Commerce (Branches at Creston, B.C. and St. Catharines, Ont.), supra,* note 126.
136   *Maclean-Hunter Cable TV Ltd.* (1979), 34 di 752, [1979] 2 Can LRBR 1.
137   *Canadian Imperial Bank of Commerce (Toronto), supra,* note 127.
138   *Eastern Provincial Airways Ltd.* (1983), 51 di 209, 3 CLRBR (NS) 75; *Eastern Provincial Airways Ltd.* (1983), 54 di 172, 84 CLLC #16,012, 5 CLRBR (NS) 368.
139   *Banque Royale du Canada (Jonquière et Kénogami)* (1980), 42 di 125.

This does not give him a free rein to do anything whatsoever at any time, because his actions fall within the framework of union activities.

In this area, the Board made a crucial distinction between union activities that are protected by the Code and those that are not.[140] The Board reasoned that provincial labour legislation and legislation enacted by Parliament protect a certain number of union activities by prohibiting any adverse employer action that is designed to interfere with the right of association and the exercise of rights that flow therefrom. Some legislation in the past qualified the words "union activities" with the adjective "legitimate". However, the latter became such a misnomer over the years that legislators have preferred to replace it with specifically enumerated protected activities, culminating in the *Canada Labour Code* with a general prohibition such as that found in the second part of s. 184(3)(a)(vi). The Board stated that none of the labour statutes gave a licence to unionized employees to disregard their normal obligations in the performance of the work owed to the employer, or to disregard the disciplinary rules in any enterprise that secure order in the work place.

This principle applies as well to union officers or representatives. The status of union officer alone combined with the unfair labour practice provisions of the Code will not protect all kinds of union activity that such an employee might exercise, nor will it exempt him from dismissal or disciplinary measures imposed by the employer.

Thus where a union president had openly and repeatedly defied the employer's management rights, the Board held that the complainant was not engaging in union activities sanctioned by the Code and dismissed a charge of unfair dismissal.[141] Where an employee organized and held meetings in the course of which he was elected an officer of the union in charge of health and safety matters, such union activities were held not to be protected by the Code because they were carried out during working hours on the premises of the employer. By participating in union activities in such a manner, the complainant had infringed upon the legitimate interest of the employer and had therefore crossed the limits of permissible conduct.[142]

11:2130   "Yellow Dog" Contracts: Section 184(3)(b)

The purpose of s. 184(3)(b) is to prevent an employer, especially when hiring an employee, from requiring him to relinquish one or more rights conferred on him by the Code as a condition of employment and in order to keep his job. An employer would violate this provision if, for

---

[140]   *Jacques Lecavalier* (1983), 54 di 100.
[141]   *Brazeau Transport Ltd.* (1979), 35 di 163.
[142]   *Jacques Lecavalier, supra,* note 140. For other cases involving dismissal of union officers, see *Transvision Magog Inc.* (1981), 43 di 56; *Services Managers Roy Ltée* (1981), 43 di 212; *Canadian Pacific Ltd.* (1981), 43 di 305; *Ed Finn* (1982), 47 di 49, [1982] 1 Can LRBR 399, 82 CLLC #16,155.

example, he had an employee sign a document to the effect that he did not have the right to join a union or take part in union activities ("yellow dog" clause).[143]

In the few cases where the Board had to determine whether a term or condition of employment amounted to a breach of s. 184(3)(b), it held[144] that the denial to striking employees of accrual of seniority for the duration of a strike could reasonably have the effect of restraining them from exercising the right to strike, but it did not constitute conduct prohibited by s. 184(3)(b). By contrast, the Board held in another decision[145] that individual contracts of employment entered into by an employer with outside workers hired in the course of a strike, and guaranteeing them preferential treatment over striking employees on the condition that they did not engage or participate in the strike, were of the nature of the yellow-dog contracts prohibited by s. 184(3)(b).

11:2140   Denial of Pension Rights or Benefits: Section 184(3)(d)(ii)

The prohibition of s. 184(3)(d)(ii) is a corollary to the prohibition contained in s. 184(3)(a). An employer may not refuse to continue to employ an employee for a reason prohibited by s. 184(3)(a)(i) to (vi). If he does, he may not deny pension rights or benefits to which the employee would be entitled were it not for his unlawful dismissal. Nor may the denial of such benefits be used as a pecuniary penalty or as a means, as prohibited by s. 184(3)(e), of compelling an employee from becoming or ceasing to be a member, officer, or representative of a trade union. The only complaint so far alleging a breach of s. 184(3)(d)(ii) was dismissed by the Board.[146]

11:2150   Acts Motivated by the Refusal of a Person to Perform a Prohibited Act: Section 184(3)(f)

Section 184(3)(f) prohibits an employer from suspending, discharging, or imposing any financial or other penalty on a person employed by him, or taking any other disciplinary action against such a person for having refused to perform an act prohibited by Part V.

The Board has not yet had the occasion to deal with complaints alleging a breach of s. 184(3)(f). The use of the word "person" indicates that it could be used by a managerial non-employee who is discriminated against for having refused to commit an unfair labour practice[147] such as,

---

143   *Murray Bay Marine Terminal Inc.* (1981), 46 di 55.
144   *Bell Canada* (1981), 42 di 298, [1981] 2 Can LRBR 148, 81 CLLC #16,083.
145   *Eastern Provincial Airways Ltd.* (1983), 51 di 209, 3 CLRBR (NS) 75.
146   *Fraser-Surrey Docks Ltd.* (1974), 3 di 14, 74 CLLC #16,102.
147   See comments made by the Board in *Mike Sheehan* (1975), 9 di 29, [1975] 2 Can LRBR 55, 75 CLLC #16,161; *Arnold Bros. Transport Ltd.* (1976), 19 di 132, [1977] 2 Can LRBR

for instance, dismissing an employee for his union activities or committing an act that would infringe upon the freedom of association enshrined in s. 110(1).

11:2200   UNION-PROHIBITED CONDUCT

11:2210   Solicitation at Place of Employment: Section 185(d)

Section 185(d) prohibits a trade union from engaging in organizing activities at an employee's place of employment during working hours, except with the consent of the employer. The purpose of this section is to recognize an employer's right to manage his enterprise and control his work force during working hours without disruption from employees exercising organizing rights.[148]

The Board's general policy under s. 185(d) with respect to company rules prohibiting the soliciting of union membership on company premises during working and non-working hours, and the distribution of union literature during such periods, has been thoroughly reviewed.[149] The Board fully endorsed the principles outlined by the Nova Scotia Labour Relations Board in *Michelin Tires (Canada) Ltd.*,[150] the British Columbia Labour Relations Board in *Cominco Ltd.*,[151] and the Ontario Labour Relations Board in *Adams Mines, Cliffs of Canada Ltd. v. United Steelworkers of America*.[152] Its policy may therefore be summarized as follows:

1. No-solicitation or no-distribution rules that prohibit union solicitation on company property by employees during their non-working time are presumptively unreasonable impediments to self-organization and are therefore invalid; however, such rules may be validated by evidence that special circumstances make the rule necessary in order to maintain production or discipline.

Thus, union solicitation and distribution of union literature by employees during their own time on company property before shifts, during coffee breaks, during lunch breaks, or after shifts is allowed if the em-

---

86; and *General Aviation Services Ltd.* (1979), 34 di 587, [1979] 1 Can LRBR 285, with respect to s. 184(3)(f).

[148] *Dome Petroleum Ltd.* (1978), 31 di 189, [1978] 2 Can LRBR 518, 78 CLLC #16,153, 79 CLLC #16,192; *Canadian Imperial Bank of Commerce (North Hills Shopping Centre)* (1979), 34 di 651, [1979] 1 Can LRBR 266, 80 CLLC #16,001. See *British Columbia Telephone Co.* (1979), 38 di 14, [1979] 1 Can LRBR 350, where s. 185(d) was found to have been breached inasmuch as solicitation of union membership during working hours on the employer's premises had taken place without the latter's consent.

[149] *Ottawa-Carleton Regional Transit Commission* (1984), 7 CLRBR (NS) 137.

[150] [1979] 2 Can LRBR 388 (N.S.L.R.B.).

[151] [1981] 3 Can LRBR 499 (B.C.L.R.B.).

[152] (1982), 1 CLRBR (NS) 384 (O.L.R.B.).

ployees' basic rights are being exercised in a manner that does not conflict with the employer's efficient operations. The employer must have compelling business reasons to prohibit employees from exercising these rights and must establish by *cogent* evidence that his purpose was to preserve property, prevent serious disturbances, ensure productivity, or preserve plant safety. Any interference with an employer's legitimate management interests must be more than a minor annoyance or inconvenience to justify no-solicitation rules during such periods.

2. No-solicitation or no-distribution rules that prohibit union solicitation by employees during working time are presumptively valid as to their promulgation in the absence of evidence that the rules were adopted for a discriminatory purpose or applied unfairly.

In this connection, the Board has determined that inasmuch as the wearing of union dress pins is part of an overall union-organizing campaign, there has to be some more positive act of persuasion in order for s. 185(d) to be violated. The wearing of such buttons does not constitute in itself a violation of this section. Rather, the whole issue of employee's rights to wear their trade union insignia turns on the same principles as the solicitation issue. Thus, the validity of restrictions on such a lawful union activity during working hours depends on the ability of the employer to show a detrimental effect on entrepreneurial interests such as negative customer reaction, security, safety, or other business considerations. In other words, he must bring evidence of compelling or justifiable business reasons.[153]

It must be stressed that the principles outlined above in 1. and 2. deal with the rights of employees to solicit on behalf of a union during working and non-working hours. They do not apply to the solicitation of employees at their place of employment during working or non-working hours by non-employees, strangers, or union organizers not part of the employer's work force. In such a situation, the principles that apply are the following:

3. No-solicitation or no-distribution rules that prohibit union solicitation by non-employee union organizers at any time on the employer's property are always valid. However, the application of such rules may, in certain circumstances, have to give way to the terms of an access order issued in accordance with s. 199.

The Board's power to issue access orders under s. 199 is studied below.

---

[153] *Ottawa-Carleton Regional Transit Commission, supra,* note 149. See also *Canadian Imperial Bank of Commerce (North Hills Shopping Centre), supra,* note 148.

11:2220   Access Orders: Section 199

Section 199 is a means of translating the intangible freedom granted in s. 110(1) of the Code into a right truly capable of exercise. History has shown that the rights granted to employees by the Code are usually only meaningful when the employees are informed of their existence, the method of their exercise, and the benefits to be derived from their exercise. In this context, s. 199 represents a limited exception to s. 185(d) by providing for union access to a place of employment without employer consent.

Canadian jurisprudence has traditionally recognized as a fundamental freedom the right of the individual to the enjoyment of property and the right not to be deprived thereof. The courts have held that, if a person is to be given the right to enter and remain on the land and property of another person, such a radical change would have to be enacted by the legislature.[154] The Board has interpreted s. 199 as constituting such a change. This section requires it to balance the property rights of the employer against the collective bargaining interests of the employees sanctioned in the Code or, in other words, to balance private property rights against the right of non-employees to gain access to certain premises for the purposes expressed in s. 199(1)(b)(ii). Consequently, an access order provides a means by which union representatives may lawfully enter rather than trespass on employer property if it is necessary to communicate with employees for the purpose of solicitation, among other purposes. Where employees are already represented by a trade union, the latter may also gain access in order to fulfil its responsibilities as exclusive bargaining agent, but the right of access is not unfettered and wholly at the choice of the union. The Board determines when access should be permitted.

The various conditions outlined below must be considered before an order under s. 199 is granted by the Board.

11:2221   Conditions for the Issuance of an Access Order

Isolated Location

First, the union must seek authorization for access to employees living "in an isolated location". There is no definition of this expression, and the Board must determine its content in each case. To date, it has considered that employees worked in isolated locations where they per-

---

154   *Carswell v. Harrison*, [1974] 4 W.W.R. 897, 17 C.C.C. (2d) 251, 74 CLLC #14,241, 48 D.L.R. (3d) 137; revd. [1976] 2 S.C.R. 200, [1975] 6 W.W.R. 673, 5 N.R. 523, 25 C.C.C. (2d) 186, 75 CLLC #14,286, 62 D.L.R. (3d) 68, cited by the Board in *Dome Petroleum Ltd.* (1977), 27 di 653, [1978] 1 Can LRBR 393, 78 CLLC #16,129, in which the Board makes the above analysis of the purpose of s. 199 in light of the Canadian jurisprudence on the right to the enjoyment of property.

formed their functions on drilling vessels in the Beaufort Sea and lived in base camps to which access was severely restricted.[155]

Ownership of the Premises

Second, the isolated location in which the employees live must be on premises owned or controlled by their employer or by any other person. Before the 1978 amendment to s. 199(1), the interest of the Code only superseded property rights over premises "owned or controlled" by the employer of the employees, and not those of other persons who were not immediately affected by the exercise of the employee rights under the Code or of those who were not a party to a collective bargaining relationship with the applicant union. Thus, where employees lived on premises owned or controlled by a person other than their employer, an access order could not be issued.[156] The union could not rely on s. 199 as an effective organizing aid and had to employ the traditional techniques used in the past.

The addition in 1978 of the words "or by any other persons" in s. 199(1) remedied that unsatisfactory result in labour relations terms and accommodated the practical realities of the maritime industry, among others. The right of access now clearly extends beyond the premises of the employer of the employees to whom the union seeks access to the premises of "any other person". In this regard, the Board has held that when it issues an order granting access to a "ship" owned by a person other than the employer of the seafarers, the ship's master or person in charge may not, under the provisions of the *Canada Shipping Act*,[157] deny permission to the union representative to board, or order him off while the latter is acting within the terms of the access order. In such circumstances the Board, exercising its authority under s. 199 and taking into consideration s. 121, may require the ship master or owner of the vessel to comply with the access order as a power incidental to the attainment of the objects of Part V.[158]

Since the amendment in 1978, the Board has twice granted applications pursuant to s. 199 that had been dismissed under the 1972 legislation to allow access to premises owned and controlled by a person other than the employer of the employees envisaged in the demand.[159]

---

[155]   *Dome Petroleum Ltd., supra,* note 154; *Dome Petroleum Ltd., supra,* note 148; *Dome Petroleum Ltd. and Canadian Marine Drilling Ltd.* (1980), 40 di 150, [1980] 2 Can LRBR 533; and *Dome Petroleum Ltd. and Canadian Marine Drilling Ltd.* (1980), 42 di 237, [1981] 1 Can LRBR 497.

[156]   *Dome Petroleum Ltd., supra,* note 154.

[157]   R.S.C. 1970, c. S-9, ss. 235, 237.

[158]   *Dome Petroleum Ltd., supra,* note 148; it was also determined that the Board also has the authority to grant an access order with respect to vessels operating beyond the territorial waters of Canada.

[159]   *Dome Petroleum Ltd., supra,* note 148; *Dome Petroleum Ltd. and Canadian Marine Drilling Ltd.* (1980), 42 di 237, [1981] 1 Can LRBR 497.

Impracticable Access

Third, the Board must determine whether the access to the employees "would be impracticable" unless permitted on premises owned or controlled by the employer of the employees or another person. The use of the word "impracticable" rather than "impractical" is significant. The Board has stated that "the shades of different connotations between 'impracticable' and 'impractical' are that the former's connotation is one of near impossibility whereas the latter is merely that access without an order would not be a practical proposition".[160] The choice of the word "impracticable" makes the test more restricted.

As the concept of impracticability is directed at the ease of contact between union representatives and the employees, the Board considers the available means or means in the near future of contacting the employees to determine whether access is impracticable. In this regard, the Board has determined that mail solicitation of union support is no substitute for face-to-face meetings, nor is the possibility of contacting persons during the off-season access in any meaningful sense, even assuming that the union knows who is to be re-employed in the coming season and where such persons live in Canada. Similarly, the possibility of contacting employees who live in isolated locations or restricted areas at the airport from which they depart when the season is over is not meaningful access.[161]

In determining whether access would be impracticable, the Board will not normally look to past failures on the part of the applicant union or missed opportunities, although it may do so, in appropriate circumstances, as a result of the 1978 amendment that rendered the granting of an access order a discretionary matter wholly within the Board's exclusive jurisdiction. Considering the range of purposes set out in s. 199(1)(b)(ii), the Board will normally look forward rather than to past failures of the union. For instance, the previous failure of a union to process a grievance may not prevent access to enable future processing of the grievance.[162] For other purposes, such as soliciting union membership, for example, the Board has held[163] that previous access may cause it to exercise its discretion so as to deny a subsequent application. In *Dome Petroleum Ltd. and Canadian Marine Drilling Ltd.*[164] an access order had been issued in favour of a union, but no certification demand had subsequently ever been filed with the Board. On a further demand under

---

160   *Dome Petroleum Ltd.*, *supra*, note 148, at p. 204 (di).
161   *British Columbia Telephone Co.* (1980), 40 di 163, [1980] 3 Can LRBR 31, 80 CLLC #16,062; *Dome Petroleum Ltd. and Canadian Marine Drilling Ltd.* (1980), 40 di 150, [1980] 2 Can LRBR 533.
162   *Dome Petroleum Ltd.*, *supra*, note 154.
163   *Dome Petroleum Ltd.*, *supra*, note 148.
164   *Supra*, note 159.

s. 199 by the same union for the same employees, the Board indicated that it had the authority to deny the access sought by the union, but since a full year had elapsed since the previous order, the union was granted a new order.

Access Reasonably Required

Fourth, access must be "reasonably required" for one or several of the purposes mentioned in s. 199(1)(b)(ii). These are "soliciting union membership, the negotiation or administration of a collective agreement, the processing of a grievance or the provision to employees of a union service". These purposes relate to the actions or needs of the applicant union.

Prior to the 1978 amendment of the Code, the Board had determined that there was no requirement to consider the employer's interests, such as ecological and security interests, or the costs incurred by the access of a union representative. Nor was there any requirement to consider the expressed wishes of the employees. The same holds true under the new legislation, but the Board may, in its discretion, consider such matters although none of them were included when s. 199 was amended. The Board has indicated that matters of ecology or health and safety can be accommodated in the order, but should not apply to deny access or defeat any meaningful opportunity to exercise the freedom granted by the Code.

For the purposes of soliciting union membership, the Board has determined that face-to-face contact is required in most industries. In this regard, it was held that access can be "reasonably required" for a union representative even if there are union members among the employees on the premises and they actively seek to persuade fellow employees to exercise their right to join a trade union. It is the union representative who is given the right of access because he is presumed to be best prepared to address employees with respect to the purposes for which access may be granted. Thus, the presence of union members already on the premises cannot be treated as a form of access. For purposes other than soliciting mentioned in s. 199(1)(b)(ii), the Board has held that alternate methods of contact, without the physical presence of a union representative, may equally promote the Code's purposes.

Nature of the Group to be Solicited and Competing Unions

Fifth, when access is sought for the purpose of soliciting union membership, the relationship between the nature of the group of employees to whom access is sought to solicit union membership and the

Board's bargaining-unit policies in various industries[165] may influence the Board in exercising its discretion to grant or deny access orders. For instance, where a demand under s. 199 sought access to premises in order to solicit "unlicensed personnel" — a common appropriate bargaining unit in the maritime industry — the Board held that in this case the nature of the group of employees was not a reason to refuse to grant the order.

In the case of applications from competing unions seeking to solicit the same group of employees, the Board may take into consideration the disruptive effect the orders would have on the employees and the employer's operation. In one case, where demands by three competing unions had been filed, the Board granted all three of them but hastened to add that, if it had granted access to one union and the latter had exercised its right, the Board would have given weight to the employer's argument about inconvenience and disruption when considering a subsequent request brought within a short time by another union.[166]

11:2222   The Content of the Order

If all the conditions described above are met, the Board may issue an order.

First, the order will grant access to "the authorized representative of the trade union designated in the order". The purpose of this requirement is that the employer will know the identity of the persons permitted to enter his premises. The Board's role is simply to endorse the person designated by the union to act on its behalf. To fulfil this purpose, the Board either names in the order a person requested by the union or it includes a condition requiring identification by the union representative.[167]

Second, the order must designate the premises owned or controlled by the employer or by such other person, as the case may be, to which the right of access is given. The purpose enumerated in s. 199(1)(b)(ii) for which the order is granted will determine the boundaries of the premises to which access is authorized.[168]

Third, under s. 199(2), the Board must also include in the order the methods of access to the employees. These include transportation as well as accommodation and meals for the union representative. The purpose of the section is not fulfilled if it can be thwarted by a refusal to provide transport when the employer has the only means thereof, or denial of meals and accommodation if the employer is the only source. Consequently, the Board may order the provision of transportation, accom-

---

165 See paragraph 4:4000.
166 *Dome Petroleum Ltd. and Canadian Marine Drilling Ltd.*, *supra*, note 159.
167 *Dome Petroleum Ltd.*, *supra*, note 154.
168 *Ibid.*

modation, and meals, but does so with the condition that the union reimburse the employer at a reasonable or prevailing cost.

Fourth, an access order is not intended to have indefinite effect. The Board must specify the times during which access is permitted and the periods of duration of the order. This is normally determined in a manner that allows union representatives to speak to employees during non-working hours and out of the presence of employer representatives. The Board does not possess, however, the power under s. 199 to authorize a union representative to contravene s. 185(d) by interfering with the work of employees. The Federal Court of Appeal has determined that the practical operation of s. 199 is limited by s. 185(d) and that, accordingly, the Board may not allow a union representative to meet with employees during their working hours.[169]

11:2223   Procedural Matters

Because s. 199 does not expressly permit the Board to make orders without notice to employers, it invites submissions from the person identified by the union as the employer. The Board may also add any other person to the proceeding, under the authority of s. 118(o), if it becomes apparent that the premises are owned or controlled by a person other than the employer.

Finally, applications pursuant to s. 199 by their very nature require expeditious treatment. Isolated locations within the domain of the Code are commonly locations in the north, where the employment season is short and subject to the vagaries of the northern climate. As a result, the Board considers a hearing to be the least effective method of administering s. 199.[170]

An example of an access order issued by the Board is reproduced in Appendix 12.

11:2300   EMPLOYER AND UNION VIOLATIONS: GENERAL PROHIBITION OF SECTION 186

Section 186 provides that "no person shall seek by intimidation or coercion to compel a person to become or refrain from becoming or to cease to be a member of a trade union". The prohibitions of that section are not limited to actions by employers and encompass those of unions and employees as well.[171] For instance, in the latter situation, the Board

---

169   *Dome Petroleum Ltd. and Canadian Marine Drilling Ltd., supra,* note 161; revd. (*sub nom. Dome Petroleum Inc. v. Canadian Merchant Service Guild*) [1981] 2 F.C. 418, 35 N.R. 243, 81 CLLC #14,076, 118 D.L.R. (3d) 335 (C.A.), and followed in *Dome Petroleum Ltd. and Canadian Marine Drilling Ltd., supra,* note 159.
170   *Dome Petroleum Ltd., supra,* note 148.
171   *Loomis Armored Car Service Ltd.* (1983), 51 di 185.

found that in attempting to persuade a co-worker to join the union, an employee had breached s. 186 by his use of threats of loss of employment if the union was certified. The use of inexperienced employees to solicit memberships among their fellow employees often results in contraventions of ss. 185(d) and 186.[172]

As against employers, the finding of a breach of the various subsections of s. 184 has often attracted a similar finding under s. 186.[173]

Prior to the 1978 amendments, s. 187(1) did not mention s. 186 of the Code and there was no recourse to the Board for a violation of that section. The avenue for redress, at that time, was by way of penal prosecution upon ministerial consent pursuant to ss. 191 to 194. This anomalous situation was clarified in the 1978 amendments to the Code, when a violation of s. 186 was expressly stated to be the subject of a complaint before the Board. Section 187 now refers specifically to s. 186. At the same time, the authority to grant consent to prosecute was transferred from the minister to the Board.[174]

---

[172] *British Columbia Telephone Co.* (1979), 38 di 14, [1979] 1 Can LRBR 350.

[173] *Brazeau Transport Inc.* (1978), 33 di 520: captive audiences held by the employer in the context of union organizing drive, resignation forms circulated among the employees, attempts to form a house union by the employer; *British Columbia Telephone Co. and Canadian Telephones and Supplies Ltd.* (1979), 38 di 205: threats of harsh consequences if employees participated in union activities, dismissal of employees; *American Airlines Inc.* (1981), 43 di 114, [1981] 3 Can LRBR 90: no compelling and justifiable business reasons for prohibiting distribution of union literature. All these actions were part of an overall strategy to intimidate or coerce employees to prevent them from becoming or ceasing to be union members. See also *Brenda Haley* (1981), 41 di 311, [1981] 2 Can LRBR 121, 81 CLLC #16,096; and *Bank of Montreal (Devonshire Mall Branch, Windsor)* (1982), 51 di 160, 83 CLLC #16,015.

[174] *Donald William Murray Movers Ltd.* (1975), 8 di 9, 75 CLLC #16,157; *Mike Sheehan* (1979), 35 di 98, [1979] 3 Can LRBR 7, 79 CLLC #16,191.

CHAPTER 12

PROTECTION OF THE INSTITUTION OF COLLECTIVE BARGAINING

12:0000 PROTECTION OF THE INSTITUTION OF COLLECTIVE BARGAINING

12:1000 STATUTORY FREEZE OF TERMS AND CONDITIONS OF EMPLOYMENT: SECTIONS 124(4) and 148(b)

There are two freeze periods provided for in the Code that relate to the terms and conditions of employment. The first one occurs in the context of certification procedures and is imposed by s. 124(4). The second is triggered by the serving of a notice to bargain after certification, whether it be for the negotiation of a first collective agreement or for the renewal of the existing agreement, and is imposed by s. 148(b).

The nature and effect of the freeze in the latter situation was settled when the Board rejected the "static freeze" theory evolved in its early decisions. Although the Board has not yet had the occasion to explore the full consequences of this new development, the immediate effects are reflected in recent decisions. Other possible effects that have not yet emerged in the Board's decisions are canvassed below. In order to better understand them, the content of the static freeze theory is also discussed.

12:1100 IN THE CONTEXT OF CERTIFICATION PROCEDURES: SECTION 124(4)

Prior to June 1, 1978, the *Canada Labour Code* did not contain any provision having the effect of freezing the terms and conditions of employment at the time an application for certification was filed. This situation was unique in the field of labour relations in Canada, since all the provincial statutes contained such provisions. Prior to 1978, unions had to rely on s. 184 to complain about modifications to the terms and conditions of employment of the employees sought to be included in the units for which they had applied.[1] Section 124(4) of the Code, which has been in effect since June 1, 1978, remedied this deficiency.[2]

12:1110   The Period Covered by Section 124(4) and the Purpose of the Protection

As soon as an application for certification is filed with the Board, the registrar notifies the employer concerned by the demand pursuant to s. 13(1) of the regulations.

The freeze imposed by s. 124(4) starts from the moment of the employer's knowledge, by means of the registrar's notification, of the application for certification filed with the Board. Knowledge of an application for certification filed with a provincial board with respect to an enterprise falling within federal jurisdiction does not trigger the application of s. 124(4).[3]

When the application of s. 124(4) is properly triggered, the freeze continues until either the application for certification has been withdrawn by the union or dismissed by the Board[4] or, in the alternative, until thirty days have elapsed from the date on which the union was certified.[5]

The purpose of the s. 124(4) freeze in that period is two-fold. First, it seeks to consolidate and protect the integrity of the right of association recognized by s. 110 of the Code, by preventing the employer from influencing his employees' decision on whether to continue to support the union or not. For example, an employer could change the terms and conditions of employment, either improving or worsening them, in order to change his employees' mind and possibly to influence them, where a representation vote is ordered, to decide against union representation. The prohibition on unilateral changes of working conditions during the sensitive period in which employees are selecting their bargaining agent ensures that an employer cannot use his privileged position over his employees to influence the freedom of their choice.

Second, s. 124(4) seeks to protect the bargaining power of the union, should it be certified, by preserving the *status quo* and the fundamental equilibrium between the parties until collective bargaining in its proper form may commence pursuant to ss. 146 and 148. It imposes a "business as usual" course of action prior to certification. During the thirty days following certification, it prevents the employer from acting in anticipa-

---

[1]   *Alitalia Airlines for Canada* (1976), 15 di 173, 76 CLLC #16,006, where an employer proceeded with the reorganization of his enterprise and laid off all the employees included in a category covered by the certification demand, after the latter had been filed but before the provisions of s. 148(b) of the *Canada Labour Code* came into effect.
[2]   *Banque Canadienne Nationale (Montréal)* (1979), 35 di 39, [1980] 1 Can LRBR 470.
[3]   *Cabano Transport Ltée* (1981), 42 di 318.
[4]   *Canada Labour Code*, s. 124(4)(a).
[5]   Section 124(4)(b).

tion of negotiations before the union has acquired the right to bargain or has had time to formulate a bargaining position.[6]

12:1120   The Scope of the freeze Imposed by Section 124(4)

Section 124(4) refers to the "rates of pay or any other term or condition of employment or any right or privilege" of the employees sought to be included in the unit.

The Board has not attempted to assign a specific definition to each of these expressions, nor has it treated them as compartmentalized subjects. Admittedly they overlap to a certain extent. The Board has said that these expressions extend generally to the normal day-to-day working conditions, including existing wage rates as well as the wage structure, hours of work, classifications, duties and functions, transfers, layoffs, and promotions.[7]

Thus far, the Board has declined to determine, however, whether the introduction of a new productivity control system of clerical employees[8] or changes in work dispatching methods[9] fall within the meaning of the expressions used in s. 124(4). Neither has the Board yet determined whether the expression "right or privilege of the employees" refers to a term or condition of employment that must be proven to have been acquired by the employees through a practice that is uniform, constant, known by both parties, general, frequent, sufficiently old to be recognized as such, and so covered by the freeze in the context of certification procedures until a first collective agreement is concluded.

Examples of what has been considered as falling within the purview of s. 124(4) are given below.[10]

12:1130   The Nature and Effect of the Freeze

As mentioned above, s. 124(4) compels the *status quo* or a "business as usual" course of action upon the employer.[11] What is frozen are the terms

---

6   *Banque Canadienne Nationale (Montréal), supra,* note 2; *Canadian Imperial Bank of Commerce (Branches at Creston, B.C. and St. Catharines, Ont.)* (1979), 35 di 105, [1980] 1 Can LRBR 307, 80 CLLC #16,002; *Bank of British Columbia* (1980), 40 di 57, [1980] 2 Can LRBR 441, 80 CLLC #16,032; *Bessette Transport Inc.* (1981), 43 di 64; *Crosbie Offshore Services Ltd.* (1982), 51 di 120.

7   *Canadian Imperial Bank of Commerce (Branches at Creston, B.C. and St. Catharines, Ont.), supra,* note 6.

8   *Brazeau Transport Inc.* (1978), 34 di 572.

9   *Maclean-Hunter Cable TV Ltd.* (1979), 34 di 752, [1979] 2 Can LRBR 1.

10   See paragraphs 12:1130 to 12:1350.

11   *Canadian Imperial Bank of Commerce (Branches at Creston, B.C. and St. Catharines, Ont.), supra,* note 6; *Bank of British Columbia* (1980), 40 di 57, [1980] 2 Can LRBR 441, 80 CLLC #16,032; *Cabano Transport Ltée, supra,* note 3; *K.D. Marine Transport Ltd.* (1982), 51 di 130, 83 CLLC #16,009.

and conditions of employment contained in the individual contracts of employment that exist when an application for certification is filed, or in other words, the way in which the employer and employee dealt with each other prior to the application for certification.[12] The employer's management rights are not affected.

12:1131   Past Practice and Customs in Effect in the Enterprise

An alteration of terms and conditions of employment, such as granting a pay increase, for example, while an application for certification is pending, may or may not constitute a prohibited alteration, depending on the circumstances. For instance, if an employer announces a general pay increase in all his branches pursuant to an established past practice by which salary adjustments are granted throughout the enterprise at recurring periods, the increase must be implemented in every branch even if an application for certification is pending in one of the branches. Indeed, as a result of such past practice, general salary increases at recurring periods have become an integral part of the employer's compensation policy for all employees. Hence, the increases are owed to them at the moment they are announced, whether or not the employees are covered by an application for certification.[13] In such circumstances, to implement the increase in the branch subject to the application for certification while the freeze period is on would be in compliance with the preservation of the *status quo* sought by s. 124(4). To withhold the increase would, on the other hand, alter the fundamental equilibrium sought by that section and constitute a violation of the Code.

12:1132   Changes Conceived and Partially Implemented Before Notification of the Application

Conversely, where no past practice of the nature mentioned above exists, granting such an increase or effecting any other alteration of terms and conditions of employment after the employer's knowledge of an application for certification would be a departure from a "business as usual" course of action. This would contravene the Code unless the alteration had been conceived and partially implemented,[14] or set in

---

12   *La Banque de Nouvelle-Ecosse (Sherbrooke et Rock Forest, Québec)* (1980), 42 di 216, [1981] 2 Can LRBR 365, 81 CLLC #16,110.
13   *Canadian Imperial Bank of Commerce (Branches at Creston, B.C. and St. Catharines, Ont.)*, *supra*, note 6.
14   *Maclean-Hunter Cable TV Ltd.*, *supra*, note 9; *Cabano Transport Ltée*, *supra*, note 3.

motion,[15] before the employer was notified of the demand for certification.

Here again, if the change conceived and set in motion before the employer's knowledge of the application is beneficial to the employees, such as a pay increase, the employer has no other alternative but to proceed with it. This is so even if the increase is scheduled to come into force while the freeze is on. If the measure conceived and set in motion prior to the employer's knowledge of the application is prejudicial to the employees, such as a reduction in hours of work, then the employer can also implement it in the freeze period without violating s. 124(4), subject, however, to other provisions of the Code prohibiting actions motivated by an anti-union animus.[16] In such circumstances, the implementation or completion of the alteration during the freeze period has been held not to violate s. 124(4), since the alteration formed an integral part of the employees' terms and conditions of employment before the application for certification was made known to the employer.[17]

Thus, "business as usual" will have varying meanings, depending on the circumstances of each case. It may mean that an alteration or modification to terms and conditions of employment must be implemented in one case, whereas in another it may mean just the contrary.

If an employer wishes to depart from his regular course of action or past practice that he would normally follow were it not for the application for certification, consent from the Board must be obtained unless the alterations are effected pursuant to a collective agreement.

12:1140   Exceptions to the Freeze

12:1141   Alterations Pursuant to a Collective Agreement

When an application for certification with respect to an enterprise is filed for the first time, it is rare and even unusual for a collective agreement to be in force. However, where a collective agreement had been concluded by a voluntarily recognized union that subsequently sought to be certified by the Board while a competing union attempted to displace it, the Board held that s. 124(4) applied, and therefore that pay increases contained in the collective agreement had to be granted.[18]

Section 124(4) also applies in circumstances where a union files an application for certification to displace a union already certified that had

---

15 *La Banque Nationale du Canada* (1981), 42 di 352, [1982] 3 Can LRBR 1; affd. (*sub nom. National Bank of Canada v. Retail Clerks International Union*) unreported, February 5, 1982, file nos. A-538-81 and A-558-81 (Fed. C.A.); revd. on other grounds [1984] 1 S.C.R. 269, 53 N.R. 203, 84 CLLC #14,037, 9 D.L.R. (4th) 10.

16 *Ibid.*

17 *Ibid.*

18 *Verreault Navigation Inc.* (1981), 45 di 72.

signed a collective agreement providing for pay increases. Such a case would arise where the raiding union applied for certification in the period provided for in s. 124(2)(d) and the collective agreement is for a term of more than three years. Again, pay increases would have to be granted regardless of the application for certification.[19]

Thus, except in circumstances where there is an existing collective agreement in which terms and conditions of employment are clearly delineated, the consent of the Board must be sought to alter conditions and terms of employment that constitute a departure from "business as usual" principles.[20]

12:1142   The Consent of the Board

In contrast to the provisions of s. 148(b), it is the consent of the Board, not that of the trade union, that is required under s. 124(4). The reason for this is that while an application for certification is pending, employers are reluctant to seek consent from a union that does not yet hold certification and that might not eventually obtain it.[21]

Although a plain reading of s. 124(4) suggests that, unless alterations are made pursuant to a collective agreement, Board consent must be obtained for any modification to the terms and conditions of employment, this is not the case. The requirement of Board consent must be viewed in the light of the "business as usual" theory.

Employers need not apply for Board consent for any and all alterations. The need for consent arises only for alterations that affect the *status quo* or depart from "business as usual" principles. In such cases, employers must apply under s. 124(4). They may argue before the Board that, in the circumstances, "business as usual" should be departed from.[22] The Board may then, in its discretion, grant consent subject to specified conditions or it may deny it.[23] This represents a brief fettering of the employer's rights, but the Board has stated that it has no intention of managing the company.[24] Except for modifications that would alter the *status quo*, the employer can continue to lay-off, dismiss, or hire employees and, subject to other provisions of the Code such as s. 184,

---

19   *Ibid.*

20   *Canadian Imperial Bank of Commerce (Branches at Creston, B.C. and St. Catharines, Ont.)* (1979), 35 di 105, [1980] 1 Can LRBR 307, 80 CLLC #16,002.

21   *Ibid.*

22   *Ibid.*

23   *Ibid.* The Board has not, however, explained the manner in which it would exercise its discretion, or spelled out the elements it would take into consideration. In this regard, a plea of economic difficulty might be well taken. See *Bessette Transport Inc.* (1981), 43 di 64, where such an element was taken into consideration, but rejected in the circumstances of the case.

24   *Canadian Imperial Bank of Commerce (Branches at Creston, B.C. and St. Catharines, Ont.), supra,* note 20.

exercise the management rights that are not affected by the filing of an application for certification.[25]

In one decision, however, the Board held that its consent under s. 124(4) was mandatory in order to implement a change even if the latter was intended and had been set in motion before the employer's knowledge of the application for certification.[26] This would seem to suggest that Board consent is mandatory for any and all modifications, whether they alter the *status quo* or not. However, it is suggested that this decision should not be read in such a fashion. To do so would have the effect of substituting a static freeze for the accepted "business as usual" approach under s. 124(4), and would be at variance with the Board's stated policy to the effect that it has no intention of acting as a temporary equal partner of the employer while the protection of s. 124(4) is in force.[27]

Employers may always, however, act in anticipation if they are in doubt and apply for a prompt determination as to whether or not a certain course of action would constitute a prohibited change. They can then argue that the action contemplated is not a prohibited alteration. For instance, an employer may fear that the denial of pay increases to employees merely because they are affected by an application for certification would result in accusations of a violation of s. 184 of the Code. On the other hand, granting the increase unilaterally may result in similar accusations. In such cases, s. 124(4) serves the purpose of removing the "damned if you do, and damned if you don't" syndrome by providing a vehicle for a speedy determination by the Board.[28]

12:1200   ONCE NOTICE TO BARGAIN HAS BEEN SERVED: SECTION 148(b)

12:1210   The Period Covered by Section 148(b) and the Purpose of the Protection

Once a trade union has been certified to represent employees in a bargaining unit, it acquires the exclusive authority to bargain collectively on behalf of the employees.[29] This acquisition of bargaining rights is the first step in the collective bargaining process. The second step is the bargaining itself, which is legislatively authorized by s. 146 for the nego-

---

25   See *La Banque de Nouvelle-Ecosse (Sherbrooke et Rock Forest, Québec), supra*, note 12; reviewed and upheld by a majority of the Board in a plenary session. See also *Bank of Nova Scotia (Sherbrooke and Rock Forest, Québec)* (1982), 42 di 398, 82 CLLC #16,158; affd. (*sub nom. Bank of Nova Scotia v. Retail Clerks' International Union*) (1982), 83 CLLC #14,007; see also note 15, *supra*.
26   *K.D. Marine Transport Ltd., supra*, note 11.
27   *Canadian Imperial Bank of Commerce (Branches at Creston, B.C. and St. Catharines, Ont.), supra*, note 20.
28   *Ibid.*
29   *Canada Labour Code*, 136(1)(a).

tiation of a first collective agreement and by s. 147 for the negotiation of a second and subsequent collective agreement. Once notice to bargain is given in accordance with s. 146 or 147 or under other sections,[30] the parties must act in accordance with the requirements of s. 148.

The freeze imposed by s. 148(b) starts from the moment the notice to bargain is served on the employer, and it continues until the right to strike or lockout is acquired pursuant to s. 180(1)(a) to (d). Like s. 124(4), it compels a "business as usual" course of action, as will be seen below, by prohibiting any alteration of terms and conditions of employment, or any right or privilege of the employees in the bargaining unit, or any right or privilege of the bargaining agent. If the notice is given in accordance with s. 146 by a newly certified bargaining agent, there will be no gap in the freeze of terms and conditions of employment from the moment of the employer's knowledge of the application for certification until the acquisition of the right to strike or lockout, provided that the notice is served within the thirty days following certification.[31]

The purpose of the freeze imposed by s. 148(b) is to protect the newly certified bargaining agent against both the internal and external pressures that would result from changes in the employees' terms and conditions of employment. By prohibiting such changes, s. 148(b) enables the bargaining agent to negotiate on the basis of a fixed reference point in time. Furthermore, it prevents the employer from obtaining tactical advantages based on the terms and conditions of employment that it could change to the employees' benefit or detriment. Such changes would undermine the employees' confidence in their bargaining agent, a confidence that is necessary if the union is to complete its task successfully.

12:1220 The Scope of the Freeze Imposed by Section 148(b)

Section 148(b) deals with the same "rates of pay or any other term or condition of employment or any right or privilege of the employees" as those referred to in s. 124(4). The meaning of these expressions is the same in the context of negotiations following the service of a notice to bargain as it is in the context of certification procedures. The only addition in s. 148(b) is a prohibition against the alteration of the rights and privileges of the bargaining agent itself.[32]

---

30   Sections 136(2), 144(3)(c), 145(5), and 152.
31   *La Banque Nationale du Canada, supra,* note 15.
32   See note 25, *supra.*

12:1230   The Nature and Effect of the Freeze

12:1231   Negotiations for the Conclusion of a First Collective Agreement

The terms and conditions of employment contained in the individual contracts of employment, which are frozen by s. 124(4) upon the filing of an application for certification, continue to be frozen in the same manner by s. 148(b) after certification, when notice to bargain is given. The "business as usual" approach under s. 124(4), transposed in the context of the freeze imposed by s. 148(b), led the Board to this conclusion after it rejected the static freeze theory.

12:1232   The Static Freeze

The static freeze theory contained two schools of thought. The first school of thought held that the freeze imposed by s. 148(b) extended to management rights. The second school held that the freeze preserved only the actual state of employment that applied when notice to bargain was given.

With respect to the latter aspect, it was determined that the pre-certification individual employer-employee relationships were replaced, as of the moment of certification, by a new collective relationship. Certification, not the conclusion of a collective agreement, abrogated the individual contracts of employment and introduced this new collective regime. As a result, the reference point for establishing the terms and conditions of employment and the rights and privileges of employees for the purposes of s. 148(b) was no longer the individual contract of employment but was, as mentioned above, the actual state of employment existing when notice to bargain was given. This meant that past arrangements or customs incorporated in the individual contracts prior to certification, or notice to bargain, did not survive the change in kind constituted by the passage to a collective relationship via certification.

Accordingly, the freeze imposed by s. 148(b) could not be interpreted as compelling the grant of an increase in benefits that had been incorporated in the individual contracts by custom. The Board held, for instance, in *Royal Bank of Canada (Kamloops and Gibsons, B.C.)*,[33] that the implementation of yearly wage increases in all branches of a bank except for the unionized branches did not violate the Code. Such improvements were a matter for negotiations, notwithstanding any disheartening effect this may have had on newly certified employees.[34]

---

[33]   (1978), 27 di 701, [1978] 2 Can LRBR 159, 78 CLLC #16,132.
[34]   *Bank of Nova Scotia (Vancouver Heights Branch)* (1978), 28 di 901, [1978] 2 Can LRBR 181.

With respect to the first aspect of the static freeze theory, the Board held[35] that once a newly certified union had served a notice to bargain, a true partnership was imposed on the parties. This meant that the employer could no longer, as of that moment, dismiss, layoff, transfer, or discipline without the consent of the union as required by s. 148(b). Hours of work, vacations, coffee breaks, and holidays could not be changed without union consent. The latter became an equal partner of the employer until the rules of employment and even management rights were established in a collective agreement as if residual management rights had never existed.

The policy underlying this interpretation of the freeze imposed by s. 148(b) was aimed at creating a tremendous pressure on both parties to settle a collective agreement as soon as possible. The assumption was that both the employer deprived of his management rights and the employees deprived of their salary increases would want to come to terms rapidly. An employer who acted unilaterally before certification would, upon the serving of a notice to bargain, require union consent to act in a manner that would affect any term and condition of employment until the rules governing transfer, layoff, and promotions had been fixed in a collective agreement. Until those rules were codified, the employer would have to consult and obtain the consent of the union if a matter was a bargainable issue. As a corollary, this approach forced the union to formulate its demands early and to specify the subjects it wished to negotiate.[36]

12:1233   "Business as Usual"

The static freeze approach was rejected by the full Board in *Bank of Nova Scotia (Sherbrooke and Rock Forest, Quebec)*.[37] The Board found that certain principles of law, enunciated in common-law court decisions and arbitral jurisprudence, could not sustain the fundamental tenet of the static freeze theory, namely that of the introduction of a new regime upon the certification of a bargaining agent elevated it to the role of an equal partner with the employer. Indeed, the individual contract of employment is revived or continues in force after the collective agreement has expired, and it incorporates the terms and conditions of the latter that are of an individual nature. It necessarily follows that it is the fact of entering into a collective agreement that at the outset abrogates the individual contract of employment to the extent of the terms of the agreement, and not the so-called new collective relationship established by certification. There is therefore a clear distinction in law between the acquisition of an exclusive power of representation upon certification,

---

35   *Bank of British Columbia* (1980), 40 di 57, [1980] 2 Can LRBR 441, 80 CLLC #16,032.
36   *Bank of British Columbia (Abbotsford)* (1980), 41 di 188, [1980] 3 Can LRBR 576, 81 CLLC #16,068.
37   See note 25, *supra*.

and the result of the exercise of that exclusive power which is the conclusion of a collective agreement.

Therefore, since the legal relationship based on the individual contract continues to exist until a first collective agreement is concluded notwithstanding certification and is revived or continues in force after the latter has expired, it was determined that s. 148(b) and s. 124(4), as they refer to the same subjects, could not be interpreted in a manner different from one another. Thus, the freeze imposed by s. 148(b) concerns only the employees' terms and conditions of employment and does not affect the employer's management rights.

Both sections impose on the employer a "business as usual" course of action. The *status quo*, or what is frozen by s. 148(b), similarly to the effect of s. 124(4), are the terms and conditions of employment, past practices and customs incorporated in the individual contracts that exist when notice to bargain is given, or the way in which the employer and employee dealt with each other before the notice. According to this interpretation, the employer may manage his enterprise in the same way as he did before receiving a notice to bargain until a collective agreement is concluded. He may discipline, discharge, and change terms of work and employment as was the custom and practice before being served the notice. But he must also, on the other hand, implement wage increases and other changes that would ordinarily have been implemented had no notice been served.

Indeed, where an employer's custom is to implement wage increases annually for all his employees, he cannot withhold such adjustments from the certified units only. In such a case, the increases are part of the terms and conditions of employment of the employees working in certified branches for which notice to bargain has been given. By failing to grant the increases to employees included in the certified branches, an employer would illegally alter their terms and conditions of employment and so violate s. 148(b) if the consent of the union had not been obtained.

12:1234   Negotiations for the Renewal of a Collective Agreement

When a notice to bargain for the renewal of a collective agreement has been given, s. 148(b) prohibits the alterations of rates of pay or any other term or condition of employment or any right or privilege of employees provided in the agreement, notwithstanding the latter's subsequent expiration, until the right to strike or lockout is acquired.

The nature of the freeze imposed by s. 148(b), in such circumstances, is the same as that when notice is given for the negotiation of a first collective agreement. Here again, the freeze does not extend to management rights that were not restricted by the agreement. It follows that the employer may manage his enterprise and discipline, discharge, layoff, and change the hours of work in the same manner as he did before receiving the notice to bargain, subject, however, to any restriction to his management's rights contained in the collective agreement to be renewed as a result of the notice to bargain.[38] Put another way, the employer's management rights must not be exercised in a manner inconsistent with the extent to which they were restricted by the agreement until the right to strike or lockout is acquired.

12:1240   Exceptions to the Freeze

12:1241   Negotiations for a First Collective Agreement

To depart from a "business as usual" course of action contemplated by s. 148(b), the employer must obtain the union's consent. It is the consent of the union and not that of the Board that is required under s. 148(b). The purpose of this is to compel the employer to recognize the authority and role of the bargaining agent. It necessitates communication between the employer and the bargaining agent, thereby fostering a joint resolution of interests of both parties.[39] As under s. 124(4), however, the need for union consent arises only for an alteration that would affect the *status quo* or depart from "business as usual".

12:1242   Negotiations for the Renewal of a Collective Agreement

In an early decision the Board expressed the view that the scope of s. 148(b) was more expansive than the scope of past collective agreements and extended to matters that were the subject of union proposals at the bargaining table even if the employer's management rights on such matters had not been restricted by the agreement sought to be renewed.[40] In that case, the Board determined that the alteration, during the freeze period, without union consent, of a privilege not provided in the agreement and attendant to a work function breached s. 148(b), because the function and the privilege were the subject of union proposals at the bargaining table.

The Board has not had the occasion to deal with this kind of issue since it rejected the static freeze theory. However, it necessarily follows from the adoption of the "business as usual" approach that s. 148(b) does

---

38   *La Banque Nationale du Canada* (1981), 42 di 352, [1982] 3 Can LRBR 1; affd. (*sub nom. National Bank of Canada v. Retail Clerks International Union*), unreported, February 5, 1982, file nos. A-538-81 and A-558-81 (Fed. C.A.); revd. on other grounds [1984] 1 S.C.R. 269, 53 N.R. 203, 84 CLLC #14,037, 9 D.L.R. (4th) 10.
39   *Air Canada* (1977), 24 di 203.
40   *Ibid.*

not extend to a privilege merely because the function to which it is attached is the subject of union proposals. To hold otherwise would be to re-introduce a mandatory union consent requirement for any matter that is a bargainable issue at variance with the accepted "business as usual" policy.

Whether the freeze imposed by s. 148(b) extends to such a privilege or to any other matter depends, according to the "business as usual" theory, on the extent to which, prior to the freeze, these matters were removed from the employer's exclusive residual managerial rights.[41] In other words, it depends on the extent to which, prior to the freeze, the employer could unilaterally remove or restrict the privilege. This determination would involve a close scrutiny of the collective agreement and a determination of whether the privilege is recognized and regulated therein. Although, as previously mentioned, the Board has not yet determined whether a privilege must be proven to have been acquired through a practice that is uniform, constant, known by both parties, general, frequent, and sufficiently old to be recognized as such, in the affirmative, the freeze would also extend to a privilege bearing such characteristics if it had been preserved by an acquired-rights clause and if no other provision of the agreement is inconsistent with the privilege.

In any case, the Board's rejection of the static freeze theory indicates that the focus for determining whether the alteration of a term of employment, without union consent, breaches s. 148(b) must be placed on the extent to which the employer's managerial rights on such subjects have been fettered or restricted by the collective agreement.[42]

As a result, a "business as usual" course of action is determined, in circumstances where a notice to bargain has been served for the renewal of a collective agreement, by the terms and conditions of employment contained in the collective agreement and the extent to which the employer's residual management rights have been restricted. It follows that if an employer wishes to alter a term or condition of employment provided in the collective agreement and the latter restricts his management rights to do so, then union consent must be obtained if the alteration is to be implemented before the right to strike or lockout is acquired. Any other alteration consistent with the employer's management rights preserved in the collective agreement could be effected without union consent, subject, however, to other provisions of the Code such as s. 184.[43]

---

41   *La Banque Nationale du Canada, supra,* note 38.
42   *Ibid.*
43   *Ibid.*

12:1300   PROCEDURAL MATTERS, PROHIBITED MOTIVE AND TIMELINESS OF A COMPLAINT UNDER SECTION 124(4) or 148(b)

A complaint alleging a breach of s. 124(4) or s. 148(b) is made pursuant to s. 187(1). Complaints alleging a breach of s. 148(b) are subject, however, to the additional requirement of the ministerial consent referred to in s. 187(5). This requirement will be dealt with in another part.[44]

The timeliness of a complaint under either section is regulated by the universal ninety-day period provided in s. 187(2). However, the alteration of terms and conditions of employment has been held to constitute a continuous offence insofar as they are not later restored, once they have been altered.[45] This question will also be dealt with in another part.[46].

The basis of a violation of s. 124(4) or 148(b) is specifically related to the basic and material requirement of an alteration in the terms and conditions, salaries, rights, and privileges of employees. It is not a question of assessing or considering the employer's reasons, in contrast with a complaint of unfair labour practices under s. 184(3), where the presence of anti-union animus has a considerable impact on the Board's appreciation of the facts. Here it is essentially an objective test by which it must be decided whether or not there have been prohibited changes or alterations and nothing more. Thus, anti-union motives are not a necessary ingredient for a finding of a contravention of the freeze provisions of s. 124(4) or 148(b).[47]

As a last matter, before reviewing the decisions rendered by the Board, it must be stressed that it has been held that an employer's actions may, in some circumstances, violate s. 184(1) as well as the provisions of either or both of the freeze mechanisms.[48] A breach of s. 148(b) may also involve a breach of the duty to bargain in good faith imposed by s. 148(a).[49]

---

[44]   See paragraph 15:1000.
[45]   *La Banque Nationale du Canada, supra,* note 38.
[46]   See paragraph 15:2300.
[47]   *Canadian Imperial Bank of Commerce (North Hills Shopping Centre)* (1979), 34 di 651, [1979] 1 Can LRBR 266, 80 CLLC #16,001; *Bessette Transport Inc.* (1981), 43 di 64; *La Banque Nationale du Canada, supra,* note 38; *Crosbie Offshore Services Ltd.* (1982), 51 di 120.
[48]   *Canadian Imperial Bank of Commerce (Branches at Creston, B.C. and St. Catharines, Ont.)* (1979), 35 di 105, [1980] 1 Can LRBR 307, 80 CLLC #16,002.
[49]   *Ottawa-Carleton Regional Transit Commission* (1983), 51 di 173, 83 CLLC #16,016.

12:1310   Cases Where No Breach of Section 124(4) Was Found

The Board has generally declined to find breaches of s. 124(4) where some alterations or changes had been conceived of and partially implemented or completed prior to the employer's knowledge of the application for certification. On this question, the Board dismissed a complaint where bargaining unit work had been subcontracted by the employer to independent technicians, as the evidence established that such a practice had been followed by the employer for years before the application for certification.[50] In one decision the Board ruled that, where the employer had initiated and completed the integration of the seniority list of drivers working out of two of the four terminals of the enterprise before he had been notified of the filing of an application for certification seeking to cover all the drivers of the company, no breach of s. 124(4) had been committed.[51] Similarly, the failure to integrate into the seniority list the drivers working out of the other two terminals did not violate s. 124(4), as such integration was held not to be part of the terms and conditions of employment before the employer learned of the application for certification.

Of course, when an alteration is effected pursuant to a consent issued by the Board, no breach of s. 124(4) is committed. On this point, the Board held in one case that the implementation of wage increases just prior to a representation vote, while several applications for certification by competing unions were pending, did not contravene s. 124(4), as the employer had properly sought and obtained the consent of the Board.[52]

12:1320   Cases Where Breaches of Section 124(4) Were Found

Where it was put in evidence that, by past practice, an employer had granted a general wage increase at least once a year, and that such an increase had been announced a few days after the filing of an application for certification, the employer's failure to implement the increase in the unit sought for certification without obtaining the consent of the Board constituted an alteration prohibited by s. 124(4). Indeed, once the announcement had been made, the increase became an integral part of the salary structure and of the conditions and terms of employment between the individual employees and the employer. Hence, the failure to implement the increase constituted an illegal alteration, as the consent of the Board had neither been asked nor granted.[53]

---

50   *Maclean-Hunter Cable TV Ltd.* (1979), 34 di 752, [1979] 2 Can LRBR 1.
51   *Cabano Transport Ltée* (1981), 42 di 318.
52   *Crosbie Offshore Services Limited, supra,* note 47.
53   *Canadian Imperial Bank of Commerce, Toronto (Branches at Creston, B.C. and St. Catharines, Ont.), supra,* note 48.

Similarly, the failure to implement payments to the employees in the bargaining unit pursuant to a profit-sharing plan, while implementing payments to others outside the bargaining unit, constituted a violation of s. 124(4) of the Code.[54]

When, after the filing of an application for certification, an employer discontinued his policy regarding payment of wages to employees on sick leave and started deducting amounts from the pay cheques of returning employees for that purpose, the Board held that s. 124(4) had been breached.[55]

Another case involving extensive violations of s. 124(4) occurred in a trucking enterprise where, after the filing of an application for certification, an employer had (i) put on call a driver who had been working on a minimal weekly hours basis; (ii) altered the time off for dinner from a half-hour with pay to one hour without pay; (iii) considerably reduced the number of local trips usually assigned to a driver and distributed them to other drivers or to brokers; (iv) imposed a set of written rules by which long-run drivers were to report for assignment at an inconvenient time; (v) stiffened the discipline for certain common misdemeanours in the trucking business; (vi) required long-run drivers to complete log books; and (vii) withdrawn from a long-run driver the truck he usually drove and assigned him an older model with a broken windshield — all of which were at odds with the past practice in that company.[56]

In another decision, the Board held that where an employer had relieved an employee of his duties and of the responsibilities, rights, and prerogatives attendant to these duties while an application for certification was pending, the employer had illegally altered the terms and conditions of employment of the complainant.[57]

12:1330   Cases Where No Breach of Section 148(b) Was Found

Leaving aside the cases in which the complaints were dismissed on the basis of the static freeze theory, the Board has rendered few decisions in which, applying the "business as usual" theory, it declined to find a violation of s. 148(b). One case where such a complaint was dismissed involved the application of s. 148(b) in the context of the renewal of a collective agreement.[58] It was determined that, by unilaterally renewing a long-term disability plan, the employer had not contravened the Code, as the coverage of the plan would have ceased had he not acted pursuant to his mandate under the collective agreement to provide such a plan. The employer's conduct fell well within the confines of "business as

---

54   *Maclean-Hunter Cable TV Ltd., supra,* note 50.
55   *Ibid.*
56   *Bessette Transport Inc., supra,* note 47.
57   *Radio-LaTuque Ltée (CFLM)* (1980), 42 di 108.
58   *Ottawa-Carleton Regional Transit Commission, supra,* note 49.

usual". In another case,[58a] where it appeared that certain changes were made in new services to passengers by an airline company during the "freeze period", the Board nevertheless rejected the complaint alleging violation of s. 148(b) after having interpreted the collective agreement and having found that it contained an implied union consent to the changes.

12:1340   Cases Where Breaches of Section 148(b) Were Found

In a case involving the renewal of a collective agreement, the Board held that an employer under federal jurisdiction who claimed to be bound by the *Inflation Restraint Act* of Ontario[59] had contravened s. 148(b) by implementing, without the incumbent union's consent, a 5 percent wage increase at the expiration of the collective agreement.[60] The same action also contravened s. 124(4) since, at the time of the implementation, applications for certification that had been filed by a competing union were pending before the Board and no consent had been sought by the employer or granted by the Board.

The other cases where breaches to s. 148(b) were found were rendered in the context of the negotiation of a first collective agreement. The Board held that the withholding or refusal to implement adjustments in wages and other conditions of employment in certified bank branches only was contrary to the employer's custom of implementing such changes annually for all his employees and so violated s. 148(b).[61]

Most of the cases[62] where the Board declined to find breaches of s. 148(b) on the basis of the static freeze theory would also constitute examples of situations in which breaches could have been found had the current "business as usual" policy been applied.

12:1350   Cases Where No Breach of Either Section 124(4) or Section 148(b) Was Found

Once a union has been certified, s. 124(4) provides for a thirty-day period during which the freeze continues to apply. If the bargaining agent does not serve a notice to bargain within that period, a legal vacuum may be created between the date of the expiration of the thirty-

---

58a   *Canadian Pacivic Airlines Ltd.* (1985), 85 CLLC #16,016.
59   *Inflation Restraint Act,* S.O. 1982, c. 55.
60   *Ottawa-Carleton Regional Transit Commission, supra,* note 49.
61   See note 25, *supra.*
62   *Royal Bank of Canada (Kamloops & Gibsons, B.C.)* (1978), 27 di 701, [1978] 2 Can LRBR 159, 78 CLLC #16,132; *Bank of Nova Scotia (Vancouver Heights Branch)* (1978), 28 di 901, [1978] 2 Can LRBR 181; *Bank of British Columbia* (1980), 40 di 57, [1980] 2 Can LRBR 441, 80 CLLC #16,032; *Bank of British Columbia (Abbotsford)* (1980), 41 di 188, [1980] 3 Can LRBR 576, 81 CLLC #16,068.

day period and the date on which s. 148(b) is triggered by the serving of a notice to bargain.

In one case where the Board was faced with such a situation, it ruled that a change conceived and set in motion during the period of the legal vacuum — the closure of a branch by a bank and the relocation of the newly certified employees to non-unionized branches — did not breach s. 124(4), since the thirty-day period had elapsed.[63] Nor had s. 148(b) been breached, although the alteration was implemented after notice to bargain had been served, since the closure had been announced during the legal vacuum and formed part of the employees' general employment situation when the freeze eventually took effect. The employer was found, however, to have breached other sections of the Code.

12:2000   THE DUTY TO BARGAIN IN GOOD FAITH: SECTION 148(a)

Once notice to bargain has been given, the parties are required to act in accordance with s. 148. They must, among other things, meet without delay — in any case, within twenty days after the notice is given, unless they agree otherwise — to bargain in good faith and make every reasonable effort to conclude a collective agreement. Such notice to bargain may be given pursuant to ss. 136(2), 144(3)(c), 145(5), 146, 147, and 152. The obligation imposed by s. 148(a) applies to all these circumstances and, as the Board has held,[64] there is no statutory basis for the proposition that the immediacy of meeting and engaging in collective bargaining is any less acute in any one of these circumstances.

12:2100   THE STANDARDS OF THE DUTY

The Board has been cautious in contributing to the wide body of literature on the duty to bargain in good faith, in view of the fact that this is one area where Board rulings may spawn countermoves requiring the creation of yet more rules. The Board seeks to minimize this fencing-in of the range of free collective bargaining. Notwithstanding this cautious approach, the Board has conceived the duty to bargain in good faith and make every reasonable effort to conclude a collective agreement in light of the principles evolved in this area by the Ontario Labour Relations Board as well as by the British Columbia Labour Relations Board. The traditional jurisprudence in these provinces holds that the two aspects of the duty — negotiation in good faith and reasonable efforts — seek two objectives: requiring the recognition of the union as the bargaining agent and the fostering of rational, informed discussions between the parties on

---

63   *La Banque Nationale du Canada, supra,* note 38.
64   *Austin Airways Ltd. / White River Air Services Ltd.* (1980), 41 di 151, [1980] 3 Can LRBR 393.

bargaining issues. According to this approach, the satisfaction of the duty to bargain in good faith and make every reasonable effort depends on the manner in which negotiations are conducted, and not upon the content of the proposals brought to the bargaining table. In turn, the conduct of the negotiations is judged not only by reference to mutual recognition, which is the first purpose of the duty, but also in terms of the quality of discussions between the parties. The British Columbia Labour Relations Board, for its part, speaks of good faith as the subjective element of the duty and reasonable efforts as the objective element.[65]

The Board evolved its general policy on this background. It must be noted, however, that in this matter, the Board is in constant evolution. It generally takes into consideration the latest Canadian and, sometimes, American jurisprudence and participates in the schools of thought that emerge in those decisions. For instance, the Board has adhered to the "illegality doctrine" according to which a breach of s. 148(a) will be found where a party advances a bargaining proposal whose content is incompatible with the policies or the scheme envisaged by the Code and insists upon its acceptance by the other party until an impasse in negotiations is reached.[66] This doctrine leads the Board to supervise, to a certain extent, as do other labour relations boards,[67] the content of demands or proposals advanced at the bargaining table. The Board may, in such instances, order the party that has been found in breach of s. 148(a), as a remedial measure, to withdraw the illegal demand from the bargaining table or to cease insisting on its acceptance by the other party as a precondition to the conclusion of a collective agreement.[68]

12:2110   General Policy

The Board has identified two competing views concerning the extent to which collective bargaining should be regulated by a labour relations board through its administration of the duty to bargain in good faith. One view holds that, once collective bargaining commences, it is a no-holds-barred exercise. The opposite view contends that the object of collective bargaining is a collective agreement, and therefore that all parties should be required to act reasonably. Among the proponents of either position there is no consensus on how rough the parties may play or on what constitutes reasonable action.

---

[65] These principles, evolved in Ontario and British Columbia, are summarized in this fashion by the Canada Board in *CKLW Radio Broadcasting Ltd.* (1977), 23 di 51, 77 CLLC #16,110.

[66] *Eastern Provincial Airways Ltd.* (1983), 51 di 209, 3 CLRBR (NS) 75; and *Les Elévateurs de Sorel Ltée* (1985), 85 CLLC #16,032 (C.L.R.B.).

[67] See D.D. Carter, "The Duty to Bargain in Good Faith: Does It Affect the Content of Bargaining?" in Swan and Swinton (eds.), *Studies in Labour Law* (Toronto: Butterworths, 1983), at 35.

[68] See paragraph 16:3200.

In order to strike a balance between these opposing views, the Board started from the proposition that although good-faith bargaining and reasonable efforts are required of the parties, the subjects or scope of bargaining are not regulated by the Code, nor does it specify that the ultimate results of the economic sanctions to which the parties have a right to resort must be the conclusion of a collective agreement.[69]

Thus, the Board does not inquire into the merits of proposals put forth at the bargaining table,[70] or judge the reasonableness of bargaining positions unless they are clearly illegal, contrary to public policy, indicative of bad faith, or inconsistent with the policies of the Code.[71] Because collective bargaining is a give-and-take process determined by threatened or exercised power, the Board has adopted the policy that it will not interfere in the balance of power and will not restrict the exercise of power by the imposition of rules designed to require the parties to act in a gentlemanly or genteel fashion.[72]

At the same time, however, the Board ensures that one party does not seek to undermine the other's right to engage in bargaining or act in a manner that prevents full, informed, and rational discussions of the issues. In the Board's view, the refusal by a party to act in a manner conducive to a full exchange of positions on issues of interest to the other party cannot be considered as fostering the development of good relations. This does not mean, however, that the parties cannot, in the exercise of collective bargaining, engage in hard or ruthless bargaining.[73]

These general principles constituted the background against which the Board evolved clearer guidelines in subsequent decisions.

12:2120   Bargaining in Good Faith: Section 148(a)(i)

12:2121   Definition

The Board discussed the meaning of the obligation to bargain in good faith in the context, particularly, of demands for the imposition of a first collective agreement pursuant to s. 171.1.[74] The good faith of the parties in collective bargaining is one of the elements the Board may take into consideration in determining whether or not it will impose an agreement. The statements it made in that context are, of course, also applicable in the context of s. 148(a) complaints.

As it is extremely difficult to establish reliable criteria to assess a situation that is essentially subjective, the Board has avoided a positive

---

69   *CKLW Radio Broadcasting Ltd.*, *supra*, note 65; *CJMS Radio Montréal Ltée* (1978), 27 di 796, [1979] 1 Can LRBR 332.
70   *CKLW Radio Broadcasting Ltd.*, *supra*, note 65.
71   *Ibid.*
72   *Ibid.*
73   *Ibid.*
74   See *CJMS Radio Montréal Ltée*, *supra*, note 69.

definition of good faith and, as in other jurisdictions, has focused rather on its opposite — that is, bad-faith bargaining. The latter exists when an examination of the conduct of one party leads to the conclusion that it has neither attempted nor intended to reach an agreement. This approach, advocated by an eminent specialist,[75] contains no suggestion that a negotiator must put the securing of an agreement ahead of the maintenance of his position concerning substantive terms and conditions of employment. It distinguishes employers who attempt to talk a union to death from those who are merely stubborn negotiators exercising their full range of bargaining powers. It allows for a distinction between bad-faith bargaining and hard bargaining conducted in good faith. The former may manifest itself by a party's "surface bargaining", which consists of going through the motions or preserving the surface indicators of negotiations without the intent of concluding a collective agreement. The Board has stated, drawing on the Ontario jurisprudence, that surface bargaining constitutes a subtle but effective refusal to recognize the trade union.[76]

On the other hand, this approach does recognize that parties to collective bargaining may act in their own individual self-interest, and in so doing are entitled to take firm positions that may be unacceptable to the other side. The obligation to bargain in good faith does not include the obligation to compromise on principles, but rather that of making reasonable efforts to reach a collective agreement.[77] The Code allows for the use of economic sanctions to resolve any bargaining impasse that is reached in the process.

12:2122   Evidence

The appreciation of such a subjective element as good-faith or bad-faith bargaining can only be made from circumstantial evidence and requires a scrutiny of the general conduct of the parties at the bargaining table, as well as their behaviour away from the table.[78]

The attitude of the parties away from the bargaining table cannot, indeed, be dissociated from their attitude at the bargaining table, since the former will reflect or motivate the positions advanced at the table, and *vice versa*.[79] Moreover, the totality of the relationship of the parties must be scrutinized by the Board even in circumstances where the allegations of bad faith are focused on a set period of time. For instance, as the parties are expected and entitled to act in the pursuit of their own self-

---

75 Archibald Cox, "The Duty to Bargain in Good Faith" in *Labour Law: Selected Essays, Harvard Law Review* (1964), at 82, quoted in *CJMS Radio Montréal Ltée, supra*, note 69, at p. 848 (di).

76 *Radio LaTuque Ltée (CFLM)* (1980), 42 di 108; *Nordair Ltd.* (1985), 85 CLLC #16,023.

77 *Ibid.*

78 *Ibid.*

79 *Banque Royale du Canada (Kénogami, Québec)* (1980), 41 di 199, [1982] 1 Can LRBR 16; *Maclean-Hunter Cable TV Ltd.* (1980), 42 di 274, [1981] 1 Can LRBR 454.

interest, the mere tendering of a proposal that is unacceptable to the other side, and even predictably so, is not sufficient of itself to allow the Board to draw an inference of surface bargaining. This conclusion can only be drawn from the totality of the evidence including, but not restricted to, the adoption of an inflexible position on issues central to the negotiations. It is only when the conduct of the parties as a whole demonstrates that one side has no intention of concluding a collective agreement, notwithstanding its preservation of the outward manifestations of bargaining, that a finding of surface bargaining and, hence, of bad-faith negotiations can be made.[80]

Conversely, to focus on a particular period of time without looking at the totality of the facts of the case could leave the Board with misleading inferences of bad faith that could be clarified by the consideration of the entire bargaining strategy and relationship between the parties.[81]

12:2130   Making Every Reasonable Effort: Section 148(a)(ii)

12:2131   Definition

The Board has not generally discussed in a distinct fashion nor dissociated the duty to make every reasonable effort from the duty to bargain in good faith when dealing with complaints under s. 148(a). Where, however, the ministerial consent under s. 187(5) had confined the Board's inquiry solely to the efforts made by a party, exclusive of the question of its good or bad faith, the Board held that the duty imposed by s. 148(a)(ii) requires a party (i) to be reasonably available to bargain, (ii) not to select a representative who is in fact too busy to take on the assignment, and (iii) to make the commitment of time and preparation necessary to fulfil its obligation to attempt to conclude a collective agreement.[82] Although in certain circumstances the Board has held otherwise,[83] a failure to meet has generally been held to be a breach of the duty imposed by s. 148(a)(ii).[84]

It must be stressed that to determine whether a bargaining agent has failed to make a reasonable effort to enter into a collective agreement for

---

80   *Banque Royale du Canada (Kénogami, Québec), supra,* note 79.

81   *General Aviation Services Ltd.* (1982), 51 di 71, [1982] 3 Can LRBR 47, 82 CLLC #16,177. The Board considers the totality of the relationship of the parties and the entire bargaining strategy, notwithstanding the fact that the ministerial consent required by s. 187(5) may have delineated a specific period within which a contravention to s. 148(a), if any, can be found. On this question, see paragraph 15:1211.

82   *North Canada Air Ltd.* (1981), 43 di 312, [1981] 2 Can LRBR 388.

83   See text accompanying notes 92, 93, and 94, *infra.*

84   *J. Phillips* (1978), 34 di 603, [1979] 1 Can LRBR 180; *Austin Airways Ltd. / White River Air Services Ltd.* (1980), 41 di 151, [1980] 3 Can LRBR 393; *Northern Telecom Canada Ltd.* (1980), 42 di 178, [1981] 1 Can LRBR 306.

the purposes of s. 138(2), in the context of applications for revocation of certification, the Board uses as its standard the expression of the duty to bargain it has developed under s. 148(a).[85]

12:2132   Evidence

The appreciation of the duty to make every reasonable effort is objectively assessed[86] and requires the same type of inquiry as does the duty to bargain in good faith.

12:2200   THE CHARACTER OF THE DUTY AND ITS CONSEQUENCES

The duty to bargain in good faith and make every reasonable effort is continuous from the time at which notice to bargain is given until a final resolution of an agreement.[87] There are three consequences to this principle, which are outlined below.

12:2210   The Duty to Bargain Pending Judicial Review or Other Proceedings Before the Board

In principle, judicial review proceedings do not interrupt or have any legal effect on orders of the Board or the consequential obligations under the Code.[88] Therefore, the Board does not accede to excuses for delay in complying with the obligations imposed by s. 148(a) that are founded on such grounds. This is so particularly when the judicial proceedings are based on issues of constitutional law, whether they be advanced by employers or unions.

As a result, such proceedings instituted with a view to having a certification order of the Board set aside will not suspend an employer's obligation to bargain in good faith and make every reasonable effort pursuant to s. 148(a),[89] nor will it relieve the union from the obligation of making a reasonable effort to enter into a collective agreement for the purposes of s. 138(2) and demands for the revocation of certification.[90]

---

[85]   *Arthur T. Ecclestone* (1978), 26 di 615, [1978] 2 Can LRBR 306, 78 CLLC #16,142; *Allan Martin* (1979), 37 di 50, [1979] 3 Can LRBR 184, 80 CLLC #16,004.

[86]   *North Canada Air Ltd.* (1981), 45 di 134, [1981] 3 Can LRBR 196.

[87]   *CKLW Radio Broadcasting Ltd.* (1977), 23 di 51, 77 CLLC #16,110; *Allan Martin, supra,* note 85; *Austin Airways Ltd./White River Air Services Ltd., supra,* note 84; *Northern Telecom Canada Ltd., supra,* note 84; *General Aviation Services Ltd., supra,* note 81.

[88]   Unless, of course, a stay of execution is issued by a court: see paragraph 19:3600.

[89]   See *Austin Airways Ltd./White River Air Services Ltd., supra,* note 84; and *Northern Telecom Canada Ltd., supra,* note 84, for cases where employers were found to have breached their duty by having refused to bargain pending judicial review.

[90]   See *Allan Martin, supra,* note 85, where a bargaining agent was decertified for having failed to make a reasonable effort as required by s. 138(2) while awaiting the outcome of judicial proceedings instituted by the employer who sought to have the certification order quashed.

The same holds true of other proceedings instituted before the Board, such as certification review proceedings under s. 119.[91]

12:2220   Survival of the Duty During Labour Disputes or Other Events

Because the duty imposed by s. 148(a) is continuous, it survives a work stoppage, a complaint of failure to bargain in good faith, and other events. The character of the duty may change, however, and may not be judged with respect to the same standards at all stages of the negotiations. The extent to which the duty alters will depend on the facts of each case. For example, the employer's refusal to meet with the union around the time of an impending strike may not be, in itself, evidence of bad faith. The Board has stated that, although the duty to bargain does not cease when a work stoppage commences, the actions of the parties must be appraised in that climate. Thus, it is quite normal for there to be a hiatus in bargaining at the outset of a strike, in order that time may pass until the effects of the strike can be felt and in the anticipation that the climate of bargaining will be sufficiently altered so as to foster a settlement of the dispute.[92]

On the same question, the Board has held that the duty imposed by s. 148(a) may differ following a request for ministerial consent made pursuant to s. 187(5) of the Code to file a complaint alleging bad-faith negotiations. The existence of the complaint may make it very difficult for the parties to meet face-to-face on their own.[93] The same holds true where an impasse at the table has been reached. The Board has held that there is no requirement on the employer to meet in the absence of any union offer reflecting a change in its position or any indication that a resumption of the dialogue will produce some movement away from the most recent position of the parties.[94]

12:2230   The Victory of One Party Does Not Result in the Demise of the Other

The reason the duty to bargain in good faith survives during a work stoppage, even though the character of the duty may change, is to ensure

---

[91]   *Austin Airways Ltd. / White River Air Services Ltd.*, *supra*, note 84; unless the Board orders otherwise pursuant to its authority under ss. 119 and 121.

[92]   *CKLW Radio Broadcasting Ltd.*, *supra*, note 87; *Arthur T. Ecclestone*, *supra*, note 85; *Nordair Ltd.*, *supra*, note 76.

[93]   *CKLW Radio Broadcasting Ltd.*, *supra*, note 87.

[94]   *Ibid.*; *Arthur T. Ecclestone*, *supra*, note 85; *Nordair Ltd.*, *supra*, note 76; *Les Elévateurs de Sorel Ltée* (1985), 85 CLLC #16,032 (C.L.R.B.).

that reasonable responses will be made in good faith to a party who puts out feelers concerning concessions as he begins to yield to economic pressure. The Board has stated that not only does the legislative scheme anticipate that one side will concede realistically under pressure but, when that occurs, the other side must act in good faith in its manner of response. Responsible consideration of the other party's position is a necessary ingredient of good-faith bargaining. The response may not be immediate and the parties may be harsh or even ruthless in the achievement of goals of self-interest, but they cannot cross over the fine line that is envisaged as a continued reasonable effort to conclude a collective agreement. Therefore, if a party takes on economic sanctions irresponsibly, it may lose valuable gains that took years to secure but it need not die. The Code anticipates that there will be an end to such a conflict without the entire demise of one of the parties.

As a result the Board held that, when a union had capitulated to the extent that it was willing to sign virtually any offer the employer might put forward, provided that the striking employees could return to their jobs, the employer's unwillingness to make such a concession constituted bad-faith bargaining.[95]

12:2300 CASES WHERE NO BREACH WAS FOUND

There is nothing unlawful about an employer approaching collective bargaining with a determination to win out or even to put together a proposed collective agreement so constructed as to make it virtually impossible for the union to accept. This is so if the motive is simply to enhance one's position and to obtain the best possible conditions in an agreement, provided that the employer stays within the bounds of good-faith bargaining.[96]

On the same issue, the Board has held that an employer did not contravene s. 148(a) by stating, at the outset of the negotiations, that his primary concern and objective was to obtain changes in the jurisdictional provisions of the agreement, and thereafter to discuss outstanding matters with the attitude that their resolution in favour of the union was contingent on the latter's acceptance of changes in the jurisdictional provisions. The character and extent of the bargaining in this case distinguished it from situations where an insistence on bargaining on jurisdictional clauses to the exclusion of all other matters was found to be a breach of the duty to bargain in good faith.[97]

---

95   *General Aviation Services Ltd.* (1982), 51 di 71, [1982] 3 Can LRBR 47, 82 CLLC #16,177.
96   *Loomis Armored Car Service Ltd.* (1983), 51 di 185.
97   *CKLW Radio Broadcasting Ltd., supra,* note 87.

In other cases, the principle that the obligation to bargain in good faith does not include the obligation to compromise on principles, provided that reasonable efforts are made, has prevailed. In one decision the Board held that an employer had not adopted an inflexible position on issues central to the negotiations, when the rationale of the position he maintained throughout the negotiations with respect to such issues was based on business considerations that he had made known to the union.[98] The employer had furthermore attempted, in so far as possible, to propose provisions in the collective agreement to allay the union's concerns. In another decision the Board determined that an employer had not failed to make every reasonable effort to conclude a collective agreement, as he had participated regularly in all the bargaining sessions called by the union or the conciliator at all stages of the process and had, on such occasions, submitted proposals or counter-proposals and had engaged in hard bargaining.[99]

In another case, the principle that the character of the duty changes after a lawful work stoppage commences was applied. The Board held that a three-month lapse in negotiations during an acrimonious dispute and strike did not constitute bargaining in bad faith or a failure to make a reasonable effort to conclude an agreement.[100]

12:2400   CASES WHERE BREACHES WERE FOUND

After the sale of a business within the meaning of s. 144 of the Code, a new employer who refused to bargain was found to have contravened s. 148(a) in spite of his allegations that the bargaining agent did not enjoy the required employee support.[101]

In the context of a demand for the imposition of a first collective agreement, the Board determined that an employer had not bargained in good faith by (i) engaging in surface bargaining, that is, doing skilfully only what, in his opinion, was sufficient to appear to be in keeping with the guidelines established by the jurisprudence in regard to the criteria of good-faith bargaining; (ii) maintaining a "take it or leave it" attitude throughout conciliation efforts, until they collapsed; and (iii) unilaterally implementing, once the right to strike or lockout was acquired, the latest wage package he had offered to the union — an action that, although technically legal, constituted bad-faith bargaining in the circumstances of that case because it was designed to render the bargaining agent impotent in the eyes of the employees.[102]

---

98   *Banque Royale du Canada (Kénogami, Québec)* (1980), 41 di 199, [1982] 1 Can LRBR 16; see also *Maclean-Hunter Cable TV Ltd.* (1980), 42 di 274, [1981] 1 Can LRBR 454.
99   *Radio CHNC Ltée*, decision no. 450, not yet reported, January 20, 1984 (C.L.R.B.).
100   *Arthur T. Ecclestone, supra*, note 85; see also *Nordair Ltd., supra*, note 76.
101   *J. Phillips* (1978), 34 di 603, [1979] 1 Can LRBR 180.
102   *Huron Broadcasting Ltd.* (1982), 49 di 68, [1982] 2 Can LRBR 227; see also *CJMS Radio Montréal Ltée* (1978), 27 di 796, [1979] 1 Can LRBR 332.

In the context of complaints under s. 148(a), the Board found, in one case,[103] that an employer had not bargained in good faith and had breached its duty by (i) attempting, at the bargaining table, to reduce the scope of the bargaining unit;[104] (ii) making public statements to the media to the effect that it would not carry on with the negotiations;[105] (iii) communicating with the employees in the course of a legal strike and inciting them to return to work on terms and conditions outlined in such communications, thereby bargaining directly with them while negotiating, at the same time, with their bargaining agent;[106] (iv) negotiating to an impasse, in a return-to-work agreement, an acceptance by the union of a no-reprisal clause to prevent union discipline against the employees who had worked during a strike;[107] and (v) adding a third year to the duration of the monetary clauses of the collective agreement, thus reneging on its previous acceptance of a two-year term and creating what was termed a "receding horizon", after the union had given in to all the employer's demands.[108] In the same case[109] the Board found that the union also breached its duty when it made public statements and negotiated through the media, making gross misstatements and contradicting offers it was advancing at the bargaining table.[110]

Breaches were found in other decisions where the employer brought the issue of voluntary deduction of union dues to impasse without plausible and justifiable business justification,[111] or where it implemented a 5

---

103 This case involves two decisions: *Eastern Provincial Airways Ltd.* (1983), 51 di 209, 3 CLRBR (NS) 75; revd. (*sub nom. Eastern Provincial Airways Ltd. v. Canada Labour Relations Board*) [1984] 1 F.C. 732, 50 N.R. 81, 2 D.L.R. (4th) 597 (C.A.) on grounds of natural justice; and *Eastern Provincial Airways Ltd.* (1983), 54 di 172, 5 CLRBR (NS) 368, 84 CLLC #16,012; affd. (*sub nom. Eastern Provincial Airways Ltd. v. Canada Labour Relations Board*) 84 CLLC #14,042 (Fed. C.A.).

104 *Ibid.* See also *British Columbia Telephone Co.* (1977), 22 di 507, [1977] 2 Can LRBR 404, 77 CLLC #16,108; and *Wardair Canada (1975) Ltd.* (1983), 53 di 26, 2 CLRBR (NS) 129, reviewed by the Board at *Wardair Canada (1975) Ltd.* (1983), 53 di 184, 84 CLLC #16,005.

105 *Eastern Provincial Airways Ltd.* (1983), 51 di 209, 3 CLRBR (NS) 75.

106 *Eastern Provincial Airways Ltd.* (1983), 54 di 172, 84 CLLC #16,012, 5 CLRBR (NS) 368.

107 *Eastern Provincial Airways Ltd., supra,* note 105. The Board stated that the negotiation of a union non-reprisal clause in a return-to-work agreement is not illegal *per se* and is quite customary. However, negotiating such a clause to impasse by an employer or insisting on it as a condition precedent to reaching a collective agreement has been held, depending on the circumstances, to constitute an interference in the administration of a trade union as well as a breach of the obligation to bargain in good faith.

108 *Eastern Provincial Airways Ltd., supra,* note 105. See also note 94, *supra.*

109 *Eastern Provincial Airways Ltd., supra,* note 106.

110 See also *CJMS Radio Montréal Ltée, supra,* note 102, for public statements and negotiations or accusations made or conducted through the media justifying the Board's policy of scrutinizing the parties' conduct at the bargaining table as well as away from the table.

111 *Austin Airways Ltd.* (1983), 54 di 49, 4 CLRBR (NS) 343. However, the recent amendment of s. 162 (by S.C. 1983-84, c. 39, s. 31) of the Code has imposed the Rand Formula and abrogated the revocable check-off of union dues. As a result, it can be anticipated that this type of issue will not arise in the future.

percent wage increase as prescribed by the *Inflation Restraint Act* of Ontario and then steadfastly refused to discuss the issue.[112]

The Board inquired into the merits or content of proposals put forth at the bargaining table and applied the "illegality doctrine" in two cases. In the first, the Board held that a clause of a return-to-work agreement proposed by an employer that purported to maintain in the active work force, out of seniority, substitutes hired during a strike, to the detriment of the employees who had participated in the work stoppage, was illegal because it contravened various dispositions of the Code.[113] In the second case, the Board held that a clause in a return-to-work agreement proposed by a union to secure the reinstatement of employees fired in the course of a strike for participation in criminal acts committed against a manager of the company was illegal and contrary to public policy.[114] Thus, in both cases, by tabling such proposals and insisting their acceptance as a condition precedent to reaching a collective agreement, the parties had failed to bargain in good faith.

With respect to the duty imposed by s. 148(a)(ii), the Board held that an employer had not made every reasonable effort to conclude a collective agreement when (i) he was represented by two law firms advancing and adopting conflicting positions at the bargaining table, although a declaration of single employer under s. 133 had been made; (ii) he was unwilling to agree to any union proposals after they had been amended to account for his concerns; (iii) he maintained two bargaining proposals so incompatible with realistic collective bargaining that they could not reasonably be viewed as efforts to enter into a collective agreement; and (iv) his representatives were unable or unwilling to meet with the union for a period of over a month and a half.[115]

12:2500   PROCEDURAL MATTERS AND TIMELINESS OF A COMPLAINT MADE UNDER SECTION 148(a)

An unfair labour practice complaint alleging a failure to bargain in good faith and make every reasonable effort is made pursuant to s. 187(1) and is subject to the universal ninety-day limitation period mentioned in s. 187(2). Various factors must be taken into consideration, however,

---

112   *Ottawa-Carleton Regional Transit Commission* (1983), 51 di 173, 83 CLLC #16,016.

113   *Eastern Provincial Airways Ltd., supra*, note 105; and *Appleton v. Eastern Provincial Airways Ltd.* (1983), 50 N.R. 99, 2 D.L.R. (4th) 147 (Fed. C.A.), quashed on grounds of natural justice. All three judges held, however, that the Board did not exceed its jurisdiction in making such a finding. The case was referred back to the Board and was reheard by a new panel, which came to the same conclusion as the one reached by the first panel: *Eastern Provincial Airways Ltd., supra*, note 106. See text accompanying note 71, *supra*.

114   *Les Elévateurs de Sorel Ltée* (1985), 85 CLLC #16,032 (C.L.R.B.).

115   *North Canada Air Ltd.* (1981), 43 di 312, [1981] 2 Can LRBR 388.

when determining the timeliness of such a complaint. These will be dealt with in another part.[116]

Like s. 148(b), a complaint under s. 148(a) is subject to the additional requirement of ministerial consent provided in s. 187(5). This requirement will also be dealt with elsewhere.[117]

12:3000   UNFAIR LABOUR PRACTICES RELATING TO LABOUR DISPUTES

A striking employee has certain protections under the Code. His employment status is preserved by s. 107(2). He cannot be dismissed or otherwise discriminated against for participating in a lawful strike (s. 184(3)(a)(vi)). Once he returns to work, his pension rights and other benefits are protected by s. 184(3)(d). While on strike he may be replaced, but other employees may lawfully refuse to perform his duties (s. 184(3)(c)).[118]

When a strike is illegal, an employee may not be disciplined or discriminated against by the union for having refused to participate in the stoppage (s. 185(h)). If a lockout is illegal, an employer may not suspend, discharge, or impose any financial or other penalty on a person employed by him for having refused to declare or institute the illegal lockout (s. 184(3)(f)). Finally, employers, trade unions, and employees are liable to fines for declaring, causing, or participating in illegal strikes or lockouts (ss. 190 and 191(1)).

12:3100   DENIAL OF PENSION RIGHTS OR BENEFITS: SECTION 184(3)(d)(i)

Section 184(3)(d)(i) expressly protects pension rights and other benefits to which employees would be entitled but for the cessation of work as a result of a lawful strike or lockout. The Board has determined, however, that Parliament did not intend to guarantee that employees would accrue employment benefits while on strike or lockout just as if they were not at work. The Board considers that s. 184(3)(d) is intended to preserve pension rights and other benefits enjoyed or acquired prior to the strike or lockout. In this respect seniority, which is usually also an integral part of pension entitlement, is preserved during a work stoppage.

As a result of this interpretation, the Board held that where employees on a legal strike are denied accrual of seniority for the duration of the work stoppage, no violation of s. 184(3)(d) occurs. The provisions of

---

116   See paragraph 15:2320.
117   See paragraphs 15:1000 and 15:1200.
118   *Bell Canada* (1981), 42 di 298, [1981] 2 Can LRBR 148, 81 CLLC #16,083.

that section do not guarantee employees the accrual of employment benefits while participating in a strike or being subject to a lockout.[119]

12:3200   DISCRIMINATION AGAINST AN EMPLOYEE BECAUSE OF A REFUSAL TO DO STRUCK WORK: SECTION 184(3)(c)

The Code protects the striking or locked-out employee through various dispositions, but only in s. 184(3)(c) does it go one step further and protect others who may be affected by a strike or a lockout. Prior to the amendments of June 1984, s. 184(3)(c) offered protection only when an employee refused to perform the duties and responsibilities of another employee who was on strike and not when the other employee was locked-out. Section 184(3)(c), unlike s. 184(3)(d) for example, spoke only of a strike and not of a lockout.[120] The new amendment remedied this deficiency by providing that an employee may refuse to perform the duties and responsibilities of another employee who is either on strike or "subject to a lockout".

Four conditions must exist before s. 184(3)(c) can be invoked. First, s. 184(3)(c) applies only to an "employee" — not all persons generally — within the meaning of s. 107(1) of the Code. Thus, an employer may call upon his unorganized employees or those in a non-striking or non-locked-out unit to do the work of the striking or locked-out employees, but he may not use disciplinary sanctions either to force them to do so or to penalize them for having refused.[121]

However, s. 184(3)(c) does not give these employees the right to work at their normal functions during the strike or lockout of other employees. It does not prohibit the employer from laying them off if there is no work available for them. Strikes and lockouts are extraordinary events. The employer who seeks to continue to operate will have to reorganize his operation to accomplish the work of those on strike or lockout. The Code does not prohibit this, nor does it forbid the engagement of outside help. The Code contemplates that employers will try to continue operating and will ask non-bargaining unit employees to assist them. If the latter refuse, the Code allows that they be laid-off during the strike. It is for this reason that there is no reference to lay-off in s. 184(3)(c) as in s. 184(3)(a), for example.

Thus, for instance, in one case, the complainant who was a non-bargaining unit supervisory employee had, prior to a strike, supervised a number of construction employees, including several junior supervisors. Once the strike began, the complainant refused to do the work of striking

---

119   *Ibid.*
120   *British Columbia Telephone Co.* (1981), 47 di 28, [1982] 1 Can LRBR 399, 82 CLLC #16,149.
121   *Ibid.*

employees and was sent home. He was off work without pay for a number of weeks. When the complainant returned to work at the conclusion of the strike, the employer instituted a unique reorganization that resulted in removing the entire complement of construction employees from the complainant's supervision. The Board found that the complainant had been laid-off during the strike in accordance with the employer's right. However, it was further held that the reorganization was intended to punish the complainant by stripping him of his responsibility, respect, and status and to reward those who had performed bargaining unit work during the strike. Such action on the part of the employer constituted prohibited disciplinary measures in contravention of s. 184(3)(c). As a result, the employer was ordered, among other things, to reverse the organizational change and to restore the complainant to his former position.[122]

Second, in order for s. 184(3)(c) to apply, the employer must have been involved in a strike or lockout situation within the meaning of the Code. The evidence must at the very least establish that the employee refused to perform some or all of the duties and responsibilities of another striking or locked-out employee.[123]

Third, the strike or lockout must be lawful under Part V of the Code, failing which the protection of s. 184(3)(c) will not be available.

Fourth, s. 184(3)(c) gives an employee the right to refuse to perform the duties of another employee who is participating in a legal strike or lockout in cases where the other employee is employed by the same employer. The protection does not apply when the striking or locked-out employee is employed by another employer, even if this other employer is under federal jurisdiction.[124] It must be noted, however, that when the other employer is subject to the federal jurisdiction, the Board could, in the proper circumstances,[125] make a finding under s. 133 to the effect that the struck and allied employers formed a single employer for the purposes of a complaint under s. 184(3)(c). Failing common control or direction between the struck and allied employers, or common employment between the striking employee and fellow employees, the protection of s. 184(3)(c) will not apply.[126]

---

[122]   *Ibid;* see also *British Columbia Telephone Co.* (1983), 52 di 88, 83 CLLC #16,048, where the Board found that the employer had contravened s. 184(3)(c).

[123]   *La Banque Nationale du Canada* (1981), 42 di 352, [1982] 3 Can LRBR 1; *British Columbia Telephone Co.* (1979), 37 di 20, [1979] 2 Can LRBR 297, 80 CLLC #16,007, reviewed and affirmed by the Board in plenary session at *British Columbia Telephone Co.* (1979), 38 di 124, [1980] 1 Can LRBR 340, 80 CLLC #16,008.

[124]   *British Columbia Telephone Co.* (1979), 37 di 20, [1979] 2 Can LRBR 297, 80 CLLC #16,007.

[125]   For a discussion of Board policy with respect to declarations of single employer during the course of economic conflicts under s. 133, see *Calgary Television Ltd.* (1977), 25 di 399, [1978] 1 Can LRBR 532.

[126]   *British Columbia Telephone Co., supra,* note 124.

12:3300   DISCRIMINATION AGAINST A PERSON BECAUSE OF PARTICIPATION IN A LEGAL STRIKE: SECTION 184(3)(a)(vi)

There are two parts to s. 184(3)(a)(vi). The second part, which relates to the exercise of any right under the Code, has been considered earlier.[127] The first part prohibits employer discrimination against any person for the reason that the person has participated in a strike that is not prohibited by Part V.

One case where a breach of s. 184(3)(a)(vi) was found involved a preference in terms of employment granted to those employees of the bargaining unit who had worked during a lawful strike.[128] During the strike, advanced payments on a profit-sharing plan had been distributed to all employees of the company except those who were participating in the work stoppage. By contrast, the denial of accrual of seniority during a work stoppage only to those employees of the unit who had participated in the strike was held not to be motivated by anti-union animus, nor was it interference in the administration of or representation by the union. Although it could have the effect of restraining an employee from exercising his right to strike, the Board found no contravention of the Code.[129]

In an earlier decision, employee dismissals resulting from activities on picket lines that involved damages to employer property were found to be in contravention of s. 184(3)(a)(vi).[130] The Board declined, however, to accept the union's argument to the effect that when there is a legal strike, an employer is precluded, *ab initio*, from the right to dismiss employees who participate in the work stoppage as long as such a situation exists. The Board also held that calls from the president of the company to employees on the first day that they exercised their right to participate in a legal strike constituted, in the particular circumstances of that case, intimidation prohibited by s. 184(3)(a)(vi).[131]

Finally, as will be discussed below, the Board has held that a bargaining proposal advanced in negotiations by which preference in employment would be granted to replacement employees over the striking employees before certain specific events have occurred contravenes s. 184(3)(a)(vi).

---

[127]   See paragraph 11:2120.
[128]   *Eastern Provincial Airways Ltd.* (1983), 54 di 172, 5 CLRBR (NS) 368, 84 CLLC #16,012; affd. in part (*sub nom. Eastern Provincial Airways Ltd. v. Canada Labour Relations Board*), 84 CLLC #14,042 (Fed. C.A.).
[129]   *Bell Canada, supra,* note 118.
[130]   *Banque Royale du Canada (Jonquière et Kénogami)* (1980), 42 di 125.
[131]   *Eastern Provincial Airways Ltd., supra,* note 128.

12:3400   THE USE OF REPLACEMENTS DURING A STRIKE

Other than s. 184(3)(c) considered above, there are no specific provisions in the *Canada Labour Code* that regulate the use by an employer operating in the federal jurisdiction of replacements in the course of a strike or a lockout. The Code does not contain anti-scab provisions, as does the *Quebec Labour Code*,[132] or professional anti-strike breaker dispositions, as do the *British Columbia Labour Code*[133] and the *Ontario Labour Relations Act*.[134]

Accordingly, the Board recognized that from the inception of a strike an employer can decide to attempt to continue operating his enterprise notwithstanding the work stoppage of his regular employees.[135] This is the very essence of the economic warfare that has been elevated in the collective bargaining system to the role of ultimate sanction for the failure to arrive peacefully and amicably at the signing or renewal of a collective agreement. It might be shocking to the strikers, but it is not forbidden under the federal labour code.

To this end an employer may call on his management personnel to perform bargaining unit work and still not contravene the Code. Subject to s. 184(3)(c), he may also use the services of employees of the bargaining unit who have decided to cross the picket lines and work during the strike. He may also, subject again to s. 184(3)(c), bring in a group of employees from other non-unionized branches or locations within the enterprise to replace the strikers. Such practices are not prohibited by the Code. A struck employer may also hire replacements from outside the bargaining unit or, in other words, newly hired workers, to fill the positions left vacant by the strikers.[136]

In such a case, however, unless an expansion has occurred in the employer's operations, a critical question concerning the employment

---

[132]   R.S.Q. 1977, c. C-27, s. 109.1.

[133]   R.S.B.C. 1979, c. 212, s. 3(3)(d).

[134]   R.S.O. 1980, c. 228, s. 71a.

[135]   *Banque Royale du Canada (Jonquière et Kénogami), supra,* note 130; *Eastern Provincial Airways Ltd.* (1983), 51 di 209, 3 CLRBR (NS) 75; revd. by *Eastern Provincial Airways Ltd. v. Canada Labour Relations Board,* [1984] 1 F.C. 732, 50 N.R. 81, 2 D.L.R. (4th) 597 (C.A.) on grounds of natural justice, and by *Appleton v. Eastern Provincial Airways Ltd.* (1983), 50 N.R. 99, 2 D.L.R. (4th) 147 (Fed. C.A.); *Eastern Provincial Airways Ltd., supra,* note 128. The policy of the Board is in keeping with the comments of the Woods Task Force: "607. As noted elsewhere, the employer's economic sanction equivalent to the union's right to strike rarely is the lockout: it is his ability to take a strike. Much of what follows in this section, therefore, relates to the strike. However, it is important to note that the employer's capacity to take a strike depends largely on his right to stockpile goods in advance of a strike and to use other employees and replacements to perform work normally done by strikers. Together with the lockout, these possibilities constitute the employer's *quid pro quo* for the workers' right to strike; this is as it should be, in our view."

[136]   *Banque Royale du Canada (Jonquière et Kénogami), supra,* note 130; *Eastern Provincial Airways Ltd.* (1983), 51 di 209, 3 CLRBR (NS) 75.

security of the outside replacements as well as that of the strikers will arise if the entire complement of jobs in the enterprise at the end of the dispute is not large enough to allow for the reinstatement of all the employees who participated in the strike while retaining at the same time the replacements hired during the conflict.

In this connection, the jurisprudence in other jurisdictions such as Ontario has determined that "as a strike endures, the commitment of an employer to the employees who have helped it resist the strike may become great and, in the usual case, it is for the negotiation process to reconcile this commitment with the interest of striking employees to return immediately to their jobs".[137] However, if the employer has, in the course of the strike, committed certain basic and flagrant unfair labour practices that have resulted in the weakening of the union's bargaining power, the latter may no longer be in a strong enough position to secure, through a negotiated settlement, the immediate return to work of the striking employees once the dispute comes to an end. In order to counter-balance the effect of the employer's unfair labour practices, the security of employment of the regular employees has been held, in such circumstances, to become a remedial issue to be handled by the Board.

These principles are consistent with the policy of the Board not to intervene in the free collective bargaining system privileged by Parliament so long as the bargaining is not tainted by violations of any of the provisions of the Code. For this reason, the Board drew upon the above principles in two decisions, *Eastern Provincial Airways Ltd.*,[138] in which it found that the employer had conferred a permanent status, upon hiring, on outside replacements engaged during the strike, in addition to having committed various unfair labour practices that had weakened the union's bargaining strength.

The Board held that "the act of conferring a permanent status on a replacement employee upon hiring, and prior to specific happenings governed and directed by the Code, constitutes an unfair labour practice which disqualifies an employer from keeping the replacement employee in his position once the strike is terminated".[139] These specific happenings, until which a permanent status cannot be conferred by the employer on a replacement employee, were described as follows:

> Absent the existence of any unfair labour practice by an employer, absent bad faith bargaining on the part of each party, absent the yielding of the bargaining agent to economic pressure, even in the face of realistic concessions by an employer, present the elapsing of at least six months from the inception date of the strike, the temporary status of the replacement em-

---

137   In Ontario, for instance, see *Fotomat Canada Ltd.* (1981), 1 Can LRBR 381, quoted in *Eastern Provincial Airways Ltd., supra,* note 136.

138   *Eastern Provincial Airways Ltd., supra,* note 136; *Eastern Provincial Airways Ltd., supra,* note 128.

139   *Eastern Provincial Airways Ltd., supra,* note 136, at p. 242 (di).

ployees could very well turn into permanency and the strikers could lose their jobs and the union's bargaining rights could be revoked.[140]

12:3410   Security of Employment of the Striking Employees

It is convenient at this point to examine the three elements that combine to protect the striking employees' security of employment. The first is s. 107(2), which preserves the striker's employee status in the course of a strike or a lockout. The second is s. 184(3)(a)(vi), which prohibits discrimination against any person in regard to employment, pay, or any other term or condition of employment because the person has participated in a legal strike. The third is the Board's remedial policy when the union's bargaining strength has been eroded by the employer's unfair labour practices, as a result of which the union is no longer in a position to secure the immediate return to work of the strikers.

The Board's construction of these sections and of others is discussed below.

12:3411   Preservation of the Employment Status of the Strikers: Section 107(2)

Section 107(2) preserves a striker's employee status with the employer being struck. In s. 184(3)(d), the Code anticipates that he will return to work. Furthermore, there is no statutory rule for when, if ever, a striking employee will lose his right to return to work.[141] In this regard, the Board has held[142] that if the Code contained only s. 107(2), which is a standard provision found in most jurisdictions, it would be open to argument that to retain "employee status" does not necessarily mean the guarantee of a job. But Parliament went much further than s. 107(2) to protect the continued employment of those who exercise their rights under the Code.

The Board stated that the construction of s. 184(3)(a)(vi) leaves no room for doubt that the mere fact that others are performing bargaining unit work is not reason enough to erase the employee's status and remove the employer's obligation to continue to employ him at the end of the strike.[143]

12:3412   Prohibition on Discriminatory Terms and Conditions of Employment: Section 184(3)(a)(vi)

The hire of a replacement employee from outside the unit in the course of a strike is based upon the conclusion of an individual contract of

---

140   *Eastern Provincial Airways Ltd., supra,* note 136, at p. 261 (di).
141   *Bell Canada* (1981), 42 di 298, [1981] 2 Can LRBR 148, 81 CLLC #16,083.
142   *Eastern Provincial Airways Ltd., supra,* note 128.
143   *General Aviation Services Ltd.* (1982), 51 di 71, [1982] 3 Can LRBR 47, 82 CLLC #16,177.

employment. If the latter is for a temporary period terminating on the same day as the strike, no violation of the Code occurs. This is the case because, as mentioned above, Part V does not contain any anti-scab or anti-strike breaker provisions. This does not mean, however, that the only replacements a struck employer can legally hire are strikebreakers. Indeed, the individual contract of employment entered into by the replacements may be for an indefinite period extending beyond the termination date of the strike. In such a case, however, the replacements must not be granted terms and conditions of employment, either in their individual contracts or through a clause of a return-to-work agreement, that amount to a guarantee not to be displaced by the returning striking employees. They also cannot, at any time, whether the specific events mentioned have occurred or not, be granted either by their individual contracts or through a return-to-work agreement, preferential terms or conditions of employment over the striking employees or advantages superior to those of the regular employees.[144]

For instance, in *Eastern Provincial Airways Ltd.*[145] the replacements had been hired on individual employment contracts of indefinite duration extending beyond the end of the strike. The employer pointed out that these contracts were identical to those entered into by the striking employees when they were originally hired and contained terms and conditions of employment no different from those offered to the union at the bargaining table. Nonetheless, the Board held that these contracts, read together with a return-to-work agreement, contravened s. 184(3)(a)(vi) by discriminating against the striking employees. The return-to-work agreement provided that (i) all remaining strikers would be placed on layoff; (ii) the laid-off strikers would be recalled to work only when vacant positions became available; and (iii) the provisions of the collective agreement regarding seniority would not affect the status of the replacements. The effect of clause (iii), in the Board's opinion, was that the strikers, upon their return to work, when and if they were recalled, would find their seniority rights subordinated to those of the replacements, so that in the event of a subsequent layoff the strikers would be dismissed before any of the replacements, and the replacements would be the first to be recalled. This contravened s. 184(3)(a)(vi) for the following reason:

> The granting of a super-seniority status to these replacements discriminates against and penalizes those employees who participated in a legal strike and

---

144   See *Eastern Provincial Airways Ltd., supra,* note 136, and the notes of Mr. Justice Mahoney in *Eastern Provincial Airways Ltd. v. Canada Labour Relations Board,* [1984] 1 F.C. 732, 50 N.R. 81, at 86, 2 D.L.R. (4th) 597 (C.A.).

145   *Eastern Provincial Airways Ltd., supra,* note 136.

146   *Ibid.,* at p. 240 (di).

attempts to, and may succeed, in dissuading them from so participating [in] a right conferred upon them by the Code.[146]

The effect of clauses (i) and (ii) of the return-to-work agreement, in the Board's opinion, was to confer a permanent status on the replacements. In the circumstances of that case, the Board held that this discriminated against the striking employees in contravention of s. 184(3)(a)(vi) for the following reasons:

> The right to participate in a legal strike is guaranteed by sections 110(1) and 180(2) of the Code. These sections grant a statutory right to an employee to suspend his service in order to participate in an activity acknowledged and sanctioned by the Code. Once the strike is over, the employee having declared himself ready to perform work according to the terms and conditions contained in the new collective agreement, it follows that if the employer refused to reinstate him for the reason that his position has been permanently filled, the withdrawal or suspension of his work or services does not depend any more upon the will of the employee, but upon that of the employer. Yet, that employer cannot refuse to accept the resuming of the services of this employee except for a reason which is not prohibited by the Code. Since the reason in these circumstances is that the services of the striking employee are not required anymore because of the presence of a replacement employee filling his position, it therefore means that the reason of the refusal of the services of the striking employee is illegal, since it is caused by the granting of a permanent status to the replacement employee. The employer is penalizing the striker because he has exercised a right acknowledged and sanctioned by the Code as belonging to him: to participate in a legal strike.
>
> If, at the end of the strike, the employer refuses to reinstate the striking pilots by reason of their positions having been filled permanently by replacements who were not in the bargaining unit represented by CALPA, it is contravening section 184(3)(a)(vi) because it penalizes the strikers who have refused to cross picket lines by discriminating against them as opposed to those employees who, in addition to the replacements from outside, decided to cross the picket lines, for the sole reason that they exercise a right conferred upon them by the Code, under the provisions of section 184(3)(c).[147]

The Board held, furthermore, that it was not enough for an employer to demonstrate that all the newly hired replacements would be placed at the bottom of the seniority list if an equivalent number of striking bargaining unit employees were not recalled to work at the end of the dispute. Indeed, although the replacements would not enjoy a super-seniority status over the employees of the bargaining unit who had returned to work during the stoppage, or who were recalled at the end of the strike, they would still enjoy such super-seniority over those employees who were not recalled to work and placed on layoff.[148]

---

[147]   *Ibid.*, at p. 241 (di).
[148]   *Eastern Provincial Airways Ltd.*, *supra*, note 128.

12:3413   The Exercise of the Remedial Powers of the Board

As in other jurisdictions,[149] the Board referred to the American doctrine of the conversion of an economic strike into an unfair labour practice strike for guidelines as to the manner in which it should exercise its remedial powers where an employer refuses to displace the replacements and reinstate the strikers and has committed various unfair labour practices that have eroded the union's bargaining strength.

According to American case law, an unfair labour practice strike is one that is caused, aggravated, or prolonged by an employer's unfair labour practices. As a general rule, an economic strike is one in support of better wages, hours, or working conditions. Furthermore, a strike can be converted from one type to another during its course. Such is the case with an economic strike that is prolonged or aggravated by an employer's unfair practices. As a result, the strikers whose jobs have been filled by replacements after the conversion to an unfair labour practice strike acquire an absolute right to reinstatement in their former positions, or to positions substantially equivalent. At the end of the work stoppage, the employer cannot refuse to displace, demote, layoff, or even fire the replacements in order to reinstate the strikers whose jobs have been filled in the unfair labour practice phase of the strike.

Drawing from these principles, the Board held that it needed not adopt all the trappings of the American doctrine but that the concept's underlying purpose had considerable relevance to the exercise of its remedial powers. The Board also drew from the decision of the Supreme Court of Canada in *C.P.R. v. Zambri*[150] further support in the exercise of its remedial powers, in a manner similar to that suggested by the American doctrine. In that case, after having reviewed the decisions of the Supreme Court of the United States that had prompted the development of the conversion doctrine of a strike, Mr. Justice Locke said the following in *obiter*:

> When employers have endeavoured to come to an agreement with their employees and followed the procedures specified by the *Labour Relations Act*, they are at complete liberty if a strike then takes place to engage others to fill the places of the strikers. At the termination of the strike, employers are not obliged to continue to employ their former employees if they have no work for them to do, due to their positions being filled.[151]

It follows that if an employer has failed to negotiate in good faith as provided by s. 148(a), or has committed, prior to or during the course of the strike, other unfair labour practices under that or other sections of

---

[149]   In Ontario, see *Fotomat Canada Ltd.*, [1981] 1 Can LRBR 381 (O.L.R.B.), quoted in *Eastern Provincial Airways Ltd.*, *supra*, note 136.

[150]   *Canadian Pacific Railway Co. v. Zambri*, [1962] S.C.R. 609, 62 CLLC #15,407, 34 D.L.R. (2d) 654.

[151]   *Ibid.*, at p. 621 (S.C.R.).

the Code, he has not "endeavoured to come to an agreement" or has not "followed the procedures specified by the Act". By being guilty of an act prohibited by statute, the employer has lost his complete liberty to hire, at least permanently, replacements to fill the jobs left vacant by the strikers.

Accordingly, as the employer in *Eastern Provincial Airways Ltd.*[152] had committed various unfair labour practices in the course of the strike that had eroded the union's bargaining strength and had conferred a preference in employment to the replacements upon their being hired, in the nature of a guarantee not to be displaced, the Board ordered the parties to "negotiate a return to work agreement which would not include any terms as to reinstatement of the striking employees to their former positions having the effect of providing them with conditions of employment or opportunities for employment or continued employment less favourable than the ones they would have been extended had they not participated in the strike". The Board further ordered the employer to reinstate each striking employee to his former or a substantially equivalent position, in accordance with the return-to-work agreement the parties will negotiate, whether or not a strike replacement employee must be transferred, laid-off, terminated, or removed from a position to which he had been promoted.[153] In the second *Eastern Provincial Airways*

---

[152]   *Supra*, note 136.

[153]   *Ibid.*; revd. (*sub nom. Eastern Provincial Airways Ltd. v. Canada Labour Relations Board*, [1984] 1 F.C. 732, 50 N.R. 81, 2 D.L.R. (4th) 597 (C.A.) on grounds of natural justice. All three judges held, however, that the Board's finding that a clause of a return-to-work agreement purporting to keep on the active work force, out of seniority, substitutes hired during a strike to the detriment of the striking employees that contravened, among others, s. 184(3)(a)(vi), was not an excess of jurisdiction.

   Upon judicial review instituted by the replacement employees against the decision of the Board, a majority of the judges held, in *Appleton v. Eastern Provincial Airways Ltd.* (1983), 50 N.R. 99, 2 D.L.R. (4th) 147 (Fed. C.A.), that the Board had breached the rules of natural justice by not affording the replacements an opportunity to be heard as parties directly affected by the order of the Board and against whom the union had taken an adverse stance. The *ratio decidendi* of the majority was two-fold. First, it held that, although the order of the Board was directed at the employer, it compelled the latter to reinstate the strikers regardless of whether by so doing the replacement would be displaced. Thus, in the court's opinion, the order affected the replacements as directly and immediately as if it had been directed at them. Second, the court held that the replacements fell within the meaning of a "party" in s. 28(2) of the *Federal Court Act*. Whether they were employees before the strike began or were hired after it began, the replacements, in the court's opinion, were all members of the bargaining unit for which the union was the recognized bargaining agent. Thus, as members of the unit for whom the union acted, they were *de facto* parties and persons whose interests were adverse to those espoused by the union. It follows that they ought to have been given an opportunity to become parties to the hearing before the order of the Board was made.

   Compare this decision of the Federal Court with the statements made by the Board in *General Aviation Services Ltd.* (1982), 51 di 71, [1982] 3 Can LRBR 47, 82 CLLC #16,177. See, to the same effect, the policy of the Ontario Labour Relations Board in *International Chemical Workers, Local 159 v. Kodak Canada Ltd.*, [1977] 2 Can LRBR 329, which distinguishes, among other, the application of *Re Hoogendoorn and Greening Metal Products & Screening Equipment Co.*, [1968] S.C.R. 30, 65 D.L.R. (2d) 641, in cases similar to the one with which the Board was confronted.

Ltd. decision[154] the Board ordered, similarly, that for the purpose of any return-to-work agreement, all the positions formerly filled by the striking employees within the bargaining unit were to be considered vacant and the return to work was to be effected by order of seniority as of the date on which the strike commenced.

12:3420　Security of Employment of the Replacements Hired From Outside the Unit

The Board had determined that the employment status of the replacements drawn from outside the bargaining unit may very well become permanent, in the absence of any unfair labour practices by an employer before and throughout the work stoppage and in the absence of bad-faith bargaining by either party. Although the Board has not expanded on this subject, the following may be drawn from its comments in the first *Eastern Provincial Airways Ltd.* decision[155] and from previous decisions.

By way of corollary, if an employer does not commit, prior to or in

---

[154]　(1983), 54 di 172, 5 CLRBR (NS) 368, 84 CLLC #16,012. On judicial review of the Board's decision, the Federal Court of Appeal concluded, in *Eastern Provincial Airways Ltd. v. Canada Labour Relations Board* (1984), 84 CLLC #14,042 (Fed. C.A.), that the Board had erred in law by finding that the employer had contravened s. 184(3)(a)(vi) of the Code by conferring a preference in employment upon the replacements hired during the strike over the striking employees through a return-to-work agreement. Nonetheless, the court upheld the decision in view of the privative clause contained in s. 122(1) of the Code. In this regard, the court said: "A prerequisite to a finding that section 184(3)(a)(vi) had been violated by E.P.A.'s insistance on clause 12 was a finding that E.P.A. insisted on it because the striking pilots had participated in the strike. The Board made no such finding. In my opinion, the Board erred in law in concluding, on the basis of the facts as it found them, that E.P.A.'s insistance on clause 12 violated section 148(a) and section 184(3)(a)(vi) of the Code. However, in view of section 122(1) of the Code and the application of that section in *Teamsters Union Local 938 v. Massicotte* [(1982) 1 S.C.R. 710], I agree that it is not a jurisdictional error."
　　Clause 12 of the return-to-work agreement referred to had the effect of preventing the reinstatement of the employees who had participated in the work stoppage until their positions occupied by replacements became vacant. It could be argued that the court failed to appreciate that there cannot be any other reason for an employer to negotiate such a clause than the participation by his employees in a strike. One would search in vain for another reason.
　　The learned judge appears to have reviewed his position on this issue. Indeed, upon judicial review of the first *Eastern Provincial Airways* decision, in which the Board had reached the same conclusion as it did in its second decision, that is, that clause 12 offended, among others, s. 184(3)(a)(vi) by conferring a permanency of employment on the replacements to the detriment of the striking employees who were put on layoff until their positions became vacant, Mr. Justice Mahoney held that there was no reviewable error, but, unlike in the extract above, he did not disagree with the correctness of the Board's decision. There he wrote: "I see no reviewable error if, as I trust, the Board intended the adjective 'permanent' only to comprehend the terms of the replacement pilots' employment it found would give them preference over the striking pilots after the strike." [*Eastern Provincial Airways Ltd. v. Canada Labour Relations Board* (1983), 50 N.R. 81, at 86].
[155]　(1983), 51 di 209, 3 CLRBR (NS) 75.

the course of the strike, any unfair labour practices and does not fail to negotiate in good faith and make every reasonable effort to conclude an agreement in any manner, the employer has not lost the "complete liberty" referred to by Mr. Justice Locke in the *Zambri* decision[156] to hire outside replacements without being obliged, at the end of the strike, to displace them, lay them off, or even fire them in order to reinstate the strikers whose jobs had been filled. By not being guilty of any act denounced by statute, the employer's actions do not affect the equilibrium of the forces of the parties and do not undermine the union's bargaining strength to negotiate the immediate return to work of the striking employees once the dispute comes to an end.

As a result, the security of employment of the striking employees does not become a remedial issue to be addressed by the Board. It is for the negotiation process to reconcile the diverging commitment of the employer to the employees who have helped him operate during the strike and the interest of the striking employees to return immediately to their jobs. As Parliament has not placed a time limit on legitimate economic conflict, if the employer withstands the pressure and is able to continue to operate with his management personnel, outside help, and bargaining unit employees who have returned to work, this state may continue for quite a while. The employees inside remain, and as the strike endures, the employees outside may gradually lose interest in continued employment in the struck enterprise and drift away to seek other employment elsewhere. In such a case, there might be fewer regular employees remaining for reinstatement at the end of the strike.

When an employer has not committed any unfair labour practices prior to and during the strike and has not failed to negotiate in good faith, the question arises, however, whether a persistant refusal in the course of negotiations for a return-to-work agreement to immediately reinstate the remaining strikers upon the conclusion of the dispute while retaining, for an indefinite period of time, the outside replacements, would be considered as bargaining in bad faith. The Board has not yet provided an answer to that question, although it is clear that a refusal to reinstate the remaining strikers at all would amount to illegal dismissals in contravention of the provisions of ss. 107(2) and 184(3)(a)(vi) of the Code, unless the employees had committed some acts in the course of the strike that would constitute a just cause for dismissal.[157]

---

156   *Supra,* note 151.
157   However, it is suggested that it follows from the Board's reasoning in *Eastern Provincial Airways Ltd.* that a proposal providing that the remaining strikers would not be immediately recalled to work but that they would (i) remain "employees", (ii) be placed on a preferential list, in order of seniority, entitling them to be recalled to work before any new employee could be hired, (iii) be recalled to work upon either the departure of replacements, the reactivation of jobs for which the strikers are qualified, or as new openings arise in the enterprise, unless they have acquired, in the meantime, regular and substantially equivalent employment elsewhere, and (iv) be entitled to full rein-

There is another consequence worth mentioning, which follows from the simple passage of time from the commencement date of the strike. It relates to the status of the incumbent bargaining agent. Indeed, although there is no actual time limit stipulated in the Code for the end of a strike, the period mentioned in ss. 124(3) and 137(5) prohibiting the filing of applications for certification or revocation within six months from the commencement of the work stoppage provides an indicator as to how long the legislator considered that such an exercise would be meaningful.[158]

An application for revocation of the certification of the bargaining agent could be filed at the expiration of such a period. This application would raise the question as to which employee would be entitled to participate in the representation vote.

In this regard, the Board has expressed the opinion that, in such circumstances, only those who were employed on the day of the commencement of the strike and who still have an interest in the issue should participate in the vote. Nonetheless, there are situations where the application could be granted. The most obvious one is where a majority of the bargaining unit employees have returned to work while a strike is still in progress.[159] Alternatively, the replacements hired in the course of a strike and the bargaining unit employees who have returned to work during the work stoppage could form an association and file an application for certification on their own at the expiration of six months from the beginning of the strike, or even earlier with the consent of the Board.

In either situation, however, whether the incumbent bargaining agent is revoked or displaced, an employer could still not discriminate against the remaining striking employees. The employment relationship between the latter and the employer would not, of course, be severed by such changes. But with the simple passage of time, there could be fewer regular employees left to reinstate at the end of the strike. A substantial number of replacements could, accordingly, secure their employment,

---

statement, including their seniority rights upon their recall to work, should not be considered as illegal. This is the solution that has been adopted in the United States with respect to the rights of economic strikers to return to work at the end of the dispute. See *Laidlaw Corp.* (1968), 68 L.R.R.M. 1252; *American Machinery Corp.* (1973), 73 L.R.R.M. 2977; *United Aircraft* (1971), 77 L.R.R.M. 1785; *Labour Spring and Electric Car Corp.* (1971), 77 L.R.R.M. 180, and generally, Douglas S. McDowell and Kenneth C. Huhn, *NLRB, Remedies for Unfair Labour Practices* (Philadelphia: University of Pennsylvania, The Wharton School, Industrial Research Unit, 1976), Labour Relations and Public Policy Series, Report No. 12. Whether the Board would be prepared to accept this kind of solution to the problem arising from the use of replacements in the course of a purely economic strike as a logical corollary of its decision in *Eastern Provincial Airways Ltd.* has yet to be determined.

158   *General Aviation Services Ltd.* (1982), 51 di 71, [1982] 3 Can LRBR 47, 82 CLLC #16,177; and *General Aviation Services Ltd.* (1982), 51 di 88, [1982] 3 Can LRBR 439, 82 CLLC #16,181.

159   This situation occurred, for instance, in *Arthur T. Ecclestone* (1978), 26 di 615, [1978] 2 Can LRBR 306, 78 CLLC #16,142.

and moreover the incumbent bargaining agent could be displaced or revoked as a result of its failure to put an end to a conflict within a meaningful period of time.

12:3430   The Status of the Replacement Originating From Within the Bargaining Unit

Once the right to strike is acquired and the operation of s. 148(b) comes to an end, if bargaining unit employees exercise their right to go on working or to return to work during the strike, there is a *de facto* contractual relationship established between the employer and such employees. The employer is then free to modify the working conditions as they previously existed in the expired collective agreement, and the employee who decides to strikebreak is free to accept them. The Board has held in the first *Eastern Provincial Airways Ltd.*[160] decision that an employer may even, in an attempt to incite the members of the bargaining unit to strikebreak, offer terms and benefits superior to those found in the expired collective agreement.

However, upon the conclusion of the strike, should the employer refuse to make the terms and conditions of employment of these non-striking employees uniform with those agreed to in the renewed collective agreement, he would violate s. 184(1)(a) and (3)(a)(vi) of the Code. Thus the employer may not attempt to impose in the return-to-work settlement a provision to guarantee or protect the advantages granted to the employees who helped him to continue operate during the strike. This would constitute discrimination against the other bargaining unit employees who decided to exercise their right to strike, guaranteed by the Code.

12:3500   THE USE OF REPLACEMENTS DURING LOCKOUTS

The Board has not yet had occasion to address this issue in the context of a lockout.

12:3600   DISCRIMINATION AGAINST A PERSON BECAUSE OF A REFUSAL TO PERFORM A PROHIBITED ACT: SECTIONS 184(3)(f) and 185(h)

Section 184(3)(f) prohibits an employer from suspending, discharging, or imposing any financial or other penalty on a "person employed by him" for having refused to perform an act contrary to the Code. The counterpart with respect to unions is found in s. 185(h), which prohibits

---

[160]   (1983), 51 di 209, 3 CLRBR (NS) 75.

the expulsion or suspension of an "employee" from membership, as well as the imposition of disciplinary action or any form of penalty for having refused to perform an act prohibited by the Code.

The Board has not yet dealt with these sections in the context of labour disputes.[161] However, s. 184(3)(f) could include a refusal to declare, cause, or participate in an illegal lockout, whereas s. 185(h) could include a refusal to declare, cause, or participate in an illegal strike.

12:3700   PENALTIES FOR DECLARING OR CAUSING AN ILLEGAL STRIKE OR LOCKOUT

The prohibition contained in s. 180(1) against employers or unions who declare a strike or lockout before the conditions set out in subparas. (a) to (d) of that section have been met is strengthened by a liability, on summary conviction, to fines as provided in ss. 190 and 191. Every employer who declares or causes an illegal lockout is liable, under s. 190(1), to a fine of up to one thousand dollars for each day of the lockout, and every person who, on behalf of an employer, declares or causes an illegal lockout is liable, pursuant to s. 190(2), to a fine of up to ten thousand dollars.

Every trade union that declares or authorizes an illegal strike is liable, pursuant to s. 190(3), to a fine of up to one thousand dollars for each day of the strike, and every officer or representative of a trade union who declares or authorizes an illegal strike is liable personally, under s. 190(4), to a fine of up to ten thousand dollars.

Finally, every employee who participates in an illegal strike is liable, pursuant to ss. 180(2) and 191(1), to a fine of up to one thousand dollars.

Any prosecution under these sections is subject to the requirement of Board consent, as provided for in s. 194. The policy of the Board in this regard is be discussed elsewhere.[162]

12:4000   **PRACTICES RELATING TO THE STATUS AND RIGHTS OF BARGAINING AGENTS**

The practices discussed in the following paragraphs concern the status of a trade union as bargaining agent. The actions of a trade union to obtain voluntary recognition are restricted by the Code. Once the

---

[161] In *Mike Sheehan* (1975), 9 di 29, [1975] 2 Can LRBR 55, 75 CLLC #16,161, and *Arnold Bros. Transport Ltd.* (1976), 19 di 132, [1977] 2 Can LRBR 86, the Board discussed the use of the expression "person employed by him [the employer]" in s. 184(3)(f), whereas the only decision in which a breach of s. 185(h) was found involved an expulsion from membership of an employee who had contravened a rule of the union's constitution prohibiting dual membership: *Terry Matus* (1980), 37 di 73, [1980] 2 Can LRBR 21, 80 CLLC #16,077; see paragraph 13:3600.

[162] See paragraph 17:2000.

status of bargaining agent is acquired according to the proper process, the union and the employer may not impede upon bargaining rights held by other bargaining agents. If the status of bargaining agent is revoked, further restrictions are placed on the employer, as discussed below.

12:4100   EMPLOYER VIOLATIONS

12:4110   One-Year Bar on Negotiations With the Former Bargaining Agent: Section 142(b)

Section 142(b) provides that where the Board revokes the bargaining rights of a trade union or a council of trade unions pursuant to s. 138, 140, or 141, "the employer shall not bargain collectively or enter into a collective agreement with such union or council for a period of one year from the date of the order" unless the Board certifies them within the year. This section seeks to safeguard the employees' wishes by preventing an employer from voluntarily recognizing, as a bargaining agent, a union that has just been rejected by the employees it represented.

However, there is no recourse to the Board for a breach of this section. When Part V was enacted in 1972, s. 142(b) was not mentioned in s. 187(1), nor was it when the 1978 amendments were adopted. The amendments of June 1984 did not address this question.[163] Recourse for a breach of s. 142(b) would therefore be obtained by means of a prosecution under s. 191(2) with Board consent as required under s. 194.

12:4200   UNION VIOLATIONS

12:4210   Illegal Action by a Trade Union to Acquire Bargaining Agent Status: Section 185(a)

In s. 107(1) the Code recognizes two kinds of bargaining agents: a certified trade union and a voluntarily recognized trade union that has entered into a collective agreement on behalf of the employees in the bargaining unit, the term of which has not expired, or in respect of which a notice to bargain for its renewal has been served on the employer. If the union cannot gain voluntary recognition from the employer, it must seek bargaining agent status by means of certification. Prior to certification, the union may not seek to compel the employer to bargain collectively with it, as prohibited by s. 185(a), nor may it wage a recognition strike.[164]

---

[163]   Bill C-34, passed by the House of Commons on June 17, 1984 (now S.C. 1983-84, c. 39).

[164]   See, for example, *Radiodiffusion Mutuelle Ltée* (1977), 18 di 56, where illegal strikes were waged while certification demands were pending before the Board.

In the only decision in which s. 185(a) was found to have been breached,[165] the Board held that, where a union had instituted a regime of economic pressure against an employer whose employees were represented by a rival union by preventing the unloading of the employer's vehicle at construction sites, the aim was to compel the employer to bargain collectively with that union rather than with the incumbent union, in contravention of s. 185(a). The Board stated that s. 185(a) does not require that the union succeed in compelling the employer to bargain collectively with it; it only stipulates that the trade union shall not seek to compel an employer to bargain collectively with it if it is not the bargaining agent for a bargaining unit that includes employees of the employer.

In *H.M. Trimble & Sons Ltd.*[166] the Board outlined a variety of situations where economic pressure with the object of forcing the employer to recognize and bargain with a union while another union is the bargaining agent of the employees in question would contravene s. 185(a). Such examples include (i) engaging in a secondary boycott of the employer's products; (ii) picketing when employees of subcontractors or suppliers arrive at the employer's site; (iii) picketing the employer's plant and inducing and encouraging employees of other employers to refuse to perform services for their respective employers; (iv) picketing the primary employer, thereby inducing employees of secondary employers working in the primary employer's plant to engage in a work stoppage; and (v) coercing and restraining secondary employers from doing business with the primary employer.

Finally, it should be noted that a complaint under s. 185(a) is subject to the requirement of ministerial consent provided for in s. 187(5).

12:4300   EMPLOYER AND UNION VIOLATIONS

12:4310   Collective Bargaining That Infringes Upon the Rights of Other Bargaining Agents: Sections 184(3)(g), 185(b)

As noted in Chapter 6,[167] the parties are free to expand the scope of the bargaining unit through voluntary recognition of additional functions or classifications. The execution of a collective agreement will amount to the voluntary recognition of the trade union as bargaining agent for the additional group of employees. Where there are two or more bargaining agents in the enterprise, however, the ability to extend bargaining units through negotiations is circumscribed by the existence of bargaining rights held by the other trade unions. Otherwise the parties

---

165   *H.M. Trimble & Sons Ltd.* (1976), 14 di 87.
166   *Ibid.*
167   See paragraph 6:2000.

will be in contravention of ss. 184(3)(g) and 185(b), which provide that no employer or trade union shall bargain collectively or enter into a collective agreement in respect of a bargaining unit if another trade union is the bargaining agent for that unit.[168] Thus, the parties cannot negotiate collective agreements extending units that result in encroachment upon other bargaining rights. Of course, there will be no such encroachment in cases where, prior to the extension of bargaining rights by voluntary recognition, the other bargaining rights had been abandoned or relinquished by the other bargaining agent.

---

168 *Eastern Provincial Airways (1963) Ltd.* (1978), 30 di 82, [1978] 2 Can LRBR 572.

CHAPTER 13

THE PROTECTION OF INDIVIDUAL RIGHTS AGAINST THE RIGHTS OF THE COLLECTIVITY

13:0000 THE PROTECTION OF INDIVIDUAL RIGHTS AGAINST THE RIGHTS OF THE COLLECTIVITY

13:1000 THE DUTY OF FAIR REPRESENTATION

Although the provisions of the *Canada Labour Code* did not expressly recognize the existence of a duty of fair representation until June 1978, the Board had already held that such a duty could be inferred from the single fact that a bargaining agent is given exclusive authority to bargain collectively on behalf of all the employees in the bargaining unit.[1] Prior to the enactment of s. 136.1, the jurisdiction over the administration of the duty lay exclusively with the courts.[2]

13:1100 THE DUTY OF FAIR REPRESENTATION IN THE ADMINISTRATION OF THE COLLECTIVE AGREEMENT

13:1110 The Scope of the Duty

The duty of fair representation is owed to all members of the bargaining unit, whether they are members of the union or not. The duty must permeate the actions of certified bargaining agents, as well as those voluntarily recognized.[3] It is applicable, as will be seen below, to the union's administration of the collective agreement, to the negotiation of

---

[1]   *British Columbia Telephone Co.* (1977), 22 di 507, [1977] 2 Can LRBR 404, 77 CLLC #16,108; *Hasan Ergen* (1979), 34 di 776, [1979] 1 Can LRBR 571; *Vincent Maffei* (1979), 37 di 102, [1980] 1 Can LRBR 90, 79 CLLC #16,202.

[2]   It was determined in *Hasan Ergen, supra,* note 1, that the duty of fair representation enacted in 1978 was intended by Parliament to be a declaratory enactment and therefore could not apply retroactively.

[3]   In *Gerald M. Massicotte* (1980), 40 di 11, [1980] 1 Can LRBR 427, 80 CLLC #16,014, the Board ruled that notwithstanding the discrepancy that existed in the 1978 French and English versions of s. 136.1, the duty applied to both certified and voluntarily recognized bargaining agents. Section 136.1 was re-enacted by s. 28 of Bill C-34, passed by the House of Commons on June 27, 1984 (now S.C. 1983-84, c. 39). The new text makes it clear that the duty of fair representation applies to both kind of bargaining agents.

the agreement,[4] and to any other action by a bargaining agent on behalf of those it represents or with respect to their interests.[5]

It must be stressed that the duty of fair representation is not concerned with, and does not apply to, internal union affairs unless they affect the representation of employees vis-à-vis the employer as employees and not as union members. Internal union discipline and decisions on applications for union membership are not governed by s. 136.1.[6]

Similarly, when the subject-matter of the complaint is an employee's dissatisfaction with the nature of the internal union procedures concerning the processing of a grievance, rather than the union's decision not to proceed to arbitration, s. 136.1 is not to be used as an avenue for appeal of internal processes; other avenues exist under s. 185.[7] Redress for the perceived or real missapplication of a union's constitution is to be found within the internal processes of the union. If these processes are deficient, attempts should be made to democratically correct them by amendments to the union's constitution. If that still does not achieve the desired results, there are other solutions, but none of those include a recourse before the Board under s. 136.1.[8]

13:1120   Status of the Complainant

A plain reading of s. 136.1 indicates that the duty is owed to "all employees" in the bargaining unit. If an individual is dismissed and the actions of the union complained of occur subsequently to the dismissal, is the duty still applicable?

A trade union's duty of fair representation toward an individual does not cease because that individual is no longer employed in the bargaining unit either by his own choice, through the employer's actions, or for any other reason. The Board has stated that where an employee has been unjustly dismissed or his employment has been terminated in some other manner contrary to the provisions of the collective agreement, to interpret s. 136.1 as meaning that a union owes no duty of fair representation to a person in this circumstance would be to conclude that Parliament intended to impose the duty of fair representation on a union in all circumstances except the one that is the most crucial to an individual.[9]

Thus, the duty of fair representation extends to persons who are no longer "employees in the unit" if the cause of their grievance arose while

---

4   See our comments about the application of the duty described in s. 136.1 in the context of the negotiation of collective agreements, at paragraph 13:1200.

5   *Len Larmour* (1980), 41 di 110, [1980] 2 Can LRBR 407.

6   *Fred J. Solly* (1981), 43 di 29, [1981] 2 Can LRBR 245, 81 CLLC #16,089.

7   *George Lochner* (1979), 37 di 114, [1980] 1 Can LRBR 149, 79 CLLC #16,209; *Fred J. Solly, supra,* note 6; *Brenda Haley* (1981), 41 di 311, [1981] 2 Can LRBR 121, 81 CLLC #16,096.

8   *Dennis Dohm* (1983), 52 di 166.

9   *John J. Huggins* (1979), 38 di 195, [1980] 1 Can. LRBR 364.

they were employees in the bargaining unit. At this point, the duty is owed to any individual included in the unit, whether he was at the time a part-time employee,[10] a probationary employee,[11] or any other type of employee within the meaning of the Code.

13:1130   Status of the Employer

No matter how quickly the Board's processes may work, it is unlikely that its decision and remedy will be rendered within the time limits of the grievance procedure of most, if not all, collective agreements. If the remedy under s. 189(a) is to have any application and effect, the Board must and does have the authority to relieve against any privately created time limit in a collective agreement.[12]

Should an employee succeed in establishing the presence of a breach of the s. 136.1 duty where, for example, the union failed to act within the time limits set in the collective agreement, the employer's expectation that the grievance will not be taken to arbitration may be affected by the Board's remedial authority. The Board will give notice of the complaint to the employer to avoid the possibility that the employer might refuse to co-operate with the union because it was not privy to the proceedings before the Board, or to avoid the possibility that the employer might insist on the time limits in the collective agreement and argue that any action in furtherance of the Board's remedy is untimely under the collective agreement.

The employer may choose not to participate or may merely supply information to the Board. In either case, it will be afforded the rights of a party. In strictly legal terms, the employer may not be properly characterized as a "party" as defined in s. 107(1) of the Code — as one against whom a complaint is made. A more precise legal description might be an "interested person". To date the Board has not chosen to make such a distinction, but in order to ensure that employers have the full right to protect their interests, especially if there should be collusion between the union and the complainant employee in order to obtain relief against time limits via the Board, the employer is added as a full party under s. 118(o).[13] The inquiry will not enter into the merits of the employer's action unless it is so intimately intertwined with the union's action as to

10   *Gerald M. Massicotte* (1980), 40 di 11, [1980] 1 Can LRBR 427, 80 CLLC #16,014; affd. (*sub nom. Masicotte v. International Brotherhood of Teamsters, Local 938*) [1982] 1 F.C. 216, 34 N.R. 611, 81 CLLC #14,084, 119 D.L.R. (3d) 193; affd. [1982] 1 S.C.R. 710, 44 N.R. 340, 82 CLLC #14,196, 134 D.L.R. (3d) 193.

11   *Larry Elliston* (1982), 47 di 103, [1982] 2 Can LRBR 241; *Manuel Silva Filipe* (1982), 52 di 20, 2 CLRBR (NS) 84.

12   *Gerald M. Massicotte, supra,* note 10.

13   *Vincent Maffei, supra,* note 1; *Brenda Haley* (1980), 41 di 295, [1980] 3 Can LRBR 501, 81 CLLC #16,070; *Robert Hogan* (1981), 45 di 43, [1981] 3 Can LRBR 389, 81 CLLC #16,132.

make it impractical or improper to separate it.[14] For this reason, the current language of the Board's notice to the employer in cases of complainants under s. 136.1 of the Code states:

> Since the interests of the employer could be affected by the outcome of a complaint of this nature, the employer has been added as a party to this complaint.[15]

13:1140   The Standards of Fair Representation[16]

The Board has stated that the policy problem in determining the standards of fair representation is that the over-extension of the duty can distort several other policies of the Code.[17] For instance, if individual rights were to gain a disproportionate ascendancy in the existing system, the exclusivity of the bargaining agent's authority could be undermined. The ability of employers to deal with and rely upon union representatives could be eroded. Thus the duty of fair representation must be viewed in a balanced context of the entire collective bargaining setting.

Because of the difficulty of combining the provisions of the Code with the intentions of Parliament and the need to protect the individual, the Board has been very cautious in definitively stating the limits of the standards in the federal jurisdiction. It has opted for an approach that recognizes the institutional needs of both the union and the employer in the overall scheme of collective bargaining established by the Code, but that also calls for a stricter enforcement of the duty of fair representation in the area of critical job interests.

The standards adopted by the Board prior to the adoption of Bill C-34 provide that a union must not act in bad faith, nor in an unfair, arbitrary, discriminatory, or seriously or grossly negligent manner in its handling of grievances or, more generally, in the administration of the collective agreement.

---

14   *Vincent Maffei, supra,* note 1.

15   *Robert Hogan, supra,* note 13, at p. 52 (di).

16   In most provincial jurisdictions the duty of fair representation is negatively phrased and provides an injunction to the effect that the union must not act "arbitrarily", "discriminatorily", or in "bad faith". In Quebec, s. 47.2 of the *Quebec Labour Code* also refers to "gross negligence". By contrast, in the federal jurisdiction, prior to the amendments of Bill C-34, the duty was affirmatively and widely phrased. This particular wording led the Board to hold that the standards by which the duty of fair representation was to be assessed might not necessarily be identical to those of any province where the duty also existed. In practice, however, the Board developed standards that closely resemble those developed by provincial boards such as the Ontario Labour Relations Board and the Quebec Labour Court. See *Kenneth Cameron* (1980), 42 di 193, [1981] 1 Can LRBR 273.

In view of that fact, it is doubtful whether the new text of s. 136.1, which is negatively phrased, will have a significant impact on the standards evolved by the Board prior to the adoption of Bill C-34. Since the Board has not yet had the occasion to address the issue, its interpretation of the old s. 136.1 is canvassed in this paragraph.

17   *Tom Forestall and Randall Hall* (1980), 41 di 177, [1980] 3 Can LRBR 491.

13:1141   "Fairly and Without Discrimination"

Disjunctive Construction

The Board has declined to read the words "fairly and without discrimination" of the old s. 136.1 conjunctively. This approach would have reduced the standard in the federal jurisdiction to one that could produce absurd results. For example, a union could act unfairly by being totally arbitrary, but without discrimination, and still not breach its duty.[18] As a result of reading the terms disjunctively, a union will breach its duty if it fails to act either fairly or without discrimination.

Fairness and Arbitrariness

It has been determined that the notion of "fairness" in the law of judicial review does not apply to determinations of whether the union has acted appropriately and met its duty under s. 136.1.[19] Such an approach would treat the union officials as if they were exercising a quasi-judicial administrative function.

In the context of the duty imposed by s. 136.1, the Board's concern is not with the rules of natural justice and the procedure to be followed, but rather with whether, prior to its decision not to process a grievance to arbitration, the bargaining agent gave the matter the attention it deserved and properly turned its mind to the question. Some conduct is so arbitrary or seriously (or grossly) negligent that it cannot be viewed as fair.[20] Union decision-makers must not act arbitrarily by making no inquiry or only a perfunctory or cursory inquiry into an employee's grievance.

Discrimination

The union decision-makers must not act fraudulently or for improper motives, such as those prohibited by human rights legislation or out of personal hostility, revenge, or dishonesty toward an employee.[21]

13:1142   Bad Faith

The Board has also declined to read the words "fairly and without discrimination" of the old s. 136.1 as requiring evidence of bad faith for a complaint to succeed. The Board rejected this approach as putting too much emphasis on the institutional needs of the union alone and as

---

18   *Ibid.*
19   *Robert Hogan, supra,* note 13.
20   *Brenda Haley, supra,* note 7.
21   *Ibid.*

overriding, to an unwarranted extent, the protection of the individual. If, as a rule, the Board were to require proof of action in bad faith for a complaint under s. 136.1 to succeed, this would mean that any union actions, as long as they were in good faith, would be valid. However, the law does not condone all actions merely because they are done in good faith. Some action or inaction, while in good faith, amounts to such a total abdication of responsibility that it is more than mere incompetence; it is a total failure to represent the members. For this reason, the Board considers that the union's duty is not discharged solely by proof of good-faith action. Conversely, bad faith is not a necessary element to establish a breach of s. 136.1.[22]

13:1143   Negligence

The propriety of this standard arose when the Board dealt, for the first time, with a complaint under s. 136.1, which alleged a union's failure to process a discharge grievance within the time limits set in the collective agreement after it had taken the decision to proceed to arbitration. In *Brenda Haley*,[23] a majority held that the standard of the duty imposed by s. 136.1 is not that of strict liability on the union when it unintentionally, but in good faith, makes a mistake such as not filing the grievance within the time limits provided in the collective agreement. The minority held that to ask a union to guarantee that it will act within the specified time limits when processing discharge grievances is not such a broad interpretation of the Code as would upset the balance of its competing policies.

The dissenting Board member reasoned that, once a decision is taken to proceed to arbitration, it can be assumed that the trade union is fully aware of the gravity of the situation. Thus it must be expected to act accordingly and be accountable in its duty to represent fairly. The dissenting member also held that it was a gross understatement to characterize a missed time limit at this crucial state as an "innocent mistake".

The decision was then referred to a plenary session of the Board, where a majority held that simple negligence is not a breach of the duty of fair representation, although seriously negligent conduct would be such a breach. The Board, however, made no rule to the effect that missed time limits or other procedural errors constitute serious or gross negligence. Missing a time limit in the grievance procedure is not automatically serious negligence even in a grievance over a discharge or any other critical job interest.[24]

---

22   *Tom Forestall and Randall Hall, supra,* note 17; *Brenda Haley, supra,* note 13; *Brenda Haley, supra,* note 7.

23   *Supra,* note 13.

24   *Brenda Haley, supra,* note 7. See paragraph 13:1170 for a more comprehensive outline of the Board's policy on this subject.

It was with reluctance, however, that the Board adopted the standard of negligence. Above all it wants to avoid inheriting the precedents created by the National Labor Relations Board in the United States concerning that standard. For example, the American jurisprudence has reached a state where even the use and/or selection of a lawyer by a union to assess a grievance and/or pilot it through arbitration can be the subject of a duty of fair representation complaint. The Board has made it clear that it wants to avoid such a stringent standard.[25]

13:1150   The Four-Fold Analysis

The above standards are not applied in a vacuum. The union's actions in discharging its duty must be assessed in the particular context within which it operates. The Board has established that any complaint filed as a result of a violation of s. 136.1 by a union must be of a very serious, obvious, and apparent nature.[26] For this reason, the Board has fashioned a four-fold test against which allegations of unfairness, arbitrariness, discrimination, bad faith, and negligence on the part of the union are to be assessed.[27] In every case, before a violation can be found, the Board analyses the facts in the light of (i) the nature of the grievance filed, (ii) the characteristics of the bargaining agent, (iii) the steps taken by the bargaining agent in fulfilling its duty toward the complainant, and (iv) the actions of the complainant in fulfilling his duty towards his union.

13:1151   The Nature of the Grievance

The Board has stated that it will always take into account the nature (the seriousness) of the grievance that eventually led to the complaint under s. 136.1.[28] As seen above, the Board has endorsed the concept of a stricter enforcement of the duty in the grievance arbitration process when the critical job interest of an individual is at stake.

The Board has not, however, exhaustively listed critical job interests. The examples of discharge, discipline, and seniority have been cited.[29] A grievance arising out of a situation where an employee's career is on the line demands the bargaining agent's full attention and energy, more so than in any other type of grievance. For example, the termina-

---

25   *Jean Laplante* (1981), 40 di 235, [1981] 3 Can LRBR 52.
26   *Andre Cloutier* (1981), 40 di 222, [1981] 2 Can LRBR 335, 81 CLLC #16,108.
27   *Ibid.; Jean Laplante, supra*, note 25; *Serge Gervais* (1983), 53 di 104; *Jacques Lecavalier* (1983), 54 di 100.
28   *Brenda Haley* (1980), 41 di 295, [1980] 3 Can. LRBR 501, 81 CLLC #16,070; *Brenda Haley* (1981), 41 di 311, 81 CLLC #16,096, [1981] 2 Can LRBR 121; *Andre Cloutier, supra*, note 26; *Yves Beaudoin* (1981), 45 di 283, [1982] 1 Can LRBR 197.
29   *Brenda Haley* (1981), 41 di 311, [1981] 2 Can LRBR 121, 81 CLLC #16,096.

tion of employment or denial of the right to promotion drastically affects an individual's career.[30]

On the other hand, a grievance resulting from a possible denial of overtime pay for working one weekend, isolated pay disputes arising out of one or only a few incidents, the loss of a union right that could be restored within a short period of time, the occasional use of supervisors to do bargaining unit work, and even a minor disciplinary action such as a verbal warning were cited by the Board as examples of minor job interests that cannot reasonably demand the same degree of attention on the part of the bargaining agent.[31]

It follows that allegations of a violation of s. 136.1 resulting from grievances where a bargaining unit member's career is at stake are more rigorously scrutinized by the Board, just as they must be by the bargaining agent. In its appreciation of the importance of the nature or seriousness of the complaint, which may vary from industry to industry or employer to employer,[32] the Board investigates whether the bargaining agent understood and respected the distinction between grievances that raise critical job interests and those that do not. This does not mean, however, that all complaints before the Board that involve the failure of a union to process a dismissal grievance to arbitration will be upheld.[33]

It is the Board's policy, then, that a decision taken by a bargaining agent not to defend a dismissal grievance, or one in which the grievor's career is at stake, if taken conscientiously after due process of thought or after the union has properly turned its mind to the subject-matter, will be upheld by the Board even if it were to conclude that, had it been in the bargaining agent's shoes, it might have come to a different decision.

13:1152   The Characteristics of the Bargaining Agent

Under the freedom guaranteed to every employee by s. 110(1) of the Code, all sorts of unions may be chosen as bargaining agents. Some unions are better equipped than others, financially and administratively. The degree of sophistication between one bargaining agent and another can vary *ad infinitum.* Accordingly, the services they are in a position to provide to their members and to the members of the bargaining unit will also vary.

The Board keeps this in mind when investigating complaints involving the duty of fair representation. It has stated that employees who,

---

30   *Brenda Haley, supra,* note 29; *Andre Cloutier, supra,* note 26.
31   *Brenda Haley* (1980), 41 di 295, [1980] 3 Can LRBR 501, 81 CLLC #16,070; *Brenda Haley, supra,* note 29; *Andre Cloutier, supra,* note 26.
32   *Brenda Haley, supra,* note 29.
33   The policy of the Board on this subject is in marked contrast to that advocated by Professor Paul Weiler to the effect that dismissal grievances should always be taken to arbitration: see Paul Weiler, *Reconcilable Differences: New Directions in Canadian Labour Law* (Toronto: Carswell, 1980), 137-39.

because of their wishes to keep union dues to a minimum, have opted for a bargaining agent who is not in a financial position to hire well-paid, permanent, full-time union officers to negotiate and administer collective agreements and the grievances that result therefrom certainly cannot demand the standards and degree of excellence as can employees who have opted for a bargaining agent having at its disposal not only well-paid, permanent, full-time union officers to fulfil the duties mentioned above, but also specialists in fields such as economics, pension plans, group insurance, labour relations, and law.[34]

The importance of this step in the Board's analysis of the facts of a complaint under s. 136.1 is that, although the same standards are applied to all unions, their stringency will depend on the bargaining agent's level of sophistication. In the Board's own words:

> We apply the same standards, but we will vary the power of our microscope, increasing it according to the degree of sophistication of the bargaining agent.[35]

Thus, a more sophisticated bargaining agent will be more closely scrutinized in the discharge of its duties that one that is smaller and less well-equipped both financially and administratively. However, the Board did not go so far as to say that it would condone any negligence or inaction for the sole reason that a certain bargaining agent has fewer resources.[36]

Where a union has taken a grievance to arbitration, however, the Board will not increase the strength of its lens to such an extent as to microscopically review the union's conduct in the preparation and presentation of an employee's grievance at arbitration.[37] The subject-matter of the complaint in this situation is no longer the union's duty as it relates to its decision to process a grievance to arbitration or its compliance with the various pre-arbitration steps provided in the collective agreement. Rather, it raises the quality of presentation of the grievance at the arbitration hearing itself. This subject will be discussed below.[38]

13:1153   Steps Taken by the Bargaining Agent

In each case, the Board will investigate in detail the steps taken by the bargaining agent in processing a grievance filed by a member of its bargaining unit. Based on the evidence before it, the Board will inquire into the practices, policies, and criteria normally followed by the union in similar cases. At the same time, the Board will bear in mind the union's abilities and talents as assessed at the preceding steps of the analysis, and

---

34   *Andre Cloutier, supra,* note 26.
35   *Ibid,* at p. 229 (di). See also *Yves Beaudoin, supra,* note 28.
36   *Paul Delorme* (1983), 52 di 46.
37   *John Semeniuk* (1981), 45 di 258; *Luccio Samperi* (1982), 49 di 40, [1982] 2 Can LRBR 207.
38   See paragraph 13:1180.

will consider how they have been put to use by the union in its handling of the case. In this fashion, the Board will determine whether the union has acted reasonably, without discrimination, in good faith, or in an arbitrary or negligent manner concerning this grievance as compared with similar ones that regularly come before it.[39]

The union must observe the spirit of the duty imposed by s. 136.1, rather than the letter of the law, when it acts on behalf of the grievor. The Board has cautioned that an exercise by a union of merely going through the motions or of putting on a charade by taking steps supposedly on behalf of a grievor, but which are simply designed to give the appearance of concern for him, or perhaps are motivated by a chance to build up a last-minute case against being accused of a failure to comply with s. 136.1, will not meet the standards of fair representation.[40]

In the final analysis, the Board's approach as outlined above has the effect of dispelling the temptation for an employee whose grievance has not been taken to arbitration by the union, to take "a second kick at the cat" via a s. 136.1 complaint.[41] This section does not constitute such a refuge. It is not a disguised way of obtaining the arbitration of a grievance that is without merit or has been so assessed in a reasonable fashion by a bargaining agent that has deployed all of its abilities.

13:1154   The Actions of the Complainant

In *Jean Laplante*[42] the Board introduced for the first time this additional step in its analysis of the facts to determine whether a union had breached its duty under s. 136.1. Bargaining unit members also have duties and obligations toward their bargaining agent, among which, as subsequently stated in *Jacques Lecavalier*,[43] is the duty to fully and loyally co-operate with the bargaining agent. No matter how sophisticated a bargaining agent may be, it cannot discharge its duties without the full and loyal co-operation of the complainant. Where, for example, the complainant had not informed his union of his problems with his employer, had readily admitted that union matters were of no importance to him, and had taken no interest in "all that business", it was held that the complainant had treated his union in such an indifferent manner that it could not be said that he came before the Board free from blame.[44]

In another case, where an employee who had been dismissed tried to secure the assistance of a Member of Parliament, sought independent legal assistance before turning to the union, and then filed an unfair

---

39   *Andre Cloutier, supra*, note 26; *Yves Beaudoin, supra*, note 28.
40   *David Alan Crouch* (1983), 55 di 48.
41   *Andre Cloutier, supra*, note 26, at p. 234 (di).
42   . (1981), 40 di 235, [1981] 3 Can LRBR 52.
43   *Supra*, note 27.
44   *Jean Laplante, supra*, note 42; *James N. Saad* (1981), 42 di 348.

labour practice complaint under s. 136.1 before the bargaining agent had even determined whether or not it would proceed to arbitration, the Board ruled that the complainant had not fulfilled his obligations toward the union. As the latter had nonetheless processed the grievance in conformity with its usual procedure, the complaint was dismissed.[45] This new step in the Board's analysis also requires an individual who claims that the union has breached its duty of fair representation to come before the Board with clean hands. The complainant must not have, by his own actions, so prejudiced his case that his union is put in the impossible position of defending him properly.[46]

13:1160   The Decision on Whether or Not to Take a Grievance to Arbitration

13:1161   General Principles

The Board does not impose upon a union the requirement to view arbitral authority to modify employer disciplinary decisions as a necessary gamble. Before the union decides not to proceed to arbitration, it need not get the prior approval of the Board, which will neither second-guess the wisdom of its decision nor supersede it.[47] Provided that the union turns its mind seriously to the problems of its members[48] and does not act in a perfunctory manner[49] or conduct merely a cursory[50] or superficial[51] inquiry or none at all, the union has the right to make a wrong decision[52] even if the Board disagrees with it.

13:1162   Discharge and Disciplinary Cases

13:1163   Cases Where No Breach Was Found

It has been accepted by the Board that a union may refuse to proceed to arbitration on the grievance of an individual's discharge, or with respect to any critical job interest, and still not breach its duty.[53] In its decision not to carry a grievance to arbitration, a union does not breach

---

45   *Jacques Lecavalier,* supra, note 27.
46   *Craig Harder,* decision no. 472, not yet reported, July 27, 1984 (C.L.R.B.).
47   *Robert Hogan* (1981), 45 di 43, [1981] 3 Can LRBR 389, 81 CLLC #16,132.
48   *Nordair Ltd.* (1982), 49 di 35; *Serge Gervais* (1983), 53 di 104.
49   *Carlton C. Caesar* (1980), 41 di 102, [1980] 3 Can LRBR 322; *Paul Godin and Robert Letang* (1984), 55 di 81.
50   *Brenda Haley,* supra, note 31.
51   *Jean-Paul Roy* (1981), 46 di 25; *Paul Godin and Robert Letang,* supra, note 49.
52   *R.V. Passero and W.G. Storry* (1982), 48 di 57.
53   *Brenda Haley* (1980), 41 di 295, [1980] 3 Can LRBR 501, 81 CLLC #16,070; *Brenda Haley* (1981), 41 di 311, [1981] 2 Can LRBR 121, 81 CLLC #16,096; *Andre Cloutier* (1981), 40 di 212, [1981] 2 Can LRBR 335, 81 CLLC #16,108; *Robert Hogan,* supra, note 47.

its duty if it takes into account its general policy not to allot funds to arbitrate grievances concerning minor disciplinary penalties such as written reprimands,[54] or the fact that to arbitrate a grievance would require it to take a stance inconsistent with its policy on health and safety matters, for example.[55] In such cases, the Board has held that it was not its role to evaluate the decisions a union, in co-operation with its members, makes in administering its funds; nor is it the Board's task to reshape union priorities for the allocation of its resources.[56]

Where the collective agreement provided that an employee could himself file a grievance, and the union gave the complainant notice that it would not take his grievance to arbitration only a few days before the deadline provided in the agreement, the Board held that such short notice was *prima facie* unreasonable and cautioned the union to act more speedily in the future. However, it found that the union had not breached its duty in view of the complainant's own actions in failing to take the proper steps to take his case to arbitration according to the procedures set out in the collective agreement, of which he was well aware.[57] In a similar case, where notice by the union that it would not take the complainant's grievance to arbitration was not given until after the time limits provided in the collective agreement had expired, the Board held that the union had not breached its duty, as the complainant was well aware of the time limits, knew that he could file the grievance himself, and the union had duly investigated the grievance.[58]

In one case, the Board held that s. 136.1 does not impose upon a bargaining agent the obligation to use the grievance procedure for a purpose other than that for which it was intended. In this case the complainant filed a grievance not so much to regain the job from which he had been dismissed as to obtain from the employer a written statement attesting to his alleged disability for purposes of workers' compensation. The Board stated that it would not tolerate such an abuse of s. 136.1.[59]

In another case, the decision not to go to arbitration on a grievance concerning several issues relating to the manner in which the grievor perceived he was treated was taken by the union's national executive after several grievance meetings at the local and national level and on the advice of legal counsel. The complaint was dismissed, as the Board found that there was no motive for the executive's decision other than to do what it thought was right.[60] The Board came to the same conclusion

---

54   *Jean-Guy Bellegarde* (1981), 45 di 292, [1982] 3 Can LRBR 378.
55   *Serge Gervais, supra,* note 48.
56   *Brenda Haley* (1980), 41 di 295, [1980] 3 Can. LRBR 501, 81 CLLC #16,070; *Brenda Haley* (1981), 41 di 311, [1981] 2 Can LRBR 121, 81 CLLC #16,096; *Jean-Guy Bellegarde* (1981), 45 di 292, [1982] 3 Can LRBR 378.
57   *Lawrence Schumph* (1980), 40 di 123.
58   *Thomas David McGrath* (1980), 42 di 120; see also *James N. Saad, supra,* note 44.
59   *Jean Laplante, supra,* note 42.
60   *Frederick B. Billington* (1981), 45 di 247.

where a grievor's claim had gone through an extensive internal union process before a decision had been made not to go to arbitration.[61]

No breach was found, either, where the evidence revealed a misunderstanding between the union and the employee that arose out of a communication failure. As the union's decision had not been improperly motivated, the complaint was dismissed.[62]

In another case a complaint was filed by a local union chairman against the union's National Appeals Committee. The latter had allegedly misinterpreted the collective agreement and, in doing so, had acted unfairly in its decision not to proceed with a grievance initiated by the complainant on behalf of an employee of the unit. Moreover, the decision of the committee, which was adverse to the interest of the employee and beneficial to the employer, was characterized by the local chairman as discriminatory. The Board held that an honest difference of opinion on the interpretation of the grievance procedure and its time limits did not constitute a violation of the standard of fair representation.[63]

However, when the interpretation of the collective agreement is at the heart of the union's decision not to proceed to arbitration, as in the above decision, a trend has emerged in the Board's jurisprudence to require a reasonably defensible interpretation of the relevant sections of the agreement that was applicable to a particular grievance. If the Board finds that the union's interpretation meets such a standard, it will not go so far as to intervene in the process of thought that eventually favours one interpretation over another.[64]

13:1164   Cases Where Breaches Were Found

The Board has stated[65] that its concern is with the process undergone by a grievance and with whether the union acts in an arbitrary, discriminatory, bad-faith, or grossly negligent manner in that process. Absent any improper motive, the union is justified in not going to arbitration if it has reasonably considered the grievance and, having reasonably turned its mind to the matter, has concluded that it has no merit. The Board will not interfere with a decision properly arrived at, even though it may hold the view that the union made a wrong decision.

Perhaps the key element in this policy is the words "properly arrived at" and "having reasonably turned its mind to the matter". It is incumbent upon the union to verify the validity of management's position in deciding the fate of the complainant's grievance. In such an endeavour

---

61   *Robert Hogan, supra,* note 47.
62   *Manuel Silva Filipe* (1982), 52 di 20, 2 CLRBR (NS) 84.
63   *John J. Huggins* (1979), 38 di 195, [1980] 1 Can LRBR 364.
64   *Frank Melia* (1983), 53 di 140.
65   *Paul Delorme* (1983), 52 di 46.

only the facts can constitute the basis of any sound decision. Before making any enlightened decision the union must satisfy itself of the validity (or lack thereof) of management's claim by examining the facts of the complainant's grievance. If those facts are not readily available, then it falls to the bargaining agent to obtain them. It must seek corroborative evidence of the complainant's alleged misdemeanour.[66]

A good example of a situation where a union did truly turn its mind to the complainant's grievance in a case of dismissal for absenteeism is found in *Frank Melia*.[67] Among the facts considered by the union there were, as a minimum, the disciplinary record of the employee, the employee's own recorded explanation of his numerous absences, which the union had sought, and the union's own counselling of the grievor to change his behaviour on the occasion of a previous discharge. The Board concluded that this was a far cry from a decision taken arbitrarily or without any factual basis whatsoever.

By contrast, in a case where a steward of a railway company had been dismissed for gross dereliction of duty, the union had decided not to process his grievance to arbitration, basing its decision only on the employer's documentation and opinion.[68] The union had not verified the statements of witnesses against the complainant, even though collusion was suspected, and had not investigated the charges of misappropriation of funds, although serious doubts were raised about the charge at the hearing. In these circumstances the Board found that the union had not represented the complainant fairly.[69]

In the same vein, the Board found that the union had breached its duty where it had either perfunctorily refused to process a grievance,[70] treated it in a superficial manner in view of the disproportion between the infraction and the penalty,[71] or had not conscientiously turned its mind to the question before it.[72]

In other cases, the Board found that the union had totally abdicated its responsibility, and held that a total lack of representation by a union, whatever its cause, was in violation of the duty of fair representation.[73] In one of these cases the union contended that it did not owe the complainant the s. 136.1 duty as he was only a probationary employee and the collective agreement barred access to the grievance procedure in the case

---

66   *Ibid.; Frank Melia, supra*, note 64.
67   *Supra*, note 64.
68   *Kenneth Cameron* (1980), 42 di 193, [1981] 1 Can LRBR 273.
69   Compare this case with the facts in *Paul Delorme, supra*, note 65, and the dissenting opinion of Board member M.M. Galipeau.
70   *Carlton C. Caesar* (1980), 41 di 102, [1980] 3 Can LRBR 322.
71   *Jean-Paul Roy* (1981), 46 di 25.
72   *David Alan Crouch* (1983), 55 di 48.
73   *Gerald M. Massicotte* (1980), 40 di 11, [1980] 1 Can LRBR 427, 80 CLLC #16,014; *Tom Forestall and Randall Hall* (1980), 41 di 177, [1980] 3 Can LRBR 491; *Brenda Haley* (1980), 41 di 295, [1980] 3 Can LRBR 501, 81 CLLC #16,070; *Larry Elliston* (1982), 47 di 103, [1982] 2 Can LRBR 241.

of dismissal of such employees.[74] The Board held this clause of the collective agreement to be invalid and found that the union's lack of representation based on such a clause constituted a breach of s. 136.1. No representation at all cannot be fair and non-discriminatory representation.

13:1165   Cases Involving Seniority

13:1166   Cases Where No Breach Was found

In one case a complainant who was the most senior employee had been denied promotion by the employer.[75] The collective agreement contained a "sufficient ability clause" and the employer contended that the complainant lacked leadership qualifications. The complainant grieved the company decision and a grievance was taken, with the assistance of union representatives, through the various steps to the final pre-arbitration level, where it was dealt with by the national chairman of the union. The latter eventually decided to drop the case. On a complaint filed under s. 136.1, a majority of the Board found that the union had not breached its duty. It determined that there was no evidence to suggest that the efforts of the union representatives who had handled the grievance before it was remitted to the national chairman were less than adequate in the initial stage of investigation. As for the national chairman's decision to drop the grievance, it was held that the union had concluded the grievance to have no merit. As there was no evidence of improper motive, the majority held that the union had taken its decision on the basis of a reasonable consideration of the matter.

This case illustrates the difficulty in assessing the union's action when the grievance has been taken through various stages of the grievance procedure short of arbitration and debated at various levels of the union's internal processes. This may create the illusion that the union has truly turned its mind to the matter, whereas it may simply have put on a charade to avoid an unfair practice charge. Conversely, it may be symptomatic of the union's genuine concern for the employee's claim. The majority in *Paul Delorme*[76] felt that the union had taken its decision on the basis of a reasonable consideration of the matter, whereas the dissenting member was prepared to go beyond the steps taken by the bargaining agent and scrutinize more closely the tangible evidence and facts on the basis of which the decision to drop the grievance was made.

In another case the complainants, who formed a minority in the bargaining unit, had grieved the employer's implementation of a demand

---

74   *Larry Elliston, supra,* note 73. For a discussion on the right of a probationary employee to grieve his dismissal, see also *Transair Ltd.* (1978), 27 di 739, [1978] 2 Can LRBR 354.
75   *Paul Delorme, supra,* note 65.
76   *Ibid.*

made by the majority of the members with respect to the interpretation of a clause of the collective agreement that adversely affected their seniority status.[77] As the union had acted upon the wish expressed by the majority of its members in a democratic fashion, the Board determined that the union had not breached its duty under s. 136.1 by refusing to forward the complainants' grievances through to arbitration. The Board came to the same conclusion where an employee's position on the seniority list had been affected by the transfer of employees from other divisions of the company and the local membership had voted that the transferred employees should retain their seniority.[78]

In a case involving a classification grievance, the employer had not adhered to a bargaining concession made with the local union to create a lower-rated position classification that would have increased the mobility of employees.[79] This prompted a difference between the officers of the local union and the regional officer of the national union over the merits of proceeding to arbitration. The Board held the regional officer's decision not to arbitrate to be in compliance with s. 136.1.

The Board also dismissed two other complaints involving call-back rights of employees on layoff.[80] The latter contended that they were not being called back to work according to their seniority, as more junior employees were allegedly put back on active payroll before them.

13:1167   Cases Where Breaches Were Found

Thus far, the board has found a breach of s. 136.1 in a case involving a seniority issue on only one occasion. In that case the complainant grieved the placement of another employee ahead of her on the seniority list.[81] The Board found that the union had breached its duty, as no one had taken any steps to assess or advance the grievance of the complainant, and no one had explained to her why there had been no local response to the grievance.

13:1170   When the Decision Is Made to Take the Grievance to Arbitration

Once the union decides to proceed to arbitration, the issue arises of missed time limits for filing a grievance, or of procedural errors preventing adjudication on the merits.

---

77   *Yves Beaudoin* (1981), 45 di 283, [1982] 1 Can. LRBR 197; see also *Wayne McLeish* (1982), 48 di 69.
78   *Wayne McLeish, supra,* note 77.
79   *R.V. Passero and W.G. Storry* (1982), 48 di 57.
80   *Wayne McLeish, supra,* note 77; *Pierre Marcotte* (1983), 53 di 150.
81   *Nordair Ltd.* (1982), 49 di 35.

The Board has made no firm rule about such mistakes constituting gross or serious negligence. Such a determination is done on the basis of the facts of each case, assessed in the light of the four-fold analysis outlined earlier.[82] However, the union is required to justify its failure to meet the deadline. In *Denis Pion*[83] the union's local president had failed to refer grievances to arbitration within the mandatory time limits provided in the collective agreement, although a firm decision had been made to forward the grievances to arbitration. The Board held that the union had the burden of proof to provide reasons why the deadline had been missed. As the union had failed to do so, the Board found that it had breached its duty.[84]

13:1180　When the Grievance Has Been Arbitrated

Where grievances had been arbitrated, subsequent complaints under s. 136.1 raised the question of the Board's role in administering the duty of fair representation in the context of assessing the quality of union representation in the preparation and presentation of an employee's grievance at arbitration. In the cases where this question arose,[85] the complainants alleged that the union had either breached its duty by not forcing the employer to adhere to time limits set in the collective agreement, or had improperly conducted the hearing by not adducing complete evidence or by not adequately cross-examining employer witnesses.

Although the duty of fair representation is applicable to any action by a bargaining agent on behalf of those it represents, the Board held that it would be a clear case of "the tail wagging the dog" if it were to quash arbitration awards because it disapproved of the manner in which a union presented a grievance at arbitration. The duty of fair representation has a role under the Code, but it must have its limits. As was stated,[86] that limit falls short of an avenue of appeal from arbitral decisions based upon a judgment by the Board's legally and non-legally trained members about the competence and performance of union representatives and their counsel. This reasoning by the Board is in accordance with its wish to avoid the type of precedents set by the National Labor Relations Board in its application of the negligence standard.

The Board has not said, however, that the duty of fair representation has absolutely no role to play in the arbitration process. It has cited the examples of extreme cases where the union merely puts on a charade with employer collusion, or where the union representative or counsel appear

---

82　*Brenda Haley, supra,* note 73. See paragraph 13:1150.
83　(1981), 43 di 254.
84　See also *Nordair Ltd., supra,* note 81.
85　*John Semeniuk* (1981), 45 di 258; *Luccio Samperi* (1982), 49 di 40, [1982] 2 Can LRBR 207; *Gary W. Craib,* decision no. 489, not yet reported, December 6, 1984 (C.L.R.B.).
86　*Luccio Samperi, supra,* note 85.

inebriated.[87] These, like all cases in this area, will turn on their facts, but the Board will not, by means of the duty imposed by s. 136.1, microscopically review union conduct during arbitration proceedings.

13:1190   Timeliness of the Complaint

A complaint alleging a violation of s. 136.1 is made pursuant to s. 187(1), and unlike complaints under s. 185(f) or (g), there is no requirement to exhaust internal union processes before complaining of a violation of s. 136.1. The Board has stated that Parliament did not intend to establish two procedural standards for employees — one that says employees who are not members of unions may complain directly to the Board and another that says employees who are union members must exhaust internal union procedures before complaining to the Board.[88]

The complaint must therefore be made not later than ninety days from the date on which the complainant knew of, or in the opinion of the Board ought to have known of, the action or circumstances giving rise to the complaint. The limitation period starts from the employee's knowledge of the union's decision not to proceed further with the grievance on his behalf, or from his knowledge of some other decision or action related to representation that he thinks violates s. 136.1.

If the complaint is not filed within ninety days of this date, further actions taking place after the date of the union's initial decision that merely serve to clarify, elaborate upon, or make more certain the union's initial decision will not be viewed as creating a later starting point for the commencement of the limitation period provided by s. 187(2).[89]

If the complaint is filed in a timely fashion, and the employee member of the union, in addition, follows the internal appeal procedure under the union's constitution, events subsequent to the union's decision to abandon the grievance with which the complainant is dissatisfied may be recounted in the presentation of his case to the Board to support or corroborate his allegations of a breach of s. 136.1. As stated above, however, there is no obligation for a complainant who is also a member of the union to follow the internal appeal procedures before resorting to the Board.

Thus far, the Board has found complaints filed under s. 136.1 to be untimely on at least three occasions.[90] By contrast, in an unusual case, although complaints under s. 136.1 had been filed six months after the complainants were forced to resign, the complaints were held to be

---

87 *Ibid.*
88 *Vincent Maffei* (1979), 37 di 102, [1980] 1 Can LRBR 90, 79 CLLC #16,202; *George Lochner* (1979), 37 di 114, [1980] 1 Can LRBR 149, 79 CLLC #16,209; *Andrew J. Startek* (1979), 38 di 228, [1980] 1 Can LRBR 577.
89 *Andrew J. Startek, supra*, note 88.
90 *Vincent Maffei, supra*, note 88; *Andrew J. Startek, supra*, note 88; *Frederick B. Billington* (1981), 45 di 247.

timely, as the complainants had not been informed of their right to file grievances and had spent much time seeking redress in other areas before being referred to the Board.[91]

13:1200   THE DUTY OF FAIR REPRESENTATION IN THE NEGOTIATION OF COLLECTIVE AGREEMENTS

Section 136.1 was introduced into the *Canada Labour Code* in 1978,[92] but it was replaced in 1984 by a new text.[93] The old and present versions of this provision respectively read:

136.1 Where a trade union is the bargaining agent for a bargaining unit, the trade union and every representative of the trade union shall represent, fairly and without discrimination, all employees in the bargaining unit.

[old text]

136.1 A trade union or representative of a trade union that is the bargaining agent for a bargaining unit shall not act in a manner that is arbitrary, discriminatory or in bad faith in the representation of any of the employees in the unit with respect to their rights under the collective agreement that is applicable to them.

[new text]

The Board has determined that the old version of s. 136.1 imposed on the bargaining agent the duty to fairly represent the employees not only in the context of the administration of the collective agreement, but also in the negotiation of a collective agreement.[94] However, since the

---

91   *Tom Forestall and Randall Hall, supra,* note 73.
92   See S.C. 1977-78, c. 27, s. 49.
93   See S.C. 1984, c. 39, s. 28.
94   See *British Columbia Telephone Co.* (1977), 22 di 507, [1977] 2 Can LRBR 404, 77 CLLC #16,108; *Len Larmour* (1980), 41 di 110, [1980] 3 Can LRBR 407; *Wayne McLeish* (1982), 48 di 69; *Luis Rivera* (1982), 49 di 86; *Captain William J. Lamore* (1982), 51 di 67; *John Valiante* (1982), 51 di 112; *Stanley Warner* (1982), 51 di 146; *Claude Latrémouille* (1983), 53 di 178; *Dennis Dohm* (1983), 52 di 160; *Buddy Lee* (1984), 7 CLRBR (NS) 56; *Nelson G. Burrows,* decision no. 488, not yet reported, December 3, 1984 (C.L.R.B.); *Claude Paquet,* decision no. 496, not yet reported, January 10, 1985 (C.L.R.B.).
      The Board did not find any violation of s. 136.1 in these cases. For instance, the Board has held that the union had not breached its duty by refusing to conduct separate negotiations for a given region of the company, by failing to present at the bargaining table proposals raised by employees of this region (*Stanley Warner*), and by refusing to hold separate ratification votes for the collective agreement ultimately concluded (*Dennis Dohm*). In *Len Larmour,* the Board dismissed a complaint where it was alleged that the complainants had been treated discriminatorily by the union because it had not negotiated for them the same privileges it had negotiated for 21 of the 32 engineers working at a railway station subsequently closed by the employer. The Board found that the union, faced with a very difficult situation, had done its utmost to minimize the adverse consequences of changes in the employer's railway operations, which involved the closure of "run-through" stations. Other cases where the complaints were dismissed involved decisions or agreements between the union and the employer adversely affecting the seniority rights of a minority of members of the

enactment of s. 136.1, one panel of the Board in a case[95] mentioned, without having to decide the question, that "whether Parliament really intended the section to have the latter effect is largely academic now; in any case, on July 18, 1984, an amendment to the Code went into force which greatly narrows the sway of section 136.1".[96] Another panel in a subsequent case[97] made the following statement:

> Similarly, given our conclusion as regards the provisions that apply in the instant case, there is no need to decide here on the actual scope, and not what some hope or anticipate is the scope, of the amendment to section 136.1. While there is no need to make this determination, we do not believe that the new text of section 136.1 supports an interpretation as narrow as that proposed by the respondent union. We would simply say that, on the strength of the new text of section 136.1, it might prove foolhardy for the union that has yet to enter into a collective agreement or whose agreement has expired to act without regard to any duty to represent its members.
>
> The duty of representation derives, not from the conclusion of a collective agreement, but from the right to bargain. Whatever interpretation is to be given to the new text of section 136.1, it may be appropriate to recall the view taken by the Supreme Court in *Canadian Merchant Service Guild and Guy Gagnon et al.* (unreported judgment no. 16891, June 7, 1984):
>
>> "The duty of representation arises out of the *exclusive power given to a union to act as spokesman for the employees in a bargaining unit.*"[98]

The latter remarks suggest that under the new text the bargaining agent still owes the duty to represent the employees fairly at the bargaining table while it negotiates a collective agreement. Yet another panel of the Board stated, in a recent decision that squarely raised the issue,[99] that s. 136.1, as currently drafted, did not permit it to deal with a complaint

---

bargaining unit. In *Luis Rivera*, the agreement complained of concerned the integration of newly certified employees into the seniority list. Another concerned the negotiation of rotating shifts, causing senior employees to lose the benefit of shift selection to which the exercise of their seniority had previously entitled them (*Captain William J. Lamore*). A more recent case concerned an agreement reached by the parties following the closure of one location of the employer whereby junior employees at relocation bases were "bumped" by senior employees and put on layoff (*John Valiante*). See *infra*, notes 95 and 97.

[95] See *Nelson G. Burrows, supra*, note 94. The Board emphasized in this case that, while the wording of s. 136.1 (as it was before the amendment went into effect on July 18, 1984) permits its application to the provisions of collective agreements, the realities of collective bargaining indicate that only in "extraordinary circumstances" where there is clear evidence of unfairness in the treatment of one member or class of members of a bargaining unit versus others should the Board intervene.

[96] *Nelson G. Burrows, supra*, note 94, at p. 13 of the unreported decision.

[97] See *Claude Paquet, supra*, note 94. In this case, the trade union negotiated a clause whereby the complainant's seniority was reduced for purposes of job security and mobility. However, the union sought and obtained for the complainant twenty years of seniority for purposes of vacation and retirement. "There was give and take in the process, and that is the essence of compromise", the Board mentioned at p. 20 of the unreported decision, and accordingly, in the light of its general policy not to intervene except in exceptional cases, the Board dismissed the complaint.

[98] *Claude Paquet, supra*, note 94, at pp. 14-15 of the unreported decision.

[99] *Gordon Parsley et al.*, decision no. 555, not yet reported, February 7, 1986 (C.L.R.B.).

arising directly from the negotiation of a collective agreement and that the duty is restricted to matters that arise from the administration of the collective agreement.

13:2000   **THE DUTY OF FAIR REFERRAL**

Extensive amendments were made to the Code in 1973, but there was no reference to the question of hiring halls. Section 185(3), (f), (g), (h), and (i) remained an incomplete legal regulation of the scheme of union security permitted by the Code in failing to address circumstances where employees had no longstanding relationship with a single employer and where, in addition, unions controlled access to employment through hiring halls. In 1978 the Code was amended to include the duty of fair representation in s. 136.1 and the duty of fair referral in s. 161.1, thereby adding new dimensions to the importance and meaning of the above subsections of s. 185.

Like any source of employment or employment agency, the union hiring hall can become an instrument of discrimination.[100] It can be operated in a manner such that it discriminates for reasons prohibited by human rights legislation. It can also be used by those controlling it as an instrument to discriminate against personal enemies, or as an instrument of favouritism and punishment to maintain control over union members or other persons seeking employment. Section 161.1 addresses such situations. As access to a union-operated referral system and, hence, to employment is often dependent on union membership status, the link between s. 161.1 and the above subsections of s. 185 clearly emerges.

13:2100   SCOPE AND INTENT OF THE DUTY

There are two aspects to union security. The first concerns the financial contribution of members of the bargaining unit, and the second concerns membership in the bargaining agent. The former is addressed by s. 162 and the latter by s. 161.

With respect to union membership, the *Canada Labour Code*, as is the case in most provincial jurisdictions, allows unions to negotiate security clauses that may range from various forms of union shop, to preferential hiring rights, to a mixture of both. These clauses have, as their common denominator, the requirement of union membership either as a condition of employment or of preferred employment. When a union is engaged in referral to employment, it has invariably negotiated some form of union security as permitted by s. 161, but such clauses may also have been negotiated without the union's being engaged in such activities. If it refers persons to employment in any manner, however, the first condition for the application of s. 161.1 will be filled.

---

[100]   *Keith Sheedy* (1980), 39 di 36, [1980] 1 Can LRBR 391, 80 CLLC #16,029.

Parliament did not restrict the duty imposed by s. 161.1 to the hiring hall mode of referral alone. It defined "referral" to include assignment, designation, dispatching, scheduling, and selection (s. 161.1(4)). Accordingly, the duty extends to all forms of employment referral and encompasses non-hiring hall situations where the acquisition of union membership is a condition of employment.[101] An obvious example occurs where a union has negotiated a closed shop clause and acts, as it usually does in such cases, as an employment agency.[102] The intent of s. 161.1 here is to regulate the effects of union security clauses permitted by s. 161 and the actions of unions resulting therefrom, rather than their internal administration.

The second condition for the application of s. 161.1 is that the union must be engaged in the activities described in s. 161.1(4) pursuant to a collective agreement concluded with an employer under federal jurisdiction. If such is the case, it does not matter whether the referral system also serves the dual purpose of fulfilling obligations under collective agreements not covered by the Code as well as one or more covered by the Code. If it operates pursuant to a collective agreement under the Code, it must operate in the manner provided in s. 161.1, regardless of whether the same system is used to make referrals to provincial as well as to federal employers.[103] That is, when both conditions are present, the rules that must be established, posted, and applied fairly and without discrimination apply to the entire referral system and to all its aspects.[104]

13:2200   STATUS OF THE COMPLAINANT

The operation of union security clauses permitted by s. 161 affects unemployed persons and persons employed in the activities of employers not regulated by the Code, as well as those who are. Section 161.1 refers to "persons" and is legislation of public order. Accordingly, anyone affected by such union security clauses who has an interest in the manner in which the union referral system is operated or in the administration of the rules may complain, pursuant to s. 187(1), that the duty imposed by s. 161.1 has been breached. Such persons have the required status whether they are employees or not, regardless of whether they may be categorized under the union rules, such as non-members, prospective members, cardholders, members, members in arrears, or transferred members.[105]

---

101   *Fred J. Solly* (1981), 43 di 29, [1981] 2 Can LRBR 245, 81 CLLC #16,089.
102   *Ronald W. Lockhart and Charles G. Wilson* (1980), 42 di 89, [1981] 1 Can LRBR 213.
103   *Keith Sheedy, supra,* note 100.
104   *Alex J. Cayer* (1980), 39 di 108, [1980] 3 Can LRBR 225, 80 CLLC #16,052.
105   *Mike Sheehan* (1980), 40 di 103, [1980] 2 Can LRBR 278, 80 CLLC #16,030.

13:2300   STATUS OF THE EMPLOYER

The Board has acknowledged that employers have an interest in the fashioning of referral rules because they have a great stake in how the rules operate to serve their needs for sufficient and qualified labour.[106] Their interests, in this regard, are better advanced at the bargaining table. Indeed, although the union establishes the rules, the employer may want to have them included in a collective agreement or have certain fundamental principles spelled out in the agreement. Employers may also pay a referral fee, or otherwise financially support the administration of the system. These are matters for negotiation between the union and the employer.[107]

However, as a remedy to a complaint under s. 161.1 the Board may order the union to accept the complainant into membership or add his name to the list of cardmen, which may subsequently lead to his acquisition of union membership. As a result, the employer's interests will be affected where past and present negotiations were based on the assumption that the union books were closed to new membership. This kind of remedy results in an expansion of the number of employees attached to and dependent on the industry and so may upset the labour balance on the basis of which the employer has negotiated. For this reason, in keeping with its practice in cases of unfair representation, the Board may and has added the employer as a party under s. 118(o) in proceedings under s. 161.1.[108]

13:2400   THE CONTENT OF THE DUTY

13:2410   The Referral Rules

A union that meets the two conditions of application of s. 161.1 is required to formulate rules for referral, regardless of whether or not it operates out of the premises referred to in s. 161.1(2).[109] A sample of the rules established by a union pursuant to an order of the Board is reproduced in Appendix 11. The rules required by s. 161.1 need not be as extensive as these, and they do not need to anticipate every hypothetical situation that can arise. Neither must they follow the exact format adopted by the union in that case.[110]

---

[106]   *Ibid.*

[107]   *David C. Nauss and Peter H. Roberts* (1981), 43 di 263.

[108]   *David C. Nauss and Peter H. Roberts* (1980), 42 di 55, [1981] 1 Can LRBR 188; *Ronald W. Lockhart and Charles G. Wilson, supra,* note 102; see also *Terrance John Matus* (1980), 41 di 278, [1981] 1 Can LRBR 155, describing the peculiarities of a hiring hall in the longshoring industry.

[109]   *Ronald W. Lockhart and Charles G. Wilson, supra,* note 102.

[110]   *David C. Nauss and Peter H. Roberts, supra,* note 107.

The Board has held that the various policy resolutions adopted by a union for the purpose of placement of employees on work boards for referral constituted rules within the meaning of s. 161.1 regardless of the failure of the union to either formally compile or post the rules as required by s. 161.1(2).[111] By contrast, the Board held that dispatch rules jointly established by the employer and the union to regulate the dispatching of employees, once they have been placed by the union on the appropriate work boards, did not constitute referral rules within the meaning of s. 161.1, since they did not regulate that portion of the union's responsibility to place employees on the various work boards so as to render them eligible for dispatch to work.[112] In the same vein, the Board also held that the requirement imposed by a union that its members sign a time sheet before entering the union referral hall was not a referral rule within the meaning of s. 161.1.[113]

When union security clauses or other arrangements make a union-operated employment referral system the only means of access to employment, then the union effectively hires employees for the employer. When union hiring or designation, selection, scheduling, assignment, and dispatching to work is dependent, in part or entirely, on union membership, then it is an integral part of the system intended to be regulated by s. 161.1. In such circumstances, the rules required under s. 161.1 must necessarily include rules regulating acquisition, retention, and loss of union membership.[114] On the other hand, if the union has established such membership rules as part of its referral system, then it must not deny membership by applying the criteria in a discriminatory manner prohibited by s. 185(f),[115] nor may it expel or suspend members by a discriminatory application of the rules as prohibited by s. 185(g).

Referral rules, once made, are not immutable. They may be remade again and again as times and circumstances change. It is not the responsibility of the Board, however, as it has stated on two occasions,[116] to write or administer the rules. The nature and content of the rules is the responsibility of the trade union. The Board must ensure that the rules are fair and non-discriminatory and are so administered. That does not mean that the Board can decide which rule is useful, good, or desirable. There are many conflicting views on how referral rules should operate in any circumstance. But the Board is not the rule-maker, nor is it a refuge for those whose views do not prevail when the rules are made.

---

[111]   *Alex J. Cayer, supra,* note 104.
[112]   *Ibid.*
[113]   *John S. Cooper* (1980), 40 di 28.
[114]   *David C. Nauss and Peter H. Roberts, supra,* note 108; *Ronald W. Lockhart and Charles G. Wilson, supra,* note 102.
[115]   *David C. Nauss and Peter H. Roberts, supra,* note 108.
[116]   *David C. Nauss and Peter H. Roberts, supra,* note 107; *Allan Richard Gray* (1982), 47 di 93.

13:2420   The Posting of Referral Rules

Section 161.1(2) provides that referral rules "shall be kept posted in a conspicuous place in every area of premises occupied by a trade union in which persons seeking referral normally gather". The union is required to comply with the spirit of subsection (2). Accordingly, if it cannot afford an office, let alone a dispatch hall in which to post its rules, it must distribute copies of the rules, and of every subsequent amendment, to its members.[117]

13:2500   THE STANDARDS OF FAIR REFERRAL

13:2510   The Role of the Board

The unilateral control by a union of important aspects of its members' employment through its referral system creates a unique situation. Matters affecting employees which, under the usual collective bargaining regime, are contained in collective agreements and therefore are subject to the grievance and arbitral procedure, are here found in the union's referral rules. In the absence of s. 161.1 the application of these rules would be totally within the union's unsupervised control.

Because the fair administration of referral systems is of public interest, the Board views its role in this area as an active one. For this reason, Board officers make occasional checks on unions to ensure that their rules have been established and posted. Uninformed unions are advised about the existence of s. 161.1.

The board does not wait for individuals to complain about the application of rules to them. Persons not adversely affected today may be adversely affected in the future. The administration of the rules may fluctuate from fair and non-discriminatory to unfair and discriminatory from season to season, year to year, or month to month. The Board assumes an ongoing role in this regard and views its task as keeping the union's administration of the rules on the straight and narrow.[118] When a complaint has been filed, the Board views its role under s. 161.1 as providing the means by which a person subject to the union's referral rules can obtain a third-party adjudication on the rules' application, in the same fashion as the unilateral decisions of the employer are subject to the scrutiny of arbitrators under a collective agreement.[119]

13:2520   Fair and Non-Discriminatory Application

Section 161.1 clearly states the standards required of union decisions. It imposes the positive requirement of fairness in the application of

---

[117]   *Gary Meagher* (1980), 41 di 95.
[118]   *Mike Sheehan* (1980), 40 di 103, [1980] 2 Can LRBR 278, 80 CLLC #16,030.
[119]   *Alex J. Cayer, supra,* note 104.

referral rules, and places a restriction against the discriminatory application of the rules.

13:2521 Duty of Fairness

The duty of fairness in s. 161.1 has been viewed by the Board as requiring a higher standard than that usually applied by labour relations boards in cases involving the duty of fair representation by a trade union.[120] The approach under the Code has not been to tie together ss. 136.1 and 161.1 as closely as they have been in other jurisdictions, such as in Ontario, for example. The s. 136.1 duty of fair representation is enacted in the division of Part V that deals with the acquisition of exclusive bargaining rights. The s. 161.1 duty of fair employment referral is enacted in the division of the Code dealing with union security and the provisions permissible in collective agreements. There is in the two sections a similarity of language, but their roots are different, and s. 161.1 goes beyond the Ontario legislation when it explicitly requires rule-making, posting, and fair administration.[121]

Thus, where a complainant under s. 161.1 alleged a refusal by the union to register him for referral to employment, the Board rejected a defence to the effect that, in the administration of referral rules, a union is entitled to make an innocent mistake, as it is under s. 136.1. Under s. 136.1 the duty and standard are measured in a myriad of circumstances as the union acts on behalf of those it represents exclusively. Under s. 161.1, however, the Board held that there is no room for or reason to accept mistakes as an excuse for deviations in the fair and non-discriminatory administration of rules. It may be an important consideration when the Board fashions a remedy, but it cannot excuse the union's wrongful actions.[122]

Finally, the duty of fairness in s. 161.1 was held to require the union to make decisions on matters of referral, impartially and in accordance with its own rules.[123]

13:2522 Discrimination

Similarly to the standards of internal union conduct regulated by s. 185(f) and (g), the Board has held that the rules established pursuant to s. 161.1 must not, in themselves, be unfair or discriminatory. If they are, no matter how even-handedly they are applied, they will contravene s. 161.1(2).[124]

---

[120] *Ibid.*
[121] *David C. Nauss and Peter H. Roberts, supra,* note 108.
[122] *Mike Sheehan, supra,* note 118.
[123] *Alex J. Cayer* (1980), 39 di 108, [1980] 3 Can. LRBR 225, 80 CLLC #16,052.
[124] *Mike Sheehan, supra,* note 118.

13:2600   CASES WHERE NO BREACH WAS FOUND

In the few cases alleging breaches of s. 161.1 that have come before the Board, it has dismissed a complaint where it found that, while the referral rules were incomplete and did not fully comply with s. 161.1(3), they were not unfair or discriminatory.[125] In the same vein, the Board rejected allegations that a union had violated s. 161.1 by failing immediately to establish rules required by s. 161.1(3) when the duty of fair referral came into force in 1978.[126]

In another decision, a complainant who had been dispatched to light duties by the union executive, in accordance with a rule concerning placement to preferred jobs or placement on compassionate grounds, contended that the subsequent reversal of that decision by a higher echelon of the union removing him from these duties constituted an unfair application of the rules. As the Board found that the union's executive had overstepped its authority in making the initial decision in favour of the complainant, the reversal of this decision did not constitute an unfair application of the rules.[127]

13:2700   CASES WHERE BREACHES WERE FOUND

Two major decisions in which breaches of s. 161.1 were found involved the longshoring industry.[128] In both decisions, the following pattern emerged. With the expanding technology and fierce competition among ports, the different locals of the union and the employer involved had sought to restrict the size of the work force permanently attached to and economically dependent upon work generated by the ports. The union and its locals had the added self-interest of preserving as much work as possible for as few employees as was required to generally service the employer's needs. For these reasons, the locals that were engaged in referral to employment under collective agreements had restricted and even suspended for long periods the admission of new employees to membership. They had created other classes of employees, such as cardholders and non-cardholders. This practice had resulted, over the years, in friction and discontent.

In the first place, there were, in some instances, no rules adopted by the local to guide a non-member or non-cardholder as to how membership could be acquired. On the other hand, when new members were occasionally admitted, the Board found that the selection of the candidates was based, in some instances, on arbitrary criteria or on nepotism

---

125   *Gary Meagher, supra,* note 117.
126   *Donald J. Jollimore* (1982), 48 di 63.
127   *Alex J. Cayer, supra,* note 123.
128   *David C. Nauss and Peter H. Roberts* (1980), 42 di 55, [1981] 1 Can LRBR 188; *David C. Nauss and Peter H. Roberts* (1981), 43 di 263; *Ronald W. Lockhart and Charles G. Wilson* (1980), 42 di 89, [1981] 1 Can LRBR 213.

rather than on fair rules. Second, preference was given to union members in work dispatching but, as between cardholders and non-members, the latter were frequently dispatched before the former on an arbitrary, unwritten, and often nepotistic basis by the local union business agent. The problem was compounded by the fact that, although in some instances non-members worked as many hours as union members, only the latter were eligible to earn, maintain, and receive health, welfare, and pension benefits.

In both decisions an earlier principle of the Board was held to govern.[129] This principle holds that, where no rules have been established regulating either employment referral or access to union membership, especially when the former is dependent in whole or in part on the latter, it cannot be said that the rules are applied fairly and without discrimination as required by s. 161.1(1), since there are simply no rules in existence.

One decision where a breach of the duty of fair referral was found involved the maritime industry.[130] In that case, the Board held that the union's refusal to register the complainant for referral to employment contravened the Code, since there was work available and the complainant was both qualified and willing to work. In another case, a breach was found where rules required by s. 161.1 had been established but had not been followed by the union.[131]

13:2800   TIMELINESS OF THE COMPLAINT

The Board has held[132] that s. 161.1 is, first and foremost, legislation with a general public purpose. The union has an obligation to the manner in which the system is operated, with those persons affected being viewed as nameless, faceless persons who may be categorized under the rules as members or members in arrears. The identity of those employees wronged is not central to the Board's inquiry into the administration of the system. That the same person is adversely affected more than once is incidental. It may be important in fashioning a remedy, but it cannot affect the Board's inquiry into how the referral system is being operated. Thus, an unfair administration practice cannot be permitted to continue to operate unfairly merely because the person complaining is personally beyond the ninety-day period imposed by s. 187(2). The administration of a referral system is a continuous process. It must be made fairly and without discrimination each time it is used. As a result, an objection based on the timeliness of a complaint under s. 161.1 will not bar the Board from inquiring into the complaint.

---

129 *Keith Sheedy* (1980), 39 di 36, [1980] 1 Can LRBR 391, 80 CLLC #16,029.
130 *Mike Sheehan, supra,* note 118.
131 *Alex J. Cayer, supra,* note 123.
132 *Mike Sheehan, supra,* note 118.

13:3000 THE RIGHT TO PARTICIPATE IN UNION ACTIVITIES: SECTION 185(f), (g), (h)

13:3100 CONSTITUTIONAL AUTHORITY OF PARLIAMENT OVER INTERNAL UNION ADMINISTRATION

The internal affairs of trade unions *prima facie* fall within the legislative authority of the provincial legislatures, as they are matters of "property and civil rights". Thus, Parliament was reluctant to embark upon a course of action that under the classical distribution of legislative powers in Canada, would leave it open to attack on constitutional grounds. Instead, it prudently chose to focus on the control of the effects of internal union administration upon employees or union members or both, in areas where such effects touch the rights and recourses created by Parliament in areas unquestionably within its competence. This is reflected, for example, in s. 134(2) of the Code. Parliament has not vested the Board with the power to rectify the policy or practice of a union seeking certification that denies membership to any employee or class of employees in a bargaining unit on the basis of their qualifications. But if the effect of the policy or practice is to deny access to union membership, the Board must refuse certification.

Further examples of Parliament's approach to internal union affairs appear in s. 185(f), (g), and (h). Parliament provided in s. 110(1) for employees to be absolutely free to participate in the lawful activities of a union. It has protected this right not by setting standards for union constitutions or practices and policies or by vesting the Board with the power to invigilate or impose these standards. Rather, Parliament has done so by instituting prohibitions against unions whose discriminatory application of their constitutions, policies, or practices has the effect of suspending or expelling an employee from membership or of denying him membership. In this regard, the Board is vested with the authority to counteract the effects of the union actions in administering its internal affairs in a discriminatory manner, for the benefit of the employees affected.[133]

As a result, where a union denies membership or expels or disciplines an employee on the basis of a rule that in itself is discriminatory because it is contrary to the *Canadian Human Rights Act*,[134] or where it contravenes a freedom guaranteed by the Code, the Board cannot order the union to delete the rule from its constitution, but it has the authority to counteract

---

[133] *Terry Matus* (1980), 37 di 73, [1980] 2 Can LRBR 21, 80 CLLC #16,022; and *Terrance John Matus* (1980), 41 di 278, [1981] 1 Can LRBR 133; affd. (*sub nom. International Longshoremen's and Warehousemen's Union, Local 502 v. Matus (No. 2)*, [1982] 2 F.C. 558, 40 N.R. 541, 82 CLLC #14,161, 129 D.L.R. (3d) 616 (C.A.).

[134] S.C. 1976-77, c. 33.

the effects of the rule's application on the complainant. Where the rule is not discriminatory in itself, the Board must decide whether it was applied in a manner that was discriminatory to the complainant. To that end, the Board has adopted various tests, which will be canvassed below.

13:3200   STATUS OF THE COMPLAINANT

An important feature of s. 185(f), (g), and (h) is that it requires the complainant to be an "employee". The use of that term is dictated by constitutional reasons[135] and proved to be a major stumbling-block in a case where a complaint was filed under s. 185(f) and (g) by an unemployed person whose registration for referral had been refused.[136] The union ran a hiring hall pursuant to a collective agreement containing a closed shop clause. Accordingly, the employer would not employ the complainant unless he had been referred through the offices of the union. The complainant had no other alternative but to bring, in addition, a complaint against the employer alleging a discriminatory refusal to hire. The status of an unemployed person to bring a complaint under s. 185(f) and (g) in the context of a union-operated referral system was dependent on a favourable disposition of the complaint against the employer. If that complaint were upheld, it would amount to a finding that the complainant would have been an "employee" of the employer, had it not been for the latter's wrongful refusal to hire him. The question of whether such a finding would also give the complainant the status of an employee for the purpose of s. 185(f) and (g) would then arise.

In this case the Board determined that the complaint against the employer had no merit. Not being an "employee", the complainant had no status to complain against the union for contravening s. 185(f) or (g). The enactment of s. 161.1, which does not require that the complainant be an "employee" and which encompasses situations where union mem-

---

135   *Gerald Abbott* (1977), 26 di 543, [1978] 1 Can LRBR 305.
136   Against the company, the complainant alleged a violation of s. 184(3)(a)(ii). The Board held that this complaint was untimely and without merit in *Mike Sheehan* (1975), 9 di 29, [1975] 2 Can LRBR 55, 75 CLLC #16,161; and *Mike Sheehan* (1976), 17 di 14, [1976] 2 Can LRBR 187, 76 CLLC #16,030. On judicial review, the Federal Court of Appeal found the complaint to be timely and meritorious: *Sheehan v. Upper Lakes Shipping Co. Ltd.*, [1978] 1 F.C. 836, 19 N.R. 456, 81 D.L.R. (3d) 208. The company then appealed and the Supreme Court of Canada reversed the appeal court's decision: *Upper Lakes Shipping Co. Ltd. v. Sheehan*, [1979] 1 S.C.R. 902, 25 N.R. 149, 79 CLLC #14,192. Against the union, the complainant alleged violations of s. 185(f) and (g). The Board determined that the alleged violation of s. 185(g) was untimely in *Mike Sheehan* (1975), 9 di 29, [1975] 2 Can LRBR 55, 75 CLLC #16,161. The Board also dismissed the complaint of a violation of s. 185(f) in *Mike Sheehan* (1976), 17 di 14, [1976] 2 Can LRBR 187, 76 CLLC #16,030. On judicial review, the Federal Court of Appeal referred the latter decision back to the Board because it found a breach of the rules of natural justice: *Sheehan v. Canadian Brotherhood of Railway, Transport and General Workers*, [1978] 1 F.C. 847, 19 N.R. 468. The Board then reheard the case and found the complaint to be untimely in *Mike Sheehan* (1979), 34 di 726, [1979] 1 Can LRBR 531.

bership is a condition of employment, subsequently provided a remedy for the complainant.[137]

Another development in the circumvention of the "employee" requirement in s. 185(f), (g), and (h), where the action complained of is an expulsion from membership in the context of a union-operated referral system, was the decision of the Supreme Court of Canada in *International Longshoremen's Association, Local 273 v. Maritime Employer's Association*.[138] Estey J., delivering the judgment of the court, determined that where a union undertakes to supply the required labour when services are requisitioned and the employer undertakes to assign work only to members of the union when work is available to be performed, members of the union are "employees" from the outset of the collective agreement. It follows that the complainant's membership in the union provides the "employee" status required by s. 185(f), (g), and (h), whether or not he was employed at the time of his expulsion.[139] Of course, if he was employed at the time of his expulsion, the complainant will have the status required by s. 185(f), (g), and (h), whether the union is engaged in employment referral or not, and whether it has negotiated union security contemplated by s. 161 or not.

13:3300   EXPULSION, SUSPENSION, AND DISCIPLINE OF MEMBERS FOR A MOTIVE PROHIBITED BY SECTION 185(f), (g).

13:3310   The Purpose and Scope of the Protection of Section 185(f), (g)

Section 185(f) and (g) concerns the right to union membership as it is affected by the application of membership rules and standards of discipline. These sections are intended to protect and advance individual rights against the previously unfettered authority of the union organization. They do not, however, abolish the right of the union to expel, suspend, or discipline members or deny membership to non-members.[140] They merely provide prohibitions against the discriminatory application of their rules and standards by unions.

The Board has determined that there is a certain amount of overlap between subsections (f) and (g). As was held,[141] s. 185(g) is addressed to all disciplinary acts, including expulsion and suspension. Section 185(f) is

---

137   *Crosbie Offshore Services Ltd.* (1983), 54 di 81.
138   [1979] 1 S.C.R. 120, 23 N.R. 386, 23 N.B.R. (2d) 458, 78 C.L.L.C. #14,171, 89 D.L.R. (3d) 289.
139   The Board applied that ruling in two cases: *Terrance John Matus, supra,* note 133; and *Roland Arsenault* (1982), 50 di 51, [1982] 3 Can LRBR 425, 82 CLLC #17,018.
140   *Fred J. Solly* (1981), 43 di 29, [1981] 2 Can LRBR 245, 81 CLLC #16,089.
141   *Gerald Abbott* (1977), 26 di 543, [1978] 1 Can LRBR 305.

addressed to expulsion and suspension that is discriminatory whether it is disciplinary or not. One is addressed to the purpose (*e.g.*, discipline) of an action, while the other is addressed to the actions (*e.g.*, expulsion, suspension, or denial of membership) without regard to their purpose. That the two subsections overlap does not negate the effect of either. Rather, it creates a greater protection against discriminatory expulsion or suspension, the harshest of acts, by providing a recourse whether the action was for disciplinary reasons or otherwise.

13:3320   The Standards of Internal Union Affairs Conduct

13:3321   Rules or Standards Applied in a "Discriminatory Manner"

In an early decision,[142] the Board defined the expression "discriminatory manner" used in s. 185(f) and (g) to mean that an individual should not be singled out for special treatment either in the decision to charge, the procedural format, or in the penalty.

These standards were evolved in cases dealing mainly with disciplinary actions taken by unions. However, as subsections (f) and (g) overlap to some extent, the standards evolved under each section complement each other.

The Decision to Charge

With respect to the decision to charge, the fact that all persons who have been charged have been treated equally is only one of the factors the Board takes into account in trying to determine whether a trade union has applied its standards of discipline in a discriminatory manner. The standards used in selecting persons against whom charges are to be laid is also an essential element considered by the Board. Otherwise, carefully selected political opponents could be harrassed and hounded out of a trade union, and yet, provided they had all been dealt with equally, the Code would give them no protection. Parliament certainly never intended such a peculiar result.

The Procedural Format

With respect to the procedural format, the Board has stated that, when assessing how the standards of trade union discipline, which may vary from one union to another, have been applied, it will look at any process that determines guilt or innocence.

---

[142]   *Ibid.*

Because of the nature and character of a trade union, the disciplinary proceedings it conducts cannot be scrutinized according to the strict criteria that must be followed by a court of law in criminal proceedings. Nevertheless, a trade union that wishes to undertake disciplinary action against its members must also take steps to ensure that union officers and members are properly informed of their rights and responsibilities, and that proceedings are conducted fairly[143] and with a minimal observance of the rules of natural justice.[144]

The Penalty

With respect to the penalty, the Board will consider not only the result of the application of disciplinary standards, but also the basis for their application and the manner in which they have been applied.[145]

13:3322   Discriminatory Rules

In more recent decisions, the Board has further refined the criteria outlined above. It has stated, more particularly with respect to membership rules, that "discriminatory" means the application of rules that distinguish between individuals or groups on grounds that are illegal, arbitrary, or unreasonable.[146]

The Definition of Membership Rules

Section 185(f) refers to membership rules, but does not mention whether these rules must be in writing or not. The Board has held that membership rules with which this section is concerned also include relevant unwritten rules. However, because the application of unwritten rules may be arbitrary, the Board requires that these rules be unambiguous before it will agree to recognize them.

Thus, the words "membership rules" in s. 185(f) include written rules as well as unambiguous unwritten rules.[147] Where such rules, established by a local union in compliance with s. 161.1 or pursuant to an order of the Board, conflict with the rules of the constitution of the international union with which it is affiliated, the Board will use as its reference point, in a complaint under s. 185(f) alleging a denial of membership, the rules established by the local union.[148]

---

143 *Ibid.; Kevin Allison MacLaren* (1982), 47 di 79.
144 *Val Udverhely* (1979), 35 di 87, [1979] 2 Can. LRBR 569; *Ronald Wheadon* (1983), 54 di 134, 5 CLRBR (NS) 192, 84 CLLC #16,004.
145 *Gerald Abbott, supra,* note 141.
146 *Gérard Casista* (1978), 28 di 955, [1979] 2 Can LRBR 149; *Terry Matus* (1980), 37 di 73, [1980] 2 Can LRBR 21, 80 CLLC #16,022.
147 *Gérard Cassista, supra,* note 146.
148 *Allan Richard Gray* (1982), 47 di 93.

Illegal Distinction

A distinction or rule is most clearly illegal when it is based on considerations prohibited by the *Canadian Human Rights Act.* The rule is discriminatory in itself, and its application is necessarily discriminatory.[149] As the Board has stated, it is not enough that a standard of selection of union members be evenly applied to everyone; the standards themselves must respect the principle of equality.[150]

We pause here to underline the fact that, if a rule or standard contravenes any one of the prohibited grounds of discrimination set out in the *Canadian Human Rights Act,* it may still be valid if it constitutes an exception recognized by law. In Canada, all human rights statutes contain such exceptions in matters related to employment. For instance, s. 14(2) of the federal Act, which provides exceptions to prohibited grounds of discrimination in matters related to employment, states that "any refusal, exclusion, expulsion, suspension, limitation, specification or preference in relation to any employment" is not a discriminatory practice if it is "established by an employer based on a *bona fide* occupational requirement". This has been interpreted by the Board to mean that, although a selection standard may contravene one of the grounds of discrimination prohibited by the Act, this standard will nevertheless be valid if it constitutes a condition of hiring directly related and relevant to the normal performance of the duties of a given job. This standard, moreover, must be truly necessary and essential to the performance of the said duties and, hence, to the normal operation of the business.

The relevance of the exceptions provided by the *Canadian Human Rights Act* in the context of a complaint under s. 185(f) alleging discriminatory membership rules and, hence, their application in a discriminatory manner is that although at first glance it appears that they can only be invoked by an employer, they may also be invoked by a union if it is engaged in referral to employment pursuant to a collective agreement.[151]

Indeed, as seen earlier, when union security clauses and other arrangements make a union referral system the only access to employment, then the union effectively hires employees for the employer.[152] Thus, in such circumstances, admission to the union ranks confers more than the status of member; it also confers that of employee. It follows that, in such circumstances, a union is entitled to invoke the legal exceptions provided in the *Canadian Human Rights Act* when rules for selection of union members are alleged to be discriminatory.

---

149   *Gérard Cassista, supra,* note 146; *Terry Matus, supra,* note 146.
150   *Roland Arsenault, supra,* note 139.
151   *Ibid.*
152   *David C. Nauss and Peter H. Roberts* (1980), 42 di 55, [1981] 1 Can LRBR 188.

Arbitrary Distinction

A distinction or rule is arbitrary when it is not based on any general rule, policy, or rationale.[153]

Unreasonable Distinction

Finally, a rule or distinction is said to be unreasonable when, although it is made in accordance with a general rule or policy, the rule or policy itself is one that bears no fair and rational relationship to the decision being made.[154]

In conclusion, the Board has cautioned that, when it is dealing with cases of alleged improper discipline, it should be clear that it is not a body for appeal from internal union discipline. The role of the Board under s. 185(g) is to ensure that disciplinary standards are applied in a non-discriminatory manner according to the criteria outlined above.[155] When it is dealing with an alleged improper denial of membership, the Board's task is not to set standards for what the union may consider to be vital institutional interests nor to dictate when those interests must yield to the interest of an individual. It is simply to ensure that the union does not act in a discriminatory manner within the meaning of s. 185(f).[156]

13:3323   Cases Where No Breach Was Found

Most cases where no breach of s. 185(f) was found were accompanied by a similar conclusion with respect to s. 185(g). The reader should refer to paragraph 13:3410 for an outline of the cases where the application of discipline standards did not offend s. 185(g). In a case where an employee was expelled from membership because he actively participated in an organizing campaign on behalf of a rival trade union,[157] the board rejected the employee complaint filed under ss. 110, 185(f), (g), and 186 since the expulsion did not offend any public interests in the scheme of the Code, and this was essentially an internal trade union matter.

Although cases where breaches of s. 185(f) were found have generally not attracted a similar conclusion with respect to s. 185(g), the converse proposition is not true. Indeed, as will be seen below, most cases in which the Board held that s. 185(g) had been breached involved a similar finding with respect to s. 185(f).

---

153 *Gérard Cassista, supra,* note 146; *Terry Matus, supra,* note 146.
154 *Ibid.*
155 *Val Udverhely, supra,* note 144; *Ronald Wheadon, supra,* note 140.
156 *Fred J. Solly, supra,* note 140.
157 *James Carbin* (1984), 85 CLLC #16,013.

13:3324   Cases Where Breaches Were Found

In one case, the expulsion from the union for non-payment of a fine would have resulted in loss of employment as a stevedore for a person on a priority list with the employer. The Board found that the expulsion of the complainant was a discriminatory application of the union's standards of discipline, in contravention of s. 185(f) and (g).[158]

More recently, the Board held that the application to the complainant of a rule prohibiting dual membership had been carried out in a discriminatory manner, in violation of s. 185(f), as the evidence had established that other employees also engaged in the same practice and had not been disciplined.[159] In another case the Board held that the union's suspension of a complainant for attempted vandalism of union property was discriminatory and in violation of s. 185(f) and (g).[160]

In an earlier case the Board determined that a complainant had not received the fair and impartial trial to which he was entitled under the union's constitution.[161] Some members who had laid the charges and who were responsible for the complainant's expulsion had taken part in the deliberations of the committee that had decided the fate of the complainant's appeal. The Board held the union's procedural format contravened s. 185(g).

13:3400   DENIAL OF MEMBERSHIP

In many decisions rendered by the Board under s. 185(f), there were elements of a job referral system present, but these cases preceded the enactment of s. 161.1 and so were not addressed to the issue of denial of membership in that context.

13:3410   Cases Where No Breach Was Found

In an early case, the Board determined that the denial of the opportunity to register at a hiring hall manned by the union did not amount to a "denial of membership" within the meaning of s. 185(f).[162] In a more recent case, a complainant, who had previously been an officer in the incumbent union that was subsequently raided and displaced by a rival union, was denied membership in the latter.[163] He had displayed open opposition to union militancy and the use of the strike weapon while in office in the displaced union. His membership application was rejected

---

[158]   *Gerald Abbott, supra,* note 141.
[159]   *Terry Matus, supra,* note 146.
[160]   *Kevin Allison MacLaren, supra,* note 143.
[161]   *Val Udverhely, supra,* note 144.
[162]   *Mike Sheehan* (1976), 17 di 14, [1976] 2 Can LRBR 187, 76 CLLC #16,030.
[163]   *Fred J. Solly* (1981), 43 di 29, [1981] 2 Can LRBR 245, 81 CLLC #16,089.

on the grounds of his prior strike-breaking activities and his public statements in opposition to strikes. A complaint brought under s. 185(f) and (g) was dismissed by the Board on the grounds that there was no evidence of discrimination in the membership procedure followed by the union.

In another case, the union's failure to credit a cardman with time while he had been on workmen's compensation in past years affected his opportunity for membership in the union.[164] As the membership rules subsequently established were not retroactive, the Board held that there was no evidence to support the contention that the union had treated the complainant differently from anyone else, or denied him membership in the union, or imposed any form of penalty on him by applying the rules of membership or standards of discipline in a discriminatory manner.

The Board also dismissed complaints filed under s. 185(f) and (g) by persons who had been dismissed from their employment with the union.[165] In this case, the Board held that trade unions, even those operating on the federal scene, are not employers within the meaning of the Code. Accordingly, the complaining senior officers of the union were held not to be employees within the meaning of the Code and could not invoke s. 185(f) or (g).

13:3420   Cases Where Breaches Were Found

In one case a rule limiting membership to longshoremen whose names appeared on a job security list forming part of a collective agreement was found not to be discriminatory in itself, since it had a legitimate purpose related to job security.[166] However, the use of this rule to deny membership to semi-skilled workers who were fully employed and whose work could not be performed by longshoremen was found to be discriminatory and in contravention of s. 185(f). In another case a rule adopted by a union, whereby relatives of active members were to be given priority in admission to membership, was found to be discriminatory in itself, because it established a distinction based on a ground prohibited by the *Canadian Human Rights Act*, namely, family status. This could not be justified as it was not relevant to the normal performance of the duties of a longshoreman.[167] Thus, its application contravened s. 185(f).

---

164   *Donald J. Jollimore* (1982), 48 di 63.
165   *Ed Finn* (1982), 47 di 49, [1982] 1 Can LRBR 399, 82 CLLC #16,155.
166   *Gérard Cassista* (1978), 28 di 955, [1979] 2 Can LRBR 149.
167   *Roland Arsenault* (1982), 50 di 51, [1982] 3 Can LRBR 425, 82 CLLC #17,018.

13:3500   THE TIMELINESS OF COMPLAINTS UNDER SECTION 185(f), (g)

13:3510   General Principles

The application of subs. (2) of s. 187 is subject to the provisions of subss. (3) and (4). The application of subs. (3), in turn, is subject to that of subs. (4). Subsections (3) and (4) set out the framework in which a complaint under s. 187(1) may be filed when subss. 185(f) and (g) have been contravened. Because of this special procedure, s. 187(2) cannot apply to such complaints.[168]

The scheme of s. 187(3) and (4) sets up a special regime of timeliness that favours the exhaustion of internal union remedies. The Board will hear a complaint under s. 185(f) or (g) where ready access to such a procedure is not available to the complainant (s. 187(4)(b)), or where the Board determines that it should be by-passed (s. 187(4)(a)).[169]

13:3520   When an Internal Union Appeal Procedure Exists and Ready Access to It is Provided

Section 187(3) deals with instances where, pursuant to the union's by-laws, the complainant may file a grievance or appeal concerning a decision that has been rendered by the union. When such a procedure exists and the complainant is given ready access to it, he must avail himself of such recourses before he takes a complaint to the Board. Although s. 187(3) does not provide for any time limit within which the complainant must avail himself of the appeal procedures, it is implicit that he must take some action within a reasonable time.[170] If he fails to do anything, that is, if the complainant does not seek internal union redress within a reasonable period of time, the right to complain to the Board under s. 187(3) will not be kept indefinitely.[171]

Although ready access to the procedure may be given to the complainant, it is not mandatory that he exhaust all avenues of internal appeal before coming to the Board under a s. 185(f) or (g) complaint.[172] Nor, where the internal union procedure includes various steps, is it necessary for the complainant to wait any longer than six months from the first step for an answer.[173] At any rate, the grievance must be dealt with in a

---

[168]   *Gérard Cassista, supra,* note 166.
[169]   *Mike Sheehan* (1979), 34 di 726, [1979] 1 Can LRBR 531.
[170]   *Ibid.*
[171]   *Gerald Abbott* (1977), 26 di 543, [1978] 1 Can LRBR 305; *Ronald Wheadon* (1983), 54 di 134, 5 CLRBR (NS) 192, 84 CLLC #16,004.
[172]   *Gerald Abbott, supra,* note 171.
[173]   *Gérard Cassista, supra,* note 166.

manner satisfactory to the complainant and answered within six months of the date on which it was originally instituted (s. 187(3)(b)). In the event that this does not occur, s. 187(3)(c) provides that the complaint to the Board must be brought within ninety days of either the day on which the union rendered its decision unsatisfactory to the employee, or of the lapse of six months from the date on which the grievance was first presented.[174]

13:3530   Where an Internal Union Appeal Procedure Exists but No Ready Access is Given, or Where the Board Decides That the Grievance Should be Dealt With Forthwith

As seen above, s. 187(2) does not apply to complaints filed under s. 185(f) or (g). It is the ninety-day period provided by s. 187(3)(c) that applies. As the latter is subject in turn to s. 187(4), then where no ready access is given to the internal procedure, or where the circumstances giving rise to the complaint are such that the Board feels it should be dealt with without delay, the limitation period of s. 187(3)(c) no longer applies. As s. 187(4) does not provide any time limit, the Board has stated that in such circumstances it would hear complaints under s. 185(f) or (g) that are filed with a reasonable period of time of the denial of ready access, or of the occurrence of such action or circumstances contemplated by s. 187(4)(a).[175]

An example of the above set of circumstances is found in *Gerald Abbott*.[176] Where the internal procedure includes various steps and access is denied at the first step, the Code does not require the complainant to try the second step.[177] This would constitute another situation envisaged by s. 187(4)(b).

13:3540   Where No Internal Union Appeal Procedure Exists

In one case it was determined that, where the union's by-laws do not provide access to a grievance or appeal procedure because such a procedure simply does not exist, then complaints under s. 185(f) and (g) are not subject to the statutory limitation of ninety days, but rather to s. 187(4).[178] Hence, they must be filed within a reasonable period of time of the alleged unfair labour practice.

---

[174] *Ibid.*
[175] *Gerald Abbott, supra,* note 171.
[176] *Ibid.*
[177] *Gérard Cassista, supra,* note 166.
[178] *Ibid.*

As a final point, although the principles outlined above apply to any type of actions prohibited by s. 185(f) or (g), the issue of the timeliness of a complaint alleging an improper denial of membership under s. 185(f) requires consideration of additional factors, which will be dealt with later.[179]

13:3600 EXPULSION, SUSPENSION, AND DISCIPLINE OF MEMBERS FOR A MOTIVE PROHIBITED BY SECTION 185(h)

The question addressed by s. 185(h), similarly to s. 185(f) and (g), is one of the right to union membership. Its general purpose is to prevent unions from demanding a loyalty that will require members to act contrary to the Code. If it does, it cannot act against the member who is unwilling to accept such a requirement.[180]

In its only decision dealing with this subsection of the Code, the Board decided that a rule in the constitution of a union that prohibited its members from belonging to any other union violated one of the basic rights set out in s. 110(1) of the Code. Although in the Code Parliament did not explicitly guarantee the rights of employees to belong to more than one union, s. 110(1) was read as creating such a basic freedom. Thus, the application of such a rule, which was held to be discriminatory in itself to an employee, and his consequent expulsion from the union that deprived him of his livelihood in the longshoring industry, violated s. 185(h). His refusal to abide by such a rule constituted a refusal to perform an act contrary to Part V.[181]

The importance of that decision is enhanced when viewed in the light of s. 161 of the Code. Although a union may have negotiated a clause requiring union membership as a condition of employment, it cannot deprive its members from exercising their freedom of association and joining a rival union during the open periods provided by s. 124(2) and (3). Simultaneous membership in more than one union is a necessary result if the union for which the employees have opted is to be successful in satisfying the Board of its majority support.

The timeliness of a complaint under s. 185(h) is subject to the universal ninety-day limitation period provided in s. 187(2).

---

179   See para. 15:2310.
180   *Gerald Abbott, supra,* note 171.
181   *Terry Matus* (1980), 37 di 73, [1980] 2 Can LRBR 21, 80 CLLC #16,022; affd. (*sub nom.* *International Longshoremen's and Warehousemen's Union, Local 502 v. Matus (No. 1)*), [1982] 2 F.C. 549, 40 N.R. 594, 82 CLLC #14,161, 129 D.L.R. (3d) 616 (C.A.).

13:4000   LOSS OF EMPLOYMENT AS A RESULT OF EXPULSION OR SUSPENSION FROM MEMBERSHIP: SECTIONS 185(e), 184(3)(a)(ii)

13:4100   PURPOSE OF THE PROTECTION

Section 185(e) relates to the continued right to employment of a person who is expelled or suspended from membership. The question is not one of the right to union membership, as it is in s. 185(f), (g), and (h), but rather of the right not to lose employment as a result of loss of union membership.

Where a union has negotiated union security provisions contemplated by s. 161, such as the requirement of membership in the union as a condition of employment or the grant of preferential hiring rights to members, the permanent or temporary loss of union membership by reason of expulsion or suspension would affect the individual's right of opportunity to employment.

Parliament considered that such a consequence was too harsh in all circumstances except those where the expulsion or suspension occurs because of the employee's failure to pay "the periodic dues, assessments and initiation fees uniformly required to be paid by all members of the trade union as a condition of acquiring or retaining membership in the trade union".[182] To buttress this prohibition against the union requiring termination of employment, a companion obligation, somewhat broader, is placed on the employer by s. 184(3)(a)(ii). The latter prohibits an employer from refusing "to employ or continue to employ, suspend, transfer, layoff or otherwise discriminate against any person in regard to employment, pay or any other term or condition of employment because the person has been expelled or suspended from membership in a trade union", except where it was for a failure to pay the dues referred to in s. 184(3)(a)(ii).[183]

The Board has yet to determine whether the fact that a union is engaged in referral to employment pursuant to a collective agreement containing a clause requiring union membership as a condition of employment relieves an employer from complying with s. 184(3)(a)(ii) when a member is expelled or suspended from membership, at least until the union has been found to have contravened s. 185(e) or 161.1. In a case where charges were brought against an employer under s. 184(3)(a)(ii) and against the union under s. 185(f) and (g), the Board declined to determine the validity of an argument to the effect that an employer is legally bound not to employ a person unless hired through the offices of

---

[182] *Canada Labour Code*, s. 185(e).
[183] *Gerald Abbott, supra,* note 171.

the union, where the latter operates a referral system pursuant to a collective agreement.[184] As no breach was found under either section in the case, the question remains open.

13:4110   Cases Where No Breach Was Found

In *Mike Sheehan*[185] the Board dismissed a complaint under s. 184(3)(a)(ii) that alleged a refusal to employ because of the employee's expulsion from membership in a trade union. The Board was satisfied that, in this case, the decision to refuse to employ the complainant did not turn on the complainant's expulsion from the union.

13:4120   Cases Where Breaches Were Found

In the only case involving a breach of s. 185(e), the Board determined that where, by application of a discriminatory rule prohibiting dual unionism, a longshoreman had been expelled from the union and, as a result, deprived of any work in the industry, the union had accomplished among other things that which is prohibited by s. 185(e).[186]

13:4200   TIMELINESS

Unlike s. 185(f) and (g), a complaint under s. 185(e) is only subject to the universal ninety-day delay of s. 187(2).[187]

A complaint under s. 184(3)(a)(ii) alleging a dismissal, refusal to continue to employ, suspension, transfer, layoff, discrimination in regard to employment, intimidation, threats, or any other form of discipline because of expulsion or suspension from membership for a reason other than a failure to pay the amounts referred to in s. 184(3)(a)(ii) is subject to the ninety-day period provided in s. 187(2). Where, however, the complaint under s. 184(3)(a)(ii) alleges a refusal to hire or to employ, the question of timeliness requires consideration of different factors, which will be dealt with later.[188]

13:5000   ACCESS TO FINANCIAL STATEMENTS OF UNIONS: SECTION 199.1

Upon the request of any of its members, every trade union must provide, free of charge, a copy of a financial statement of its affairs to the

---

184   *Mike Sheehan* (1976), 17 di 14, [1976] 2 Can LRBR 187, 76 CLLC #16,030.
185   *Ibid.*
186   *Terrance John Matus* (1980), 41 di 278, [1981] 1 Can LRBR 133; affd. (*sub nom. International Longshoremen's and Warehousemen's Union, Local 502 v. Matus (No. 2)*), [1982] 2 F.C. 558, 40 N.R. 541, 82 CLLC #14,161, 129 D.L.R. (3d) 616 (C.A.).
187   *Gerald Abbott, supra,* note 171.
188   See paragraph 15:2310.

end of the last fiscal year, certified by its president and treasurer or by its president and any other officer responsible for the handling and administration of the union's funds to be a true copy.[189]

The financial statement must be sufficiently detailed to disclose accurately the financial conditions and operations of the trade union for the fiscal year for which it was prepared.[190]

If the union refuses to provide the member with the statements required, a complaint can be laid before the Board, which may pursuant to the powers conferred by s. 199.1(3) and (4) make an order requiring the trade union to file with the Board, within the time set out in the order, a statement in such form and with particulars as the Board may determine. In addition the Board may require the trade union to provide a copy of the statements to such other members of the union as in its discretion it may direct.[191]

---

[189]   *Canada Labour Code*, s. 199.1(1).
[190]   Section 199.1(2).
[191]   The provisions of s. 199.1 may also be invoked by every member of an employers' organization wishing to obtain from the latter a copy of its financial statements: see s. 199.1(1).

CHAPTER 14

PROTECTION OF ACCESS TO THE BOARD: SECTIONS 184(3)(a)(iii) to (v), 184(3)(e)(i) to (iii), and 185(i)(i) to (iii)

14:0000   **PROTECTION OF ACCESS TO THE BOARD: SECTIONS 184(3)(a)(iii) to (v), 184(3)(e)(i) to (iii), and 185(i)(i) to (iii)**

Section 185(1) of the *Canada Labour Code* is a companion section to s. 184(3)(a)(iii) to (v) and (e)(i) to (iii), which prohibit employer action against persons who have participated in Board or other proceedings under Part V of the Code. These provisions of the Code have at least a two-fold purpose. First, they are intended to ensure that rights under the Code are real and not merely illusory and capable of being frustrated by acts designed to discourage their exercise.[1] Employees may be subject to many pressures exerted by an employer or union to discourage the exercise of the rights that Parliament has given them. One form of pressure is to discourage the utilization by an employee of the remedies designed to protect against interference with his rights. By interfering with access to the remedy, the right is effectively denied.[2]

The second purpose of these provisions is closely related to the first. This purpose is to encourage and hopefully to ensure honest and candid testimony and disclosure to the Board in its administration of Part V. The function delegated to the Board by Parliament would be rendered nugatory if its proceedings could be interfered with by pressures exerted on those who may seek access to it or participate in Board proceedings.[3]

As with other anti-discrimination provisions of the Code, motive is a constituent element of an infraction of s. 184(3)(a)(iii) to (v) and (e). The prohibited motive is a desire to punish an individual for participating in proceedings under the Code.[4] A common characteristic of these sections and of s. 184(3)(a)(i) is that the Board must be satisfied that the activities described therein were not part of the reason for any disciplinary or

---

[1]   *Frank J. Nowotniak and Gordon E. Ostby* (1979), 34 di 835, [1979] 2 Can LRBR 466.
[2]   *Giant Yellowknife Mines Ltd.* (1977), 19 di 147, [1977] 1 Can LRBR 483, 77 CLLC #16,082.
[3]   *Ibid.*
[4]   *Claude Latrémouille* (1983), 50 di 197. The desire to punish is also a motive prohibited by s. 185(i).

other prejudicial action by the employer. Thus, the prohibited consideration in these sections need not be the sole one. The onus of establishing that such motivation did not exist rests with the employer under s. 188(3).[5]

In *Fraser Surrey Docks Ltd.*[6] the Board dismissed a complaint under s. 184(3)(a)(iii) and (v) as the complainant failed to establish that it was well known to management that he was going to be a chief witness for the union in a certification before the Board. In another decision, the Board rejected a complaint of unjust dismissal because the dismissal was the result of the complainant's refusal to follow directives and not of her participation in a hearing before the Board.[7] In a subsequent decision a complaint filed by a retired employee under s. 184(3)(a)(i) and (iii), alleging that his former employer had denied him an employment opportunity because of his past union activities and testimony in certain proceedings before the Board, was dismissed.[8]

By contrast, the Board found a contravention of s. 184(3)(a)(v) where a newly hired employee was dismissed for having filed an unfair labour practice complaint against a previous employer. The Board stated that the form of interference prohibited by s. 184(3)(a)(v) is even more serious when an employee is subject to pressure by an employer because he has sought a remedy against another employer.[9] In another decision,[10] a supervisory employee had exercised his right under s. 184(3)(c) to refuse to perform work of other unionized employees who were participating in a legal strike. He was penalized by the company for his behaviour and complained to the Board, which found the company in violation of s. 184(3)(c). The complainant subsequently filed an unfair practice charge under s. 184(3)(a)(iii) and (v), alleging that he was being penalized by the company for making the earlier complaint. The Board upheld the complaint and ordered that the employee be offered a promotion commensurate with his training and experience and financial assistance to relocate elsewhere in the territory of the company.

Under s. 185(i), the Board determined that a union may not use an amendment of its by-laws as a cloak of legitimacy for reprisals against employees who had tried to displace it as bargaining agent by filing a certification demand with the Board.[11] The union's refusal to reinstate the complainant's membership was discriminatory and constituted an

---

[5]   *Frank J. Nowotniak and Gordon E. Ostby, supra,* note 1; *Northern Telecom Canada Ltd.* (1982), 48 di 78.
[6]   (1974), 3 di 14, 74 CLLC #16,102.
[7]   *Brazeau Transport Inc.* (1979), 35 di 158.
[8]   *Northern Telecom Canada Ltd., supra,* note 5; see also *CHUM Western Ltd., Radio CKVN* (1974), 3 di 18.
[9]   *Giant Yellowknife Mines Ltd., supra,* note 2.
[10]   *British Columbia Telephone Co.* (1983), 52 di 88, 83 CLLC #16,048.
[11]   *Frank J. Nowotniak and Gordon E. Ostby, supra,* note 1.

unfair labour practice under s. 185(i). In *Claude Latrémouille*[12] the Board found that the complainant had been expelled from the administrative board of directors of the union not because he had participated in proceedings before the Board but because his participation revealed a state of mind that rendered him unsuitable for continued occupation of his executive position in the union. Thus, s. 185(i) had not been contravened.

---

[12] *Supra*, note 4; affd. not yet reported, February 22, 1983, file no. A-244-83 (Fed. C.A.).

CHAPTER 15

UNFAIR LABOUR PRACTICES COMPLAINTS: PROCEDURE AND TIMELINESS

15:0000   **UNFAIR LABOUR PRACTICES COMPLAINTS: PROCEDURE AND TIMELINESS**

This chapter deals with the information that must be included in an unfair labour practice complaint, the procedure for filing it, and the way in which it is processed and disposed of by the Board.

15:1000   COMPLAINTS REQUIRING MINISTERIAL CONSENT: SECTION 187(5)

A complaint alleging a violation of ss. 148(a) and (b), 184(3)(g), and 185(a) and (b) requires the authorization of the minister as provided by s. 187(5).

In respect of complaints alleging bad-faith bargaining, the requirement for ministerial consent has a two-fold purpose. First, upon receipt of a request, officials of Labour Canada contact both parties and seek a resolution of the impasse. As there is no formal complaint at this stage, they can focus their efforts on the mediation of a resolution of the bargaining impasse. In this process the officials may also gather information on the basis of which, should their efforts at mediation fail, they can advise the minister on whether granting consent to the complaint would merely promote frivolous proceedings or whether efforts at settlement and adjudication by the Board would further the interests of either party and the objects of the Code. This constitutes the second purpose. Once the minister's consent is given and a complaint is made, the Board's officers seek a resolution of the complaint. They enter very late on the scene, but have the added leverage of the immediacy of a Board determination and a possible remedial order. The final step is Board adjudication.

Throughout this process, until adjudication, the focus is on efforts to resolve the bargaining impasse. Even at the adjudication stage, the Board may attempt settlement efforts.[1]

---

[1]   *CKLW Radio Broadcasting Ltd.* (1977), 23 di 51, 77 CLLC #16,110.

15:1100   APPLICATION TO THE MINISTER

The application to the minister must be in writing and state the following:

(a) the name and address of the party making the request;

(b) the name and address of the person or organization against whom it is desired to make a complaint;

(c) the nature of the alleged failure to comply;

(d) the section of the Act in respect of which it is alleged there has been a failure to comply;

(e) the date or dates upon which and the place where the alleged failure to comply occurred or, in the case of an alleged continuing failure to comply, the date upon which the alleged continuing failure to comply commenced and the period of time during which it continued, and

(f) the facts upon which the party making the requests relies as constituting the alleged failure to comply. . . .[2]

The application must be signed on behalf of the party making the request and must be verified by a statutory declaration. In this connection, a party drafting the request to the minister must take care with the facts alleged therein, since they must be verified by affidavit. As the facts alleged in the request are usually the same as those alleged in the complaint filed with the Board, the affidavit could come back to haunt the complainant and undermine his credibility if the evidence adduced during the hearing before the Board does not support or contradicts the allegations made in the request.[3] A careful drafting of the request to the minister is also warranted by the fact (as will be seen below) that the period within which the Board may make a finding of a breach can be limited by the wording used by the minister in its authorization to file the complaint.

Although s. 35(2) of the Board's regulations provides that the consent required by s. 187(5) must be filed with the complaint, the Board's practice is to accept the complaint but not to deal with it until the consent is provided. When the Board is ready to hear the case, however, the consent must be filed.[4] The Board has taken the position that the absence of consent is unquestionably fatal to an application that requires it. However, the existence of a consent that bears a date posterior to that of the complaint is a simple defect in form or a technical irregularity curable under s. 203 of the Code and s. 6 of the Board's regulations.[5] Furthermore, where it was argued that the consent itself was invalid and, hence, that the Board did not have jurisdiction to embark upon an inquiry to

---

2   *Canada Industrial Relations Regulations*, C.R.C. 1978, c. 1012, s. 7.

3   *Le Banque Nationale du Canada* (1981), 42 di 352, [1982] 3 Can LRBR 1.

4   *Ibid.*

5   *Canadian Imperial Bank of Commerce (Branches at Creston, B.C. and St. Catharines, Ont.)* (1979), 35 di 105, [1980] 1 Can LRBR 307, 80 CLLC #16,002.

determine whether the complaint was founded or not, the Board held[6] that it was not its role to second-guess the minister and that it had to assume that he had acted in accord with his general mandate, provided in s. 197.

15:1200   EFFECT OF CONSENT ON BOARD'S JURISDICTION

As outlined above, the requirement for ministerial consent under s. 187(5) is not a mere procedural step. If it were, the minister would not be vested with a discretionary power either to grant or refuse it.[7] Where the minister has granted the required consent, he has in some cases exercised his discretion so as to restrict either the object of the Board's inquiry or the time period within which a violation can be found.

15:1210   Restriction as to the Time Period

15:1211   Complaints Under Section 148(a)

Open-Ended Time Period

The following consent, authorizing a complaint under s. 148(a), was issued by the minister in *Northern Telecom:*[8]

> Pursuant to subsection 187(5) of the *Canada Labour Code,* I consent to a complaint being made to the Canada Labour Relations Board by the Complainant against the Respondent for an alleged violation of section 148 paragraph (a) of the *Canada Labour Code* in that notice to bargain collectively having been given by the Complainant to the Respondent on or about the 26th day of January, 1977, the Respondent refused, within twenty days of that date, and still refuses to meet and commence, or cause its authorized representatives on its behalf to meet and commence to bargain collectively in good faith and make every reasonable effort to enter into a collective agreement.

The words "and still refuses" have not been read by the Board as though they meant "and still refuses to this date", that is, the date on which the consent was granted by the minister so as to restrict the period in which a contravention could be found. In the above case that period commenced on January 26, 1977, and continued until the complaint was heard by the Board. In the particular circumstances of this case, the complaint, which was filed with ministerial consent on the day the latter was granted, was not heard by the Board until three and one-half years later. Seeking to avoid procedural objections, the union had obtained a

---

6   *North Canada Air Ltd.* (1981), 43 di 312, [1981] 2 Can LRBR 388; affd. (1983), 46 N.R. 422.

7   *CKLW Radio Broadcasting Ltd., supra,* note 1.

8   *Northern Telecom Canada Ltd.* (1980), 42 di 178, at 180, [1981] 1 Can LRBR 306.

second ministerial consent in 1979 to the same effect as the first one. The Board held that the second consent was strictly unnecessary and found that the employer had failed to meet and bargain as required by s. 148(a) throughout the period of 1977 to 1979.

Limited Time Period

By contrast, the minister issued the following consent in *Eastern Provincial Airways Ltd.*:[9]

> Pursuant to subsection 187(5) of the Canada Labour Code, I consent to a complaint being made to the Canada Labour Relations Board by the Complainant against the Respondent for an alleged violation of paragraph (a) of section 148 of the Canada Labour Code, in that on and after the 6th day of July, 1982, when the Complainant gave notice to the Respondent pursuant to subsection 147(1) of the Canada Labour Code to bargain collectively in order to revise their collective agreement and continuing to this date, the Respondent has failed to bargain collectively in good faith and make every reasonable effort to enter into a collective agreement.

The effect on the Board's jurisdiction of such a wording was discussed in *North Canada Air Ltd.*,[10] in which a similar consent had been granted by the minister. It read, in part, as follows:

> Pursuant to subsection 187(5) of the Canada Labour Code, I consent to a complaint being made to the Canada Labour Relations Board by the Complainant against the Respondent for an alleged violation of paragraphs (a) and (b) of section 148 of the Canada Labour Code, in that:
>
> (i) since on or about the 18th day of June, 1980 and continuing to this date the Respondents have failed to make every reasonable effort to enter into a collective agreement.

This consent had been granted on September 18, 1980. The Board held that, in his discretion, the minister had restricted the basis of the complaint under s. 148(a) to the period from June 18 to September 18, 1980, and therefore that a contravention could only be found, if at all, within that narrow period. However, in view of the continuous character of the duty to bargain in good faith, the Board may consider events that have occurred prior to and subsequent to the time period delineated by the ministerial consent and may inquire into the entire collective bargaining relationship in order to properly interpret and put in true perspective the events that have occurred within that period.[11]

---

9   *Eastern Provincial Airways Ltd.* (1983), 51 di 209, 3 CLRBR (NS) 75.
10   (1981), 43 di 312, at 315, [1981] 2 Can LRBR 388.
11   *North Canada Air Ltd. v. Canada Labour Relations Board* (1982), 46 N.R. 422, at 425, 117 D.L.R. (3d) 206 (Fed. C.A.).

15:1212   Complaints Under Section 148(b)

Open-Ended Time Period

As for consents granted in respect of complaints under s. 148(a), limited and open-ended time periods may be defined by the minister in consents authorizing complaints alleging a breach of the statutory freeze imposed by s. 148(b). An example of a consent with an open-ended time period in which such a contravention could be found is given in *North Canada Air Ltd.*[12] It read, in part, as follows:

> Pursuant to subsection 187(5) of the Canada Labour Code, I consent to a complaint being made to the Canada Labour Relations Board by the Complainant against the Respondent for an alleged violation of paragraphs (a) and (b) of section 148 of the Canada Labour Code in that: . . .
>
> (ii) after notice to commence bargaining had been given to the Respondents by the Complainants, the Respondents granted pay increases to their employees without the requirements of paragraphs 180(1)(a) to (d) having been met and without the consent of the Complainants having been obtained.

The time period here is open-ended, but the only alterations for which the consent is granted and which, accordingly, may be found to be in contravention of s. 148(b) are those related to pay increases. Illegal alterations that may have been made in that period to any other term and condition of employment could not be the object of a finding by the Board.

Limited Time Period

In *Canadian Imperial Bank of Commerce (Branches at Creston, B.C. and St. Catharines, Ont.)*[13] the following consent was granted:

> Pursuant to subsection 187(5) of the Canada Labour Code, I consent to a complaint being made to the Canada Labour Relations Board by the Complainant against the Respondent for an alleged violation of paragraphs (a) and (b) of section 148 of the Canada Labour Code, in that in or about the month of December 1978 the Respondents refused to make every reasonable effort to enter into a collective agreement and did alter the rates of pay for certain employees effective January 1st, 1979 without the requirements of paragraphs 180(1)(a) to (d) having been met.

Here, the consent to a complaint with respect to the alleged violation of s. 148(b) is restricted solely to the alteration of rates of pay of January 1, 1979. Of course, the Board may consider events subsequent to the alleged date of the alteration and will obviously consider events that have occurred prior to January 1, 1979, such as the compensation policy estab-

---

[12] *Supra*, note 6.
[13] *Supra*, note 5.

lished by the employer in previous months or years, or past practice, in order to determine whether the employer acted in accordance with the status quo, or "business as usual". However, the time period within which the Board may find a contravention of s. 148(b) is restricted to the single date of January 1, 1979, when the alteration was allegedly implemented.

By contrast, the consent issued in *La Banque Nationale du Canada*[14] defined the period within which a breach could be found in the following manner:

> Pursuant to subsection 187(5) of the Canada Labour Code, I consent to a complaint being made to the Canada Labour Relations Board by the Complainant concerning an alleged violation of paragraph (b) of section 148 of the Canada Labour Code by the Respondent who, during the week of August 4, 1980, or on or about this time, announced, after receiving from the Complainant the notice to commence collective bargaining, its intention to amalgamate its branch located at 1354 Maguire Street, Sillery, Quebec, which action would have the effect of reducing the personnel of the Maguire Street branch, without the requirements of paragraphs 180(1)(a) to (d) of the Canada Labour Code having been met and without the consent of the Complainant having been obtained.

The employer argued that the terms of the above consent related only to the amalgamation announcement, which the Bank had allegedly made during the week of August 4, 1980. The consent did not concern any other aspect, such as the actual closing of the Maguire Street branch or the lay-off of employees. In such circumstances, according to the employer, the Board was restricted to deciding whether the announcement of the amalgamation of the Maguire Street branch violated s. 148(b).

The Board held that an alteration of terms and conditions of employment contrary to the provisions of s. 148(b) is a continuing offence so long as, once the conditions have been altered after a notice to bargain has been sent, they are not thereafter restored. The offence continues in such circumstances until the terms and conditions are restored or, failing this, until the right to declare a strike or lockout is acquired. Thus the date referred to in the consent simply marked the point in time at which the Bank had allegedly begun to commit the offence. The Board held, furthermore, that it was entitled to consider the events following or preceding the week of August 4, 1980, insofar as they related, on the one hand, to the amalgamation of the branch and, on the other, to the alteration of terms and conditions of employment, if any, referred to in the consent (lay-off of personnel), which remained in effect subsequently. Accordingly, in this case the period within which a contravention of s. 148(b) could be found was not limited to the single week of August 4, 1980, but could extend to the date on which the right to declare a strike

---

14   *Supra*, note 3, at p. 356 (di).

or lockout was acquired by the parties. Thus, the only limit on the time period was that defined by the starting date of the offence.

15:1220   Restriction as to the Subject Matter

15:1221   Complaints Under Section 148(a)

The minister may also restrict the object of the Board's inquiry. His role under ss. 187(5) and 194 is not limited to granting or withholding his consent; he may give a modified consent. In a case where the latter had occurred and where there was a substantial lack of correspondence between the consent requested and that granted by the minister, the Board held that this did not constitute a mere defect in form or technical irregularity that it could cure under s. 203. As a result, the Board will not broaden its inquiry beyond the issues set by the minister. Accordingly, where the request to the minister sought a consent to file a complaint under s. 148(a) and the consent granted restricted the object of the Board's inquiry to an alleged failure to make every reasonable effort and excluded any inquiry into the good faith of the employer, the Board held that it was bound by the terms of the ministerial consent and restricted the object of its inquiry solely to this aspect of the duty imposed by s. 148(a).[15]

15:1222   Complaints Under Section 148(b)

The consents issued by the minister authorizing the filing of a complaint alleging a breach of s. 148(b) usually determine the particular term or condition of employment alleged to have been altered and restrict to this extent the object of the Board's inquiry. For instance, in *La Banque Nationale du Canada*[16] the consent authorized the union to file a complaint in respect of the amalgamation of the Maguire Street branch of the bank that would have the effect of reducing the personnel, but it did not include any other alterations such as modifications of the employees' wages or the reduction of their normal hours of work.

15:2000   TIMELINESS

The Code sets out two regimes for the timeliness of unfair labour practice complaints: the exceptional rule in s. 187(3) and (4) for complaints filed under s. 185(f) and (g), which has been dealt with previ-

---

[15]   The wording of this consent, issued in *North Canada Air Ltd.* (1981), 43 di 312, at 315, [1981] 2 Can LRBR 388, is reproduced at the text accompanying note 10.

[16]   (1981), 42 di 352, [1982] 3 Can LRBR 1. The wording of this consent is reproduced at the text accompanying note 14.

ously,[17] and a general regime provided in s. 187(2) for complaints under all the other sections referred to in s. 187(1)(a) and (b). The latter accordingly governs complaints under ss. 124(4), 148, 184, 185, and 186. It also governs complaints alleging a breach of the duty of fair representation in s. 136.1 and the duty of fair referral in s. 161.1 but, in view of the particularity of the Board's policy with respect to the timeliness of such complaints, these have been treated elsewhere.[18]

A complaint filed pursuant to s. 187(1) must fall within the ninety-day period prescribed by s. 187(2). The latter states that a complaint "shall be made to the Board not later than ninety days from the date on which the complainant knew, or in the opinion of the Board ought to have known of the action or circumstances giving rise to the complaint".

15:2100   ENLARGEMENT OF THE TIME LIMITS

The Board had always considered that it had the authority under s. 118(m) to enlarge the time limit prescribed in s. 187(2) in order to consider important and meritorious complaints.[19] The need for flexibility in this area clearly emerges when one considers the administrative difficulties involved in cases of complaints alleging a failure to bargain in good faith. These were described in *Giant Yellowknife Mines Ltd.*[20] in the following manner:

> Let us examine an alleged violation of the duty to bargain in good faith contrary to section 148. The complaining party may become aware of the violation but seek to alter the other party's attitude through private negotiations. This approach is contemplated in the collective bargaining regime. Failing this the party may seek ministerial consent. The presence of the consent requirement has its purpose. The Minister does not give his consent as a matter of form. If he did there would be no need to have this step before Board proceedings. The Minister through his office and the resources of his department seeks to mediate a resolution of the problem. Failing a satisfactory resolution, he may give his consent. Then the party may complain to the Board. It is not inconceivable, indeed it may the norm, that such a complaint would be untimely under section 187(2). In those circumstances, if the complaint were a nullity the provisions of section 187(2) would militate against encouraging co-operative labour-management resolution of differences. It would encourage parties to rush to the Minister rather than seek self resolution in the spirit of collective bargaining and it would unduly constrain the Minister because delay, no matter how much success appeared imminent, would serve the interest of the offending party.

---

17   See paragraph 13:3500.
18   See paragraphs 13:1190 and 13:1270 with respect to complaints alleging a breach of s. 136.1, and paragraph 13:2800 with respect to s. 161.1 complaints.
19   *Mike Sheehan* (1975), 9 di 29, [1975] 2 Can LRBR 55, 75 CLLC #16,161; *Giant Yellowknife Mines Ltd.* (1977), 19 di 147, [1977] 1 Can LRBR 483, 77 CLLC #16,082; *Air Canada* (1977), 24 di 203; *Bank of Nova Scotia (Vancouver Heights Branch)* (1978), 28 di 901, [1978] 2 Can LRBR 181; *La Société Radio-Canada* (1978), 31 di 144.
20   *Supra*, note 19.

These results were avoided by enlarging the ninety-day time limit pursuant to s. 118(m). In 1979, however, the Supreme Court of Canada in *Upper Lakes Shipping Ltd. v. Sheehan*,[21] disagreed with the Board's interpretation of its powers under s. 118(m). Laskin C.J.C., speaking for the majority of the court, concluded that that section did not empower the Board to alter a substantive provision of the statute prescribing a time limit for filing complaints:

> I read this provision as empowering the Board to abridge or enlarge the time for taking steps in a proceeding which is properly before it, as, for example, a certification proceeding. If, however, the issue is whether a proceeding is timely under the Board's governing statute, that is, whether the Board can lawfully entertain it at all in the light of section 187(2), I do not regard its powers under section 118(m) as entitling it to give latitude to a complainant who is out of time under the statute. The correlative would be that if it can enlarge it can abridge, and that would be absurd. A complainant is entitled to the advantage and is subject to the limitation of the ninety day period under s. 187(2). It can neither be restricted to a lesser period by any direction of the Baord nor be allowed a greater period.[22]

15:2200   TWO-STEP PROCESS IN CALCULATING THE LIMITATION PERIOD

The Board followed the judgment of the Supreme Court of Canada and declared in subsequent decisions[23] that it did not have the authority to enlarge the time limit set out in s. 187(2) pursuant to s. 118(m) nor, even, pursuant to s. 121. Nonetheless, the Board may achieve some flexibility in the exercise of its discretion under s. 187(2) allowing it to determine when the complainant "ought to have known of the action or circumstances giving rise to the complaint". That section contemplates a two-step process. One must first determine when the action or circumstances giving rise to the complaint occurred. Then one must determine when the complainant became aware of the action. The ninety-day period starts to run when, "in the opinion of the Board", the complainant ought to have become aware of the action or of the elements comprising the alleged unfair labour practice.

The application of this formula is simple enough when the date on which the complainant became aware of the action complained of coincides with the date of implementation. For instance, in *Air Canada*,[24] where a complainant alleged that he had been suspended by his employer for five days without pay in contravention of s. 184(3)(a)(i), the Board held

---

[21] [1979] 1 S.C.R. 902, 25 N.R. 149, 79 CLLC #14,192; revg. [1978] 1 F.C. 836, 19 N.R. 456, 77 CLLC #14,111, 81 D.L.R. (3d) 208; revg. *Mike Sheehan* (1976), 17 di 14, [1976] 2 Can LRBR 187, 76 CLLC #16,030.

[22] *Ibid.*, at p. 915 (S.C.R.).

[23] *Ralph Gordon Chatwin* (1979), 34 di 707, [1979] 1 Can LRBR 481, 79 CLLC #16,176.

[24] (1975), 11 di 5, [1975] 2 Can LRBR 193, 75 CLLC #16,164; see, however, *William Gallivan* (1981), 45 di 180, [1982] 1 Can LRBR 241.

that the decision of the employer to suspend the complainant without pay constituted the action or circumstances giving rise to the complaint. The ninety-day period began to run when the complainant was informed of the decision by letter. The complaint, having been filed more than ninety days from the date on which the complainant was informed of the decision, was held to be untimely.

Where, however, the date on which the complainant acquires the requisite knowledge of the action does not coincide with the date of its implementation, the starting point for the calculation of the ninety-day period may be determined by taking into consideration the context in which the particular unfair labour practice has been committed. This is one situation where the Board may use its discretion to determine when the complainant "ought to have known" of "the action or circumstances giving rise to the complaint" so as to achieve some flexibility. For example, in *Société Radio-Canada*[25] the date on which a complainant was informed, in the midst of a union organizing campaign, that his individual contract of employment set to expire some two weeks later would not be renewed was held to be the date on which the ninety-day period began to run. The date of the expiration of the contract two weeks later or, in other words, the date of the actual non-renewal of the contract, was not accepted as the starting point for the calculation of the time limit.

An examination of the purpose behind the unfair labour practice provision of the Code invoked by the complainant in that case sheds some light on the rationale of the decision of the Board.[26] The complainant alleged a dismissal for union activities contrary to s. 184(3)(a)(i) committed within the context of a union organizing campaign. The Code protects an employee's right to join and participate in the lawful activities of a trade union without fear of being disciplined or discriminated against as a consequence. Thus the Code prohibits the employer from using a decision not to rehire someone as a tactic in an anti-union campaign. The non-renewal of an employee's contract may affect other employees. Fearing for their jobs, they may be discouraged from joining the union. Although the Code is aimed at the decision to discipline as well as to its implementation or, as in this case, the expiration of the contract, the Board took the view that in the context of an organizing campaign, the decision to discipline is the action that may improperly influence the employees and may thus have a chilling effect on the union drive.[27] Consequently, in this case the decision not to rehire — as opposed to its implementation — was held to be the circumstances giving rise to the

---

[25]   (1978), 31 di 144.

[26]   This is the argument made by Carl Peterson, "Timeliness of Unfair Labour Practice Complaints Under the Canada Labour Code" (1982), 14 *Ottawa Law Review* 100, at 110.

[27]   *Ibid.* Peterson points out that the fact that the employer may later change his mind before the actual expiration of the contract does not lessen the potential impact of the original decision not to rehire upon the organizing drive.

complaint, and the date on which the complainant was so informed marked the starting point for the calculation of the limitation period.

By contrast, in another *Air Canada* case,[28] during the negotiations for the renewal of a collective agreement, the employer announced, on March 14, 1977, his plan, effective May 1, 1977, to terminate a first-class travel privilege enjoyed by pilots and officers when deadheading to or from flight duty prior to the statutory freeze of working conditions. The union became aware of this decision of March 28 of that year. It objected to the change in policy and requested ministerial consent pursuant to s. 187(5) to complain under s. 148(b). The latter was granted on June 16, but the complaint was not filed with the Board until July 11. Viewed from another angle, the dates revealed that the ministerial consent had not been granted until more than ninety days after the announcement of the termination of the privilege, but it had been granted before ninety days had elapsed from the date of implementation of the policy.

In view of the purpose of the statutory freeze imposed by s. 148(b), which is to enforce the exclusive authority of the bargaining agent, the employer's decision to change its policy appeared to constitute the action giving rise to the complaint. It was the unilateral decision to alter the privilege of the pilots that undermined the exclusivity of the union's bargaining authority. If, however, the limitation period had been calculated from the date on which the union became aware of the employer's decision, the complaint would have been untimely.

The Board resolved the matter by determining that the earliest date on which the union could have known of the action giving rise to the complaint was May 1, 1977, the date of implementation of the change. Until that date, in the Board's opinion, the union could not have known whether the employer would carry out its proposal or be deterred by the union's refusal to grant its consent under s. 148(b). Thus, although the employer's decision to change his policy constituted the action and the union became aware of it on March 28, the Board exercised its discretion to determine when the complainant ought to have known of it so as to achieve the flexibility required in the administration of the duty imposed by s. 148(b).[29]

---

[28]   (1977), 24 di 203.

[29]   The basis of this decision has been explained by Peterson, *supra*, note 26, at p. 112, by reference to the context within which the unfair practice had allegedly been committed: "Given the context, this conclusion makes sense. During the negotiation stances will be taken and harsh tactics will be employed to force the other party to settle. From this perspective, Air Canada's announcement could have been perceived by the union as just another ploy during hard bargaining. The union counter-punched, so to speak, by requesting Ministerial consent. In addition, the CLRB in exercising its discretion in this way is not discouraging private resolution of disputes. The Board is attempting to give the parties more time to settle their disputes privately and, in the process, alleviate the administrative difficulties outlined in *Giant Yellowknife Mines Ltd.*"

In conclusion, in calculating the time period one must determine the constituent elements of the action and ascertain when the complainant knew or ought to have known of the action within the context of the particular alleged unfair labour practice.

15:2300   SIMILAR REPEATED VIOLATIONS AND CONTINUING OFFENCES

15:2310   Refusal to Hire [Section 184(3)(a)], Denial of Membership [Section 185(f)], and Union Discipline [Section 185(g)]

In calculating the time period for filing an unfair labour practice complaint, the distinction between similar repeated violations and continuing offences must be kept in mind. The Board dealt with this question in *Mike Sheehan*,[30] where it dismissed as untimely a complaint alleging an improper refusal to hire for a reason other than the failure to pay union dues contrary to s. 184(3)(a)(ii).

The Board concluded that as between an employer and a person, unlike a dismissal, a refusal to hire is not necessarily a single event taking place at a definite moment in time. There is, indeed, an obvious distinction between a refusal to hire and a dismissal. Legally, the dismissal terminates the employer-employee relationship and, as such, it can occur only once and at a point in time that is normally easily ascertainable. Of course, if the employer-employee relationship is found not to have been terminated or is later re-established, a new dismissal can later take place, and it will be a distinct event that may give rise to a new complaint. A dismissal or the imposition of discipline on an employee by an employer in contravention of the Code is closely akin to the taking of disciplinary action against or the imposition of a penalty on an employee by a union in contravention of s. 185(g). Such incidents are, by definition, single incidents taking place at a definite moment in time. Therefore, a complaint alleging such wrongful dismissals or discipline filed more than ninety days from the date on which the complainant knew, or in the opinion of the Board ought to have known, of the action or circumstances giving rise to the complaint will be dismissed as untimely.[31]

A refusal to hire, however, can be renewed many times. In this connection it must be noted that one rebuff or a succession of rebuffs does not make subsequent complaints timely by the mere fact of their being filed within ninety days of the latest rebuff. Indeed, the limitation period runs against a refusal to employ where the latter occurred more

---

[30]   (1975), 9 di 29, [1975] 2 Can LRBR 55, 75 CLLC #16,161.
[31]   *Ibid.*

than ninety days before a complaint is made in respect of a subsequent refusal based on the same circumstances.[32] In other words, when a complaint alleging a refusal to hire is not made within the required limit of ninety days from the date on which the complainant became aware of the refusal and no change in circumstances can be shown to have occurred between the original and subsequent renewed refusals, the Board will consider the complaint as untimely.[33] One set of circumstances cannot, by multiplying requests followed by refusals, give rise to a continuous unfair practice. The same rationale also applies to a complaint alleging a denial of membership by a union in contravention of s. 185(f).[34]

On the other hand, successive refusals to hire or denials of membership caused by different prohibited considerations or based on different discriminatory grounds can give rise to more than one violation of the provisions of the Code, giving rise, in turn, to different complaints. In such a case, a complaint filed within ninety days from the date on which the complainant became aware of the latest refusal or denial will be timely.[35]

15:2320　Employer Financial Contributions [Section 184(1)(b)] and Duty to Bargain in Good Faith [Section 148(a)]

Where the purpose of a duty or a prohibition imposed by the Code is of general public interest, a failure to comply has been held by the Board

---

32　*Mike Sheehan* (1976), 17 di 14, [1976] 2 Can LRBR 187, 76 CLLC #16,030; affd. (*sub nom. Upper Lakes Shipping Ltd. v. Sheehan*) [1979] 1 S.C.R. 902, 25 N.R. 149, 79 CLLC #14,192, 95 D.L.R. (3d) 25; revg. [1978] 1 F.C. 836, 19 N.R. 456, 77 CLLC #14,111, 81 D.L.R. (3d) 208 (C.A.).

33　*Mike Sheehan* (1979), 34 di 726, [1979] 1 Can LRBR 531.

34　*Mike Sheehan, supra,* note 30; *Mike Sheehan, supra,* note 33.

35　*Mike Sheehan, supra,* note 30. The problem with this approach is well expressed in *Mike Sheehan, supra,* note 33, at pp. 747, 749: "Suppose an employer in a seasonal business in our jurisdiction (such as employment in the Territories or maritimes industries) makes a blanket decision not to employ a person because he is a union member. If that person does not complain within ninety days of his knowledge of that reason for the refusal to employ he is precluded from complaining about any subsequent refusal in later years. . . . A denial of union membership can be more serious than a refusal to employ. There may be other employers, but there may not be other unions, even other local unions. In some industries it is common to find one union and only one union representing particular tradesmen or types of employees. The result is that, for example, if a new immigrant to Canada seeks membership in a union that represents people with his skill or trade and it denies him membership because of his ancestry he has only one ninety day period within which he can complain. If he misses that period because of his ignorance of Canadian law and institutions the union can continue to discriminate so long as the circumstances do not change." The Board expressed the opinion, however, that where such blanket decisions are made by a union or an employer, the intervention of a new ground prohibited by the Code upon which a subsequent refusal or denial is based could constitute a changed or new set of circumstances.

to give rise to a continuing offence. Even with no change of circumstances between the original and subsequent contraventions, repeated violations will give rise to different complaints and each will start the limitation period anew.

For example, s. 184(1)(b) prohibits an employer from contributing financial or other support to a trade union. If such financial support is given on a monthly basis, it would be absurd, the Board has held,[36] to interpret the provisions of s. 187(2) to mean that if a complaint is not filed ninety days after the first payment is made, a complaint cannot be filed later. In such a case it is more consistent with the wording and intent of the Code to find that a complaint can be timely provided that it is filed within ninety days of the date on which the complainant became aware of the latest payment. Each payment would amount to a new violation of the provisions of s. 184(1)(b) and could lead to the filing of a new complaint in accordance with the provisions of s. 187(2).

A refusal to bargain and bargaining in bad faith contrary to s. 148(a) can also constitute continuing offences. The duty imposed by s. 148(a) is continuous from the time when notice to bargain is given until a final resolution of an agreement.[37] It follows that a refusal to bargain, which can be repeated many times, will give rise to different complaints. If a complaint is filed within ninety days of the date on which the bargaining agent became aware of the latest refusal, it will be timely even if more than ninety days have elapsed since the previous or the original refusal to bargain.

It must be kept in mind, however, that a complaint under s. 148 is subject to the requirement of ministerial consent provided in s. 187(5). Since the Board does not have the power to enlarge the time limits prescribed by s. 187(2), a complainant would be well advised not to follow the course outlined in *Giant Yellowknife Mines Ltd.*[38] and to file the complaint within the limitation period even if the consent has not yet been granted. This would constitute a simple technical irregularity curable by the Board under s. 203 of the Code and s. 6 of its regulations. If a party has followed the course outlined in the decision above and the consent is granted on the eve of the expiration of the limitation period, a copy of the consent may be filed with the Board as a last-minute recourse to be treated without further formality as the complaint. This procedure may prevent a meritorious complaint from being dismissed as out of time.[39]

---

[36]   *Mike Sheehan* (1975), 9 di 29, [1975] 2 Can LRBR 55, 75 CLLC #16,161.

[37]   *CKLW Radio Broadcasting Ltd.* (1977), 23 di 51, 77 CLLC #16,110; *Allan Martin* (1979), 37 di 50, [1979] 3 can LRBR 184, 80 CLLC #16,004; *Austin Airways Ltd. / White River Air Services Ltd.* (1980), 41 di 151, [1980] 3 Can LRBR 393; *Northern Telecom Canada Ltd.* (1980), 42 di 178, [1981] 1 Can LRBR 306; *General Aviation Services Ltd.* (1982), 51 di 71, [1982] 3 Can LRBR 47, 82 CLLC #16,177.

[38]   *Supra,* note 19.

[39]   This method was accepted by the Board in *Northern Telecom Canada Ltd., supra,* note 37.

15:3000   **DRAFTING AND FILING THE**
                          COMPLAINT

15:3100   FORM AND CONTENT OF THE
             COMPLAINT

The complaint must be in writing[40] and must state:

(a) the full name and address of the complainant;

(b) the full name and address of the person who is alleged to have failed to comply with a subsection or section of the Code;

(c) the particular provisions of the subsection or section of the Code that are alleged to have been violated;

(d) the whole name and address of the person alleged to have been prejudicially affected;

(e) a statement of the facts and circumstances on which the complainant relies in support of the complaint;

(f) a statement of the order sought from the Board;

(g) where a failure to comply with paragraphs 185(f) or (g) of the Code is alleged, details of the facts on which the complainant relies in claiming that the conditions set out in subsection 187(3) of the Code have been met;

(h) the date on which the complainant knew of the action or circumstances giving rise to the complaint; and

(i) where a collective agreement was in effect at the time of the incidents giving rise to the complaint, full particulars of the attempts, if any, made to have the complaint submitted to arbitration under the collective agreement.[41]

Furthermore, when the consent of the minister is required under s. 187(5), a copy of the authorization must be filed,[42] but this requirement must be read in the light of the Board's practice, canvassed above.[43]

The purpose of s. 35(1) of the *Canada Labour Relations Board Regulations* is to provide information concerning the basis of the complaint to the Board and the respondent, but the requirements set out therein have not been interpreted in a formalistic or strict manner.[44] By way of illustration, the Board ruled in one case[45] that where a complaint filed by employees dismissed for participating in union activities alleged that their employer had "violated section 184(1) et seq. of the Code", the complainants intended to invoke both subss. (1) and (3) of s. 184 and that, accordingly, the employer's objection to having to lead evidence first could not be upheld in view of the reverse onus provisions of s. 188(3). On

---

40   *Canada Labour Code*, s. 187(1), and *Canada Labour Relations Board Regulations*, S.O.R./78-499, s. 4.

41   Regulations, s. 35(1).

42   Regulations, s. 35(2).

43   See paragraph 15:1100.

44   *Mike Sheehan*, *supra*, note 36.

45   *Banque Royale du Canada (Jonquière et Kénogami)* (1980), 42 di 125.

the same question, the Board has also ruled[46] that an error in the designation of a vessel to which the union sought access pursuant to s. 199 of the Code was no more than a minor point curable under s. 203 of the Code and s. 6 of the regulations, and that it did not affect the application.

Where, however, a complaint did not disclose the facts or circumstances upon which it was based, the Board granted the employer's preliminary motion and dismissed the complaint on the grounds that it failed to comply with the spirit and the letter of s. 35(1)(e) of the regulations.[47] By contrast, it has been determined that a complaint that does not specify the remedy sought as required by s. 35(1)(f) of the regulations is not invalid, since the Board can remedy the violation of the Code pursuant to the broad powers given it by s. 189.[48]

If the complaint is filed on behalf of a trade union, an association of trade unions, or an association of employers,[49] it must be signed by the secretary or president of the organization or by two of its other officers or by a person authorized in writing to sign on behalf of the organization. If it is filed on behalf of an employer,[50] it must be signed by the employer himself, the general manager, the principal chief executive officer, or by a person authorized in writing to do so. When the complaint is filed on behalf of an employee,[51] it must be signed by the employee himself or by a person authorized to do so in writing by him. If a person is acting on behalf of a trade union, an employer, or an employee, a copy of the authorization must be filed with the Board.[52]

On a number of occasions, respondents have raised preliminary objections alleging that the person acting on behalf of the complainant had not obtained his authorization or if he had, the latter had not been filed with the Board. The Board has treated these objections as a matter of form and has consistently refused to invalidate the complaint on such a basis.[53]

---

[46]   *Dome Petroleum Ltd.* (1978), 31 di 189, [1978] 2 Can LRBR 518, 78 CLLC #16,153, 79 CLLC #16,192.

[47]   *Bank of Nova Scotia (Vancouver Heights Branch)* (1978), 28 di 901, [1978] 2 Can LRBR 181. See also *Murray Bay Marine Terminal Inc.* (1981), 46 di 55, where the Board refused to make a finding against the employer in respect of facts that had not been alleged in the complaint.

[48]   *Maclean-Hunter Cable TV Ltd.* (1979), 34 di 752, [1979] 2 Can LRBR 1.

[49]   *Canada Labour Relations Board Regulations*, s. 9(1)(a).

[50]   Section 9(1)(b).

[51]   Section 9(1)(c).

[53]   In *Canadian Imperial Bank of Commerce (Branches at Creston, B.C. and St. Catharines, Ont.)* (1979), 35 di 105, [1980] 1 Can LRBR 307, 80 CLLC #16,002, the Board said that one of the primary objectives of s. 9 of the regulations was to ensure that persons, corporations, or organizations implicated in applications are aware of their contents. It ensures the *"bona fides"* of the application. The Board thus dismissed a preliminary objection to the effect that the complaints had not been signed on behalf of the various local unions. The Board ruled, in that case, that where counsel and a qualified representative were responsible for the filing, the purpose of the regulations had been served and its requirements met.

In *A & M Transport Ltd.* (1983), 52 di 69, the Board said the purpose of s. 9 of the

15:3200 FILING THE COMPLAINT WITH THE BOARD

The properly completed complaint must be filed with the Board by addressing it by mail or delivering it by hand to the Board's head office in Ottawa or to one of its regional offices.[54] If it is not delivered by hand, it is preferable to use registered mail so that the complaint may be deemed to have been filed on the date it was registered. If the complaint is sent by regular mail, the date it is received by the Board will be considered as the date of filing.[55] This may be important, given that complaints of unfair labour practices must be filed within specified delays[56] and that failure to do so may result in the dismissal of the complaint.

15:3300 REPLY TO THE COMPLAINT

A person against whom a complaint is made must file his reply within five days of receipt of the copy of the complaint sent by the Board registrar.[57] If for some reason a person cannot reply within the five days, he may require an extension from the Board. The reply must contain:

(a) the full name and address of the person replying;

(b) an admission or denial of each of the statements made in the complaint; and

(c) a statement of the grounds and facts relied on in reply to the complaint.[58]

---

regulations was to ensure that the complaints filed with the Board are screened for genuineness by requiring those who are in fact the direct subjects of such complaints to provide written authorizations for them if they do not actually file them themselves. Section 9 is intended to minimize the possibility of frivolous complaints, but not to make it difficult for prejudicially affected persons to obtain industrial relations justice. Section 9 of the regulations does not say precisely when the requisite authorization for a complaint submitted on behalf of a complainant must be filed. It does not say that the authorization must come into the Board's hands before the application or complaint is filed, nor that it must accompany the application or complaint or that it must somehow be filed at the same moment as the application or complaint. Thus, the Board stated that it may permit a period of time to elapse between the actual filing of the complaint and the subsequent filing of the complainant's authorization. That this period time might extend beyond the ninety days mentioned in Code s. 187(2) does not make the complaint itself untimely if the complaint was filed within the ninety days. The Board's decision was upheld by the Federal Court of Appeal in an unreported decision, July 27, 1983, file no. A-1129-83, where the court held that, by virtue of s. 203 of the Code and s. 6 of the regulations, a lack of written authorization is no more than a defect in form or a technical irregularity that does not render the proceeding void or deprive the Board of its jurisdiction to entertain the complaint. On the same subject, see also *Ronald Wheadon* (1983), 54 di 134, 5 CLRBR (NS) 192, 84 CLLC #16,004.

54 *Canada Labour Relations Board Regulations*, s. 11. See Appendix 1 for a list of the Board's head offices and regional centres' addresses.

55 Regulations, s. 8(1).

56 *Canada Labour Code*, s. 187(2), (3), and (4). See paragraph 15:2000.

57 Regulations, s. 36(1).

58 Section 36(2).

A respondent wishing to raise preliminary objections would be well advised to raise them in his reply, rather than at the hearing, as the Board does not easily grant postponements[59] unless there is a compelling reason to do so and serious prejudice would result from denying the adjournment. The Board may dismiss the objection on grounds of tardiness.[60]

15:4000   PROCESSING THE COMPLAINT

15:4100   BY THE INVESTIGATING OFFICER

When a complaint has been filed with the Board it is assigned to an investigating officer, whose mandate is to meet with the parties involved and seek a settlement.[61] The discussions between the investigating officer and the parties are confidential and are not divulged to Board members.[62] On this issue, the Board refuses to deal with allegations that a complaint has been settled where the settlement has not been confined to writing and the testimony of the Board's investigating officer would be required to establish whether the parties have, in fact, reached a settlement.[63] If no written settlement is reached, the officer files a report to the Board, with a copy to the parties, stating that no settlement was reached.

15:4200   BY THE BOARD

When no written settlement is reached, the file is referred to a panel of the Board.

---

[59]   The Board's attitude in this regard is dictated by the fact that it must travel to the place of the hearing and sit as a three-member panel. To organize another hearing is costly and administratively difficult, as suitable dates must be found to accommodate the members who may already be scheduled months in advance on other cases. This, in turn, causes delays which may result in a denial of justice for the parties involved.

[60]   This is particularly true of last-minute motions for details.

[61]   The mediative involvement of the investigating officer is rooted in the provisions of s. 188(1)(a) of the Code. The officers exercise the powers provided by s. 118(k) under the authorization of the Board. The Board is not obliged to designate an investigating officer. See *Bank of British Columbia* (1983), 52 di 98.

[62]   The information gathered by the investigating officer is privileged, because by virtue of Code s. 208 he is not a compellable witness. In *A.J. (Archie) Goodale Ltd.* (1977), 21 di 473, [1977] 2 Can LRBR 309, the Board determined that, in the course of a hearing on an unfair labour practice charge, it would not allow evidence of conversations held between its investigating officer and an employer with respect to the settlement of the complaint. Accepting evidence of conversations associated with settlement efforts would seriously undermine the ability of the Board through its officers to perform its wider mandate for the constructive settlement of disputes. If statements made to officers of the Board could be the subject of testimony before the Board, the officers would not enjoy the frank and full discussions that are necessary for the successful settlement of complaints. Section 208 is a legislative recognition of the necessity of confidentiality in labour relations matters. That acceptance reflects the well-known fact that if the intermediary does not have the confidence of both parties, he cannot effectively perform his role. See *Bank of British Columbia, supra,* note 61.

[63]   *Bank of Montreal (Carrall and Hastings Street Branch)* (1980), 39 di 122.

15:4210   Hearing

As a general rule, if the complaint is not settled the Board will dispose of it after a formal hearing.[64] A hearing date is fixed by the Board, and the parties are notified of the time and location. The Board will give at least ten days' notice of the hearing, although it may abridge that delay in exceptional circumstances.[65]

15:4220   Exceptions to the Rule

There are three exceptions to the general rule, where the Board will dispose of an unfair labour practice complaint without a hearing. These are outlined below.

15:4221   Referral to Arbitration Pursuant to Section 188(2)

The Board may refuse to hear and determine a complaint if it is of the opinion that the matter should be referred to arbitration pursuant to its powers under s. 188(2).[66] In *Bell Canada*[67] the Board identified five factors that it would examine to determine whether it should exercise its discretion to refer a matter to arbitration. First, the board verifies the existence of a collective agreement. Second, the Board considers the presence or absence in the collective agreement of concrete provisions concerning anti-union discrimination. Third, the Board examines the actual text of the grievance procedure, the universality of its application to employees, and the possibility of filing a grievance for a violation of an anti-union discrimination provision. Fourth, the Board examines the connection that exists between the grievance procedure and the arbitration procedure itself, that is, the possibility of a grievance reaching arbitration. Some collective agreements limit the number and type of disputes that may be referred from grievance to arbitration. Fifth, the jurisdiction of the arbitrator must be examined. Some collective agreements limit his power to grant redress. If the Board is satisfied that each of the above factors are met, it is likely that it will exercise its discretion pursuant to s. 188(2) of the Code and refer the matter to arbitration.

---

[64] *Canada Labour Code*, s. 188(b).
[65] *Canada Labour Relations Board Regulations*, s. 20.
[66] See *Air Canada* (1975), 11 di 5, [1975] 2 Can LRBR 193, 75 CLLC #16,164, where the Board explained its policy under s. 188(2). In that case the Board refused to adjudicate a complaint because it was of the opinion that the matter should have been dealt with through the grievance procedure. The Board decided that the decision of the trade union not to refer the grievance to arbitration was not a reason for the Board to intervene.
[67] (1977), 20 di 356, [1978] 1 Can LRBR 1, 78 CLLC #16,126. See also, on the same subject, *Bank of Montreal (Devonshire Mall Branch, Windsor)* (1982), 51 di 160, 83 CLLC #16,015; and *Loomis Armored Car Service* (1983), 51 di 185. In these three cases, the Board refused to defer the matter to arbitration.

In conclusion, it is not sufficient to plead the existence of a collective agreement or that of a grievance clause, an arbitration procedure, or an arbitration decision to persuade the Board to exercise its discretion to refer complaints of unfair practice to arbitration. Even if all the factors listed above are present, the Board will still analyse the case to determine whether the concern raised in the complaint can be dealt with effectively in arbitration. For instance, in *Canada Post Corp.*[68] the union had filed three policy grievances and two thousand individual grievances in relation to the employer's decision to alter the rotation of days off during the Christmas period of 1982. In addition, the union had filed various complaints before the Board alleging the violation of many sections of the Code. The Board found that the complaints were based on the same facts and were aimed at obtaining the same remedies as those sought in the grievances. It therefore refused to hear the matters referred to in the complaints.

15:4222   Denial of a Public Hearing

Since the enactment of Bill C-34 in June 1984, the Board may dispose of complaints alleging a violation of ss. 136.1 (duty of fair representation) and 161.1 (duty of fair referral) without a hearing as provided for by s. 188(1.1).

15:4223   Consent of the Parties to Dispense With a Formal Hearing

Where a statement of facts agreed to by the parties and written argument had been filed with the Board, the complaints were disposed of without a hearing. Thus, where the parties so agree, the Board may dispense with hearings in unfair labour practice complaints.[69]

15:5000   PROCEDURE AND EVIDENCE AT THE HEARING

15:5100   PRE-HEARING MEETING

The Board's practice is to call the parties to a pre-hearing meeting held immediately before the commencement of the hearing. At this meeting, the Board will discuss procedural matters such as preliminary objections and the manner in which it intends to deal with the issues during the hearing, the duration of the session, and the administration of the evidence. The three questions most often dealt with are those related to (i) preliminary objections to the Board's jurisdictions; (ii) which party

---

[68]   (1983), 52 di 106, 83 CLLC #16,047.
[69]   *Bell Canada* (1981), 42 di 298, [1981] 2 Can LRBR 148, 81 CLLC #16,083. A similar procedure was followed in *Air Canada* (1977), 24 di 203.

bears the onus and has to lead evidence first; and (iii) verbal amendments presented at the last minute. These are discussed below.

15:5110   Preliminary Objections

Although preliminary objections must be raised in writing by way of reply,[70] they are sometimes not submitted until the hearing. At the pre-hearing meeting, however, the Board requires the parties to identify all preliminary issues they intend to raise and the grounds therefor. The Board may then provide directions as to whether the objections must be argued orally or in writing, and at what stage of the hearing they must be raised. Frequently, if the objections are argued orally, a general outline will be required at the outset, followed by full argument at the conclusion of the hearing.

As a general rule, regardless of whether an objection goes to its statutory or constitutional jurisdiction, the Board will take it under advisement and proceed to hear evidence on the merits of the application.[71] However, in exceptional cases[72] where a review of the file had produced serious doubts about the Board's constitutional competence, the parties were notified that the hearing would be confined solely to this question in order to avoid unnecessary expenses and inconvenience to witnesses summoned from across Canada, should the objection be sustained.

Save for these few cases, the Board will not usually make interlocutory decisions and will not delay hearing evidence on the merits of the application or complaint. Where the latter involves charges of unfair labour practices and no bargaining certificate has yet been issued by either the federal or a provincial board, the Board will normally deal, in its reasons for decision, with the constitutional issue before addressing the merit of the complaint.[73] By contrast, where the union has previously been certified in the federal jurisdiction, the Board will not discuss the merit of a preliminary objection concerning its constitutional jurisdiction in its reasons for decision, but will address the merits of the unfair labour practice complaint. The Board takes the view that it would be destructive to question the validity of an existing bargaining certificate and collective agreement in this manner.[74] The Code provides for this at more appro-

---

[70]   Regulations, s. 36(2).
[71]   The rationale for this Board practice is explained in *Purolator Courier Ltd.* (1982), 48 di 32. In short, it is based on operational and hearing practices considerations.
[72]   *Ed Finn* (1982), 47 di 49, [1982] 1 Can LRBR 399, 82 CLLC #16,155.
[73]   *Scotian Shelf Traders Ltd.* (1983), 52 di 151, 4 CLRBR (NS) 278, 83 CLLC #16,070. At the hearing, as in all cases requiring a constitutional characterization of an enterprise, the employer will be required to lead evidence on this question before the complainant, since it has better knowledge of the facts relating to the proper classification of the enterprise.
[74]   *Services Ménagers Roy Ltée* (1981), 43 di 212.

priate times in order not to disrupt a situation that has been stabilized by a collective agreement.

Conversely, where a union has been certified under provincial legislation and an application or a complaint with respect to the same employer is lodged before both the provincial and federal boards, the Board will address the constitutional question at the outset of its reasons for decision. The Board has no discretion to refuse to decide a constitutional issue for the sole reason that a provincial board has previously asserted jurisdiction over the employer's operations and that sound labour relations would be negatively affected if it were to conclude that the enterprise comes under federal jurisdiction.[75] Thus, in cases where the operations of the employer fall clearly within the provincial jurisdiction and a complaint has been filed in both jurisdictions, the policy of the Board is to limit its reasons for decision to the constitutional question. The matter may then be dismissed on the threshold constitutional issue and referred to the provincial board for a judgment on the merits.[76]

It should also be remembered that objections to the jurisdiction of the Board to proceed to hear a complaint based on the existence of a voluntary settlement will be dismissed unless a written settlement accepted by both parties is produced.[77]

15:5120   Object of the Evidence

In Canada, the remedy for unfair labour practices in the past has been by way of a prosecution before the common-law courts. In this forum motive, characterized as anti-union animus, was considered an essential element of many unfair labour practices. The Board reconsidered this approach after the Code was amended in June 1978. As a result of these amendments, the labour relations process was decriminalized to the extent that the Board became the single agency with remedial authority on the federal scene. It was vested with wide discretionary remedial authority under s. 189 and given a clear legislative mandate to exercise this authority so as to further the objectives of the Code, and not primarily to punish.

15:5121   Practices Concerned with Effects

In the context described above, the Board held that many unfair practices no longer required evidence of a prohibited motive as an essential element of a contravention. For instance, the prohibitions of ss. 124(4) and 148(b) dealing with statutory freezes of terms and conditions of employment have as their primary focus the objectives they seek

---

75   *Seafarers International Union of Canada v. Crosbie Offshore Services Ltd.*, [1982] 2 F.C. 855, 82 CLLC #14,180, 135 D.L.R. (3d) 485 (C.A.).
76   *Baron W. Lewers* (1982), 48 di 83, 82 CLLC #16,179.
77   *Bank of Montreal (Carrall and Hastings Street Branch), supra*, note 63.

to achieve rather than the employer's motive.[78] Sections 136.1 and 161.1 are similar.[79] Nor is there any need to prove motive to establish a violation of s. 185(d). The act itself is prohibited because of the effect it may have on the employer's right to manage his enterprise and control his work force without disruption from employees engaged in an organizing campaign.[80] Effect as a more important factor than motive is also reflected in s. 184(3)(b).[81]

With respect to s. 184(1)(a), the Board hesitated for a while[82] and eventually adopted the American test, according to which if it can reasonably be concluded that the employer's discriminatory conduct was inherently destructive of important employee rights, no proof of anti-union motivation is needed.[83] The trend in favour of this approach culminated in a subsequent decision in which the Board affirmed without reservation that motive was not a necessary ingredient of a contravention of s. 184(1)(a).[84]

Among unfair labour practices concerned more with effects than with the employer's motives, there are those that require a delicate balancing of legitimate union, employee, and employer interests in any given case to determine whether or not a breach has been committed. Section 184(1)(a) falls into this category.[85] Because motive is not an essential element of a contravention of that section, a practice prohibited by the latter consists of otherwise lawful activities that become unlawful because of their effects or consequences on employee rights. To measure such effects the Board balances, on the one hand, business justification or legitimate reasons for the employer's conduct, and on the other, the individual employee's or the union's right to pursue freedoms under the Code. These are assessed in the realistic light of the adversarial economic conflict of collective bargaining.[86] In cases where the balance is equal, motive becomes the determining factor.[87]

---

78   *Bank of Nova Scotia (Vancouver Heights Branch)* (1978), 28 di 901, [1978] 2 Can LRBR 181; *Canadian Imperial Bank of Commerce (North Hills Shopping Centre)* (1979), 34 di 651, [1979] 1 Can LRBR 266, 80 CLLC #16,001; *Canadian Imperial Bank of Commerce (Branches at Creston, B.C. and St. Catharines, Ont.)* (1979), 35 di 105, [1980] 1 Can LRBR 307, 80 CLLC #16,002; *Banque Nationale du Canada* (1981), 42 di 352, [1982] 2 Can LRBR 1.

79   *Canadian Imperial Bank of Commerce (North Hills Shopping Centre), supra,* note 78.

80   *Ibid.*

81   *Ibid.*

82   See *Bank of Nova Scotia (Vancouver Heights Branch), supra,* note 78, where a Board member, J. Archambault, wrote in a dissenting opinion that motive in the form of anti-union animus had no application in the context of s. 184(1)(a) complaints, and see the comments his opinion prompted in *Canadian Imperial Bank of Commerce (North Hills Shopping Centre), supra,* note 78, which expanded further on this subject.

83   *Banque Canadienne Nationale (Montréal)* (1979), 35 di 39, [1980] 1 Can LRBR 470.

84   See *Wardair Canada (1975) Ltd.* (1983), 53 di 26, 2 CLRBR (NS) 129, and decisions cited therein.

85   *Canadian Imperial Bank of Commerce (North Hills Shopping Centre), supra,* note 78.

86   As the Board did, for example, in *Royal Bank of Canada (Kamloops & Gibsons, B.C.)* (1978), 27 di 701, [1978] 2 Can LRBR 159, 78 CLLC #16,132.

87   *Wardair Canada (1975) Ltd., supra,* note 84.

15:5122   Practices Requiring a Motive

In other provisions of the Code that render otherwise legitimate employer actions unlawful, such as discipline in s. 184(3)(a) or penalizing in s. 184(3)(e), motive or anti-union animus is an essential element[88] because without it the actions fall within the employer's managerial prerogatives and therefore do not come under Part V of the Code.[89] In determining whether such an animus exists where the employee's actions are alleged to constitute union activities protected by the Code, the Board keeps in mind that legitimate employer interests are not swept aside by the legislation. The latter must be interpreted in the context of an employment relationship and the reciprocal responsibilities of such a relationship. It follows that the requisite unlawful motive is absent in an unfair labour practice charge when it is found that by his actions the employer was merely seeking to protect his legitimate interests. Thus, where the very actions of the employee to which the employer objects are alleged to constitute union activities protected by the statute, the Board will balance the respective interests in the light of the purpose of the *Canada Labour Code* to determine the limits of the employee or employer freedom claimed.[90]

15:5123   Classification of Employer and Union Unfair Practices

In summary, the general approach evolved by the Board recognizes at least two classes of employer unfair practices. First are those that require a motive as an element of an offence under the Code (s. 184(3)(a)). The required motive may be an anti-union animus, as in s. 184(3)(a)(i), or a desire to punish employee participation in proceedings under the Code (s. 184(3)(a)(iii)). Thus the nature of the motive may vary.

The second class of employer unfair practices is concerned with the effect of the employer's actions. Those are divided in two sub-categories. The first sub-category includes unfair practices such as employer actions prohibited by s. 184(1)(a) that interfere with legitimate employee or union rights and collective bargaining interests without sufficient or legitimate managerial, entrepreneurial, or collective bargaining justification. In such kinds of unfair practices, motive is a relevant factor only if the balance of competing interests is equal. The second sub-category

88   *Canadian Imperial Bank of Commerce (North Hills Shopping Centre)*, *supra*, note 78; *Banque Royale du Canada (Jonquière et Kénogami)* (1980), 42 di 125.
89   *Canadian Imperial Bank of Commerce (North Hills Shopping Centre)*, *supra*, note 78; *Road Runner Courrier Services* (1979), 34 di 783, [1979] 2 Can LRBR 20; *Canadian Imperial Bank of Commerce (Branches at Creston, B.C. and St. Catharines, Ont.)*, *supra*, note 78; *Air Mistassini Inc.* (1982), 48 di 73.
90   *Jacques Lecavalier* (1983), 54 di 100.

includes unfair practices such as entering into "yellow dog" contracts prohibited by s. 184(3)(b). This kind of unfair practice is also concerned with effects, but does not require the delicate balancing mentioned above. Here the act itself is prohibited.[91]

There are also two classes of union unfair practices. First are those that require a motive as an element. Such is the case, for example, with practices prohibited by s. 185(i), which, similarly to s. 184(3)(a)(iii), require a desire to punish participation in proceedings under the Code.[92] The second class includes unfair practices prohibited by sections of the Code that have as their primary focus the objective they seek to achieve rather than the union's motive. Such is the case with ss. 136.1, 161.1, and 185(f), (g), and (h), which are concerned with the effect of the union's actions.[93]

15:5130   Onus of Proof

As a general rule, the onus of proof rests with the complainant, who must be prepared to lead evidence first. An exception is found in complaints alleging a violation of s. 184(3) where, in accordance with s. 188(3), the onus is on the party who alleges that no violation has occurred.[94] At the pre-hearing meeting, the Board may be called upon to determine the main thrust of a complaint for purposes of the application of the onus created by s. 188(3) where the same facts are alleged to constitute a violation of more than one section.[95]

---

[91]   This classification is slightly different from that outlined by the Board in *Canadian Imperial Bank of Commerce (North Hills Shopping Centre)*, *supra*, note 78. The latter needed to be brought up to date, since at the time the Board issued its decision, it had not yet determined whether s. 184(1)(a) was concerned with effects only or with motive. From subsequent decisions which settled that issue, it can be determined that unfair practices that require a balancing of respective employee, union, and employer interests (as does s. 184(1)(a)) do not form a third category, but rather are part of those concerned with effects.

[92]   *Claude Latrémouille* (1983), 50 di 197.

[93]   For ss. 136.1 and 161.1, see *Canadian Imperial Bank of Commerce (North Hills Shopping Centre)*, *supra*, note 78. For s. 185(f), (g), and (h), see *Terry Matus* (1980), 37 di 73, [1980] 2 Can LRBR 21, 80 CLLC #16,022; and *Banque Royale du Canada (Jonquière et Kénogami)*, *supra*, note 88.

[94]   The decisions of the Board dealing with s. 188(3) and the reverse onus are numerous. See, among others, *Canadian Imperial Bank of Commerce (Sioux Lookout)* (1978), 33 di 432, [1979] 1 Can LRBR 18; *Banque Canadienne Nationale (Montréal)* (1979), 35 di 39, [1980] 1 Can LRBR 470; *G. Courchesne Transport Inc.* (1979), 36 di 63; *Banque Nationale du Canada (Fermont, Québec)* (1979), 36 di 69; *Bank of Montreal (Carrall and Hastings Street Branch)* (1980), 39 di 122; *Bessette Transport Inc.* (1981), 43 di 64; *American Airlines Inc.* (1981), 43 di 156; *Purolator Courier Ltd.* (1982), 48 di 32; *Northern Telecom Canada Ltd.* (1982), 48 di 78; *National Bank of Canada* (1982), 51 di 60; *A & M Transport Ltd.* (1983), 52 di 69; *Scotian Shelf Traders Ltd.* (1983), 52 di 151, 4 CLRBR (NS) 278, 83 CLLC #16,070.

[95]   *Oshawa Flying Club* (1981), 42 di 306, [1981] 2 Can LRBR 95.

The policy of the Board with respect to the onus of proof is dealt with more extensively below.

15:5131   Unfair Practices Subject to the Reverse Onus of Section 188(3)

Effect of Section 188(3)

The Board has determined[96] that, unlike the case in some jurisdictions where the legislation requires a complainant to first establish certain facts in order to shift the onus of proof onto the employer, under s. 188(3) of the *Canada Labour Code* a presumption results from the simple fact of filing with the Board a written complaint made pursuant to s. 187 alleging a violation of s. 184(3). In this respect, the Code differs significantly from various provincial labour statutes since, upon a strict construction of the provisions of s. 188(3), there is no legal requirement that the complainant establish a *prima facie* case. The mere filing of a complaint under s. 184(3) is sufficient to place on the employer the burden of adducing evidence in order to dispel the presumption thus created. The Board has stated[97] that rules such as those found in s. 188(3) are rules of evidence establishing a procedure to be followed where the evidence of the opposing parties is evenly balanced. The trier of fact in such a situation must make an evidential finding against the party upon whom the burden rests, and the complaint must be considered to be well founded.[98] As a result, subject to what is said below, the Board's practice is to require the employer to lead evidence first.

---

[96]   *CHUM Western Ltd., Radio CKVN* (1974), 3 di 18; *Fraser-Surrey Docks Ltd.* (1974), 3 di 14, 74 CLLC #16,102; *Aéro-Club de Montréal Inc.* (1974), 4 di 44, 74 CLLC #16,106; *Air Canada* (1975), 11 di 5, [1975] 2 Can LRBR 193, 75 CLLC #16,164; *Central Broadcasting Co. Ltd.* (1975), 10 di 8, [1975] 2 Can LRBR 65, 75 CLLC #16,169.

[97]   *Banque Canadienne Nationale (Montréal), supra,* note 94.

[98]   Under the old s. 188(3), as enacted in 1972, the Supreme Court of Canada held, in *Central Broadcasting Co. Ltd. v. Canada Labour Relations Board,* [1977] 2 S.C.R. 112, 9 N.R. 345, 76 CLLC #14,029, 67 D.L.R. (3d) 538, at 543, that the Board's interpretation of that section as creating a presumption against the employer was wrong. The effect of that decision on the Board's practices is reflected in *CKOY Ltd.* (1976), 17 di 24, [1976] 2 Can LRBR 329; *A.J. (Archie) Goodale Ltd.* (1977), 21 di 473, [1977] 2 Can LRBR 309; and *Oshawa Flying Club* (1981), 42 di 306, [1981] 2 Can LRBR 95. The reaction of Parliament after the above decision of the Supreme Court of Canada was to amend s. 188(3) in June 1978 by adding the words: "and, if any party to the complaint proceedings alleges that such failure did not occur, the burden of proof thereof is on that party". This amendment gave status to the written complaint itself as evidence of the alleged violation and made it clear that the onus to disprove such a violation rested with the employer.

On this point, it is worth mentioning that the Board has recently determined that the new s. 188(3) does not offend the "innocent until proven guilty" guarantee of s. 11(d) of the *Canadian Charter of Rights and Freedoms.* See *Scotian Shelf Traders Ltd.* (1983), 52 di 151, 4 CLRBR (NS) 278, 83 CLLC #16,070. Section 11(d) is directed at alleged offences that are criminal or quasi-criminal, not at alleged unfair labour practices that are in the civil and remedial realm.

Board Practice of Requiring a Prima Facie Case

The Board somewhat tempered its interpretation of s. 188(3) by requiring a complainant to establish a *prima facie* case before the presumption can be triggered.[99] Various concerns led the Board to adopt this practice. In the first place, it was the intent of Parliament that the Board should avoid undue technical or procedural requirements. Yet, to give effect to s. 188(3) without infringing on the rights of employers, it became necessary to require that a complaint alleging a violation of s. 184(3) meet certain basic requirements.

However, this rule to require a *prima facie* case is only a procedural device evolved by the Board and is not a requirement of law. Therefore the Board's practice is not to be construed as limiting in any way the full extent of the legal presumption created by s. 188(3). The purpose of this practice is not to limit the rights of a complainant or to create rights in favour of the respondent. For instance, the Board may require evidence of union membership as part of a *prima facie* case, but the fact that for technical or legal reasons the membership may not be valid cannot be used by the employer to rebut a complaint filed under s. 184(3)(a)(i) of the Code alleging that the complainant was dismissed because of his membership in a union. Moreover, since this procedural device is simply a practice evolved by the Board, it can be interpreted and applied solely by the Board. The latter will not interpret this practice in such a manner as to defeat the purpose of the provisions of s. 188(3).

The elements that may be required as part of a *prima facie* case have been outlined by the Board. They include:

1. The name and address of the person who has been refused employment or who has been terminated or otherwise discriminated against as well as evidence of the relationship (in most cases, evidence of a contract of employment with the respondent) between that person and the respondent.

2. The name, address and status of the complainant if he is not the person referred to above.

3. The name, address and status of the person who is alleged to have committed the unfair labour practice.

4. Information and, where it is available, evidence concerning the action or circumstances giving rise to the complaint. For example, if the complaint results from disciplinary action taken by the employer, there may be a letter addressed by the employer to the employee informing him of the action taken; the filing of such a document with the Board is evidence of the identity of the parties and of the employer-employee relationship, as well as evidence of the disciplinary sanction imposed upon the employee.

---

[99] On this subject, see *CHUM Western Ltd., Radio CKVN* (1974), 3 di 18; *Aéro-Club de Montréal Inc.* (1974), 4 di 44, 74 CLLC #16,106; *Les Ailes du Nord Ltée, Northern Wings Ltd.* (1974), 5 di 17, 74 CLLC #16,136; *Air Canada* (1975), 11 di 5, [1975] 2 Can LRBR 193, 75 CLLC #16,164; and *Central Broadcasting Co. Ltd.* (1975), 10 di 8, [1975] 2 Can LRBR 65, 75 CLLC #16,169.

5. Information and, where possible, evidence of the element listed in the relevant sub-paragraph of Section 184(3)(a). For example, if it is alleged that a person has been dismissed because she was a union member, the Board will look for evidence of union membership, such as a union membership card, or of activities which may have led the employer to believe that the person was a union member.

6. Information and, where possible, evidence concerning the possible existence of a recourse under a collective agreement in order to allow the Board to determine whether it should exercise the power given to it by Section 188(2) of the *Canada Labour Code* (Part V).[100]

Often, this information will be provided in the complaint or will be filed with the Board prior to the hearing. If in the opinion of the Board there is insufficient information, the complainant will be required to adduce supplementary evidence at the commencement of the hearing in order to satisfy the Board by the establishment of a *prima facie* case that the onus has been shifted. When such a case is established, the Board will simply announce that fact at the commencement of the hearing, after having disclosed to the respondent the supplementary information provided by the applicant.

Rebuttal of the Presumption Created by Section 188(3)

Once the Board has determined that the onus of proof has shifted to the employer, which may occur at the start of the hearing, the latter must lead evidence to rebut the legal presumption created by s. 188(3). If the employer fails to adduce any evidence, the "fact" of which the written complaint is evidence is deemed to be established.[101] If the employer leads evidence, the complainant will submit his own evidence, if any, after the employer has rested his case. The employer may then reply.

The Board is of the opinion that, because the employer is required to proceed first without the advantage of hearing the complainant's case, few restrictions can in fairness be applied to his right of rebuttal at the conclusion of the complainant's evidence. Although this may result in lengthy hearings, due to the requirements of natural justice, the Board is exceedingly reluctant to impose restraints upon a respondent employer who, as a result of the procedure imposed by s. 188(3), is initially required to adduce evidence without having heard from the complainant the entire case he has to meet.[102] In this area, and generally, at all stages of the hearing, the Board is extremely lenient:

> Since it does not feel bound by the same strict procedure as common law courts do in the hearing of evidence, this Board is well known for its

---

[100]   *Air Canada* (1975), 11 di 5, at 10, [1975] 2 Can LRBR 193, 75 CLLC #16,164.

[101]   *Upper Lakes Shipping Ltd. v. Sheehan*, [1979] 1 S.C.R. 902, at 923, 25 N.R. 149, 79 CLLC #14,192, 95 D.L.R. (3d) 25.

[102]   *Bank of Montreal (Carrall and Hastings Street Branch)* (1980), 39 di 122; *Scotian Shelf Traders Ltd.*, *supra*, note 98.

readiness to entertain rebutting evidence, additional evidence, proof in reply and proof in rebutting reply, if one dares call them that.

We want to learn all the facts as expeditiously as possible, regardless of how they arrive on the record, provided that this method does not deprive the opposing party from learning them, challenging them, refuting them or adding to them through cross-examination and rebutting evidence.[103]

The object of the evidence the employer must lead to offset the presumption imposed upon him varies, depending on whether his alleged unfair practice requires a motive or not. The classification of unfair practices prohibited by the Code has been outlined above.

If the unfair practice requires a motive as an essential element of a contravention, the employer must satisfy the Board, on a preponderance of evidence,[104] that the impugned action was not taken because of one of the prohibited considerations or motives listed in s. 184(3). Even if such a prohibited consideration or motive was not the sole reason for the action but merely a proximate cause among other proximate causes, the complaint will be upheld. In other words, if one of the prohibited considerations or motives was present in the mind of the employer in his decision to take the impugned action, either as the main reason or one incidental to it or as one of many reasons, regardless of priority, a breach of the *Canada Labour Code* has occurred.[105] In the board's view, an employer must not be permitted to achieve a discriminatory objective because he coupled his discriminatory motive with other non-discriminatory reasons for his act. Thus, if an employer acts with anti-union animus, even only incidentally, and if his act is one contemplated by s. 184(3), he will be found to have committed an unfair labour practice. Needless to say that the Code will all the more have been breached if a prohibited reason was the determining, principal, or intrinsic cause of the action taken by the employer.

Scope of Section 188(3) and Mixed Burden of Proof

The reverse onus clause of s. 188(3) applies only to the unfair labour practices listed in s. 184(3). In the Board's view, the reason for this singling-out by Parliament of a subparagraph of s. 184 to apply a major

---

103   *Banque Royale du Canada (Jonquière et Kénogami)* (1980), 42 di 125, at 151.

104   The presumption created by s. 188(3) is a presumption *juris tantum*, that is, a rebuttable presumption. Since the proceedings before the Board are civil and not criminal in nature, the Board must render its decisions according to the standard of the preponderance of evidence. The employer must, accordingly, adduce evidence that is strong enough to outweigh the presumption created in favour of the complainant: *Aéro-Club de Montréal Inc., supra,* note 99; *Canadian Imperial Bank of Commerce (Sioux Lookout)* (1978), 33 di 432, [1979] 1 Can LRBR 18; *Banque Canadienne Nationale (Montréal)* (1979), 35 di 39, [1980] 1 Can LRBR 470; *Bank of Montreal (Carrall and Hastings Street Branch), supra,* note 102; *Banque Royale du Canada (Jonquière et Kénogami), supra,* note 103; *Cabano Transport Ltée* (1981), 42 di 318.

105   See *Yellowknife District Hospital Society* (1977), 20 di 281, 77 CLLC #16,083; and *R. v. Bushnell Communications Ltd.* (1973), 1 O.R. (2d) 442, 14 C.C.C. (2d) 426, 45 D.L.R. (3d) 218; affd. 4 O.R. (2d) 288, 18 C.C.C. (2d) 317, 47 D.L.R. (3d) 668 (C.A.).

exception to the general rule of law that he who claims to have been wronged has the burden of proving his allegations, is a clear indication of the importance attached to the provisions of the Code prohibiting employer unfair labour practices. A scrutiny of the elements contained in the various divisions of s. 184(3) underlines the fact that it was paramount in the legislator's concern to protect the fundamental right and freedom of employees to join the trade union of their choice and to participate in its lawful activities as enshrined in s. 110(1) of the Code. Sections 184, 185, and 186 ensure that the exercise of these rights will not be tampered with by improper or undue pressure brought to bear by employers, unions, or any other person. But it is only in s. 184(3) that the onus is reversed.[106]

Complaints before the Board often allege violations of various sections of the Code, among which some are subject to the reverse onus of s. 188(3) and others are not. The Board has the authority under s. 24 of its regulations to consolidate or combine such matters into one hearing notwithstanding the different burden of proof attached to the various complaints. In such a situation where, for example, unfair labour practice complaints are filed under ss. 148(a) and 184(3), the Board may order the employer to proceed first with his evidence, although s. 188(3) imposes no burden of proof with respect to the first complaint. The Board distinguishes between the imposition of a burden of proof such as that mentioned by the legislator in s. 188(3) and the obligation to lead evidence, at the request of the Board itself. The Board has stated that it seems obvious and logical that the party having the burden of proof should begin.[107]

At this stage, it is only a matter of administering the evidence. If, after hearing all the evidence the Board concludes that s. 184(3) does not apply but that s. 148(a) does, it is clear that even though the employer has assumed a certain burden of proof by proceeding first, the Board will not rely on the provisions of s. 188(3) in making its determination. There is a major difference between the administration of the evidence or determining who will proceed first, and the application of a burden of proof on the basis of which it may be concluded, where the evidence is evenly balanced that the Code has been contravened.[108]

---

[106] *Canadian Imperial Bank of Commerce (Branches at Creston, B.C. and St. Catharines, Ont.)* (1979), 35 di 105, [1980] 1 Can LRBR 307, 80 CLLC #16,002.

[107] *Banque Royale du Canada (Jonquière et Kénogami), supra,* note 103.

[108] *Purolator Courier Ltd.* (1982), 48 di 32. This policy has recently received implicit judicial recognition by the Federal Court of Appeal in *Eastern Provincial Airways Ltd. v. Canada Labour Relations Board* (1984), 84 CLLC #14,042 (Fed. C.A.), in which the consolidation into a single hearing of various complaints under ss. 148(a) and 184(1)(a) and (3)(a)(vi) has been raised by the applicant as a ground for review, but was dismissed by the court as not deserving of consideration.

15:5132 Unfair Practices Not Subject to the Reverse Onus of Section 188(3)

Where a complaint filed before the Board is not subject to the statutory reverse onus, the Board will determine which party is to begin first. Such a determination becomes a matter of rationality. It may happen that it is more logical that either one or the other party begin first. It must be kept in mind that the Board alone determines its own procedure and, depending on the circumstances of each case, either one or the other party may be asked to lead evidence.[109]

15:5140 Amendments

Complainants and respondents occasionally request the Board, either at the pre-hearing or sometimes during the hearing itself, to amend their procedures. Each case is dealt with according to its particular circumstances. As a general rule, it may be said that the Board will refuse an amendment if it changes the nature of the complaint or has the effect of taking the other party by surprise and causing it prejudice.[110] For instance, when the facts outlined in a complaint are alleged to constitute a violation of a section of the Code to which the reverse onus does not apply, and the same facts are also capable of substantiating a contravention of a subparagraph of s. 184(3), an amendment adding this additional conclusion may be allowed by the Board. However, if such an amendment is intended primarily to place on the employer's shoulders the burden of presenting evidence first, and if it is presented on the eve or the opening of a hearing, the Board may refuse the amendment or, if it is allowed, the complainant will be required to proceed first.

For instance, in *Bessette Transport Inc.*[111] the Board allowed an amendment of a complaint alleging a violation of s. 124(4) to add the additional conclusion of a violation of s. 184(3) because the facts outlined in the complaint were capable of substantiating a contravention to both sections. The Board refused a request for a postponement because it considered that the employer was not substantially prejudiced by the amendment, but the complainant was directed to lead evidence first notwithstanding s. 188(3).

Amendments presented at this late stage may also raise the issue of timeliness.

15:5200 EVIDENCE AT THE HEARING

The usual rules applicable in civil litigation are followed by the Board. The parties in turn can call witnesses, who are subject to cross-

---

109 *Banque Royale du Canada (Jonquière et Kénogami), supra,* note 103.
110 *Mike Sheehan* (1975), 9 di 29, [1975] 2 Can LRBR 55, 75 CLLC #16,161; *Banque Canadienne Nationale (Montréal), supra,* note 104.
111 (1981), 43 di 64.

examination. The parties leading evidence always maintain the right to call rebuttal evidence and, as seen earlier, "additional evidence, proof in reply and proof in rebuttal reply".[112] As to the admissibility of evidence, the Board has a wide discretion.[113]

In practice, the Board follows basically the same rules as those used by provincial labour relations boards. A party wishing to discuss a particular procedural problem may always do so by raising the question at the preliminary hearing.

---

[112] *Banque Royale du Canada (Jonquière et Kénogami), supra,* note 103.
[113] See *Canada Labour Code,* s. 118(c).

CHAPTER 16

REMEDIAL AUTHORITY OF THE BOARD AND REMEDIES

16:0000   REMEDIAL AUTHORITY OF THE BOARD AND REMEDIES

16:1000   GENERAL CONTEXT AND LEGISLATIVE EVOLUTION

Before the 1973 amendments[1] the Board's authority to remedy unfair labour practices was nonexistent. The only recourse open to the parties to sanction unfair practices was by way of penal prosecution. Moreover, ministerial consent had to be obtained before such proceedings could be instituted.[2] The only exception provided by the Code concerned complaints alleging a breach of the duty to bargain in good faith. The latter could be referred by the minister to the Board, which could issue an order requiring the parties to comply with their obligation to negotiate in good faith.[3] However, the Code did not provide for any procedure to secure the enforcement of such an order. Thus, again, the only recourse open to the parties was a penal prosecution[4] or the issuance of an injunction in common-law courts. Illegal strikes and lockouts were also sanctioned in the same manner.

The Prime Minister's Task Force on Labour Relations, chaired by the late H.D. Woods, submitted its report in December 1968. It recommended an expanded role for the Board and also recommended that it be vested with jurisdiction over unfair labour practices and the authority to consent to penal prosecution with broad remedial power. At the same time, the Board was to become the body to which unions would be accountable for illegal work stoppages and unlawful picketing.

The 1972 amendments that followed[5] failed to implement all the recommendations of the Woods Report, but they nonetheless radically modified the powers of the Board and shaped it into a modern labour

---

1   S.C. 1972, c. 18 (in force in 1973).
2   *Canada Labour Code*, R.S.C. 1970, c. L-1, s. 152(1).
3   Section 152(2) of R.S.C. 1970, c. L-1.
4   Pursuant to the general provisions of s. 148 of R.S.C. 1970, c. L-1.
5   The R.S.C. 1970 Act was abrogated and the new Part V of the *Canada Labour Code* enacted by S.C. 1972, c. 18.

relations forum. In s. 189, Parliament entrusted the Board with the authority to issue compliance orders in addition to specific remedies for various unfair practices.[6] This power, read in conjunction with s. 121, considerably broadened the authority of the Board in this area.[7] Furthermore, s. 123 provided a procedure for the enforcement of the remedies and orders issued by the Board.

The Board's remedial authority was restricted, however, to contraventions of the provisions of ss. 148, 184, and 185. In respect of illegal strikes or lockouts, the Board's authority was also very limited. Sections 182 and 183 only enabled it to issue a declaration on the legality of the work stoppage or lockout, but did not empower the Board to enjoin a party from any further illegal activities. At the same time, the 1972 Code retained penal prosecutions for illegal strikes and lockouts and contraventions to the provisions of the Code other than those of ss. 148, 184, and 185. Nor had the Board been transferred the authority to consent to penal prosecutions; this still had to be obtained from the minister. Thus, on entering the 1970s, the Board's remedial authority was incomplete and its ability to manage industrial relations conflicts limited.

It was not until the 1978 amendments[8] that the Board's remedial powers were finally expanded to their current scope. Section 189 was amended to provide remedial authority and specific remedies with respect to contraventions of the provisions of ss. 124(4), 136.1, 161.1, and 186, in addition to those of ss. 148, 184, and 185. The opening words of s. 189 maintained the power to issue compliance orders. Under the powers conferred by the last paragraph of s. 189, the Board could issue cease and desist orders and, within the parameters outlined below, any other remedial order in addition to or in lieu of the specific remedies listed in s. 189(a) to (e).[9]

The 1978 amendments also conferred upon the Board an expanded jurisdiction over illegal strikes or lockouts. Sections 182 and 183 were amended to enable the Board to issue cease and desist orders in such matters. At the same time, penal prosecutions for illegal strikes and lockouts and contraventions of the provisions of the Code other than

---

6   The 1972 version of s. 189 did not include the last paragraph of the current text. Nonetheless, the Board had been given the authority to issue orders requiring the party who had contravened s. 148, 184, or 185 to comply with that section. In addition, the Board could order various remedies specifically spelled out in s. 189(a) to (e). It could not, however, order any other positive actions to counteract the consequences of the breach or issue "cease and desist" orders requiring a party to refrain from doing something to remedy the contravention of the Code.

7   See, however, note 14, *infra*.

8   S.C. 1977-1978, c. 27.

9   The authority of the Board to issue cease and desist orders was further entrenched by the June 1984 amendments (Bill C-34, passed by the House of Commons, June 27, 1984, s. 37(1)), which modified the opening words of s. 189 so as to read: "the Board may, by order, require the party to comply with or cease contravening" the section of the Code prohibiting an unfair labour practice.

those of ss. 148, 184, and 185 were maintained, but the authority to grant consents to institute such proceedings was transferred to the Board.[10] Finally, s. 123 was amended to confer a discretion upon the Board to determine whether it should file its orders in the Trial Division of the Federal Court of Canada for enforcement.

16:2000   PARAMETERS OF THE EXERCISE OF THE BOARD'S REMEDIAL AUTHORITY

The Board's wide remedial authority[11] under s. 189 must be exercised within certain parameters. In describing the effect of the 1978 amendments, the Board spelled out the cardinal rules it must respect in fashioning remedies. In the *Banque Royal du Canada (Jonquière et Kénogami)*[12] the Board stated:

> We said earlier that it was obvious, especially since the June 1978 amendments, that Parliament sought to decriminalize labour relations and that it expressed the wish that the Board find solutions truly aimed at the establishment of sound labour relations between the parties. The provisions of section 189 that we just detailed are proof thereof.
>
> Therefore, in applying remedies, the Board neither wants to be, nor should be, perceived as inflicting punishment. It wants to find remedies that will ensure *"the objectives"* of Parliament in Part V of the Code.

Thus, the purpose and effect of the remedy must be "to remedy or counteract any consequences of such contravention or failure to comply that is adverse to the fulfillment" of the objectives of Part V as expressed in the Preamble of the Code. In practical terms, this means that equitable and consequential considerations in the Board's choice of a particular remedy are not to be so remote from reparation of an established breach as to exceed any rational parameters.[13] In other words, there must be a rational relationship between the unfair labour practice, its consequences, and the remedy ordered by the Board.[14]

---

10   *Canada Labour Code*, s. 194.
11   See *Canadian Union of Public Employees v. Nova Scotia Labour Relations Board*, [1983] 2 S.C.R. 311, 49 N.R. 107, 60 N.S.R. (2d) 369, 128 A.P.R. 369, 83 CLLC #14,069, 1 D.L.R. (4th) 1, at p. 122 of Mr. Justice Dickson's notes; and *Eastern Provincial Airways Ltd. v. Canada Labour Relations Board* (1984), 84 CLLC #14,042 (Fed. C.A.), at p. 6 of Mr. Justice Pratte's notes.
12   (1980), 42 di 125, at 167.
13   *Canada Labour Relations Board v. Halifax Longshoremen's Association, Local 269*, [1983] 1 S.C.R. 245, 46 N.R. 324, 83 CLLC #14,022, at pp. 12,100-101, 144 D.L.R. (3d) 1.
14   *National Bank of Canada v. Retail Clerks' International Union*, [1984] 1 S.C.R. 269, 53 N.R. 203, 84 CLLC #14,037, 9 D.L.R. (4th) 10. In regard to s. 121 of the Code, the Board believed that that section could be relied on as an additional source of remedial authority. The rationale was that since one of the objects of Part V of the *Canada Labour Code* expressed in the preamble is the establishment of good labour relations, s. 121 constituted an additional source of authority because it enables the Board to "exercise such powers and perform such duties as are conferred or imposed upon it by, or as may be incidental to the attainment of the objects of this Part . . .". However, in *Le Syndicat des employés de production du Québec et de l'Acadie v. Canada Labour Relations*

16:3000   EXAMPLES OF REMEDIES ORDERED BY THE BOARD

The wide variety of remedies ordered by the Board makes it difficult to fashion a complete inventory. However, the very nature of many unfair labour practices dictates the kind of remedy that will counteract their consequences. As a result, some remedies are fairly common and consistently reoccur in the Board's decisions. Some examples are listed below to give an idea of the kind of remedy the Board may order.

16:3100   STATUTORY FREEZES: SECTIONS 124(4), 148(b)

Where the Board determines that an employer has failed to comply with the statutory freeze provisions of s. 124(4) or 148(b), it may require the contravenor, pursuant to s. 189(a.1), to "pay to any employee compensation not exceeding such sum as, in the opinion of the Board, is equivalent to the remuneration that would, but for that failure, have been paid by the employer to the employee". Thus, where an employer

---

Board, [1982] 1 F.C. 471, at 476-77, Mr. Justice Pratte, in a unanimous decision, disagreed with the Board's interpretation. He wrote, in part: "I cannot agree with this argument. If section 121 were given such a scope, the many provisions of the Act that specify the Board's powers would be rendered useless. In my view, the scope of section 121 is more modest. I consider that . . . this section relates only to the powers necessary to perform the duties expressly imposed by the Act on the Board; however, as I understand it the Act does not impose on the Board a duty to resolve labour disputes which may be the cause of strikes."

On appeal to the Supreme Court of Canada, Mr. Justice Beetz, for a unanimous court, endorsed the decision of the Federal Court of Appeal. In *Syndicat des employés de production du Québec et de l'Acadie v. Canada Labour Relations Board*, [1984] 2 S.C.R. 412, at 432, Mr. Justice Beetz underlined the extreme consequences of the interpretation proposed by the Board: ". . . adopting the argument made by counsel for the Board in their submission as to the powers conferred on the Board by s. 121 of the Canada Labour Code in conjunction with the preamble to Part V of the said Code would amount to a recognition that the Board has complete power and authority in the field of labour relations in Canada (except for powers specifically conferred on other bodies or jurisdictions), even powers which the legislator has not conferred on it, and make the said preamble a source of power and authority.

"The legislator intended that the Board's powers should be extensive: he did not intend that they should be practically unlimited.

"It is quite possible that s. 121 covers only the powers necessary to perform the tasks expressly conferred on the Board by the Code, as Pratte J. indicated. Nevertheless, I consider that even if it covers autonomous or principal powers, like that of ordering a reference to arbitration, and not merely incidental or collateral powers, it cannot cover autonomous powers designed to remedy situations which the Code has dealt with elsewhere, and for which it has prescribed specific powers, as is the case with unlawful strikes. Here, the legislator has not only specified the principal powers of the Board in s. 182, but its collateral powers as well in s. 183.1. These two sections contain an exhaustive description of the Board's authority over unlawful strikes and cover it completely."

As a result, s. 121 cannot be relied on as an autonomous source of authority to remedy situations that the Code has dealt with elsewhere and for which specific powers were prescribed.

had failed to implement wage increases, contrary to his past practice or compensation policy, the Board ordered that the wage increase be implemented and that the employees be compensated for the wages lost.[15] Pursuant to the last paragraph of s. 189, the Board may also require an employer to do or refrain from doing anything equitable to remedy or counteract the consequences of the failure to comply with the freeze provisions. Thus, in addition to any compensation, the Board usually orders the employer to re-establish the *status quo ante* as of the date of the commencement of the statutory freeze. It has ordered, for example, the resumption of the normal work schedule of an employee,[16] the reinstatement of an employee's rights and prerogatives associated with his job,[17] the reinstatement of the practice of not deducting wages for persons on sick leave,[18] and so forth.

16:3200   THE DUTY TO BARGAIN IN GOOD FAITH: SECTION 148(a)

The Board's policy with respect to the manner in which it will exercise its remedial powers when unfair labour practices have been committed during collective bargaining is to exercise caution and to refrain from using s. 189 in a way that would result in one party or the other gaining economic concessions it could not ordinarily secure through the normal process of negotiations. In other words, in fashioning its remedies, the Board takes a "hands off" approach.[19] It will go only as far as is needed to provide the parties with an opportunity to settle their own disputes.[20] This means that it will not tip the balance more than is required to restore the bargaining power held by a party before it was weakened by unlawful means.

Thus, in some cases, a simple declaration that the employer had failed to comply with s. 148(a) was issued by the Board.[21] In others, the Board ordered the parties to meet and commence collective bargaining[22] and to make every reasonable effort to conclude a collective agreement. Such remedy has, depending on the circumstances, been accompanied by an order to the employer to discontinue communicating with his em-

---

15   For instance, see *Canadian Imperial Bank of Commerce (Branches at Creston, B.C. and St. Catharines, Ont.)* (1979), 35 di 105, [1980] 1 Can LRBR 307, 80 CLLC #16,002; and *La Banque de Nouvelle-Ecosse (Sherbrooke et Rock Forest, Québec)* (1980), 42 di 216, [1981] 2 Can LRBR 365, 81 CLLC #16,110.
16   *Bessette Transport Inc.* (1981), 43 di 64.
17   *Radio LaTuque Ltée (CFLM)* (1980), 42 di 108.
18   *Maclean-Hunter Cable TV Ltd.* (1979), 34 di 752, [1979] 2 Can LRBR 1.
19   *Eastern Provincial Airways Ltd.* (1983), 54 di 172, 5 CLRBR (NS) 368, 84 CLLC #16,012.
20   *General Aviation Services Ltd.* (1982), 51 di 71, [1982] 3 Can LRBR 47, 82 CLLC #16,177.
21   *J. Phillips* (1978), 34 di 603, [1979] 1 Can LRBR 180.
22   See *Austin Airways Ltd. / White River Air Services Ltd.* (1980), 41 di 151, [1980] 3 Can LRBR 393; *Ottawa-Carleton Regional Transit Commission* (1983), 51 di 173, 83 CLLC #16,016; *Austin Airways Ltd.* (1983), 54 di 49, 4 CLRBR (NS) 343.

ployees and so undermining the union's representation,[23] and an order to the union to inform employees on the current state of negotiations and to follow their wishes on the future course of negotiations.[24]

In one case, the Board ordered the employer to pay to the union an amount equal to the union dues it would have received but for a two-month stoppage caused primarily by the company's failure to bargain in good faith.[25]

In other decisions the Board fashioned more persuasive remedies by ordering the parties to engage in good-faith bargaining with the further requirement that if no agreement was reached, the parties would file a copy of their most recent bargaining proposals with the Board. A hearing would then be convened to ascertain the extent to which progress had been made and to hear representations on the adequacy of the Board's remedy.[26] A more compelling variation of this kind of remedy consists in an order to reach a collective agreement within a specific time limit set by the Board, failing which the parties must meet and bargain in the Board's offices in the presence of a Board member,[27] or an order directing the employer to table a complete collective agreement that it would be prepared to sign within a specific time limit set by the Board.[28]

The Board has shown its willingness to order even more substantial remedies, given the proper circumstances, by ordering an employer (i) to withdraw surprise demands introduced at the eleventh hour at a moment when final settlement was in sight, thus creating what has been referred to as a "receding horizon" and unduly prolonging a long and bitter strike; (ii) to cease and desist from making proposals that had been put forward in violation of the Code; and (iii) to execute the agreement the employer had agreed to before the surprise demands and illegal proposals were introduced.[29] The Board has, furthermore, ordered the parties to meet to conclude a return-to-work agreement for the purpose of which all positions within the bargaining unit formerly occupied by the striking employees were to be considered vacant.[30] In another decision, it also imposed a return-to-work procedure of its own.[31] In exceptional cases, where the dispute had been referred to it by the minister under

---

23   *Austin Airways Ltd. / White River Air Services Ltd., supra,* note 22.

24   *Télévision Saint-François Inc.* (1981), 43 di 175.

25   *Austin Airways Ltd.* (1984), 5 CLRBR (NS) 239, 84 CLLC #16,019.

26   *North Canada Air Ltd.* (1981), 43 di 312, [1981] 2 Can LRBR 388.

27   *Northern Telecom Canada Ltd.* (1980), 42 di 178, [1981] 1 Can LRBR 306.

28   *General Aviation Services Ltd., supra,* note 20.

29   *Eastern Provincial Airways Ltd.* (1983), 54 di 172, 5 CLRBR (NS) 368, 84 CLLC #16,012; affd. (*sub nom. Eastern Provincial Airways Ltd. v. Canada Labour Relations Board*) 84 CLLC #14,042 (Fed. C.A.). For similar remedies in Ontario and the United States, see Michael Bendel, "A Rational Process of Persuasion: Good Faith Bargaining in Ontario" (1980), 30 *University of Toronto Law Journal* 1.

30   *Ibid.*

31   *General Aviation Services Ltd.* (1982), 51 di 88, [1982] 3 Can LRBR 439, 82 CLLC #16,181.

s. 171.1, the Board exercised its discretion and imposed a first collective agreement on the parties.[32]

16:3300   THE DUTY OF FAIR REPRESENTATION: SECTION 136.1

Section 189(a) provides that the Board may, in respect of a failure to comply with s. 136.1, "require a trade union to take and carry on on behalf of any employee affected by the failure or to assist any such employee to take and carry on such action or proceeding as the Board considers that that union ought to have taken and carried on on the employee's behalf or ought to have assisted the employee to take and carry on".

While the Board has used its authority in one case[33] to direct that an investigation be carried by one of its officers to decide what remedy would be appropriate (in view of a possible conflict between the *Canada Labour Code* and the *Canadian Human Rights Act*, under which unsuccessful proceedings had also been instituted), the usual remedy ordered by the Board is to send the complainant's grievance directly to arbitration.[34] To achieve this result, the Board has the power to relieve against any privately created time limit in a collective agreement.[35] However, in one case[36] the Board has found it more appropriate to order the union to file a grievance and process it all the way to arbitration, if necessary, rather than ordering it directly to arbitration, while in another[37] the Board has merely directed that the merit of the grievance be reconsidered and debated at the various levels of the union's internal processes, but has left the union free to decide whether or not the grievance should go to arbitration. The union was also ordered, in similar cases, not to reach any settlement without the employee's consent,[38] and it has been ordered that the employee be represented by counsel of his choice to present the merits of his grievance at the final level of the union's internal process.[39]

---

[32]   *CJMS Radio Montréal Ltée* (1978), 27 di 796, [1979] 1 Can LRBR 332; *Huron Broadcasting Ltd.* (1982), 49 di 68, [1982] 2 Can LRBR 227.

[33]   *Carlton C. Caesar* (1980), 41 di 102, [1980] 1 Can LRBR 322.

[34]   See, for instance, *Gerald M. Massicotte* (1980), 40 di 11, [1980] 1 Can LRBR 427, 80 CLLC #16,014; *Kenneth Cameron* (1980), 42 di 193, [1981] 1 Can LRBR 273; *Denis Pion* (1981), 43 di 254; *Jean-Paul Roy* (1981), 46 di 25; *David Alan Crouch* (1983), 55 di 48; *Paul Godin and Robert Letang* (1984), 55 di 81.

[35]   The Supreme Court of Canada found this to be "a power incidental or ancillary to the powers granted to the Board by section 189(a)": *Massicotte v. International Brotherhood of Teamsters, Local 938*, [1982] 1 S.C.R. 710, 44 N.R. 340, 82 CLLC #14,196, 134 D.L.R. (3d) 193.

[36]   *Tom Forestall and Randall Hall* (1980), 41 di 177, [1980] 3 Can LRBR 491.

[37]   *Larry Elliston* (1982), 47 di 103, [1982] 2 Can LRBR 241.

[38]   *Kenneth Cameron, supra,* note 34.

[39]   *Larry Elliston, supra,* note 37.

Where the Board ordered the grievance sent directly to arbitration, it has also ordered some or all of the following measures: (i) that the complainant be represented at arbitration by independent counsel of his choice;[40] (ii) that the legal fees, disbursements, and expenses of the complainant's counsel be paid by the union;[41] (iii) that the union pay the amount of compensation from the date of discharge to the date of the decision of the Board, and that the employer pay the amount from the date of the decision of the Board to the date of reinstatement, should the arbitrator determine that the complainant be reinstated and compensated,[42] or that the union assume liability for payment of any compensation to the employee in the event of a favourable ruling by the arbitrator,[43] or that the union pay the complainant a given number of months' gross salary;[44] and (iv) that the amount of compensation payable by the union not be decreased by any application of a duty to mitigate.[45] In one case, the Board also ordered that, if and when the complainant was reinstated, he must be offered the opportunity to attend a union-conducted educational program for local shop stewards and officers.[46]

16:3400   THE DUTY OF FAIR REFERRAL: SECTION 161.1

There is no specific remedy prescribed in s. 189(a) to (e) for a failure to comply with the duty of fair referral in s. 161.1. Accordingly, the Board may require the union to comply with that section, may issue cease and desist orders, and in addition may require the union "to do or refrain from doing any thing that it is equitable to require the trade union to do or refrain from doing in order to remedy or counteract any consequences" of the failure to comply with s. 161.1.

Thus, where a union engaged in referral to employment had established rules that were incomplete and did not fully comply with s. 161.1(3), the union was ordered to finalize the rules and distribute copies to its members to comply with the spirit of s. 161.1(2), since it could not afford a dispatch hall in which to post them.[47] Where a union had applied its rules in a manner unfair and discriminatory to the complainant, it was ordered

---

40   *Gerald M. Massicotte, supra,* note 34; *Kenneth Cameron, supra,* note 34; *Jean-Paul Roy, supra,* note 34.

41   *Larry Elliston, supra,* note 37.

42   See, for instance, *Gerald M. Massicotte, supra,* note 34; and *Kenneth Cameron, supra,* note 34. See also *Jean-Paul Roy, supra,* note 34; affd. not yet reported, June 22, 1983, file no. A-749-81 (Fed. C.A.), in which the court held that the Board had not exceeded its jurisdiction under s. 189 by ordering the union to compensate the employee whom it had wrongfully refused to represent.

43   *Denis Pion, supra,* note 34.

44   *Tom Forestall and Randall Hall, supra,* note 36.

45   *Gerald M. Massicotte, supra,* note 34.

46   *Tom Forestall and Randall Hall, supra,* note 36.

47   *Gary Meagher* (1980), 41 di 95.

to (i) discontinue such practice, (ii) compensate the complainant for the loss incurred by reason of the failure to be registered for referral, (iii) register the complainant at the top of the list for referral in the coming season, and (iv) refer him to an employer for a full-time job.[48]

Where the union had completely failed to comply with s. 161.1, the Board ordered that rules be established and posted or distributed, that they include rules for the obtaining of membership, and that they be filed with the Board along with any subsequent amendments. Furthermore, the Board ordered the union to admit one complainant to membership and to promote another to the status of union cardholder.[49]

16:3500   UNFAIR PRACTICES RELATING TO UNION MEMBERSHIP OR ACTIVITIES: SECTION 184(3)(a), (c), (e), (f)

The Board has specific authority in s. 189(b) and (c) to remedy contraventions of s. 184(3)(a), (c), (e), and (f). It may order the reinstatement of a dismissed employee, rescind the discipline, and order that a person be employed and compensated. Under this authority and that conferred by the last paragraph of s. 189, the Board has fashioned remedies that vary with the particular circumstances of each case.

16:3510   Dismissal, Discipline, and Refusal to Employ

Where an employee is illegally dismissed or disciplined, the Board usually orders the reinstatement of the complainant or rescission of the discipline, depending on the case, accompanied by a removal from the complainant's file of any reference to the disciplinary action[50] and full compensation.[51] The Board may add teeth to such an order if the employer refuses to comply. For instance, where an employer refused to reinstate the complainant in defiance of a previous order to that effect, the Board ordered the reinstatement and compensation implemented by a fixed date, failing which a formal order would be automatically filed in the Federal Court of Canada for enforcement at the union's request.[52]

---

48 *Mike Sheehan* (1980), 40 di 103, [1980] 2 Can LRBR 278, 80 CLLC #16,030.

49 *David C. Nauss and Peter H. Roberts* (1980), 42 di 55, [1981] 1 Can LRBR 189; *Ronald W. Lockhart and Charles G. Wilson* (1980), 42 di 89, [1981] 1 Can LRBR 213. The Federal Court of Appeal held that the Board had exceeded its jurisdiction and set aside the part of the Board's decision ordering admittance to membership and union cardholder status: see *Halifax Longshoremen's Association v. Nauss*, [1981] 2 F.C. 827, 37 N.R. 242, 124 D.L.R. (3d) 171. The Supreme Court of Canada reversed the decision of the Federal Court of Appeal and reinstated the Board's decision: see *Canada Labour Relations Board v. Halifax Longshoremen's Association, Local 269*, [1983] 1 S.C.R. 245, 46 N.R. 324, 83 CLLC #14,022, 144 D.L.R. (3d) 1.

50 *Bell Canada* (1977), 20 di 312.

51 However, in some cases, only partial monetary compensation was awarded, on account of the complainant's behaviour: see *CJRF Radio Provinciale Ltée* (1977), 19 di 136.

52 *T.E. Quinn Truck Lines Ltd.* (1982), 47 di 87.

Organizational changes to the employer's enterprise that are completed before the Board could schedule a hearing and render a decision have not prevented it from remedying illegal dismissals that had resulted from such a reorganization. For instance, in one case the Board ordered an employer to transfer the operations of one of his departments back to the complainant's home-town division of the enterprise, in order to reinstate her in the position she had held before being illegally dismissed.[53] In another, the Board ordered an employer to reverse organizational changes that had been designed to oust the complainant from his duties and authority and to replace him in his former status.[54] On a further complaint filed by the same employee alleging that he was being penalized in contravention of s. 184(3)(a)(iii) to (v) for making the earlier complaint, the Board ordered that he be offered a promotion commensurate with his training and experience, together with financial assistance to relocate elsewhere in the territory of the company.[55] These decisions illustrate that, in some cases, reinstatement orders or rescission of discipline with monetary awards are not always sufficient to fully compensate an employee illegally discriminated against.

Another example is that of the dismissal of a probationary employee in contravention of the Code. In such cases the Board has ordered reinstatement with monetary compensation and, in addition, ordered that the period of dismissal be considered as time worked for the purpose of the complainant's probation period.[56]

However, reinstatement may not always be possible or be the proper solution. For instance, where a subcontractor employer had illegally refused to employ a person, the Board held that the respondent employer was responsible for the complainant's loss of an opportunity to be trained for a particular trade and, accordingly, for his failure to be engaged by the successor subcontractor. As the respondent had lost the contract to the new subcontractor, the Board was unable to order that the complainant be employed. As a result, the Board ordered that the complainant be paid a sum equivalent to that which he would have earned for the whole period during which the respondent held the contract and, in addition, a sum of money equivalent to that which the complainant would have earned had he been employed by the new subcontractor from the date the latter was awarded the contract to the date of the hearing before the Board.[57]

---

53   *Purolator Courier Ltd.* (1982), 48 di 32.
54   *British Columbia Telephone Co.* (1981), 47 di 28, [1982] 1 Can LRBR 326, 82 CLLC #16,149.
55   *British Columbia Telephone Co.* (1983), 52 di 88, 83 CLLC #16,048.
56   See, for example, *American Airlines Inc.* (1981), 43 di 156, where the complainant's probation period was thereby completed.
57   *Scotian Shelf Traders Ltd.* (1983), 52 di 151, 4 CLRBR (NS) 278, 83 CLLC #16,070. This is the only case in which a refusal to employ was found to contravene the provisions of s. 184(3). It must be emphasized that the respondent employer's enterprise was not

Where an employee had been illegally dismissed but had secured employment with another employer before his complaint was heard and decided by the Board, the respondent was ordered to make a *bona fide* offer of employment to the complainant and to compensate him for the period beginning with the date of his termination and ending with the commencement of his employment with his new employer.[58]

16:3520   Discrimination in Terms and Conditions of Employment

Where, for a motive prohibited by s. 184(3)(a), an employer had cancelled an employee's right to use a company truck outside working hours, the Board ordered that the complainant be allowed to use the truck and other pieces of equipment without any restriction on the duration of the use, in accordance with the past practice in the enterprise.[59] But changes in the employee's terms and conditions of employment for prohibited reasons may have more serious economic consequences. Where, for instance, in combining lists of seniority, an employer had singled-out an employee for special favourable treatment, thereby detrimentally affecting the opportunity of other employees to be assigned trips, the Board ordered that they be compensated for the trips they would have been attributed had their position on the seniority list not been reshuffled.[60] In another decision, where an employer had cancelled the regular overtime assignment of an employee, which by past practice had become a regular part of his work week, the Board ordered full compensation for all earnings the employee would have received had the employer not refused him the continued assignment of overtime.[61]

16:3530   Threats and Intimidation

Where an employer uses threats or other means to intimidate employees in contravention of s. 184(3)(a) and the first part of s. 184(3)(e), the Board seeks to cure the direct effects as well as the side-effects of the employer's violations. For example, the Board will order the reinstatement of an illegally dismissed employee, if such was the means used by the employer. In order to counteract or dispel the side-effects the illegal dismissal may have had upon other employees, the Board's most common remedy is to order the distribution of its reasons for decision.[62]

---

unionized, and accordingly the successor provisions of s. 144 did not apply. Of course, had the respondent employer not lost the contract to the new subcontractor, there is no doubt that the Board would have had the authority to order that the complainant be employed.

58   *Canadian Imperial Bank of Commerce (Toronto)* (1979), 34 di 677, [1979] 1 Can LRBR 391.
59   *Sorel-O-Vision Inc.* (1981), 46 di 73.
60   *Cabano Transport Ltée* (1981), 42 di 318.
61   *Road Runner Courrier Services* (1979), 34 di 783, [1979] 2 Can LRBR 20.
62   See paragraph 16:3600.

16:3600   INTERFERENCE IN ADMINISTRATION AND UNION REPRESENTATION: SECTION 184(1)

A breach of various sections of the Code such as s. 184(3)(a)(i) and (e) in the case of an illegal dismissal, or a breach of the freeze mechanism provided in ss. 124(4) and 148(b), or a failure to bargain in good faith as prescribed in s. 148(a) often involves a breach of s. 184(1)(a) as well.[63] A breach of s. 184(1)(a) may also be independent of a failure to comply with another section of the Code. The nature of the remedy ordered by the Board is dependent on the extent of the damage visited by the employees on their right to organize and to join a union of their choice. In some cases[64] a simple cease-and-desist order directing the employer to refrain from interfering with the formation of a trade union may be sufficient. In others, more positive action may be required where, for instance, at the organizing stage of a trade union, an employer displays open opposition to the unionization of his employees in various written or oral communications and commits flagrant unfair labour practices.

In such cases, the Board has often ordered, among other remedies, the distribution to employees of its reasons for the decision finding the employer in breach of the Code.[65] Those may be accompanied by a covering letter that must be signed by an officer of the company. The determination of which person in the hierarchy of the enterprise will be ordered to sign the covering letter is usually dependent on the level of the enterprise at which the illegal action was conceived or condoned.[66]

The covering letter written by the Board generally states that (i) the Board has found the employer in breach of the Code, (ii) the provision of the Board's attached reasons for decision is in compliance with the Board's order, (iii) the employer will comply with the remedial order, and in some cases, (iv) he will comply with the legislation in the future.[67]

---

[63]   See paragraph 11:1121.

[64]   *City and Country Radio Ltd.* (1975), 11 di 22, [1975] 2 Can LRBR 1, 75 CLLC #16,171; *Amok Ltd.* (1981), 43 di 289.

[65]   *Canadian Imperial Bank of Commerce (Toronto), supra,* note 58; *Road Runner Courrier Services, supra,* note 61; *Frank J. Nowotniak and Gordon E. Ostby* (1979), 34 di 835, [1979] 2 Can LRBR 466; *Banque Canadienne Nationale (Montréal)* (1979), 35 di 39, [1980] 1 Can LRBR 470; *Canadian Imperial Bank of Commerce (Branches at Creston, B.C. and St. Catharines, Ont.)* (1979), 35 di 105, [1980] 1 Can LRBR 307, 80 CLLC #16,002; *Transx Ltd.* (1980), 40 di 214; *Austin Airways Ltd. / White River Air Services Ltd.* (1980), 41 di 151, [1980] 3 Can LRBR 393; *Banque Royale du Canada (Jonquière et Kénogami)* (1980), 42 di 125; *Cabano Transport Ltée, supra,* note 60; *American Airline Inc.* (1981), 43 di 114, [1982] 3 Can LRBR 90; *Television Saint-François Inc.* (1981), 43 di 175; *La Banque Nationale du Canada* (1981), 42 di 352, [1982] 3 Can LRBR 1; *Loomis Armored Car Service Ltd.* (1983), 51 di 185.

[66]   *La Banque Nationale du Canada, supra,* note 65; revd. (*sub nom. National Bank of Canada v. Retail Clerks' International Union*) [1984] 1 S.C.R. 269, 53 N.R. 203, 84 CLLC #14,037, 9 D.L.R. (4th) 10, in view of the content of the covering letter the employer was ordered to sign. See note 69, *infra.*

[67]   See, for instance, *Canadian Imperial Bank of Commerce (Branches at Creston, B.C. and St.*

The range of distribution is usually coextensive with the extent to which the deterring effect of the illegal means used by the employer has spread in the enterprise. For instance, where the intimidating effects had not spread any further than the branch in which the illegal action or means used by the employer had occurred, the Board limited the distribution of its decision solely to the employees of that particular branch.[68] By contrast, where the deterring effect on the exercise of the freedom enshrined in s. 110(1) had spread throughout the Canada-wide operations of the employer, the latter was ordered to provide a copy of the decision of the Board to each and every one of his employees in the country.[69]

In another case, the Board has ordered that a statement be read, rather than written and sent, to the employees by a high-ranking representative of the employer at a meeting of all staff, in the course of which the company would undertake to comply with the obligations of the Code in the future.[70]

In order to restore employee confidence in the freedom of association and free collective bargaining, the employer has been ordered, in exceptional cases, to post in a conspicuous place a notice to the employees

---

Catharines, Ont.), *supra*, note 65; and *Banque Royale du Canada (Jonquière et Kénogami)*, *supra*, note 65.

[68] *Canadian Imperial Bank of Commerce (Toronto)*, *supra*, note 58; *Banque Royale du Canada (Jonquière et Kénogami)*, *supra*, note 65.

[69] *International Sea-Land Shipping Services Ltd.* (1983), 54 di 63. This kind of remedy — distribution of reasons for decision accompanied by a covering letter — is not unique to the federal jurisdiction: see George Adams, "Labour Remedies on Entering the 80's," in K.P. Sward and K.E. Swinton, *Studies in Labour Law* (Toronto: Butterworths, 1982), 55-79. As pointed out by the Ontario Labour Relations Board in *Valdi Inc.*, [1980] 3 Can LRBR 299, at 314, the origin of this kind of remedy in labour law can be traced as far back as 1937 in the United States: see *Johns and Laughlin Steel Corp.* (1937), 301 U.S. 1, 1 LRRM 703, at 715. It has been ordered many times by other Canadian labour relations boards also: see *Radio Shack*, [1979] OLRB Rep. 1220; affd. (*sub nom. Re Tandy Electronics Ltd. and United Steelworkers of America* (1980), 115 D.L.R. (3d) 197; *Westinghouse Canada Ltd.*, [1980] OLRB Rep. 577, [1980] 2 Can LRBR 469, 80 CLLC #16,053; affd. 80 CLLC #14,062 (Ont. Div. Ct.); *Fotomat Canada Ltd.*, [1981] 1 Can LRBR 381 (O.L.R.B.); *K-Mart Canada Ltd.*, [1981] 2 Can LRBR 5, [1981] OLRB Rep. 60, 81 CLLC #16,084; *United Steelworkers of America v. Homeware Industries Ltd.* (1981), 81 CLLC #16,087 (O.L.R.B.); *Sunnylea Foods Ltd.*, [1982] 1 Can LRBR 125, 82 CLLC #16,144, [1981] OLRB Rep. 1640. Nonetheless there are limits to the content of the statement a board may order an employer to make, as the Supreme Court of Canada has pointed out in *National Bank of Canada v. Retail Clerks Employees' International Union*, [1983] 1 S.C.R. 269, 53 N.R. 203, 84 CLLC #14,037, 9 D.L.R. (4th) 10.

[70] *Banque Royale du Canada (Jonquière et Kénogami)* (1980), 42 di 125. This remedy resembles the one ordered by the National Labor Relations Board in *United Dairy Farmers*, 101 L.R.R.M. 1278. In that case the American Board ordered the employer to post a notice in a conspicuous location in the work place and to mail a notice to each employee, stating that he had been found guilty of violating the *National Labor Relations Act* and that he would henceforth conform with its requirements. In addition, the Board ordered the employer to read the notice to the employees at a special meeting called for that purpose and to publish it in local newspapers twice a week for a one-month period. Enforcement of this remedy was granted by the Court of Appeal of the third circuit: see 105 L.R.R.M. 3034.

in which were listed all the remedies fashioned by the Board.[71] These included (i) the immediate distribution by the employer to all employees and management of a copy of the Board's decision and copies of the *Canada Labour Code;* (ii) the creation of a permanent labour management committee to discuss labour relations problems involving the employees, the employer, and the union; and (iii) the compulsory enrollment of all representatives of the permanent labour management committee in a specialized or intensive course in labour relations.

In other cases, the Board has ordered the employer to provide the union with a list of all the names and addresses of his employees.[72] Where, in an attempt to dilute the union's membership support, an employer had entered into individual contracts of employment with various employees that cast them into managerial positions out of the bargaining unit, the Board ordered the employer to rescind the individual contracts of employment and to recognize the union as the bargaining agent for all the employees in the unit.[73] In another decision where, in the context of a certification demand, the employer's actions were also aimed at diluting the union's membership support, the Board exercised its remedial authority by determining, pursuant to its discretion under s. 126(c), that the date on which the wishes of the employees would be ascertained was a date on which the union had a clear majority.[74]

In a more recent decision[75] the Board issued its most comprehensive order by requiring the employer to (i) provide the names and addresses of the employees, (ii) allow the union to hold meetings during working hours on employer premises and to install a bulletin board to which the union could have free access, (iii) pay for the cost of organizing the meetings and installing the bulletin board, and (iv) establish a trust fund to be jointly administered by the union and employer to further the objectives of Part V of the Code.[76]

The Board has declined, however, to award unions their costs incurred in organizational campaigns even if they had been hampered by the employer's actions.[77]

---

[71]   *Banque Royale du Canada (Jonquière et Kénogami), supra,* note 70.
[72]   *Transx Ltd.* (1980), 40 di 214; and *National Bank of Canada* (1981), 42 di 352, [1982] 3 Can LRBR 1.
[73]   *Manitoba Pool Elevators* (1980), 42 di 27, [1981] 1 Can LRBR 44; affd. (*sub nom. Manitoba Pool Elevators v. Canada Labour Relations Board*) [1982] 2 F.C. 659, 39 N.R. 387, 82 CLLC #14,160 (C.A.).
[74]   *Canadian Imperial Bank of Commerce (Sioux Lookout)* (1978), 33 di 432, [1979] 1 Can LRBR 18.
[75]   *National Bank of Canada, supra,* note 72.
[76]   The trust fund remedy as well as that of the letter drafted by the Board to be signed by the bank's president were quashed by the Supreme Court of Canada in *National Bank of Canada v. Retail Clerks Employees' International Union, supra,* note 69.
[77]   *Canadian Imperial Bank of Commerce (Toronto)* (1979), 34 di 677, [1979] 1 Can LRBR 391.

16:3700   CONTRAVENTIONS OF SECTION 185(a), (d)

In cases of violations of s. 185(a) and (d), the Board has declined to issue any remedy against the employees who had participated in the unlawful actions but ordered the union to cease and desist from any further act that would contravene the provisions of those sections.[78]

16:3800   CONTRAVENTIONS OF SECTION 185(f), (g), (h)

Unions who had failed to comply with s. 185(f), (g), or (h) were ordered either to admit the complainant to membership[79] or to rescind disciplinary actions taken against him[80] and reinstate the complainant retroactively to the date of his suspension.[81] The Board ordered, furthermore, that the complainant be compensated for the wages he would have earned had he not been illegally suspended or expelled from membership;[82] that the complainant be retroactively credited for the purpose of the welfare plan and other membership benefits;[83] that the employee not pay union dues for the period during which he was expelled or suspended;[84] and that the union take all necessary measures to have the employee restored to his position on the seniority list with the employer[85] or reinstated in the exact position he occupied prior to his expulsion regarding work opportunity at the hiring hall.[86] In addition, some unions were also ordered to post a copy of the Board's reasons for decision in the hiring hall they operated,[87] or to post a notice stating that their criteria for admission to membership were found by the Board to be discriminatory.[88]

The Board has clear authority to order such measures in subss. (d) and (e) and the last paragraph of s. 189.

---

[78]   *Government of the Northwest Territories and Housing Corp. of the Northwest Territories* (1978), 31 di 165, [1979] 2 Can LRBR 521, 78 CLLC #16,171; *North Canada Air Ltd.* (1978), 35 di 129, [1979] 3 Can LRBR 239, 79 CLLC #16,194.

[79]   *Gérard Cassista* (1978), 28 di 955, [1979] 2 Can LRBR 149; *Terry Matus* (1980), 37 di 73, [1980] 2 Can LRBR 21, 80 CLLC #16,022.

[80]   *Kevin Allison MacLaren* (1982), 47 di 79; *Ronald Wheadon* (1983), 54 di 134, 5 CLRBR (NS) 192, 84 CLLC #16,004.

[81]   *Gerald Abbott* (1977), 26 di 543, [1978] 1 Can LRBR 305; *Val Udvarhely* (1979), 35 di 87, [1979] 2 Can LRBR 569.

[82]   *Gerald Abbott, supra,* note 81; *Terry Matus, supra,* note 79.

[83]   *Gerard Cassista, supra,* note 79.

[84]   *Terry Matus, supra,* note 79.

[85]   *Gerald Abbott, supra,* note 81.

[86]   *Terry Matus, supra,* note 79.

[87]   *Ibid.*

[88]   *Roland Arsenault* (1982), 50 di 51, [1982] 3 Can LRBR 425, 82 CLLC #17,018.

16:4000   THE BOARD'S PRACTICE WITH RESPECT TO COMPENSATION, INTERESTS, AND COSTS

As seen earlier,[89] when the Board reinstates and awards compensation to an illegally dismissed employee, it leaves the determination of the quantum to be settled by the parties with the assistance of an investigating officer. However, the Board always reserves jurisdiction on this question, whether the parties consent to it or not. Furthermore, the complainant does not have the obligation to show that he has attempted to mitigate his losses, but any sums that may have been earned during the period of dismissal will be deducted from the total amount of compensation.

The Board has never awarded interests on monetary compensation,[90] but it has not made any pronouncement on its jurisdiction to do so. However, it has recently[91] determined that it has jurisdiction under s. 189 to award costs in favour of a successful complainant. The Board may also award costs against an unsuccessful complainant pursuant to its authority under s. 121. As a matter of policy, however, the Board's practice is not to award legal costs, whether the complaint is dismissed or allowed. In support of this policy the Board has pointed out that (i) awarding costs labels a winner and a loser, which is counterproductive in an industrial relations relationship; (ii) the exercise of assessing the reasonableness of costs is not one to which a labour board's processes are well suited; (iii) the exercise of assessing the reasonableness of legal costs would detract from the Board's primary labour relations functions; (iv) the awarding of costs has a punitive connotation that is inappropriate in the context of labour board remedies; (v) to award costs in certain kinds of cases would raise difficult questions of when or when not to order costs; and (vi) awarding costs does not respond to the real harm done.

---

[89]   See paragraph 11:2112.
[90]   See, for instance, *American Airlines Inc.* (1981), 43 di 156.
[91]   *National Bank of Canada* (1984), 84 CLLC #16,038.

CHAPTER 17

PENAL PROSECUTION

17:0000   PENAL PROSECUTIONS

17:1000   GENERALLY

The 1972 Code maintained penal prosecutions for illegal strikes and lockouts and contraventions to the provisions of the Code other than those of ss. 148, 184, and 185. The Board had not been transferred the authority to grant or withhold consents for penal prosecutions that had to be obtained from the minister. The 1978 amendments maintained penal prosecutions for illegal strikes and lockouts and contraventions to the provisions of the Code other than those of ss. 148, 184, and 185, but the authority to grant consents to institute such proceedings was transferred to the Board under the provisions of s. 194.

In practical terms this means that, according to s. 191, penal prosecutions for breaches of ss. 124(4), 136.1, 161.1, 186, 190, 192, 193, 199.1, and any other provision of Part V other than those of ss. 148, 184, and 185 can be instituted if the Board grants its consent pursuant to s. 194.

Section 190 strengthens the prohibition contained in s. 180(1) against illegal strikes or lockouts. Every employer who declares or causes an illegal lockout is liable, under s. 190(1), to a fine of up to one thousand dollars for each day of the lockout; and every person who, on behalf of an employer, declares or causes an illegal lockout is liable, pursuant to s. 190(2), to a fine of up to ten thousand dollars. Every trade union that declares or authorizes an illegal strike is liable, pursuant to s. 190(3), to a fine of up to one thousand dollars for each day of the strike; and every officer or representative of a trade union who declares or authorizes an illegal strike is liable personally, under s. 190(4), to a fine of up to ten thousand dollars. Finally, every employee who participates in an illegal strike is liable, pursuant to ss. 180(2) and 191(1), to a fine of up to one thousand dollars.

Section 192 strengthens the authority of the Board under s. 118(a) and that of a conciliation board (s. 175(b)), a conciliation commissioner (s. 175(b)), and an arbitrator and arbitration board (s. 157(b)), which have also been granted the authority to exercise the powers of s. 118(a). Every person who fails to appear as a witness, produce documents, be sworn, or

411

affirm or answer a question before the Board, a conciliation commissioner or board, or an arbitrator or arbitration board is liable to a fine of up to four hundred dollars. In the 1978 Code the conciliation officer appointed under s. 164(1)(a) had not been granted the authority to exercise the powers of s. 118(a), but he was referred to in s. 192(d). The amendments of June 1984 did not enlarge the authority of the conciliation officer. On the contrary, the reference to the conciliation officer was removed from s. 192(d).[1]

Section 193(2) provides that an employer's organization, a trade union, and a council of trade unions shall be deemed to be a person and may be prosecuted for their acts and those of their officers or agents acting within the scope of their authority. Such a prosecution may be brought, according to s. 193(1), against and in the name of an employer's organization, a trade union, or a council of trade unions.

Finally, it must be kept in mind that for the purpose of ss. 180 to 193, an "employer" includes an employer's organization and "trade union" includes a council of trade unions.[2]

17:2000 BOARD CONSENT

The Board has not yet discussed the criteria it will take into consideration when an application under s. 194 is made to prosecute general offences under s. 191 or breaches of the provisions of ss. 192 and 193. However, in *Conseil des Ports Nationeaux*[3] the Board has outlined its policy in disposing of applications under s. 194 made in the context of an illegal strike. In that case, the union waged illegal work stoppages and instituted an overtime ban. On an application by the employer under s. 182, a cease-and-desist order was issued by the Board, re-establishing the status quo.[4] The union complied for a short period but eventually waged new illegal work stoppages and reinstituted an overtime ban, in spite of the Board's order. The Board granted consent to the employer pursuant to s. 194 to prosecute the union but not its officers or members, stipulating that the prosecution must be initiated within the period preceding the conclusion of the collective agreement. The Board stated that although an employer may seek an authorization to prosecute at the same time as a declaration of an unlawful strike and a cease-and-desist order, the Board's general policy in such circumstances will be to deny automatic authorization to lay criminal charges. When the board declares that a union has violated

---

1   See s. 38 of S.C. 1983-84, c. 39, passed by the House of Commons on June 27, 1984, re-enacting s. 192(d) of Part V of the *Canada Labour Code*.
2   *Canada Labour Code*, s. 179.
3   (1979), 33 di 530, [1979] 3 Can LRBR 502, 79 CLLC #16,204.
4   *Ibid.*

s. 180 and orders the union to put an end to such unlawful acts by issuing a cease-and-desist order, which may be accompanied by directives addressed to one or the other or both parties, the Board expects the union to understand that what it was doing was forbidden and ran counter to the spirit of the Code.

Thus, when an order has been issued under s. 182 or 183 and an application under s. 123 or 194 is subsequently filed, the Board stated that

> it is necessarily obliged to verify whether the ordinance rendered under section 182 or 183, together with the directives added thereto, have been observed and whether the directives it has issued have been understood by one or both parties and have yielded the anticipated results. This is why as a general rule, we will not grant consent under section 194 before we know not only whether the order issued under section 182 has been observed but also what the parties' behaviour has been in terms of healthy labour relations. If order has been restored and the true cause of the dispute has been eliminated, it is highly unlikely that it would be in the interest of good labour relations to authorize prosecution.[5]

However, when a party refuses without reason to comply with the provisions of the Code and has been warned of the consequences, the authorization to prosecute may serve the purposes of healthy labour relations if it has the effect of making the parties concerned and everyone in the labour relations sphere as a whole understand and it is in everyone's interest that the rules of the game be observed.

---

5   *National Harbours Board* (1979), 33 di 557, at 562, [1979] 3 Can LRBR 513, 79 CLLC #16,204.

CHAPTER 18

OCCUPATIONAL HEALTH AND SAFETY

18:0000 OCCUPATIONAL HEALTH AND SAFETY

18:1000 APPLICATION OF PART IV

Since the mid-1960s there have been provisions in the *Canada Labour Code* with respect to health and safety. They form the subject-matter of Part IV of the Code. This Part underwent major amendments in 1978 and in 1984.[1] Although the 1978 amendments were extensive and important, Part IV was completely remodelled in 1984. When these last amendments come into force, all its provisions will be replaced and the scope of application will be different.[2] However, at the time of writing, the 1984 amendments had not yet been proclaimed in force.[3]

Pursuant to s. 80(1), as it existed prior to the 1984 amendments, Part IV generally applied to all federal enterprises and Crown corporations (excluding government departments), but this was "*subject* to any other Act of the Parliament of Canada and any regulations thereunder". The new s. 80(1) provides that this Part will apply "notwithstanding any other Act of Parliament or any regulations thereunder". However, pursuant to the new s. 80.1, "the Governor in Council may by order exclude, in whole or in part, from the application of this Part or any specified provision thereof employment on or in connection with any work or undertaking that is regulated pursuant to the *Atomic Energy Control Act*".

---

[1] *Canada Labour Code*, R.S.C. 1970, c. L-1, ss. 79-106, as amended by *An Act to Amend the Canada Labour Code*, S.C. 1977-78, c. 27, ss. 27.1-35; *An Act to Amend the Canada Labour Code and the Financial Administration Act*, S.C. 1983-84, c. 39, ss. 17-20. See notes 2 and 3, *infra*.

[2] Pursuant to S.C. 1983-84, c. 39, s. 17, the headings preceding s. 79 of the *Canada Labour Code* are repealed and substituted with new headings and with new ss. 79 and 79.1. Pursuant to s. 18, s. 80 of the *Canada Labour Code* is repealed and replaced by a new s. 80. Pursuant to s. 19, a new s. 80.1 is added to the *Canada Labour Code*. Pursuant to s. 20, ss. 81-106.1 of the *Canada Labour Code* are repealed and replaced by new ss. 81-106. See note 3, *infra*. Pursuant to s. 44, the *Financial Administration Act* is to be amended so as to bring the public service within the scope of Part IV of the Code.

[3] According to information received by the authors, by March 31, 1986, ss. 17, 19, 20, and 41 of S.C. 1983-84, c. 39 will be proclaimed in force. It is planned that s. 18 will be proclaimed later in 1986.

18:2000 **OVERVIEW OF THE BOARD'S JURISDICTION**

18:2100   AFTER THE 1978 AMENDMENTS

Prior to the 1978 amendments the Board exercised no jurisdiction under Part IV of the Code. In 1978, Parliament conferred on the persons to whom Part IV applied the right to refuse to work in case of an "imminent danger" to their safety or health, and it established mechanisms under which this right could be exercised once a safety officer had determined that an "imminent danger" existed.[4] By virtue of these amendments the Board was given an appellate jurisdiction in two situations:

1. where an employee who has exercised the right to refuse to work for reason of imminent danger is not satisfied with the safety officer's decision that the use or operation of the machine, device, or thing does not constitute an imminent danger to the employee's health or safety (s. 82.1(8));[5] and

2. where the employer or the operator of the enterprise is not satisfied with the safety officer's decision to issue directions in a case where the latter has concluded that a place, matter, or thing, or any part or parts thereof, constitute a source of imminent danger to the employees' safety or health (s. 95).[6]

Furthermore, the Board was given jurisdiction to act in cases where employees made complaints alleging that they had been illegally penalized by their employer because they had exercised their right to refuse to work in situations of imminent danger (s. 96.1).[7]

---

[4]   Section 82.1, repealed by s. 20 of S.C. 1983-84, c. 39, notes 2 and 3, *supra.* See, however, our comments at paragraphs 18:2200 and 18:3000.

[5]   This provision is repealed by s. 20 of S.C. 1983-84, c. 39, notes 2 and 3, *supra.* The following decisions of the Board were rendered pursuant to the existing s. 82.1: *Brian Beeson* (1981), 46 di 82, [1981] 1 Can LRBR 268; *Ernest L. Labarge* (1981), 47 di 18, 82 CLLC #16,151; *Richard McIlveen* (1983), 52 di 26, 2 CLRBR (NS) 67; and *Jean M. Sibley* (1983), 52 di 137, 3 CLRBR (NS) 409. See our comments at paragraphs 18:2200 and 18:3341.

[6]   This provision is repealed by s. 20 of S.C. 1983-84, c. 39, notes 2 and 3, *supra.* The Board has rendered one decision under s. 95: *Bell Canada,* decision no. 469, not yet reported, July 9, 1984 (C.L.R.B.). See our comments at paragraphs 18:2200 and 18:3342.

[7]   This provision is replaced by s. 20 of S.C. 1983-84, c. 39, notes 2 and 3, *supra.* The following Board decisions have been rendered pursuant to s. 96.1: *Alan Miller* (1980), 39 di 93, [1980] 2 Can LRBR 344, 80 CLLC #16,048; *Alan Miller* (1980), 39 di 168, [1980] 3 Can LRBR 377, 80 CLLC #16,049; *Michel Bisson* (1981), 45 di 197; *M. Gaétan Froment* (1982), 46 di 125; *Christine Nugent* (1982), 47 di 72, [1982] 1 Can LRBR 416; *Samuel John Snively* (1982), 48 di 93; *Michael McKye* (1983), 52 di 118, 4 CLRBR (NS) 167; and *Samuel John Snively* (1984), 8 CLRBR (NS) 309. See our comments at paragraphs 18:2200 and 18:4200.

18:2200   AFTER THE COMING INTO FORCE OF THE 1984 AMENDMENTS

When the 1984 amendments are eventually brought into force,[8] the Board will lose a part of its appellate jurisdiction now exercised under ss. 82.1 and 95. The jurisdiction granted by the present provision will be transferred to the regional safety officers by the new s. 103.[9] However, pursuant to the new s. 86(5), the Board will continue to hear appeals from employees in cases where safety officers have refused to permit them to exercise their right to refuse to work.[10]

Under the new s. 90, the Board will also continue to decide complaints from employees who allege that they have been penalized by their employer because they have exercised the right to refuse to work.[11]

18:3000   REFUSAL TO WORK FOR REASON OF DANGER

18:3100   WHAT CONSTITUTES A "DANGER"

The new s. 85(1) of the Code reads as follows:

85.(1) Subject to this section, where an employee while at work has reasonable cause to believe that

(a) the use or operation of a machine or thing constitutes a danger to himself or another employee, or

(b) a condition exists in any place that constitutes a danger to the employee,

the employee may refuse to use or operate the machine or thing or to work in that place.

The same right is currently conferred by s. 82.1(1), which reads:

82.1(1) Where a person employed upon or in connection with the operation of any federal work, undertaking or business has reasonable cause to believe that

(a) the use or operation of a machine, device or thing would constitute an imminent danger to the safety or health of himself or another employee, or

(b) a condition exists in any place that would constitute an imminent danger to his own safety or health,

that person may refuse to use or operate the machine, device or thing or to work in the place.

The present provision uses the expression "imminent danger", while the new provision refers simply to "danger". The expression

---

8   See notes 2 and 3, *supra.*
9   See paragraph 18:3342.
10   See paragraph 18:3341.
11   See paragraph 18:4200.

"imminent danger" was not defined. The new s. 79 will now define the word "danger". In Board cases decided under the 1978 provisions,[12] the following definition given by Labour Canada has been accepted:

> A threat of injury to your safety or health which is likely to happen at any moment without warning. This would usually refer to a situation where the injury might occur before the hazard could be removed.

The new definition of "danger" now provided by s. 79 is very similar to the earlier definition given by Labour Canada, which has been accepted by the Board. It reads:

> "danger" means any hazard or condition that could reasonably be expected to cause injury or illness to a person exposed thereto before the hazard or condition can be corrected.

However, as explained below,[13] an employee may still be deprived of his right to refuse to work, even where a situation of danger exists.

18:3200   CASES WHERE AN EMPLOYEE IS NOT PERMITTED TO REFUSE TO WORK

18:3210   Where the Life, Health, or Safety of Another Person Is in Danger

Pursuant to the new s. 85(2)(a), an employee may not exercise the right to refuse to work if his refusal puts the life, health, or safety of another person directly in danger.

Although employees on a ship or aircraft are not automatically deprived of the right to refuse to work in case of danger, the new s. 85(3), (4), and (5) will provide that the person in charge of the ship or aircraft be empowered to suspend the exercise of this right while the ship or aircraft is in operation because of the necessity of the safe operations of the vessel or aircraft.

18:3220   Where the Danger Is Inherent in the Employee's Work or Is a Normal Condition of Employment

Pursuant to the new s. 85(2)(b), an employee may not exercise the right to refuse to work if the danger is inherent in his work or if it is a normal condition of employment. The present s. 82.1(12) similarly

---

12   See *Alan Miller* (1980), 39 di 93, [1980] 2 Can LRBR 344, 80 CLLC #16,048; *Brian Beeson, supra*, note 5; *Ernest L. Labarge, supra*, note 5; *Richard McIlveen, supra*, note 5; *Jean M. Sibley, supra*, note 5; *Canadian Imperial Bank of Commerce* (1985), 85 CLLC #16,021.
13   See paragraph 18:3200.

provides that there can be no "imminent danger" in situations where a particular condition or circumstance is normal in that occupation. However, "imminent danger" will be found to exist any place where the radiation safety level set by the federal or provincial government has been exceeded.

18:3300　MULTI-STEP PROCEDURE

A multi-step procedure has been established in cases of refusals for reason of danger. This procedure is currently contained in s. 82.1, which will be repealed when the 1984 amendments come into force.[14] The new ss. 85 to 87 will establish a procedure that is fundamentally the same. However, as mentioned earlier, the Board will lose the appellate jurisdiction provided by the present s. 95. The multi-step procedure established by the new ss. 85 to 87 is described in detail below. It must be remembered however, that pursuant to the new s. 88 (currently s. 82.2), the Minister of Labour, on the joint application of the parties, may exclude the employees from the application of these sections for the period during which the agreement remains in force where he is satisfied that the provisions of the agreement are at least as effective as the provisions of the Code.

18:3310　First Step: Report of the Employee to the Employer: New Section 85(6) (Present Section 82.1(2))

The employee who refuses to work must immediately report the circumstances to his employer and to a member of the health and safety committee or to the health and safety representative, if one has been appointed for the work place (s. 86(6)). Unless the employer's work place falls into an exempted category or has been exempted by ministerial order, employers are obliged to establish a health and safety committee for each work place at which twenty or more employees are employed (s. 92). A health and safety representative is appointed in cases where the work place employs five or more employees if no health and safety committee has been established (s. 93).

18:3320　Second Step: The Employer's Investigation: New Section 85(7) (Present Section 82.1(3))

Following the employee's refusal to work and report, the employer must investigate the complaint. The investigation is executed in the presence of the employee and at least one member of the health and

---

14　See notes 2 and 3, *supra.*

safety committee (who does not exercise a managerial function), or in the presence of the health and safety representative, if any, or of a representative chosen by the employee (s. 85(7)).

The employee may continue to refuse to use or operate the allegedly dangerous machine or thing or to work in that area if he still has reasonable cause to believe that a danger exists, notwithstanding the fact that the employer may dispute the report following his investigation or that he may have taken steps to protect the safety of the employee (s. 85(8)).

18:3330   Third Step: Investigation by a Safety Officer: New Section 86(1) (Present Section 82.1(5))

In case of a continued refusal to work, at a third stage, the matter will be investigated by a safety officer in the presence of the employer and the employee or his representative. Prior to the investigation and decision of the safety officer, the employer may require that the employee concerned remain at a safe location near the place in respect of which the investigation is being made, or he may assign the employee reasonable alternate work (s. 86(3)(a)). Furthermore, during this period the employer is not authorized to assign any other employee to use or operate the machine or thing, or to work in that area unless that other employee has been advised of the refusal of the employee concerned (s. 86(3)(b)).

After this investigation, the safety officer must decide whether or not a danger exists (s. 86(2)), and, if so, he may take measures to isolate the source of the danger or to protect any person from the danger. He may direct that the place, machine, or thing shall not be used or operated until his directions have been complied with (ss. 86(4) and 102(2)). The employee may continue to refuse to use or operate the machine or thing, or to work in the area until the direction has been complied with or until it has been varied or rescinded under Part IV (s. 86(4)).

18:3340   Fourth Step: Review of the Safety Officer's Decision

18:3341   Reference to the Board: New Section 86(5) (Present Section 82.1(8))

Where the safety officer decides that a danger does not exist, the employee is not permitted to continue to refuse to work. If the latter is unsatisfied he may, by notice in writing given within seven days of receiving notice of the decision, require the safety officer to refer his decision to the Board (s. 86(5)). The Board must without delay and in a summary fashion inquire into the circumstances of the decision. Notwithstanding s. 115(1) of the Code, one member of the Board may dispose of such a reference (s. 105.8(1)). The Board's (or member's) powers are not limited to the confirmation or quashing of the decision, but they include the issuance of any direction the safety officer was authorized to make (ss. 87(1)(b) and 105.8(1)). The Board's directions are posted at or near the machine, thing, or place in respect of which the direction is given and may not be removed without the authorization of a safety officer or the Board (s. 87(2)). The machine, thing, or place cannot be used until the Board's directions have been complied with (s. 87(3)). The provisions of Part V respecting orders and decisions of the Board will apply in respect of all orders and decisions of the Board (or any member) under this Part (s. 105.8(2)). Accordingly, in a case of non-compliance, the Board can file its order or decision in the Federal Court of Canada (s. 123).

18:3342 Reference to a Regional Safety Officer: Section 103

The new s. 103(1) provides:

103.(1) Any employer, employee or trade union that considers himself or itself aggrieved by any direction issued by a safety officer under this Part may, within fourteen days of the date of the direction, request that a regional safety officer for the region in which the place, machine or thing in respect of which the direction was issued is situated, review the direction.

However, pursuant to s. 103(5), subs. (1) does not apply in respect of a direction of a safety officer that is based on a decision of the safety officer that has been referred to the Board pursuant to s. 86(5). Accordingly, if an employer wishes to contest the validity of a safety officer's direction issued after the exercise of the right to refuse to work, he must address himself to a regional safety officer within fourteen days of the date of the direction.[15] This request may be made orally, although the regional officer may require that it be made in writing as well (s. 103(2)). The regional officer must make a summary inquiry into the directions (s. 103(3)). A request for a review of a direction does not operate to stay the direction (s. 103(4)). The regional officer has the power to vary, rescind, or confirm the direction (s. 103(3)).

18:4000 PROTECTION OF EMPLOYEES' RIGHTS UNDER PART IV

18:4100 GENERAL PROHIBITION

The new s. 104(a) establishes a general prohibition. Pursuant to this section, no employer shall

---

[15] Prior to the 1984 amendments, this jurisdiction was exercised by the Board pursuant to s. 95. See paragraph 18:2100 and note 6, *supra*.

(a) dismiss, suspend, lay off or demote an employee or impose any financial or other penalty on an employee or refuse to pay the employee remuneration in respect of any period of time that the employee would, but for the exercise of his rights under this Part, have worked or take any disciplinary action against or threaten to take any such action against an employee because that employee

(i) has testified or is about to testify in any proceeding taken or inquiry held under this Part,

(ii) has provided information to a person engaged in the performance of duties under this Part regarding the conditions of work affecting the safety or health of that employee or any of his fellow employees, or

(iii) has acted in accordance with this Part or has sought the enforcement of any of the provisions of this Part . . .

As we can see, the application of the prohibition is not limited to any particular case of reprisal but it includes any action taken against an employee because the latter "has acted in accordance with this Part or has sought the enforcement of any of the provisions of this Part" (s. 104(a)(iii)). The present s. 97 is not drafted in such a broad fashion.

18:4200   COMPLAINT TO THE BOARD

18:4210   Right to Complain

Pursuant to the new s. 90, an employee has the right to make a complaint to the Board where he alleges that he has been the object of illegal action by the employer because he has acted in accordance with s. 85 or 86, that is, where he has refused to work because he had reasonable cause to believe that a situation of danger existed.[16] The employee may not make a complaint under s. 90 if he has failed to comply with s. 85(6) or 86(1) in relation to the matter that is the subject-matter of the complaint (s. 90(3)).

In relation to the present provision of the Code dealing with the right to refuse to work in case of imminent danger (present s. 82.1), the Board has determined that the most important factor is not primarily the degree of danger present but rather the reasonableness of the employee's belief in its existence.[17] The Board has also said that an employee's right to refuse to do work for reasons of health or safety should be used only in the true interests of safety and not to further other interests, such as to gain an advantage in collective bargaining.[18] However, where the employee has reasonable grounds to believe in the existence of a danger and

---

16   See paragraph 18:3000.

17   See *Alan Miller, supra,* note 12; *M. Gaétan Froment, supra,* note 7; *Canadian Imperial Bank of Commerce, supra,* note 12.

18   *William Gallivan* (1981), 45 di 180, [1982] 1 Can LRBR 241.

where he acts in good faith, the protection offered by the Code is absolute.[19]

18:4220   Time Limits

Pursuant to the present s. 96.1, the complaints must be made within thirty days of the date on which the complainant knew, or in the opinion of the Board ought to have known, of the action or circumstances giving rise to the complaint, unless the minister has granted an extension of time (present s. 96.1(2)).[20] The delay has now been increased to ninety days, in the new text, but the ministerial discretion to extend this delay has been removed by the new s. 90(2).

18:4230   Investigation of the Complaint

The Board may attempt to settle the complaint before the hearing (new s. 90(5)). Notwithstanding s. 115(1), one member of the Board may dispose of the complaint. The Board or the Board member have all the powers, rights, and privileges (except for the regulatory powers contained in s. 117) conferred on the Board by the Code (s. 105.8(1)). By virtue of s. 90(6), "a complaint made pursuant to subsection (1) in respect of an alleged contravention of paragraph 104(a) by an employer is itself evidence that such contravention actually occurred and, if any party to the complaint proceedings alleges that such contravention did not occur, the burden of proof thereof is on that party".

18:4240   Remedial Authority of the Board

The remedial authority of the Board is found in the new s. 91. It is the same as that under the present s. 96.3. The Board has the power to order the employer to cease contravening s. 90. It may make an order of reinstatement, with or without compensation (which may not in any case exceed the equivalent of the remuneration lost). It may also rescind any disciplinary action and order the payment of compensation (not exceeding the equivalent of the penalty).[21] The Board's order may be filed pursuant to s. 123 of the Code (s. 105.8(2)), which refers to the provisions of Part V respecting orders, decisions, and proceedings before the Board.

---

[19]   See *Michael McKye, supra,* note 7; and *Samuel John Snively* (1984), 8 CLRBR (NS) 309.
[20]   See *Michel Bisson, supra,* note 7.
[21]   See *Alan Miller* (1980), 39 di 168, [1980] 3 Can LRBR 377, 80 CLLC #16,049; *Christine Nugent, supra,* note 7; and *Samuel John Snively* (1982), 48 di 93.

18:4250   Exclusion of Arbitration

Pursuant to the new s. 90(4) (present s. 96.1(4)), notwithstanding any law or agreement to the contrary, such a complaint may not be referred by an employee to arbitration.

18:5000   REMEDIES IN CASE OF A CONTRAVENTION OF PART IV

18:5100   SAFETY OFFICERS' DIRECTIONS

Several provisions of Part IV impose duties on the employer and the employee in order to prevent accidents and injury to health (see new ss. 79.1, 81, 82, 83, 84).

The safety officer has the power to direct an employer or an employee to cease actions that contravene any provision of this Part (s. 102(1)). Specific directions can be issued in dangerous situations (see s. 102(2)). These directions may be reviewed by a regional safety officer (s. 103).

18:5200   PENAL PROSECUTION

A person who breaches any provision of Part IV is guilty of an offence (s. 105(1)). Specific offences are also created (s. 105(2) to (5)). However, no proceeding in respect of an offence under this Part may be instituted if the minister has not given his consent (s. 105.1(1)).

18:5300   INJUNCTION PROCEEDINGS

Pursuant to the new s. 105.4, the Minister of Labour may apply or cause an application to be made to a judge of a superior court or of the Federal Court, Trial Division, for an order enjoining any person from contravening a provision of this Part, whether or not a prosecution has already been instituted. The order may also enjoin the person from continuing any act or lack of action for which he was convicted of an offence under this Part. The present s. 105 is limited to the latter situation.

18:5400   COMPENSATION UNDER OTHER LAWS

Pursuant to s. 89, the fact that an employer or employee has complied with or failed to comply with any of the provisions of this Part shall not be construed so as to affect any right of the employee to compensation for a work-related injury under any other statute or to affect any liability or obligation of the employer or employee under any other statute.

CHAPTER 19

JUDICIAL REMEDIES

19:0000   JUDICIAL REMEDIES

In this chapter we examine the role played by the courts in the judicial review of Board decisions and orders. The last section deals with judicial enforcement of such decisions and orders.

19:1000   LEGISLATIVE RESTRAINTS IMPOSED ON JUDICIAL AUTHORITY

19:1100   THE PRIVATIVE CLAUSE – SECTION 122

The exercise of the Board's functions and duties under Part V of the Code is enhanced and protected by the powerful privative clause in s. 122. It reads as follows:

122.(1) Subject to this Part, every order or decision of the Board is final and shall not be questioned or reviewed in any court, except in accordance with paragraph 28(1)(a) of the *Federal Court Act*.

(2) Except as permitted by subsection (1), no order, decision or proceeding of the Board made or carried on under or purporting to be made or carried on under this Part shall be

(a) questioned, reviewed, prohibited or restrained, or

(b) made the subject of any proceedings in or any process of any court, whether by way of injunction, *certiorari*, prohibition, *quo warranto* or otherwise,

on any ground, including the ground that the order, decision or proceeding is beyond the jurisdiction of the Board to make or carry on or that, in the course of any proceeding, the Board for any reason exceeded or lost its jurisdiction.

The actual form of the present privative clause was introduced with the legislative reform of 1978. Prior to this reform, Board decisions and orders could be reviewed on all three grounds mentioned in s. 28(1) of the *Federal Court Act:*

28.(1) Notwithstanding section 18 or the provisions of any other Act, the Court of Appeal has jurisdiction to hear and determine an application to review and set aside a decision or order, other than a decision or order of an administrative nature not required by law to be made on a judicial or quasi-judicial basis, made by or in the course of proceedings before a federal board, commission or other tribunal, upon the ground that the board, commission or tribunal

(a) failed to observe a principle of natural justice or otherwise acted beyond or refused to exercise its jurisdiction;

(b) erred in law in making its decision or order, whether or not the error appears on the face of the record; or

(c) based its decision or order on an erroneous finding of fact that it made in a perverse or capricious manner or without regard for the material before it.

Grounds (b) and (c) provided open invitations to either party to seek review of the merits of a Board decision on questions clearly within its jurisdiction. Accordingly, the courts did not hesitate to examine the Board's interpretations of the definitions found in the Code, or the Board's appreciation of the intent of other provisions of the Code in view of their purpose in a labour relations context. In *Bank of Montreal v. Canada Labour Relations Board*[1] the issue was whether or not the Board had erred in law in interpreting and applying the words "matters relating to industrial relations" found in the definition of "employee". In *Bank of Nova Scotia v. Canada Labour Relations Board*[2] a similar issue relating to the inclusion of loan officers in the bargaining units was raised by the employer as an alleged error of law by the Board.[3] In *CKCH Radio Ltée v. Canada Labour Relations Board*,[4] although the Court dismissed an application to review a decision handed down under the old text of s. 155 of the Code, it mentioned in conclusion that emphasis should be placed on the fact that the applicant had not argued that the impugned decision was illegal for any reason other than that which the court had dismissed. The court then indicated that s. 155(2) of the Code did not entitle the Board to make an order that did not comply with all the requirements of s. 155(1). It further concluded that, in the case at bar, doubts concerning the validity of the decision handed down by the Board had arisen *inter alia*, because it appeared that the collective agreement, as amended by the Board's order, did not permit the employer to present a grievance or submit a dispute to arbitration.

Judicial interference on the grounds mentioned in s. 28(1)(b) led to unhappy results for the administration of the Code in *CKOY Ltd. v. Ottawa Newspaper Guild, Local 205*,[5] a 1977 case. The Federal Court of Appeal determined here that the Board had made a reviewable error of law within the meaning of s. 28(1)(b) when it decided that, for the purposes of s. 126(c), the time to decide whether the majority of employees in a

---

1   [1979] 1 F.C. 87, 21 N.R. 214 (C.A.).

2   [1978] 2 F.C. 807, 21 N.R. 1, 78 CLLC #14,145 (C.A.).

3   See also: *Empire Stevedoring Co. Ltd. v. International Longshoremen's and Warehousemen's Union, Local 514*, [1974] 2 F.C. 742, 6 N.R. 485, 75 CLLC #14,262 (C.A.); *Public Service Alliance of Canada v. Francis*, [1982] 2 S.C.R. 72, 44 N.R. 136, [1982] 4 C.N.L.R. 94, 82 CLLC #14,208, 139 D.L.R. (3d) 9; revg. [1981] 1 F.C. 225.

4   [1976] 1 F.C. 3 (C.A.).

5   [1977] 2 F.C. 412, 14 N.R. 264, 77 CLLC #14,093, 74 D.L.R. (3d) 229 (C.A.).

bargaining unit wish to be represented by the union seeking certification was the date on which the application for certification was made. The court was of the opinion that, pursuant to this section, the Board should have been satisfied that this majority existed at the time of rendering its decision and not at the time of filing the application for certification. In 1978, ss. 118.1 and 126(c) were specifically enacted in order to nullify the effects of this judgment.[6]

Furthermore, before the 1978 amendment, proceedings in the nature of writs or prohibition or other writs could be brought before the Trial Division of the Federal Court under s. 18 of the *Federal Court Act* to prevent the Board from pursuing an inquiry for lack of jurisdiction.[7] At that time it was generally recognized that the pre-1978 form of the privative clause was in no way exceptional. It would have been illogical to assume that, merely by inserting in the Board's constitutive Act a privative clause and by outlining its jurisdiction, Parliament had authorized the Board to deal with matters or persons over which it had not been given jurisdiction or to engage in otherwise unauthorized hearings. In *British Columbia Packers Ltd. v. Canada Labour Relations Board*[8] Mr. Justice Addy of the Federal Court issued a writ of prohibition under s. 18(a) of the *Federal Court Act* to restrain the Board from proceeding with certain applications for certification. He held that the terms of the Code did not encompass the definition of fishing crews as employees and the applicant companies as their employers, since the fishermen were not employed upon or in connection with the operation of any federal work, undertaking, or business within s. 108 of the *Canada Labour Code*. He further concluded that if the Code did cover them, its provisions were in that respect *ultra vires*. The Federal Court of Appeal affirmed the judgment of Addy J. on the above constitutional ground.[9] The Supreme Court of Canada confirmed both judgments, but only on the single ground that Part V of the Code did not bring crew members and the companies into an employee-employer relationship so as to authorize the Board to entertain applications for certification.[10]

---

6   The outcome was different in *Canada Labour Relations Board v. Transair Ltd.*, [1977] 1 S.C.R. 722, 9 N.R. 181, 76 CLLC #14,024, 67 D.L.R. (3d) 421; revg. [1974] 2 F.C. 832, 6 N.R. 123, 75 CLLC #14,261, 51 D.L.R. (3d) 709, where the Board succeeded in having a Federal Court decision overturned wherein the latter had held that the Board had erred in determining the unit as of the date of the application for certification.

7   See *British Columbia Packers Ltd. v. Canada Labour Relations Board*, [1974] 2 F.C. 913, 50 D.L.R. (3d) 602; affd. [1976] 1 F.C. 375, 75 CLLC #14,307, 64 D.L.R. (3d) 522; affd. [1978] 2 S.C.R. 97, 19 N.R. 320, [1978] 1 W.W.R. 621, 82 D.L.R. (3d) 182; *Maritime Telegraph & Telephone Co. Ltd. v. Canada Labour Relations Board*, [1976] 2 F.C. 343, 67 D.L.R. (3d) 55 (T.D.); *Transportaide Inc. v. Canada Labour Relations Board*, [1978] 2 F.C. 660, 86 D.L.R. (3d) 24 (C.A.); *Télévision St-François Inc. (CKSH-TV) v. Canada Labour Relations Board*, [1977] 2 F.C. 294 (T.D.).

8   *Supra*, note 7.

9   *Ibid.*

10   *Ibid.*

The 1978 version of s. 122 was specifically designed to overcome some of the problems of previous court decisions. The actual wording of this section shows a clear intention to remove any jurisdiction the Trial Division may wish to claim under s. 18 of the *Federal Court Act.* Furthermore, the privative clause limits the jurisdiction of the Federal Court of Appeal to the grounds of review mentioned in s. 28(1)(a) of the *Federal Court Act.*

19:1200   EFFECTIVENESS OF THE PRIVATIVE CLAUSE

As explained above, s. 122 of the Code has two objectives: the limiting of the grounds of judicial intervention to those contained in s. 28(1)(a), and the elimination of parallel interventions by courts other than the Federal Court of Appeal.

Although it may not be easy to determine what is or is not "jurisdictional" and hence reviewable within the meaning of s. 28(1)(a), the Federal Court of Appeal has accepted without any resistance the limitation of its role by the 1978 amendments of the privative clause. As a preliminary question to examining the question raised by a litigant, the court will qualify the question within the terms of s. 28(1)(a), (b), and (c) of the Act, and only if it comes within the scope of the section will it hear argument on the merits.[11]

With regard to the elimination of parallel intervention by courts other than the Federal Court of Appeal, the privative clause has been effective in part. The Trial Division of the Federal Court has disclaimed jurisdiction to issue writs of prohibition or other writs under s. 18 of the *Federal Court Act.* However, the superior courts of the provinces have successfully claimed review jurisdiction where a constitutional issue has been raised before the Board.

In *CJMS Radio Montréal (Québec) Ltd. v. Canada Labour Relations Board,*[12] shortly after the adoption of the present version of the privative clause, a party brought before the Trial Division of the Federal Court an application for a writ of prohibition to prevent the Board from inquiring into an industrial dispute and establishing the terms of an initial collective agreement pursuant to s. 171.1 of the *Canada Labour Code.* The court rejected this application for want of jurisdiction in view of the revised text

---

[11]   *La Banque Provinciale du Canada v. Syndicat National des employés de commerce et de bureau du comté Lapointe (CSN),* [1979] 2 F.C. 439, 30 N.R. 564, 79 CLLC #14,214, 102 D.L.R. (3d) 720 (C.A.); *Dome Petroleum Inc. v. Canadian Merchant Service Guild,* [1981] 2 F.C. 418, 35 N.R. 243, 81 CLLC #14,076, 118 D.L.R. (3d) 335 (C.A.); *St. Lawrence Seaway Authority v. Canada Labour Relations Board* (1979), 31 N.R. 196 (Fed. C.A.); *Uranerz Explorations & Mining Ltd. v. Canada Labour Relations Board,* [1980] 1 F.C. 312, 28 N.R. 431, 79 CLLC #14,215, 102 D.L.R. (3d) 519 (C.A.); *Eastern Provincial Airways Ltd. v. Canada Labour Relations Board,* [1984] 1 F.C. 732, 50 N.R. 81, 2 D.L.R. (4th) 597 (C.A.).

[12]   [1979] 1 F.C. 501, 78 CLLC #14,163, 91 D.L.R. (3d) 388 (T.D.).

of s. 122. It did not find this section to be unconstitutional, since the right of review by the Federal Court of Appeal under s. 28(1)(a) of the *Federal Court Act* was preserved so as to protect the parties should the Board fail to observe a principle of natural justice, act beyond its jurisdiction, or refuse to exercise its jurisdiction.[13] The *CJMS* judgment no doubt has discouraged litigants from bringing proceedings against the Board under s. 18 of the *Federal Court Act.*

However, a major breakthrough against the impermeability of s. 122 was achieved by a judgment rendered in 1981 by the Quebec Court of Appeal in *Paul L'Anglais Inc.*[14] The appeal court confirmed the issuance of a writ of evocation under art. 846 of the *Code of Civil Procedure* of Quebec against the Board's preliminary finding that it had constitutional jurisdiction to make a declaration of a single employer under s. 133.

At the outset the applicant employer had been unsuccessful in having the Board's finding reversed by the Federal Court of Appeal. The latter determined that it lacked jurisdiction under s. 28 of the *Federal Court Act,* since the Board's decision was not "final" within the meaning of that section.[15] The employer then applied to the Superior Court of Quebec for the issuance of a writ of evocation against the Board to have the constitutionality of the application of the Code to the employees decided by the court before the Board proceeded to the merits of the issue. The application was dismissed by the Superior Court, which was of the opinion that the supervisory jurisdiction of the superior courts had been transferred to the Federal Court.[16]

The Court of Appeal subsequently reversed this judgment and decided that s. 122 of the Code should not prevent the superior courts from hearing an application against the Board that contested the constitutional validity of legislation. Parliament, it was held, had no authority to clothe the Federal Court with an exclusive jurisdiction over such a question under s. 18 of the *Federal Court Act.* Finally, the Court of Appeal extended this reasoning to cases of constitutional applicability and declared that they constituted a properly justiciable issue before the Superior Court seized of a judicial review application.[17]

Two years later, the Supreme Court of Canada confirmed the appeal court's judgment.[18] The reasons of the appeal court were adopted by the

---

[13] *Ibid.,* at pp. 506-07 (F.C.). The court did not discuss the constitutional issue raised as one of the grounds by the petitioner in light of the evidence placed before it.

[14] *Paul L'Anglais Inc. v. Le Conseil canadien des relations du travail,* [1981] C.A. 62, 81 CLLC #14,090, 122 D.L.R. (3d) 583; affd. [1983] 1 S.C.R. 147, 47 N.R. 351, 83 CLLC #14,033, 146 D.L.R. (3d) 202.

[15] *Paul L'Anglais Inc. v. Canada Labour Relations Board,* [1979] 2 F.C. 444, 79 CLLC #14,217 (C.A.).

[16] *Paul L'Anglais Inc. v. Le Conseil canadien des relations du travail,* unreported, November 8, 1979, file no. 500-05-01206-793 (Que. S.C.), Justice André G. Biron.

[17] [1981] C.A. 62, at 67-68, 81 CLLC #14,090, 122 D.L.R. (3d) 583.

[18] *Canada Labour Relations Board v. Paul L'Anglais Inc.,* [1983] 1 S.C.R. 147, 47 N.R. 351, 83 CLLC #14,033, 146 D.L.R. (3d) 202.

Supreme Court, which in the interim had rendered another important constitutional judgment in *Attorney General of Canada v. Law Society of British Columbia.*[19] In the latter case it was held that proceedings in the nature of a declaratory judgment that raised constitutional issues could properly be brought before the superior courts of the provinces, notwithstanding the alleged effect of s. 18 of the *Federal Court Act.*

In a more recent case, the Divisional Court of the Supreme Court of Ontario determined that it was competent to review a final order of the Board that held that it had constitutional jurisdiction over the applicant enterprise and had found that the applicant had contravened ss. 124 and 148 of the Code.[20]

Prior to the 1978 amendments to s. 122, the Trial Division of the Federal Court had not hesitated to intervene in cases where a constitutional question as to the applicability of the Code was raised by an applicant.[21] However, the latter court has since then expressed the opinion that the new text of s. 122 could effectively prevent it from issuing a prohibition order even where a constitutional question was raised, and that the privative clause was not unconstitutional.[22]

It is too early to assess what effects the new *Canadian Charter of Rights and Freedoms* may have on the Code, although there have been some attempts to bring the rights guaranteed by the Charter within the context of the limitations placed by s. 122 of the Code. In *Vergis v. Canada Labour Relations Board,*[23] the Trial Division decided that s. 24(1) of the Charter did not give it jurisdiction to stay the execution of orders of the Board. The stay of execution would have protected the employment of the affected employees pending the outcome of litigation concerning the Board orders. Nor did the Trial Division have the power to provide injunctive relief of both a negative and mandatory nature against the acts of the employer and the union, in order to prevent any lay-off or termination of employees during the legal proceedings. The court concluded that s. 122 of the Code deprived it of any jurisdiction to grant the relief asked for under the Charter.

The court also rejected the argument that s. 122 is inoperative or *ultra vires* because it restricts or interferes with the jurisdiction over

---

19   [1982] 2 S.C.R. 307, 43 N.R. 451, 37 B.C.L.R. 145, [1982] 5 W.W.R. 289, 19 B.L.R. 234, 66 C.P.R. (2d) 1, 137 D.L.R. (3d) 1.

20   *Ottawa-Carleton Regional Transit Commission v. Amalgamated Transit Union, Local 279* (1983), 83 CLLC #14,034, 144 D.L.R. (3d) 581; affd. 44 O.R. (2d) 560, 1 O.A.C. 77, 84 CLLC #14,006, 4 D.L.R. (4th) 452 (C.A.).

21   See *British Columbia Packers Ltd. v. Canada Labour Relations Board, supra,* note 7; *Maritime Telegraph & Telephone Co. Ltd. v. Canada Labour Relations Board, supra,* note 7; *Transportaide Inc. v. Canada Labour Relations Board, supra,* note 7; *Télévision St-François Inc. (CKSH-TV) v. Canada Labour Relations Board, supra,* note 7.

22   *CJMS Radio Montréal (Québec) Ltd. v. Canada Labour Relations Board, supra,* note 12; *Speaker of the House of Commons v. Canada Labour Relations Board,* not yet reported, May 30, 1984, file no. T-751-84 (Fed. T.D.).

23   [1983] 1 F.C. 482, 142 D.L.R. (3d) 747 (T.D.).

judicial review that belongs to the Federal Court under the Charter. Since s. 122 permits s. 28 review by the Federal Court of Appeal, the court held that this provision could not be *ultra vires*, and it further suggested, without expressing a conclusion, that s. 122 might well be sustainable under the exception in s. 1 of the Charter.[24]

In *Re Crosbie Offshore Services Ltd. and Canada Labour Relations Board*,[25] it was held by the Trial Division that it was not a court of competent jurisdiction within s. 24(1) of the Charter to decide whether or not the directives imposed by the Board, which concerned electioneering, campaigning, or propaganda to influence or persuade an employee to vote in a certain way, constituted an infringement of s. 2(b) of the Charter. The court held that, in any case, it was not an infringement.[26]

19:2000 JURISDICTION OF THE FEDERAL COURT OF APPEAL

19:2100 APPLICATIONS TO REVIEW AND SET ASIDE A DECISION OR ORDER

When s. 28(1)(a) of the *Federal Court Act* is read together with s. 122 of the Code, the Federal Court of Appeal is given jurisdiction "to hear and determine an application to review and set aside a decision or order of the Board other than a decision or order of an administrative nature not required by law to be made on a judicial or quasi-judicial basis . . . upon the ground that the Board failed to observe a principle of natural justice or otherwise acted beyond or refused to exercise its jurisdiction". Section 52(d) of the *Federal Court Act* provides that in such a case the Court of Appeal may either dismiss the application, set aside the decision, or refer the matter back to the Board for determination in accordance with such directions as it considers to be appropriate.

Over the years, the Federal Court of Appeal has maintained that only final decisions or orders could be reviewed under s. 28. Interim or administrative decisions that do not determine an issue are not "final" within the meaning of this provision. It has been held that a position taken by the Board as to its jurisdiction is not a "decision" within the meaning of this section, except where, in taking this position, it has exhausted its jurisdiction.[27] Therefore, where the Board not only declares that it is not competent to hear an application but decides to dismiss

---

24 *Ibid.*, at p. 485 (F.C.).
25 (1983), 3 D.L.R. (4th) 694 (Fed. T.D.).
26 *Ibid.*, at p. 703.
27 *British Columbia Packers Ltd. v. Canada Labour Relations Board*, [1973] F.C. 1194 (C.A.); *Paul L'Anglais Inc. v. Canada Labour Relations Board*, [1979] 2 F.C. 444, 79 CLLC #14,217 (C.A.); *Peterson v. Sheedy*, unreported, February 2, 1981 (Fed. C.A.).

it as a result, this becomes a final decision within the meaning of s. 28, since the Board has then exhausted all its powers under the Code.[28]

It has been decided that the refusal of the Board to admit evidence is not a decision subject to review, although it may invalidate the final decision taken by the Board.[29] The Board's decision to order a representation vote is an administrative decision that may not be disputed.[30] An order of the Board to produce documents is also an administrative order of an interlocutory nature, and therefore it is not final.[31]

Since June 1, 1978, s. 120.1 of the Code has provided as follows:

120.1(1) Where, in order to dispose finally of an application or complaint it is necessary for the Board to determine two or more issues arising therefrom, the Board may, if it is satisfied that it can do so without prejudice to the rights of any party to the proceeding, issue a decision resolving only one or some of those issues and reserve its jurisdiction to dispose of the remaining issues.

(2) A decision referred to in subsection (1) is, except as stipulated by the Board, final.

(3) In this section, "decision" includes an order, a determination and a declaration.

The Federal Court of Appeal considers that a Board's decision stating that it has jurisdiction to undertake an inquiry is not final within the meaning of s. 120.1[32]

19:2200   REFERENCE BY THE BOARD OF CERTAIN QUESTIONS

Pursuant to s. 28(4) of the *Federal Court Act*, the Board may at any stage of its proceedings refer any question or issue of law, jurisdiction, practice, or any procedure to the Court of Appeal for hearing and determination. The possibility of a referral of a constitutional question to the Federal Court of Appeal was raised in *British Columbia Packers Ltd. v. Canada Labour Relations Board*,[33] where the court suggested that the Board could avail itself of the procedure set out in s. 28(4) of the *Federal Court Act*. A few years later, the Board followed this advice and asked the Court of Appeal to determine whether it had constitutional jurisdiction

---

28   *Le Syndicat international des marins canadiens CLC-ALF-CIO v. Crosbie Offshore Services Ltd.*, unreported, May 15, 1981, file no. A-2-81 (Fed. C.A.).

29   *Syndicat des employés de CJRC (CNTU) v. Canada Labour Relations Board* (1978), 24 N.R. 454, 78 CLLC #14,179 (Fed. C.A.).

30   *Voyageur Inc. v. Syndicat des chauffeurs de Voyageur Inc.*, [1975] F.C. 533 (C.A.); *Crosbie Offshore Services Ltd. v. Canadian Merchant Service Guild*, unreported, November 21, 1983, file no. A-1162-82 (Fed. C.A.).

31   *Transportaide Inc. v. Canada Labour Relations Board*, [1978] 2 F.C. 660, at 670, 86 D.L.R. (3d) 24 (C.A.).

32   *Paul L'Anglais Inc. v. Canada Labour Relations Board, supra*, note 27.

33   *Supra*, note 27.

to grant an application for certification with respect to the installers employed by Northern Telecom Canada Limited.[34] The constitutional validity of s. 28(4) was examined by the Supreme Court of Canada in an appeal from the Federal Court decision holding that the installers of Northern Telecom came under federal jurisdiction. In a majority judgment written by Justice Estey, the Supreme Court confirmed the Federal Court's decision.[35] However, the court was unanimous on the point that the Federal Court of Appeal did have jurisdiction to entertain the question referred under s. 28(4).

19:3000   PROCEEDINGS UNDER SECTION 28 OF THE FEDERAL COURT ACT

19:3100   ORIGINATING NOTICE

Rules 1400 to 1409 of the *Federal Court Rules* apply to s. 28 proceedings.[36] An application to set aside and review a decision or order of the Board is made by the filing of a notice entitled "Originating Notice under section 28 of the Federal Court Act" and containing, as precisely and concisely as possible, a description of the order or decision that is the subject of the application. Once filed, the originating notice must be served on the Deputy Attorney General of Canada and on the Board, and it must be served personally on all interested persons.[37]

19:3200   THE TIMELINESS OF THE APPLICATION

Pursuant to s. 28(2) of the *Federal Court Act,* "an application to set aside and review a decision or an order of the Board must be made within ten days of the time the decision or order was first communicated to the office of the Deputy Attorney General of Canada or to that party by the Board, or within such further time as the Court of Appeal or a judge thereof may, either before or after the expiry of those ten days fix or allow". In *National Association of Broadcast Employees and Technicians v. Western Ontario Broadcasting Ltd.*[38] an application to extend the time for a s. 28 application was granted, although eight months had passed, because the case was "exceptional".

---

34   *Re Canada Labour Relations Board and Communications Workers of Canada,* [1982] 1 F.C. 191, 37 N.R. 145, 123 D.L.R. (3d) 483.
35   *Northern Telecom Canada Ltd. v. Communications Workers of Canada (No. 2)* (1983), 48 N.R. 161, 147 D.L.R. (3d) 1 (S.C.C.).
36   See C.R.C. 1978, c. 663, as amended.
37   Section 28(2) of the *Federal Court Act* and *Federal Court Rules* 1401(2) and (3). For the manner in which a notice is served personally, see Rules 304 and 309.
38   (1978), 25 N.R. 471 (Fed. C.A.).

19:3300   WHO MAY BRING THE APPLICATION

Section 28(2) of the *Federal Court Act* provides that an application to review and set aside a decision of the Board can be made by the Attorney General of Canada or by any party directly affected by the decision. In *Canadian Telecommunications Union, Division No. 1 of United Telegraph Workers v. Canadian Brotherhood of Railway, Transport and General Workers*[39] the applicant union, who wished to attack a Board decision on the ground that in future proceedings it might be affected by a subsequent decision, was not permitted to bring an application to set aside and review the first decision.

In *Appleton v. Eastern Provincial Airways*[40] the court (with a dissenting opinion) determined that replacement employees hired during a strike had the right to be given an opportunity to be heard by the Board in proceedings brought by the bargaining agent against the employer, which resulted in an order by the Board that the employer refrain from conferring permanent status on the replacement employees and reinstate striking employees regardless of whether a replacement employee would have to be displaced as a result. These replacement employees, as members of the bargaining unit for which the bargaining agent acted, were *de facto* parties, and they had sufficient interest to bring an application under s. 28 complaining that they should have been given a notice of the Board's hearing.

19:3400   MATERIAL UPON WHICH THE APPLICATION WILL BE DECIDED

The application must be decided upon the material mentioned in Rule 1402(1), or on any other material if an application is made to vary the contents of the case in accordance with Rule 1402(2). Pursuant to Rule 1402(3) it is the Board registrar who prepares the material listed in Rule 1402(1) and sends it to the court. However, this Rule does not require the Board to supply material that is part of the file if such material is "not in its possession or control".[41] In cases where an applicant alleges that the rules of natural justice have been breached by the Board, it may be necessary to adduce additional evidence. That evidence should be by affidavit.[42]

---

[39]   [1982] 1 F.C. 603, 42 N.R. 243, 81 CLLC #14,126, 126 D.L.R. (3d) 228 (C.A.).

[40]   (1983), 50 N.R. 99, 2 D.L.R. (4th) 147 (Fed. C.A.).

[41]   See *Grain Handlers' Union No. 1 v. Grain Workers' Union, Local 333*, [1978] 1 F.C. 762 (C.A.), where the court rejected an application seeking an order that the Board provide a written transcript of the verbal testimony given at the hearing for use in the s. 28 application, for the reason that the Board had no such transcript in its possession.

[42]   See Rule 332 for the manner of making such affidavits.

19:3500   HEARING BY THE COURT

Pursuant to Rule 1403(1) the applicant must, "within three weeks after he has received a copy of the material in the case, file four copies of a memorandum of the points to be argued by him, including a list of cases intended to be cited; and he shall serve a copy thereof upon each of the other interested persons". Rule 1407(1) provides that "the Court may on application or, having regard to subsection 28(5) of the Act, on its own motion, dismiss an application by reason of the applicant's undue delay in prosecuting it". Pursuant to Rule 1404 a person wishing to participate in the argument must first file a notice of intention to participate and then, in accordance with Rule 1403(2), file and serve a memorandum of the points to be argued by him within three weeks after being served with the applicant's memorandum of points or argument, or of the expiration of the time fixed for the filing of the applicant's memorandum, whichever is the earlier. Under Rule 1405(1), the court may, in its discretion, upon an application before the hearing or during the course of a hearing, decide which persons shall be heard on the argument. Pursuant to Rule 1409 an "interested person" is a person who appeared as a party in the proceeding that gave rise to the decision or the order that is the subject of the s. 28 application and any person who has been granted leave to be heard in the matter by an order under Rule 1405.

19:3600   STAY OF EXECUTION OF BOARD DECISIONS OR ORDERS

Prior to the 1978 amendments to the privative clause,[43] the courts had decided that, pending a s. 28 application before the Court of Appeal, the Trial Division was the competent authority and had the power to stay the execution of a Board order or to vary the time for its compliance.[44] The filing of a Board order in the Federal Court in accordance with s. 123 gave the order the same force and effect as a judgment rendered by the Federal Court. Federal Court Rules 1904 and 1909 were accordingly held to be applicable. They are as follows:

Rule 1904

(1) Notwithstanding that a judgment or order requiring a person to do an act specifies a time within which the act is to be done, the Court may make an order requiring the act to be done within another time, being such time after service of that order, or such other time, as may be specified therein.

(2) Where a judgment or order requiring a person to do an act does not specify a time within which the act is to be done, the Court may subse-

---

[43]   See paragraph 19:1100.

[44]   *Communications Workers of Canada v. Bell Canada*, [1976] 1 F.C. 282, 64 D.L.R. (3d) 171 (T.D.); *Central Broadcasting Co. Ltd. v. Canada Labour Relations Board*, [1975] F.C. 310 (C.A.).

quently make an order requiring the act to be done within such time after service of that order, or such other time, as may be specified therein.

Rule 1909

A party against whom a judgment has been given or an order made may apply to the Court for a stay of execution of the judgment or order or other relief against such judgment or order, and the Court may by order grant such relief, and on such terms, as it thinks just.

In 1981 the appeal court, in *Nauss v. International Longshoremen's Association, Local 269*,[45] in light of the revised privative clause, reversed a judgment of the Trial Division staying the execution of a Board order and varying the time within which the respondent had to demonstrate compliance. The Court of Appeal expressed the opinion that, in view of the clear language of ss. 119 and 122 of the Code, equally clear language would be required to confer on the Trial Division the power to stay the execution of a Board order, particularly in a case such as the one before the court, where the stay of execution implied a variation of that order.[46]

In *Purolator Courrier Ltée v. Canada Labour Relations Board*[47] the Trial Division made an attempt to distinguish *Nauss* on the ground that the latter judgment varied the Board order, but that no variation was required where the court was simply asked to suspend the execution of the order. Therefore, in *Purolator* the court ordered that the Board order be stayed until the decision of the Federal Court of Appeal on the s. 28 application had been rendered. On appeal, the Court of Appeal found that the Trial Division had wrongly interpreted its own earlier judgment, and that accordingly the lower court was without jurisdiction to order a stay of execution.[48] Following these two Court of Appeal judgments, the Trial Division has subsequently refused to issue a stay of execution of a Board order while judicial review proceedings were pending, even where s. 24(1) of the *Canadian Charter of Rights and Freedoms* was invoked against s. 122 of the Code.[49]

However, an unusual development occurred in 1984 when, for the first time, doubts were entertained by the Court of Appeal itself about the *Nauss* judgment. In *Banque Nationale du Canada v. Granda*[50] the court was asked to annul a Trial Division judgment[51] refusing to stay the execution

---

45   [1982] 1 F.C. 114, 36 N.R. 238, 122 D.L.R. (3d) 573 (Fed. C.A.).

46   See Justice Pratte's comments *ibid.* at p. 117 (F.C.).

47   [1983] 1 F.C. 472 (T.D.).

48   *Union des employés de commerce, Local 503 v. Purolator Courrier Ltée,* [1983] 2 F.C. 344, 53 N.R. 330 (C.A.).

49   *Vergis v. Canada Labour Relations Board,* [1983] 1 F.C. 482, 142 D.L.R. (3d) 747 (T.D.).

50   [1984] 2 F.C. 249 (C.A.).

51   The Trial Division, in an unreported judgment dated January 9, 1984, file no. T-2921-83, had rejected the stay application for the sole reason that in *Nauss* and *Purolator* it had been decided that the court had no jurisdiction to grant a stay. The same reasoning was also applied by the Trial Division in *National Association of Broadcast Employees and Technicians (NABET) v. Inland Broadcasters,* [1983] 1 F.C. 786 to reject a stay application concerning an arbitrator's award filed in court pursuant to s. 159(1) of the Code.

of an arbitrator's award rendered under Part III of the Code in an unjust dismissal case. The award had been filed pursuant to s. 61.5(12) of the Code, which is a provision very similar to s. 123 of the Code.

The appeal court, with a dissenting opinion, rejected the appeal. Justice Pratte, who spoke for the majority, expressed the opinion that although the Trial Division had no power to modify a Board decision or order filed in the court, this did not mean that it could not grant a stay, since in this case the court does not modify the decision of an order but merely prescribes that the failure to conform to the decision or order during the stay will not lead to the issuance of writs of execution by the court. Therefore, in this case, pursuant to s. 50(1)(b) of the *Federal Court Act*, the court should only exercise its discretionary power to stay proceedings where it is in the interests of justice that the proceedings be stayed. Accordingly, Mr. Justice Pratte concluded that *Nauss* and *Purolator* had been wrongly decided.[52] However, His Lordship came to the conclusion that a stay should not be ordered in this particular case since the evidence did not show that the employer who was ordered to take back the concerned employee would suffer a serious prejudice if the stay was not granted. Mr. Justice Marceau, on the other hand, not only agreed with the majority of the court that the Trial Division had jurisdiction to consider the employer's application, but he would have ordered a stay in the circumstances.

In this case the court was also seized with an application to stay the execution of the arbitrator's award that was the object of an application pursuant to s. 28 of the *Federal Court Act.* This was rejected by the court, but each judge gave his own reasons for doing so.[53] Justice Marceau clearly considered that the appeal court had no jurisdiction to grant a stay, except in appeal proceedings against a judgment of the Trial Division that refused or granted a stay of execution. Mr. Justice Hugessen preferred not to express any opinion on this question since, in any case, he felt that it was not a proper case for a stay. Mr. Justice Pratte suggested that although the appeal court might not possess the same power to order a stay as does the Trial Division, it may find that where it is asked to review a decision or order under s. 28, this power is held implicitly if it appears necessary for the exercise of the express jurisdiction granted under s. 28.

Between *Nauss* and *Banque Nationale du Canada*, it was thought that neither division of the Federal Court had the power to stay the execution of a Board order or decision pending judicial review under s. 28 of the

---

52 *Banque Nationale du Canada v. Granda, supra,* note 50, at p. 255. In another judgment rendered in the same affair ([1984] 2 F.C. 157), the Federal Court of Appeal concluded that the Trial Division had jurisdiction to supervise proceedings in execution of an adjudicator's decision filed pursuant to s. 61.5(12) of the Code, just as it could supervise the execution of its own decision. Accordingly, the Trial Division had the power to allow the appellant's application (and indeed it should have allowed it) to vacate a seizure made pursuant to the decision of the adjudicator.

53 *National Bank of Canada v. Granda,* not yet reported, April 19, 1984, file no. A-1690-83.

Federal Court Act.[54] The judgment rendered by the Court of Appeal in *Banque Nationale du Canada* attempted to correct that situation by at least conferring on the Trial Division the power to stay the execution of a Board order or decision. However, even if it is assumed that the Court of Appeal was right in the first place in *Nauss* and that s. 122 of the Code effectively prevents the Federal Court from making an order of stay pending review, it may be argued that in any case a superior court of a province would have this power.

In *Wah Shing Television and Partners Ltd. Partnership v. Chinavision Canada Corp.,*[55] the Supreme Court of Ontario decided that it had jurisdiction to grant injunctive relief restraining the defendant Chinavision Canada Corporation and its employees from broadcasting until final disposition of *certiorari* proceedings in the Trial Division and review proceedings in the Federal Court of Appeal against a decision made by the Canadian Radio and Television Commission (CRTC) that granted a broadcast licence to the defendant. The court came to the conclusion that jurisdiction to grant injunctive relief had not been ousted by the jurisdiction over the subject-matter given to the Federal Court. Considering that the applicant corporation had a clear statutory right to appeal the order of the CRTC, that no interim remedy was available in the Federal Court, and that no express ouster of the inherent jurisdiction of the court to grant the injunctive relief was sought, the Supreme Court of Ontario concluded that it retained jurisdiction to do so.

19:4000   GROUNDS TO SET ASIDE A BOARD DECISION OR ORDER

Pursuant to s. 28(1)(a) of the *Federal Court Act,* there are two grounds justifying the setting-aside of a decision or order of the Board: the failure to observe a principle of natural justice, and excess of jurisdiction or a refusal to exercise jurisdiction by the Board.

19:4100   FAILURE TO OBSERVE A PRINCIPLE OF NATURAL JUSTICE

The concept of natural justice involves two primary principles: "that [the tribunal] be disinterested and unbiased (*nemo judex in causa sua*) and that the parties be given adequate notice and opportunity to be heard (*audi alteram partem*)." The right to be heard by a disinterested tribunal may involve "the rights to notice, to examine reports and other secret evidence, to particulars, to adjournment, to cross-examination, to coun-

---

54   *General Aviation Service Ltd. v. Canada Labour Relations Board,* unreported, August 9, 1982, file no. A-762 (Fed. C.A.); June 15, 1982 (Fed. T.D.). In this case each level of the Federal Court had been asked to stay the execution of an order of the Board pending review; both divisions held that no such authority existed.

55   Not yet reported, September 19, 1984 (Ont. H.C.).

sel, to open court, to be heard by the person who decides, to know reasons for the decision, and to have a disinterested and unbiased judge."[56] However, it is also recognized that these particular rights may be restricted by statute and that, by its conduct, a party may waive some of them and so forfeit its rights to allege a breach of the rule of *audi alteram partem*.[57] It is also agreed that the rules of natural justice are flexible and must be applied according to the exigencies of each particular case that the tribunal has to decide. On the other hand, they are to be applied, *inter alia*, to remedy any real possibility of injustice through failure to afford any party a reasonable opportunity to meet the case against him.[58]

19:4110   Notice

The Board regulations provide for the sending of notices to persons affected or to the parties.[59] Pursuant to s. 13 of the regulations, on receipt of an application the registrar must give notice in writing to any person who, in his opinion, may be affected by the outcome of the proceedings. The registrar may also require an employer to immediately post notices or to do anything in lieu of a notice to bring to the attention of the employees an application that may affect them. Where the Board directs that a hearing be held, s. 19 obliges the registrar, unless the Board orders otherwise, to give not less than ten days notice to all persons who have asked for notice of the hearing, or who are parties thereto.

In *St. Lawrence Seaway Authority v. Canada Labour Relations Board*,[60] although the Federal Court of Appeal was of the opinion that the Board could not exercise the power conferred by s. 144 without first giving the purchaser of the business an opportunity to make his case, it nevertheless concluded that the absence of notice to the purchaser was not fatal and did not amount to a breach of natural justice where the purchaser was a subsidiary of the vendor company and had received proper notice.

In *R. v. Canada Labour Relations Board; Ex parte Martin*[61] the Ontario Court of Appeal, sitting in review in 1966 on a certification order issued by the federal Board, held unanimously that the latter had not violated the requirements of natural justice when it certified a union without a vote, despite its failure to post notice of the application, since the Board

---

56   W. Wesley Pue, *Natural Justice in Canada* (Toronto: Butterworths, 1981), at 4 and 93-94. Pue quotes the two principles from S.A. de Smith's *Judicial Review of Administrative Action*, 3rd ed. (London: Stevens & Sons Ltd., 1973). He notes that the ten "rights" were distilled by F.A. Laux in *The Administration Process*, 4th ed. (Edmonton: The University of Alberta, 1978).

57   See comments *ibid.*, at pp. 63 *ff.* and 74 *ff.*

58   See comments of Justice Jackett in *Bell Canada v. Communications Workers of Canada*, [1976] 1 F.C. 459, at 477-78, 13 N.R. 91 (C.A.).

59   S.O.R./78-499, June 2, 1978.

60   (1979), 31 N.R. 196 (Fed. C.A.).

61   [1966] 2 O.R. 684, 66 CLLC #14,144, 58 D.L.R. (2d) 134 (C.A.).

had been satisfied that a majority of employees was in favour of the union. Two of the three judges who rendered the decision, including Chief Justice Laskin (as he then was), were of the opinion that employees, employers, or other trade unions can be "interested parties", entitled to notice of certification applications and hearings, only if either: (1) the statute so prescribes; or (2) the Board's rules so provide; or (3) the Board so treats them; or (4) they ask to be so treated and are then recognized. Since none of the applicant employees who were seeking an order of *certiorari* against the Board fell into the first three of these categories, and since they had failed to seek status as parties as was open to them, the court concluded that the Board had not breached the rules of natural justice. Although, in the opinion of the two justices, a posting should have been directed, the Board's rules permitted it to decide otherwise, and this was a decision within its jurisdiction.[62]

However, in *Appleton v. Eastern Provincial Airways*[63] the Federal Court of Appeal decided that the Board should have given notice of proceedings taken by the union against the employer to employees whom he had hired to replace strikers. The employer was found to have committed a number of unfair labour practices when he conferred permanent status on the newly hired employees. The court held that the Board had breached the rules of natural justice with regard to the new employees in that it had issued orders directing the employer to cease and desist from conferring permanent status on the employees and directing the employer to reinstate the striking employees in either their former or substantially equivalent positions, regardless of whether the replacement employees would thereby be transferred, laid off, terminated, or otherwise removed from their positions.[64]

19:4120　　Hearing

The rules of natural justice also require that the Board give an opportunity of being heard to the parties before it. However, this does not necessarily oblige the Board to hold an oral hearing in every case. What is adequate will depend on all the circumstances surrounding the exercise of the particular power in issue. Under s. 19 of the regulations, a party wishing to be heard by the Board must make a written request stating the circumstances that it feels warrant a hearing, but the Board is not obliged to accede to such a request. The Board holds hearings only when it deems it to be advisable. Otherwise it may dispose of an application on the basis of the written material filed before it by the parties. The only situation in which natural justice imposes on the Board an obligation

---

62　See *ibid.*, at pp. 697-98 (O.R.).
63　(1983), 50 N.R. 99, 2 D.L.R. (4th) 147 (Fed. C.A.).
64　See also comments made about this case at paragraph 19:3300.

to hold a hearing prior to a decision is where the parties must present oral arguments.[65]

Once the Board has decided to hold a hearing in a particular case, it may or it may not record its proceedings, although it has been the Board's tradition to record its proceedings at hearings since the 1940s, when a judge of the Appellate Division of the Supreme Court of Alberta became the Board's first chairman. However, in the fall of 1979, after evaluating the impact that the legislative reform of 1978 had on judicial authority, the Board decided to discontinue the recording of its proceedings. At the same time it also decided not to allow one party to use recording facilities at a hearing.

The rationale for this policy was explained by the Board in *Canadian Pacific Ltd.*[66] The Board recognized that there could be exceptions to this practice as, for example, in constitutional cases,[67] or where two Board members acted as authorized persons under s. 118(k) to hear evidence in the absence of the third member of the Board who was unable to be present at the hearings.[68]

In *Eastern Provincial Airways Ltd. v. Canada Labour Relations Board*[69] the Federal Court of Appeal was asked if the Board's refusal to permit the parties to make a verbatim record of the proceedings by any practical means whatsoever constituted a breach of the rules of natural justice. The court carefully reviewed the rationale of the Board's policy, mentioned above, and noted that it was fair to conclude that the Board had determined that it could do its job better if those before it were discouraged from resorting to the court. The court commented that an obvious reason for a party record, but one that had not been previously mentioned, is to facilitate the pursuit of its subsequent right to judicial review. A verbatim record would unquestionably make the court's fulfilment of its duty easier. However, the court concluded that the refusal by the Board to permit the applicant to make a verbatim record was not, *per se*, a denial of natural justice even though it was intended, *inter alia*, to render more difficult the pursuit of its remedy in the court. Applicable as it was to both parties in the dispute, and to all parties in all disputes

---

65 See comments by Mr. Justice Pratte in *Canadian Arsenals Ltd. v. Canada Labour Relations Board*, [1979] 2 F.C. 393, at 399 (C.A.). In this case, an applicant employer attacked a decision of the Board certifying a union on the sole basis of the written materials in the file. The court rejected the challenge to the Board's decision. See also *Durham Transport Inc. v. International Brotherhood of Teamsters* (1978), 21 N.R. 20 (Fed. C.A.); *Re Greyhound Lines of Canada Ltd. and Office and Professional Employees International Union, Local 458* (1979), 24 N.R. 382 (Fed. C.A.); *C.S.P. Foods Ltd. v. Canada Labour Relations Board*, [1979] 2 F.C. 23, 25 N.R. 91 (C.A.); *Komo Construction Inc. v. Quebec Labour Relations Board*, (1967), 68 CLLC #14,108, 1 D.L.R. (3d) 125 (S.C.C.); *Labour Relations Board v. Traders' Services Ltd.*, [1958] S.C.R. 672, 15 D.L.R. (2d) 305.
66 (1980), 39 di 138, [1980] 3 Can LRBR 87, 80 CLLC #16,059.
67 See *Northern Telecom Canada Ltd.* (1980), 41 di 44, [1980] 2 Can LRBR 122.
68 See *Air West Airlines Ltd.* (1980), 39 di 56, [1980] 2 Can LRBR 197.
69 [1984] 1 F.C. 732, 50 N.R. 81, 2 D.L.R. (4th) 597 (C.A.).

generally, the implementation of this policy could not have been procedurally unfair to the applicant. Nevertheless, the court cautioned the Board that this refusal exposed it to the determination of issues of natural justice solely on evidence of what happened, which would be led by the parties, while the Board itself could not be heard on the subject unless it elected to file Board affidavits and offered their deponents for cross-examination.[70]

19:4130   Examination of Evidence

It is generally agreed that an administrative tribunal cannot rely on evidence that a party has not had a chance to examine or to answer. The normal rule is that persons whose interests will be affected have a right to see all the evidence available to the decision maker.[71] Accordingly, in *Sheehan v. Canadian Brotherhood of Railway, Transport and General Workers*[72] the Federal Court of Appeal held that the Board had failed to meet the requirements of the rule of *audi alteram partem* when it allowed a s. 185(f) complaint on the basis of the evidence adduced in relation to another complaint alleging a s. 184 violation.

The normal rule that a person is entitled to know all of the evidence before the tribunal may be modified for reasons of public policy. This is the case with regard to certain information concerning union membership.

Under s. 117(m) of the Code the Board is authorized to prescribe by regulations the circumstances in which the Board may receive confidential evidence as to the membership of any employees in a trade union, any objection by employees to the certification of a trade union, or any signification by employees that they no longer wish to be represented by a trade union. Section 28 of the Board regulations prescribes that such evidence shall not be made public by the Board unless the Board is of the opinion that disclosure would be in furtherance of the purposes and intent of the Code or of its administration. Accordingly, it has been held by the Supreme Court of Canada that the Board did not commit any

---

70   The fact that the Board records its proceedings on tape does not oblige it to make a transcript for use in a s. 28 application. This is the responsibility of the applicant if he wishes to have included a transcript of these proceedings in the Court file. See *Grain Handlers' Union No. 1 v. Grain Workers' Union, Local 333*, [1978] 1 F.C. 762 (C.A.). See our comments in paragraph 19:3400. It may be very difficult for the Board to produce affidavit evidence where allegations of a breach of the principles of natural justice are at issue, since the Board has only limited standing before the courts: *Canada Labour Relations Board v. Transair Ltd.*, [1977] 1 S.C.R. 722, 9 N.R. 181, 76 CLLC #14,024, 67 D.L.R. (3d) 421; *Re Northwestern Utilities Ltd. and Edmonton*, [1979] 1 S.C.R. 684, 23 N.R. 565, 7 Alta. L.R. (2d) 370, 12 A.R. 449, 89 D.L.R. (3d) 161; *Bibeault v. McCaffrey* (1984), 52 N.R. 241, (*sub nom. Vassart v. Carrier*) 84 CLLC #14,026, 7 D.L.R. (4th) 1 (S.C.C.).

71   See W. Wesley Pue, *Natural Justice in Canada, supra*, note 56, at p. 98.

72   [1978] 1 F.C. 847, 19 N.R. 468 (C.A.).

breach of the rule of natural justice by its refusal in certification proceedings to permit the employer's counsel to cross-examine a union officer as to the number of employees within the proposed bargaining unit who were union members.[73]

19:4140   Refusal to Receive Evidence or to Permit Cross-Examination

An administrative tribunal such as the Board is master of its own procedure. Section 117(a) of the Code confers on the Board the power to make regulations of general application respecting the establishment of rules of procedure. A tribunal or any court certainly has the right to refuse to receive evidence that is not pertinent to the case. Furthermore, a person has no right to cross-examination as such, but what he does have is a right to rebut opposing evidence and to correct or contradict prejudicial statements.[74]

Accordingly, in *Bank of Nova Scotia v. Canada Labour Relations Board*[75] it was held by the Federal Court of Appeal that the Board did not breach the rules of natural justice when it failed to give the applicant an opportunity to answer material that was not relevant to the issue being heard. However, in *Eastern Provincial Airways v. Canada Labour Relations Board*[76] the same court ruled that the refusal of the Board to receive evidence was a breach of the rules of natural justice where it appeared that, by this refusal, the applicant was deprived of the opportunity to lead evidence on events that the Board specifically found to have been unfair labour practices. But where, in a certification proceeding, employees presented a counter-petition nine months after the original application at which it was directed had been filed, and where notices had been posted on the employer's premises, the Supreme Court of Canada found no breach of natural justice in the Board's decision to refuse to consider the petition.[77]

19:4150   Bias

The rule that a tribunal should be impartial and free from bias is considered to be one of the most fundamental elements of natural justice. The courts are authorized to intervene where an application demonstrates that a "reasonable apprehension" of bias exists.[78]

---

73   *Canada Labour Relations Board v. Transair Ltd.;* [1977] 1 S.C.R. 722, 9 N.R. 181, 76 CLLC #14,024, 67 D.L.R. (3d) 421.
74   W. Wesley Pue, *Natural Justice in Canada, supra,* note 56, at p. 106.
75   [1978] 2 F.C. 807, 21 N.R. 1, 78 CLLC #14,145.
76   [1984] 1 F.C. 732, 50 N.R. 81, 2 D.L.R. (4th) 597 (C.A.).
77   *Canada Labour Relations Board v. Transair Ltd.,* [1977] 1 S.C.R. 722, 9 N.R. 181, 76 CLLC #14,024, 67 D.L.R. (3d) 421.
78   See W. Wesley Pue, *Natural Justice in Canada, supra,* note 56, at pp. 119-24.

It has been held that "[t]here will, however, be a 'reasonable apprehension bias' where a person sits on the appeal from his own decision, and this will be so even though he in fact only answers questions put by other members of the appellate tribunal and does not attempt to influence the outcome".[79]

Section 119 of the Code provides that "the Board may review, rescind, amend, alter or vary any order or decision made by it, and may rehear any application before making an order in respect of the application". The Board, like an appellate tribunal, had been willing in certain circumstances to review the merits of its decisions under s. 119 and had in the past seen nothing objectionable in the fact that members who sat on the original decision participated in the reconsideration of their own decision, or took part in a debate on the policy involved when the matter was reheard by the Board sitting as a whole.[80]

Since the statute does not provide a specific procedure for applications under s. 119 and certainly does not require that they be dealt with by Board members other than those involved in the original decision, the Federal Court has indicated that it is not contrary to natural justice that a review application be dealt with by the same members who formed the original panel.[81]

However, in *Eastern Provincial Airways Ltd. v. Canada Labour Relations Board*,[82] where the court found a breach of the principles of natural justice and accordingly directed a new Board hearing, it was thought to be unwise for the same members of the Board to undertake any rehearing of the complaints, in view of the vehemence with which the original Board decision had been expressed. The court therefore directed that the panel rehearing the matter should not include any of the original members. But in the same case it was also held that a public statement made by an employee of the Board, who was not a member, concerning the possible disposition of a complaint before it had even been received, was no basis for imputing bias or a reasonable apprehension of bias by the Board itself, however ill-advised and improper it may have been and whatever its actual impact on the patently sensitive situation of a bitter strike.

---

79   *Ibid.*, at p. 122, where the author cites cases in support for this statement: *Re Alberta Securities Commission and Albrecht* (1962), 38 W.W.R. 430, 36 D.L.R. (2d) 99 (Alta. T.D.); *Kane v. Board of Governors of the University of British Columbia*, [1980] S.C.R. 1105, 31 N.R. 214, [1980] 3 W.W.R. 125, 18 B.C.L.R. 124, 110 D.L.R. (3d) 311.

80   *British Columbia Telephone Co.* (1979), 38 di 124, [1980] 1 Can LRBR 340, 80 CLLC #16,008; *Canadian Air Line Flight Attendants' Association v. Wardair Canada (1975) Ltd.* (1983), 84 CLLC #16,005 (C.L.R.B.).

81   *Air B.C. Ltd. v. International Association of Machinists and Aerospace Workers*, unreported, June 9, 1981, file no. A-225-81 (Fed. C.A.); *Canadian Brotherhood of Railway, Transport and General Workers v. Canada Labour Relations Board*, unreported, August 7, 1981, file no. T-3165-81 (Fed. T.D.).

82   *Supra*, note 76.

19:4160   Curing by the Board of a Breach of Natural Justice

It has been suggested by the Board that it could use its review power under s. 119 of the Code to correct a decision tainted by a breach of the rules of natural justice.[83] However, in *St. Lawrence Seaway Authority v. Canada Labour Relations Board*[84] the Federal Court of Appeal mentioned that the mere existence of this power given to the Board by s. 119 of the Code did not have the effect of validating such a decision and of placing it beyond the power of review given to the court by s. 28 of the *Federal Court Act*. Furthermore, while the Board's revocation of its decision might render a s. 28 application unnecessary, a mere offer to review the decision does not. Accordingly, in *Eastern Provincial Airways Ltd. v. Canada Labour Relations Board*[85] the Federal Court of Appeal held that once a court challenge to the Board's decision was underway, an offer by the Board to permit the parties to call evidence and make new representations could not validate the decision *ex post facto*, nor could it prevent the applicant from pursuing his right to judicial review.

19:4200   ACTIONS OF THE BOARD THAT CONSTITUTE AN EXCESS OF JURISDICTION OR A REFUSAL TO EXERCISE JURISDICTION

Pursuant to s. 28(1)(a) of the *Federal Court Act*, the second ground for setting aside a Board decision or order is an excess of jurisdiction, or the Board's refusal to exercise its jurisdiction.

The latter ground of review can be raised where the Board rejects an application for want of jurisdiction and erroneously concludes that there is no federal work, undertaking, or business involved, or decides that the case concerns "employment by Her Majesty in Right of Canada", which falls under the scope of legislation other than the *Canada Labour Code*. The Board's practice of rejecting a certification application without seriously considering the applicability of the Code to the employer and the employees involved, for reasons of administrative convenience re-

---

[83]   *British Columbia Telephone Co., supra,* note 80; *Cablevision Nationale Ltée* (1978), 25 di 422, [1979] 3 Can LRBR 267.

[84]   (1979), 31 N.R. 196 (Fed. C.A.).

[85]   *Supra,* note 76.

sulting from the fact that a provincial labour board acted more quickly in assuming jurisdiction, has been questioned.[86]

A refusal by the Board to entertain an application or a complaint would also amount to a refusal to exercise jurisdiction if it wrongfully decided that the application or the complaint had not been filed within the time delays imposed by the Code. In *Upper Lakes Shipping Ltd. v. Sheehan*[87] the Supreme Court of Canada reversed a judgment of the Federal Court of Appeal setting aside a Board decision that held that a complaint of an unfair labour practice should be dismissed because it was untimely under s. 187(2) of the Code and was ill-founded in fact. In this case, the issue was whether this complaint had been made not later than ninety days from the date on which the complainant knew of, or in the opinion of the Board ought to have known of, the action or circumstances giving rise to the complaint.

The Federal Court of Appeal, on a s. 28 application, set aside the Board's decision and held that the complaint was in fact timely, that the alleged violation of the Code had been established, and that the case should be remitted to the Board for a remedy under s. 189 of the Code. However, on appeal, the Supreme Court of Canada unanimously reversed this judgment, although the judges differed among themselves as to the reasons. A majority of six felt that the Board had correctly rejected the contention that one refusal or a succession of refusals does not make subsequent applications untimely so long as the complaint is filed within ninety days of the latest one. The minority expressed the view that the Federal Court of Appeal was correct in holding that each refusal of a request for employment, if in breach of s. 184, might become the subject of a complaint.

On the other hand, the Board is not always obliged by law to exercise certain statutory powers. It may be vested with a discretionary jurisdiction, as for instance where it is asked to review an earlier decision under s. 119, or to file an order or decision in the Federal Court pursuant to s. 123, or to settle the terms and conditions of a first collective agreement under s. 171.1 of the Code. In the case of unfair labour practices complaints, pursuant to s. 188(2) the Board can refuse to hear and determine any complaint in respect of a matter that, in its opinion, could be referred by the complainant to an arbitrator or arbitration board as provided for

---

[86]   The Board's policy of accepting as valid the decision of another labour board to assume jurisdiction was explained in *Verrault Navigation Inc.* (1981), 45 di 72, at 81. The Board claimed that the opting of a group of employees for collective bargaining should take priority over any dispute over the appropriate jurisdiction where there are grey areas of constitutional law. However, this policy seems to be no longer sustainable since the Federal Court of Appeal judgment rendered in *Seafarers International Union v. Crosbie Offshore Services Ltd.*, [1982] 2 F.C. 855, 82 CLLC #14,180, 135 D.L.R. (3d) 485 (C.A.) [leave to appeal to S.C.C. refused at 135 D.L.R. (3d) 485n, 43 N.R. 266n].

[87]   [1979] 1 S.C.R. 902, 25 N.R. 149, 79 CLLC #14,192, 95 D.L.R. (3d) 25; revg. [1978] 1 F.C. 836, 19 N.R. 456, 77 CLLC #14,111, 81 D.L.R. (3d) 208.

in a collective agreement. In other instances, such as unfair labour practices or illegal strikes or lockouts, the Board may be entitled to choose among different remedies to correct the situation. Where the refusal of the Board to exercise its jurisdiction concerns the refusal of a discretionary power, it seems doubtful that the decision of the Board could be reviewed under s. 28(1)(a) of the *Federal Court Act* unless it can be demonstrated that in so doing the Board acted in bad faith or in an arbitrary or capricious manner amounting to a flagrant injustice, which would amount to an abuse of its powers.

It is conceded that the Board would exceed its jurisdiction if it undertook an inquiry after having made an error on a preliminary matter upon which the existence of its jurisdiction depended. However, the Supreme Court of Canada has also recognized that, in the case of labour tribunals such as this one, the characterization of preliminary or collateral questions is not very helpful, since it artificially fragments the functions of these boards. In *Canadian Union of Public Employees, Local 963 v. New Brunswick Liquor Corp.*, Mr. Justice Dickson, speaking for the court, said:

> The question of what is and is not jurisdictional is often very difficult to determine. The courts, in my view, should not be alert to brand as jurisdictional, and therefore subject to broader curial review, that which may be doubtfully so.[88]

These comments were cited with approval and explained by the late Chief Justice Laskin for the court in *International Brotherhood of Teamsters, Local 938 v. Massicotte*,[89] a case that concerned a Board decision and orders made under the authority of s. 189 of the Code.

In *Service Employees' International Union, Local 333 v. Nipawin District Staff Nurses Association*,[90] decided before *New Brunswick Liquor Corporation* and *Massicotte*, Mr. Justice Dickson, speaking again for the court, had already elaborated these important general principles:

> There can be no doubt that a statutory tribunal cannot, with impunity, ignore the requisites of its constituent statute and decide questions any way it sees fit. If it does so, it acts beyond the ambit of its powers, fails to discharge its public duty and departs from legally permissible conduct. Judicial intervention is then not only permissible but requisite in the public interest. But if the Board acts in good faith and its decision can be rationally

---

88 [1979] 2 S.C.R. 227, at 233, 25 N.B.R. (2d) 237, 51 A.P.R. 237, 26 N.R. 341, 79 CLLC #14,209.
89 [1982] 1 S.C.R. 710, at 721-22, 44 N.R. 340, 82 CLLC #14,196, 134 D.L.R. (3d) 193.
90 [1975] 1 S.C.R. 382, at 388-89, [1974] 1 W.W.R. 653, 41 D.L.R. (3d) 6. These cases are often cited in support of an allegation of loss of jurisdiction following an error on a preliminary matter, or where the tribunal has asked itself the "wrong question": *Anisminic Ltd. v. Foreign Compensation Commission*, [1969] 2 A.C. 147, [1969] 1 All E.R. 208 (H.L.); *Metropolitan Life Insurance Co. v. International Union of Operating Engineers, Local 796*, [1970] S.C.R. 425, 70 CLLC #14,008, 11 D.L.R. (3d) 336; *Jacmain v. Attorney General of Canada*, [1978] 2 S.C.R. 15, 18 N.R. 361, 78 CLLC #14,117, 81 D.L.R. (3d) 1.

supported on a construction which the relevant legislation may reasonably be considered to bear, then the Court will not intervene.

A tribunal may, on the one hand, have jurisdiction in the narrow sense of authority to enter upon an inquiry but, in the course of that inquiry, do something which takes the exercise of its powers outside the protection of the privative or preclusive clause. Examples of this type of error would include acting in bad faith, basing the decision on extraneous matters, failing to take relevant factors into account, breaching the provision of natural justice or misinterpreting provision of the Act so as to embark on an inquiry or answer a question not remitted to it. If, on the other hand, a proper question is submitted to the tribunal, that is to say, one within its jurisdiction, and if it answers that question without any errors of the nature of those to which I have alluded, then it is entitled to answer the question rightly or wrongly and that decision will not be subject to review by the Courts. . . .

There are two familiar types of jurisdictional errors: errors on preliminary matters upon which the existence of jurisdiction depends, and errors of law that are so patently unreasonable that they result in a loss of jurisdiction.

19:4210   Errors on Preliminary Matters

It becomes difficult for an applicant in judicial review proceedings to sustain an allegation that an excess of jurisdiction has been committed by a tribunal on a preliminary matter upon which the existence of jurisdiction depends where the tribunal is specifically empowered to decide certain collateral questions. This is the case in the questions mentioned in s. 118(p) of the Code, which reads:

118. The Board has, in relation to any proceeding before it, power . . .

(p) to decide for all purposes of this Part any question that may arise in the proceeding, including, without restricting the generality of the foregoing, any question as to whether

(i) a person is an employer or employee,

(ii) a person performs management functions or is employed in a confidential capacity in matters relating to industrial relations,

(iii) a person is a member of a trade union,

(iv) an organization or association is an employers' organization, a trade union or a council of trade unions,

(v) a group of employees is a unit appropriate for collective bargaining,

(vi) a collective agreement has been entered into,

(vii) any person or organization is a party to or bound by a collective agreement, and

(viii) a collective agreement is in operation.

Therefore, it is doubtful that an applicant could successfully plead that a wrong answer given by the Board to anyone of the questions within s. 118(p) constitutes a jurisdictional error, where the Board otherwise has jurisdiction to undertake an inquiry or make an order.[91] In *International Brotherhood of Teamsters, Local 938 v. Massicotte*[92] the Supreme Court of Canada was concerned with the validity of a decision of the Board allowing a complaint made under s. 136.1 of the Code. A part-time employee complained that his union had refused to file a grievance contesting his dismissal on the ground that part-time employees had no grievance rights under the collective agreement. At p. 714 (S.C.R.) the court commented:

> Certainly the Board had authority to enter upon the inquiry based upon the complaint made by Massicotte under s. 187 of the *Canada Labour Code* . . . alleging a violation of s. 136.1. Moreover, it had the fortification provided by s. 118(p) (vii) of the *Canada Labour Code* . . . . That provision empowers the Board to decide any question as to whether any person or organization is a party to or bound by a collective agreement and it is authorized to decide this for all purposes of Part V of the *Canada Labour Code*, being the part concerned with industrial relations and the role of the Board in that respect, including the entire process of certification, negotiation of collective agreements and arbitration.

And at p. 716:

> To the extent to which the Canada Labour Relations Board was entitled to examine the collective agreement (not to administer it but to assess its reach to part-time employees), there can be no basis for saying that it committed a jurisdictional error in finding that part-time employees were in the bargaining unit delineated by the agreement. If it was wrong in that assessment, the error would be one committed within its jurisdiction and hence would be at the most a non reviewable error of law.[93]

A finding of a sale of business under s. 144(1) or a determination of the identity of the purchaser of the business may not be termed a preliminary question related to jurisdiction, since the Board is expressly empowered to determine those questions. Section 144(5) provides that

> Where any question arises under this section as to whether or not a business has been sold or as to the identity of the purchaser of a business, the Board shall determine the question.

The Supreme Court of Canada in *National Bank of Canada v. Retail Clerks' International Union*[94] rejected the argument raised by the appellant to the effect that the Board had made an error preliminary to its jurisdiction in deciding that it was not necessary to have two distinct employers, one of the predecessor and the other the successor, to declare that a sale

---

[91] *North Canada Air Ltd. v. Canada Labour Relations Board*, [1981] 2 F.C. 407, at 409-10, 34 N.R. 560, 81 CLLC #14,072, 117 D.L.R. (3d) 216 (C.A.); *Manitoba Pool Elevators v. Canada Labour Relations Board*, [1982] 2 F.C. 659, 39 N.R. 387, 82 CLLC #14,160 (C.A.).

[92] [1982] 1 S.C.R. 710, 44 N.R. 340, 82 CLLC #14,196, 134 D.L.R. (3d) 193.

[93] *Ibid.*, at p. 714 (S.C.R.).

[94] [1984] 1 S.C.R. 269, 53 N.R. 203, 84 CLLC #14,037, 9 D.L.R. (4th) 10.

had occurred under s. 144, as was the case in these circumstances of the integration of the operations of two branches of the same employer.[95]

19:4211   Necessity of an Application

However, the necessity of an application or a demand may in certain circumstances be considered a preliminary condition to the exercise of the Board's jurisdiction. For example, this would be the case in certification proceedings,[96] in revocation proceedings,[97] or where, following a sale or business, employees are intermingled in one bargaining unit.[98] A complaint may also be necessary in cases of unfair labour practices,[99] but the Board may not be limited in its inquiry to the particular breaches alleged to have been committed in the complaint and may validly find a party in breach of other sections of the Code if it offers the party an opportunity to be heard. Furthermore, the Board would have ample authority to initiate, on its own motion, a review of an earlier decision or an order after having given the parties a reasonable opportunity to be heard.[100]

19:4212   Necessity of Ministerial Consent

The necessity of ministerial consent is a condition preliminary to the exercise of the Board's jurisdiction to inquire into the alleged breach of s. 148 or 184(3)(g) or 185(a) or (b) of the Code.[101] However, the Board is not precluded from considering evidence of facts that have occurred outside of the time period specified in the ministerial consent so given.[102]

19:4213   Time Limits

Where a complainant alleges a failure to comply with ss. 124(4), 136.1, 148, 161.1, 184, 185, and 186, pursuant to s. 187(2) the complaint must be made not later than ninety days from the date "on which the complainant knew, or in the opinion of the Board ought to have known,

---

95   *Ibid.*, at p. 12,153 (CLLC). To the same effect, see *Québec Sol Services Ltée v. Canada Labour Relations Board*, unreported, November 1, 1982, file no. A-612-81 (Fed. C.A.); see also the pertinent comments of Mr. Justice Reid in *Hughes Boat Works Inc. v. United Auto Workers, Local 1620*, (1979), 26 O.R. (2d) 420, 79 CLLC #14,230, 102 D.L.R. (3d) 661, at 672-73 (Div. Ct.) which were quoted with approval by the Supreme Court in *National Bank of Canada v. Retail Clerks' International Union, supra*, note 94.
96   Canada Labour Code, s. 126(a).
97   Sections 138, 140.
98   Section 144(3)(a).
99   Section 188(1).
100   *Television St-François Inc. (CKSH-TV) v. Canada Labour Relations Board*, [1977] 2 F.C. 294 (T.D.); *North Canada Air Ltd. v. Canada Labour Relations Board, supra*, note 91.
101   *Canada Labour Code*, s. 187(5).
102   *North Canada Air Ltd. v. Canada Labour Relations Board*, unreported, June 7, 1982, file no. A-454-81 (Fed. C.A.).

of the actions or circumstances giving rise to the complaint". The decision of the Board on whether a complaint is late is not, in our opinion, jurisdictional in nature, and accordingly is not a basis for judicial review unless it is patently unreasonable.[103] However, the Board would exceed its jurisdiction if it regarded its power to abridge or enlarge the time for instituting the proceedings under s. 118(m) as entitling it to give latitude to a complainant who is late. In this regard, the late Chief Justice Laskin, speaking in the name of five other judges in *Upper Lakes Shipping Ltd. v. Sheehan*[104] concerning the use of the power given to the Board by s. 118(m) of the Code, said:

> I read this provision [s. 118(m) of the Code] as empowering the Board to abridge or enlarge the time for making steps in a proceeding which is properly before it, as, for example, a certification proceeding. If, however, the issue is whether a proceeding is timely under the Board's governing statute, that is, whether the Board can lawfully entertain it at all in the light of s. 187(2), I do not regard its powers under s. 118(m) as entitling it to give latitude to a complainant who is out of time under the statute. The correlative would be that if it can enlarge it can abridge, and that would be absurd. A complainant is entitled to the advantage and subject to the limitation of the ninety day period under s. 187(2). It can neither be restricted to a lesser period by any direction of the Board nor be allowed a greater period.

On the other hand, the mere absence of a document authorizing the complainant's lawyers to sign a complaint of unfair labour practice validly made in writing within the ninety-day period prescribed by the statute would not deprive the Board of jurisdiction to entertain the complaint. Section 203 of the Code and s. 6 of the Board regulations provide that no proceeding is invalid by reason only of a defect in form or a technical irregularity.[105]

19:4214   Employees' Wishes in Certification or Review Proceedings

In certification proceedings brought under the Code, the Board must be satisfied before issuing certification that, as of the date of the filing of the application or of such other date as the Board considers appropriate, a majority of the employees in the unit wish to have the trade union represent them as their bargaining agent.[106] The Federal

---

[103]   By analogy, see *Syndicat des professeurs du collège de Lévis-Lauzon v. College d'enseignement général et professionel de Lévis-Lauzon*, [1985] 1 S.C.R. 596.

[104]   [1979] 1 S.C.R. 902, at 915, 25 N.R. 149, 79 CLLC #14,192, 95 D.L.R. (3d) 25.

[105]   If the signing and making of the complaint were in fact authorized by the complainants, even though not in writing, the lack of a written authorization would be no more than a technical irregularity that does not render the proceeding void or deprive the Board of its jurisdiction to entertain the complaint: *A & M Transport Ltd. v. Black*, unreported, October 29, 1983, file no. A-1129-83 (Fed. C.A.).

[106]   Canada Labour Code, ss. 126(c), 118.1.

Court of Appeal stated in *Banque Provinciale du Canada v. Syndicat National des employés de commerce et de bureau du comté Lapointe (CSN)*[107] that the provision establishing this requirement was not a "jurisdiction provision". The court concluded in this case that it had no power to set aside a certification order on the ground that the order was based on an error of the Board in interpreting the effect of the change in s. 126(c), since this was a question of law that would fall under s. 28(1)(b) of the *Federal Court Act* but did not fall under s. 28(1)(a).

However, in *Uranerz Exploration and Mining Ltd. v. Canada Labour Relations Board*,[108] decided a few weeks before *La Banque Provinciale*, the same court (but differently constituted) held that it was a condition precedent to the Board's power to grant certification that it be satisfied that a majority of the employees in the bargaining unit wish to have the trade union represent them. Therefore, in the court's opinion the Board had exceeded its jurisdiction where, in an endeavour to satisfy itself as to the wishes of a majority of the employees, it directed that a second representation vote be taken between two competing unions, but failed to give the employees a choice as to a particular union or no union at all, as the court felt it was required to do so where a vote was ordered. Accordingly, in the court's opinion, the Board asked the employees the wrong question and based the certification on the answers given by the employees to that wrong question. Since the proper question was never asked, it was impossible for the Board to determine what the true wishes of the employees were, and it therefore exceeded its jurisdiction.[109] The court found that the taking of a second representation vote without permitting the employees to express their wishes on the option of no union representation violated the provisions of s. 128(2), which read as follows:

> Where the Board orders that a representation vote be taken on an application by a trade union for certification as the bargaining agent for a unit in respect of which no other trade union is the bargaining agent, the Board shall include on the ballots a choice whereby an employee may indicate that he does not wish to be represented by any trade union named on the ballots.

However, in 1984 Parliament adopted s. 128(3) to rectify the situation:

> Notwithstanding subsection (2), where the employees in a unit have cast ballots in favour of all trade unions involved in a representation vote totalling more than fifty per cent of the ballots cast but have not given majority support to one trade union in that vote and, as a result, a second or subsequent representation vote is required, the Board shall not be required

---

107 [1979] 2 F.C. 439, 30 N.R. 564, 79 CLLC #14,214, 102 D.L.R. (3d) 720 (C.A.).
108 [1980] 1 F.C. 312, 28 N.R. 431, 79 CLLC #14,215, 102 D.L.R. (3d) 519 (C.A.).
109 *Ibid.*, at p. 438 (N.R.). The court referred to *Toronto Newspaper Guild v. Globe Printing Co.*, [1952] O.R. 345, [1952] 2 D.L.R. 302, 102 C.C.C. 318; affd. [1953] 2 S.C.R. 18, [1953] 3 D.L.R. 561, 106 C.C.C. 225.

to include the choice referred to in subsection (2) in the ballots for the second or subsequent vote.[110]

Furthermore, s. 126 makes it unnecessary for the union to establish membership in the union as a condition of certification. Thus, it was held by the Federal Court of Appeal that neither s. 127(2) nor 134(2) indicated the necessity of proof of membership in the applicant union as a condition precedent to the exercise of the Board's power under s. 126. It further held that the obligation of the Board under s. 126 was merely to satisfy itself that a majority of the employees in the unit wished the union to represent them, regardless of their membership status in the union.[111]

In review proceedings under s. 119 of the Code where the applicant seeks to enlarge an already certified bargaining unit, it has been suggested that the Board must exercise its power so as not to circumvent the requirements of s. 126. It follows that the Board cannot expand a bargaining unit as defined in a previous order of the Board without being satisfied that the bargaining agent enjoys the support of the majority of the employees in the proposed enlarged unit, but this does not oblige the Board specifically to ascertain the wishes of the employees to be added to the unit.[112]

19:4220   Errors of Law That are Patently Unreasonable

Errors of law are, since the 1978 reform, no longer reviewable by the Federal Court of Appeal. Any error by the Board in the construction or application of the Code should be considered, *prima facie*, to be no more than an error of law if the Board has embarked upon an inquiry that it is authorized to pursue.[113] It has also been suggested by the Supreme Court of Canada that a mere doubt as to the correctness of the Board's interpretation of its statutory power is no ground for finding jurisdictional error, especially when it is exercising powers conferred on it in wide terms to resolve competing contentions.[114] However, this does not entitle the Board to abuse its powers or act with unfettered discretion. Although the Supreme Court has recognized the very broad remedial powers conferred on the Board by s. 189, it has also recognized that these powers are not totally free from examination on equitable grounds. In *Canada*

---

110   Enacted by S.C. 1983-84, c. 39, s. 27, proclaimed in force July 18, 1984.
111   *Toronto Dominion Bank v. Canada Labour Relations Board*, [1979] 1 F.C. 386, 22 N.R. 504, 78 CLLC #14,150, 88 D.L.R. 3d 256 (C.A.).
112   *Proulx v. Conseil canadien des relations du travail*, unreported, October 3, 1980, file no. A-514-79 (Fed. C.A.); *Téléglobe Canada v. Syndicat canadien des télécommunications transmarines*, unreported, October 3, 1980, file no. A-487-79 (Fed. C.A.); *Northwestell Inc. v. International Brotherhood of Electrical Workers, Local 1574*, unreported, May 5, 1983, file no. A-895-82 (Fed. C.A.).
113   *International Brotherhood of Teamsters, Local 938 v. Massicotte*, [1982] 1 S.C.R. 710, at 717, 44 N.R. 340, 82 CLLC #14,196, 134 D.L.R. (3d) 193.
114   *Ibid.*, at p. 724 (S.C.R.).

Labour Relations Board v. Halifax Longshoremen's Association, Local 269,[115] the Supreme Court decided that the Board had validly exercised its remedial powers where it ordered a union that had breached s. 161.1 on the establishment of referral rules for hiring halls to adopt rules for the administration of the hiring hall, including rules regarding the admission of members and the issuing of cards. It had also ordered that three of the complainants be admitted to the union as members and that a card be issued to the fourth. However, the late Chief Justice Laskin, on behalf of the court, pointed out:

> Even more in fashioning a remedy conferred in such broad terms is the Board's discretion to be respected than when it is challenged as exceeding its jurisdiction to determine whether there has been a breach of a substantive provision of the Code. At the same time, equitable and consequential considerations are not to be so remote from reparation of an established breach as to exceed any rational parameters.[116]

Therefore, even where the Board is called upon to exercise its broad remedial powers under s. 189, the relationship between the act alleged, its consequences, and the remedy ordered by the Board can be scrutinized by the courts. In *National Bank of Canada v. Retail Clerks' International Union*[117] the Supreme Court of Canada unanimously decided that an order of the Board forcing an employer to create a trust fund to promote the objectives of the Code among all its employees, as well as an order concerning a letter written by the Board sent by the company president to all employees and informing them of its decision and of the creation of the fund, constituted an excess of jurisdiction and should be quashed. Furthermore, Justice Beetz commented that the remedy forcing the president to sign the above-mentioned letter was totalitarian in nature and as such was alien to the tradition of free nations like Canada. The relationship between the alleged unfair practice, an illegal closing of one of the employer's branches and its consequences on the one hand, and the creation of the fund on the other hand was, in the court's opinion totally lacking. Mr. Justice Chouinard, speaking for the court, stated:

> However, remedy no. 6, regarding the creation of a trust fund to promote the objectives of the Code among other employees of the Bank, which in my view means promoting the unionization of those other employees, is not something intended to remedy or counteract the consequences harmful to the realization of those objectives that may result from closure of the Maguire Street Branch and its incorporation in the Sheppard Street Branch. The fact that a large number of the bank's other employees are not unionized is not a consequence of closure of the Maguire Street Branch, where the union continued to exist and had its certificate extended. Thus I consider that this remedy should be set aside.[118]

---

[115]   [1983] 1 S.C.R. 245, 46 N.R. 324, 83 CLLC #14,022, 144 D.L.R. (3d) 1.
[116]   *Ibid.*, at p. 255 (S.C.R.).
[117]   [1984] 1 S.C.R. 269, 53 N.R. 203, 84 CLLC #14,034, 9 D.L.R. (4th) 10.
[118]   *Ibid.*, at p. 12,160 (CLLC).

Subsequently, the Supreme Court of Canada, affirming a judgment of the Federal Court of Appeal, held in *Le Syndicat des employés de production du Québec et de l'Acadie v. Canada Labour Relations Board*[119] that the Board had exceeded its jurisdiction when it ordered the parties to an illegal strike to submit to arbitration the question as to whether overtime was voluntary or compulsory since s. 183.1(a) did not permit the Board to render orders other than those encompassed specifically by ss. 182 and 183, dealing with illegal strikes and lock-outs.

However, leaving aside the exercise of the Board remedial powers, it may be more difficult to determine what error of law will be considered "patently unreasonable" where the court is confronted with a Board's interpretation of its statute and its policy. The reviewing courts themselves may not and do not always agree on the "patent reasonableness" of Board decisions and orders, and differing opinions on the actual scope of this concept may be found where different cases concerning the Board are compared.[120]

19:5000 ENFORCEMENT OF BOARD ORDERS AND DECISIONS

The court's jurisdiction is not limited to the judicial review of Board actions. The Trial Division of the Federal Court plays a role[121] in the enforcement of Board orders and decisions once they have been filed by the Board pursuant to s. 123 of the Code, which reads:

123.(1) The Board shall, on the request in writing of any person or organization affected by any order or decision of the Board, file a copy of the order or decision, exclusive of the reasons therefor, in the Federal Court of Canada, unless, in the opinion of the Board,

(a) there is no indication of failure or likelihood of failure to comply with the order or decision, or

(b) there is other good reason why the filing of the order or decision in the Federal Court of Canada would serve no useful purpose.

(2) Where the Board files a copy of any order or decision in the Federal Court of Canada pursuant to subsection (1), it shall specify in writing to the Court that the copy of the order or decision is filed pursuant to subsection

---

119   [1984] 2 S.C.R. 412. See comments at paragraphs 9:2310 and 16:2000.
120   *International Longshoremen's and Warehousemen's Union, Local 502 v. Matus (No. 2)*, [1982] 2 F.C. 558, at 568-70, 40 N.R. 541, 82 CLLC #14,161, 129 D.L.R. (3d) 616 (C.A.); *International Longshoremen's and Warehousemen's Union, Local 502 v. Matus (No. 1)*, [1982] 2 F.C. 549, at 554, 40 N.R. 594, 82 CLLC #14,161, 129 D.L.R. (3d) 616 (C.A.); *Dome Petroleum Inc. v. Canadian Merchant Service Guild*, [1981] 2 F.C. 418, 35 N.R. 243, 81 CLLC #14,076, 118 D.L.R. (3d) 335 (C.A.); *Canadian Airline Employees' Association v. Eastern Provincial Airways (1963) Ltd.*, [1980] 2 F.C. 512, 33 N.R. 419, 80 CLLC #14,033, 108 D.L.R. (3d) 743 (C.A.).
121   In view of s. 26 of the *Federal Court Act*, it is within the jurisdiction of the Trial Division to enforce and execute decisions and orders filed by the Board under s. 123 of the Code. See *Central Broadcasting Co. Ltd. v. Canada Labour Relations Board*, [1975] F.C. 310 (C.A.).

(1) and, where the Board so specifies, the copy of the order or decision shall be accepted for filing by, and registered in, the Court without further application or other proceeding and, when the copy of the order or decision is registered, the order or decision has the same force and effect and, subject to this section and section 28 of the *Federal Court Act*, all proceedings may be taken thereon by any person or organization affected thereby as if the order or decision were a judgment obtained in the Court.

As set out above, the Board orders are filed by the Board itself upon a request in writing from any person or organization affected by any such order or decision. The Code provides that the copy of the order or decision shall be accepted for filing by, and registered in, the Court without further application or other proceeding once the Board has specified in writing that the filing is made pursuant to the appropriate subsection of the Code. Section 201(1) further provides that

Any document purporting to contain or to be a copy of any order or decision of the Board and purporting to be signed by a member of the Board is receivable in any court in evidence without proof of the signature or of the official character of the person appearing to have signed the document and without further proof thereof.

Before the 1978 legislative amendments to the provisions, the parties themselves were responsible for the filing of Board orders and decisions in the Federal Court. The parties had to satisfy the court registrar that the decision could in fact be filed under s. 123, for example, by producing an affidavit to prove the existence of the circumstances described in that section.[122]

The Board may refuse to file a decision or order where, in its opinion, there is no indication of failure or likelihood of failure to comply with the order or decision, or where there is another good reason why the filing of the order or decision would serve no useful purpose. This second situation in which the Board may refuse to file an order or decision is very broad. The Board in its discretion to refuse to file will take account of the objectives and purposes of the Code, particularly if it is of the opinion that such filing would not further future good relations between the parties or that another Board intervention could achieve the same results. Accordingly, in *Seaspan International Ltd.*[123] the Board refused an application to file the order on the ground that there was no indication of failure or likelihood of failure to comply with the order, and on the added ground

---

[122] *Paradis v. Verrault Navigation Inc.*, [1978] 2 F.C. 147, 22 N.R. 75, 87 D.L.R. (3d) 547. In this decision, the Federal Court of Appeal reversed a number of decisions which held that the filing should be preceded by a judgment of the Trial Division itself confirming the existence of the circumstances justifying the filing of the order or decision, and more particularly, that non-compliance had occurred. See *International Brotherhood of Electrical Workers, Local 529 v. Central Broadcasting Company Ltd.*, [1977] 2 F.C. 78, 78 CLLC #14,045 (T.D.); *Public Service Alliance of Canada Local 660 v. Canadian Broadcasting Corp.*, [1976] 2 F.C. 151; *International Longshoremen's Association, Local 375 v. Maritime Employers' Association* (1974), 52 D.L.R. (3d) 293 (Fed. T.D.).

[123] (1979), 33 di 544, [1974] 2 Can LRBR 493.

that filing would serve no useful purpose, since the purpose for which filing was sought was to seek a stay of the Board's order.[124] In *Dome Petroleum Ltd.*[125] the Board granted the union's application to file where the employer had not disclosed why in its opinion such filing would serve no useful purpose.

Finally, when the copy of the order or decision has been registered, it has the same force and effect as a decision of the court, "and subject to this section and section 28 of the *Federal Court Act*, all proceedings may be taken thereon by any person or organization affected thereby as if the order or decision were a judgment obtained in the Court" (s. 123(2)). Enforcement proceedings are taken before the Trial Division of the Federal Court pursuant to the provisions of the *Federal Court Act* and the rules made under it, which prescribe the procedure to be followed.[126] The court may be called upon to decide whether the decision or order was carried out, and if it was not, whether this failure is excusable before penalizing or ordering the remedies opened against a party in such cases.[127] Furthermore, the order or decision must be capable of enforcement through the means provided in the Rules of the Federal Court. Some of these means of execution may not be available where the order or decision is too vague, uncertain, imprecise, or ambiguous.[128]

---

[124] See paragraph 19:3600.

[125] *Dome Petroleum Ltd.* (1980), 41 di 169, [1980] 3 Can LRBR 570.

[126] See *Federal Court Rules* 1900 and following.

[127] *Paradis v. Verreault Navigation Inc.*, [1979] 2 F.C. 147, at 150, 22 N.R. 75, 87 D.L.R. (3d) 547 (C.A.).

[128] *International Brotherhood of Electrical Workers, Local 529 v. Central Broadcasting Co. Ltd.*, [1977] 2 F.C. 78, 76 CLLC #14,045 (T.D.).

APPENDICES

APPENDIX 1

CANADA LABOUR RELATIONS BOARD OFFICES

HEAD OFFICE

Canada Labour Relations Board
C.D. Howe Building
240 Sparks Street, 4th floor West
Ottawa, Ontario
K1A 0X8
Telephone: (613) 996-9466
Telex no: 053-4426
Answer back code: CLRB OTT
Facsimile installation type dex telephone no: 995-9493

ATLANTIC REGION

Queen Square
14th Floor
45 Alderney Drive
Dartmouth, Nova Scotia B2Y 2N6
Telephone: (902) 426-7068
Facsimile installation type dex telephone no: 426-7397

QUEBEC REGION

Guy Favreau Complex
Suite 1202 — East Tower
200 Dorchester Blvd. West
Montreal, Quebec
H2Z 1X4
Telephone: (514) 283-3258
Telex no: 05-25706
Answer back code: CLRB MTL
Facsimile installation type dex telephone no: 283-3590

ONTARIO REGION

19th Floor
Toronto-Dominion Bank Tower
Suite 1905
P.O. Box 190
Toronto, Ontario
M5K 1H6
Telephone: (416) 369-3782
Facsimile installation type dex telephone no: 369-6543

CENTRAL REGION

One Lakeview Square
Suite 1040
155 Carlton Street
Winnipeg, Manitoba
R3C 3H8
Telephone: (204) 949-3145
Facsimile installation type dex telephone no: 949-3170

WESTERN REGION

1090 West Pender Street
12th Floor
Vancouver, B.C.
V6E 2N7
Telephone: (604) 666-6001
Facsimile installation type dex telephone no: 666-6071

APPENDIX 2
CANADA LABOUR RELATIONS BOARD

APPLICATION FOR CERTIFICATION AS BARGAINING AGENT PURSUANT TO SECTION 124 OF THE CANADA LABOUR CODE

Read carefully the information and directions relating to this form.

1. Full name and address of applicant trade union:

_____

_____

2. Full name and address of employer:

_____

_____

3. General nature of employer's business:

_____

_____

4. Description and location of the proposed bargaining unit which the applicant trade union considers appropriate for collective bargaining and for which certification is sought:

_____

_____

_____

_____

_____

_____

5. Approximate number of employees in the proposed bargaining unit:

_____

_____

_____

6. Give the full name and address of any trade union known to the applicant which is the certified bargaining agent or which has been or is a party to a collective agreement covering part or all of the employees affected by this application:

_____

_____

_____

_____

_____

7. Give the terms as to the effective date, renewal and termination of an existing or recently expired collective agreement:

_____

_____

_____

_____

8. Additional information that the applicant thinks will be of assistance to the Board:

_____

_____

_____

_____

_____

_____

_____

_____

_____

_____

_____

_____

_____

_____

_____

9. The applicant trade union hereby makes application pursuant to section 124 of the Canada Labour Code to be certified by the Canada Labour Relations Board as the bargaining agent of the employees in the bargaining unit described in paragraph 4 above.

Made and signed on behalf of the applicant trade union this   day of
           , 19 . . . .

           19 . . . .

       by

Name of Trade Union: _____

Signature (name) _____

Trade union office held: _____

Address: _____

Signature (name) _____

Trade union office held: _____

Address: _____

N.B. — Section 9 of the Board's Regulations provides that an application made by a trade union shall be signed by the president or secretary thereof, by two other officers thereof or by a person authorized in writing to sign on behalf of the trade union.

INFORMATION AND DIRECTIONS FOR COMPLETION OF APPLICATION FOR CERTIFICATION AS BARGAINING AGENT

(Each paragraph number corresponds to its counterpart in the application.)

1. If application is made by a local union the number and address of the local should be given. If no office is maintained by the applicant, the address given may be that of a person signing the application.

2. The full name and head office address of the employer is required.

3. Section 108 of the Code provides for its application to employees of employers who may be engaged in any federal work, business or undertaking and section 109 provides for its application to employees of certain corporations established to perform function or duty on behalf of the Government of Canada.

   A "Federal work, undertaking or business" is defined in section 2 of the Code.

   If possible, relate the general nature of the employer's business to one of the activities outlined in sections 2 or 109 of the Code.

4. The applicant may describe the proposed bargaining unit as: "all employees, except . . . . . (list the classifications excepted)".

APPENDIX 3
CANADA LABOUR RELATIONS BOARD

NOTICE TO EMPLOYEES

File No. _____

TAKE NOTICE THAT _____

_____ (Applicant)

has on _____ 19 ____ filed with the CANADA LABOUR
RELATIONS BOARD an application (copy attached hereto) for

in respect of employees of _____

_____

In accordance with the usual procedures, the Board has appointed an
Officer to investigate this application.

ANY CORRESPONDENCE IN RESPECT OF THIS APPLICATION
SHOULD BE SENT BY REGISTERED MAIL OR DELIVERED TO THE
ADDRESS SHOWN BELOW NOT LATER THAN TEN DAYS FROM THE
POSTING OF THIS NOTICE. THE FOLLOWING EXTRACTS FROM THE
CANADA LABOUR RELATIONS BOARD REGULATIONS ARE
APPLICABLE:

9. (1) An application, reply or intervention filed with the Board shall be signed as follows:

(a) where it is filed on behalf of a trade union, a council of trade unions or an employers' organization, it shall be signed by the president or secretary thereof, by two other officers thereof or by a person authorized in writing to sign on behalf of the trade union, council of trade unions or employers' organization;

(b) where it is filed on behalf of an employer, it shall be signed by the employer himself, by the general manager or principal executive officer of the employer or by a person authorized in writing to sign on behalf of the employer; and

(c) where it is filed on behalf of an employee, it shall be signed by the employee himself or by a person authorized by the employee in writing to sign on his behalf.

(2) Where a person has been authorized to sign an application, reply or intervention on behalf of another person, a copy of the authorization shall be filed with the Board.

10. Where a person has been authorized to act on behalf of another person and a copy of the authorization has been filed with the Board, any document required to be given to that other person may be given to the person so authorized to act.

NOTICE OF APPLICATIONS

13. (1) Subject to subsection (2), the Registrar shall, on receipt of an application, give notice in writing thereof to any person who, in his opinion, may be affected thereby.

(2) The Registrar may, in writing, require an employer to immediately post notices of an application in places where those notices are most likely to come to the attention of the employees who may be affected by the application and to keep the notices posted for a period of seven days.

(3) The Registrar may, in writing, require the employer, in addition to posting the notices referred to in subsection (2), or in lieu thereof, to bring the application to the attention of the employees who may be affected thereby in such other manner as the Registrar may direct.

(4) Where an employer has complied with a requirement of the Registrar under subsection (2) or (3), the employer shall, on request from the Registrar, file a statement to that effect with the Board.

14. When notices of an application are posted by an employer as required by the Registrar pursuant to subsection 13(2), any person employed by that employer who wishes to file a reply to or intervene in the application is deemed to have received notice of the application as of the first day the notices are posted unless, before that day, he has been notified pursuant to subsection 13(1) or (3).

REPLIES

15. A person who wishes to reply to an application shall file with the Board a written reply containing
(a) his full name and address;
(b) a clear identification of the application to which the reply relates;
(c) the admission or denial of each of the statements made in the application;
(d) a concise statement of the facts relied on; and
(e) a statement as to whether or not a hearing before the Board is requested for the purpose of making oral representations or presenting evidence in respect of the issues raised in the reply.

INTERVENTIONS

16. A person who wishes to intervene in an application shall file with the Board a signed intervention setting out
(a) his full name and address;
(b) his grounds for intervening; and
(c) the facts relied on.

17. On receipt of an intervention filed pursuant to section 16, the Board shall, where it is of the opinion that the intervention would be in furtherance of the purposes and intent of the Code or its administration, accept the intervention.

TIME FOR REPLYING OR INTERVENING

18. (1) No person shall file a reply or an intervention in an application later than ten days from the date on which he received notice of the application.

(2) If a person who wishes to reply to or intervene in an application fails to comply with subsection (1), he shall not, without the consent of the Board, be permitted to make any representations to the Board in relation to the application, and the Board may dispose of the application without notice to the person.

HEARINGS

19. (1) Any party may request a hearing to be held by filing a request therefor in writing, stating the circumstances that the party considers warrants the holding of the hearing.

(2) The Board may hold such hearings as it deems advisable and may dispose of any application without a hearing notwithstanding the filing of a request therefor pursuant to paragraph 15(e) or subsection (1).

20. Unless the Board directs otherwise, the Registrar shall give not less than ten days notice of a hearing to all persons who have asked for notice of the hearing or who are parties.

21. Where a person who has been given notice of a hearing fails to attend

before the Board in accordance with the notice, the Board may proceed with the hearing and dispose of the matter in the absence of and without further reference to that person.

28. Evidence presented to the Board in respect of
(a) the membership of any employees in a trade union,
(b) any objection by employees to the certification of a trade union, or
(c) any signification by employees that they no longer wish to be represented by a trade union

shall not be made public by the Board unless the Board is of the opinion that disclosure would be in furtherance of the purposes and intent of the Code or its administration.

Signed _____

_____

As directed by the Canada Labour Relations Board, this notice was

posted by me on the _____ day of _____ 19 _____

Name _____ Title _____

(To be completed at the time the notice is posted)

APPENDIX 4
CANADA LABOUR RELATIONS BOARD

CERTIFICATE OF POSTING

File No. _____

In connection with the application for certification by _____

_____

_____

_____

_____ applicant, in respect of employees of _____

_____

_____ employer, I hereby certify that I am the

_____(title) of the employer and that I have had posted and kept posted for a period of seven (7) days a copy of the NOTICE TO EMPLOYEES in the following conspicuous place(s) in the employer's establishment(s) where they were most likely to come to the attention of the employees who could be affected by the application, namely:

Name of establishment and Location(s)	1st day of posting

(Attach list if space is not sufficient)

Date _____ Signature _____

THIS REPORT OF POSTING TO BE COMPLETED SEVEN (7) DAYS AFTER POSTING OF NOTICE AND MAILED TO

_____

APPENDIX 5
CANADA LABOUR RELATIONS BOARD

ATTESTATION BY A UNION OFFICIAL APPLYING FOR CERTIFICATION

File: . . . .

IN THE MATTER OF an Application by (name of trade union) . . . .

. . . .

. . . .

concerning a bargaining unit of employees of (name of employer) . . . .

. . . .

comprising (description of bargaining unit) . . . .

. . . .

. . . .

I, ...

(name of union officer and office held)

of the applicant (or intervener) union, do hereby report and certify to the Canada Labour Relations Board as follows:

1.   That I have been provided with a copy of the Canada Labour Relations Board Regulations, and that I have read and understand section 27 thereof.

2.   That I have custody of and am familiar with the membership records and the financial receipts and deposits in connection with the above-cited application.

3.   That the membership application forms provided to the investigating officer were in fact signed by the employees indicated on the dates shown thereon and that their applications were accepted on behalf of the union.

4.   That the amounts shown as having been paid as union dues and/or initiation fees were actually paid by the employees concerned on their own behalf and on the dates indicated.

5.   That I have produced to the investigating officer resignations or revocations of membership up to date of application which have been submitted to the union by employees claimed as members for the purpose of this application.

6.   That I understand that the investigating officer has the authority to investigate and verify all documents and statements made by the parties to this application.

7.   That the bank deposit records produced to the investigating officer are a true record of monies deposited to the credit of the union in respect of dues and/or initiation fees paid on their own behalf by the employees covered by this application, at the time indicated in the records shown.

8.   That I understand that any misrepresentation or irregularities in the membership evidence provided to the investigating officer could result in the rejection of all or part of the evidence submitted and the rejection of the application or intervention.

9.   That I have read the provisions of sections 139 and 140 of the Canada Labour Code and that I understand their implications.

Dated this . . . . day of . . . . 19 . . . .

. . . .

(Signature of Witness)   (Signature of Union Official)

APPENDIX 6
CANADA LABOUR RELATIONS BOARD

ATTESTATION TO BE SIGNED BY AN EMPLOYEE
APPLYING FOR REVOCATION

File: . . . .

IN THE MATTER OF an Application for revocation made by . . . .

. . . .

. . . .

concerning a bargaining unit of employees of (name of employer)

. . . .

comprising (description of bargaining unit) . . . .

. . . .

. . . .

for which the . . . .
is the certified bargaining agent.

I, ...
(name of applicant)

do hereby report and certify to the Canada Labour Relations Board as follows:

1. That I have been provided with a copy of the Canada Labour Code (Part V – Industrial Relations) and the Canada Labour Relations Board Regulations.

2. That I am an employee of the respondent employer in the bargaining unit covered by this application.

3. That I represent a majority of the employees in the bargaining unit.

4. That to my knowledge all signatories in support of this application are expressing their true wishes.

5. That I understand that the investigating officer has the authority to investigate and verify all documents and statements made by parties to this application.

6. That I understand that any misrepresentations or irregularities in evidence provided to the Investigating Officer could result in the rejection of all or part of the evidence submitted and the rejection of the application.

Dated this . . . . day of . . . . 19 . . . .

. . . .
(Signature of Witness)　　　　　　　　　(Signature of Applicant)

APPENDIX 7
CANADA LABOUR RELATIONS BOARD

NOTICE OF VOTE

A representation vote among certain employees (described below) of . . . .

. . . .

will be conducted by the Canada Labour Relations Board in order to determine if the employees eligible to vote wish

to act as their bargaining agent in matters of collective bargaining with their employer.

REPRESENTATION VOTE

The vote will be by secret ballot. Voters will be allowed to vote without interference, restraint or coercion from any source. Electioneering will not be permitted at or near the voting place. A representative of the Canada Labour Relations Board will hand a ballot to each eligible voter presenting himself to vote at his proper voting place. The voter will then mark the ballot in secret and fold it. The voter will then promptly deposit the folded ballot in a ballot box under the supervision of the representative of the Board.

This is a SECRET BALLOT and MUST NOT BE SIGNED

SCRUTINEERS

Scrutineers representing each of the parties named by the Board on the ballot may be appointed by the parties for each voting place. These scrutineers will have the following duties and privileges:

1. To assist in the identification of voters.
2. To act as checkers at the voting place and at the counting of the ballots.
3. To otherwise assist the representative of the Canada Labour Relations Board.

ELIGIBLE VOTERS

Employees eligible to vote are:

TIME AND PLACE OF VOTE

The vote will be held on . . . .

between the hours of . . . . and . . . . at the following place(s):

. . . .

BALLOT

Reproduced below is a sample of the ballot to be used.

. . . .

Secretary

Canada Labour

Relations Board

APPENDIX 8
LISTING OF CERTIFICATION ORDERS

Lists of Canada Labour Relations Board files in which certification orders were issued from 1973 to the end of fiscal 1983-84. Grouped by industries or subject-matters, referenced by employers' names, and cross-referenced with the Board's publication, *Decisions Information* (di), in which the reader will find a description of the bargaining unit. Orders that were not reproduced in *di* have been omitted.

AIR TRANSPORT

File	Employer	di
555-1224	ADGA Systems International Ltd.	32 di 223
C-98	Aero-Club de Montréal (Montreal Flying Club)	1 di 9
555-1952	Aero Photo (1961) Inc., Ste-Foy, (Québec)	51 di 18
555-1457	Air B.C. Division of Air B.C. Ltd. (formerly Airwest Airlines Ltd.)	41 di 11
555-1445	Air B.C. Division of Air B.C. Ltd. (formerly West Coast Air Services)	41 di 11
555-1851	Air B.C. Division of Jim Pattison Industries Ltd., Richmond, B.C.	50 di 16
555-596	Air Canada	16 di 220
555-1329	Air Fecteau Ltée	38 di 4
555-1642	Air Mistassini Inc.	45 di 7
555-1983	Air Satellite Inc., Hauterive, (Québec)	51 di 19
555-453	Aircon Aviation Services	11 di 3
555-338	Airtransit Canada	8 di 5
555-609	Airwest Airlines Ltd.	18 di 39
555-478	Alitalia Linee Aeree Italianee S.P.A.	12 di 5
555-488	Alitalia Linee Aeree Italianee S.P.A.	12 di 5
555-450	Austin Airways Ltd./White River Air Services Ltd.	12 di 4
555-763	Austin Airways Ltd./White River Air Services Ltd.	22 di 493
555-1309	Austin Airways Ltd./White River Air Services Ltd.	36 di 9
555-1444	Austin Airways Ltd./White River Air Services Ltd.	39 di 20
555-1634	British Airways	44 di 5
555-1898	British Airways, Toronto, Ontario	51 di 14
C-175	Butler Aviation of Canada Ltd.	5 di 6
555-1757	Burns International Security Services Ltd.	48 di 14
555-716	BWIA International (British West Indian Airways)	19 di 99
555-1841	CAFAS Inc.	50 di 15
555-1280	Canadian Pacific Air Lines Ltd.	33 di 352
555-1357	Canadian Pacific Airlines Ltd.	36 di 13
555-1460	Canadian Pacific Airlines Ltd.	41 di 12
555-1779	Canadian Pacific Airlines	48 di 16
555-1564	Carrier Canada Ltd.	42 di 14
555-1536	Cité de Rouyn	42 di 12

555-776	City of Kelowna	20 di 227
555-1065	Conair Aviation Ltd.	27 di 642
C-19	Consolidated Aviation Fueling and Services (Pacific) Ltd.	1 di 6
555-830	Consolidated Aviation Fueling and Services (Pacific) Ltd.	21 di 376
555-871	Consolidated Aviation Services Alberta Ltd.	22 di 497
555-1154	Consolidated Aviation Services Alberta Ltd.	30 di 68
555-1468	Consolidated Aviation Services of Alberta Ltd.	41 di 13
555-689	Corporation of the City of Castlegar (Castlegar Airport)	18 di 41
555-921	Corporation of the City of Cranbrook	24 di 135
555-1424	D.B. Services des Avion Inc.	39 di 19
555-391	Eastern Provincial Airways (1963) Ltd.	9 di 7
555-410	Eastern Provincial Airways (1963) Ltd.	10 di 3
555-495	Eastern Provincial Airways (1963) Ltd.	13 di 3
555-1055	Eastern Provincial Airways (1963) Ltd.	28 di 868
555-1607	El Al Israel Airlines	43 di 12
555-1429	Evidence Research Associates Ltd.	38 di 8
555-1436	Evidence Research Associates Ltd.	38 di 8
555-412	Field Aviation Co. Ltd.	11 di 3
555-1854	Fort-Net Inc., Mtl., Québec	50 di 17
555-555	General Aviation Services Ltd.	15 di 156
555-884	General Aviation Services Ltd.	22 di 498
555-931	General Aviation Services Ltd.	29 di 2
555-874	Gilles Grandmaison	22 di 497
C-220	Great Lakes Airlines Ltd.	5 di 8
555-278	Great Lakes Airlines Ltd.	6 di 5
555-1110	Great Lakes Airlines Ltd.	30 di 66
555-1188	Great Lakes Pilotage Authority Ltd.	30 di 71
555-886	Haida Airlines Ltd.	22 di 498
555-1830	Héli-Québec Limitée, Bellefeuille (Québec)	50 di 14
555-1829	Hélicoptères Trans-Québec Ltée, Les Cèdres (Québec)	50 di 14
555-1574	Highland Helicopters Ltd.	42 di 14
555-1080	I.M.P. Aviation Services Ltd.	28 di 869
555-1871	Innotech Aviation Ltd., Dorval, Quebec	51 di 12
C-125	Island Airlines Ltd.	3 di 5
555-318	KLM Royal Dutch Airlines	7 di 5
555-367	KLM Royal Dutch Airlines	9 di 5
555-1892	La Cie de Pavage d'Asphalte Beaver Ltée, Montréal (Québec)	51 di 14
555-1378	La Compagnie de Pavage d'Asphalte Beaver Ltée	36 di 16
555-1448	La Sarre Air Services Ltée	43 di 7
555-457	Labrador Airways Ltd.	12 di 4
555-1542	Labrador Airways Ltd.	42 di 12
555-1900	Labrador Airways Ltd., Goose Bay, Labrador	51 di 14
555-1928	Labrador Airways Ltd., Goose Bay, Newfoundland	53 di 4
555-1950	Labrador Airways Ltd., Goose Bay, Newfoundland	53 di 4
555-1561	Labrador Aviation Services Ltd., Goose Bay, Newfoundland	43 di 9
	Labrador Aviation Services Ltd., Goose Bay, Newfoundland	53 di 4
555-249	Lavergne L'Italien	8 di 4

C-54	Les Ailes du Nord Ltée (Northern Wings Ltd.)	1 di 7
555-681	Les Ailes du Nord Ltée	18 di 40
555-781	Lcs Ailcs du Nord Ltée	21 di 374
555-782	Les Ailes du Nord Ltée	21 di 374
555-933	Modern Building Cleaning, Division of Dustband Enterprises Ltd.	25 di 331
555-456	Newfoundland and Labrador Air Transport Ltd.	12 di 4
555-1248	Norcanair Limited, North Canada Air Ltd., (Carrying on business under the name of "Norcanair Electronics Ltd.")	35 di 3
555-678	Nordair Ltd.	18 di 14
555-1381	Nordair Ltée	43 di 6
	Northern Air Services Ltd., Stephenville, Newfoundland	53 di 4
	Northern Air Services Ltd., Stephenville, Newfoundland	53 di 4
555-1200	Northern Thunderbird Air Ltd.	33 di 351
555-1407	Okanagan Helicopters Ltd.	41 di 11
555-1302	Ontario Worldair Ltd.	35 di 5
555-1373	Ontario Worldair Ltd.	37 di 4
555-1422	Oshawa Flying Club	38 di 7
555-1325	Pacific Coastal Airlines Ltd.	35 di 6
555-1108	Pacific Western Airlines Ltd.	29 di 3
555-1132	Pacific Western Airlines Ltd.	29 di 9
555-1353	Pacific Western Airlines Ltd.	38 di 5
555-924	Pacific Western Airlines Ltd.	25 di 331
555-925	Pacific Western Airlines Ltd.	24 di 136
555-1479	Powell Air Ltd.	41 di 14
555-1370	Provincial Investigation Services Ltd.	36 di 15
555-394	Québecair	10 di 3
555-592	Québecair	15 di 159
555-1576	Québecair	43 di 10
555-1008	Shell Canada Ltd.	26 di 497
555-1595	Société d'amémagement de l'Outaouais	43 di 11
555-1794	Société d'aménagement de l'Outaouais	49 di 9
555-1683	Société de Protection et Enquête du Québec Inc. (SOPEQ)	46 di 8
555-500	Taylor Aircraft Services Ltd.	12 di 5
555-1126	The Corporation of the City of Cranbrook	29 di 8
555-764	Time Air Ltd.	20 di 226
C-126	Trans Mountain Air Services Ltd.	2 di 6
555-598	Trans-Provincial Airlines Ltd.	16 di 220
555-1408	Trans-Provincial Airlines Ltd.	37 di 5
C-90	Transair Ltd.	4 di 6
555-863	Transair Ltd.	22 di 496
555-1865	Tri-L Flight Service Ltd., Calgary, Alberta	50 di 17
555-754	Tyee Airways Ltd.	20 di 225
C-78	United Air Lines Inc.	1 di 8
555-1670	Venezuelan International Airways	45 di 9
555-616	Victoria Flying Services Ltd.	17 di 2
555-1903	Ville de Rouyn, Rouyn (Québec)	51 di 15
555-983	Wardair Canada (1975) Ltd., a Subsidiary of Wardair International Ltd.	25 di 333
555-1018	Wardair Canada (1975) Ltd.	26 di 497

555-1197	Wardair Canada (1975) Ltd.	31 di 129
555-1333	Wardair Canada (1975) Ltd.	36 di 11
555-1170	West Coast Air Services Ltd.	30 di 70
C-161	Western Airlines Inc.	5 di 6
555-937	Western Airlines Inc. (Calgary, Vancouver & Edmonton)	25 di 331
555-1766	Western Airlines Inc.	48 di 15
555-1174	Woodward's Oil Ltd.	32 di 221
555-1526	Worldways Airlines Ltd.	41 di 18
555-569	Yellow Coach Lines Ltd.	15 di 158

BANKS

File	Employer	di
555-1102	Bank of British Columbia	29 di 3
555-1332	Bank of British Columbia	36 di 10
555-626	Bank of Montreal (Langley, B.C. Branch)	20 di 223
555-630	Bank of Montreal (Saltspring Island, B.C. Branch)	20 di 223
555-634	Bank of Montreal	20 di 223
555-658	Bank of Montreal	20 di 223
555-785	Bank of Montreal	20 di 227
555-788	Bank of Montreal	20 di 228
555-819	Bank of Montreal	21 di 375
555-814	Bank of Montreal (Montréal, Québec)	21 di 375
555-821	Bank of Montreal (Royal Oak Branch)	21 di 375
555-832	Bank of Montreal	21 di 376
555-842	Bank of Montreal	21 di 376
555-852	Bank of Montreal	22 di 496
555-882	Bank of Montreal	22 di 498
555-901	Bank of Montreal	23 di 4
555-902	Bank of Montreal	24 di 134
555-919	Bank of Montreal	24 di 135
555-1011	Bank of Montreal	26 di 497
555-1019	Bank of Montreal	26 di 497
555-1022	Bank of Montreal	26 di 498
555-1038	Bank of Montreal	26 di 499
555-1104	Bank of Montreal	29 di 3
555-1124	Bank of Montreal	29 di 8
555-1125	Bank of Montreal	29 di 8
555-1127	Bank of Montreal	29 di 8
555-1128	Bank of Montreal	29 di 8
555-1161	Bank of Montreal	30 di 69
555-1164	Bank of Montreal	30 di 70
555-1165	Bank of Montreal	30 di 70
555-1166	Bank of Montreal	30 di 70
555-1171	Bank of Montreal	30 di 70
555-1184	Bank of Montreal	31 di 128
555-1185	Bank of Montreal	31 di 128
555-1186	Bank of Montreal	31 di 128
555-1212	Bank of Montreal	32 di 222
555-1261	Bank of Montreal	35 di 352
555-1291	Bank of Montreal	35 di 4

555-1406	Bank of Montreal	38 di 7
555-1426	Bank of Montreal	37 di 6
555-1437	Bank of Montreal	38 di 8
555-1443	Bank of Montreal	39 di 20
555-1656	Bank of Montreal	45 di 8
555-1777	Bank of Montreal	48 di 16
555-1890	Bank of Montreal (Montréal, Québec)	50 di 19
555-2017	Bank of Montreal, Montreal Quebec	53 di 7
555-611	Bank of Nova Scotia	19 di 96
555-612	Bank of Nova Scotia (Norfolk Street Branch, Simcoe, Ontario)	19 di 96
555-618	Bank of Nova Scotia (Main Street Branch, Jarvis, Ontario)	19 di 96
555-624	Bank of Nova Scotia (Simon Fraser U. Branch)	21 di 373
555-632	Bank of Nova Scotia	21 di 373
555-643	Bank of Nova Scotia	21 di 373
555-845	Bank of Nova Scotia	21 di 377
555-1156	Bank of Nova Scotia	30 di 68
555-1260	Bank of Nova Scotia	33 di 351
555-1290	Bank of Nova Scotia	35 di 4
555-1394	Bank of Nova Scotia	37 di 4
555-1441	Bank of Nova Scotia	39 di 20
555-1647	Bank of Nova Scotia	44 di 5
555-1811	Bank of Nova Scotia	49 di 10
555-1821	Bank of Nova Scotia	49 di 11
555-1853	Bank of Nova Scotia (Toronto, Ontario)	50 di 16
555-889	Banque Canadienne Nationale	24 di 133
555-899	Banque Canadienne Nationale	24 di 133
555-930	Banque Canadienne Nationale	31 di 127
555-939	Banque Canadienne Nationale	25 di 331
555-943	Banque Canadienne Nationale	24 di 136
555-970	Banque Canadienne Nationale	26 di 494
555-997	Banque Canadienne Nationale	26 di 496
555-999	Banque Canadienne Nationale	26 di 496
555-1017	Banque Canadienne Nationale	26 di 497
555-1024	Banque Canadienne Nationale	26 di 498
555-1027	Banque Canadienne Nationale	31 di 127
555-1037	Banque Canadienne Nationale	26 di 499
555-1040	Banque Canadienne Nationale	27 di 640
555-1096	Banque Canadienne Nationale	28 di 870
555-1176	Banque Canadienne Nationale	32 di 221
555-1249	Banque Canadienne Nationale	32 di 223
555-1301	Banque Nationale du Canada	35 di 5
555-1303	Banque Nationale du Canada	35 di 5
555-1328	Banque Nationale du Canada	36 di 10
555-1340	Banque Nationale du Canada	36 di 11
555-1355	Banque Nationale du Canada	36 di 13
555-1364	Banque Nationale du Canada	36 di 14
555-1379	Banque Nationale du Canada (succursale Sillery, Qué.)	36 di 16
555-1388	Banque Nationale du Canada	37 di 4
555-1418	Banque Nationale du Canada	38 di 7
555-1419	Banque Nationale du Canada	38 di 7
555-1469	Banque Nationale du Canada	41 di 13

555-1553	Banque Nationale du Canada	43 di 9
555-1603	Banque Nationale du Canada	43 di 12
555-1626	Banque Nationale du Canada	43 di 14
555-1788	Banque Nationale du Canada	48 di 17
555-1819	Banque Nationale du Canada	49 di 11
555-1825	Banque Nationale du Canada	50 di 14
555-1915	Banque Nationale du Canada (Montréal, Québec)	51 di 15
555-986	Banque Provinciale du Canada	28 di 868
555-1013	Banque Provinciale du Canada	28 di 868
555-1084	Banque Provinciale du Canada	28 di 869
555-631	Canadian Imperial Bank of Commerce	21 di 373
555-671	Canadian Imperial Bank of Commerce	20 di 223
555-777	Canadian Imperial Bank of Commerce	20 di 227
555-784	Canadian Imperial Bank of Commerce	20 di 227
555-872	Canadian Imperial Bank of Commerce	22 di 497
555-929	Canadian Imperial Bank of Commerce	24 di 136
555-1010	Canadian Imperial Bank of Commerce	26 di 497
555-1016	Canadian Imperial Bank of Commerce	27 di 638
555-1041	Canadian Imperial Bank of Commerce	27 di 641
555-1091	Canadian Imperial Bank of Commerce	28 di 870
555-1100	Canadian Imperial Bank of Commerce	28 di 871
555-1114	Canadian Imperial Bank of Commerce	29 di 7
555-1129	Canadian Imperial Bank of Commerce	29 di 9
555-1137	Canadian Imperial Bank of Commerce	30 di 67
555-1160	Canadian Imperial Bank of Commerce	30 di 69
555-1505	Canadian Imperial Bank of Commerce	41 di 16
555-1702	Canadian Imperial Bank of Commerce	46 di 9
555-1804	Canadian Imperial Bank of Commerce	49 di 10
555-783	Royal Bank of Canada	22 di 493
555-826	Royal Bank of Canada	22 di 493
555-847	Royal Bank of Canada	22 di 495
555-971	Royal Bank of Canada	26 di 494
555-979	Royal Bank of Canada	27 di 637
555-1030	Royal Bank of Canada	27 di 639
555-1031	Royal Bank of Canada	27 di 640
555-1035	Royal Bank of Canada	27 di 640
555-1086	Royal Bank of Canada	28 di 869
555-1087	Royal Bank of Canada	28 di 870
555-1138	Royal Bank of Canada	30 di 67
555-1146	Royal Bank of Canada	30 di 67
555-1365	Royal Bank of Canada	36 di 14
555-1417	Royal Bank of Canada	37 di 5
555-1625	Royal Bank of Canada	43 di 14
555-1652	Royal Bank of Canada	44 di 6
555-1671	Royal Bank of Canada	45 di 10
555-1722	Royal Bank of Canada	47 di 5
555-1787	Royal Bank of Canada	48 di 17
555-868	Toronto-Dominion Bank	22 di 497
555-879	Toronto-Dominion Bank	22 di 498
555-907	Toronto-Dominion Bank	23 di 4
555-913	Toronto-Dominion Bank	23 di 4
555-1430	Toronto-Dominion Bank	39 di 20
555-1511	Toronto-Dominion Bank	41 di 17
555-1691	Toronto-Dominion Bank	45 di 10

BRIDGES

File	Employer	di
C-100	Niagara Falls Bridge Commission	1 di 9
C-103	Niagara Falls Bridge Commission	2 di 5

BROADCASTING

File	Employer	di
555-1592	5440 Cable Ltd.	42 di 15
555-652	ATV Cape Breton Ltd.	18 di 39
555-462	Allview Cable Services Ltd.	11 di 3
555-1150	Allview Cable Service Ltd. (a division of Cablebroadcasting Ltd.)	30 di 67
555-1470	Anslon Cablevision Ltd.	39 di 21
555-2001	Bimcor Inc., Mtl. Quebec	52 di 6
555-258	CFQC Broadcasting Ltd. (A.A. Murphy & Sons Ltd.)	7 di 3
555-1539	CHEM TV Inc.	43 di 8
555-454	CHLT Télé-7 Ltée	14 di 69
555-1762	CHLT-TV Inc.	48 di 15
555-686	CHYR Radio (Dancy Broadcasting Ltd.) and Essex Cable T.V. Rogers Management Services Ltd.	18 di 41
C-145	CJBR Radio Ltée	4 di 7
C-146	CJBR Radio Ltée – CJBR TV Ltée	4 di 7
C-147	CJBR TV Ltée	4 di 7
C-148	CJBR TV Ltée	4 di 7
555-1651	CJMD Chibougamau Inc.	45 di 8
555-690	CJMS Radio Montréal Ltée	19 di 98
555-1271	CJMS Radio Montréal Ltée	35 di 3
555-698	CJMT Radio Ltée	18 di 42
555-1316	CJOH Broadcasting Ltd., CJOH-TV	36 di 9
555-836	CJPM-TV Inc.	22 di 494
555-701	CJRC Radio Capitale Ltée	19 di 99
555-301	CJRP Radio Provinciale Ltée	10 di 3
555-316	CJRP Radio Provinciale Ltée	10 di 3
555-644	CJRS Radio Sherbrooke Ltée	17 di 3
555-697	CJTR Radio Trois-Rivières Ltée	18 di 42
555-1265	CJTR Radio Trois-Rivières Ltée	35 di 3
555-1803	CJTR Radio Trois-Rivières Ltée	49 di 10
555-1643	CKCV (Québec) Ltée	45 di 7
555-674	CKRV Radio des Plaines Ltée	18 di 40
555-674	CKRV Radio des Plaines Ltée	18 di 40
555-1153	Cable TV Ltée	30 di 68
555-1782	Cable T.V. Inc.	48 di 16
555-1704	Cable West TV Ltd.	46 di 10
555-372	Cablevision Nationale Ltée	10 di 3
555-579	Cablevision Nationale Ltée (Channel 9)	17 di 2
555-719	Cablevision Nationale Ltée	20 di 224
555-720	Cablevision Nationale Ltée	20 di 224

555-877	Cablevision Nationale Ltée	22 di 498
555-1337	Cablevision Nationale Ltée	38 di 4
555-365	Cambrian Broadcasting Ltd. CKSO-TV	10 di 3
555-1003	Can West Broadcasting Ltd. (CKND-TV)	26 di 496
555-327	Canadian Broadcasting Corp.	8 di 5
555-437	Canadian Broadcasting Corp.	19 di 95
555-849	Canadian Broadcasting Corp.	24 di 131
555-1023	Canadian Broadcasting Corp.	30 di 65
555-1409	Canadian Broadcasting Corp.	42 di 9
C-199	Canadian Wirevision Ltd.	4 di 8
555-1149	Cape Breton Cablevision Ltd.	30 di 67
555-2026	Cariboo Broadcasters Ltd., Quesnel, British Columbia	53 di 7
C-173	Central Broadcasting Co. Ltd.	4 di 7
555-355	Coopérative de Télevision de l'Outaouais (CFV-TV)	9 di 5
555-350	Coquitlam Cablevision Ltd.	9 di 5
555-546	Courtenay-Comox Television Ltd. (C-C. TV) (Cable TV)	14 di 72
C-50	Delta Cable Television Ltd.	1 di 7
555-1005	Dolbeau Télévision Service Inc.	26 di 496
C-215	Edmundston Radio Ltd.	5 di 8
555-1144	Entreprises Télé-Capitale Ltée (Division CFCM-TV et CKMI-TV)	32 di 220
555-1389	Entreprises Télé-Capitale Ltée, Division Rimouski (CFER-TV)	38 di 6
555-1455	Entreprises Télé-Capitale Ltée, Division CFCM-TV/CKMI-TV	44 di 4
555-1735	Entreprises Télé-Capitale Ltée, "Division CHRC-CHOI-FM"	48 di 12
C-183	Four Seasons Radio Ltd. (CKIQ)	4 di 7
C-97	Frontenac Broadcasting Co. Ltd. CKWS	3 di 4
555-1076	Halifax Cablevision Ltd.	28 di 869
555-1374	Halifax Cablevision Ltd.	36 di 15
555-1493	Hineson Entreprises Ltd.	41 di 15
555-1555	Huron Broadcasting Ltd.	42 di 13
555-1155	Island Broadcasters (1969) Ltd. & Twin Cities Radio Ltd.	30 di 68
555-1538	Kamloops Cablenet Ltd.	41 di 18
555-601	Kelowna Cable TV Ltd.	16 di 220
C-135	Kootenay Broadcasting Co. Ltd. and E.K. Radio Ltd.	5 di 5
555-1617	La Belle Vision Inc.	43 di 13
C-210	La Compagnie de Radio-diffusion de Shawinigan Falls Ltée, (CKSM)	5 di 7
555-1039	La Voix de l'Est (Departement Radio – CHEF)	27 di 640
555-1061	Les Entreprises Télé-Capitale Ltée	27 di 642
555-415	Lethbridge Television Ltd., CJOC-TV	10 di 3
555-1085	MacLean Hunter Cable Television	30 di 66
555-1278	MacLean-Hunter Cable T.V. Ltd.	35 di 3
C-24	Metro Cable T.V. Ltd.	1 di 6
555-235	Moffat Communications Ltd. CKLG	5 di 9
555-364	Multiple Access Ltd. (Broadcast Division)	9 di 5
555-242	Niagara Television Ltd.	5 di 10

C-231	North West Community Video Ltd.	5 di 8
555-483	North West Community Video Ltd.	12 di 5
555-390	Northern Television Systems Ltd.	14 di 69
C-207	Okanagan Radio Ltd.	4 di 8
555-1703	Okanagan Valley Television Co. Ltd. (CHBC-Television)	46 di 9
555-292	Ottawa Valley Broadcasting Co. Ltd. (CKOV RADIO)	8 di 4
555-1562	Peelcraft Quebec Ltée	42 di 14
555-964	Placements Claude St. Annault Inc. (CHVD Radio)	27 di 637
555-969	Powell River Television Co. Ltd.	25 di 333
C-133	QCTV Ltd.	2 di 6
555-1168	Radio Acadie Ltée	30 di 70
555-1344	Radio CKBM Inc.	36 di 12
555-283	Radio CKML Inc.	7 di 4
555-704	Radio Communautaire du Saguenay Lac Saint-Jean	18 di 42
555-1718	Radio Communautaire M.F. de la Haute Gatineau (CHGA)	48 di 11
555-548	Radio Côte-Nord Inc.	17 di 2
555-691	Radiodiffusion Mutuelle Ltée	18 di 41
555-1532	Radio Edmundston Ltée	42 di 11
555-758	Radio La Baie CKPB Ltée	20 di 226
555-965	Radio Lac Saint-Jean	26 di 494
555-679	Radio Lachute, Québec	18 di 40
555-1398	Radio Le Tuque Ltée	38 di 6
555-1134	Radio Mégantic Ltée	32 di 220
555-1135	Radio Plessisville Ltée (CKTL)	32 di 220
555-1700	Radio Roberval Inc. (CHRL)	46 di 9
555-1351	Radio Saguenay Ltée	36 di 12
C-172	Radio Sainte-Agathe Inc., (CJSA)	4 di 7
555-1054	Radio St.-Hyacinthe (1978) Ltée	16 di 641
C-203	Radio Station CHQM, Division of Q Broadcasting Ltd.	9 di 3
555-510	Radio Station CJDC (Dawson Creek, B.C.) Ltd.	13 di 4
555-1738	Radio Station CKPG Ltd. and CKPG Television Ltd.	48 di 12
555-866	Radio Témiscamingue Inc. Ville-Marie, Qué. (CKVM Ville-Marie et CKTV Témiscamingue)	22 di 497
555-1090	Radio Valleyfield Ltée (CFLV 1370)	29 di 2
555-1133	Radio Victoriaville Ltée (CFDA)	32 di 220
555-336	Radio Windsor Canadian Ltd. (CKWW-AM)	8 di 5
555-727	Seaside Cable Television Ltd.	19 di 100
555-335	Skyline Cablevision Ltd.	8 di 5
C-174	Ralph Snelgrove Television Ltd., CKVR-TV	3 di 5
555-1662	Société d'édition et de transcodage Ltée.	45 di 9
555-1524	Sorel-O-Vision Inc.	42 di 11
555-746	Télé-Câble Charlevoix Inc.	20 di 225
555-240	Télé-Métropole Inc.	6 di 4
555-241	Télé-Métropole Inc.	6 di 4
555-347	Télé-Métropole Inc.	9 di 4
555-735	Télé-Métropole Inc. (CFTM-CANAL 10) Montréal	20 di 225
555-1450	Télé-Métropole Inc.	41 di 12

555-824	Télécable de Québec, Inc.	21 di 376
555-1036	Télésaq Inc.	26 di 499
555-428	Télévision Saint-François Inc. (CKSH-TV)	10 di 4
C-212	Télévision Saint-Maurice Inc. CKTM-TV	5 di 7
555-1638	Television St.-Maurice (1976) Inc. (CKTM-TV)	45 di 7
C-121	The Niagara District Broadcasting Co. Ltd.	3 di 4
555-1203	Transvision Magog Inc.	32 di 222
555-480	Tri Co Broadcasting Ltd. (CJSS)	12 di 5
555-949	Vancouver Co-Operative Radio	24 di 136
555-471	Vercom Cable Service Ltd.	11 di 4
555-946	West Coast Cablevision Ltd.	25 di 332
555-1120	Western Approaches Ltd.	29 di 7
555-1602	White Rock Cablevision	43 di 12
555-1795	Yorkton Television Co. Ltd.	49 di 9

COMMUNICATIONS

File	Employer	di
555-1209	ADGA Systems International Ltd.	32 di 222
555-1356	Artel Leasing Ltd. Distacom Communications Ltd. and Pacific Comtel Ltd.	36 di 13
555-494	Bell Canada	14 di 69
555-1183	Bell Canada	32 di 221
555-323	British Columbia Telephone Co.	9 di 3
555-610	Canadian Pacific Ltd., Telecommunications Department	19 di 96
555-835	Canadian Pacific Telecommunications	22 di 493
555-702	Canadian Pacific Telecommunications Department	19 di 99
555-685	Canadian Telephones and Supplies Ltd.	18 di 41
555-246	Northern Telecom Ltd. (formerly Northern Electric Co. Ltd.)	14 di 69
555-1507	NorthwesTel Inc.	42 di 10
555-1616	NorthwesTel Inc.	43 di 13
555-557	Reuters Ltd.	15 di 156
555-649	TASCO Telephone Answering Exchange Ltd.	19 di 97
555-404-A	The Canadian Press	11 di 3
555-479	Téléglobe Canada	13 di 2
555-486	Téléglobe Canada	14 di 69

CONSTRUCTION IN NORTH

File	Employer	di
555-1810	A & M Johnson Contracting Ltd.	49 di 10
C-224	Aishihik Constructors	5 di 8
555-608	Argus Installations Ltd.	16 di 221
555-508	Atco Construction, a Division of Atco Structures Ltd.	13 di 4

555-558	Atco Construction, a division of Atco Structures Ltd.	15 di 156
555-1151	Atco Structures Ltd.	30 di 67
555-1742	Avonmore Heating & Airconditioning Ltd.	48 di 13
555-967	BACM Construction Co. Ltd.	25 di 332
555-968	BACM Construction Co. Ltd.	25 di 332
555-1560	Bresett Construction Ltd.	42 di 14
555-1696	Bresett Construction Ltd.	46 di 8
C-93	Burke Integrated Ceilings Ltd.	1 di 8
555-519	Walter Cabott Construction Ltd.	13 di 5
C-101	Canadian Longyear Ltd.	2 di 4
555-542	Canadian Longyear Ltd.	14 di 72
555-1698	Canievi Entreprises Ltd.	46 di 9
555-541	D.W. Coates Enterprises Ltd.	14 di 72
555-619	Co-Val Developments Ltd.	16 di 221
C-115	Connors Drilling Ltd.	2 di 5
555-640	Dinsmore Construction Ltd.	16 di 222
555-1324	Doey Construction Ltd.	35 di 6
555-396	Dominion Bridge Co. Ltd.	9 di 7
555-695	Duncan's Ltd.	18 di 42
555-1015	Excelsior Building Maintenance Ltd.	26 di 497
555-530	Flanders Installation Ltd.	14 di 71
555-1741	Fuller and Knowles Co. Ltd.	48 di 13
555-1428	Geddes Contracting Co. Ltd.	38 di 7
555-1431	Geddes Contracting Co. Ltd.	38 di 8
555-431	General Enterprises Ltd.	10 di 5
555-1342	Guran Construction Co. Ltd.	36 di 12
555-1727	HMW Constructors Ltd.	47 di 6
555-948	Herschel Construction Ltd.	25 di 332
C-102	Inspiration Drilling, Dresser Industrial	2 di 4
555-1092	Interior Contracting Co. Ltd.	28 di 870
555-1159	Keith Plumbing & Heating Co. Ltd.	30 di 69
555-313	Klondike Enterprises Ltd.	9 di 3
555-298	KRM Construction Ltd.	8 di 4
555-429	R.J. Keen Construction (1966) Ltd.	10 di 4
666-1791	L & W. Steel Ltd.	48 di 17
555-1543	Loram International Ltd.	41 di 18
555-1780	M & R. Mechanical Contractors	48 di 16
555-736	Majestic Wiley Contractors Ltd.	19 di 100
555-737	Majestic Wiley Contractors Ltd.	19 di 100
555-748	Majestic Wiley Contractors Ltd.	19 di 101
555-1807	Malamuti Saloon Ltd.	49 di 10
555-755	Manson Bros. Construction Ltd.	20 di 226
555-1028	Mitchell Installations Ltd.	26 di 498
555-1476	Mitchell Installations Ltd.	39 di 22
555-1520	Mitchell Installations Ltd.	41 di 17
555-1323	Moon Construction Co. (Yukon) Ltd.	35 di 6
555-848	North American Construction Ltd.	22 di 496
555-1056	North American Construction Ltd.	27 di 641
555-743	North American Road Ltd.	19 di 101
555-760	North American Road Ltd.	20 di 226
C-159	Stuart Olson Construction Ltd.	3 di 5
555-1697	P.C.L. Construction Ltd.	46 di 8
555-326	Packard Construction Ltd.	9 di 4

555-531	Pine Tree Construction Co. Ltd.	14 di 71
555-1556	Pipe Line Contractors Association of Canada (member employees: Loram International Ltd. & Bannister Pipe Lines)	41 di 19
555-1786	Pitts Engineering	48 di 16
555-1765	Pitts Engineering Construction Ltd.	48 di 15
555-1844	Pitts Engineering Construction Ltd.	50 di 15
555-675	J. Raab Plumbing & Heating Ltd.	18 di 40
555-496	Saturn Contracting Ltd.	13 di 3
555-1815	Sheafer-Townsend Ltd.	49 di 11
555-1025	South Grove Gravel Ltd.	26 di 498
555-520	State Construction Ltd.	13 di 5
C-139	Tompkins Contracting Ltd.	2 di 6
C-158	Work Arctic	2 di 6

CROWN CORPORATIONS

File	Employer	di
C-124	Atomic Energy of Canada Ltd.	3 di 4
C-225	Atomic Energy of Canada Ltd.	7 di 3
555-236	Atomic Energy of Canada Ltd.	5 di 9
555-392	Atomic Energy of Canada Ltd.	9 di 7
555-563	Atomic Energy of Canada Ltd.	15 di 157
555-873	Atomic Energy of Canada Ltd.	24 di 132
555-982	Atomic Energy of Canada Ltd.	25 di 333
555-1007	Atomic Energy of Canada Ltd.	27 di 637
555-1674	Canada Mortgage and Housing Corp.	46 di 7
C-110	Canadian Arsenals Ltd.	5 di 5
555-880	Canadian Arsenals Ltd. Division du remplissage	22 di 498
555-436	Canadian Saltfish Corp.	10 di 4
C-67	Cape Breton Development Corp.	1 di 8
555-694	Cape Breton Development Corp.	18 di 42
555-770	Cape Breton Development Corp., Coal Division	23 di 2
555-1207	Cape Breton Development Corp.	32 di 222
555-1930	Cape Breton Development Corp., Sydney, Nova Scotia	51 di 17
C-162	Central Mortgage and Housing Corp.	2 di 7
C-164	Central Mortgage and Housing Corp.	5 di 6
555-461	Central Mortgage and Housing Corp.	12 di 4
555-589	Central Mortgage and Housing Corp. (Grenet-De-Guire)	16 di 219
555-590	Central Mortgage and Housing Corp.	16 di 220
555-657	Central Mortgage and Housing Corp.	16 di 222
555-699	Central Mortgage and Housing Corp.	21 di 373
555-984	Central Mortgage and Housing Corp.	26 di 495
555-1070	Central Mortgage and Housing Corp.	28 di 868
555-369	Eldorado Nuclear Ltd.	9 di 6
555-741	Eldorado Nuclear Ltd.	21 di 374
555-1320	Eldorado Nuclear Ltd. (carrying on business under the firm name and style of Club Eldorado)	35 di 6
555-1552	Eldorado Nuclear Ltd. (formerly Eldorado Mining & Refining Ltd.)	43 di 8

C-230	Jeunesse Canada Monde (Canada World Youth)	5 di 8
555-1096	Les ponts Jacques Cartier et Champlain Inc.	28 di 870
555-337	National Arts Centre Corp.	8 di 5
555-521	National Arts Centre Corp.	13 di 5
555-1710	National Arts Centre	47 di 4
C-142	National Harbours Board	4 di 7
C-185	National Harbours Board	5 di 6
555-300	National Harbours Board	8 di 4
555-351	National Harbours Board	9 di 5
555-379	National Harbours Board	9 di 6
555-812	National Harbours Board	21 di 375
555-813	National Harbours Board	21 di 375
555-1251	National Harbours Board	32 di 223
555-1494	National Harbours Board	41 di 15
555-386	Northern Transportation Co. Ltd.	12 di 4
555-385	The Company of Young Canadians	9 di 7
C-63	The St. Lawrence Seaway Authority	4 di 5
555-1026	Toronto Harbour Commission	27 di 638
555-1052	The Toronto Harbour Commissioners	28 di 868

FEED AND GRAIN

File	Employer	di
555-1386	Alberta Terminals Ltd.	36 di 16
555-1585	Allstate Grain Co. Ltd.	43 di 10
555-684	B.C. Terminal Elevator Operator's Association	19 di 98
C-91	Burns Food Ltd.	1 di 8
555-928	C.S.P. Foods Ltd.	24 di 136
555-1083	Canbra Foods Ltd.	28 di 869
555-252	Cowichan Co-operative Services	5 di 10
C-228	Delta Food Processors Ltd. (Melograin Milling Co. Division)	5 di 8
555-575	Farines Phénix Ltée	15 di 158
555-1021	Feed-Rite Ltd.	27 di 638
555-1173	William A. Flemming Ltd.	31 di 128
555-497	Fortress Formula Feed Co. Ltd.	13 di 3
555-1653	Gainers Inc.	45 di 8
555-1608	Les Minoteries Rozon (1980) Inc.	43 di 12
C-17	Manitoba Pool Elevators	1 di 6
555-309	Manitoba Pool Elevators	7 di 4
555-883	Manitoba Pool Elevators	23 di 3
555-307	Maple Leaf Mills Ltd. Master Feeds Plant	7 di 4
555-311	Maple Leaf Mills Ltd. Master Feeds Branch	7 di 5
555-534	Maple Leaf Mills Ltd. (Prescott)	14 di 71
555-535	Maple Leaf Mills Ltd.	15 di 156
555-567	Maple Leaf Mills Ltd.	15 di 157
555-759	Maple Leaf Mills Ltd.	20 di 226
555-1392	Maple Leaf Mills Ltd.	36 di 16
555-1818	Maple Leaf Mills Ltd.	49 di 11
555-1962	Maple Leaf Mills Ltd.	51 di 18
555-1147	Maple Leaf Ltd.	30 di 67
555-1427	Maple Leaf Ltd.	39 di 20

555-769	Maritime Co-operative Services Ltd.	20 di 227
555-607	Master Feeds, A Division of Maple Leaf Mills Ltd.	16 di 221
555-1130	Master Feeds, Division of Maple Leaf Mills Ltd.	29 di 9
555-1581	Memco Processors Ltd.	42 di 15
555-911	Moulins Maple Leaf Ltée (Maple Leaf Mills)	24 di 134
555-1006	Newfield Seeds Ltd.	26 di 496
555-1575	Ogilvie Flour Mills Co. Ltd.	43 di 10
555-1832	Ogilvie Flour Mills Co. Ltd.	40 di 14
555-975	Preston Feed and Seed Ltd.	25 di 333
555-308	Robin Hood Multifoods Ltd.	7 di 4
555-532	Robin Hood Multifoods Ltd.	15 di 156
555-914	Robin Hood Multifoods Ltd.	24 di 135
555-1679	Robin Hood Multifoods Ltée	45 di 10
555-1287	The Great Lakes Elevator Co. Ltd.	35 di 4
555-1537	United Co-Operatives of Ontario, Parent Firm of wholly owned subsidiary Patrons Elevators, Ltd.	41 di 18
C-120	United Grain Growers Ltd.	2 di 5

INDIAN BANDS

File	Employer	di
555-1577	Conseil des Montagnais du Lac St.-Jean	50 di 14
555-414	Indian claims Commissioner	10 di 3
C-87	Manitou Community College	7 di 3
C-58	Qu'Appelle Indian Residential School Council	2 di 4
C-75	Walpole Island Council	3 di 4
555-1873	Fort Alexander School Board of the Sagkeeng Education Authority, Fort Alexander Reserve, Pine Falls, Manitoba	51 di 13
555-1861	Nelson House Education Authority, Nelson House (Manitoba)	50 di 17
555-1856	Southeast Tribal Division School Inc.	50 di 17
C-195	The Professional Institute of the Public Service	5 di 7

LONGSHORING

File	Employer	di
555-1863	W.S. Anderson & Co. Ltd.	52 di 4
555-459	Annacis Marine Terminals Ltd.	10 di 4
555-1322	Arrimage de Gros Cacouna Inc.	35 di 6
555-1158	Arrow Stevedoring Inc.	30 di 69
C-2	Associated Stevedoring Co. Ltd.	5 di 4
555-1208	Bayside Stevedoring Ltd.	31 di 130
555-1122	British Columbia Forest Products Ltd.	30 di 66
C-73	British Yukon Navigation Co. Ltd.	5 di 5
555-803	Brown & Ryan Ltd.	24 di 131

555-808	Brown & Ryan Ltd.	24 di 131
C-109	Brunterm Ltd. (Container Terminal Operators)	4 di 6
555-799	Brunterm Ltd.	24 di 131
555-806	Brunterm Ltd.	24 di 131
555-1672	C.N. Marine Inc.	45 di 10
555-1664	Canada Enterprises Stevedoring Ltd.	47 di 4
C-3	Canadian Stevedoring Co. Ltd.	5 di 4
C-4	Casco Terminals Ltd.	5 di 4
C-5	Cassiar Asbestos Corp. Ltd.	
	(Asbestos Wharf Division)	5 di 4
555-956	Cérès Stevedoring Co. Ltd.	24 di 131
555-1753	Cérès Stevedoring Co.	50 di 14
555-800	Cullen Stevedoring Co. Ltd.	24 di 131
555-809	Cullen Stevedoring Co. Ltd.	24 di 131
C-6	Empire Stevedoring Co. Ltd.	5 di 4
555-802	Empire Stevedoring Co. Ltd.	24 di 131
555-807	Empire Stevedoring Co. Ltd.	24 di 131
555-1258	Fibreco Export Inc.	33 di 351
555-1416	Fibreco Export Inc.	37 di 5
C-7	Fraser-Surrey Docks Ltd. (Nanaimo Stevedoring)	5 di 4
555-958	Furness Canada (1975) Ltd.	24 di 131
555-1178	Johnston Terminals and Storage Ltd.	36 di 8
555-804	Logistic Corp., Stevedoring Division	24 di 131
555-811	Logistic Corp., Stevedoring Division	24 di 131
C-72	Lynn Stevedoring Co. Ltd.	5 di 5
555-1334	Maritime and Gulf Stevedores Ltd.	36 di 11
555-1289	Marime Employers' Association	35 di 4
555-1318	Marime Employers' Association	35 di 6
555-1529	Maritime Employers' Association	44 di 4
C-116	Murray Bay Marine Terminal Inc.	2 di 5
555-1733	Murray Bay Marine Terminal Inc.	49 di 8
555-1759	Murray Bay Marine Terminal Inc.	49 di 8
555-1701	National Harbours Board (Port of Montreal)	46 di 9
C-9	Neptune Terminals Ltd.	5 di 4
C-170	New Brunswick International Paper Co.	5 di 6
C-83	North Sydney Warehouse Ltd.	2 di 4
C-10	Northland Shipping (1962) Co. Ltd.	5 di 4
C-11	Pacific Coast Terminals Co. Ltd.	8 di 4
C-9A	Squamish Terminals Ltd.	5 di 4
555-383	Squamish Terminals Ltd.	9 di 6
555-959	Stevco Marine Corp.	24 di 131
555-960	Stevco Terminals Operators Ltd.	24 di 131
555-1216	Task Terminal Ltée	44 di 4
555-293	Vancouver Island Stevedoring Co. Ltd.	9 di 3
C-12	Vancouver Wharves Ltd.	3 di 4
C-184	F.K. Warren Ltd.	5 di 6
555-815	Waterfront Terminals Ltd.	21 di 375
C-15	Westcan Terminals Ltd., Westcan Stevedoring	
	Ltd.	5 di 4
C-13	Western Stevedoring Co. Ltd.	5 di 4
C-14	Westshore Terminals Ltd.	5 di 4
555-909	Williams and Simpson Pulpwood Ltd.	24 di 134
555-801	Wolfe Stevedores Ltd.	24 di 131
555-810	Wolfe Stevedores Ltd.	24 di 131

NORTH TERRITORIES

File	Employer	di
555-1902	Aklavik Housing Association, Aklavik, Northwest Territories	51 di 15
555-1912	Arctic House, Yellowknife, N.W.T.	51 di 15
555-1910	Cambridge Bay Housing Association, Cambridge Bay, Northwest Territories	51 di 15
555-1984	Chesterfield Inlet Housing Association, Chesterfield Inlet, Northwest Territories	52 di 5
555-1923	Custom Structures (a division of Bralorne Resources Limited), Spruce Grove, Alberta	51 di 16
555-1985	Hamlet of Chesterfield Inlet, Chesterfield Inlet, N.W.T.	53 di 5
555-1934	ICG Utilities (Plains-Western) Ltd., Leduc, Alberta	51 di 17
555-1857	Inuvik Housing Association, Inuvik, Northwest Territories	51 di 12
555-1917	Northern Loram Joint Venture, Norman Wells (T.N.O.)	51 di 16
555-1883	Partec Lavalin Inc., Calgary, Alberta	51 di 13
555-1986	Repulse Bay Housing Association, Repulse Bay, N.W.T.	53 di 5
555-1876	Super A Foods (Porter Creek) Ltd.	50 di 18
555-1918	Tarfu Holdings Ltd., Whitehorse, Yukon	51 di 16

RAILWAYS

File	Employer	di
555-245	Algoma Central Railway	5 di 10
C-18	Canadian National Railways	1 di 6
C-45	Canadian National Railway Co.	5 di 5
555-900	Canadian National Railways	30 di 65
555-1464	Canadian National Railway Co.	41 di 13
555-295	Canadian Pacific Ltd.	7 di 4
555-331	Canadian Pacific Ltd.	8 di 5
555-851	Canadian Pacific Ltd. (CP Rail) Dominion Atlantic Railway Co.	23 di 3
555-917	Canadian Pacific Ltd.	30 di 65
555-1483	Canadian Pacific Ltd. (& Quebec Central Railway Co., Dominion Atlantic Railway Co. & Esquimalt & Nanaimo Railway)	46 di 7
C-144	Cannet Freight Cartage Ltd.	6 di 4
555-1669	Cape Breton Development Corp. (Devco Railway)	45 di 9
555-1744	Chesapeake & Ohio Railway Co.	48 di 14
555-1745	Chesapeake and Ohio Railway Co.	48 di 14
555-1858	Crawley & McCracken Co. Ltd., Montreal, Quebec	50 di 17
555-1859	Crawley & McCracken Co. Ltd., Montreal, Quebec	50 di 17
C-112	Dominion Atlantic Railway Co.	3 di 4
C-113	Dominion Atlantic Railway Co.	3 di 4

C-209	Essex Terminal Railway Co. Windsor, Ont. Morton Warehouses Inc., Windsor, Ont. Morton Terminal Ltd.	5 di 7
555-850	Ontario Northland Railway	22 di 496
555-443	Quebec Central Railway	10 di 4
555-341	Quebec North Shore and Labrador Railway Co.	9 di 4
555-348	Quebec North Shore and Labrador Railway Co.	9 di 4
555-368	Quebec North Shore and Labrador Railway Co.	9 di 5
555-904	Quebec North Shore and Labrador Railway Co.	24 di 134
555-1648	The British Yukon Railway Co.	45 di 7
555-1663	Toronto Terminals Railway Co.	45 di 9
555-1814	R.F. Welch (B.C.) Ltd.	49 di 11

ROAD TRANSPORT

File	Employer	di
555-1599	97236 Canada Inc.	43 di 11
555-1472	A & H Express Lines (Canada) Ltd.	39 di 21
555-1728	A & H Express Lines (Canada) Ltd.	47 di 6
555-1988	A & H Express Lines (Canada) Ltd., Mississauga, Ontario	52 di 5
555-1528	A & M Transport Ltd.	41 di 18
555-717	A.J. (Archie) Goodale Ltd.	19 di 99
555-1169	A.L. Transport Inc.	31 di 127
555-1533	Able Moving & Storage Ltd.	42 di 12
555-1901	Acadian Express Service Ltd., Scarborough, Ontario	51 di 14
555-1551	Advance Transport (operated by Stan's Cartage Movers & Storage Ltd.)	42 di 12
555-523	Al's Trucking and Livestock Transport	13 di 5
555-334	All Province Auto Terminals Ltd.	8 di 5
555-1798	Alltrans Express Ltée	49 di 9
555-1062	Armstrong the Mover (Yorkton) Ltd., and Armstrong Martin Moving and Storage Co. Ltd.	29 di 2
555-573	Arnold Brothers Transport Ltd.	16 di 219
C-226	Arrow Transfer Company Ltd.	5 di 8
555-339	Atlantic Automobile Transport Ltd.	8 di 5
555-565	Atomic Interprovincial Transportation System Ltd.	15 di 157
555-538	Auto Haulaway Ltd.	14 di 72
555-1240	Autocar Rive-Sud Ltée	35 di 3
555-1658	Autocars Jasmin Inc.	45 di 9
555-524	Automobile, Transport Ltd.	14 di 71
555-885	B. & H. Transport Ltd.	23 di 4
C-1	B.D.C. Ltd.	1 di 6
C-26	B.D.C. Ltd.	1 di 6
C-76	B.D.C. Ltd.	1 di 8
555-564	B.D.C. Ltd.	14 di 73
555-1330	B.D.C. Ltée	41 di 11
555-1557	B.M.A. Couriers Ltd.	42 di 13
555-469	A. & F. Baillargeon Express Inc.	12 di 4

555-1721	A & F Baillargeon Express Ontario Inc.	47 di 5
555-1361	C. Barber Ltée	36 di 14
C-117	Bekins Moving & Storage Co. Ltd.	2 di 5
555-1891	Bel-Mont Transit Inc., Mont Joli, Quebec	51 di 14
555-1432	Bessette Transport Inc.	41 di 11
555-1855	Bestway Household Movers Ltd., Richmond, B.C.	50 di 17
555-266	Big Valley Supply and Enterprises Ltd.	7 di 4
C-136	Black Ball Transport Inc. and/or Black Ball	4 di 9
555-1177	Borisko Brothers Ltd.	36 di 8
555-371	Bowes Moving & Storage Ltd.	9 di 6
555-1033	Brazeau Transport Inc.	27 di 640
555-1454	Brocklesby, Heavy Haul Division of Kingsway Transports Ltd.	41 di 12
C-74	Byer Transport Ltd.	4 di 6
555-1405	Byers Transport Ltd.	37 di 5
555-837	Cabano Transport Ltd.	22 di 494
555-1440	Cabano Transport Ltée	41 di 11
C-178	Cana Mark Transportation Ltd.	5 di 6
555-1375	Canadian Auto Carriers Ltd.	36 di 15
555-1936	Capitaine Courrier Corp., Ville St. Laurent (Quebec)	52 di 5
555-1113	Cascade Carriers Ltd.	29 di 7
555-1310	Cascade Carriers Ltd.	35 di 5
555-1057	Cast North America Ltd.	29 di 2
555-1053	Champlain Sept-Iles Express Interprovincial	28 di 868
C-129	Charlton Transport Ltd.	4 di 6
C-61	Charterways Company Ltd.	1 di 7
555-798	Charterways Transport Ltd. (Air Terminal Transport Division)	21 di 375
C-69	Charterways Transportation Ltd.	1 di 8
555-721	Charterways Transportation Ltd. (carrying on business as Two Cities Transit)	20 di 224
555-1001	Charterways Transportation Ltd.	25 di 334
555-1094	Christie Transport Ltd.	28 di 870
555-269	City Express Ltd.	6 di 5
555-1911	Classic Moving & Storage Ltd., Calgary, Alberta	51 di 15
555-441	Colossal Carriers Ltd.	11 di 3
555-615	Columbia Containers Ltd.	16 di 221
555-1509	Columbia Stage Lines Ltd.	41 di 17
555-1051	Columbia-Western Transportation Systems Inc.	27 di 641
555-1548	Comanche Road Transport Ltd.	41 di 19
555-751	Commission de Transport de la Communauté Régionale de l'Outaouais	19 di 101
555-1591	Cooney Haulage Ltd., and Brownlee Cartage Ltd.	43 di 11
555-1535	J.G. Cotnoir Transport Ltée	42 di 12
555-1269	G. Courchesne Transport Inc.	33 di 352
555-1692	D & F Equipment Rentals Ltd.	46 di 8
555-1078	D.H.L. International Express Ltd.	28 di 869
555-511	Déménagement Cartier Inc.	14 di 70
555-1484	Déménagements Cartier Inc.	41 di 14
555-1485	Déménagement Côté (1977) Ltée	41 di 14
555-1252	Déménagement G. Roy Inc.	33 di 351
555-1665	Déménageurs Pilon Inc.	45 di 9
555-1846	P. Dickson Trucking Ltd.	50 di 16

555-1366	Direct Transportation Systems Ltd., and/or Millar and Brown Ltd.	36 di 14
555-947	Diversified Transportation Ltd.	25 di 332
555-1840	Divnich Management Ltd.	50 di 15
555-1451	Georges O. Dubois Inc.	41 di 12
555-718	Durham-Walker Transport, Division of DURHAM Trans.	20 di 223
555-502	Emslie Bros. Ltd.	13 di 3
555-1313	Forget Transport Inc.	36 di 9
C-131	Frederick Transport Ltd.	4 di 6
555-1947	Frederick Transport Ltd., Chatham, Ontario	51 di 18
555-1953	Frederick Transport Ltd., Chatham, Ontario	51 di 18
555-1957	Frederick Transport Ltd., Chatham, Ontario	51 di 18
555-1630	Freeport Transport Inc.	43 di 14
555-1628	Gardewine & Sons Ltd.	45 di 6
555-1397	Glenncoe Transport Ltd.	37 di 4
C-89	Gonder & Sons Ltd.	2 di 4
555-233	Gray Coach Lines Ltd.	5 di 9
555-1784	Great West Transport Co. Ltd.	49 di 9
555-934	Greyhound Lines of Canada Ltd.	25 di 331
555-288	Grimshaw Trucking and Distributing Ltd.	8 di 4
555-916	Hall's Motor Transit Co. Ltd.	24 di 135
555-1465	Harkema Express Lines Ltd.	41 di 13
555-1927	Harkema Express Lines Ltd., Mississauga, Ontario, owned and operated by Roadway Express, Inc. Ohio, U.S.A.	51 di 16
555-1067	Hart and Page Ltd. (carrying on business under the name Road Runner Courier)	27 di 642
555-838	Hemingway Transport Inc.	22 di 495
555-303	Hennis Freight Lines of Canada Ltd.	7 di 4
555-1498	Hill and Hill Transport of Canada Inc.	41 di 16
555-525	Holmes Transport (Québec) Ltée	19 di 95
555-855	Hub Transportation Services Ltd.	22 di 496
555-1123	Humphrey's Transfer Ltd.	29 di 8
555-1187	Humphrey's Transfer Ltd.	31 di 129
555-1193	Humphrey's Transfer Ltd.	31 di 129
555-1367	Humphrey's Transfer Ltd.	36 di 14
555-1734	Hurdman Bros. Ltd.	48 di 12
555-570	Husband Transport Ltd.	16 di 219
555-1241	Husband Transport Ltd.	32 di 223
C-119	Imperial Railways Ltd.	2 di 5
555-411	Imperial Roadways Ltd.	10 di 3
555-1606	Imperial Roadways Ltd.	43 di 12
555-1118	Inter-City Truck Lines (Canada) Inc.	31 di 127
555-1376	Inter-City Truck Lines (Canada) Inc.	36 di 15
555-1402	Jeffrey's Cartage Ltd.	37 di 5
555-1645	Jeffrey's Cartage Ltd.	45 di 7
555-310	K.R.M. Construction Ltd.	8 di 5
555-1306	Kaps Transport Ltd.	35 di 5
C-96	Kindersley Transport Ltd.	1 di 8
555-498	Kingsboro Couriers Ltd.	3 di 3
555-1518	Kingsway Freightlines Ltd.	41 di 17
555-514	Kingsboro Couriers Ltd.	13 di 4
555-439	Kleysen Transport Ltd.	13 di 2

555-729	Kleysen Transport Ltd.	19 di 100
555-1689	Kohlman Industries Ltd.	45 di 10
555-1720	Kohlman Transport Ltd.	47 di 5
555-1354	Kourier, The Small Package Division of Kingsway Transport Ltd.	36 di 13
555-1550	Kourier, The Small Package Division of Kingsway Transport Ltd.	42 di 12
555-1657	Kwikasair Express Ltd.	45 di 8
555-1723	La Cie de Transport Great West Ltée	48 di 11
C-44	La Porte's Van & Storage Ltd.	1 di 7
555-1423	Lacaille (Rouville) Transport Inc.	39 di 19
555-296	Lakeshore Movers and Warehousing (Can.) Ltd.	8 di 4
555-854	Lamothe Transport Corp.	23 di 3
555-1554	Maurice Lamoureux Ltd.	42 di 13
555-1371	Les Déménagements et Entreposage Lapointe Ltée et des Aviseurs en Déménagements du Québec Inc.	43 di 5
555-1372	Les Déménagements et Entreposage Lapointe Ltée et des Aviseurs en Déménagements du Québec Inc.	43 di 5
555-1939	Les Déménagements et Entreposage Lapointe Ltée et Des Aviseurs en Déménagements du Québec Inc., Longueil, Québec	51 di 17
555-1724	Les Déménagements Rimouski Ltée	47 di 5
555-1675	Les Déménagements Trans-Québec Inc.	45 di 10
555-1377	Les Déménagements Tremblay Express Ltée	36 di 16
C-47	Les Déménagements Trumblay Express Ltée	1 di 7
555-1487	Les Services Sanitaire de l'Outaouais Inc.	41 di 15
555-1965	Les Transports Provost Inc., Ville d'Anjou, Québec	53 di 5
555-517	Leslie's Storage Ltd.	13 di 4
555-1471	Lewis Movers Ltd.	39 di 21
555-1299	Liftlock Bus Lines	35 di 5
555-254	Loiselle Transport Ltd.	6 di 5
555-1385	Loomis Armored Car Service Ltd.	36 di 4
555-1989	Loomis Armored Car Service Ltd., Winnipeg, Manitoba	52 di 6
555-1514	Loomis Courier Service Ltd.	43 di 8
555-1349	Loomis Courier Service Ltd., and Trans Canada Parcel Service Ltd.	36 di 12
555-1847	Loomis Courier Service Ltd. and Trans Canada Parcel Service Ltd., Vancouver, B.C.	50 di 16
555-1549	Loram International Ltd.	41 di 19
C-132	Lou's Transport Ltd.	2 di 6
555-1348	Loughead Express Ltd.	38 di 5
555-1774	M.H. Transport Ltd.	48 di 16
555-1748	MacCosham Van Lines Ltd.	48 di 14
555-1751	MacCosham Van Lines Ltd.	48 di 14
555-1242	MacCosham Van Lines (Canada) Ltd.	33 di 351
555-1488	MacCosham Van Lines (Canada) Ltd.	41 di 15
555-1489	MacCosham Van Lines (Canada) Ltd.	41 di 15
555-1914	MacCosham Van Lines (Canada) Ltd., Edmonton, Alberta	51 di 15
C-122	MacCosham Van Lines (Saskatchewan) Ltd.	2 di 5
555-1523	MacDonald Moving and Storage Co. Ltd.	41 di 17

555-373	Keith MacKinnon Transport Ltd.	9 di 6
555-1711	Marks Transport Ltd.	46 di 10
555-1162	K.F. Marshall Ltd.	30 di 69
C-134	Martel Express Ltée et/ou R. Martel Express	5 di 5
555-858	R. Martel Express Ltd.	22 di 496
555-556	Raoul Martineau Inc.	15 di 156
555-1510	Maverick Coach Lines Ltd.	41 di 17
555-447	L.J. McDonald & Sons Trucking Ltd.	10 di 4
555-581	Melchin Auto Transport Ltd.	16 di 219
555-582	Melchin Auto Transport Ltd.	15 di 158
C-202	Merchant's Speedy Delivery Ltd.	5 di 7
555-1288	Merchant's Speedy Delivery (1978) Ltd.	35 di 4
555-1860	Mercury Tanklines Ltd., Calgary, Alberta	52 di 4
C-55	Midland Superior Express	2 di 4
555-1106	Midland Superior Express Ltd.	29 di 3
555-1504	Midland Superior Express Ltée	41 di 16
555-833	Midland Transport Ltd.	22 di 493
555-1732	Miller Bros. Feed Lot Co. Ltd. d/b/a Hub City Transport	48 di 12
555-1462	Moffat Bros. Moving & Storage Ltd.	39 di 21
555-1897	Moffatt Bros. Moving and Storage Ltd., Truro, Nova Scotia	51 di 14
555-1941	Moffat Bros. Moving & Storage Ltd., Truro, Nova Scotia	51 di 17
555-1981	Moffatt Bros. Moving & Storage Ltd. (Moffatt Express Freight Division-Truro Dock/City Operation), Truro, Nova Scotia	51 di 19
555-1940	Monarch Carriers Ltd., c/o Melburn Truck Lines Ltd., Clarkson, Ontario	51 di 17
555-1190	Moncton Moving & Storage Ltd.	31 di 129
555-1869	Monson Trucking Inc., Duluth, Minnesota	50 di 18
555-1273	Morgan Storage and Moving Ltd.	33 di 352
555-1307	Municipal Tank Lines Ltd.	36 di 8
555-696	National Freight Consultants Inc.	18 di 42
555-409	Cal Nichols Movers Ltd.	12 di 5
555-1888	François Nolin Ltée Gerard Nolin (1975) Ltée a/s Les Transports Provost Inc., St. Jean Chrysostôme (Québec)	51 di 13
555-1870	North Star Transport Ltd., Calgary, Alberta	50 di 18
555-1272	Ojibwae Equipment Operators Inc.	35 di 3
555-1069	Oldham's Transport Ltd.	27 di 642
555-655	Orlick Transport Ltd.	18 di 40
555-1929	Orlick Transport Ltd., Edmonton, Alberta	51 di 16
555-1629	Ottawa-Carleton Regional Transit Commission	44 di 5
555-1837	Ottawa-Carleton Regional Transit Commission	50 di 15
555-1838	Ottawa-Carleton Regional Transit Commission	50 di 15
555-1839	Ottawa-Carleton Regional Transit Commission	50 di 15
555-305	Ottor Freightways Ltd.	8 di 4
555-322	Ottor Freightways Ltd.	7 di 5
555-1474	Overnite Express (1980) Inc.	41 di 14
555-1481	Overnite Express (1980) Inc.	41 di 14
555-1196	Overnite Express Ltée	32 di 221
555-1284	Overnite Express Ltée	35 di 4
555-1326	Overnite Express Ltée	36 di 10

555-1072	Oxford Warehousing Ltd.	35 di 3
555-1655	G.M. Patry Ltée	49 di 8
555-1908	Phénix Limousines Ltée, Montreal (Québec)	51 di 15
555-460	Pioneer Transfer Ltd.	10 di 4
555-1414	Purolator Courier Ltd.	39 di 19
555-1482	Purolator Courier Ltée	42 di 10
555-1864	Purolator Courier Ltée, Ville St. Laurent, Québec	52 di 4
555-1189	Quebec Parcel Services Inc.	31 di 129
C-92	Queensway Tank Line Ltd.	2 di 4
555-1641	T.E. Quinn Truck Lines Ltd.	44 di 5
555-1495	Quirion Transport Inc.	41 di 16
555-843	Red Star Express Lines of Quebec (1976) Ltd.	22 di 495
555-1415	Red's Transfer Ltd.	37 di 5
555-1213	Reimer Express Lines Ltd., Reimer Express Lines (Western) Ltd.	36 di 8
555-1614	Reliable Transfer of Victoria Ltd., Dowell's Moving & Storage Ltd., Butterworths Moving & Storage Ltd., Blue & White and Ferridays Moving & Storage Co. Ltd., James Bay Movers Ltd.	43 di 13
555-1403	Reliable-Scott Transport Ltée	38 di 6
555-1456	Reliable-Scott Transport Ltée	39 di 21
555-1736	Rigaud Transport Inc.	48 di 12
555-509	Ringsby Truck Lines Inc.	13 di 4
555-1390	Riverdale Transfer Ltd.	36 di 16
555-543	Riverside Marine Ltd.	14 di 72
555-239	Roadway Transport Ltd.	7 di 3
555-1597	Roys Midway Ltd.	43 di 11
555-1452	Salivrac Services Inc.	41 di 12
555-1368	Raoul Sénécal Transport Ltée	36 di 15
C-205	Siemens Transport & Service Ltd.	5 di 7
C-189	SMT (Eastern) Ltd. (baggage-express agent & ticket agent)	3 di 6
C-188	SMT (Eastern) Ltd. (drivers & maintenance personnel)	3 di 5
555-444	H.G. Snyder Trucking Inc.	12 di 4
555-738	H.G. Snyder Trucking Inc.	20 di 225
C-190	Soo-Security Motorways Ltd.	5 di 6
555-726	Soo-Security Motorways Ltd.	19 di 100
555-472	Soulanges Cartage & Equipment Co. Ltd.	12 di 4
555-473	Soulanges Cartage & Equipment Co. Ltd.	12 di 4
555-522	Speedway Express Ltd.	14 di 71
555-1706	St-Lambert Transport Inc.	46 di 10
555-285	Star Transfer Ltd.	7 di 4
C-27	Swan River - The Pas Transfer Ltd.	3 di 4
555-1712	Swan River, The Pas Transfer Ltd.	47 di 5
555-1678	Taggart Service Ltd.	46 di 7
555-317	Territorial Transport (1968) Ltd.	8 di 5
555-953	Texport Division of Oxford Warehousing Ltd.	25 di 332
555-1073	Texport Ltd. (A division of Oxford Warehousing)	35 di 3
555-1916	Texport Ltd. (Division of TNT Canada Inc.), Winnipeg, Manitoba	51 di 16
555-731	Texport Ltd. and Texport	20 di 224
C-20	The British Yukon Navigation Co. Ltd.	1 di 6

555-1512	J.E. Thompson Transport Ltd.	42 di 11
555-1996	Tilt-N-Load Transport (Québec) Ltée, Montreal (Quebec)	52 di 6
555-234	Tippet-Richardson (Ottawa) Ltd.	5 di 9
555-1725	TNT Courier/Air Express	47 di 6
C-151	Trailways of Canada Ltd.	2 di 6
555-270	Trans Western Express	5 di 11
555-1894	Trans-Spec Outaouais Ltée, Hull (Québec)	50 di 19
555-2013	Transport Asbestos Eastern Inc., Candiac, Quebec	53 di 6
555-248	Transport d'Anjou Inc.	6 di 5
555-1547	Transport Ducharme Inc.	42 di 12
555-580	Transport Gérald Roy Waterloo Inc.	17 di 2
555-1079	Transport Holmes (Québec) Ltée	30 di 66
555-1866	Transport McNeil-McGrath Inc., Toronto, Ontario	51 di 1250
555-1943	Transport Parchemin Inc., Mirabel, Québec	52 di 5
555-1654	Transport Vincent Pelletier Inc.	45 di 8
555-1768	Transport Super Rapide Inc.	48 di 15
555-1163	Travelways Maple Leaf Ltd.	30 di 70
555-637	Travelways Maple Leaf Ltd. (Orillia Division), formerly Stock Bros. Bus Lines Ltd., and Stock Algar Coach Lines Ltd.	19 di 97
C-223	H.M. Trimble & Sons Ltd.	5 di 8
555-1767	Trumbler Ridge Transport Ltd.	48 di 15
555-433	Tymos Cartage and Storage Ltd.	10 di 4
555-238	Valihora Transport Ltd.	5 di 10
555-1686	Van De Hogen Cartage Ltd.	46 di 8
555-1717	Vedder Transport (1974) Ltd.	47 di 5
555-237	Voyageur Inc. (Division de l'Abitibi)	9 di 3
555-1446	Voyageur Inc.	41 di 12
555-1478	Voyageur Inc.	41 di 14
555-1497	Voyageur Inc.	41 di 16
555-1746	Voyageur Transport Inc.	48 di 14
555-377	Waddick Transport Ltd.	9 di 6
555-1191	Wallace Warehouse & Cartage Ltd.	31 di 129
C-107	Wells Fargo Armoured Express Ltd.	2 di 5
555-574	Wells Fargo Armoured Express Ltd.	15 di 158
555-712	Wells Fargo Armoured Express Ltd.	18 di 43
555-856	West Rim Express Lines DMR Transport	23 di 3
555-470	Western Crating and Moving Ltd.	12 di 4
555-1836	Westrux Timber Transit Inc.	50 di 14
555-922	Wholesale Delivery Service (1972) Ltd.	24 di 135
555-642	Williams Moving & Storage (B.C.) Ltd. & Robertson Moving & Storage Ltd.	18 di 39
C-217	B. Williamson Trucking and Leasing Ltd.	8 di 4
C-138	Yukon Territorial Ventures Ltd.	2 di 6
555-1352	Zavitz Brothers Ltd.	36 di 12

SHIPPING

File	Employer	di
555-1763	114037 Canada Inc.	48 di 15

555-1266	ADGA Systems International Ltd.	33 di 352
C-156	Algoma Central Railway, Marine Division	2 di 6
555-987	Algoma Central Railway	26 di 495
555-1571	Algoma Central Railway (Marine Division)	43 di 10
555-993	Algoma Steel Corp. Ltd.	26 di 495
555-1567	Algoma Steel Corp. Ltd.	42 di 14
C-150	American Can of Canada Ltd.	4 di 7
555-272	Arctic Navigation and Transportation Ltd.	6 di 5
555-976	Arctic Navigation and Transportation Ltd. Now Lindberg Transportation Ltd.	25 di 333
555-823	Arctic Transportation Ltd.	21 di 376
555-944	Arctic Transportation Ltd.	25 di 332
555-1600	Atlantic Freight Lines Ltd.	43 di 11
555-329	Atlantic Pilotage Authority	8 di 5
555-1004	Atlantic Pilotage Authority	25 di 334
555-1889	Beaver Dredging Company Ltd. Toronto, Ontario, and Beaver Dredging (Western) Ltd., Calgary, Alberta	51 di 13
C-160	Bomar Navigation Ltd.	2 di 7
C-196	Bomar Navigation Ltd.	4 di 8
555-1167	Boréal Navigation Inc.	31 di 127
555-1305	Boréal Navigation Inc.	35 di 5
555-1558	Boréal Navigation Inc.	42 di 13
555-505	British Columbia Steamship Co. (1975) Ltd.	14 di 70
555-1682	C.N. Marine Inc.	46 di 8
C-168	Canada Cement Lafarge Ltd.	3 di 5
555-282	Canada Steamship Lines, Ltd.	6 di 5
555-562	Canada Steamship Lines (1975) Ltd.	15 di 157
555-1047	Canada Steamship Lines (1975) Ltd.	27 di 641
555-402	Canadian Dredge and Dock Co. Ltd.	9 di 7
C-21	Canadian Offshore Marine Ltd.	1 di 6
555-831	Canadian Offshore Marine Ltd.	22 di 493
555-761	Canadian Pacific Ltd.	20 di 226
555-895	Canadian Pacific Ltd. British Columbia	23 di 4
555-923	Canadian Pacific Ltd.	24 di 136
555-1221	Canadian Pacific Steamships Ltd.	45 di 6
C-214	Cargill Grain Co. Ltd.	5 di 8
555-1752	Carino Co. Ltd.	48 di 14
C-169	Carryore Ltd.	3 di 5
555-1569	Carryore Ltd.	43 di 9
555-827	C.H. Cates & Sons Ltd.	21 di 376
555-1175	Centennial Leasing Ltd.	31 di 128
555-259	Christensen Canadian Enterprises Ltd.	5 di 11
555-380	Christensen Canadian Enterprises Ltd.	9 di 6
555-1620	Coastal Shipping Ltd.	43 di 13
555-1572	Consolidated-Bathurst Shipping Ltd.	43 di 10
555-912	Council of Marine Carriers and its 32 Member Cos.	24 di 134
555-1566	Dale Transports Ltd.	43 di 9
555-972	Eastern Canada Towing Ltd.	26 di 494
C-166	Federal Off-shore Services Ltd.	5 di 6
C-66	Fraser River Pile Driving Co. Ltd.	1 di 7
555-617	Geophysical Service Inc.	17 di 2
666-1615	Granel and Lake Services Ltd.	43 di 13

C-53	Great Lakes Pilotage Authority Ltd.	1 di 7
555-549	Great Lakes Pilotage Authority, Cornwall	16 di 219
C-177	H & W Towing Co. Ltd.	3 di 5
C-187	Halidon (Canada) Ltd.	7 di 3
555-988	Hall Corporation Shipping Ltd.	26 di 495
C-182	Hindman Transportation Co. Ltd.	3 di 5
555-359	Hodder Tugboat Co. Ltd.	9 di 5
555-1993	Husky Oil Operations Ltd.	53 di 5
555-244	Imperial Marine Industries Ltd.	7 di 3
555-547	Imperial Marine Industries Ltd.	14 di 73
555-279	Incan Ships Ltd.	6 di 5
555-280	Incan Ships Ltd.	6 di 5
555-1601	Intercan Marine Services Ltd.	43 di 12
555-1899	International Sea-Land Shipping Service Ltd., Vancouver, B.C.	51 di 14
555-1589	Jensen Shipping Ltd.	43 di 10
555-1590	Jensen Shipping Ltd.	43 di 11
555-1750	Jensen Shipping Ltd.	48 di 14
555-1380	Jourdain Navigation Ltée	37 di 4
555-1800	K.D. Marine Transport Ltd.	49 di 9
555-261	Kaps Transport Ltd.	7 di 3
555-778	Kelly Towing	20 di 227
555-1817	Kerr Steamship Co. Ltd.	49 di 11
555-1152	La Cie Minière Québec Cartier	31 di 127
555-1961	Lake Ontario Cement Ltd.	51 di 18
555-1635	Lakespan Marine Inc.	45 di 7
555-328	Laurentian Pilotage Authority	8 di 5
555-492	Laurentian Pilotage Authority	13 di 3
555-1812	Les Rimorqueurs du Québec Ltée	49 di 11
555-273	Lindberg Transportation Ltd.	6 di 5
555-400	Macnamara Marine	9 di 7
555-370	Marine Industries (Salvage) Ltd.	9 di 6
555-419	McAllister Towing & Salvage Ltd.	10 di 4
555-757	McAllister Towing & Salvage Ltd.	21 di 374
555-633	McGregor Johnston Contracting Ltd.	17 di 3
555-841	McGregor Johnston Contracting Ltd.	22 di 495
555-1565	Misener Transportation	43 di 9
C-165	Montreal Boatman Ltd.	4 di 7
555-1425	Navigation Jouradin Ltée	38 di 7
555-1951	Navimar Corporation Ltée	51 di 17
555-1399	Noble Towing Ltd.	37 di 4
555-1611	Nonia Navigation Inc.	43 di 13
555-250	North Arm Transportation Ltd.	7 di 3
555-1404	North Arm Transportation Ltd.	38 di 6
555-455	Northern Construction Co., Division of Morrison-Knudsen Company Inc.	13 di 2
555-481	Northern Construction Co., Division of Morrison-Knudsen Company Inc.	13 di 2
555-482	Northern Construction Co., Division of Morrison-Knudsen Co. Inc.	13 di 2
555-978	Northern Construction Co., Division of Morrison-Knudsen Co. Inc.	26 di 495
555-977	Northern Transportation Co. Ltd.	26 di 494
555-2006	Northlake Shipping Ltd., Halifax, Nova Scotia	52 di 6

555-876	Northland Shipping (1962) Co. Ltd.	22 di 497
C-23	Oceanic Tankers Agency Ltd.	2 di 4
555-1764	P.K.B. Sconia Cargo Surveyors Ltd.	48 di 15
555-560	N.M. Paterson & Sons Ltd.	15 di 157
555-990	N.M. Paterson and Sons Ltd.	26 di 495
555-887	Port Bécancour Inc.	23 di 4
555-398	J.P. Porter Company Ltd.	9 di 7
555-401	J.P. Porter (Ontario) Ltd.	9 di 7
555-561	Quebec and Ontario Transportation Co. Ltd.	15 di 157
555-991	Quebec and Ontario Transportation Co. Ltd.	26 di 495
555-399	Richelieu Dredging Corporation Inc.	9 di 7
555-1584	Riley's Boat Service Ltd.	42 di 15
555-974	Sault Marine Services Ltd.	25 di 333
555-1205	Sceptre Dredging Ltd.	31 di 130
555-992	Scott Misener Steamship Ltd.	26 di 495
555-358	Sea Island Towing Co. Ltd.	9 di 5
555-1609	Sea-West Holdings Ltd.	44 di 4
555-1623	Sea-West Holdings Ltd.	43 di 14
555-324	Seaspan International Ltd.	9 di 3
555-325	Seaspan International Ltd.	9 di 3
555-1582	Seaspan International Ltd.	42 di 15
555-1690	Sefel Geophysical Ltd.	46 di 8
555-1885	Sefel Geophysical Ltd., Calgary, Alberta	50 di 19
555-1809	Service de traversiers Masson et Cumberland Inc., et les Services Maurice Bourbonnais Ltée	49 di 10
555-466	Shields Navigation Ltd.	11 di 3
555-973	Smit & Cary International Port Towage Ltd.	26 di 494
555-1182	Société d'Electrolyse et de Chimie Alcan Ltée (Division d'Aluminium du Canada Ltée)	31 di 128
555-572	Société Maritime de Baillon Inc.	16 di 219
555-1568	Soo River Co.	42 di 14
555-1875	Standard Towing Ltd., Burnaby, B.C.	50 di 18
555-1879	Standard Towing Ltd., Burnaby, B.C.	50 di 18
555-491	Streeper Brothers Marine Transport Ltd.	12 di 5
555-1874	Tap Catering & Management Ltd., St. John's Nfld.	51 di 13
555-980	The British Yukon Navigation Co. Ltd.	25 di 333
555-1776	The Ottawa River Boat Co. Ltd.	49 di 8
555-1968	Toronto Harbour Commissioners	51 di 19
555-243	Triangle Pacific Forest Products Ltd.	5 di 10
555-1559	Upper Lakes Shipping Ltd.	42 di 13
555-1499	Verreault Navigation Inc.	43 di 8
555-654	Wakeham & Son Ltd.	17 di 3
555-1636	Wakeham & Son Ltd.	44 di 5
555-1639	Wakeham & Son Ltd.	44 di 5
555-1098	Wakeham Shipping Ltd.	29 di 3
555-1046	Wakeham Shipping Ltd.	27 di 641
C-186	Westdale Shipping Ltd.	3 di 5
555-994	Westdale Shipping Ltd.	26 di 496
555-1043	Western Engineering Service Ltd.	27 di 641
555-333	Westshore Terminals Ltd.	9 di 4
C-28	Wildwood Transportation Ltd. (Towing Division)	1 di 7
555-1880	Wolf Offshore Transport Ltd., St. John's, Newfoundland	50 di 19

URANIUM MINING

File	Employer	di
555-1097	Agnew Lake Mines Ltd.	38 di 871
555-1740	Amok Ltd.	48 di 13
555-786	Cassiar Asbestos Corp. Ltd.	21 di 374
555-1709	Combustion Engineering – Superheater Ltd.	46 di 10
C-194	Denison Mines Ltd.	9 di 3
C-229	Denison Mines Ltd.	8 di 4
555-1121	Denison Mines Ltd.	29 di 8
555-1438	Key Lake Mining Corp.	39 di 20
555-881	Uranerz Exploration and Mining Ltd.	26 di 494
555-1640	Westinghouse Canada Inc.	45 di 7

APPENDIX 9
CONCILIATION UNDER THE CANADA LABOUR CODE (PART V – INDUSTRIAL RELATIONS)

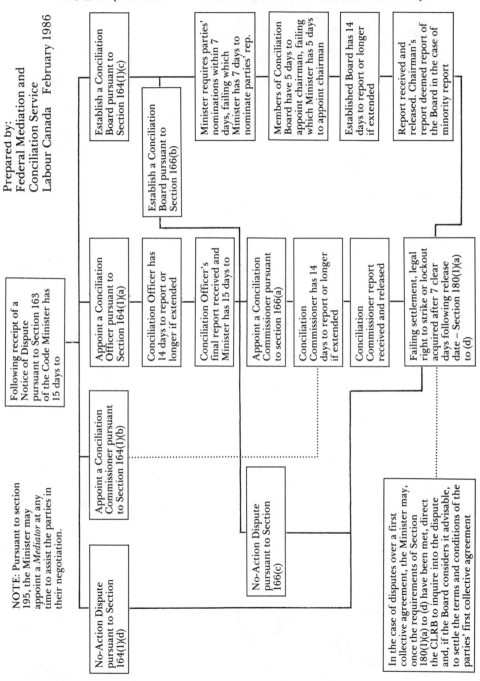

Prepared by:
Federal Mediation and
Conciliation Service
Labour Canada   February 1986

NOTE: Pursuant to section 195, the Minister may appoint a *Mediator* at any time to assist the parties in their negotiation.

Following receipt of a Notice of Dispute pursuant to Section 163 of the Code Minister has 15 days to

Establish a Conciliation Board pursuant to Section 164(1)(c)

Establish a Conciliation Board pursuant to Section 166(b)

Minister requires parties' nominations within 7 days, failing which Minister has 7 days to nominate parties' rep.

Members of Conciliation Board have 5 days to appoint chairman, failing which Minister has 5 days to appoint chairman

Established Board has 14 days to report or longer if extended

Report received and released. Chairman's report deemed report of the Board in the case of minority report

Appoint a Conciliation Officer pursuant to Section 164(1)(a)

Conciliation Officer has 14 days to report or longer if extended

Conciliation Officer's final report received and Minister has 15 days to

Appoint a Conciliation Commissioner pursuant to section 166(a)

Conciliation Commissioner has 14 days to report or longer if extended

Conciliation Commissioner report received and released

Failing settlement, legal right to strike or lockout acquired after 7 clear days following release date – Section 180(1)(a) to (d)

Appoint a Conciliation Commissioner pursuant to Section 164(1)(b)

No-Action Dispute pursuant to Section 166(c)

No-Action Dispute pursuant to Section 164(1)(d)

In the case of disputes over a first collective agreement, the Minister may, once the requirements of Section 180(1)(a) to (d) have been met, direct the CLRB to inquire into the dispute and, if the Board considers it advisable, to settle the terms and conditions of the parties' first collective agreement

505

APPENDIX 10
SAMPLES OF CEASE AND DESIST ORDERS GRANTED BY THE CANADA LABOUR RELATIONS BOARD IN CASES OF ILLEGAL STRIKES OR LOCKOUTS

Board File: 725-37

IN THE MATTER OF THE

> *Canada Labour Code*

> > *— and —*

> *Syndicat des employés de Service*
> *Technique de Cable TV (CNTU),*

> > > > > > > *applicant,*

> > *— and —*

> *Cable TV Limited,*
> *Montreal, Quebec,*

> > > > > > > *employer.*

WHEREAS the union claimed that on March 5, 1979 the employer had declared or caused a lockout of the following employees:

> Serge Bélanger, Normand Chabot, Claude Chartrand, Nancy Degauque, Gétano Ditrapini, Gilles Doin, Jean-Yves Doin, Robert Fortin, Raymond Lecours, Gaétan Leduc, Marcel Legault, Léonard Lerede, René Paulet, Michel Ricard, Tom Roobroeck, Pierre St-Laurent, Gilles Vallée,

in violation of the provisions of the *Canada Labour Code* (Part V — Industrial Relations);

AND WHEREAS the union claimed that the employer was about to declare, as of April 30, 1979, a lockout of all its service employees, represented by the union, in violation of the provisions of the *Canada Labour Code* (Part V — Industrial Relations);

AND WHEREAS on March 20, 1979, the parties were called to a hearing during which the employer was heard on the union's application;

AND CONSIDERING the evidence submitted by the union and the employer;

AND CONSIDERING the provisions of the *Canada Labour Code* (Part V — Industrial Relations) and more particularly the provisions of sections 183, 183.1, 180 and 107;

NOW, THEREFORE, the Board declares that:

(a) the layoff of Serge Bélanger, Normand Chabot, Claude Chartrand, Nancy Degauque, Gétano Ditrapini, Gilles Doin, Jean-Yves Doin, Robert Fortin, Raymond Lecours, Gaétan Leduc, Marcel Legault, Léonard Lerede, René Paulet, Michel Ricard, Tom Roobroeck, Pierre St-Laurent, and Gilles Vallée by the employer on March 5, 1979 constitutes an unlawful lockout in violation of the provisions of the *Canada Labour Code* (Part V — Industrial Relations);

(b) the layoff of all service employees represented by the union, set for April 30, 1979, will constitute an unlawful lockout in violation of the provisions of the *Canada Labour Code* (Part V — Industrial Relations);

AND, in addition, the Board orders the employer:

(a) to immediately terminate the unlawful lockout commenced on March 5, 1979;

(b) to immediately take back into its employ Serge Bélanger, Normand Chabot, Claude Chartrand, Nancy Degauque, Gétano Ditrapini, Gilles Doin, Jean-Yves Doin, Robert Fortin, Raymond Lecours, Gaétan Leduc, Marcel Legault, Léonard Lerede, René Paulet, Michel Ricard, Tom Roobroeck, Pierre St-Laurent and Gilles Vallée, and to maintain them in their positions, in accordance with the provisions of the collective agreement signed on September, 3, 1976 and amended on March 17, 1978, until such time as the said collective agreement is renewed or the right to strike or lockout is acquired in accordance with the provisions of the *Canada Labour Code* (Part V — Industrial Relations);

(c) not to cause or order the lockout set for April 30, 1979;

(d) to apply to the above-mentioned employees all the benefits provided for in the said collective agreement, which they could have lost as a result of the unlawful lockout undertaken by the employer. The Board names Mr. Alfred Pedneault, Board officer, or any other person that he shall designate, to assist the parties in reaching agreement on item (d) of the present Order. Should the parties fail to agree within ten days following receipt of this Order, our officer shall provide us with a written report on the matter and the Board shall subsequently issue a final Order on this item (d). In accordance with the provisions of section 120.1, item (d) of this Order does not constitute a final decision;

(e) to proceed without delay to bring the present Order to the attention of all the employees covered by the collective agreement signed on September 3, 1976 and amended on March 17, 1978.

ISSUED at Ottawa, this 21st day of March 1979, by the Canada Labour Relations Board.

_____

(Signed, Vice-chairman)

Board File: 725-39

IN THE MATTER OF THE

    Canada Labour Code

— and —

    National Harbours Board,
      Port of Montreal,

applicant,

— and —

    Syndicat National des Employés
      du Port de Montréal,

respondent union,

— and —

    The Officers and Representatives
      of the respondent union,

respondents,

— and —

    The employee members of the
      bargaining unit for which the
      respondent union is certified,

respondents.

WHEREAS, le Syndicat National des Employés du Port de Montréal is the certified bargaining agent for employees of the applicant covered by a collective agreement dated October 24, 1978;

AND WHEREAS, following a hearing of an application pursuant to Section 182 of the Code the Board has found that:

(a) the respondent union and its officers have declared and authorized illegal strikes on April 12th, 1979 and May 4th, 1979;

(b) the respondent union and its officers have declared and authorized an unlawful concerted refusal to perform overtime; and

(c) representatives and members of the respondent union have participated in these unlawful activities;

NOW, THEREFORE, the Canada Labour Relations Board hereby orders the employees of the applicant who are members of the bargaining unit concerned to perform the duties of their employment and to refrain from any concerted illegal activity designed or intended to restrict output;

AND, FURTHER, the respondent union is hereby ordered to refrain from authorizing or declaring any strike or concerted activity designed or intended to restrict output;

509

AND, FURTHER, the respondent union is hereby ordered to distribute forthwith a copy of this order to each employee in the bargaining unit for which the union is certified. The applicant employer is ordered to forthwith post copies of this order in prominent places where they are likely to come to the attention of the employees affected.

THIS ORDER IS IN FULL FORCE AND EFFECT UNTIL THE CONDITIONS SET OUT IN SECTION 180(1), (a) to (d) of the Canada Labour Code HAVE BEEN MET.

ISSUED at Ottawa, this 8th day of May 1979, by the Canada Labour Relations Board.

_____

(Signed, Chairman or Vice-Chairman)

Board File: 725-44

IN THE MATTER OF THE

> *Canada Labour Code*

> > *— and —*

> *Canadian Broadcasting Corporation,*

> > > > > > > > > *applicant,*

> > *— and —*

> *National Association of Broadcast*
> *Employees and Technicians,*

> > *— and —*

> *Syndicat des Techniciens du Réseau*
> *Français de Radio-Canada,*

> > *— and —*

> *named employees of the applicant,*

> > > > > > > > > *respondents.*

WHEREAS, the Canada Labour Relations Board following a hearing of a previous application dated June 20, 1979 by the Canadian Broadcasting Corporation issued an order enjoining the National Association of Broadcast Employees and Technicians and the employees in the bargaining unit which they represented from strikes which would affect the televising of the Canadian Open Golf Tournament on June 22nd, 1979, and obtained confirmation of an agreement between the parties that there would be no interruption of the television coverage of the Pan American Games from July 1st to 15th, 1979;

AND WHEREAS, the respondent unions are certified bargaining agents for employees of the applicant employer covered by current collective agreements in force until June 29, 1980;

AND WHEREAS, extensive efforts by officers of the Board failed to secure agreement or resolve the problems;

AND WHEREAS, the Board heard the current application at a public hearing on July 27th, 1979;

AND WHEREAS, on consideration of the evidence and argument of the parties the Board has determined that employees of the applicant in the bargaining unit represented by National Association of Broadcast Employees and Technicians have participated in an unlawful strike by refusing to work in mixed crews in Calgary on July 18th, 1979 and that employees of the applicant in the bargaining units represented by both respondent unions are likely to participate in unlawful strike action contrary to the provisions of Section 180 of the *Canada Labour Code*;

NOW, THEREFORE, the Canada Labour Relations Board pursuant to the provisions of Section 182 and 183.1 of the Code hereby declares that strike activity by the respondent unions or the employees of the applicant in the bargaining units represented by the respondent unions would be unlawful;

AND FURTHER, it is hereby ordered that the respondent unions shall forthwith direct their officers, representatives and members to work in mixed crews when so scheduled by the employer unless the parties otherwise agree;

AND FURTHER, the respondent unions, their officers, representatives and members are hereby enjoined from declaring, authorizing or participating in any strike action contrary to the provisions of the Code;

AND FURTHER, it is hereby ordered that the employees of the Canadian Broadcasting Corporation in the bargaining units represented by the respondent unions shall refrain from participating in a strike in contravention of the *Canada Labour Code* and shall continue to perform the duties of their employment and refrain from any refusal to work or to continue to work or any other concerted activity contrary to the provisions of Section 180 of the *Canada Labour Code*.

THIS ORDER OF THE BOARD SHALL CONTINUE IN FULL FORCE AND EFFECT UNLESS MODIFIED OR REVOKED BY THE BOARD ON A SUBSEQUENT APPLICATION PURSUANT TO SECTION 183.1(2) OF THE CODE.

ISSUED at Ottawa, this 27th day of July 1979, by the Canada Labour Relations Board.

(Signed, Vice-Chairman)

Board File: 725-54

IN THE MATTER OF THE

> *Canada Labour Code*

> > *— and —*

> *Canadian Broadcasting Corporation,*

> > > > > > *applicant,*

> > *— and —*

> *Le Syndicat des employés de
> production du Québec et de
> l'Acadie,*

> > > > > *respondent union,*

> > *— and —*

> *Roger Cuerrier,   — and —
> Francis André
> Georges Beaudoin,
> Serge Chapu,
> Jean Henquet,
> Adélard Lavoie,
> Hervé Ouimet,
> Denis Paquette,
> Maurice Poirier,
> Jean-Claude Rozec,
> Roland Théberge,
> Jean-Marie Wuatelet,
> Charles Boulay,*

> > > > *respondent procurement specialists.*

WHEREAS the Canada Labour Relations Board received an application on November 30, 1979 from the Canadian Broadcasting Corporation, Montreal, Quebec, pursuant to section 182 of the Canada Labour Code (Part V — Industrial Relations), alleging that the respondents had violated and continue to violate the said section;

AND WHEREAS the Board held a public hearing on December 3, 4 and 5, 1979 to which the parties involved had been summoned and at which they appeared and during which the Board received the submissions of the parties involved;

AND WHEREAS, after examining and considering the submissions of the parties involved, the Board is convinced that after affording the union and the respondent employees an opportunity to be heard on the application:

1. The work stoppage by the procurement specialists constitutes a strike which is unlawful within the meaning of the *Canada Labour Code*. Accord-

ingly, the said procurement specialists are notified that they are enjoined from participating in the said strike, and are ordered to perform their duties, and the respondent union is ordered forthwith to give notice of the above prohibition and orders to all the respondent procurement specialists.

Moreover, the said procurement specialists shall perform their duties by the beginning of their respective shifts on Thursday, December 6, 1979, at the latest;

2. The problem of the procurement specialists and the set designers shall be dealt with on a priority basis between the respondent union and the Canadian Broadcasting Corporation, French Services Division, by the conciliation commissioner, Pierre Dufresne, at a special conciliation hearing to be held on Thursday, December 6, 1979;

3. Moreover, the ban on overtime constitutes an unlawful strike within the meaning of the Code and the Board so declares.

However, the Board has decided in the present circumstances and for the time being to exercise its discretion and not issue an order in this regard with respect to the corporation's employees in Montreal, but hereby orders that the said ban be ended immediately in Moncton and Quebec City, that all the employees in the bargaining unit and the respondent union in these two locations comply with this order immediately, as well, the respondent union shall give notice of this order to all its members immediately;

4. The two parties, namely, the respondent union and the Canadian Broadcasting Corporation, French Services Division, are ordered to immediately submit the problem of whether or not overtime is voluntary, according to the provisions of the collective agreement now in force, to an arbitrator appointed pursuant to the provisions of section 155(2)(c) and/or (d) of the *Canada Labour Code*, by means of one of the grievances which is now pending and which deals with this question. The arbitrator shall give priority to this matter, in accordance with the expedited arbitration procedure, and his decision should resolve this problem until the signing of a collective agreement which will replace the present one, which may contain different provisions on this subject.*

ISSUED at Ottawa, this fifth day of December, 1979 by the Canada Labour Relations Board.

_____

(Signed, Chairman or Vice-Chairman)

(Our translation)

ISSUED at Ottawa, this 18th day of March, 1980.

*Remedy number 4 was quashed by the appeal court. See *Syndicat des Employés de Production du Québec et de l'Acadie v. Canada Labour Relations Board*, [1984] 2 S.C.R. 412.

Board File: 725-56

IN THE MATTER OF THE

> *Canada Labour Code (Part V —*
> *Industrial Relations) and an*
> *application for a declaration of an*
> *unlawful strike and for an order filed*
> *under Section 182 of the said Code and*
> *Section 37 of the Canada Labour*
> *Relations Board Regulations (1978)*
> *concerning:*

> *Clarke Transport Canada Inc.,*
> *1155, Dorchester Boulevard West,*
> *Montreal, Province of Quebec,*
> *H3B 3Z5*

Applicant,

— and —

> *International Longshoremen's*
> *Association, whose address, for the*
> *purposes of this document, is the one for*
> *its Local 1932, that is*
> *6700 Sherbrooke Street East,*
> *P.O. Box 150, Postal Station "K",*
> *Montreal, Province of Quebec,*
> *H1N 3K9*

Union,

— and —

> *International Longshoremen's*
> *Association, Local 1932,*
> *6700 Sherbrooke Street East,*
> *P.O. Box 150, Postal Station "K",*
> *Montreal, Province of Quebec,*
> *H1N 3K9,*

Respondent Union,

— and —

> *Serge Longpre, President and Business*
> *Manager of the International*
> *Longshoremen's Association, Local*
> *1932, domiciled and residing at*
> *137 Cherrier Street, Repentigny,*
> *Province of Quebec, J6A 3Z6,*

Respondent,

— and —

*Pierre Bernard, Vice-president and
Business Manager of the International
Longshoremen's Association, Local
1932, domiciled and residing at
7245 Toulon Street, Brossard,
Province of Quebec, J4W 2X2,*

Respondent,

— and —

*Roger Lamy, Secretary-Treasurer and
Business Manager of the International
Longshoremen's Association, Local
1932, domiciled and residing at
144 McDuff Street, Repentigny,
Province of Quebec, J6A 6L2,*

Respondent.

WHEREAS the International Longshoremen's Association, Local 1932, is the bargaining agent certified by this Board, for a unit of the applicant's employees and that they are party to a collective agreement concluded between the applicant and the said Association dated June 5, 1979, the said collective agreement to remain in effect until March 31, 1981;

WHEREAS, following a hearing of an application under Section 182 of the *Canada Labour Code* (Part V — Industrial Relations), a hearing which was transformed into verbal representations submitted to the Board by their respective counsel,

The Board, on the basis of the application and the documents attached to it, as well as on the basis of the representations of the said counsel, has come to the conclusion that:

(a) the employees who are members of the bargaining unit took concerted action to refuse to carry out their work assignments since December 12, and have done so in a continuous fashion since, thereby participating in a strike in violation of Part V — Industrial Relations of the *Canada Labour Code,* the said strike being therefore unlawful;

(b) the alleged cause of this concerted refusal to continue to carry out their work assignments would be the instituting by the employer of a punch clock system, that this cause does not justify the said employees of the bargaining unit violating the provisions of the Code, more specifically the provisions of Section 180, subparagraph 2 of the *Canada Labour Code.*

NOW, THEREFORE, the Canada Labour Relations Board, hereby orders, after having heard the parties and especially the representations of the bargaining unit employees according to the provisions of the preamble to Section 182, the employees who are members of the International Longshoremen's Association, Local 1932, and of the bargaining unit determined by this Board, to continue to carry out their respective functions and to abstain from any unlawful concerted activity, the purpose of which is the refusal to work or to continue to work;

AND MOREOVER, the Canada Labour Relations Board orders the respondent union, Local 1932, as well as the union, to distribute as soon as is reasonably possible, a copy of this Order to each of the employees who are part of the bargaining unit for which the respondent union, Local 1932, is certified;

IT IS ALSO ORDERED that the employer post copies of this Order forthwith in prominent areas in his establishments, so that it may be examined by the employees governed by it;

AND MOREOVER, after consultation with the parties through their respective counsel, the Canada Labour Relations Board, in its desire to resolve the real cause of this unlawful concerted refusal to work, orders the parties to submit the question of the employer's right to institute a punch clock system, to accelerated arbitration before Mr. René Lippé, Q.C., the arbitrator agreed upon by counsel for the parties who, following consultation by the Canada Labour Relations Board, has accepted to act as arbitrator and to proceed by way of accelerated arbitration, said arbitration to begin on December 15, 1979 at 2:00 p.m. The parties have agreed not to raise any objections as to the jurisdiction personae nor as to the said arbitrator's jurisdiction and to plead this case on the merit only and by means of a grievance.*

THIS ORDER SHALL BE IN FULL FORCE AND SHALL BE IN EFFECT UNTIL MR. RENE LIPPE, Q.C., RENDERS HIS FINAL ARBITRAL AWARD.

ISSUED at Ottawa, this 14th day of December 1979, by the Canada Labour Relations Board.

_____

(Signed, Chairman)

* The Supreme Court of Canada, in *Syndicat des employes de production du Québec et de l'Acadie v. Canada Labour Relations Board*, [1984] 2 S.C.R. 412, struck down a similar remedy, and it is unlikely that the Board would now apply such a remedy without the parties' consent.

Board File: 725-63

IN THE MATTER OF THE

> *Canada Labour Code*

> — *and* —

> *Giant Yellowknife Mines Limited*

> > > *Applicant*

— and —

*Canadian Association of Smelter and
Allied Workers, Local No. 4*

Respondent Union

— and —

*The Officers and Representatives of the
Respondent Union*

Respondents

— and —

*The Employee Members of the
Bargaining Unit for which the
Respondent Union is Certified*

Respondents.

WHEREAS, Canadian Association of Smelter and Allied Workers, Local No. 4 is the certified bargaining agent for employees of the Applicant covered by a collective agreement dated June 19, 1978;

AND WHEREAS, following a hearing of an application pursuant to Section 182 of the Code the Board has found that the representatives and members of the Respondent Union have participated in an unlawful strike which commenced on April 15, 1980;

AND WHEREAS, the Applicant has agreed not to take any disciplinary or civil action against the Respondent Union, its officers or members arising out of the said unlawful strike;

NOW, THEREFORE, the Canada Labour Relations Board hereby orders the employees of the Applicant who are members of the bargaining unit concerned to perform the duties of their employment and to refrain from any concerted illegal activity designed or intended to restrict output;

AND, FURTHER, the Respondent Union is hereby ordered to distribute forthwith a copy of this order to each employee in the bargaining unit for which the union is certified. The Applicant employer is ordered to forthwith post copies of this order in prominent places where they are likely to come to the attention of the employees affected.

NOW THEREFORE, AND FURTHER the Applicant employer is hereby ordered to meet with the Respondent Union and the Concilliation officer appointed by the Minister as and when required by the Concilliation Officer.

THIS ORDER IS IN FULL FORCE AND EFFECT UNTIL THE CONDITIONS SET OUT IN SECTION 180(1), (a) to (d) of the Canada Labour Code HAVE BEEN MET.

ISSUED at Yellowknife, Northwest Territories, this 29th day of April, 1980, by the Canada Labour Relations Board.

_____
(Signed, Vice-Chairman)

Board File: 725-66

IN THE MATTER OF THE

> *Canada Labour Code*

> > *— and —*

> *Thibodeau-Finch Express Ltd.,*

> > > > *applicant,*

> > *— and —*

> *Transport Drivers, Warehousemen and*
> *General Workers, Local 106 of the*
> *International Brotherhood of Teamsters,*
> *Chauffeurs, Warehousemen and*
> *Helpers of America,*

> > > > *respondent union,*

> > *— and —*

> *Gaétan Morin,*
> *Jean-Guy Lévesque,*
> *Denis Ouellet,*
> *Stanley Tremblay,*
> *Robert Arsenault,*
> *Alain Bussières,*
> *Yvon Raymond,*
> *Robert Oakes,*
> *Gilles Lefebvre,*

> > > > *respondents.*

WHEREAS, the Transport Drivers, Warehousemen and General Workers, Local 106 of the International Brotherhood of Teamsters, Chauffeurs, Warehousemen and Helpers of America is the certified bargaining agent for a unit of employees of the applicant covered by a collective agreement dated April 1, 1978;

AND WHEREAS, following a hearing of an application made pursuant to Section 182 of the *Canada Labour Code*, the Board has found that:

(a) there has been no agreement between locals 69 and 106 of the International Brotherhood of Teamsters, Chauffeurs, Warehousemen and Helpers of America, and the company members of General Freight Division of the Motor Transport Industrial Relations Bureau of Quebec Inc. on the renewal of the collective agreement to which they are parties, expiring March 31, 1980; and

(b) that the employees of the applicant not being at work as they may be scheduled or called at or after 10 p.m., May 25, 1980, will constitute an illegal strike;

NOW, THEREFORE, the Canada Labour Relations Board hereby orders pursuant to the provisions of Sections 182 and 183.1 of the *Canada Labour Code* (Part V — Industrial Relations) that the employees of the applicant who are members of the bargaining unit concerned to report to work as they may be scheduled or called at or after 10 p.m., May 25, 1980, and to perform the duties of their employment and to refrain from any concerted illegal activity designed or intended to restrict output;

AND, FURTHER, the respondent union, its officers and officials are hereby ordered to refrain from authorizing or declaring any strike or concerted activity designed or intended to restrict output;

AND, FURTHER, the respondent union is hereby ordered to distribute forthwith a copy of this order to each employee in the bargaining unit for which the union is certified. The applicant employer is ordered to forthwith post copies of this order in prominent places where they are likely to come to the attention of the employees affected.

THIS ORDER IS IN FULL FORCE AND EFFECT UNTIL THE CONDITIONS SET OUT IN SECTION 180(1)(a) to (d) OF THE *CANADA LABOUR CODE* HAVE BEEN MET.

ISSUED at Montreal, this 25th day of May 1980, by the Canada Labour Relations Board.

_____

(Signed, Vice-Chairman)

Board File: 725-96

IN THE MATTER OF THE

    Canada Labour Code

— and —

Quebecair

applicant,

— and —

Parenteau Suzanne
12100 Boul. Pierrefonds
Pierrefonds, P.Q.

— and —

Eighty other named employees

respondents.

WHEREAS, the Canada Labour Relations Board has received an application pursuant to Section 182 of the *Canada Labour Code* (Part V — Industrial Relations) alleging that certain employees, members of the International Association of Machinists and Aerospace Workers, Local 2413, covered by a collective agreement dated February 1, 1978 and which expired on July 31, 1980, did engage in an unlawful strike beginning on June 7, 1981;

AND WHEREAS, the requirements of Section 180(1) of the Code have not been fulfilled in order to engage in a legal strike as the report of the conciliator appointed by the Minister of Labour, has not yet been released by the Minister, nor has the latter made a decision to appoint or not, a commissioner conciliator to assist the parties in arriving at an agreement to renew said collective agreement;

AND WHEREAS, such strike activity is therefore prohibited by Section 180 of the Canada Labour Code;

NOW THEREFORE, the Canada Labour Relations Board hereby orders all of the employees of the applicant covered by the aforementioned collective agreement and members of the bargaining unit represented by local 2413 of the International Association of Machinists and Aerospace Workers to perform the duties of their employment and to refrain from strike activity until all requirements of Section 180(1) of the Code have been fulfilled;

FURTHERMORE, local 2413 of the International Association of Machinists and Aerospace Workers, through its officers, will instruct its members in the aforementioned bargaining unit to refrain from engaging in any illegal strike in violation of Section 180(1) of the Code;

For the purpose of clarification, it is recorded that the Board has not heard any formal evidence in regard to this application and no finding is made on the merit of the application but that an informal meeting was held at which time both the applicant and International Representative of the International Association of Machinists and Aerospace Workers were present and that some of the facts were not in dispute.

ISSUED at Ottawa, this 8th day of June 1981, by the Canada Labour Relations Board.

_____

(Signed, Chairman)

Board File: 725-106

IN THE MATTER OF THE

    Canada Labour Code

               — *and* —

    Canadian National Railway Company,

                        applicant (employer)

— and —

Canadian Council of Railway Shopcraft
Employees and Allied Workers, and
unnamed employees of the employer,

respondents

WHEREAS, the Canada Labour Relations Board received from the applicant an application pursuant to section 182 of the Canada Labour Code (Part V — Industrial Relations) alleging that certain of its employees, represented by the respondent council of trade unions, have and were participating or were about to participate in an unlawful strike;

AND WHEREAS, having heard evidence and argument by the parties at Vancouver on the 24th day of March, 1982, the Canada Labour Relations Board has found that the employees of the applicant represented by the respondent council of trade unions are subject to the provisions of a collective agreement and that the provisions of section 180 of the Code have not been satisfied, therefore the actions of certain employees involved in work stoppages and overtime bans constitute an unlawful strike within the meaning of the Code;

AND WHEREAS, the Canada Labour Relations Board further finds that the respondent council of trade unions did not authorize or declare such an unlawful strike;

NOW, THEREFORE, the Canada Labour Relations Board dismisses the application against the Canadian Council of Railway Shopcraft Employees and Allied Workers;

AND FURTHER, the Canada Labour Relations Board hereby orders all employees of Canadian National Railway Company represented by the respondent council of trade unions to perform the duties of their employment and to cease and desist from participating in such unlawful activities.

This Order is made pursuant to the provisions of section 182 of the Canada Labour Code and shall remain in full force and effect until the provisions of section 180 of the Code have been met unless it is continued, modified or revoked pursuant to an application under section 183.1(2) of the Code.

ISSUED at Vancouver, this 24th day of March, 1982 by the Canada Labour Relations Board.

_____
(Signed, Vice-chairman)

Board File: 725-106

Canada Labour Relations Board
Statement Accompanying Board Order

The Canadian Council of Railway Shopcraft Employees and Allied Workers and the Canadian National Railway are engaged in difficult collective bargaining. Notwithstanding the union's efforts to keep the employees informed and encouraging them to be patient many employees in Alberta and British Columbia have undertaken job action to demonstrate their unhappiness with negotiations. Because of these actions, the employer asks for certain orders against the union and its employees.

These actions, neither authorized nor condoned by the Canadian Council, are illegal under the Canada Labour Code. Collective bargaining is now at the conciliation stage and the Canadian Council and employer must be able to direct their energies to matters at the bargaining table and not to fighting operational bush fires and legal battles.

The Board has determined the Canadian Council has not acted contrary to the Code and makes no order against it. The employees' actions are clearly an organized illegal wildcat strike. They and others contemplating future actions must clearly understand that work stoppages and overtime bans are not permitted at this stage of the bargaining process. To make this clear and dispel any misconceptions the employees may have, the Board has issued the attached order.

The Board expects the employer to distribute the order and this statement to its employee.

ISSUED at Vancouver this 24th day of March, 1982.

_____

(Signed, Vice-chairman and Two Members)

Board File: 725-138

IN THE MATTER OF THE

    Canada Labour Code

— *and* —

Canada Post Corporation,

applicant,

— *and* —

Canadian Union of Postal Workers,

respondent.

WHEREAS the Canada Labour Relations Board conducted a hearing on December 5th and 6th, 1983, into an application pursuant to Section 182 of the Canada Labour Code by the Canada Post Corporation, applicant, alleging violation of Section 180 of the Code by the Canadian Union of Postal Workers, respondent;

AND WHEREAS, the Board found that the identification and taxing of items bearing insufficient postage by members of the respondent employed by the applicant, constituted a portion of the normal duties of their employment;

522

AND WHEREAS, the Board found that by news release dated November 25th, 1983, the respondent union unlawfully declared or authorized that its members employed by the applicant would process letters bearing insufficient postage, mailed between December 11th and 17th, 1983, without taxing them;

AND WHEREAS, the Board found that the participation of the members of the respondent employed by the applicant in such concerted refusal to perform in the normal manner this portion of their duties would constitute an unlawful strike;

NOW, THEREFORE, the Canada Labour Relations Board hereby orders, pursuant to Section 182 and subject to Section 183.1 of the Canada Labour Code:

THAT the Canada Post Corporation is hereby ordered to post forthwith on its premises in locations where they are most likely to come to the attention of employees represented by the respondent and to keep posted in such prominent places until January 31st, 1984, copies of this order and the other orders issued by the Canada Labour Relations Board relating to the unlawful strike declaration or authorization made by the respondent.

THIS ORDER shall remain in full force and effect until January 31st, 1984, unless continued, modified or revoked pursuant to Section 183.1 of the Canada Labour Code.

ISSUED at Ottawa, this 6th day of December 1983, by the Canada Labour Relations Board.

_____

(Signed, Chairman)

Board File: 725-138

IN THE MATTER OF THE

　　Canada Labour Code

— *and* —

Canada Post Corporation,

applicant,

— *and* —

Canadian Union of Postal Workers,

respondent.

WHEREAS, the Canada Labour Relations Board conducted a hearing on December 5th and 6th, 1983, into an application pursuant to Section 182 of the Canada Labour Code by the Canada Post Corporation, applicant, alleging violation of Section 180 of the Code by the Canadian Union of Postal Workers, respondent;

AND WHEREAS, the Board found that the identification and taxing of items bearing insufficient postage by members of the respondent employed by the applicant, constituted a portion of the normal duties of their employment;

AND WHEREAS, the Board found that by news release dated November 25th, 1983, the respondent union unlawfully declared or authorized that its members employed by the applicant would process letters bearing insufficient postage, mailed between December 11th and 17th, 1983, without taxing them;

AND WHEREAS, the Board found that the participation of the members of the respondent employed by the applicant in such concerted refusal to perform in the normal manner this portion of their duties would constitute an unlawful strike;

NOW, THEREFORE, the Canada Labour Relations Board hereby orders, pursuant to Section 182 and subject to Section 183.1 of the Canada Labour Code:

THAT the employees of the applicant represented by the respondent are hereby ordered to refrain from participating in unlawful concerted activity and to continue to perform in a normal manner the duties of their employment.

IT IS HEREBY FURTHER ORDERED that, without limiting the generality of the foregoing, the decision and orders of the Board do not in any way restrict the applicant from its normal function of determining the priorities as between various aspects of an employee's duties at any given time or the employee's normal obligation to follow the direction of the applicant in the carrying out of his or her duties.

THIS ORDER shall remain in full force and effect until January 31st, 1984, unless continued, modified or revoked pursuant to Section 183.1 of the Canada Labour Code.

ISSUED at Ottawa, this 6th day of December 1983, by the Canada Labour Relations Boards.

_____

(Signed, Chairman)

Board File: 725-138

IN THE MATTER OF THE

    Canada Labour Code

— and —

    Canada Post Corporation,

applicant,

— and —

    Canadian Union of Postal Workers,

respondent.

WHEREAS the Canada Labour Relations Board conducted a hearing on December 5th and 6th, 1983, into an application pursuant to Section 182 of the Canada Labour Code by the Canada Post Corporation, applicant, alleging violation of Section 180 of the Code by the Canadian Union of Postal Workers, respondent;

AND WHEREAS, the Board found that the identification and taxing of items bearing insufficient postage by members of the respondent employed by the applicant, constituted a portion of the normal duties of their employment;

AND WHEREAS, the Board found that by news release dated November 25th, 1983, the respondent union unlawfully declared or authorized that its members employed by the applicant would process letters bearing insufficient postage, mailed between December 11th and 17th, 1983, without taxing them;

AND WHEREAS, the Board found that the participation of the members of the respondent employed by the applicant in such concerted refusal to perform in the normal manner this portion of their duties would constitute an unlawful strike;

NOW, THEREFORE, the Canada Labour Relations Board hereby orders, pursuant to Section 182 and subject to Section 183.1 of the Canada Labour Code:

THAT the respondent union, through its National President, is hereby ordered to revoke the declaration or authorization of an unlawful strike contained in its news release of November 25th, 1983, declaring that members of the bargaining unit would not perform a portion of their duties relating to the processing of items bearing insufficient postage;

IT IS FURTHER HEREBY ORDERED that the respondent union give forthwith to all employees of the applicant affected by the unlawful declaration or authorization of November 25th, 1983, notice of said revocation and to order the display of the notice of revocation on all union bulletin boards and at all union offices and premises and to keep such notices posted until January 31st, 1984;

IT IS HEREBY FURTHER ORDERED that the respondent union shall, no later than 2:00 p.m., December 7th, 1983, deliver to the Board in Ottawa evidence supported by Affidavit of the procedures followed to secure full compliance with the letter and intent of these orders, including the full text of communications to the officers and membership of the respondent.

THIS ORDER shall remain in full force and effect until January 31st, 1984, unless continued, modified or revoked pursuant to Section 183.1 of the Canada Labour Code.

ISSUED at Ottawa, this 6th day of December 1983, by the Canada Labour Relations Board.

_____

(Signed, Chairman)

APPENDIX 11
REFERRAL RULES PURSUANT TO SECTION 161.1

The following referral rules required by s. 161.1 were established by a union pursuant to an order of the Board in *David Nauss and Peter Roberts*, 43 di 263 (No. 313) (April 22, 1981).

Rules for Employment Referral Established by Halifax Longshoremen's Association, Local 269 of the International Longshoremen's Association

(Effective March 1, 1981)

Part 1: General
A. Rules of Conduct

1. No person shall interfere with the dispatcher nor create a disturbance during dispatch.
2. No person shall drink alcoholic beverages or be under the influence of alcohol in the hiring hall or on the job.
3. No person shall pilfer or unlawfully be in possession of any cargo at any time.
4. No person shall destroy or deface union property.
5. No person shall leave the job area without first obtaining the permission of his foreman or his representative.
6. No person shall be insubordinate or fail to carry out orders from his foreman or his representative.
7. No person shall give the dispatcher another person's number.
8. No person shall communicate directly with any of the employers on the Halifax Waterfront — all communications shall be through the elected representatives.
9. No person shall interfere with the dispatcher at any time.

B. Penalties

Any person interfering with the dispatcher or creating a disturbance during dispatch shall not be dispatched for that period. Any recurrence of such behaviour shall subject the person to a suspension, fine, or complete dismissal from the hiring hall.

Any person who breaches or violates any of the hiring hall rules shall, depending upon the circumstances, be subject to suspension, fine, or complete dismissal from the hall.

C. Right of Appeal

Any union member who is penalized under these rules has the right to appeal to the Executive of the Union under Article XIX — Section 3 of the International Constitution.

Any cardman penalized under these rules shall have the right to appeal to the Executive of the Union.

Any bullpen member who has been penalized under these rules has the right to appeal to the Executive of the Union.

D. Complaints

Any person wishing to complain about the hiring hall or its rules shall make his complaint in writing and shall submit it to the President and/or Vice-President. Any complaint which is not in writing shall not be dealt with.

Part 2: General Rules for Hiring Hall

1. Any active union member with ten years' or more seniority shall be given first preference to all available man hours on the Halifax Waterfront, all training or upgrading programs and first preference to join all gangs and basic work forces. (This rule is restricted to skills only.)
2. The following sequence shall be followed when labour is being reduced or checked in anywhere on the Halifax Waterfront:
   1. Bullpen members
   2. Cardmen
   3. Union members

Within each of the groups referred to above, persons shall be checked in or reduced in the reverse order of their hiring. In other words, the last man hired within the group shall be the first man checked in or reduced.

3. After the last dispatch of the day, the dispatcher shall call each of the job sites working on the Halifax Waterfront giving to Management the names of at least three persons who are next eligible to be dispatched and these persons shall be called if fill-ins are required after the hiring hall closes. This procedure applies to the following: 6:00 p.m. to 8:00 p.m.; 6:00 p.m. to 5:00 a.m.; midnight to start; and 6:00 p.m. to a finish.
4. No person under sixteen years of age shall be dispatched from the hiring hall.
5. Each foreman shall have the right, regardless of a person's place on the dispatch slip, to reduce or check in any person not performing his work.
6. Each foreman is responsible for the men that work for him.
7. Any person not intending to return to the job for the following work period shall notify his foreman.
8. A person shall become registered for a skill on the union board or the card board after a foreman has notified the hiring hall that the person has the required skills.
9. Any person requesting to have a skill removed from either the union board or the card board shall not be registered for that skill for a period of one year after the skill has been removed.
10. High climb lashing shall be considered a skill on the Halifax Waterfront and shall be registered on the union board and card board, for persons having such skills.
11. The dispatcher shall have the right to refuse employment to any person who is not capable of performing the job or who is intoxicated.

Part 3: Sequence of Hiring

1. Cement, only when new order. (Otherwise regular spot)
2. Grain, marine legge. (Otherwise regular spot)
3. Shed, only on first order of week. (Otherwise regular spot)
4. Gantry Crane
5. Karricon

6. Winchmen
7. Crane Operators
8. Hatch Tenders
9. Machine, Shed, Hold, Other Jobs, Pushers
10. High Climb Lashers
11. Gangs, farthest pier first, low to high rotation. Brow first, hold last.
12. Extra men for gangs, farthest pier first.
13. All other jobs, farthest pier first.
14. Locations in order for gang hiring are: Autoport, Pier 9, Pier 39, and back up to Pier 20. (One difference, Pier 33 ahead of 34) (Farthest pier first)
15. Where there are new gangs and old gangs, the new gangs are ordered first even if they are closer or not.
16. All orders start from original nail on first call. Each skill has its own starting point for the duration of that period only.
17. The only time the original nail moves is when it moves for general work.

Part 4: Union Board Rules

A union board system has been established in the hiring hall for all union workers, who are members of the Halifax Longshoremen's Association, Local 269. All persons on the board are listed alphabetically and as each new person is taken as a member of the union, he is placed on this board in accordance with an alphabetical listing. This board is controlled by "the nail". This nail indicates where the dispatcher shall start and stop hiring labour during any hiring period. After each hiring period, the nail is placed into the board by the dispatcher to indicate the last man hired for general labour and this also indicates where the hiring will start at the beginning of the next hiring period.

The rules for hiring from the union board shall be as follows:

1. Union men will have first preference for all jobs on the Halifax Waterfront.
2. To obtain employment, the union member shall plug into the board and shall be present in the hall to be dispatched.
3. Skilled jobs shall be hired first by the dispatcher calling the skill and proceeding alphabetically around the board until he reaches a member who has plugged in for the job. This procedure continues for all skilled jobs. If additional skilled labour is required after exhausting the union board, the dispatcher shall go to the card board and dispatch in the same manner.
4. After skills have been hired, the dispatcher shall start hiring for general labour commencing at the place where the nail was located at the start of the hiring period. The dispatcher shall then proceed according to the alphabetical listing for each job. If the dispatcher makes a complete rotation of the board to the place of beginning without filling the job requirements, he shall proceed to the card board to obtain labour. Once having filled the job order, he will return to the union board for the next job. This procedure is then continued for each new job.
5. Once a job is offered to the card board, it shall not be re-offered to the union board.
6. After all jobs have been first offered to the union members, the additional orders shall be filled from the card board in accordance with the card board rules.
7. If additional labour is required, after hiring from the card board, the dispatcher shall go to the bullpen to hire labour in accordance with the bullpen rules.

8. The rules of dispatch, as contained in Article 15 of the collective agreement, shall apply to all jobs placed through the hiring hall.
9. Each union member once hired has the responsibility to know his foreman's name and the pier dispatched to and shall report directly to the job.
10. If, during a work period, a vacancy occurs for a skilled job, the foreman shall place an order to the hiring hall for such vacancy. If the order for the skilled job cannot be filled through the hiring hall, the foreman may shift a person from an unskilled job to fill the skilled job requirement.
11. The dispatcher shall have the right to refuse employment to any person that is not capable or intoxicated.
12. No union member shall quit a job and return to the hall to obtain another job.
13. No union member shall be insubordinate to his foreman or fail to carry out orders from his foreman.
14. A foreman requiring men for his gang shall not select a union member with less than 10 years' seniority in the union, without first posting a notice in the hiring hall for a period of one week. If a union member, with less than 10 years' seniority in the union, is selected to become a member of a gang, he cannot be replaced by another union member, unless he terminates his employment or is terminated for just cause.
15. No foreman shall shift a member of his gang with less than 10 years' seniority in the union to a position of winchman, hatch tender, machine man or brow man, without first posting a notice of such vacancy in the hiring hall for a period of one week.

Part 5: Card Board Rules

A card board system has been established in the hiring hall for a group of non-union workers, referred to as card board members, who shall be given the second opportunity for employment after union members. This card board is an alphabetical listing which is controlled by "the nail". This nail indicates where the dispatcher shall start and stop hiring labour, during any hiring period. After each hiring period, the nail is placed into the board by the dispatcher to indicate the last man hired, which also indicates where the hiring will start at the beginning of the next hiring period.

To maintain a position on the card board, each cardman shall work at least 75 percent of the total average hours worked by all cardmen. Every three months, commencing March 1st, a review of the card board shall be carried out by office staff or a committee designated to carry out such review by the Executive of the Union.

The rules for hiring from the card board shall be as follows:

1. Cardmen shall be given second opportunity for employment after union members.
2. To obtain employment, a cardman shall plug in to the board and shall be present in the hall to be dispatched.
3. Skilled jobs shall be hired first, following the same procedure as is used for the union members' board. If no cardmen are available for work with the registered skill required, the dispatcher shall ask if any cardmen are interested before the skilled job is offered to the bullpen.
4. After skills have been hired, the dispatcher shall start hiring for general labour commencing at the nail designating the next person to be dispatched. The dispatcher shall then proceed according to the alphabetical listing on the board to obtain labour. After hiring, the dispatcher shall place the nail

identifying where the hiring has stopped for that period. This procedure shall be followed for all hiring from the card board.

5. The dispatcher shall only go around the card board once during each dispatch period.
6. The general nail does not move for skilled jobs. Any cardman obtaining a skilled job shall have his nail reversed and it shall remain reversed until the general nail passes his name. When this occurs, his nail shall be removed entitling that cardman to plug his nail in for employment.
7. Any cardman who is late for dispatch, but receives a job after all other cardmen have been dispatched, shall have his nail placed in backwards against him whether the dispatcher goes to the bullpen or not. His nail shall remain reversed until the general nail passes his name. When this occurs, his nail shall be removed entitling that cardman to plug his nail in for employment.
8. Cardmen may be checked in at the end of each work period in accordance with Article 15:12 of the collective agreement.
9. No cardman shall quit a job and return to the hall to obtain another job.
10. When a cardman obtains a job at the hall, he shall not trade jobs with another cardman.
11. After all available cardmen are dispatched from the hall and additional labour is required, the dispatcher shall proceed to the bullpen for hiring in accordance with the bullpen rules.

Part 6: Bullpen Rules

A. General

1. Any person who is not a member of the Association or is not on the card board list of persons eligible to be admitted to the union shall be known as a bullpen man.
2. To obtain a job from the bullpen, persons must be seated in the proper area in the hiring hall.
3. Once a person is hired from the bullpen, he shall go directly to the job site and report to the foreman or his representative for whom he is hired.
4. All bullpen men shall be checked in before cardmen or union men.
5. Any person who is dispatched to the job and he cannot or will not do that job, will be sent back to the hall and he shall inform the dispatcher why he was sent back.
6. For proper performance of the job and for safety reasons, bullpen men shall do as requested when on the job whether instructed by a foreman or any other union member.

B. Hiring

1. A duplicate tag system shall be established on a board located in the hiring hall and numbered consecutively.
2. At the commencement of each hiring time, the dispatcher shall check the board to determine if all numbers are in place with a duplicate tag for each number.
3. If any member is missing or if a duplicate tag is missing, that number will not be used for hiring purposes at the hiring time.
4. Each person entering the hall for bullpen privileges shall take a number by removing both tags from a nail on the board, deposit one of the numbered tags in a box provided in the hall and retain the other duplicate tag on his person.

5. After the dispatcher has hired from the union board and card board and additional men are required from the bullpen, the dispatcher shall make an announcement to the hall indicating the foreman's name, the pier where work is to be carried out, and the number of men required.
6. The dispatcher shall then place the box containing the tags in open view to the hall and remove a tag calling out the number drawn. The person having the matching duplicate number shall be dispatched from the hall upon presenting the duplicate tag to the dispatcher.
7. This procedure shall be followed without exception during all hiring times from the bullpen.
8. If skills are required from the bullpen, the dispatcher shall use his discretion in filling the orders taking into account the skill required, the experience and the ability of persons available in the bullpen.
9. After the hiring from the bullpen is completed, the dispatcher shall request that all tags be placed in the box. Any person who does not return a tag is subject to a penalty including a fine, suspension, or dismissal from the hall.

Part 7: Cement Vessels

Starting next vessel there shall be a specific nail for cement only. Last man out of original five, nail will stop there regardless of where general board nail is. Additional men for rigging and unrigging to come from general nail.

1. Any man that is under the gun for the cement nail and his nail is backwards loses his turn on that cement vessel, unless the board makes complete turn.
2. Any man ordered out and/or ordered back must follow those orders.
3. Any man that does not follow his orders, (gangs and/or basic work forces) and/or quits the job he was working on will be subject to a fine which could include the amount he made on the cement.
4. Any man reported drinking on the cement vessels will be subject to a fine and a removal from that job.
5. If any foreman keeps a man that is drinking he too will be subject to a fine.

Part 8: Card Board Membership

A. General

The following rules apply to obtaining membership on the card board:

1. No new members shall be accepted or placed on the card board until the Manpower Committee, established under the collective agreement, has completed a study of the manpower requirements on the Halifax Waterfront and determines that it is necessary to have new members placed on the card board to meet the manpower requirements in the Port of Halifax.
2. A present member of the card board may lose his status on the card board if he fails to maintain at least 75 percent of the total average hours worked by all other cardmen, or is otherwise suspended or expelled from the hiring hall in accordance with the rules established by Local 269 of the Halifax Longshoremen's Association.
3. A cardman who has been injured on the Halifax Waterfront and is in receipt of benefits under the Workers' Compensation Act of Nova Scotia shall receive a credit of twenty-five hours per week, while in receipt of Workers' Compensation benefits.
4. Every three months, commencing March 1, 1981, a review of the card board shall be carried out by office staff or a committee designated to carry out such

reviews by the Executive of the Union to determine if members of the card board are maintaining the required number of hours. Any member of the card board who is not maintaining the required number of hours is subject to losing his membership on the card board and his status and ranking for obtaining membership in Local 269 of the Halifax Longshoremen's Association.

B. Leave of Absence

1. Cardmen may make applications for leave of absence in circumstances where they will not be available for work on the Waterfront.
2. The applications are to be made out on an approved form and submitted to the Office Staff.
3. No leave of absence shall exceed a period of more than three (3) months, although additional applications may be made to the Union Executive.
4. Cardmen who are granted a leave of absence shall not have their status on the Cardboard affected in any way.
5. After being granted a leave of absence, a cardman wants to return to work on the Waterfront before his leave is up shall give two (2) weeks notice to the Office Staff before returning.

Application for Leave

Name: . . . .

No.: . . . .

I . . . ., a Cardman, hereby request a Leave of Absence for the period of . . . . to . . . .

The reason for this request is:

Explanation: . . . .

I have a total of . . . . hours of employment to the date of this application.

. . . .
          Dated   Signature

APPENDIX 12
ACCESS ORDERS

The following access order was issued by the Board pursuant to its authority under s. 199 in Dome Petroleum, 42 di 237, at 244-245.

1. Access to the jetty and the base camp of Dome Petroleum Limited and its wholly owned subsidiary Canadian Marine Drilling Limited located at Tuktoyaktuk Harbour in the vicinity of Tuktoyaktuk, N.W.T. and to the vessels Canmar Explorer, Canmar Explorer II, Canmar Explorer III and Canmar Explorer IV, be granted to an authorized representative of each of the two unions to be named by each union.

2. Access is to be for the purpose of permitting the authorized representative of the SIU to meet with unlicensed personnel and the authorized representative of the CMSG to meet with licensed personnel employed by the employer on all its vessels, including:

    Canmar Explorer
    Canmar Explorer II
    Canmar Explorer III
    Canmar Explorer IV
    Canmar Carrier
    Canmar Supplier
    Canmar Supplier II
    Canmar Supplier III
    Canmar Supplier IV
    Canmar Supplier V
    Canmar Supplier VI
    Canmar Supplier VII
    Canmar Supplier VIII
    Canmar Jet Barge
    Kigoriak
    Arctic Sun

3. Access to the jetty and base camp is to be permitted, for a period not exceeding six hours per day, with the right to board all the vessels, including the following:

    Canmar Supplier
    Canmar Supplier II
    Canmar Supplier III
    Canmar Supplier IV
    Canmar Supplier V
    Canmar Supplier VI
    Canmar Supplier VII
    Canmar Supplier VIII
    Canmar Jet Barge
    Arctic Sun

    while any of these vessels are docked thereat.

4. If access to the employees employed aboard a vessel listed in paragraph 3 cannot be achieved in the manner set out therein before August 1, 1981 then access shall be obtained in the manner and under the terms relating to access to the employees employed aboard the vessels listed in paragraph 5.

5. Access to the vessels Canmar Explorer, Canmar Explorer II, Canmar Explorer III, Canmar Explorer IV, Kigoriak and Canmar Carrier is to be

permitted for a period not exceeding eighteen hours on each vessel and representatives of each union shall have access at the same time.

6. Access to the vessels Canmar Explorer, Canmar Explorer II, Canmar Explorer III, Canmar Explorer IV, Kigoriak and Canmar Carrier is to be by means of transportation provided by Dome Petroleum Limited or Canadian Marine Drilling Limited for which each union must make reasonable reimbursement.

7. During access to the vessels Canmar Explorer, Canmar Explorer II, Canmar Explorer III, Canmar Explorer IV, Kigoriak and Canmar Carrier, Dome Petroleum Limited or Canadian Marine Drilling Limited must provide each authorized representative with meals and sleeping accommodation, for which the union must make reasonable reimbursement.

8. Access by the authorized representative of each union to the employees aboard the vessels is solely for purposes relating to soliciting union membership and must not interfere with the operation of any of the vessels or the performance by the crew of their duties.

9. Each union shall submit to Dome Petroleum Limited and Canadian Marine Drilling Limited an identification of its authorized representative and Dome Petroleum Limited and Canadian Marine Drilling Limited shall issue appropriate instructions to its on site representative or representatives and the masters of the vessels to permit the applicant's authorized representative, on the presentation of the identification, access to the base camp, jetty, and vessels.

10. Dome Petroleum Limited or Canadian Marine Drilling Limited shall on one occasion with respect to each vessel notify the union at least eight hours prior to the estimated time of arrival at the base camp and jetty of the vessel.

11. The right of access will commence on June 1, 1981 and continue until the authorized representative of the SIU has had an opportunity to meet the unlicensed personnel on each of the vessels and the authorized representative of the CMSG has had an opportunity to meet the licensed personnel on each of the vessels or until October 1, 1981, whichever date is earlier.

The following access order was issued by the Board pursuant to its authority under s. 199 in Dome Petroleum Ltd. and Canadian Marine Drilling Ltd., 40 di 150, [1980] 2 Can LRBR 533. Note, however, that paragraph 11 of the order was set aside by the Federal Court of Appeal in Dome Petroleum Ltd. and Canadian Marine Drilling Ltd. v. Canadian Merchant Service Guild, [1981] 2 F.C. 418, 35 N.R. 243, 81 CLLC #14,076, 118 D.L.R. (3d) 335, as being contrary to s. 185(d) of the Code.

We have decided to grant all three applications and issue an order in the following terms:

1. Access to the jetty and the base camp of Dome Petroleum Limited and its wholly owned subsidiary Canadian Marine Drilling Limited located at Tuktoyaktuk Harbour in the vicinity of Tuktoyaktuk, N.W.T. and to the vessels Canmar Explorer, Canmar Explorer II, Canmar Explorer III and Canmar Explorer IV, be granted to an authorized representative of each of the three unions to be named by each union.

2. Access is to be for the purpose of permitting the authorized representative of the CBRT & GW and SIU to meet with unlicensed personnel and the authorized representative of the CMSG to meet with licensed personnel employed by the employer on the vessels —

    Canmar Explorer
    Canmar Explorer II
    Canmar Explorer III
    Canmar Explorer IV
    Canmar Carrier
    Canmar Supplier
    Canmar Supplier II
    Canmar Supplier III
    Canmar Supplier IV
    Canmar Supplier V
    Canmar Supplier VI
    Canmar Supplier VII
    Canmar Supplier VIII
    Canmar Jet Barge
    Kigoriak
    Arctic Sun

3. Access to the jetty and base camp is to be permitted, for a period not exceeding six hours per day, with the right to board the following vessels:
    Canmar Supplier
    Canmar Supplier II
    Canmar Supplier III
    Canmar Supplier IV
    Canmar Supplier V
    Canmar Supplier VI
    Canmar Supplier VII
    Canmar Supplier VIII
    Canmar Jet Barge
    Arctic Sun

    while any of these vessels are docked thereat.

4. If access to the employees employed aboard a vessel listed in paragraph 3 cannot be achieved in the manner set out therein within the period specified in paragraph 12, then access shall be obtained in the manner and under the

terms relating to access to the employees employed aboard the vessels listed in paragraph 5.

5. Access to the vessels Canmar Explorer, Canmar Explorer II, Canmar Explorer III, Canmar Explorer IV, Kigoriak and Canmar Carrier is to be permitted for a period not exceeding eighteen hours on each vessel and representatives of each union shall have access at the same time.

6. Access to the vessels Canmar Explorer, Canmar Explorer II, Canmar Explorer III, Canmar Explorer IV, Kigoriak and Canmar Carrier is to be by means of transportation provided by Dome Petroleum Limited or Canadian Marine Drilling Limited for which each union must make reasonable reimbursement.

7. During access to the vessels Canmar Explorer, Canmar Explorer II, Canmar Explorer III, Canmar Explorer IV, Kigoriak and Canmar Carrier, Dome Petroleum Limited or Canadian Marine Drilling Limited must provide each authorized representative with meals and sleeping accommodation for which the union must make reasonable reimbursement.

8. Access by the authorized representative of each union to the employees aboard the vessels is solely for purposes relating to soliciting union membership and must not interfere with the operation of any of the vessels or the performance by the crew of their duties, except as set out in paragraph 11.

9. Each union shall submit to Dome Petroleum Limited and Canadian Marine Drilling Limited an identification of its authorized representative and Dome Petroleum Limited and Canadian Marine Drilling Limited shall issue appropriate instructions to its on site representative or representatives and the masters of the vessels to permit the applicant's authorized representative, on the presentation of the identification, access to the base camp, jetty, and vessels.

10. Dome Petroleum Limited or Canadian Marine Drilling Limited shall on one occasion with respect to each vessel notify the union at least eight hours prior to the estimated time of arrival at the base camp and jetty of the vessel.

11. If the licensed or unlicensed personnel of each vessel are not off-duty for at least two hours of the time the vessel on which they are employed is docked at the base camp and jetty and the unions have been given prior notice of its arrival in accordance with paragraph 10, then the authorized representatives may meet with the employees, out of the presence of other persons, for two hours during the employees' normal working hours.

12. The rights of access will commence on July 1, 1980 and continue until the authorized representative of the CBRT & GW and SIU have had an opportunity to meet the unlicensed personnel on each of the vessels and the authorized representative of the CMSG has had an opportunity to meet the licensed personnel on each of the vessels or until October 1, 1980, whichever date is earlier.

INDEX

All references are to paragraph numbers.

S

W